Philosophy Then and Now

Philosophy
THEN AND NOW

EDITED BY

N. SCOTT ARNOLD, THEODORE M. BENDITT, AND GEORGE GRAHAM

BLACKWELL
Publishers

MAI 4174985√

Copyright © Blackwell Publishers Ltd 1998

First published 1998
2 4 6 8 10 9 7 5 3 1

Blackwell Publishers Inc.
350 Main Street
Malden, Massachusetts 02148
USA

Blackwell Publishers Ltd
108 Cowley Road
Oxford OX4 1JF
UK

Library of Congress Cataloging-in-Publication Data

Philosophy then and now / edited by N. Scott Arnold, Theodore M. Benditt, George Graham.
p.   cm.
Includes bibliographical references and index.
ISBN 1–55786–741–0 (alk. paper). — ISBN 1–55786–742–9 (pbk. : alk. paper)
1. Philosophy—Introductions.   I. Arnold, N. Scott.   II. Benditt, Theodore M.   III. Graham, George, 1945–.
BD21.P483   1998
100—dc21   97–47396
                                        CIP

British Library Cataloguing in Publication Data

A CIP catalogue record for this book is available from the British Library.

Typeset in 10.5 on 13 pt Bembo
by Graphicraft Typesetters Limited, Hong Kong
Printed in Great Britain by T. J. International, Padstow, Cornwall

This book is printed on acid-free paper

Contents

Editors and Contributors

N. Scott Arnold received his PhD from the University of Massachusetts in 1979. Currently, he is Professor of Philosophy at the University of Alabama at Birmingham. He has been a visiting scholar at the Hoover Institution at Stanford University and at the Social Philosophy and Policy Center at Bowling Green State University in Ohio. Professor Arnold is the author of *Marx's Radical Critique of Capitalist Society* (Oxford, 1990) and *The Philosophy and Economics of Market Socialism* (Oxford, 1994).

Theodore M. Benditt received his law degree from the University of Pennsylvania in 1965 and his PhD in philosophy from the University of Pittsburgh in 1971. He has been Dean of the School of Arts and Humanities at the University of Alabama at Birmingham since 1984 and a member of its Philosophy Department since 1978. He is the author of *Law as Rule and Principle* (Stanford, 1978) and *Rights* (Rowman and Littlefield, 1982).

George Graham received his PhD from Brandeis University in 1975. He is Professor of Philosophy and Psychology and Chair of the Department of Philosophy at the University of Alabama at Birmingham. Professor Graham is the former editor of the journal *Behavior and Philosophy* and the author of *Philosophy of Mind* (Blackwell, 1998). He has edited (with Hugh LaFollette) *Person to Person* (Temple, 1989), *Philosophical Psychopathology* (MIT Press, 1994) with G. Lynn Stephens, and *Companion to Cognitive Science* (Blackwell, 1998) with William Bechtel.

Harold Kincaid is Professor of Philosophy at the University of Alabama at Birmingham. He received his PhD from Indiana University in 1983. Professor Kincaid has published articles in journals such as *Synthese* and *Philosophy of Science*. He is the author of *Philosophical Foundations of the Social Sciences* (Cambridge, 1996) and *Individualism and the Unity of Science* (Rowman and Littlefield, 1997).

G. Lynn Stephens received his PhD from the University of Massachusetts at Amherst (1978). Currently, he is Associate Professor of Philosophy at the University of Alabama at Birmingham. He is the co-author (with Gregory Pence) of *Seven Dilemmas of World Religions* (Paragon House, 1994) and the co-editor (with George Graham) of *Philosophical Psychopathology* (MIT Press, 1994).

James Rachels is University Professor of Philosophy at the University of Alabama at Birmingham and is a former dean of its School of Arts and Humanities. Professor Rachels has taught at New York University, Duke University, and the University of Miami. He is the author of *The End of Life: Euthanasia and Morality* (Oxford, 1986), *The Elements of Moral Philosophy* (McGraw-Hill, 1993) and *Created from Animals: The Moral Implications of Darwinism* (Oxford, 1990).

Gregory Pence is Professor of Philosophy in the Philosophy Department and the School of Medicine at the University of Alabama at Birmingham. He is the author of *Who's Afraid of Human Cloning?* (Rowman and Littlefield, 1998), *Classic Cases in Medical Ethics* (McGraw-Hill, 1995) and (with G. Lynn Stephens) *Seven Dilemmas of World Religions* (Paragon House, 1994).

N. Scott Arnold, Theodore M. Benditt, and George Graham can be contacted at http://www.uab.edu/philosophy.

Acknowledgments

Chapter 1: Plato. Death scene from "Phaedo." *The Last Days of Socrates*, trans. Hugh Tredennick. Penguin Books Ltd, 1954. Reprinted by permission. / Descartes, René. "Letter to Princess Elizabeth," selections from *Principles of Philosophy* and *The Passions of the Soul*. *The Philosophical Writings of Descartes*, trans. John Cottingham, Robert Stoothoff, and Dugald Murdoch. Copyright 1984. Reprinted by permission of Cambridge University Press. / Nagel, Thomas. "Death." *Mortal Questions*, ed. Thomas Nagel. Copyright 1979. Reprinted by permission of Cambridge University Press. / Matthews, Gareth B. "Life and Death as the Arrival and Departure of the Psyche." *American Philosophical Quarterly* 16. Reprinted by permission of *American Philosophical Quarterly*, copyright holder, and the author. / Fodor, Jerry A. "The Mind–Body Problem." *Scientific American*, January 1981. Text copyright 1981 by Scientific American, Inc. All rights reserved. Illustration copyright 1981 by Jerome Kuhl. Reprinted by permission of Scientific American, Inc., and Jerome Kuhl. / *Chapter 2*: Sartre, Jean-Paul. *Being and Nothingness*, trans. H. H. Barnes. New York: Philosophical Library, 1956. Reprinted by permission. / Laplace, Pierre Simon de. "Philosophical Essay on Probability," trans. J. Cottingham. *Western Philosophy: An Anthology*, ed. John Cottingham, 1996. Reprinted by permission of Blackwell Publishers, Oxford. / Dennett, Daniel. "On Giving Libertarians What

They Say They Want." *Brainstorms*, ed. Daniel Dennett. Copyright 1981. Reprinted by permission of MIT Press. / Kane, Robert. "Free Will: The Elusive Ideal." *Philosophical Studies* 75. Copyright 1994. Reprinted by permission of Kluwer Academic Publishers and the author. / *Chapter 3*: Aquinas, Thomas. *The Basic Writings of St. Thomas Aquinas*, ed. Anton C. Pegis, 1945. Reprinted by permission of the A. C. Pegis Estate. / Mackie, J. L. "Arguments For Design." *The Miracle of Theism*. Copyright Joan Mackie 1982. Reprinted by permission of Oxford University Press. / Rowe, William L. "The Cosmological Argument." *Philosophy of Religion*, 1978, reprinted in *Reason and Responsibility*, 7th edn, ed. Joel Feinberg, 1989. Reprinted by permission of William L. Rowe. / Adams, Robert Merrihew. "Kierkegaard's Arguments Against Objective Reasoning in Religion." *The Monist* 60. Copyright 1977, *The Monist*, La Salle, Illinois 61301. Reprinted by permission. / Dostoevsky, Fyodor. *The Brothers Karamazov*, trans. Constance Garnett. Copyright 1923 by Macmillan Publishing Company. Reprinted by permission of Simon & Schuster and Random House UK Ltd on behalf of William Heinemann Ltd, publishers, for Constance Garnett. / *Chapter 4*: Descartes, René. *Meditations on First Philosophy. The Philosophical Writings of Descartes*, vol. 2, trans. John Cottingham, Robert Stoothoff, and Dugald Murdoch. Copyright 1984. Reprinted by permission of Cambridge University Press. / Quine, W. V. O. "Posits and Reality." *The Ways of Paradox and Other Essays*, rev. edn, ed. W. V. O. Quine, 1976. Copyright 1966, 1976 by the President and Fellows of Harvard College. Reprinted by permission of Harvard University Press, Cambridge, MA. / Aune, Bruce. "Is There a Problem About Knowledge of the External World?" *Knowledge, Mind, and Nature*, Random House, 1967. Reprinted with permission of The McGraw-Hill Companies. / *Chapter 5*: Mill, John Stuart. *A System of Logic. Collected Works of John Stuart Mill*, vol. 7, ed. J. M. Robson. Reprinted by permission of the University of Toronto Press. / Hempel, Carl G. *Philosophy of Natural Science*, 1966. Reprinted by permission of Prentice-Hall, Inc., Upper Saddle River, New Jersey. / Popper, Karl. "Philosophy of Science: A Personal Report." *British Philosophy in Mid-Century: A Cambridge Symposium*, ed. C. M. Mace. Copyright Karl R. Popper 1957. Reprinted with permission from the estate of Sir Karl Popper. / Kuhn, Thomas. *The Structure of Scientific Revolutions*, 2nd edn, copyright 1970. Reprinted with permission of the University of Chicago Press. / Smart, J. J. C. "Physics and Reality." *Our Place in the Universe* (1989). Reprinted with permission of Blackwell Publishers, Oxford. / *Chapter 6*: Nietzsche, Friedrich. *Beyond Good and Evil*, trans. Walter Kaufmann. Copyright 1966 by Random House, Inc. Reprinted by permission. / Nietzsche, Friedrich. *On the Genealogy of Morals*, trans. Walter Kaufmann and R. J. Hollingdale. Copyright 1967 by Random House, Inc. Reprinted by permission. / Ayer, A. J. *Philosophical Essays*. Copyright 1954. Reprinted by permission of Macmillan Press Ltd. / Bambrough, Renford. "A Proof of the Objectivity of Morals." *American Journal of Jurisprudence*, 1969. Reprinted by permission of the American Journal of Jurisprudence. / Dworkin, Ronald. "Lord Devlin and the Enforcement of Morals." *The Yale Law Journal*, vol. 75, no. 5, 1966. Reprinted by permission of The Yale Law Journal Company and Fred B. Rothman & Company.

/ *Chapter 7*: Plato. *The Republic*, trans. G. M. A. Grube. Reprinted by permission of Hackett Publishing Co., Inc. All rights reserved. / Hobbes, Thomas. *Leviathan*, ed. Michael Oakeshott. Copyright 1962 by Macmillan Publishing Company. Reprinted with the permission of Simon & Schuster. / Dargo, George. *Law in the New Republic: Private Law and the Public Estate*. Copyright 1983. Reprinted with permission of The McGraw-Hill Companies. / Reich, Charles A. "The New Property." *The Yale Law Journal*, vol. 73, 1964. Reprinted by permission of The Yale Law Journal Company and Fred B. Rothman & Company. / Sandel, Michael. "Morality and the Liberal Ideal." *The New Republic*, vol. 190. Copyright 1984, The New Republic, Inc. Reprinted by permission. / Young, Iris Marion. "Impartiality and the Civic Public." *Feminism as Critique*, ed. Seyla Benhabib and Drucilla Cornell. Copyright 1987. Reprinted by permission of the University of Minnesota Press and Blackwell Publishers, Oxford, for Polity Press. / *Chapter 8*: Marx, Karl. Preface to *A Contribution to the Critique of Political Economy*, trans. Maurice Dobb. Progress Publishers, Moscow, 1970. / Marx, Karl and Engels, Friedrich. *The Communist Manifesto*, 1948. Reprinted by permission of International Publishers Co. / Marx, Karl. *Critique of the Gotha Program*. Progress Publishers, Moscow, 1971. / Rawls, John. *A Theory of Justice*. Copyright 1971 by the President and Fellows of Harvard College. Reprinted by permission of Harvard University Press, Cambridge, MA. / Nozick, Robert. *Anarchy, State, and Utopia*. Copyright 1974 by Basic Books, Inc. Reprinted by permission of Basic Books, a division of HarperCollins Publishers, Inc.

The editors wish to thank Steve Smith, the commissioning editor at Blackwell, for suggesting this project. It is unusual for members of a department to collaborate in this way, and we are grateful to Steve for his confidence in us and for his support for the book. Thanks also go to Mary Riso who saw the book through the various stages up to publication and to Sherry Ledbetter for secretarial assistance. Finally, we were blessed by a superb chief copy-editor, Margaret Aherne, whose careful and informed reading of the manuscript improved it immeasurably.

Introduction

A person's first exposure to philosophy can be like entering an unfamiliar room in which a conversation has been going on for quite some time. Even if one knows the general topic that is under discussion, one does not know how the discussion got started or what the most important people have had to say.

Assumption: You are someone who has never studied philosophy. The room you are entering, as it were, is unfamiliar. So before you pick this book up, you have little idea of what's to be found inside. You know that the book is an introduction to philosophy, but you know almost nothing of the subject. Perhaps you think philosophy has something to do with taking a resigned or stoical attitude towards life's misfortunes, being "philosophical" in the face of difficulty. Or perhaps you think it has something to do with religion. Either way, your conception of philosophy is quite uninformed. Before you put this book down, if it has done its job, you should be well informed about philosophy. This book is designed to introduce you to philosophy – to make the room familiar. It is about how philosophers think and reason; it is about what philosophers as philosophers say and believe.

Let's get started.

What's in a Word?

"Philosophy" is one word but we must distinguish two primary meanings. We must distinguish between philosophy as a possession or something *had*, and philosophy as an activity or something *done*. In the first sense, "philosophy" refers to the substance of people's beliefs, attitudes, and concepts. In the second it refers to reflective criticism of the substance of people's beliefs, attitudes, and concepts. One may engage in the activity in order to secure the possession. One may do philosophy to have a philosophy.

"Substance" means elementary or basic. It refers to the elements out of which something is constructed and without which it cannot be maintained. Just as a house or car has elements, people's beliefs, attitudes, and concepts have elements. So when we say that "philosophy," in its first sense, means the substance of people's beliefs, we mean elementary beliefs or basic attitudes out of which other beliefs and attitudes are formed and through which they are maintained.

Consider, for example, the issue of free will. Some people believe that we always are free in our decisions and actions; whatever you decide and do is up to you. Others believe that human behavior is unfree; nothing you decide or do is up to you. Still others claim that some of what we do is free, some is unfree. Ideally, philosophically, these beliefs about freedom have a basis in other beliefs: they rest on more elementary attitudes about the nature and purpose of decision and the character of natural laws. Even if your elementary beliefs about decisions and the laws of nature are vague and not fully determinate, that is no reason to stunt their emergence or to refuse to acknowledge their potential existence and need for development. However, this raises issues about what it means to do philosophy, to which we now turn.

On Doing Philosophy

You are introduced to philosophy as a possession when you are introduced to elementary beliefs of philosophers; when you are introduced to Sartre's libertarianism, St Thomas Aquinas's theism, and Marx's critique of capitalism. You are introduced to philosophy as an activity when you are trained to do philosophy. As you will quickly discover, however, it is difficult to distinguish between being introduced to philosophy as something possessed and as something done, for, in truth, there is no sharp line between possessing and doing philosophy. Suppose, for example, you read Jean-Paul Sartre (1905–80) to find out what he thinks about human freedom. You try to discover his views and opinions on the topic, but the possibilities of classification and interpretation are difficult and vexing. Is Sartre's version of libertarianism the same as that of other philosophers who call themselves libertarians? Does Sartre really mean it when he says that we choose to be born? What could he possibly mean by that and why would he say it? A careful reading of a philosopher plunges you into doing philosophy: plunges you into thinking for yourself about the issues the philosopher discusses.

So what, then, does it mean to *do philosophy*? Philosophical activity often focuses on the meaning of elementary beliefs, their rational basis and coherence, and their connections with other beliefs or convictions; it involves assessing, creating, design-ing, and refining the substance of one's beliefs. Being trained to do philosophy is, as a contemporary teacher of philosophy puts it:

> learning how to ask and re-ask questions until meaningful answers begin to appear. It is learning how to relate materials . . . It is learning how to reject fallacious . . . claims – to reject them no matter how prestigious the authority who holds them or how deeply one would personally like to believe them.[1]

"Pretend what we may," wrote William James (1842–1910), one of the great figures of late nineteenth- and early twentieth-century philosophy, "the whole person within us is at work when we do philosophy."[2]

Every person has *some* elementary beliefs or convictions even if the scope of most people's convictions is limited to issues of daily bread. Most of us, for example, have beliefs about the life we desire and the values to which we aspire, but our deliberations about these matters usually fall short of *doing* philosophy. When you do philosophy you try to render those beliefs and values systematic and informed, to discover alternatives that might be overlooked, and to investigate what rational support might exist for them.

Another illustration will clarify the above remarks. Asked whether you believe that people cease to exist at death, you may reply, "Yes, death ends our existence." Asked what you mean by ending existence, you may respond by saying that you have not given the idea much thought, but you are convinced that people are extinguished at death. Or you may offer the beginnings of an articulate response: you may refer to the brain. You may claim that once the human brain dies, the person is extinguished; no living brain, no person. Much in either response may stem from accidents of your birth. You inherit a conception of death from your surrounding culture or sub-culture. People born in the Middle Ages, say, in Eng-land at the end of the thirteenth century, believed in the soul and its immortality; those sitting next to you in class may believe in brain and mortality. Someone from a devout Christian family may believe in death and resurrection; someone raised as a Hindu may believe in death and reincarnation. Your cultural inheritance may give you many of your elementary beliefs, but it does not give you a clear arti-culation of the meaning of these beliefs or their rational basis. For that, you need to do philosophy.

Accidents of birth aside, it is unwise to hold unexamined, inexplicit elementary beliefs; it is imprudent not to give the substance of your beliefs some careful thought and perhaps even to replace or revise your beliefs, if their credentials seem weak or identities nebulous. If your basic commitments, unbeknownst to you, are

---

[1] James L. Christian, *Philosophy: An Introduction to the Art of Wondering* (New York: Holt, Rinehart & Winston, 1977), p. xvii.

[2] William James, *Essays in Pragmatism* (New York: Hafner, 1965), p. 24.

incoherent or riddled with inconsistencies, there is a good chance your life will be messy and haphazard. This is because you will live according to those commitments. To mix metaphors, "a healthy garden of beliefs requires well-nourished roots."[3] You may live more satisfyingly – healthily, as it were – if you make explicit and examine your elementary beliefs and convictions at some time in your life. Indeed, as you hold this book in your hands, now might be a good time to begin to do that.

We can express this idea another way. Life is full of conflicts. Some conflicts get in our way and cause confusion. The most bothersome are internal conflicts – conflicts within yourself. For example, is death something I can survive or does it extinguish me? You are pulled in two directions. Part of you says that death extinguishes; part of you hopes to survive. Some types and amounts of internal conflict count as amiable characteristics of a person; they contribute to curiosity, tolerance, and open-mindedness. However, certain types and degrees of internal conflict wreak havoc. William James observes:

> There are persons whose existence is little more than a series of zigzags, as now one tendency and now another gets the upper hand. Their spirit wars with their flesh, they wish for incompatibles, wayward impulses interrupt their most deliberate plans, and their lives are one long drama of repentance and of effort to repair misdemeanors and mistakes.[4]

Philosophy can render personal conflict less intense and dramatic. As the twentieth-century American philosopher John Dewey (1859–1952) said, "it does not offer a table of commandments in a catechism."[5] But it does encourage greater coherence and consistency in belief and conviction.

Accidents of Birth or Circumstance

What about accidents of birth or circumstance? How much do they shape a philosopher's work? The answer is complex, and only in part because the influence of these accidents varies from one individual to another. It is impossible to *completely* dissociate philosophical reflection – doing philosophy – from accidents of birth. Even among professional philosophers of the sorts represented in this book, doing philosophy is tied to personal and social circumstance.

Philosophy was born in ancient Greece, and some of its first practitioners, like Plato (428–348 BC), were people of leisure. Plato was also wealthy; his mentor, Socrates (469–399 BC), was not. The discipline and study of philosophy played a critical role in setting up universities in the Middle Ages, where it was inseparably

---

[3] W. V. Quine and J. S. Ullian, *The Web of Belief* (New York: Random House, 1978), p. 126.

[4] William James, *Varieties of Religious Experience* (New York: Penguin, 1982), p. 169.

[5] John Dewey, *Theory of the Moral Life* (New York: Holt, Rinehart & Winston, 1970), p. 7f.

connected with Christian theology. At the University of Paris, for example, in the mid-thirteenth century "natural philosophy" (philosophy without theology) was prohibited as heretical, though the ban was dropped when the Dominican priest, Thomas Aquinas (*c.*1224–74), who had sympathies for the natural philosophy of Aristotle (384–322 BC), joined the faculty. "Scholasticism," as medieval philosophy was called, meant the pursuit of philosophy under the guidance and authority of the Scriptures. By contrast, in the seventeenth and eighteenth centuries philosophers tended to be persons of commerce, politics, and public affairs, not priests or clerics. Towards the end of the nineteenth century, philosophical journals and professional philosophical societies began to proliferate, and an intimate relationship formed between doing philosophy and teaching philosophy. The norm now at the end of the twentieth century is for professional philosophers to belong to philosophy departments in colleges and universities. Spinoza (1632–77) was a lens grinder; Leibniz (1646–1716) was supported by the patronage of kings and princes. However, philosophers today, such as Jerry Fodor and Daniel Dennett, whose work appears in this text, engage in the discipline as faculty in universities.

One thing that the academic housing of professional philosophy has meant is that the Church has lost its position in the philosophical world. Arguably, its place has been taken by science. Much of contemporary philosophy consists of adding clarity and understanding to the foundations and methods of empirical science. The scientific world-view provides the materials for many of the basic beliefs that contemporary philosophy examines, just as religion provided the materials for many of the basic beliefs that medieval philosophy examined. The case of Bertrand Russell (1872–1970), one of the most important philosophers of the twentieth century, is representative.

Before studying philosophy, Russell was a mathematician, and he became interested in philosophical problems that arose in mathematics. He wrote the monumental three-volume *Principia Mathematica* on the foundations of mathematics with A. N. Whitehead in 1910–13 and his *Introduction to Mathematical Philosophy* in 1918. Throughout his life, he was much taken up with issues in mathematics, physics, and experimental psychology. "Philosophy," he once said, "has not achieved positive results" as compared with empirical science.[6]

Russell did not mean to demean philosophy; he loved it. His remark about positive results was a way of saying that philosophy is not a search for scientific facts: results about the genetic determination of eye color, the speed of light, the fertility of the soil, or the set of natural numbers. Philosophy, for Russell, involved searching for reasoned attitudes towards scientific facts, attitudes which, though defended by analysis and argument, are not provable mathematically or by laboratory experiment. Russell, for example, knew all sorts of facts in mathematics, even facts about esoteric numbers such as transfinite cardinals. (Transfinite cardinals measure the size of infinite sets.) He sometimes worried, however, about whether mathematicians' talk about numbers was talk about things which exist only in their

---

[6] Bertrand Russell, *The Problems of Philosophy* (Oxford: Oxford University Press, 1954), p. 154.

minds. Knives and forks are concrete things located in space and time. But what about the number 7? What about transfinite cardinals?

Russell argued that numbers are just as real as knives and forks, though real in a different way than concrete physical objects. A person can create or invent an idea; but mathematicians cannot create numbers. Numbers are "out there" waiting to be discovered and described. They are not mere ideas. He said, "Arithmetic must be discovered in just the same sense in which Columbus discovered the West Indies, and we no more create numbers than he created West Indians."[7] There is no mathematical or experimental proof of the mind-independence of numbers, according to Russell, but he believed that there are good philosophical arguments for this mind-independence. For Russell, philosophy of mathematics was the search for reasoned attitudes to take towards the nature and reality of numbers.

Accidents of birth or culture provide circumstances which influence how philosophy is done. Because of the overwhelming social and intellectual presence of the Catholic Church in the Middle Ages, for medieval philosophers doing philosophy began with ideas found in the Scriptures. Russell's interest in philosophy of mathematics is explained by the fact that he came to the study of philosophy through mathematics. For many influential philosophers of today, the study of philosophy means taking science seriously. Either they have had an antecedent interest in science, or they have been impressed by the theoretical and practical successes of science, especially in the twentieth century.

Circumstances of culture and accidents of birth may be very influential without completely determining either how philosophers work or the topics on which they write. One way to achieve some measure of impersonal objectivity, of truth independent of birth and culture, is to examine philosophies developed in other places and times. Philosophers find common ground in their shared conceptual heritage. The great philosophers of all ages, almost without exception, have engaged the ideas and arguments of their predecessors. For example, Aristotle's writings are filled with discussions of his predecessors – and this includes not only his teacher Plato but a host of lesser figures whose works have not survived the ravages of time. Immanuel Kant (1724–1804), the greatest philosopher of the Enlightenment, tells us that the turning-point in his intellectual life was his engagement with the ideas of the Scottish philosopher David Hume (1711–76). The influential twentieth-century American philosopher Wilfrid Sellars (1912–89) saw himself as restating Kantian themes in a manner appropriate for the twentieth century. Throughout history, philosophers have found a framework for their own positions in the work of predecessors. Predecessors provide contemporary philosophers with models of philosophic reasoning that can be assessed and reassessed, added to and subtracted from.

It is a curious feature of philosophy that it takes its predecessors so seriously and yet often disagrees so profoundly with those very thinkers. No mathematician would say that Newton was wrong about calculus; no biologist would say that Pasteur was fundamentally mistaken about the causes of disease. By contrast, this

---

[7] Bertrand Russell, "Is Position in Space and Time Absolute or Relative?" *Mind* 10 (1901), p. 312.

sort of thing happens in philosophy all the time. Aristotle rejected Plato's views about universals; Kant maintained that Hume was fundamentally mistaken about the relation of cause and effect; almost every philosopher after Descartes believes that Descartes failed in his attempt to show that we do in fact have knowledge about the world. The explanation for this feature of philosophy is to be found in the dual nature of philosophy as an activity and a set of fundamental or elementary beliefs. An important part of doing philosophy is critically evaluating the philosophical belief systems of others. For someone aspiring to make an original contribution to philosophy, this is an indispensable first step in developing his or her own views. The imperfections of human reason and the profound nature of the questions under discussion make it likely that even the greatest philosophers have made important errors. Discovery of those errors, like the falsification of an important hypothesis in science, can be an indispensable step on the journey toward the truth.

Three Rules of Thumb and One Special Number

How to get started? A useful rule of thumb in doing philosophy as a beginner is to consider Big Ideas, those that stand out like great mountains from the plain – concepts like God, Death, Mind, Freedom, Knowledge, and Morality. Once we consider them, they naturally suggest whole areas of philosophical inquiry. Another useful rule of thumb is to examine Big Names, figures in the history of philosophy commonly classified as major contributors – philosophers like Nietzsche, Socrates, and Locke. Both rules become one rule embraced by the editors and collegial authors of this book: *consider big ideas of big names*. Examine the basic beliefs of major philosophers. Some of their philosophies are cast in an iconoclastic vein: Friedrich Nietzsche's (1844–1900), for example, attempts to call into question our most basic beliefs about morality. Some are reverent theories: Socrates, for example, urges respect for religious attitudes about survival of bodily death. Still others strive to offer credentials for trusting direct experience: John Stuart Mill (1806–73), for instance, puts forward a defense of observation-based scientific method, while others, such as René Descartes (1596–1650), search for basic beliefs which are absolutely secure against doubt or skepticism.

How should we consider or examine the big ideas of big names? Another good rule of thumb may be called The Rule of Comparative Philosophy. To follow this rule is to meet the basic beliefs and arguments of one philosopher with those of others. A natural way to do this is to put a major philosopher of the past in conversation with other philosophers, especially contemporary figures. The aim is twofold: to appreciate the philosophical insights of a major historical figure and to assess the significance of his contribution by measuring it against successive developments – in effect, to compare philosophy *then* with philosophy *now*.

Which big ideas? Which big names? There is no list that all philosophers would agree on. But there may be a non-arbitrary number if one just is beginning to learn about philosophy. What number?

For the answer we rely on numerology, so to speak. In 1956 George Miller, a psychologist at Princeton University, published in the *Psychological Review* a paper with the engaging title of "The Magical Number Seven, Plus or Minus Two: Some Limits on Our Capacity to Process Information." Miller claimed that people's ability to remember and adequately process information seemed to undergo a critical change at about the level of seven items. Beneath that number, in units or chunks of less than seven, people could readily deal with information; but above it, people were likely to fail. Miller suggested that the number 7 was no random accident. It identified natural constraints of the human mind: in his words, "a limit that keeps our channel capacities in this general range."

We may have hoped for a Miller's Tale of seven thinkers with seven ideas or basic convictions. However, perhaps beginning students could manage eight (remember, plus or minus two) and their instructors may then, if they wish, subtract to seven. So we offer Seven Plus One.

Surely there are more or other philosophical figures and ideas that could be included. We have tried to assemble a mix of those that reflect some of the best work done in past and current philosophy, work which should both deepen a student's daily reflections and broaden the scope of his or her intellectual interests.

Philosophy done comparatively enables us to transcend the accidental moment. It enlarges the present to years, decades, centuries, and to other cultures. Instead of being locked into our own time and circumstance, philosophy done comparatively and historically offers access to basic or elementary convictions that we are unlikely to have entertained or employed on our own.

How to Read and Use this Book

The beginner needs someone to pull her aside and say, "Here's what's going on in philosophy." Each chapter begins with a lead essay designed to do this – to make its corner of the room, as it were, familiar. It introduces a traditional philosophical problem or gives an overview of a particular philosophical issue and one historically important philosopher's contribution to it. Each chapter also includes selections from the writings of the historical figure who is the subject of the lead essay and selections from the writings of other philosophers, some contemporary, some not. The selections, along with some discussion questions, are introduced at the end of the lead essay by a brief discussion of how they relate to the major themes of the chapter; there are also suggestions for further reading. What, then, are the issues and problems by which this book introduces philosophy?

Chapter 1 is about mind, body, and death. Are persons immaterial souls or minds who could survive the deaths of their bodies, or are they purely material objects who perish when the body dies? Chapter 1 considers what both Socrates and Descartes had to say about this and explores how contemporary philosophers have thought about the nature of the mind and what death really means. The selection from Jerry Fodor considers the impact of developments in modern psychology and computer science on the traditional question of the nature of mind.

Chapter 2 is about free will. Is everything we do completely determined by our heredity and environment or are some of our actions genuinely free? This question is nearly as old as the question about the nature of mind. Despite that fact, the historical figure who anchors this chapter is the twentieth-century philosopher and novelist Jean-Paul Sartre. Although the school of philosophy that Sartre is most closely associated with – Existentialism – is no longer active, his contribution to this perennial philosophical problem is an enduring one. The lead essay in chapter 2 explains that contribution and outlines alternative views on the issue. The readings include selections from Sartre's *magnum opus*, *Being and Nothingness*, a brief selection from the arch-determinist of the Enlightenment, Pierre Simon de Laplace, and two readings from contemporary philosophers. The latter include extensive reflections on the nature of freedom that is in dispute in the debate.

Chapter 3 confronts the central question of philosophical theology: Can the existence of God be proved? The thought of the greatest of all the medieval philosophers, St Thomas Aquinas, serves as a point of departure for the lead essay and for the readings in this chapter. The essay and the readings of chapter 3 articulate and critically evaluate traditional arguments for the existence of God. They also discuss the main argument against the existence of God, the so-called Problem of Evil, which can be framed as a question: If there is evil in the world, how is it possible for there to be an all-perfect God? The chapter also considers a variety of ways in which believers have responded to the problem of evil.

Chapter 4 concerns the fundamental question of the branch of philosophy known as epistemology: can the human mind really know anything at all? Without doubt, we have a variety of beliefs and opinions about the world, but do any of them count as real knowledge? The skeptic denies that we have any real knowledge, and the challenge of skepticism as it arises in the philosophy of René Descartes is the main subject of the lead essay in chapter 4. Substantial excerpts from Descartes' *Meditations* are also included in this chapter, as well as selections from the writings of three philosophers (Russell, Quine, and Aune) whose professional lives span the twentieth century.

One of the most important developments in the Western intellectual tradition is the rise of modern science beginning around the late sixteenth century. Modern science raises a number of philosophically important questions that are addressed in chapter 5. One of those concerns the scientific method. What is distinctive about the kind of reasoning employed in the sciences? And does science tell us about the true nature of physical reality? The latter question is pressing in light of two facts: (i) contemporary science describes entities and processes on both the large and the small scale that are literally unobservable. No one has ever seen an electron, much less the more exotic elementary particles posited by contemporary physicists. Nor has anyone ever observed the processes of stellar evolution or continental drift. So, how do we know that such entities exist and such processes have really occurred? (ii) The history of science is the history of radical change in fundamental theories about the nature of physical reality. Like a suspect who keeps changing his story, scientists have told us very different stories over time about the nature of physical reality. Are they telling us the truth now? And if so, how do we – or for that matter, how do they – know? Questions about the scientific method and what science tells us about the nature of physical reality dominate chapter 5.

Historically important philosophers often challenge conventional thinking. For example, in the first Meditation, Descartes disputes our claims to know anything at all about the world. Chapter 6 is about perhaps the most radical challenge to conventional views about morality in the history of philosophy – that posed by Friedrich Nietzsche. Nietzsche expresses contempt for what conventional morality praises and celebrates what it condemns. The lead essay in this chapter explains why and evaluates his challenge to conventional morality. In the process, it raises broader questions about the nature and foundations of morality. Those questions are further pursued in the readings, which come from a variety of historical and contemporary sources.

Since the time of the ancient Greeks, philosophers have debated the proper role of the state, that is, the government, in the life of a society. This is the main topic of chapter 7. Plato, for example, held that the purpose of the state is to promote harmony and virtue among its citizens. A popular modern view, first fully articulated in the late seventeenth century by John Locke (1632–1704), is rather different. It holds that the purpose of government is to protect and enforce certain natural rights that each of us has simply in virtue of the fact that we are human. On Locke's view (and those of the American Founding Fathers who took their cue from Locke), those rights include the right to life, liberty, and property. These rights have a divine origin in that they are bestowed on us by God. Even if Locke and others are right in holding that the main purpose of government is to protect and enforce people's rights, there remain important unresolved questions. In particular, the content of these rights, especially the right to private property, has always been a contentious matter. Some have held that the right to private property is virtually absolute, which implies that the role of government in the life of a society should be strictly limited to the criminal law and the enforcement of contracts. By contrast, others have held that it is the right of private property that is strictly limited and that the public interest can legitimately constrain private property rights. This controversy, and how it has informed the American system of government, are the main themes of the lead essay in chapter 7. The readings in this chapter are of two sorts. The first four are from historically important figures on the traditional philosophical question about the purpose of government and its role in the life of a society. The other readings are from contemporary sources. They explore some of the controversies within and about the philosophical tradition of natural rights associated with Locke.

Chapter 8 is about the question of justice in the distribution of wealth and income. How should wealth and income be distributed in a society? Many critics of the existing system have claimed that the current distribution of wealth and income is unjust, typically on the grounds that this distribution is highly unequal.

A few have enormous economic and political power while the vast majority has very little of either. It is perhaps surprising that Karl Marx, perhaps the most famous and influential critic of the existing order – what he called the capitalist system – did *not* make this charge of injustice. Instead, Marx believed that large-scale social change was coming that would render the question of distributive justice obsolete. The lead essay in this chapter explains why Marx thought this and criticizes his dismissive attitude toward the issue of distributive justice and related questions about rights. The readings in this chapter include selections from Marx and from the writings of two of the most influential contemporary philosophers on the topics of distributive justice and rights. Chapters 7 and 8 complement each other, coming at some of the same issues from somewhat different angles.

This book may be used in a number of different ways. Although the lead essays are designed to introduce the readings, an instructor may prefer to take over this task himself or herself, in which case these essays may be treated as optional rather than required readings. Or, the essays could be the main focus with less attention to the collateral readings. In addition, though the chapters are topically arranged in one natural order, they are independent of one another and can be read and studied in any order.

We've gotten started. Let's continue.

1

Mind, Body, and Death

George Graham, "Socrates and the Soul of Death"

Readings

Plato, *Phaedo* (selection)

Thomas Nagel, "Death"

Gareth B. Matthews, "Life and Death as the Arrival and Departure of the Psyche"

René Descartes, *Letter to Princess Elizabeth, Principles of Philosophy, The Passions of the Soul* (selections)

Jerry A. Fodor, "The Mind–Body Problem"

Jacques Louis David, *The Death of Socrates*. The Metropolitan Museum of Art, Catharine Lorillard Wolfe Collection, Wolfe Fund, 1931 (31.45)

GEORGE GRAHAM

Socrates and the Soul of Death

Now it is time that we were going. I to die and you to live. But which of us has the happier prospect is unknown to anyone but God.
Socrates, *Apology*

That we die frightens many of us. In life the whiff of lilacs, the warmth of the sun, the taste of honey, then death. It stings.

This chapter is about what the first truly famous philosopher, Socrates, thought about death. It is about whether death is bad for the person who is dead. It is also about whether persons, including dead persons, are something over and above their brains and bodies.

Is it possible, as Socrates believed, for people to survive death? If persons, as Socrates also believed, are something over and above brains and bodies, personal survival seems possible. However, if we are nothing over and above brains and bodies, death snuffs us out.

1 The Most Famous Death in the History of Philosophy

No other death in the history of philosophy has left so lasting an impression on Western philosophical consciousness as the death of Socrates. Socrates faced death with complete and total equanimity, free of fear, anxiety, or remorse. In the words of one intellectual historian:

The picture of the dying Socrates must have afforded his pupils, in the highest degree, what it now after centuries affords to us – a simple testimony to the greatness of the human mind, to the power of philosophy, and to the victory of a spirit pious and pure. (Zeller 1962: 236)

Who was Socrates? Why did he face death with equanimity?

Who was Socrates?

Socrates was born in the city of Athens in Greece in 469 BC. His life was brought to an end in prison there, by his own hand, in 399 BC at the age of 71. A death sentence had been meted out in court for him. He elected to end his life by drinking poison rather than staining the conscience of his executioner with the knowledge that he had killed Socrates.

Socrates was an immensely influential teacher of philosophy though he wrote nothing. We know of Socrates primarily through his most talented pupil, the world's second most famous philosopher, Plato (428–348 BC), who admired him as only a deeply appreciative student admires a teacher. In various writings of Plato, which are called "dialogues" because they are written in the form of conversations on philosophical topics, Socrates is the chief speaker or interlocutor. This is especially true in a series of three dialogues describing the last days of his life, which are entitled the *Apology*, *Crito*, and *Phaedo*. The first is Plato's version of Socrates' speech to the jury at his trial. The second and third depict conversations which Socrates had with friends who visited him in prison, including his last conversation, after which he drank the poison to end his life.

The mind and heart of Plato inform his depiction of Socrates. So it is not easy to distinguish Socrates' philosophy from Plato's or to view Socrates' life apart from his student's appreciative reconstruction. Caution about such distinctions aside, the following picture of Socrates emerges in the dialogues.

According to Plato the political leaders of Athens believed that Socrates undermined the support and allegiance which they needed to rule the city. He was found guilty, or framed guilty, of a kind of intellectual civil disobedience: of disrespect for what the leaders perceived to be the central and necessary interests of their leadership.

Two of Socrates' teachings in particular got him politically into trouble. The first is that people should think less about trying to get ahead in the world and more about moral character and being good people. The second is that the only sure way to protect one's character is to be prepared to die when that character is threatened or jeopardized. Ordinary Athenian citizens, Socrates feared, valued material possessions, safety, and comfort more than character. Socrates maintained that one must prize character above life itself. As he said:

You are mistaken . . . if you think that a man who is worth anything ought to spend his time weighing up the prospects of life and death. He has only one thing to consider in performing any action; that is, whether he is acting rightly or wrongly, like a good man or a bad one. (A: 28)

And again:

The difficulty is not . . . to escape death; the real difficulty is to escape from doing wrong, which is far more fleet of foot. (A: 39)

Moral character. Personal sacrifice. Hardly the material for a death sentence. However, the city leaders believed that these two teachings masked a deep personal skepticism in Socrates about the gods of the official state polytheistic religion. Thereby, they feared, he exerted negative influence on young pupils, encouraging them to question authority in all of its forms including political. According to Plato the deposition against Socrates at his trial read:

Socrates is guilty of corrupting the minds of the young, and of believing in deities of his own invention instead of the gods recognized by the State. (A: 24)

These and related charges against Socrates had little or nothing to do with the truth. Socrates respected religion. However, political power does not always track the truth. So Socrates was condemned to death.

True, Socrates' respect for religion was ambiguous. According to Socrates, reasons for believing in gods do not *prove* or demonstrate the truth of some particular religious conception (such as Athenian polytheism). Socrates maintained that there are two kinds of truths, which may be called "provable" and "unprovable." Truths about, for example, which diets contribute to bodily health or whether two sides of a triangle intersect are provable, whereas truths about gods are unprovable. At most, when in the domain of the unprovable, we may entertain *plausible* or *reasonable* beliefs or expectations, but we never can demonstrate the truth of those beliefs or expectations. On matters of the unprovable, he said, "we must brace ourselves and do our best" (P: 90).

Socrates claimed that the unprovable includes much that is near and dear to the human heart. It includes questions about not just the divine but death and what happens to persons who are dead.

No one knows with regard to death whether it is really the greatest blessing that can happen to a man; but people dread it as though they were certain that it is the greatest evil . . . If I were to claim to be wiser than my neighbor in any respect, it would be in this – that not possessing any real knowledge of what comes after death, I am also conscious that I do not possess it. (A: 29)

What happens after death cannot be proven. People tend to fear it. But its real nature is uncertain. Since its real nature is uncertain, argued Socrates, there will always be some attitudes towards it which have to be accepted without proof. There may be reasons to believe one thing rather than another. However, these reasons must fall short of demonstration.

Socrates' deadly equanimity

Let's turn to our second question. Why did Socrates face death with equanimity?

Socrates faced death with equanimity because of two convictions. Though he classified them as unprovable, he felt safe and secure in living, and dying, in accord with them.

1. The most fundamental conviction is that *we*, as persons, or "souls" (or "psyches") as Socrates called us, despite bodily death and decay, continue to exist after death. Personal survival does not mean that persons are necessarily happy after death. Socrates used popular Athenian religious imagery to convey his sense that people who live lives unworthy of themselves – people who bring dishonor or indignity upon themselves – may be cycled after death through unhappy reincarnations until they merit and achieve a happy afterlife. Was his talk of reincarnation intended merely as forceful metaphor or to illustrate literal transformations after death? Scholars and historians of Greek philosophy don't know. Regardless, however, of whether Socrates really did believe in reincarnation, the point is that for him there is no *guarantee* of happiness after death. Happiness has to be earned.

2. Socrates' second conviction is related to, but distinguishable from, the first conviction about post-mortem survival. He variously stated the conviction. It is a conviction about whether death is bad – an evil or misfortune – for the person who is dead. At his trial he announced: "We are quite mistaken in supposing death to be an evil" (A: 40).

The conviction can be expressed as follows:

Being dead is not bad for the person who is dead.

Many readers of Plato's dialogues find the second conviction implausible. Death in the minds of many is something fearful. How can it not be bad?

What may be said on behalf of Socrates' two convictions? Let us examine the second first.

2 Why Death is Not Bad

Although Socrates denied that death extinguishes, in the history of Western philosophy one of the most popular arguments in support of the thesis that death is not bad for the person who is dead rests on the premise that death is extinction. The argument is owed to the Greek philosopher Epicurus (341–271 BC). It was later reiterated and refined by the Roman philosopher and poet Lucretius (c.96–55 BC). If the argument is strong, it provides solid ground for holding that death is not bad for the person who is dead. Examining the Epicurus–Lucretius argument from a Socratic point of view will eventually help us to understand Socrates' own position.

The Epicurus–Lucretius argument may be called *the argument from extinction* and can be expressed as follows:

1   Each and every person stops existing at death. Death extinguishes. Epicurus
     said, "when death comes, then we do not exist."
2   If a person does not exist, he or she does not have experiences (good or bad).
     No you, no your experience.
3   So, being dead is not an experience. It is a complete blank.
4   Meanwhile, the only things that are bad for a person are bad experiences. What
     you don't experience is not bad for you.
5   Therefore, being dead is not bad for the person who is dead. In the words of
     Lucretius, "he who exists not, cannot become miserable."

If the extinction argument is sound, then death is not bad for the dead. Consider, for illustration, the bad of suffering. Some people fear that the dead suffer in
an afterlife. However, according to the extinction argument suffering is not part of
being dead (although of course it may be part of dying) because no experience is
part of being dead. The dead don't exist. Families remember the dead. Tombs house
their remains. Monuments honor them. But all the while dead people themselves
are non-existent. There is no afterlife and no suffering after death.

Is the extinction argument's way of picturing death correct? There are three
main assumptions (premises #1, #2, and #4) behind the argument. Let's look at
them as Socrates would have looked at them.

According to Socrates the first assumption is false. Granted, Socrates admitted
that he could not *disprove* the first assumption; nevertheless he denied that we are
snuffed out just because our brains and bodies die and decay. He believed that we
survive death. Since survival is a big topic, we will turn to it later in the chapter.

What about the second premise? It is hard to imagine anyone sensibly opposing
the second premise. Existence is a precondition of experience. No you, no your
experience.

This brings us to the fourth premise. The fourth premise captures some common-
sense folk wisdom – "what you don't know can't hurt you", "ignorance is bliss" –
however Socrates, for one, flatly rejected the fourth premise. The assumption that
only bad experiences are bad for a person is, certainly, a central piece of the argument. If some *other* matter is bad, as Socrates himself claimed, then the extinction
argument is hollow at its core.

The question therefore to be asked is: What things other than bad experiences
are bad for people? Socrates offered the following answer.

One of the most striking facts about Socrates is that he insisted that people
should not focus on escaping from bad experiences but should prepare themselves
"to be as good as possible" (A: 39). "The really important thing," he claimed, "is
not to live but to . . . live honorably or rightly" (C: 48). "One must not even do
wrong when one is wronged" (C: 48).

Socrates had no criticism of people enjoying themselves and having good experiences. He himself loved libations. He maintained, however, that persons should
carry themselves throughout their lives with dignity and honor or sound moral
character (these notions were interchangeable for him). Failing to live honorably,

he believed, is bad for a person *even if* the person is not aware of (does not experience) their own dishonor. People, in the words of Michael Walzer in his book *Spheres of Justice* (1983):

> can't ignore standards, and we can't juggle the verdict. We do measure up, or we don't. Measuring up is a way of . . . holding one's head high. (Walzer 1983: 278)

According to Socrates, people should hold their heads high: make something of themselves: measure up. Being unable to hold one's head high, doing things which devalue or dishonor one's person, is bad for a person. And it is no good saying in the manner of the fourth premise that the dishonor isn't bad for us if we do not experience it. It is bad for us that we are dishonorable *period*. Such behavior diminishes ourselves as persons. It lessens us or stains our character.

Does Socrates' answer contain a valid reason for objecting to the fourth premise? To help to answer this question, consider the following imaginary experiment.

Suppose that there exists a machine in a room at Harvard University Medical School, the Harvard philosopher Robert Nozick's (1974: 42–5) imaginary "experience machine," with electrodes that can be attached to your brain so that you *feel* exactly as if you are having and doing whatever you want. You want to perform brilliantly on your first philosophy exam? The machine gives you sensations of writing a stunning exam and receiving the highest grade in the class. You wish an ideal marriage? Raise children who are the envy of the neighborhood? The experience machine is up to the task. It will give you the feelings of doing these things, day or night or for a lifetime.

Being hooked to the machine means that your life is a kind of fake. Your experience *to you* will seem just like the experience of acing the exam and marrying the person of your dreams. This is because the machine is responsible for the experience, which is why it is called an "experience machine," and not the exam or marriage.

Suppose you enter the room and hook yourself to the machine. Suppose your experience has all the subjective qualities of acing an exam and marrying the person of your dreams. But also suppose that without your knowing this, while hooked to the machine you miss the exam and your spouse deserts you. You become the laughingstock of everyone around you. Socrates would claim that this means you are severely diminished. You are not living as you should. You are failing to make something of yourself. In the *Phaedo*, for example, Socrates says that every "pleasure . . . has a sort of rivet" which nails the person to the pleasure and "pins" the person down. Socrates would object that being hooked to the experience machine means you are "riveted" or "pinned" to its pleasure. True, no bad experience happens to you. However, that's precisely his point. Experience aside, the bad of not measuring up happens to you. Consider how demeaning it is to say of someone, "His life is a disaster, but so what? He thinks he's a success."

If we concede Socrates' point, then we must reject the fourth premise that only bad *experiences* are bad for a person. Once we reject the fourth premise the entire argument from extinction is unglued. Death *may* be bad for the person who is dead even assuming that it extinguishes. This can be shown by the following line of reasoning, whose third premise is endorsed by both Epicurus and Lucretius (although not Socrates):

1   Suppose a person dies in a state or condition of dishonor. Then *either* (a) he or she can do something to regain their honor *or* (b) he or she can do nothing.
2   There is no way to regain honor – to measure up – if you do not exist.
3   Death extinguishes the person who is dead.
4   So, a person who dies in dishonor dies permanently dishonored.
5   Being dishonored is bad for a person even if she or he does not experience it.
6   Therefore, death is bad for the person who dies in dishonor.

However, what about Socrates himself? Didn't *he* say that death is *not* bad? Why did Socrates say *that*?

Remember a second troublesome feature of the Epicurus–Lucretius extinction argument from the Socratic point of view is that it assumes (premise #1 in the extinction argument, repeated as premise #3 in the second argument just above) that persons stop existing at death. They are snuffed out. Socrates rejected that assumption. So what argument for the non-badness of death did he offer in Epicurus' place?

If a person dies in dishonor beyond all capacity to make something of herself – if death is extinction – let's call such a death *irrevocably* dishonorable. If a person dies in dishonor but with the capacity still to make something of herself (perhaps by cycling through reincarnations) – that is, if death is not extinction – let's call such a death *revocably* dishonorable.

The distinction is important because it helps to explain why Socrates said that death is not bad, that is, not evil or a misfortune for the person who is dead. What Socrates meant is that death is not irrevocably dishonorable. It is dishonorable (when a person dies in dishonor) only revocably and revocable dishonor is not *really* bad as far as Socrates is concerned. It is a kind of pseudo-badness, for at a later time the person may restore her honor or dignity.

This brings us to the edge of the topic which I said earlier requires separate treatment: Socrates' conviction that people survive death. For him survival means that any dishonor which attaches to a person at death is revocable. People get, as it were, another chance to make something of themselves. This is partly why he said that death may be a "blessing" for the dead person. So let us now turn to Socrates' first conviction concerning survival of death.

3   Survival of Death

One can only wait and see, or alternately (which is not less likely) wait and not see.
(C. D. Broad)

21

Socrates' most famous and fundamental belief about death is that it is survived. People persist beyond the grave.

What is survival?

Before considering what Socrates said in favor of belief in survival, let us examine what Socrates meant by survival of death. The idea of personal survival is not transparently intelligible or unambiguous, as Socrates admitted to friends during his prison conversations. What, exactly, did he intend by the notion?

Unfortunately it is not always clear in Socrates (i.e. in Plato's depiction of Socrates) what survival is or means. This is partly because Socrates does not speak specifically of "persons" surviving. He speaks instead of "souls" which he equates with persons, and it is not always clear what souls – that is, persons – are supposed to be. Here, however, is how we shall describe the Socratic conviction that souls or persons survive.

Consider the following words or phrases:

- "Socrates"
- "the former teacher of Plato"
- "I" (spoken by Socrates)
- "you" (spoken by someone addressing Socrates)

According to Socrates, each and every one of these words or phrases stands for or denotes the same thing, namely a soul, the person Socrates. If Socrates survives death this means that he does so as himself: as Socrates: as the "I" spoken by him: as the former teacher of Plato: as the "you" (when addressed to Socrates).

Moreover, to survive death is to survive in such a manner that one is conscious of oneself *as oneself* after death. To *be* Socrates surviving – that is, more generally, to be a soul after death – is to survive self-consciously. Personal (soulful) survival is self-conscious survival.

To bring out what self-consciousness means, imagine that I am reading a newspaper and the paper reports that the Mafia have a contract on George Graham, a philosopher who teaches at the University of Alabama at Birmingham. But suppose I do not read carefully or attentively. I spot my name in the paper but I do not recognize the individual living under the shadow of the Mafia contract as me. I do not recognize the name *as mine*. I do not think "That's me!"

However, now let us suppose that it suddenly occurs to me that "George Graham" refers to me. I think, "I may be killed by the Mafia!" According to Socrates, in surviving death I am capable *after* death of thinking "I": of thinking "I was killed by the Mafia." To survive self-consciously is to survive with such thoughts, I-thoughts or self-reflexive thoughts, as it were.

Socrates' notion of survival is not out of the dictionary yet. At least one other component in the concept needs to be defined. Since the body, including the brain, decays and decomposes after death, in *my* surviving death in addition to me there is my body, a physical organism. So the question arises, what does Socrates think of the body, the organism? What role, if any, does it play in survival?

For Socrates, none. Socrates maintains that persons or souls are intimately related to bodies but do not need them to survive. Quite the contrary, the soul – the person – leaves or separates and becomes independent of the body at death. So although people and bodies are associated for a person's biological lifetime, body and soul are not one and the same thing. There is an important feature of souls which bodies lack. This is the capacity for post-mortem survival.

So what does Socratic survival mean? To sum up, in maintaining that persons or souls survive death Socrates means that persons or souls, that Socrates, you, and I, survive as ourselves. We survive with self-awareness (with self-recognition or I-thoughts). We survive without bodies.

Such is his idea. However, why endorse *that*? Why, one may ask, is Socrates so confident that people are capable of survival? Some philosophers hold that belief in personal survival is, to put it simply, a lot of sentimental hogwash. Bertrand Russell (1872–1970) wrote:

> Brief and powerless is Man's life; on him his race is slow, sure doom falls pitiless and dark. (Russell 1903: 172)

Why believe in survival rather than extinction at death? Why endorse Socrates over Russell?

Why believe in survival?

Irenaeus, a second-century Christian bishop, wrote: "our survival forever comes from His greatness, not from our nature." According to Irenaeus there is nothing about us, nothing inherent in us, which explains why we survive bodily death. We survive only because God miraculously makes us survive. Apart from God's intervention death is extinction.

Socrates would have disagreed with Irenaeus. Socrates contended that, divine intervention or no divine intervention, we survive death. This is because there is something about us, inherent in us, which explains why we survive. What is that something?

The something responsible for our survival is identified by Socrates in the *Phaedo* as the "simplicity" or "incompositeness" of the soul or of the "I" or person. Indeed, one of Socrates' main arguments for survival is sometimes called the *simplicity of the soul* argument. In order to learn whether we wish to side with Socrates, let us examine this argument. It goes as follows:

1   For anything to go out of existence it must have parts. It must be composite. Things cease to exist only by coming undone: by being dissolved or resolved into their parts.

2   The soul – that is, the person – has no parts. Souls are simple or incomposite.

3   So, persons or souls cannot go out of existence. When bodies including brains with which persons are associated die and decay, persons survive.

Is this a good argument? It represents a dramatically different position from that found in, say, the Christian religious tradition represented by Irenaeus. However, other religious believers, Christians included, are pleased to agree with Socrates, as the following remark of the Catholic philosopher Jacques Maritain makes clear. The soul, he says,

> cannot be disintegrated, since it has no . . . parts. . . . Once it exists, it cannot disappear. (Maritain 1953: 60)

Maritain did not mean to flout Irenaeus but his sympathies were with Socrates.

As for the simplicity of the soul argument, let's start by inspecting the initial premise. The initial premise seems intuitively satisfactory. We often talk and act as if when things go out of existence this is because they come apart. We say things like, "When my house burned down, there was nothing left but ashes," "I tore the book up and threw the pieces of paper that were left away," or "The toy wooden horse which she received for Christmas smashed all to bits." This suggests that our concept of going out of existence is the concept of something possessing parts, which, in some sense, come undone or break up.

In *The Monadology*, Gottfried Leibniz (1646–1716), the great German philosopher, scientist, mathematician, and historian, offers an imaginary experiment relevant to the issue of the simplicity of the soul. He asks us to imagine that we are reduced to the size of the smallest mite, and enter inside the human brain as a person may enter a giant mechanical mill, filled with levers and gears – or neurons and ganglia. However diligently we observe the brain's internal mechanisms, or parts, claims Leibniz, it is clear that we would never observe the person whose brain it is. The person, he thus says, must belong to a higher order of reality.

Higher order? For Socrates as well as Leibniz, the person or soul is simple; the brain is composite. The brain is not the right stuff for being a soul. As Leibniz writes in *The Monadology*, "Perception must be sought in simple substance, not in what is composite."

So let us now move to the second premise. What about the second premise? Persons are simple.

Contrary to Leibniz the second premise seems intuitively *un*satisfactory. Much about us is complex. Our thoughts and deeds are complex. Our personalities and characters are complex. The societies and cultures in which we live are complex. But we, according to Socrates, are simple. Why think *that*? Or perhaps even more to the point, what does that mean?

4   The Simplicity of the Soul

The brilliant French philosopher and mathematician René Descartes (1596–1650) championed the thesis of the simplicity of the soul in his *Meditations*:

I am unable to distinguish any parts within myself; I understand myself to be something . . . single and complete. (Descartes 1984: 59)

And again:

The soul is utterly indivisible. (Descartes 1984: 59)

Descartes did not leave the thesis unexplained. He tried to clarify just what it means to say that something (the soul) is simple. His explanation took the form of the following principle:

Physical Principle: Something has parts only if it is physical; if something is not physical it does not have parts but is simple.

So for Descartes simplicity means non-physicality. In Descartes' terms, Socrates' simplicity of the soul argument may be recast as follows:

1D. For something to go out of existence it must be physical.
2D. Souls or persons are not physical.
3D. So souls or persons do not go out of existence. They survive bodily death and decay.

Descartes' notion of simplicity would have pleased Socrates – indeed, arguably, non-physicality is implicit in Socrates' very idea of the simplicity of the soul. So I shall adopt it in what follows. However, the notion immediately raises a second question. Are souls or persons simple (read: non-physical)?

Persons certainly seem physical. Consider, for example, the following remarks made of Socrates.

• Socrates weighs 200 lbs.
• The teacher of Plato is sitting in the middle of his prison cell.
• "I" (spoken by Socrates) am sitting next to Crito, my friend.
• "You" (spoken by Crito to Socrates) need to escape from prison.

Doesn't our ability to refer to persons with language like the above presuppose that persons are physical and made of flesh and blood? What are the relevant senses of "weighs," "middle," "next to," and "escape"? Aren't these physical notions? Descartes admits that they are. However, he denies that they refer, strictly speaking, to Socrates or to persons. Although we *seem* to be physical, we are not physical.

We must be careful, according to Descartes, to distinguish between terms which refer indirectly or non-strictly to persons and terms which apply directly or strictly. Terms which apply indirectly apply by referring to something which is intimately associated with persons but nevertheless is distinct from them. Suppose, by analogy, you are looking at fruit on a vine. In pointing to the fruit you also may seem to point to the vine, since the two are tangled together, although the fruit is something different from the vine. Likewise, in referring to the body of a person you also may seem to refer to the person, though according to both Descartes and Socrates the person is something different from the body.

Terms which apply directly to persons apply without referring to something else. They strike the soul, as it were, on the head. Suppose, for example, Socrates says "I think that the death sentence which I have received is unjust"; he does, according to Descartes, speak directly of himself. The "I think" applies to him without referring to anything else. But suppose Socrates also says, "I am sitting next to Crito"; he does, according to Descartes, speak indirectly of himself. The "I am sitting" refers to the body with which he is intimately connected. It is the body, Socrates' body, which strictly speaking is perched next to Crito (Crito's body).

According to Descartes, although persons are distinct from bodies, nothing is wrong with saying things like "Socrates weighs 200 lbs." These and similar statements are simply philosophically uninformed shorthand for saying things like "Socrates' body weighs 200 lbs." Shorthands are common in ordinary speech. In the same way I may say "I am living on a shoe-string." I don't mean to assert that, strictly, I exist on a string. I mean that I am living with very little money.

What leads Descartes to hold that the "I think" applies directly to Socrates? In its most bare form, his answer goes as follows: An expression applies directly to a person just when it refers to the person as a person or to something essential to the person as a person (such as his capacity for thought). So when Socrates says "I think," this expression applies directly to himself; it refers to him as a person. By contrast, when he claims "I am sitting" he does not refer directly to himself. The ability to sit is not essential to him as a person. "Thinking," says Descartes in the *Meditations*, "cannot be separated from me." We exist, so to speak, as thinking, as conscious; but we do not exist as bodies. We exist, for Descartes, *in* bodies.

What then can be said for the (2D) thesis that persons or souls are non-physical?

Why we are not physical

The British philosopher John Locke (1632–1704) wrote in his *An Essay Concerning Human Understanding*: "Matter, incogitative Matter and Motion, whatever changes it might produce of Figure and Bulk, could never produce Thought." What Locke meant may be expressed thus:

Locke's Thesis: Persons are by nature self-conscious (cogitative) and neither self-consciousness nor self-conscious behavior can be understood or explained in physical terms (in terms of matter and motion).

Descartes agreed. As he remarked, "when I examine the body I just do not find anything in it which savours of thought." He shared Locke's view that self-consciousness cannot be understood or explained in physical terms and this supplied him with an argument that persons are not physical. I dub it the *limits of physical science* argument. The argument goes as follows:

1   If something is physical, it is understandable or explainable in physical scientific terms, that is, in terms of sciences such as physics, chemistry, and biology. If something is not understandable or explainable in terms of physical science, it is not physical.

2   Persons or souls – the "I" of which we are self-conscious – cannot be understood or explained in physical scientific terms.

Therefore,

3   Persons or souls are not physical.

Is it a strong argument? The first premise, which I shall call *the distinction principle* since it distinguishes the physical from the non-physical, while not uncontroversial is immensely popular among contemporary philosophers. In addition, it makes intuitive sense. Just when something is physical, physical science understands it, if not now at least in principle or eventually. We think of the electricity which pulses through our homes, for instance, as physical. Exactly why? Certainly not because we see it with the naked eye; we don't. Here is the answer supplied by the distinction principle: because physical science – and in particular James Clerk Maxwell's theory of electric and magnetic fields – understands or explains it. Whether something (electricity) counts as physical depends on physical science.

How about the second premise? The main idea behind it is that there is a categorical difference between what can and cannot be understood in physical scientific terms – that is, in terms of physical science – which leaves persons outside physical science. The soul or person defies physical scientific understanding. Does it? Is there any reason here for the escape of the soul, the person, from the grasp of science?

Why the soul escapes science

Is the "I" or person (for Socrates, the soul) the sort of thing which can be understood by physical science?

According to Descartes the object of self-consciousness – the soul, "I," or person – is *private* or subjective. Being private it is in principle impossible for physical science to describe or understand such a thing. Why is that? This is because physical science is *un*subjective; it studies things that are public and open to inspection by multiple observers. The objects of science are, in a relevant sense, objective. These include things like chemical substances and biological organisms, mountains and molehills, lightning and gold. The "I" therefore is something that physical science just is not equipped to understand. Persons abide in a subjective world of thought and consciousness rather than in the physical scientific world of, as Locke put it, figure and bulk, matter and motion.

Imagine a case – derived loosely from a story of the philosopher Frank Jackson (1982) – of Harry, the world's greatest physicist. Harry knows everything physical science knows about persons when they are self-conscious. Harry is, for example, totally familiar with the behavior of neurons in the brain of a self-conscious person.

He knows all about their electrical states and the mechanisms by which they release chemicals. He knows about synchronized oscillations in the cortex, firing patterns of cells, spike trains, the complete works. However, suppose, for whatever strange reason, Harry has never been self-conscious. He has never thought "It's my brain I'm studying" or "I myself am thinking."

Now consider what would happen if Harry suddenly, for whatever reason, became self-conscious. Descartes would claim that in becoming self-conscious Harry learns something he did not know before: something neurophysics cannot teach him. Harry comes to know facts about what it is or means to be a person: an "I": a soul. These facts about what it is or means to be a person are inaccessible to physical science in the sense that physical science is incapable of uncovering them. They have a subjective character or appearance and can be acquired only by being self-conscious. They are "inside" facts as opposed to the "outside" facts uncovered by physical science.

Consider, by analogy, two different descriptions of infantry fighting in the Battle of the Bulge in the Second World War. We may rely on the PhD dissertation of a history doctoral candidate at Princeton or on the autobiographical descriptions of a soldier who actually fought in the battle. To Descartes, Harry, prior to becoming self-conscious, is like the doctoral candidate. He may write an awful lot about the battle but he is not in a position really to *know* the fighting (the "soul" of combat infantry). The soldier, by contrast, has an inside story; he knows first-hand what it was like to confront the enemy. The hunger, the cold, the fright, the pain and hurt.

When it comes to the brain of a self-conscious person, Harry knows everything about it prior to being self-conscious. But grasping the character of soulhood: that, for Descartes, requires self-consciousness.

Descartes' limits argument is controversial. It is far from being universally endorsed by philosophers. However, Descartes is not alone in holding that the "I" escapes physical science. Thomas Nagel of New York University writes:

> Methods of objective physical understanding cannot be successfully applied to the [subjective] ... The method can be used on the body, including its central nervous system ... But for the subjective ... we need a different form of understanding. (Nagel 1994: 66)

Having just offered Descartes' thesis that persons escape science, let's return to the entire limits of physical science argument.

Physicalism and dualism

Is Descartes' limits of physical science argument a good argument? There are different ways of assessing it. One is in terms of the contrast between *physicalism* and *dualism*.

Suppose with Descartes that by "physical" thing we mean something that is entirely composed of things understandable by physical science. Accordingly toys, houses, and paper qualify as physical, and the human body and brain count as physical. Suppose again with Descartes that a "non-physical" thing is something not understandable by physical science. Perhaps this is because such things are private and therein methodologically resistant to physical science, although there may be other reasons. In any case do persons or souls qualify as non-physical?

Many contemporary philosophers find it completely congenial to believe both that "physical" means understandable by physical science and that persons can be studied and understood in physical scientific terms. The person, that is, the subject of I-thoughts, the "soul," is amenable to physical scientific examination. Persons, says Paul Churchland in his book *Matter and Consciousness*, "are creatures of matter." "And we should learn to live with that fact." Such a view is called *physicalism* or *materialism*.

Descartes, of course, was an anti-physicalist. The thesis to which he was sympathetic, the thesis that persons or souls are non-physical and cannot be understood physically scientifically, is called *dualism*. This word derives from the Latin word for "two." The dualist believes that persons exhibit a twofold character; more exactly, persons are non-physical though intimately associated with something physical, viz. their brains and bodies. My brain/body lends itself to study by physical science; *I* do not.

According to dualism the association between person and body is so intimate that persons may believe of themselves, falsely, that they are indistinguishable from their bodies. However, says Descartes in *Replies to Objections*, this illusion occurs only because:

> they have never had the experience of being without a body, and . . . have frequently been obstructed by the body in its operation. It is just as if someone had had his legs permanently shackled from infancy: he would think that the shackles were part of his body and that he needed them for walking. (Descartes 1641: 96)

These two theses about persons, the one dualist, the other physicalist, are deeply opposed. How one compares the merits of physicalism and dualism will dictate whether one agrees with Socrates and Descartes that persons are non-physical. How one compares their merits will also determine whether one agrees that someone like Harry cannot understand himself as a person or soul without abandoning the language and perspective of physical science.

So how do dualism and physicalism compare? Which "ism" is better?

Physicalism has at least one advantage over dualism. It does not have to worry about any kind of interactive relationship between soul and brain/body. It does not have to worry about the association between the non-physical and physical. This is because to the physicalist there is no relationship or association. Persons are physical through and through. The person is in fact physical. Freedom from worry about interaction helps to make physicalism a more attractive doctrine than dualism to many contemporary philosophers. Let's briefly examine the worry.

Dualism's worry: how should person/body association be understood?

Socrates said:

> When the soul and the body are both in the same place, nature teaches the one to serve and be subject, the other to rule and govern. (P: 80)

On one tempting interpretation of Socrates' remark, I, the soul, am housed in my body as a ship's captain is housed in his vessel. The vessel moves at the captain's command. However, this surely is the wrong comparison. Duke University's Owen Flanagan remarks:

> My experience of my twisted ankle is far more intimate than the pilot's observation that his ship's rudder needs repair. (Flanagan 1991: 19)

With twisted ankle I moan in agony. Often we are at our body's beck and call. Socrates also said:

> So long as we keep to the body . . . our soul is contaminated with imperfection. (P: 66)

On one tempting interpretation of Socrates' statement, I, the soul, am poisoned by my body. However, once again this is the wrong comparison. People use their bodies to build, plant, paint, dance, eat – to enrich life. The body is no poison, although in poor health it may contain toxins.

According to Socrates and Descartes, soul and body are intimately associated. However, what is the nature of that association? If it is not Soul Rule/Body Pollute, what is it? The most common answer given by dualists, and favored by Descartes (and arguably also by Socrates, except for some Socratic–Platonic antipathy towards the body evidenced by remarks like those just above), is that the association is "direct interaction." The general idea behind direct interaction is twofold:

1   Persons bring about changes in their bodies (including brains) without causing changes in any body but their own. I typically can, for example, wave my hand or speak just by deciding or trying to perform these actions. My soul directly affects my body.
2   Changes in a person's body affect the person without immediately affecting any other person; for example, if I step on a nail, the resulting feeling of pain is no one else's but mine. My body directly affects my soul.

Is the direct interaction thesis credible? Physicalists claim that the direct interaction thesis just is not credible. How exactly are we to understand direct interaction? Physicalists charge that it is extremely difficult – some even say impossible – to conceive of what interaction is supposed to look like in a dualist framework. To take an example, suppose that you have an ice-cold bottle of apple juice in the refrigerator. Being thirsty, you pour yourself a glass of the liquid and drink it. Most likely all sorts of physical changes take place in your body from grasp to swallow.

Worry for dualism: The changes, being physical, can be explained in terms of physical science. This is a consequence of the distinction principle (the first premise of Descartes' limits of science argument). According to the principle, if something is physical it can be physically explained. *But* that is very different from the conclusion of the interaction thesis. The interaction thesis says that you, the soul, bring about these changes because you are thirsty; the changes are *from* you even if they are not in you but in your body.

Presumably there cannot be *two* independent sources or explanations of one and the same bodily changes. Either non-physical you (the soul) brings about the changes or something physical (the brain or body itself perhaps) brings about the changes, but not both. So which is it? You? Or the body? The answer is something physical if the physicalist thesis is correct. But the answer is something non-physical (you, the soul) if the interaction thesis is correct.

Having a dualist conception of interaction means, among other things, having to explain how a non-physical soul can bring about changes in a brain/body which being physical can (also?) be explained in terms of physical science. There is a widespread and deeply rooted conviction among physicalists that this just cannot be done. If persons are something "over and above" brains/bodies, they cannot act on their brains/bodies in any direct way. Only something physical can act on something physical. Dualism appears to physicalism as a conceptual blind alley. In the words of Jaegwon Kim, a physicalist philosopher who teaches at Brown University, there is a "sheer impossibility of coherently imagining the details of what might have to be the case if some nonphysical agent is going to affect the course of purely physical events" (Kim 1984: 104). "Even if the idea of the soul's influencing [the body] were coherent, the postulation of such a causal agent would seem neither necessary nor helpful in understanding why and how our [bodies] move" (Kim 1996: 132).

Descartes tried with the limits of science argument to establish that persons – souls, "I's" – are non-physical. But in order for dualists to make a convincing case for dualism, physicalists are right to insist that dualists must say how souls can affect bodies directly. Physicalists regard the project with skepticism. The philosophical jury still is out.

For Socrates the jury is no longer out. Condemned to death he waits in prison, but expects to survive the death of his body.

5   The Motivational Argument for Believing in Survival

A man who has devoted his life to philosophy should be cheerful in the face of death, and confident of finding the greatest blessing in the next world when his life is finished. (Socrates, *Phaedo*)

In Socrates' conversations about personal survival, he mentions to his friends that even though warrant or evidence for survival falls short of proof (dualism does have problems), it is better to believe in survival than not to believe or to disbelieve. Why so?

Philosophers sometimes distinguish between two sorts of reasons for believing something. This is the distinction between "evidential" and "motivational" reasons. Evidential reasons are reasons purporting to establish the truth (or likely truth) of a belief. Motivational reasons are considerations attempting to establish a legitimate purpose or psychological advantage in believing.

Evidential reasons – the simplicity of the soul was an evidential reason for Socrates – are truth-focused. Thus, for example, if the soul is simple and simple things do not go out of existence, then it is *true* that people survive death. Of course, those are two big "ifs". Socrates did not claim to *prove* that the soul is simple or that simple things never extinguish; he merely tried to render these two assumptions reasonable or comparatively intellectually secure.

Motivational reasons have no direct bearing or focus on truth. They don't mean that something is true; they mean that believing in some sense is good for the believer. The distinction between the two sorts of reason calls for illustration.

Suppose Harry has to decide between two actions: asking Bernice (the woman he loves) to marry him or not asking her. If he decides one way, he will utter the words, "Bernice, will you marry me?", and if his decision goes the other way, he will retreat back to his laboratory and remain silent. He loves Bernice and wants to marry her. So suppose his decision rests on what he believes will happen if he asks her. Let us suppose that he has evidence that she will accept and evidence that she will decline, but he takes the evidence that she will accept to be slightly stronger than that she will decline. He wishes the positive evidence was much stronger, for its mere slight superiority makes him nervous and anxious.

Now let Harry wonder: "Overall what should I believe? That Bernice will accept or that she will refuse?" He formulates the following argument to himself:

> It would be self-defeating or demoralizing not to believe Bernice is going to accept my proposal. It would cause me to lose my resolve and to dampen my courage in asking Bernice. By contrast, believing that she will accept will secure my resolve. Since I want Bernice so much, I should believe that she will accept – even if I am not absolutely convinced by the evidence that she will.

Bernice aside, Harry is lucky, for his motivational reasons are matched by evidential reasons. The belief better evidenced that Bernice will accept is recommended also by considerations of emotional advantage.

Socrates was lucky. It seemed true to him that souls survive. However, he warned one of his friends not to boast too loudly about the seeming success of his (Socrates') pro-survival simplicity argument "lest some misfortune upset the argument" (P: 94). The evidence is strong, he thought, but not certain. So in case he wobbled in the face of death, he inspected motivational reasons. What he found was this. He sensed three reasons to buttress his courage in the face of death: his needs to keep his spirits high, to boost the morale of his friends, and to trust that no matter how much his honor or character may have led him personally to sacrifice in Athens he ultimately would not be demeaned. Believing in survival would accomplish these ends. Therefore, he realized, there is advantage in believing in survival; he should believe.

Concerning Big Questions in life over death, marriage, family, loyalties to others and such, intelligent believers reason just like Socrates. They care about the effects which believing likely will have on their mood, behavior, and resolve. However, people are not always as lucky as Socrates (or Harry). For what happens when evidence rubs *against* motive? Suppose in facing death you sense that better evidence favors the hypothesis of extinction, although you also think that it would be helpful to believe in survival. What then?

The apple did not fall far from the tree. When Bertrand Russell denied that persons survive death he expressed a sentiment which he independently shared with his godfather, the philosopher John Stuart Mill (1806–73). In writing, for example, of Socrates' arguments for survival in the *Phaedo*, Mill wrote:

> They are for the most part such as have no adherents, and need not be seriously refuted. (Mill 1874: 172)

Mill was dismissive. He regarded Socrates' arguments as weak and shabby. More generally, he said, there is insufficient evidence of survival and plenty of evidence against it. However, unlike Russell, Mill had tolerance for the fact that persons are psychologically complicated creatures and that an ideal of pure and unalloyed allegiance to evidence and truth, especially on the Big Questions about life, is often neither possible nor desirable. So, he added, while we should adjust and proportion *beliefs* to evidence and thus (given his construal of the evidence) disbelieve in survival, we should not let this derail our hopes. Hopes are different sorts of psychological beasts from beliefs. It may be reasonable to *hope* for survival even if we are unwarranted in believing in it. Mill wrote:

> To anyone who feels it conducive either to his satisfaction or to his usefulness to *hope* for a future state, there is no hindrance to his indulging in that hope. (Ibid.)

Hope, according to Mill, is a more evidentially slack attitude than belief. Belief consists in attending to how things seem: to where the truth appears to reside. Hope, on the other hand, can subsist on a more evidentially spartan diet. Hope may grant that there is contrary evidence but (provided the contrariety is not too severe) persist in the teeth of the evidence. In hope, for example, we are invited to trust in possibilities that we cannot defend or perhaps even describe adequately just because they answer to our aspirations, desires, and needs.

What about death? Many people face death having had much more sorrow than happiness in life for no fault of their own. Many feel terribly let down by the world. Hoping in an afterlife – thinking that death may be, just may be, a journey to a better world – may give some people power to confront death. True, death may sting with extinction, but hope in post-mortem survival may ennoble a person's last days.

"I should only make myself ridiculous in my own eyes," said Socrates, "if I clung to life." "Come," he said to his friend Crito, "do as I say and don't make difficulties."

References

Socrates in Plato's works

Socrates left no print. His ideas are contained in Plato's dialogues written over 2,300 years ago. For convenience of reference it is common to refer to passage numbers of individual dialogues rather than to page numbers of particular translations. Passage numbers are affixed to most translations. For example, the quotation which begins the chapter is taken from (A: 42), which means the forty-second passage in Plato's *Apology*.

Numerous translations and editions of Plato are available in English. The dialogues considered in the present essay include the *Apology* (A), *Crito* (C), and *Phaedo* (P). These are available, along with two other dialogues, in *Five Dialogues*, translated by G. M. A. Grube (Indianapolis: Hackett Publishing Company, 1981). They are also available in *Plato: The Last Days of Socrates*, translated with an introduction by Hugh Tredennick (Harmondsworth, England: Penguin Books, 1954). The complete dialogues of Plato (including Tredennick's "last days") are available in *The Collected Dialogues of Plato including the Letters*, edited by Edith Hamilton and Huntington Cairns (New York: Pantheon, 1961). The present essay uses the Tredennick translations.

Other works cited

For reasons of space, only works insufficiently identified in the preceding essay (or in the recommended readings section which follows) are listed below:

Descartes, René. [1641] 1984. *The Philosophical Writings of Descartes*, vol. 2. Translated by John Cottingham, Robert Stoothoff, and Dugald Murdoch. Cambridge: Cambridge University Press.

Flanagan, Owen. 1991. *The Science of Mind*, 2nd edition. Cambridge, MA: MIT Press.

Jackson, Frank. [1982] 1990. Epiphenomenal qualia. Reprinted in William Lycan (ed.), *Mind and Cognition: A Reader*. Oxford: Blackwell.

Kim, Jaegwon. [1984] 1993. Epiphenomenal and supervenient causation. Reprinted in Jaegwon Kim (ed.), *Supervenience and Mind*. New York: Cambridge University Press.

Kim, Jaegwon. 1996. *Philosophy of Mind*. Boulder, CO: Westview Press.

Maritain, Jacques. 1953. *The Range of Reason*. New York: Scribners.

Mill, John Stuart. [1874] 1992. Immortality. In Paul Edwards (ed.), *Immortality*. New York: Macmillan.

Nagel, Thomas, 1994. Consciousness and objective reality. In R. Warner and T. Szubka (eds), *The Mind–Body Problem: A Guide to the Current Debate*. Oxford: Blackwell.

Nozick, Robert. 1974. *Anarchy, State, and Utopia*. New York: Basic Books.

Russell, Bertrand. [1903] 1989. A free man's worship. Reprinted in Terence Penelhum (ed.), *Faith*. New York: Macmillan.

Walzer, Michael. 1983. *Spheres of Justice*. New York: Basic Books.

Zeller, E. 1962. *Socrates and the Socratic Schools*. Translated by O. J. Reichel. New York: Russell and Russell.

Suggestions for further reading

A good place to read about Socrates is F. M. Cornford's *Before and After Socrates* (Cambridge: Cambridge University Press, 1968). Cornford explains the source of Socrates' fame and describes the Greek philosophical culture within which he worked and which he revolutionized.

The trial of Socrates is explored from two very different vantage points in T. C. Brickhouse and N. D. Smith's *Socrates on Trial* (Oxford: Oxford University Press, 1988); and the less reverent and more provocative *The Trial of Socrates* by I. F. Stone (New York: Little & Brown, 1988).

Two good student-oriented commentaries on Platonic dialogues in which Socrates' views of survival of death figure prominently are: *Socrates in The Apology*, by C. D. C. Reeve (Indianapolis: Hackett Publishing Company, 1989); and David Bostock's *Plato's Phaedo* (Oxford: Oxford University Press, 1986). The "simplicity of the soul argument" presented in the present chapter is part of a larger argument which Bostock dubs the "affinity argument."

Plato wrote more than twenty dialogues, including the magisterial *Republic*. When Socrates was condemned to death (in 399 BC) Plato was almost 30. Although Socrates is the chief speaker in many of the dialogues, the consensus of most historians is that Plato often uses Socrates – or the character of Socrates – as mouthpiece for his own philosophical views. (I am inclined to believe that much of Socrates' antipathy towards the body in the *Phaedo* actually is Plato's antipathy.) The issue of the two philosophies, the one Socratic, and the other Platonic, is nicely sorted out in the introductory chapter in Bostock.

Descartes left much print and a lot has been written about his philosophy. A good short introduction to his philosophy of soul, mind, and consciousness is chapter 1 on "Minds and Bodies: René Descartes and the Possibility of a Science of Mind" in Owen Flanagan's *The Science of Mind*, 2nd edn (Cambridge, MA: MIT Press, 1991). Skepticism about how interaction between person (soul, mind) and body could occur is not unique to contemporary materialism/physicalism. It was voiced by Descartes' own contemporaries, as discussed in a short but historically informative chapter on dualism (chapter 5) in William Bechtel's *Philosophy of Mind: An Overview for Cognitive Science* (Hillsdale, NJ: Erlbaum, 1988). The intellectually ambitious student may enjoy Gordon Baker and Katherine Morris's *Descartes' Dualism* (London: Routledge, 1996) for its detailed attempt to explain how Descartes pictured his own brand of dualism.

Dualism/anti-physicalism is defended in John Foster's *The Immaterial Self: A Defense of the Cartesian Dualist Conception of the Mind* (London: Routledge, 1991) as well as in J. P. Moreland's *Scaling the Secular City* (Michigan: Baker Books, 1987). Moreland argues that commitment to dualism is best understood as part of a religious commitment to theism. Physicalism/anti-dualism is defended in Paul Churchland's *Matter and Consciousness*, rev. edn (Cambridge, MA: MIT Press, 1988) as well as in J. J. C. Smart's *Our Place in the Universe*

(Oxford: Blackwell, 1989). To understand general issues in philosophy of mind and consciousness, a book by the present author may be helpful: George Graham, *Philosophy of Mind: An Introduction* (Oxford: Blackwell, 1998).

Introduction to Selected Readings

The selected readings begin with the closing passages of Plato's *Phaedo*, sometimes known as "the death scene." Despite its brevity, the scene reveals three important elements in Socrates' view of death: (i) that it is survived, (ii) that reasons for believing in survival are both motivational and evidential, and (iii) that things other than bad experiences can be bad for a person.

In the second selection, "Death," Thomas Nagel, a philosopher who teaches at New York University, shares the Socratic conviction that things other than bad experiences can be bad for a person. Nagel, however, views the effect of death on persons through the eyes of Lucretius. Death extinguishes. Denying Socratic survival while embracing the hypothesis that non-experiences can be bad still permits, Nagel contends, saying that death can be bad for the person who dies. How so? Death is bad when it strips a person of the positive good of life, which is, as he says, "all that one has."

What value is the idea of the soul if the Socratic hypothesis that persons survive bodily death is rejected or suspended from judgment? According to Gareth Matthews, a philosopher at the University of Massachusetts at Amherst, in the third reading entitled "Life and Death as the Arrival and Departure of the Psyche," the notion remains useful because it helps to determine when persons or souls are alive in a human body.

In the death scene Socrates refers to Crito's worry about his (Socrates') burial. Crito is anxious, says Socrates, about "how . . . to bury me." To Socrates such anxiety is unwarranted. It stems, he thinks, from mistakenly equating persons with bodies. After death Socrates' body will no longer be the body of Socrates; it will be the *former* body of Socrates. *He* – Socrates – is not buried.

Two questions now suggest themselves. These are Matthews' questions. One is about when human life ends: When in the history of a body does death of its person occur? The second is the symmetrical question about the start of life: When in the history of a body does its person first live?

Boiled down to essentials Matthews' position is this: Personal death occurs when the body is de-animated by the soul; life of the person begins in the body when it is animated by the soul. When is that? According to Matthews, we should treat the issue of when the soul animates/de-animates a body as a scientific problem to be tackled using data from experimental psychology and neurobiology. Physically scientific criteria can and should be used to determine when the body is "ensouled."

Descartes made various stabs at solving the problem of dualistic interactionism, including speculation about the location of interaction in the brain and the involvement of God in mind–body union. To be sure, since for Descartes there is no equation of soul or mind with brain, this forced him to speculate on how conscious functions and activities could be carried out independently of the exact kind of brain structure or neurophysiology that we have – which also forced him to speculate about our neurophysiology. Rather than being a philosopher with no interest in scientific work, he became (for his time) an accomplished theorist about the nervous system. The fourth reading contains selections from various of his writings and should help to clarify not only why he favored dualism but why he thought it perfectly legitimate to disconnect description of subjective mental phenomena from talk of nerves and tissues. Further reading on this topic can be found in the sixth of Descartes' *Meditations on First Philosophy*, which meditation is reprinted (along with much of the rest of that work) in chapter 4 of this book.

In the fifth selection, a survey article entitled "The Mind–Body Problem" and written for *The Scientific American*, Jerry Fodor, a philosopher at both Rutgers University and the City University of New York, reiterates the physicalist lament that dualistic interaction is a failure – no matter its alleged location in the brain. So, where does that leave the understanding of persons?

Fodor explores recent philosophical ideas for how best to understand the relationship between the subjective or mental features of persons and our physical structure. One of these ideas – so-called "functionalism" – is remarkably like Descartes' dualism in freely encouraging the notion that the subjective or psychological constitution of a person depends not on the brain or body but on conscious, intelligent activities. According to Fodor, conscious, intelligent activities, such as perception, thought, and motor control, are best understood by picturing persons as *representing* or *processing information about* the world. Our perceptions and thoughts are *about* things and our actions are *towards* things. Furthermore, perceptions, thoughts, and so on regulate behavior in virtue of what they are about, that is, because of what information they contain. For example, because of my desire to introduce the reading from Fodor, I type letters on my keyboard – I move my fingers in physical space because I perceive *the keyboard* and act *towards* the keys. Information about such things helps to explain why I behave as I do. However, whatever Descartes' and Fodor's particular points of agreement may be, Fodor clearly distances himself from dualism. He believes that traditional questions about what it means to be a person can be solved only within the confines of a materialism which reflects the best in current psychological and cognitive science.

Something else to note in Fodor is his claim that conscious experience – what Fodor calls "qualitative content" – is not all there is to the subjectivity or minds of persons. Psychological and cognitive science deal mainly with why we behave as we do, and for science, and thus for Fodor, numerous psychological states or characteristics of a person may be nonconscious and lack any sort of qualitative content or "conscious feel" whatsoever.

Discussion questions

1   Explain how it is possible, if Socrates is correct that the soul (mind) survives bodily death, to witness one's own funeral. (Caution: A disembodied soul will not have sense organs.)

2   In each pair, which of the following ways of speaking would Socrates and Descartes find preferable, and why?
    (i)   "I am a person who has a soul and a body" or "I am a soul who has a body."
    (ii) "I lost my soul" or "I lost my body."

3   Imagine that the science of artificial intelligence has advanced to the point where a program is written which allows a robot with a "brain" consisting of a computer running on the program to behave like a human being. Now imagine something really quite fantastic. Imagine that instead of running the program in a machine, the entire

population of the USA is enlisted to act out the program. Each citizen is given a precise set of instructions about how to behave so that they mimic the inner workings of the computer. In effect, although it would take a trans-global visual perspective to recognize the behavior, the "computerized" set of citizens behaves like the robot. Which of the following set of assertions is true?

(i)   Persons think but neither the robot nor the population as a whole thinks.

(ii) Persons think; the robot thinks; but the population as a whole does not think.

(iii) Persons think; the robot thinks; and the population as a whole thinks.

4   Why would a functionalist endorse (iii) above? How could Matthews endorse (i) and reject both (ii) and (iii)?

5   Read the next chapter on human freedom before answering the following question: Some philosophers have held that there are "basic facts" in the universe – facts that cannot be explained. They just are. For example, it may be a basic fact that human beings are free; it may be a basic fact that human beings fail to survive bodily death. But other philosophers have claimed that no fact is basic; every fact somehow is connected with other facts which help to explain it. If we are free, something must explain why we are free rather than unfree; if we are extinguished when we die, something must explain why we are extinguished rather than survive. In your opinion, does our world contain basic facts or are all facts non-basic? If you believe there are basic facts, which facts are basic?

Readings

Plato, death scene from *Phaedo* (114d–118)

"Of course, no reasonable man ought to insist that the facts are exactly as I have described them. But that either this or something very like it is a true account of our souls and their future habitations – since we have clear evidence that the soul is immortal – this, I think, is both a reasonable contention and a belief worth risking; for the risk is a noble one. We should use such accounts to inspire ourselves with confidence; and that is why I have already drawn out my tale so long.

"There is one way, then, in which a man can be free from all anxiety about the fate of his soul; if in life he has abandoned bodily pleasures and adornments, as foreign to his purpose and likely to do more harm than good, and has devoted himself to the pleasures of acquiring knowledge; and so by decking his soul not with a borrowed beauty but with its own – with self-control, and goodness, and

From *Plato: The Last Days of Socrates*, translated by Hugh Tredennick (Harmondsworth: Penguin Books, 1954).

courage, and liberality, and truth – has fitted himself to await his journey to the next world. You, Simmias and Cebes and the rest, will each make this journey some day in the future; but 'for me the fated hours' (as a tragic character might say) 'calls even now'. In other words, it is about time that I took my bath. I prefer to have a bath before drinking the poison, rather than give the women the trouble of washing me when I am dead."

When he had finished speaking, Crito said "Very well, Socrates. But have you no directions for the others or myself about your children or anything else? What can we do to please you best?"

"Nothing new, Crito," said Socrates; "just what I am always telling you. If you look after yourselves, whatever you do will please me and mine and you too, even if you don't agree with me now. On the other hand, if you neglect yourselves and fail to follow the line of life as I have laid it down both now and in the past, however fervently you agree with me now, it will do no good at all."

"We shall try our best to do as you say," said Crito. "But how shall we bury you?"

"Any way you like," replied Socrates, "that is, if you can catch me and I don't slip through your fingers." He laughed gently as he spoke, and turning to us went on: "I can't persuade Crito that I am this Socrates here who is talking to you now and marshalling all the arguments; he thinks that I am the one whom he will see presently lying dead; and he asks how he is to bury me! As for my long and elaborate explanation that when I have drunk the poison I shall remain with you no longer, but depart to a state of heavenly happiness, this attempt to console both you and myself seems to be wasted on him. You must give an assurance to Crito for me – the opposite of the one which he gave to the court which tried me. He undertook that I should stay; but you must assure him that when I am dead I shall not stay, but depart and be gone. That will help Crito to bear it more easily, and keep him from being distressed on my account when he sees my body being burned or buried, as if something dreadful were happening to me; or from saying at the funeral that it is Socrates whom he is laying out or carrying to the grave or burying. Believe me, my dear friend Crito: mis-statements are not merely jarring in their immediate context; they also have a bad effect upon the soul. No, you must keep up your spirits and say that it is only my body that you are burying; and you can bury it as you please, in whatever way you think is most proper."

With these words he got up and went into another room to bathe; and Crito went after him, but told us to wait. So we waited, discussing and reviewing what had been said, or else dwelling upon the greatness of the calamity which had befallen us; for we felt just as though we were losing a father and should be orphans for the rest of our lives. Meanwhile, when Socrates had taken his bath, his children were brought to see him – he had two little sons and one big boy – and the women of his household – you know – arrived. He talked to them in Crito's presence and gave them directions about carrying out his wishes; then he told the women and children to go away, and came back himself to join us.

It was now nearly sunset, because he had spent a long time inside. He came and sat down, fresh from the bath; and he had only been talking for a few minutes when the prison officer came in, and walked up to him. "Socrates," he said, "at any rate I shall not have to find fault with you, as I do with others, for getting angry with me and cursing when I tell them to drink the poison – carrying out Government orders. I have come to know during this time that you are the noblest and the gentlest and the bravest of all the men that have ever come here, and now especially I am sure that you are not angry with me, but with them; because you know who are responsible. So now – you know what I have come to say – goodbye, and try to bear what must be as easily as you can." As he spoke he burst into tears, and turning round, went away.

Socrates looked up at him and said "Goodbye to you, too; we will do as you say." Then addressing us he went on "What a charming person! All the time I have been here he has visited me, and sometimes had discussions with me, and shown me the greatest kindness; and how generous of him now to shed tears for me at parting! But come, Crito, let us do as he says. Someone had better bring in the poison, if it is ready prepared; if not, tell the man to prepare it."

"But surely, Socrates," said Crito, "the sun is still upon the mountains; it has not gone down yet. Besides, I know that in other cases people have dinner and enjoy their wine, and sometimes the company of those whom they love, long after they receive the warning; and only drink the poison quite late at night. No need to hurry; there is still plenty of time."

"It is natural that these people whom you speak of should act in that way, Crito," said Socrates, "because they think that they gain by it. And it is also natural that I should not; because I believe that I should gain nothing by drinking the poison a little later – I should only make myself ridiculous in my own eyes if I clung to life and hugged it when it has no more to offer. Come, do as I say and don't make difficulties."

At this Crito made a sign to his servant, who was standing near by. The servant went out and after spending a considerable time returned with the man who was to administer the poison; he was carrying it ready prepared in a cup. When Socrates saw him he said "Well, my good fellow, you understand these things; what ought I to do?"

"Just drink it," he said, "and then walk about until you feel a weight in your legs, and then lie down. Then it will act of its own accord."

As he spoke he handed the cup to Socrates, who received it quite cheerfully, without a tremor, without any change of colour or expression, and said, looking up under his brows with his usual steady gaze, "What do you say about pouring a libation from this drink? Is it permitted, or not?"

"We only prepare what we regard as the normal dose, Socrates," he replied.

"I see," said Socrates. "But I suppose I am allowed, or rather bound, to pray the gods that my removal from this world to the other may be prosperous. This is my prayer, then; and I hope that it may be granted." With these words, quite calmly and with no sign of distaste, he drained the cup in one breath.

Up till this time most of us had been fairly successful in keeping back our tears; but when we saw that he was drinking, that he had actually drunk it, we could do so no longer; in spite of myself the tears came pouring out, so that I covered my face and wept broken-heartedly – not for him, but for my own calamity in losing such a friend. Crito had given up even before me, and had gone out when he could not restrain his tears. But Apollodorus, who had never stopped crying even before, now broke out into such a storm of passionate weeping that he made everyone in the room break down, except Socrates himself, who said:

"Really, my friends, what a way to behave! Why, that was my main reason for sending away the women, to prevent this sort of disturbance; because I am told that one should make one's end in a tranquil frame of mind. Calm yourselves and try to be brave."

This made us feel ashamed, and we controlled our tears. Socrates walked about, and presently, saying that his legs were heavy, lay down on his back – that was what the man recommended. The man (he was the same one who had administered the poison) kept his hand upon Socrates, and after a little while examined his feet and legs; then pinched his foot hard and asked if he felt it. Socrates said no. Then he did the same to his legs; and moving gradually upwards in this way let us see that he was getting cold and numb. Presently he felt him again and said that when it reached the heart, Socrates would be gone.

The coldness was spreading about as far as his waist when Socrates uncovered his face – for he had covered it up – and said (they were his last words): "Crito, we ought to offer a cock to Asclepius. See to it, and don't forget."

"No, it shall be done," said Crito. "Are you sure that there is nothing else?"

Socrates made no reply to this question, but after a little while he stirred; and when the man uncovered him, his eyes were fixed. When Crito saw this, he closed the mouth and eyes.

Such was the end of our comrade, who was, we may fairly say, of all those whom we knew in our time, the bravest and also the wisest and most upright man.

Thomas Nagel, "Death"

If death is the unequivocal and permanent end of our existence, the question arises whether it is a bad thing to die.

There is conspicuous disagreement about the matter: some people think death is dreadful; others have no objection to death *per se*, though they hope their own will be neither premature nor painful. Those in the former category tend to think those in the latter are blind to the obvious, while the latter suppose the former to be prey to some sort of confusion. On the one hand it can be said that life is all we have and the loss of it is the greatest loss we can sustain. On the other hand

From Thomas Nagel (ed.), *Mortal Questions* (Cambridge: Cambridge University Press, 1979), pp. 1–10.

it may be objected that death deprives this supposed loss of its subject, and that if we realize that death is not an unimaginable condition of the persisting person, but a mere blank, we will see that it can have no value whatever, positive or negative.

Since I want to leave aside the question whether we are, or might be, immortal in some form, I shall simply use the word "death" and its cognates in this discussion to mean *permanent* death, unsupplemented by any form of conscious survival. I want to ask whether death is in itself an evil; and how great an evil, and of what kind, it might be. The question should be of interest even to those who believe in some form of immortality, for one's attitude toward immortality must depend in part on one's attitude toward death.

If death is an evil at all, it cannot be because of its positive features, but only because of what it deprives us of. I shall try to deal with the difficulties surrounding the natural view that death is an evil because it brings to an end all the goods that life contains. We need not give an account of these goods here, except to observe that some of them, like perception, desire, activity, and thought, are so general as to be constitutive of human life. They are widely regarded as formidable benefits in themselves, despite the fact that they are conditions of misery as well as of happiness, and that a sufficient quantity of more particular evils can perhaps outweigh them. That is what is meant, I think, by the allegation that it is good simply to be alive, even if one is undergoing terrible experiences. The situation is roughly this: There are elements which, if added to one's experience, make life better; there are other elements which, if added to one's experience, make life worse. But what remains when these are set aside is not merely *neutral*: it is emphatically positive. Therefore life is worth living even when the bad elements of experience are plentiful, and the good ones too meager to outweigh the bad ones on their own. The additional positive weight is supplied by experience itself, rather than by any of its contents.

I shall not discuss the value that one person's life or death may have for others, or its objective value, but only the value it has for the person who is its subject. That seems to me the primary case, and the case which presents the greatest difficulties. Let me add only two observations. First, the value of life and its contents does not attach to mere organic survival: almost everyone would be indifferent (other things equal) between immediate death and immediate coma followed by death twenty years later without reawakening. And second, like most goods, this can be multiplied by time: more is better than less. The added quantities need not be temporally continuous (though continuity has its social advantages). People are attracted to the possibility of long-term suspended animation or freezing, followed by the resumption of conscious life, because they can regard it from within simply as a *continuation* of their present life. If these techniques are ever perfected, what from outside appeared as a dormant interval of three hundred years could be experienced by the subject as nothing more than a sharp discontinuity in the character of his experiences. I do not deny, of course, that this has its own disadvantages. Family and friends may have died in the meantime; the language may have changed; the comforts of social, geographical, and cultural familiarity would be lacking. Nevertheless these inconveniences would not obliterate the basic advantage of continued, though discontinuous, existence.

If we turn from what is good about life to what is bad about death, the case is completely different. Essentially, though there may be problems about their specification, what we find desirable in life are certain states, conditions, or types of activity. It is *being* alive, *doing* certain things, having certain experiences, that we consider good. But if death is an evil, it is the *loss of life*, rather than the state of being dead, or nonexistent, or unconscious, that is objectionable.[1] This asymmetry is important. If it is good to be alive, that advantage can be attributed to a person at each point of his life. It is a good of which Bach had more than Schubert, simply because he lived longer. Death, however, is not an evil of which Shakespeare has so far received a larger portion than Proust. If death is a disadvantage, it is not easy to say when a man suffers it.

There are two other indications that we do not object to death merely because it involves long periods of nonexistence. First, as has been mentioned, most of us would not regard the *temporary* suspension of life, even for substantial intervals, as in itself a misfortune. If it ever happens that people can be frozen without reduction of the conscious lifespan, it will be inappropriate to pity those who are temporarily out of circulation. Second, none of us existed before we were born (or conceived), but few regard that as a misfortune. I shall have more to say about this later.

The point that death is not regarded as an unfortunate *state* enables us to refute a curious but very common suggestion about the origin of the fear of death. It is often said that those who object to death have made the mistake of trying to imagine what it is like to *be* dead. It is alleged that the failure to realize that this task is logically impossible (for the banal reason that there is nothing to imagine) leads to the conviction that death is a mysterious and therefore terrifying prospective *state*. But this diagnosis is evidently false, for it is just as impossible to imagine being totally unconscious as to imagine being dead (though it is easy enough to imagine oneself, from the outside, in either of those conditions). Yet people who are averse to death are not usually averse to unconsciousness (so long as it does not entail a substantial cut in the total duration of waking life).

If we are to make sense of the view that to die is bad, it must be on the ground that life is a good and death is the corresponding deprivation or loss, bad not because of any positive features but because of the desirability of what it removes. We must now turn to the serious difficulties which this hypothesis raises, difficulties about loss and privation in general, and about death in particular.

Essentially, there are three types of problem. First, doubt may be raised whether *anything* can be bad for a man without being positively unpleasant to him: specifically, it may be doubted that there are any evils which consist merely in the deprivation or absence of possible goods, and which do not depend on someone's *minding* that deprivation. Second, there are special difficulties, in the case of death,

---

[1] It is sometimes suggested that what we really mind is the process of *dying*. But I should not really object to dying if it were not followed by death.

about how the supposed misfortune is to be assigned to a subject at all. There is doubt both as to *who* its subject is, and as to *when* he undergoes it. So long as a person exists, he has not yet died, and once he has died, he no longer exists; so there seems to be no time when death, if it is a misfortune, can be ascribed to its unfortunate subject. The third type of difficulty concerns the asymmetry, mentioned above, between our attitudes to posthumous and prenatal nonexistence. How can the former be bad if the latter is not?

It should be recognized that if these are valid objections to counting death as an evil, they will apply to many other supposed evils as well. The first type of objection is expressed in general form by the common remark that what you don't know can't hurt you. It means that even if a man is betrayed by his friends, ridiculed behind his back, and despised by people who treat him politely to his face, none of it can be counted as a misfortune for him so long as he does not suffer as a result. It means that a man is not injured if his wishes are ignored by the executor of his will, or if, after his death, the belief becomes current that all the literary works on which his fame rests were really written by his brother, who died in Mexico at the age of 28. It seems to me worth asking what assumptions about good and evil lead to these drastic restrictions.

All the questions have something to do with time. There certainly are goods and evils of a simple kind (including some pleasures and pains) which a person possesses at a given time simply in virtue of his condition at that time. But this is not true of all the things we regard as good or bad for a man. Often we need to know his history to tell whether something is a misfortune or not; this applies to ills like deterioration, deprivation, and damage. Sometimes his experiential *state* is relatively unimportant – as in the case of a man who wastes his life in the cheerful pursuit of a method of communicating with asparagus plants. Someone who holds that all goods and evils must be temporally assignable states of the person may of course try to bring difficult cases into line by pointing to the pleasure or pain that more complicated goods and evils cause. Loss, betrayal, deception, and ridicule are on this view bad because people suffer when they learn of them. But it should be asked how our ideas of human value would have to be constituted to accommodate these cases directly instead. One advantage of such an account might be that it would enable us to explain *why* the discovery of these misfortunes causes suffering – in a way that makes it reasonable. For the natural view is that the discovery of betrayal makes us unhappy because it is bad to be betrayed – not that betrayal is bad because its discovery makes us unhappy.

It therefore seems to me worth exploring the position that most good and ill fortune has as its subject a person identified by his history and his possibilities, rather than merely by his categorical state of the moment – and that while this subject can be exactly located in a sequence of places and times, the same is not necessarily true of the goods and ills that befall him.[2]

---

[2] It is certainly not true in general of the things that can be said of him. For example, Abraham Lincoln was taller than Louis XIV. But when?

These ideas can be illustrated by an example of deprivation whose severity approaches that of death. Suppose an intelligent person receives a brain injury that reduces him to the mental condition of a contented infant, and that such desires as remain to him can be satisfied by a custodian, so that he is free from care. Such a development would be widely regarded as a severe misfortune, not only for his friends and relations, or for society, but also, and primarily, for the person himself. This does not mean that a contented infant is unfortunate. The intelligent adult who has been *reduced* to this condition is the subject of the misfortune. He is the one we pity, though of course he does not mind his condition – there is some doubt, in fact, whether he can be said to exist any longer.

The view that such a man has suffered a misfortune is open to the same objections which have been raised in regard to death. He does not mind his condition. It is in fact the same condition he was in at the age of three months, except that he is bigger. If we did not pity him then, why pity him now; in any case, who is there to pity? The intelligent adult has disappeared, and for a creature like the one before us, happiness consists in a full stomach and a dry diaper.

If these objections are invalid, it must be because they rest on a mistaken assumption about the temporal relation between the subject of a misfortune and the circumstances which constitute it. If, instead of concentrating exclusively on the oversized baby before us, we consider the person he was, and the person he *could* be now, then his reduction to this state and the cancellation of his natural adult development constitute a perfectly intelligible catastrophe.

This case should convince us that it is arbitrary to restrict the goods and evils that can befall a man to nonrelational properties ascribable to him at particular times. As it stands, that restriction excludes not only such cases of gross degeneration, but also a good deal of what is important about success and failure, and other features of a life that have the character of processes. I believe we can go further, however. There are goods and evils which are irreducibly relational; they are features of the relations between a person, with spatial and temporal boundaries of the usual sort, and circumstances which may not coincide with him either in space or in time. A man's life includes much that does not take place within the boundaries of his body and his mind, and what happens to him can include much that does not take place within the boundaries of his life. These boundaries are commonly crossed by the misfortunes of being deceived, or despised, or betrayed. (If this is correct, there is a simple account of what is wrong with breaking a deathbed promise. It is an injury to the dead man. For certain purposes it is possible to regard time as just another type of distance.) The case of mental degeneration shows us an evil that depends on a contrast between the reality and the possible alternatives. A man is the subject of good and evil as much because he has hopes which may or may not be fulfilled, or possibilities which may or may not be realized, as because of his capacity to suffer and enjoy. If death is an evil, it must be accounted for in these terms, and the impossibility of locating it within life should not trouble us.

When a man dies we are left with his corpse, and while a corpse can suffer the kind of mishap that may occur to an article of furniture, it is not a suitable object for pity. The man, however, is. He has lost his life, and if he had not died, he would have continued to live it, and to possess whatever good there is in living. If we apply to death the account suggested for the case of dementia, we shall say that although the spatial and temporal locations of the individual who suffered the loss are clear enough, the misfortune itself cannot be so easily located. One must be content just to state that his life is over and there will never be any more of it. That *fact*, rather than his past or present condition, constitutes his misfortune, if it is one. Nevertheless if there is a loss, someone must suffer it, and *he* must have existence and specific spatial and temporal location even if the loss itself does not. The fact that Beethoven had no children may have been a cause of regret to him, or a sad thing for the world, but it cannot be described as a misfortune for the children that he never had. All of us, I believe, are fortunate to have been born. But unless good and ill can be assigned to an embryo, or even to an unconnected pair of gametes, it cannot be said that not to be born is a misfortune. (That is a factor to be considered in deciding whether abortion and contraception are akin to murder.)

This approach also provides a solution to the problem of temporal asymmetry, pointed out by Lucretius. He observed that no one finds it disturbing to contemplate the eternity preceding his own birth, and he took this to show that it must be irrational to fear death, since death is simply the mirror image of the prior abyss. That is not true, however, and the difference between the two explains why it is reasonable to regard them differently. It is true that both the time before a man's birth and the time after his death are times when he does not exist. But the time after his death is time of which his death deprives him. It is time in which, had he not died then, he would be alive. Therefore any death entails the loss of *some* life that its victim would have led had he not died at that or any earlier point. We know perfectly well what it would be for him to have had it instead of losing it, and there is no difficulty in identifying the loser.

But we cannot say that the time prior to a man's birth is time in which he would have lived had he been born not then but earlier. For aside from the brief margin permitted by premature labor, he *could* not have been born earlier: anyone born substantially earlier than he was would have been someone else. Therefore the time prior to his birth is not time in which his subsequent birth prevents him from living. His birth, when it occurs, does not entail the loss to him of any life whatever.

The direction of time is crucial in assigning possibilities to people or other individuals. Distinct possible lives of a single person can diverge from a common beginning, but they cannot converge to a common conclusion from diverse beginnings. (The latter would represent not a set of different possible lives of one individual, but a set of distinct possible individuals, whose lives have identical conclusions.) Given an identifiable individual, countless possibilities for his continued existence are imaginable, and we can clearly conceive of what it would be for him to go on existing indefinitely. However inevitable it is that this will not come about, its possibility is still that of the continuation of a good for him, if life is the good we take it to be.[3]

We are left, therefore, with the question whether the nonrealization of this possibility is in every case a misfortune, or whether it depends on what can naturally be hoped for. This seems to me the most serious difficulty with the view that death is always an evil. Even if we can dispose of the objections against admitting misfortune that is not experienced, or cannot be assigned to a definite time in the person's life, we still have to set some limits on *how* possible a possibility must be for its nonrealization to be a misfortune (or good fortune, should the possibility be a bad one). The death of Keats at 24 is generally regarded as tragic; that of Tolstoy at 82 is not. Although they will both be dead for ever, Keats' death deprived him of many years of life which were allowed to Tolstoy; so in a clear sense Keats' loss was greater (though not in the sense standardly employed in mathematical comparison between infinite quantities). However, this does not prove that Tolstoy's loss was insignificant. Perhaps we record an objection only to evils which are gratuitously added to the inevitable; the fact that it is worse to die at 24 than at 82 does not imply that it is not a terrible thing to die at 82, or even at 806. The question is whether we can regard as a misfortune any limitation, like mortality, that is normal to the species. Blindness or near-blindness is not a misfortune for a mole, nor would it be for a man, if that were the natural condition of the human race.

The trouble is that life familiarizes us with the goods of which death deprives us. We are already able to appreciate them, as a mole is not able to appreciate vision. If we put aside doubts about their status as goods and grant that their quantity is in part a function of their duration, the question remains whether death, no matter when it occurs, can be said to deprive its victim of what is in the relevant sense a possible continuation of life.

---

[3] I confess to being troubled by the above argument, on the ground that it is too sophisticated to explain the simple difference between our attitudes to prenatal and posthumous nonexistence. For this reason I suspect that something essential is omitted from the account of the badness of death by an analysis which treats it as a deprivation of possibilities. My suspicion is supported by the following suggestion of Robert Nozick. We could imagine discovering that people developed from individual spores that had existed indefinitely far in advance of their birth. In this fantasy, birth never occurs naturally more than a hundred years before the permanent end of the spore's existence. But then we discover a way to trigger the premature hatching of these spores, and people are born who have thousands of years of active life before them. Given such a situation, it would be possible to imagine *oneself* having come into existence thousands of years previously. If we put aside the question whether this would really be the same person, even given the identity of the spore, then the consequence appears to be that a person's birth at a given time *could* deprive him of many earlier years of possible life. Now while it would be cause for regret that one had been deprived of all those possible years of life by being born too late, the feeling would differ from that which many people have about death. I conclude that something about the future *prospect* of permanent nothingness is not captured by the analysis in terms of denied possibilities. If so, then Lucretius' argument still awaits an answer. I suspect that it requires a general treatment of the difference between past and future in our attitudes toward our own lives. Our attitudes toward past and future pain are very different, for example.

The situation is an ambiguous one. Observed from without, human beings obviously have a natural lifespan and cannot live much longer than a hundred years. A man's sense of his own experience, on the other hand, does not embody this idea of a natural limit. His existence defines for him an essentially open-ended possible future, containing the usual mixture of goods and evils that he has found so tolerable in the past. Having been gratuitously introduced to the world by a collection of natural, historical, and social accidents, he finds himself the subject of a *life*, with an indeterminate and not essentially limited future. Viewed in this way, death, no matter how inevitable, is an abrupt cancellation of indefinitely extensive possible goods. Normality seems to have nothing to do with it, for the fact that we will all inevitably die in a few score years cannot by itself imply that it would not be good to live longer. Suppose that we were all inevitably going to die in *agony* – physical agony lasting six months. Would inevitability make *that* prospect any less unpleasant? And why should it be different for a deprivation? If the normal lifespan were a thousand years, death at 80 would be a tragedy. As things are, it may just be a more widespread tragedy. If there is no limit to the amount of life that it would be good to have, then it may be that a bad end is in store for us all.

Gareth B. Matthews, "Life and Death as the Arrival and Departure of the Psyche"

Then tell me, what must be present in a body to make it alive?
Soul. [*Psyche.*]
Is this always so?
Of course.
So whenever soul [*psyche*] takes possession of a body, it always brings life with it?
Yes, it does. (*Phaedo* 105cd)

Do we believe that there is such a thing as death?
Most certainly, said Simmias, taking up the role of answering.
Is it simply the release of the soul [*psyche*] from the body?
. . . Is death anything else than this?
No, just that. (*Phaedo* 64c)[1]

Among theoretical questions of great practical import perhaps none is more significant, or more vexing, than the pair of questions, "When does human life begin?" and "When does human life end?" I propose to defend an answer to these perplexing questions that is perhaps as old as the questions themselves: the life of a human being begins when a human body is first invested with a soul or psyche, and it ends when that body is last invested with a soul or psyche. Since the Latin

From *American Philosophical Quarterly* 16 (1979), pp. 151–7.
[1] Tr. H. Tredennick (Loeb Classical Library).

for "soul" or "psyche" is "anima," one could put this traditional view in the following, tautology-like formulation: a human being is animate so long as, and only as long as, the appropriate human body has an anima.

Historically three further doctrines have been associated with the idea of life and death as the arrival and departure of the soul. One is the doctrine that the soul is a distinct substance. A second is the doctrine that the soul pre-exists, perhaps even eternally pre-exists, the point at which it comes to animate any given body. And the third is the doctrine that, after it has ceased to animate any given human body, the soul continues to exist, perhaps eternally. I shall not discuss these further doctrines. Since I want to talk about the arrival and departure of the soul without being committed either to the soul's pre-existence or to its survival, I shall be using "arrival" and "departure" in a loose, or perhaps in a figurative, way.

The doctrines I want to consider are really two. The first links being alive with having a psyche, in this way:

(A1) For any body, b, and any time, t, b is alive at t if, and only if, b has a psyche at t.

The second takes the period during which a human being exists to coincide with the period during which a certain body is animated, that is:

(A2) For any human being, h, there is a human body, b, such that h comes into existence when b is first alive and h passes out of existence immediately after b is last alive.

From (A1) and (A2) together one may deduce this corollary:

(C1) For any human being, h, there is a human body, b, such that h comes into existence when b first has a psyche and h passes out of existence immediately after b last has a psyche.[2]

Although I have said I do not wish to discuss either the idea that a soul might exist before it begins to animate a given body or the idea that a soul might exist after it ceases to animate a given body, (A1) and (A2) could be thought to rule out both. In fact they do not, though they do rule out, given certain natural assumptions, the identification of a soul with the human being whose soul it is.

I realize that the project of refurbishing and defending this very traditional view will strike many reasonable people as either perverse or else naive. What help could the ancient concept of a psyche possibly be in the contemporary discussion of life and death? We know so much more about embryology than the ancients did, it strains credulity to suggest that their soul-concept could help us to understand what

---

[2] "... among living things, living is existing, and the psyche is the cause and the first principle of this" (Aristotle, De anima B4 415b13–4). I take (C1) to be a way of applying these ideas to (among living things) human beings.

it is for human life to begin. And we know so much more than they of the physiology of death that their picture of the departure of the psyche – memorable as it is in Homer, Plato and ancient art – surely cannot help us grapple with the contemporary debate over criteria for death.

And yet I propose – perverse or naive as it may seem – to return for enlightment to what is perhaps the oldest way of thinking about life and death.

For centuries now doctors have pronounced their patients dead when, and not until, the patient's heart stops beating and the lungs stop expanding and contracting. Only in the last few years has there been significant dissatisfaction with this traditional "cardiopulmonary" indicator of death. Two related developments are chiefly responsible for the new dissatisfaction. First, it is now possible to keep a heart beating and a pair of lungs expanding and contracting under many conditions of disease and injury that would formerly have ended the functioning of both heart and lungs. In the most extreme of these cases the patient is sometimes called (whether appropriately remains to be discussed) "a ventilated corpse." The second and related development is the improved technology of organ transplantation that makes even, or especially, these "ventilated corpses" a valuable source of fresh organs suitable for transplantation.

These two developments have inspired a number of suggestions for new indicators of death. Perhaps the most important two – often, unfortunately, not distinguished – are irreversible coma and "brainstem death." Brainstem death is the state of a brainstem that has become permanently and completely nonfunctional. One might add that when the brainstem becomes completely nonfunctional, so do the higher parts of the brain as well – including the cerebral cortex, the seat of consciousness. Thus a person whose brainstem is dead has no possibility of regaining consciousness. By contrast, the brainstem of a person in irreversible coma may remain functional for an indefinitely long period of time.

How are these competing indicators to be conceived? What is one doing when one looks for an indicator of human death? Presumably one is looking for a sign of that state in which a human body has become permanently inoperative. The eye is permanently inoperative if one can no longer use it to see with. The kidney is permanently inoperative if one can never use it again to collect urine to send on to the bladder. But when is the human body permanently inoperative? To answer that question we need to think about what makes a human body count as operative, that is, alive.

Aristotle seems to suggest that the Greek word for "to live" has one sense in which both plants and animals can be said to live, another in which animals, but not plants, can be said to live, and a third in which human beings, but not other animals or, of course, plants, can be said to live (De anima B2). In a similar spirit it is tempting to view the three competing indicators of human death as pointing to, respectively, (1) capacities common to the functioning of plants and animals, (2) capacities distinctive of the functioning of animals and (3) capacities distinctive of the functioning of human beings. This thought suggests that, in the present controversy over indicators of death, it may be that "dead" is being given three different and noncompeting senses.

Common to functioning plants and animals is, perhaps, the ability to take in nourishment, to eliminate wastes and to preserve a degree of homeostasis. It is perhaps this common functioning that Lawrence Becker has in mind when, in a defense of the cardiopulmonary indicator, he says this about human death:

> . . . a human organism is dead when, for whatever reason, the system of those recip-rocally dependent processes which assimilate oxygen, metabolize food, eliminate wastes, and keep the organism in relative homeostasis are arrested in a way which the organism itself cannot reverse. (Becker [3], p. 353)

Distinctive of functioning animals, as opposed to plants, is psychological control. In vertebrates the total breakdown of psychological control is perhaps most plaus-ibly linked to permanent and complete loss of function in the base of the brain – hence the brainstem indicator.

What functions are distinctive of human beings, as opposed to other animals? Henry K. Beecher, who chaired the Harvard Ad Hoc Committee to Examine the Definition of Brain Death includes these functions in the essential nature of human beings:

> the individual's personality, his conscious life, his uniqueness, his capacity for remem-bering, judging, reasoning, acting, enjoying, worrying, and so on . . . (Veatch [16], p. 39)

It is plausible to think that these features, or most of them, are seated in the cerebral cortex and that any disablement of the cortex sufficient to produce irre-versible coma would, in turn, eliminate these functions.

Should one say that both "is alive" and "is dead" have three different senses and that the apparent disagreement over indicators of death is only a sham disagreement that really rests on an equivocation?

No, I don't think so. And there are many reasons for saying "No." Perhaps the most important is this. We have no plausible candidate for a capacity distinctive of human beings, as opposed to all other animals.[3] Speech has been the most popular candidate.[4] But being capable of speaking is not a necessary condition for being a human being – as newborn infants, mutes and certain stroke victims demonstrate. Nor is it even sufficient – as the recent sign-language experiments with higher primates make clear.

Certainly consciousness is not distinctive of human beings. If human infants are sometimes conscious – as, surely, they are – then so are other animals – higher

---

[3] For a detailed and expert consideration of the most popular suggestions, see Thorpe [15].

[4] As in Descartes: ". . . speech is the only certain sign of thought hidden in a body. All men use it, however stupid and insane they may be, and though they may lack tongue and organs of voice; but no animals do. Consequently it can be taken as a real specific difference between men and dumb animals" (Descartes [8], p. 245). See also, e.g., Blumenfeld [4], p. 263.

primates, certainly, but also, I should say, all other therian mammals, as well as birds.

So one of the three alleged senses (the one in which only human beings could be said correctly to be alive) is suspect. What about the other two? Is there a distinctive sense of "alive" in which only animals can be said correctly to be alive? Or is there only a general sense in which plants, too, can correctly be said to be alive?

Here it is well to remember that not only plants and animals but also proto-plants and proto-animals (that is, seeds and embryos) and parts of plants and parts of animals can be said to be alive. Once one allows for a different sense in which animals may be said to be alive from that in which plants, too, can be correctly said to be alive, it may be hard to deny, reasonably, that it is in yet other senses that a heart, a bit of tissue, a neuron, a seed or an embryo can be correctly said to be alive. I'd rather say this:

> x is alive = df
> (1) x is an organism (i.e. plant or animal) or x is a part of an organism (organ, bit of organic tissue or cell) or x is an organic seed or embryo and (2) x is capable of regulating itself in the way distinctive of plants, if x is a plant; animals, if x is an animal; organs, if x is an organ; bits of organic tissue, if x is a bit of organic tissue; seeds or embryos, if x is a seed or embryo.

What mode of self-regulation is distinctive of animals? I have already said that it is psychological control. Psychological control in an organism is certainly something that depends in some way on a capacity to take in nourishment, to eliminate wastes and to preserve a degree of homeostasis. Heartbeat and breathing in a mammal or bird may together be a sufficient sign of that underlying capacity. But a decerebrate cat that is kept functioning by external stimulation, though it contains living organs, living tissue and thousands of living cells, is not, I should say, itself alive. And the reason is that it has no psychology; it cannot regulate itself psychologically. As it is with cats, so it is also with human beings. I do not mean, of course, that a cat can do everything that any human being can do. Far from it. I do mean that what a cat has to be capable of doing, for the cat to be alive, is no more than what a human being has to be capable of doing, for the human being to be alive, but that in each case the requirement comes to more than what a plant, or an organ, or a cell, has to be capable of doing for it to be alive.

The discussion so far is intended to give both content and support to (A1), and through it to, especially, the second half of (C1) – namely, "For any human being, h, there is a human body, b, such that . . . h passes out of existence immediately after b last has a psyche." What now about the first half of (C1) – "h comes into being when b first has a psyche"?

If one links, as I do, having a psyche with being alive, one can see the first half of (C1) as a version of the old common-law doctrine of "quickening." According to that doctrine there is a state in the development of a human fetus at which it first comes to life. A recent historical study, *Abortion in America*, by James C. Mohr (New York and Oxford, 1978), gives impressive evidence that the doctrine of quickening lay behind widespread acceptance in the 19th Century of first-trimester abortions. Aborting a fetus before 90 to 120 or so days' gestation was not considered homicide because the little being was thought to be not yet alive and therefore not capable of being killed. Only when the mother could feel movements in her womb was the fetus first considered alive.

In the last three or four decades of the 19th Century the medical profession seems to have convinced the public, including the clergy, that the embryo is alive from the very moment of conception. The question then became, not "when exactly is the human embryo first alive?," but rather "when exactly is the living and developing organism first a human being?" There was, we might say, a shift from the idea that human genesis is the *quickening* of a previously nonliving human body to the idea that human genesis is the *metamorphosis* of an already living organism into a full-fledged human being.[5] Much, though certainly not all, of the abortion debate today concerns when in human embryology (or infancy!) this metamorphosis takes place; such debate presupposes that human genesis is a metamorphosis, rather than a quickening.

In calling, as I want to, for a return to the notion of quickening, I am not proposing that we, like our ancestors, identify quickening as that point in embryology when the embryo or fetus first makes movements with its arms and legs that are perceptible to the mother. Rather I propose that we look for a point at which there is first a being with a psychology – a being that can act to satisfy desire in accordance with perception.[6] But before I say a little more about when that might be, let me say something about what makes the metamorphosis debate so maddeningly frustrating.

Among the points that have been singled out as the point at which a proto-human being first turns into a full-fledged human being the most popular have been these three: (1) conception; (2) viability and (3) birth.

Roger Wertheimer brings out the attractiveness of conception as the point of human genesis in this passage:

> [The newly fertilized zygote] and it alone can claim to be the beginning of the spatio-temporal-causal chain of the physical object that is a human body. . . . Neither the sperm nor the egg could be, by itself, a human being, any more than an atom of sodium or an atom of chlorine could by itself properly be called salt. (Wertheimer [17], p. 79)

Yet there is a decisive objection to taking conception as the point at which there is first a human being. It rests on the phenomenon of twinning. Twinning takes

---

[5] I take the metamorphosis language from Becker [3].

[6] Each part of this crucial phrase ("can," "act," "desire," "in accordance with," and "perception") is philosophically problematic. To make any substantial progress in clarifying the phrase one would need to discuss a range of cases in the literature of animal psychology to get clear about whether, and if so, on what reasonable basis, an amoeba or an earthworm can be correctly said to act to satisfy desire in accordance with perception.

place during the first two weeks or so of gestation. Current research suggests that whether a given zygote twins is a question of its chemical environment and not a question of its genetic make-up. Every zygote, so far as we know, has within itself the potentiality to twin. (See Balmer [2], especially chapter 2.) Reflection on the phenomenon of twinning thus suggests this argument:

(1) No human being has within itself the potentiality to become two human beings.
(2) Every one-celled zygote has within itself the potentiality to become two human beings.

∴(3) No one-celled zygote is a human being.

Several recent discussions of personal identity might provide reason to reject the first premise of this argument (most notably, perhaps, Parfit [11]). But I shall suppose, for present purposes, that such reasoning is faulty. If that is right, then we have quite a devastating objection to the claim that the newly-fertilized ovum is a human being.

What about viability? Viability is meant to be that point in embryology when the fetus is first capable of living on its own, outside the mother's womb.

Perhaps the most troubling thing about viability as the point of human genesis is that the notion of independence it incorporates is objectionably vague. Suppose that a fetus of m months (or g grams) is capable, with probability p, of surviving outside the womb (perhaps with severe birth defects). Is it capable of living on its own? And how long does the infant need to survive for it to be shown to have been viable? A month? A week? A day? An hour? A minute? Was the infant that was able to take only two breaths thereby shown to have been viable?

There is also another worry about viability. Whether an infant will survive outside the mother's womb has as much to do with the development of medical technology and the availability of medical service as with intrinsic developments in the fetus. But most of us recoil from the suggestion that whether a fetus of m months has achieved full human status is a question of the development of medical technology or the availability of medical service. So viability seems unsatisfactory.

Among the three popular candidates for the point at which an already living proto-human being might be said to turn into a full-fledged human being, only birth is left. There are lots of good reasons to say that birth marks the point at which the fetus becomes a legal person. But the metamorphosis idea suggests that an F turns into a G by taking on the form of a G. Birth is certainly one of the most dramatic changes in external circumstance that there is. But it is not a change in form. The butterfly that is ready to break out of the cocoon has already metamorphosed. So also, presumably, has the full-term fetus waiting to be born.

Are there any good suggestions as to when the point of metamorphosis might be that the general public has so far overlooked?

In an impressively well-worked-out paper Lawrence C. Becker has developed an interesting position according to which there is first a human being when

(1) the organism has assumed its basic gross anatomical form, normal or not (by which I mean its basic skeletal structure, musculature, arrangement of organ masses, and distribution of tissues); (2) the organism's inventory (normal or not) of histologically differentiated organs is complete. (Becker [3], p. 343)

Becker supposes that, by his criterion, there is a human being from about the seventh or eighth month of gestation.

In and of itself, Becker's position is attractive. But I become troubled when I lay it alongside reasoning that would have us conclude that there is a human being much, much earlier – perhaps even six months earlier.

Consider a view which G. E. M. Anscombe once outlined to me tentatively in conversation. To determine when in human embryology there is first a human being, Professor Anscombe suggested, one should look to see when there is first a little animal. (Difficulties arising from identical twinning prevented her from going confidently back to conception as immediately yielding a human being, a *Mensch*, *homo* or *anthropos*.) To discover when there is first a little animal one should look to see when there is enough differentiation to mark off recognizable organs and limbs – a functioning heart, liver (etc.), little arms and legs (etc.). When there is that much differentiation (perhaps by the end of the first month, certainly before the end of the second), there is an animal. To find out what kind of animal it is, the reasoning continues, one looks to see what this little animal will naturally become. A *human* child is what it will naturally become; so the little animal is a *human* animal.

I find this line of reasoning attractive, too, but it leads to quite a different conclusion from that of the Becker argument. It leads to saying that a human embryo turns into a human being after the first month or two, whereas Becker's argument would lead us to say that there is first a human being after about seven, or perhaps, eight, months' gestation.

Which is right? Is there first a human being when there are first limbs and a few functioning organs? Or is there first a human being when there is first a complete inventory of organs? I don't know how to choose between these alternatives. My indecision gives the matter a, to me, frightening air of arbitrariness.

Inability to fill out the metamorphosis view in a way that commands assent leads me to reconsider quickening as the point of human genesis – where "quickening" is now taken to mean that point in embryology when a human fetus first comes to "animal life," that is, first becomes a psychological being. Is the idea of quickening plagued with an equally serious indeterminacy?

Perhaps not. The plausibility of taking brainstem death, the point of complete loss of psychological control, as the mark of death in higher animals seems to argue for taking the onset of psychological control as the point at which there is first a living animal (as distinct from a living cell, tissue or even embryo). To die is, after all, to cease to live.[7] But is there actually a point in human embryology (or the

---

[7] This point about a symmetry between the onset and the termination of life is developed nicely in Brody [6] (see especially p. 72) and is stressed by Pluhar [12], p. 161. The point had been considered earlier by Callahan [7], p. 334.

embryology of other higher animals, for that matter) at which psychological self-control begins?

If it were really true, as embryologists have sometimes supposed, that ontogeny recapitulates phylogeny, then there would be psychological control from conception; the one-celled zygote would have the psychology of a protozoon, perhaps that of an amoeba, whereas the embryo or fetus of w weeks might have the psychology of a fish. In fact what we know about the maturation of the central nervous system and about the behavior of the embryo and fetus in the womb rules out such a picture.[8]

But is there any well-defined point in human embryology at which there is first a psychological being? Certainly the newly fertilized ovum is not a psychological being. On the other end, the newborn infant certainly is a psychological being. Recent research indicates that the neonate is already capable of learning on its first day and moreover that its motivation for learning may be simple curiosity.[9] So sometime between conception and birth a psychological being emerges. I expect that research now underway in developmental psychobiology will soon give us reason to fix a point within parameters of a month or so. I predict that that point will be sometime early in the second trimester.

It will be a point well beyond the first emergence of reflexes in the embryo (about $7\frac{1}{2}$ weeks; see Hooker [9], pp. 56, 62–3, 78–9). An amputated frog's leg can be made to jerk upon being stimulated electrically, but an amputated frog's leg does not have a psychology.

It will be a point at which there is sufficient development in the sensory systems (especially, no doubt, taste and touch) and sufficient maturation in the central nervous system to enable the fetus to act to satisfy desire in accordance with perception. Evidence such as the following will help establish the point more exactly:

> The human fetus in utero becomes capable of swallowing as early as the fifth month of development and normally begins to swallow small amounts of amniotic fluid. One obstetrician . . . took advantage of the ability of the fetus to swallow and its preference for sweet-tasting substances to treat expectant mothers suffering from an excess accumulation of fluid within the amniotic sac . . . The obstetrician injected a small amount of saccharine directly through the abdominal wall into the amniotic sac. The fetus almost immediately started swallowing larger-than-usual amounts of the sweetened fluid, which was then absorbed through the intestine into the general circulation of the fetus. Eventually much of the fluid was returned as a waste product

[8] On the psychology of the amoeba, see Jennings [10], chapter 1, esp. pp. 17–25, and chapter 20, esp. pp. 335–7. On the behavior of the human embryo and fetus, see Hooker [9]. Even though human ontogeny does not recapitulate phylogeny, it is well, I think, to link (1) the problem of saying when on the "vertical" scale of human growth and development there is first a being with a psychology with (2) the problem of saying where on the "horizontal" or evolutionary scale of nature there is first a species with a psychology. Each problem puts constraints on dealing with the other, and each problem invites us to try to get clearer about what it is, exactly, that we need a psychological theory to account for (which is a worthwhile project in itself).

[9] Bower [5], pp. 8–9.

to the mother through the placenta and was excreted through her urinary tract. The very beneficial result was a reduction in the painful swelling of the pregnant woman's abdomen. It thus appears that the fetus is capable of discriminatory taste behavior, preferring the sweetened to the normally unsweetened amniotic fluid.[10]

The human embryo is, of course, made up of living organs and living tissue. Moreover, it is itself a living embryo long before it, or its successor, the fetus, takes on a psychology. But there is no human being, I suggest, until that little fetal body comes to psychological, that is, animal, life. Amending Plato somewhat, "There is human life whenever psyche takes possession of a human body; and human death is simply the withdrawal of psyche from that same human body."[11]

Bibliography

[1] Annis, Linda Ferrill, *The Child Before Birth* (Ithaca, 1978).

[2] Balmer, M. G., *The Biology of Twinning* (Oxford, 1970).

[3] Becker, Lawrence C., "Human Being: The Boundaries of the Concept," *Philosophy and Public Affairs*, vol. 4 (1975), pp. 334–59.

[4] Blumenfeld, Jean Beer, "Abortion and the Human Brain," *Philosophical Studies*, vol. 32 (1977), pp. 251–68.

[5] Bower, T. G. R., *Development in Infancy* (San Francisco, 1974).

[6] Brody, Baruch, "On the Humanity of the Foetus," in Robert L. Perkins (ed.), *Abortion: Pro and Con* (Cambridge, Mass., 1974), pp. 69–90.

[7] Callahan, Daniel, *Law, Choice and Morality* (New York, 1970).

[8] Descartes, René, *Philosophical Letters*, ed. and tr. by Anthony Kenny (Oxford, 1970).

[9] Hooker, Davenport, *The Prenatal Origin of Behavior* (Lawrence, Kansas, 1952).

[10] Jennings, H. S., *Behavior of the Lower Organisms* (New York, 1906).

[11] Parfit, Derek, "Personal Identity," *The Philosophical Review*, vol. 80 (1971), pp. 3–27.

[12] Pluhar, Werner S., "Abortion and Simple Consciousness," *The Journal of Philosophy*, vol. 74 (1977), pp. 159–72.

[13] Mohr, James C., *Abortion in America* (New York, 1978).

[14] Montagu, M. F. Ashley, *Prenatal Influences* (Springfield, Ill., 1962).

[15] Thorpe, W. H., *Animal Nature and Human Nature* (New York, 1974).

[16] Veatch, Robert M., *Death, Dying and the Biological Revolution* (New Haven, 1976).

[17] Wertheimer, Roger, "Understanding the Abortion Argument," *Philosophy and Public Affairs*, vol. 1 (1971), pp. 67–95.

[10] Annis [1], pp. 50–1. The obstetrician, Dr. Karl de Snoo, used this procedure, apparently with success, on twenty different fetuses. (See Montagu [14], pp. 106–7.)

[11] This paper is part of a rather ambitious project aimed at recommending the traditional concept of the psyche as an alternative to the Cartesian concept of mind. Here are two crucial differences between the concept of a psyche and the (Cartesian) concept of a mind: (1) whereas a psyche is an animator, a mind has nothing essential to do with life (see my "Consciousness and Life," *Philosophy*, vol. 52 (1977), pp. 13–26); (2) whereas every living animal has a psyche, only human beings, angels and God, according to Descartes, have minds (see my "Animals and the Unity of Psychology," *Philosophy*, vol. 53 (1978), pp. 437–54).

René Descartes, *Letter to Princess Elizabeth* (28 June 1643); selections from *Principles of Philosophy* and *The Passions of the Soul*

To Princess Elizabeth, 28 June 1643

I am very obliged to Your Highness because although she saw how badly I explained myself in my last letter about the question she was good enough to put me, she still has enough patience to listen to me on the same subject and to give me the opportunity to mention the things I left out. The principal omissions seem to me as follows. First of all I distinguished three kinds of primitive ideas or notions, each of which is known in its own proper manner and not by comparison with any of the others: the notions we have of the soul, of body and of the union between the soul and the body. After that I should have explained the difference between these three kinds of notion and between the operations of the soul by which we acquire them. I should have explained also how to make each of them familiar and easy to us. Finally, after saying why I used the analogy of heaviness, I should have explained how, although one may wish to conceive of the soul as material (which is, strictly speaking, to conceive of its union with the body), one may still recognize afterwards that it is separable from the body. I think this covers the topics which Your Highness proposed for me in her letter.

First of all then, I observe one great difference between these three kinds of notions. The soul is conceived only by the pure intellect; body (i.e. extension, shapes and motions) can likewise be known by the intellect alone, but much better by the intellect aided by the imagination; and finally what belongs to the union of the soul and the body is known only obscurely by the intellect alone or even by the intellect aided by the imagination, but it is known very clearly by the senses. That is why people who never philosophize and use only their senses have no doubt that the soul moves the body and that the body acts on the soul. They regard both of them as a single thing, that is to say, they conceive their union; because to conceive the union between two things is to conceive them as one single thing. Metaphysical thoughts, which exercise the pure intellect, help to familiarize us with the notion of the soul; and the study of mathematics, which exercises mainly the imagination in the consideration of shapes and motions, accustoms us to form very distinct notions of body. But it is the ordinary course of life and conversation, and abstention from meditation and from the study of the things which exercise the imagination, that teaches us how to conceive the union of the soul and the body.

I am almost afraid that Your Highness may think that I am not now speaking seriously; but that would go against the respect which I owe her and which I will never cease to show her. I can say with truth that the chief rule I have always

From *The Philosophical Writings of Descartes*, translated by John Cottingham, Robert Stoothoff, and Dugald Murdoch (Cambridge: Cambridge University Press, 1984).

observed in my studies, which I think has been the most useful to me in acquiring what knowledge I have, has been never to spend more than a few hours a day in the thoughts which occupy the imagination and a few hours a year on those which occupy the intellect alone. I have given all the rest of my time to the relaxation of the senses and the repose of the mind. And I include among the exercises of the imagination all serious conversations and anything which needs to be done with attention. This is why I have retired to the country. In the busiest city in the world I could still have as many hours to myself as I now employ in study, but I could not spend them so usefully if my mind was tired by the attention required by the bustle of life. I take the liberty of writing this to Your Highness, so that she may see how genuinely I admire her ability to devote time to the meditations needed to appreciate the distinction between the mind and the body, despite all the business and cares which attend people who combine great minds with high birth.

I think it was those meditations rather than thoughts requiring less attention that have made Your Highness find obscurity in the notion we have of the union of the mind and the body. It does not seem to me that the human mind is capable of forming a very distinct conception of both the distinction between the soul and the body and their union; for to do this it is necessary to conceive them as a single thing and at the same time to conceive them as two things; and this is absurd. This is why I made use earlier of the analogy with heaviness and other qualities which we commonly imagine to be united to certain bodies in the way that thought is united to ours. I supposed that Your Highness still had in mind the arguments proving the distinction between the soul and the body, and I did not want to ask her to put them aside in order to represent to herself the notion of the union which everyone invariably experiences in himself without philosophizing. Everyone feels that he is a single person with both body and thought so related by nature that the thought can move the body and feel the things which happen to it. I did not worry about the fact that the analogy with heaviness was lame because such qualities are not real, as people imagine them to be. This was because I thought that Your Highness was already completely convinced that the soul is a substance distinct from the body.

Your Highness observes that it is easier to attribute matter and extension to the soul than to attribute to it the capacity to move and be moved by the body without having such matter and extension. I beg her to feel free to attribute this matter and extension to the soul because that is simply to conceive it as united to the body. And once she has formed a proper conception of this and experienced it in herself, it will be easy for her to consider that the matter she has attributed to the thought is not thought itself, and that the extension of this matter is of a different nature from the extension of the thought, because the former has a determinate location, such that it thereby excludes all other bodily extension, which is not the case with the latter. And so Your Highness will easily be able to return to the knowledge of the distinction between the soul and the body in spite of having conceived their union.

I believe that it is very necessary to have properly understood, once in a lifetime, the principles of metaphysics, since they are what gives us the knowledge of God and of our soul. But I think also that it would be very harmful to occupy one's intellect frequently in meditating upon them, since this would impede it from devoting itself to the functions of the imagination and the senses. I think the best thing is to content oneself with keeping in one's memory and one's belief the conclusions which one has once drawn from them, and then employ the rest of one's study time to thoughts in which the intellect co-operates with the imagination and the senses.

The great devotion which I feel to Your Highness's service gives me hope that my frankness will not be disagreeable to her. I would have written at greater length, and tried to clarify on this occasion all difficulties on this topic, but I am forced to stop by a piece of tiresome news. I learn from Utrecht that I am summoned before the Magistrates to justify what I have written about one of their ministers. This despite the fact that he has slandered me very unworthily, and that everything that I wrote about him for my just defence was only too well known to everyone. I must proceed to find a way of freeing myself from their quibblings as soon as I can.

From *Principles of Philosophy*

71   *The chief cause of error arises from the preconceived opinions of childhood*
It is here that the first and main cause of all our errors may be recognized. In our early childhood the mind was so closely tied to the body that it had no leisure for any thoughts except those by means of which it had sensory awareness of what was happening to the body. It did not refer these thoughts to anything outside itself, but merely felt pain when something harmful was happening to the body and felt pleasure when something beneficial occurred. And when nothing very beneficial or harmful was happening to the body, the mind had various sensations corresponding to the different areas where, and ways in which, the body was being stimulated, namely what we call the sensations of tastes, smells, sounds, heat, cold, light, colours and so on — sensations which do not represent anything located outside our thought.[1] At the same time the mind perceived sizes, shapes, motions and so on, which were presented to it not as sensations but as things, or modes of things, existing (or at least capable of existing) outside thought, although it was not yet aware of the difference between things and sensations. The next stage arose when the mechanism of the body, which is so constructed by nature that it has the ability to move in various ways by its own power, twisted around aimlessly in all directions in its random attempts to pursue the beneficial and avoid the harmful; at this point the mind that was attached to the body began to notice that the objects of this pursuit or avoidance had an existence outside itself. And it attributed to them not only sizes, shapes, motions and the like, which it perceived as things or

[1] ". . . but which vary according to the different movements which pass from all parts of our body to the part of the brain to which our mind is closely joined and united" (added in French version).

60

modes of things, but also tastes, smells and so on, the sensations of which were, it realized, produced by the objects in question. Moreover, since the mind judged everything in terms of its utility to the body in which it was immersed, it assessed the amount of reality in each object by the extent to which it was affected by it. As a result, it supposed that there was more substance or corporeality in rocks and metals than in water or air, since it felt more hardness and heaviness in them. Indeed, it regarded the air as a mere nothing, so long as it felt no wind or cold or heat in it. And because the light coming from the stars appeared no brighter than that produced by the meagre glow of an oil lamp, it did not imagine any star as being any bigger than this. And because it did not observe that the earth turns on its axis or that its surface is curved to form a globe, it was rather inclined to suppose that the earth was immobile and its surface flat. Right from infancy our mind was swamped with a thousand such preconceived opinions; and in later childhood, forgetting that they were adopted without sufficient examination, it regarded them as known by the senses or implanted by nature, and accepted them as utterly true and evident. [. . .]

From *The Passions of the Soul*

30 *The soul is united to all the parts of the body conjointly*

But in order to understand all these things more perfectly, we need to recognize that the soul is really joined to the whole body, and that we cannot properly say that it exists in any one part of the body to the exclusion of the others. For the body is a unity which is in a sense indivisible because of the arrangement of its organs, these being so related to one another that the removal of any one of them renders the whole body defective. And the soul is of such a nature that it has no relation to extension, or to the dimensions or other properties of the matter of which the body is composed: it is related solely to the whole assemblage of the body's organs. This is obvious from our inability to conceive of a half or a third of a soul, or of the extension which a soul occupies. Nor does the soul become any smaller if we cut off some part of the body, but it becomes completely separate from the body when we break up the assemblage of the body's organs.

31 *There is a little gland in the brain where the soul exercises its functions more particularly than in the other parts of the body*

We need to recognize also that although the soul is joined to the whole body, nevertheless there is a certain part of the body where it exercises its functions more particularly than in all the others. It is commonly held that this part is the brain, or perhaps the heart – the brain because the sense organs are related to it, and the heart because we feel the passions as if they were in it. But on carefully examining the matter I think I have clearly established that the part of the body in which the soul directly exercises its functions is not the heart at all, or the whole of the brain. It is rather the innermost part of the brain, which is a certain very small gland situated in the middle of the brain's substance and suspended above the passage through which the spirits in the brain's anterior cavities communicate with those in its posterior cavities. The slightest movements on the part of this gland may alter very greatly the course of these spirits, and conversely any change, however slight, taking place in the course of the spirits may do much to change the movements of the gland.

32 How we know that this gland is the principal seat of the soul

Apart from this gland, there cannot be any other place in the whole body where the soul directly exercises its functions. I am convinced of this by the observation that all the other parts of our brain are double, as also are all the organs of our external senses — eyes, hands, ears and so on. But in so far as we have only one simple thought about a given object at any one time, there must necessarily be some place where the two images coming through the two eyes, or the two impressions coming from a single object through the double organs of any other sense, can come together in a single image or impression before reaching the soul, so that they do not present to it two objects instead of one. We can easily understand that these images or other impressions are unified in this gland by means of the spirits which fill the cavities of the brain. But they cannot exist united in this way in any other place in the body except as a result of their being united in this gland. [. . .]

34 How the soul and the body act on each other

Let us therefore take it that the soul has its principal seat in the small gland located in the middle of the brain. From there it radiates through the rest of the body by means of the animal spirits, the nerves, and even the blood, which can take on the impressions of the spirits and carry them through the arteries to all the limbs. Let us recall what we said previously about the mechanism of our body. The nerve-fibres are so distributed in all the parts of the body that when the objects of the senses produce various different movements in these parts, the fibres are occasioned to open the pores of the brain in various different ways. This, in turn, causes the animal spirits contained in these cavities to enter the muscles in various different ways. In this manner the spirits can move the limbs in all the different ways they are capable of being moved. And all the other causes that can move the spirits in different ways are sufficient to direct them into different muscles. To this we may now add that the small gland which is the principal seat of the soul is suspended within the cavities containing these spirits, so that it can be moved by them in as many different ways as there are perceptible differences in the objects. But it can also be moved in various different ways by the soul, whose nature is such that it receives as many different impressions — that is, it has as many different perceptions as there occur different movements in this gland. And conversely, the mechanism of our body is so constructed that simply by this gland's being moved in any way by the soul or by any other cause, it drives the surrounding spirits towards the pores of the brain, which direct them through the nerves to the muscles; and in this way the gland makes the spirits move the limbs.

35   *Example of the way in which the impressions of objects are united in the gland in the middle of the brain*

Thus, for example, if we see some animal approaching us, the light reflected from its body forms two images, one in each of our eyes; and these images form two others, by means of the optic nerves, on the internal surface of the brain facing its cavities. Then, by means of the spirits that fill these cavities, the images radiate towards the little gland which the spirits surround: the movement forming each point of one of the images tends towards the same point on the gland as the movement forming the corresponding point of the other image, which represents the same part of the animal. In this way, the two images in the brain form only one image on the gland, which acts directly upon the soul and makes it see the shape of the animal. [. . .]

Jerry A. Fodor, "The Mind–Body Problem"

Could calculating machines have pains, Martians have expectations and disembodied spirits have thoughts? The modern functionalist approach to psychology raises the logical possibility that they could.

Modern philosophy of science has been devoted largely to the formal and systematic description of the successful practices of working scientists. The philosopher does not try to dictate how scientific inquiry and argument ought to be conducted. Instead he tries to enumerate the principles and practices that have contributed to good science. The philosopher has devoted the most attention to analyzing the methodological peculiarities of the physical sciences. The analysis has helped to clarify the nature of confirmation, the logical structure of scientific theories, the formal properties of statements that express laws and the question of whether theoretical entities actually exist.

It is only rather recently that philosophers have become seriously interested in the methodological tenets of psychology. Psychological explanations of behavior refer liberally to the mind and to states, operations and processes of the mind. The philosophical difficulty comes in stating in unambiguous language what such references imply.

Traditional philosophies of mind can be divided into two broad categories: dualist theories and materialist theories. In the dualist approach the mind is a nonphysical substance. In materialist theories the mental is not distinct from the physical; indeed, all mental states, properties, processes and operations are in principle identical with physical states, properties, processes and operations. Some materialists, known as behaviorists, maintain that all talk of mental causes can be eliminated from the language of psychology in favor of talk of environmental stimuli and behavioral responses. Other materialists, the identity theorists, contend that there are mental causes and that they are identical with neurophysiological events in the brain.

From *Scientific American* (January 1981), pp. 114–23.

In the past 15 years a philosophy of mind called functionalism that is neither dualist nor materialist has emerged from philosophical reflection on developments in artificial intelligence, computational theory, linguistics, cybernetics and psychology. All these fields, which are collectively known as the cognitive sciences, have in common a certain level of abstraction and a concern with systems that process information. Functionalism, which seeks to provide a philosophical account of this level of abstraction, recognizes the possibility that systems as diverse as human beings, calculating machines and disembodied spirits could all have mental states. In the functionalist view the psychology of a system depends not on the stuff it is made of (living cells, metal or spiritual energy) but on how the stuff is put together. Functionalism is a difficult concept, and one way of coming to grips with it is to review the deficiencies of the dualist and materialist philosophies of mind it aims to displace.

The chief drawback of dualism is its failure to account adequately for mental causation. If the mind is nonphysical, it has no position in physical space. How, then, can a mental cause give rise to a behavioral effect that has a position in space? To put it another way, how can the nonphysical give rise to the physical without violating the laws of the conservation of mass, of energy and of momentum?

The dualist might respond that the problem of how an immaterial substance can cause physical events is not much obscurer than the problem of how one physical event can cause another. Yet there is an important difference: there are many clear cases of physical causation but not one clear case of nonphysical causation. Physical interaction is something philosophers, like all other people, have to live with. Nonphysical interaction, however, may be no more than an artifact of the immaterialist construal of the mental. Most philosophers now agree that no argument has successfully demonstrated why mind–body causation should not be regarded as a species of physical causation.

Dualism is also incompatible with the practices of working psychologists. The psychologist frequently applies the experimental methods of the physical sciences to the study of the mind. If mental processes were different in kind from physical processes, there would be no reason to expect these methods to work in the realm of the mental. In order to justify their experimental methods many psychologists urgently sought an alternative to dualism.

In the 1920s John B. Watson of Johns Hopkins University made the radical suggestion that behavior does not have mental causes. He regarded the behavior of an organism as its observable responses to stimuli, which he took to be the causes of its behavior. Over the next 30 years psychologists such as B. F. Skinner of Harvard University developed Watson's ideas into an elaborate world view in which the role of psychology was to catalogue the laws that determine causal relations between stimuli and responses. In this "radical behaviorist" view the problem of explaining the nature of the mind–body interaction vanishes; there is no such interaction.

Radical behaviorism has always worn an air of paradox. For better or worse, the idea of mental causation is deeply ingrained in our everyday language and in our ways of understanding our fellow men and ourselves. For example, people commonly attribute behavior to beliefs, to knowledge and to expectations. Brown puts gas in his tank because he believes the car will not run without it. Jones writes not "acheive" but "achieve" because he knows the rule about putting *i* before *e*. Even when a behavioral response is closely tied to an environmental stimulus, mental processes often intervene. Smith carries an umbrella because the sky is cloudy, but the weather is only part of the story. There are apparently also mental links in the causal chain: observation and expectation. The clouds affect Smith's behavior only because he observes them and because they induce in him an expectation of rain.

The radical behaviorist is unmoved by appeals to such cases. He is prepared to dismiss references to mental causes, however plausible they may seem, as the residue of outworn creeds. The radical behaviorist predicts that as psychologists come to understand more about the relations between stimuli and responses they will find it increasingly possible to explain behavior without postulating mental causes.

The strongest argument against behaviorism is that psychology has not turned out this way; the opposite has happened. As psychology has matured, the framework of mental states and processes that is apparently needed to account for experimental observations has grown all the more elaborate. Particularly in the case of human behavior psychological theories satisfying the methodological tenets of radical behaviorism have proved largely sterile, as would be expected if the postulated mental processes are real and causally effective.

Nevertheless, many philosophers were initially drawn to radical behaviorism because, paradoxes and all, it seemed better than dualism. Since a psychology committed to immaterial substances was unacceptable, philosophers turned to radical behaviorism because it seemed to be the only alternative materialist philosophy of mind. The choice, as they saw it, was between radical behaviorism and ghosts.

By the early 1960s philosophers began to have doubts that dualism and radical behaviorism exhausted the possible approaches to the philosophy of mind. Since the two theories seemed unattractive, the right strategy might be to develop a materialist philosophy of mind that nonetheless allowed for mental causes. Two such philosophies emerged, one called logical behaviorism and the other called the central-state identity theory.

Logical behaviorism is a semantic theory about what mental terms mean. The basic idea is that attributing a mental state (say thirst) to an organism is the same as saying that the organism is disposed to behave in a particular way (for example to drink if there is water available). On this view every mental ascription is equivalent in meaning to an if–then statement (called a behavioral hypothetical) that expresses a behavioral disposition. For example, "Smith is thirsty" might be taken to be equivalent to the dispositional statement "If there were water available, then Smith would drink some." By definition a behavioral hypothetical includes no mental terms. The if-clause of the hypothetical speaks only of stimuli and the then-clause speaks only of behavioral responses. Since stimuli and responses are physical events, logical behaviorism is a species of materialism.

The strength of logical behaviorism is that by translating mental language into the language of stimuli and responses it provides an interpretation of psychological explanations in which behavioral effects are attributed to mental causes. Mental causation is simply the manifestation of a behavioral disposition. More precisely, mental causation is what happens when an organism has a behavioral disposition and the if-clause of the behavioral hypothetical expressing the disposition happens to be true. For example, the causal statement "Smith drank some water because he was thirsty" might be taken to mean "If there were water available, then Smith would drink some, and there was water available."

I have somewhat oversimplified logical behaviorism by assuming that each mental ascription can be translated by a unique behavioral hypothetical. Actually the logical behaviorist often maintains that it takes an open-ended set (perhaps an infinite set) of behavioral hypotheticals to spell out the behavioral disposition expressed by a mental term. The mental ascription "Smith is thirsty" might also be satisfied by the hypothetical "If there were orange juice available, then Smith would drink some" and by a host of other hypotheticals. In any event the logical behaviorist does not usually maintain he can actually enumerate all the hypotheticals that correspond to a behavioral disposition expressing a given mental term. He only insists that in principle the meaning of any mental term can be conveyed by behavioral hypotheticals.

The way the logical behaviorist has interpreted a mental term such as thirsty is modeled after the way many philosophers have interpreted a physical disposition such as fragility. The physical disposition "The glass is fragile" is often taken to mean something like "If the glass were struck, then it would break." By the same token the logical behaviorist's analysis of mental causation is similar to the received analysis of one kind of physical causation. The causal statement "The glass broke because it was fragile" is taken to mean something like "If the glass were struck, then it would break, and the glass was struck."

By equating mental terms with behavioral dispositions the logical behaviorist has put mental terms on a par with the nonbehavioral dispositions of the physical sciences. That is a promising move, because the analysis of nonbehavioral dispositions is on relatively solid philosophical ground. An explanation attributing the breaking of a glass to its fragility is surely something even the staunchest materialist can accept. By arguing that mental terms are synonymous with dispositional terms, the logical behaviorist has provided something the radical behaviorist could not: a materialist account of mental causation.

Nevertheless, the analogy between mental causation as construed by the logical behaviorist and physical causation goes only so far. The logical behaviorist treats the manifestation of a disposition as the sole form of mental causation, whereas the physical sciences recognize additional kinds of causation. There is the kind of causation where one physical event causes another, as when the breaking of a glass is attributed to its having been struck. In fact, explanations that involve event–event causation are presumably more basic than dispositional explanations, because the manifestation of a disposition (the breaking of a fragile glass) always involves event–event causation and not vice versa. In the realm of the mental many examples of event–event causation involve one mental state's causing another, and for this kind of causation logical behaviorism provides no analysis. As a result the logical behaviorist is committed to the tacit and implausible assumption that psychology requires a less robust notion of causation than the physical sciences require.

Event–event causation actually seems to be quite common in the realm of the mental. Mental causes typically give rise to behavioral effects by virtue of their interaction with other mental causes. For example, having a headache causes a disposition to take aspirin only if one also has the desire to get rid of the headache, the belief that aspirin exists, the belief that taking aspirin reduces headaches and so on. Since mental states interact in generating behavior, it will be necessary to find a construal of psychological explanations that posits mental processes: causal sequences of mental events. It is this construal that logical behaviorism fails to provide.

Such considerations bring out a fundamental way in which logical behaviorism is quite similar to radical behaviorism. It is true that the logical behaviorist, unlike the radical behaviorist, acknowledges the existence of mental states. Yet since the underlying tenet of logical behaviorism is that references to mental states can be translated out of psychological explanations by employing behavioral hypotheticals, all talk of mental states and processes is in a sense heuristic. The only facts to which the behaviorist is actually committed are facts about relations between stimuli and responses. In this respect logical behaviorism is just radical behaviorism in a semantic form. Although the former theory offers a construal of mental causation, the construal is Pickwickian. What does not really exist cannot cause anything, and the logical behaviorist, like the radical behaviorist, believes deep down that mental causes do not exist.

An alternative materialist theory of the mind to logical behaviorism is the central-state identity theory. According to this theory, mental events, states and processes are identical with neurophysiological events in the brain, and the property of being in a certain mental state (such as having a headache or believing it will rain) is identical with the property of being in a certain neurophysiological state. On this basis it is easy to make sense of the idea that a behavioral effect might sometimes have a chain of mental causes; that will be the case whenever a behavioral effect is contingent on the appropriate sequence of neurophysiological events.

The central-state identity theory acknowledges that it is possible for mental causes to interact causally without ever giving rise to any behavioral effect, as when a person thinks for a while about what he ought to do and then decides to do nothing. If mental processes are neurophysiological, they must have the causal properties of neurophysiological processes. Since neurophysiological processes are presumably physical processes, the central-state identity theory ensures that the concept of mental causation is as rich as the concept of physical causation.

The central-state identity theory provides a satisfactory account of what the mental terms in psychological explanations refer to, and so it is favored by psychologists who are dissatisfied with behaviorism. The behaviorist maintains that mental terms refer to nothing or that they refer to the parameters of stimulus–response relations.

Either way the existence of mental entities is only illusory. The identity theorist, on the other hand, argues that mental terms refer to neurophysiological states. Thus he can take seriously the project of explaining behavior by appealing to its mental causes.

The chief advantage of the identity theory is that it takes the explanatory constructs of psychology at face value, which is surely something a philosophy of mind ought to do if it can. The identity theory shows how the mentalistic explanations of psychology could be not mere heuristics but literal accounts of the causal history of behavior. Moreover, since the identity theory is not a semantic thesis, it is immune to many arguments that cast in doubt logical behaviorism. A drawback of logical behaviorism is that the observation "John has a headache" does not seem to mean the same thing as a statement of the form "John is disposed to behave in such and such a way." The identity theorist, however, can live with the fact that "John has a headache" and "John is in such and such a brain state" are not synonymous. The assertion of the identity theorist is not that these sentences mean the same thing but only that they are rendered true (or false) by the same neurophysiological phenomena.

The identity theory can be held either as a doctrine about mental particulars (John's current pain or Bill's fear of animals) or as a doctrine about mental universals, or properties (having a pain or being afraid of animals). The two doctrines, called respectively token physicalism and type physicalism, differ in strength and plausibility. Token physicalism maintains only that all the mental particulars that happen to exist are neurophysiological, whereas type physicalism makes the more sweeping assertion that all the mental particulars there could possibly be are neurophysiological. Token physicalism does not rule out the logical possibility of machines and disembodied spirits having mental properties. Type physicalism dismisses this possibility because neither machines nor disembodied spirits have neurons.

Type physicalism is not a plausible doctrine about mental properties even if token physicalism is right about mental particulars. The problem with type physicalism is that the psychological constitution of a system seems to depend not on its hardware, or physical composition, but on its software, or program. Why should the philosopher dismiss the possibility that silicon-based Martians have pains, assuming that the silicon is properly organized? And why should the philosopher rule out the possibility of machines having beliefs, assuming that the machines are correctly programmed? If it is logically possible that Martians and machines could have mental properties, then mental properties and neurophysiological processes cannot be identical, however much they may prove to be coextensive.

What it all comes down to is that there seems to be a level of abstraction at which the generalizations of psychology are most naturally pitched. This level of abstraction cuts across differences in the physical composition of the systems to which psychological generalizations apply. In the cognitive sciences, at least, the natural domain for psychological theorizing seems to be all systems that process information. The problem with type physicalism is that there are possible information-processing systems with the same psychological constitution as human beings but not the same physical organization. In principle all kinds of physically different things could have human software.

This situation calls for a relational account of mental properties that abstracts them from the physical structure of their bearers. In spite of the objections to logical behaviorism that I presented above, logical behaviorism was at least on the right track in offering a relational interpretation of mental properties: to have a headache is to be disposed to exhibit a certain pattern of relations between the stimuli one encounters and the responses one exhibits. If that is what having a headache is, however, there is no reason in principle why only heads that are physically similar to ours can ache. Indeed, according to logical behaviorism, it is a necessary truth that any system that has our stimulus–response contingencies also has our headaches.

All of this emerged 10 or 15 years ago as a nasty dilemma for the materialist program in the philosophy of mind. On the one hand the identity theorist (and not the logical behaviorist) had got right the causal character of the interactions of mind and body. On the other the logical behaviorist (and not the identity theorist) had got right the relational character of mental properties. Functionalism has apparently been able to resolve the dilemma. By stressing the distinction computer science draws between hardware and software the functionalist can make sense of both the causal and the relational character of the mental.

The intuition underlying functionalism is that what determines the psychological type to which a mental particular belongs is the causal role of the particular in the mental life of the organism. Functional individuation is differentiation with respect to causal role. A headache, for example, is identified with the type of mental state that among other things causes a disposition for taking aspirin in people who believe aspirin relieves a headache, causes a desire to rid oneself of the pain one is feeling, often causes someone who speaks English to say such things as "I have a headache" and is brought on by overwork, eyestrain and tension. This list is presumably not complete. More will be known about the nature of a headache as psychological and physiological research discovers more about its causal role.

Functionalism construes the concept of causal role in such a way that a mental state can be defined by its causal relations to other mental states. In this respect functionalism is completely different from logical behaviorism. Another major difference is that functionalism is not a reductionist thesis. It does not foresee, even in principle, the elimination of mentalistic concepts from the explanatory apparatus of psychological theories.

The difference between functionalism and logical behaviorism is brought out by the fact that functionalism is fully compatible with token physicalism. The functionalist would not be disturbed if brain events turn out to be the only things with the functional properties that define mental states. Indeed, most functionalists fully expect it will turn out that way.

Since functionalism recognizes that mental particulars may be physical, it is compatible with the idea that mental causation is a species of physical causation. In other words, functionalism tolerates the materialist solution to the mind–body problem provided by the central-state identity theory. It is possible for the functionalist to assert both that mental properties are typically defined in terms of their relations and that interactions of mind and body are typically causal in however robust a notion of causality is required by psychological explanations. The logical behaviorist can endorse only the first assertion and the type physicalist only the second. As a result functionalism seems to capture the best features of the materialist alternatives to dualism. It is no wonder that functionalism has become increasingly popular.

Machines provide good examples of two concepts that are central to functionalism: the concept that mental states are interdefined and the concept that they can be realized by many systems. The illustration [opposite] contrasts a behavioristic Coke machine with a mentalistic one. Both machines dispense a Coke for 10 cents. (The price has not been affected by inflation.) The states of the machines are defined by reference to their causal roles, but only the machine on the left would satisfy the behaviorist. Its single state (*S0*) is completely specified in terms of stimuli and responses. *S0* is the state a machine is in if, and only if, given a dime as the input, it dispenses a Coke as the output.

The machine on the right in the illustration has interdefined states (*S1* and *S2*), which are characteristic of functionalism. *S1* is the state a machine is in if, and only if, (1) given a nickel, it dispenses nothing and proceeds to *S2*, and (2) given a dime, it dispenses a Coke and stays in *S1*. *S2* is the state a machine is in if, and only if, (1) given a nickel, it dispenses a Coke and proceeds to *S1*, and (2) given a dime, it dispenses a Coke and a nickel and proceeds to *S1*. What *S1* and *S2* jointly amount to is the machine's dispensing a Coke if it is given a dime, dispensing a Coke and a nickel if it is given a dime and a nickel and waiting to be given a second nickel if it has been given a first one.

Since *S1* and *S2* are each defined by hypothetical statements, they can be viewed as dispositions. Nevertheless, they are not behavioral dispositions because the consequences an input has for a machine in *S1* or *S2* are not specified solely in terms of the output of the machine. Rather, the consequences also involve the machine's internal states.

Nothing about the way I have described the behavioristic and mentalistic Coke machines puts constraints on what they could be made of. Any system whose states bore the proper relations to inputs, outputs and other states could be one of these machines. No doubt it is reasonable to expect such a system to be constructed out of such things as wheels, levers and diodes (token physicalism for Coke machines). Similarly, it is reasonable to expect that our minds may prove to be neurophysiological (token physicalism for human beings).

Nevertheless, the software description of a Coke machine does not logically require wheels, levers and diodes for its concrete realization. By the same token, the software description of the mind does not logically require neurons. As far as functionalism is concerned a Coke machine with states *S1* and *S2* could be made of ectoplasm, if there is such stuff and if its states have the right causal properties. Functionalism allows for the possibility of disembodied Coke machines in exactly the same way and to the same extent that it allows for the possibility of disembodied minds.

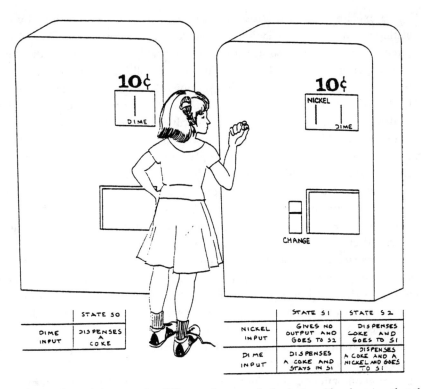

	STATE S0
DIME INPUT	DISPENSES A COKE

	STATE S1	STATE S2
NICKEL INPUT	GIVES NO OUTPUT AND GOES TO S2	DISPENSES COKE AND GOES TO S1
DIME INPUT	DISPENSES A COKE AND STAYS IN S1	DISPENSES A COKE AND A NICKEL AND GOES TO S1

Two Coke machines bring out the difference between behaviorism (the doctrine that there are no mental causes) and mentalism (the doctrine that there are mental causes). Both machines dispense a Coke for 10 cents and have states that are defined by reference to their causal role. The machine at the left is a behavioristic one: its single state ($S0$) is defined solely in terms of the input and the output. The machine at the right is a mentalistic one: its two states ($S1$, $S2$) must be defined not only in terms of the input and the output but also in terms of each other. To put it another way, the output of the Coke machine depends on the state the machine is in as well as on the input. The functionalist philosopher maintains that mental states are interdefined, like the internal states of the mentalistic Coke machine.

To say that $S1$ and $S2$ are interdefined and realizable by different kinds of hardware is not, of course, to say that a Coke machine has a mind. Although interdefinition and functional specification are typical features of mental states, they are clearly not sufficient for mentality. What more is required is a question to which I shall return below.

Some philosophers are suspicious of functionalism because it seems too easy. Since functionalism licenses the individuation of states by reference to their causal role, it appears to allow a trivial explanation of any observed event E, that is, it appears to postulate an E-causer. For example, what makes the valves in a machine open? Why, the operation of a valve opener. And what is a valve opener? Why, anything that has the functionally defined property of causing valves to open.

In psychology this kind of question-begging often takes the form of theories that in effect postulate homunculi with the selfsame intellectual capacities the theorist set out to explain. Such is the case when visual perception is explained by simply postulating psychological mechanisms that process visual information. The behaviorist has often charged the mentalist, sometimes justifiably, of mongering this kind of question-begging pseudo explanation. The charge will have to be met if functionally defined mental states are to have a serious role in psychological theories.

The burden of the accusation is not untruth but triviality. There can be no doubt that it is a valve opener that opens valves, and it is likely that visual perception is mediated by the processing of visual information. The charge is that such putative functional explanations are mere platitudes. The functionalist can meet this objection by allowing functionally defined theoretical constructs only where mechanisms exist that can carry out the function and only where he has some notion of what such mechanisms might be like. One way of imposing this requirement is to identify the mental processes that psychology postulates with the operations of the restricted class of possible computers called Turing machines.

A Turing machine can be informally characterized as a mechanism with a finite number of program states. The inputs and outputs of the machine are written on a tape that is divided into squares each of which includes a symbol from a finite alphabet. The machine scans the tape one square at a time. It can erase the symbol on a scanned square and print a new one in its place. The machine can execute only the elementary mechanical operations of scanning, erasing, printing, moving the tape and changing state.

The program states of the Turing machine are defined solely in terms of the input symbols on the tape, the output symbols on the tape, the elementary operations and the other states of the program. Each program state is therefore functionally defined by the part it plays in the overall operation of the machine. Since the functional role of a state depends on the relation of the state to other states as well as to inputs and outputs, the relational character of the mental state is captured by the Turing-machine version of functionalism. Since the definition of a program state never refers to the physical structure of the system running the program, the Turing-machine version of functionalism also captures the idea that the character of a mental state is independent of its physical realization. A human being, a roomful of people, a computer and a disembodied spirit would all be a Turing machine if they operated according to a Turing-machine program.

The proposal is to restrict the functional definition of psychological states to those that can be expressed in terms of the program states of Turing machines. If this restriction can be enforced, it provides a guarantee that psychological theories will be compatible with the demands of mechanisms. Since Turing machines are very simple devices, they are in principle quite easy to build. Consequently by formulating a psychological explanation as a Turing-machine program the psychologist ensures that the explanation is mechanistic, even though the hardware realizing the mechanism is left open.

There are many kinds of computational mechanisms other than Turing machines, and so the formulation of a functionalist psychological theory in Turing-machine notation provides only a sufficient condition for the theory's being mechanically realizable. What makes the condition interesting, however, is that the simple Turing machine can perform many complex tasks. Although the elementary operations of the Turing machine are restricted, iterations of the operations enable the machine to carry out any well-defined computation on discrete symbols.

An important tendency in the cognitive sciences is to treat the mind chiefly as a device that manipulates symbols. If a mental process can be functionally defined as an operation on symbols, there is a Turing machine capable of carrying out the computation and a variety of mechanisms for realizing the Turing machine. Where the manipulation of symbols is important the Turing machine provides a connection between functional explanation and mechanistic explanation.

The reduction of a psychological theory to a program for a Turing machine is a way of exorcising the homunculi. The reduction ensures that no operations have been postulated except those that could be performed by a familiar mechanism. Of course, the working psychologist usually cannot specify the reduction for each functionally individuated process in every theory he is prepared to take seriously. In practice the argument usually goes in the opposite direction; if the postulation of a mental operation is essential to some cherished psychological explanation, the theorist tends to assume that there must be a program for a Turing machine that will carry out that operation.

The "black boxes" that are common in flow charts drawn by psychologists often serve to indicate postulated mental processes for which Turing reductions are wanting. Even so, the possibility in principle of such reductions serves as a methodological constraint on psychological theorizing by determining what functional definitions are to be allowed and what it would be like to know that everything has been explained that could possibly need explanation.

Such is the origin, the provenance and the promise of contemporary functionalism. How much has it actually paid off? This question is not easy to answer because much of what is now happening in the philosophy of mind and the cognitive sciences is directed at exploring the scope and limits of the functionalist explanations of behavior. I shall, however, give a brief overview.

An obvious objection to functionalism as a theory of the mind is that the functionalist definition is not limited to mental states and processes. Catalysts, Coke machines, valve openers, pencil sharpeners, mousetraps and ministers of finance are all in one way or another concepts that are functionally defined, but none is a mental concept such as pain, belief and desire. What, then, characterizes the mental? And can it be captured in a functionalist framework?

The traditional view in the philosophy of mind has it that mental states are distinguished by their having what are called either qualitative content or intentional content. I shall discuss qualitative content first.

It is not easy to say what qualitative content is; indeed, according to some theories, it is not even possible to say what it is because it can be known not by description but only by direct experience. I shall nonetheless attempt to describe it. Try to imagine looking at a blank wall through a red filter. Now change the filter to a green one and leave everything else exactly the way it was. Something about the character of your experience changes when the filter does, and it is this kind of thing that philosophers call qualitative content. I am not entirely comfortable about introducing qualitative content in this way, but it is a subject with which many philosophers are not comfortable.

The reason qualitative content is a problem for functionalism is straightforward. Functionalism is committed to defining mental states in terms of their causes and effects. It seems, however, as if two mental states could have all the same causal relations and yet could differ in their qualitative content. Let me illustrate this with the classic puzzle of the inverted spectrum.

It seems possible to imagine two observers who are alike in all relevant psychological respects except that experiences having the qualitative content of red for one observer would have the qualitative content of green for the other. Nothing about their behavior need reveal the difference because both of them see ripe tomatoes and flaming sunsets as being similar in color and both of them call that color "red." Moreover, the causal connection between their (qualitatively distinct) experiences and their other mental states could also be identical. Perhaps they both think of Little Red Riding Hood when they see ripe tomatoes, feel depressed when they see the color green and so on. It seems as if anything that could be packed into the notion of the causal role of their experiences could be shared by them, and yet the qualitative content of the experiences could be as different as you like. If this is possible, then the functionalist account does not work for mental states that have qualitative content. If one person is having a green experience while another person is having a red one, then surely they must be in different mental states.

The example of the inverted spectrum is more than a verbal puzzle. Having qualitative content is supposed to be a chief factor in what makes a mental state conscious. Many psychologists who are inclined to accept the functionalist framework are nonetheless worried about the failure of functionalism to reveal much about the nature of consciousness. Functionalists have made a few ingenious attempts to talk themselves and their colleagues out of this worry, but they have not, in my view, done so with much success. (For example, perhaps one is wrong in thinking one can imagine what an inverted spectrum would be like.) As matters stand, the problem of qualitative content poses a serious threat to the assertion that functionalism can provide a general theory of the mental.

Functionalism has fared much better with the intentional content of mental states. Indeed, it is here that the major achievements of recent cognitive science are found. To say that a mental state has intentional content is to say that it has certain semantic properties. For example, for Enrico to believe Galileo was Italian apparently involves a three-way relation between Enrico, a belief and a proposition that is the content of the belief (namely the proposition that Galileo was Italian). In particular it is an essential property of Enrico's belief that it is about Galileo (and not about, say, Newton) and that it is true if, and only if, Galileo was indeed Italian. Philosophers are divided on how these considerations fit together, but it is widely agreed that beliefs involve semantic properties such as expressing a proposition, being true or false and being about one thing rather than another.

It is important to understand the semantic properties of beliefs because theories in the cognitive sciences are largely about the beliefs organisms have. Theories of learning and perception, for example, are chiefly accounts of how the host of beliefs an organism has are determined by the character of its experiences and its genetic endowment. The functionalist account of mental states does not by itself provide the required insights. Mousetraps are functionally defined, yet mousetraps do not express propositions, and they are not true or false.

There is at least one kind of thing other than a mental state that has intentional content: a symbol. Like thoughts, symbols seem to be about things. If someone says "Galileo was Italian," his utterance, like Enrico's belief, expresses a proposition about Galileo that is true or false depending on Galileo's homeland. This parallel between the symbolic and the mental underlies the traditional quest for a unified treatment of language and mind. Cognitive science is now trying to provide such a treatment.

The basic concept is simple but striking. Assume that there are such things as mental symbols (mental representations) and that mental symbols have semantic properties. On this view having a belief involves being related to a mental symbol, and the belief inherits its semantic properties from the mental symbol that figures in the relation. Mental processes (thinking, perceiving, learning and so on) involve causal interactions among relational states such as having a belief. The semantic properties of the words and sentences we utter are in turn inherited from the semantic properties of the mental states that language expresses.

Associating the semantic properties of mental states with those of mental symbols is fully compatible with the computer metaphor, because it is natural to think of the computer as a mechanism that manipulates symbols. A computation is a causal chain of computer states, and the links in the chain are operations on semantically interpreted formulas in a machine code. To think of a system (such as the nervous system) as a computer is to raise questions about the nature of the code in which it computes and the semantic properties of the symbols in the code. In fact, the analogy between minds and computers actually implies the postulation of mental symbols. There is no computation without representation.

The representational account of the mind, however, predates considerably the invention of the computing machine. It is a throwback to classical epistemology, which is a tradition that includes philosophers as diverse as John Locke, David Hume, George Berkeley, René Descartes, Immanuel Kant, John Stuart Mill and William James.

Hume, for one, developed a representational theory of the mind that included five points. First, there exist "Ideas," which are a species of mental symbol. Second, having a belief involves entertaining an Idea. Third, mental processes are causal associations of Ideas. Fourth, Ideas are like pictures. And fifth, Ideas have their semantic properties by virtue of what they resemble: the Idea of John is about John because it looks like him.

Contemporary cognitive psychologists do not accept the details of Hume's theory, although they endorse much of its spirit. Theories of computation provide a far richer account of mental processes than the mere association of Ideas. And only a few psychologists still think that imagery is the chief vehicle of mental representation. Nevertheless, the most significant break with Hume's theory lies in the abandoning of resemblance as an explanation of the semantic properties of mental representations.

Many philosophers, starting with Berkeley, have argued that there is something seriously wrong with the suggestion that the semantic relation between a thought and what the thought is about could be one of resemblance. Consider the thought that John is tall. Clearly the thought is true only of the state of affairs consisting of John's being tall. A theory of the semantic properties of a thought should therefore explain how this particular thought is related to this particular state of affairs. According to the resemblance theory, entertaining the thought involves having a mental image that shows John to be tall. To put it another way, the relation between the thought that John is tall and his being tall is like the relation between a tall man and his portrait.

The difficulty with the resemblance theory is that any portrait showing John to be tall must also show him to be many other things: clothed or naked, lying, standing or sitting, having a head or not having one, and so on. A portrait of a tall man who is sitting down resembles a man's being seated as much as it resembles a man's being tall. On the resemblance theory it is not clear what distinguishes thoughts about John's height from thoughts about his posture.

The resemblance theory turns out to encounter paradoxes at every turn. The possibility of construing beliefs as involving relations to semantically interpreted mental representations clearly depends on having an acceptable account of where the semantic properties of the mental representations come from. If resemblance will not provide this account, what will?

The current idea is that the semantic properties of a mental representation are determined by aspects of its functional role. In other words, a sufficient condition for having semantic properties can be specified in causal terms. This is the connection between functionalism and the representational theory of the mind. Modern cognitive psychology rests largely on the hope that these two doctrines can be made to support each other.

No philosopher is now prepared to say exactly how the functional role of a mental representation determines its semantic properties. Nevertheless, the functionalist recognizes three types of causal relation among psychological states involving mental representations, and they might serve to fix the semantic properties of mental representations. The three types are causal relations among mental states and stimuli, mental states and responses and some mental states and other ones.

Consider the belief that John is tall. Presumably the following facts, which correspond respectively to the three types of causal relation, are relevant to determining the semantic properties of the mental representation involved in the belief. First, the belief is a normal effect of certain stimulations, such as seeing John in circumstances that reveal his height. Second, the belief is the normal cause of certain behavioral effects, such as uttering "John is tall." Third, the belief is a normal cause of certain other beliefs and a normal effect of certain other beliefs. For example, anyone who believes John is tall is very likely also to believe some-one is tall. Having the first belief is normally causally sufficient for having the second belief. And anyone who believes everyone in the room is tall and also believes John is in the room will very likely believe John is tall. The third belief is a normal effect of the first two. In short, the functionalist maintains that the proposition expressed by a given mental representation depends on the causal properties of the mental states in which that mental representation figures.

The concept that the semantic properties of mental representations are determined by aspects of their functional role is at the center of current work in the cognitive sciences. Nevertheless, the concept may not be true. Many philosophers who are unsympathetic to the cognitive turn in modern psychology doubt its truth, and many psychologists would probably reject it in the bald and unelaborated way that I have sketched it. Yet even in its skeletal form, there is this much to be said in its favor: It legitimizes the notion of mental representation, which has become increas-ingly important to theorizing in every branch of the cognitive sciences. Recent advances in formulating and testing hypotheses about the character of mental rep-resentations in fields ranging from phonetics to computer vision suggest that the concept of mental representation is fundamental to empirical theories of the mind.

The behaviorist has rejected the appeal to mental representation because it runs counter to his view of the explanatory mechanisms that can figure in psychological theories. Nevertheless, the science of mental representation is now flourishing. The history of science reveals that when a successful theory comes into conflict with a methodological scruple, it is generally the scruple that gives way. Accordingly the functionalist has relaxed the behaviorist constraints on psychological explanations. There is probably no better way to decide what is methodologically permissible in science than by investigating what successful science requires.

2
Freedom and Determinism

George Graham and Harold Kincaid, "Sartre on Being Free"

Readings

Jean-Paul Sartre, *Being and Nothingness* (selections)

Pierre Simon de Laplace, *Philosophical Essay on Probability* (selection)

Daniel Dennett, "On Giving Libertarians What They Say They Want"

Robert Kane, "Free Will: The Elusive Ideal"

Jean-Paul Sartre. Magnum Photos Inc. Copyright © 1995 Henri
Cartier-Bresson.

GEORGE GRAHAM
and
HAROLD KINCAID

Sartre on Being Free

In freedom the human being is his own past as also his own future.
Jean-Paul Sartre, *Being and Nothingness*

Our mental and physical deeds – the things we decide and do – often appear to be under our personal control. How we behave seems *up to us*. Consider the following mundane example. I have the impression that there are several things I could do next with my right index finger: type the letter "w" with it, dial a telephone number, put it under my chin and so on.[1] The situation at the moment leaves each of those alternatives *up to me*. Nothing that exists up to the moment necessitates any one of these actions. In brief: I am free. I type "w."

If we are free, just how often are we free? When is it up to us how to choose and act? Jean-Paul Sartre (1905–80) once said that he had chosen to be born. Sartre of course did not mean this literally. Yet he did believe that humans are unrestrictedly or radically free, and that there is an important sense in which I have control over all facets of my life. This chapter is about Sartre's claims and the larger issues they raise about human freedom and action.

[1] Purely for stylistic reasons, the first-person pronoun is occasionally used in the chapter, though the chapter is co-authored.

1 Who Was Sartre?

Sartre is one of the most famous philosophers of the twentieth century. His funeral in 1980 attracted 50,000 mourners; he had been an institution in French intellectual and political life since the Second World War. Born of upper economic class parents in Paris in 1905, Sartre faced adversity early on. His father died when he was one year old. At age four an infection left him with one eye that wandered and gave him what some thought was a distinctly unhandsome appearance. Sartre grew up in the household of his grandparents. Though he eventually came to despise their upper-class values and way of life, Sartre did take from them a deep appreciation of literature and writing. He began writing short stories as a young child, did well at an exclusive secondary school, and attended university at the Ecole Normale in Paris. There he studied philosophy, and in 1929 placed first on the stiff graduation exams. Placing second was Simone de Beauvoir, who became his life-long love and companion and was also destined to be a major figure in twentieth-century literature. *The Second Sex* is her best-known book.

After university Sartre took a teaching position at a French secondary school outside Paris. He was known as a lively and unorthodox teacher. His teaching duties were minimal (ten hours a week), however, and he began in earnest as a writer. He worked on both fiction and philosophical treatises. He also spent many hours at the movies (he especially liked the Marx brothers), many hours listening to jazz, and many hours writing in Parisian cafés, a habit he would continue throughout his life.

This pleasant existence was interrupted twice by military duties. In the early 1930s he served 18 months in the army, fulfilling his obligation by running a weather station. With the German invasion of Poland in 1939 he was called up for active duty and was taken prisoner by the Germans in 1940. He was placed in a prisoner-of-war camp. No doubt the experience was frightening; yet it turned out rather well for Sartre. He organized his fellow prisoners to put on plays, and he escaped in 1941. He did so by convincing the prison camp doctor that his imprisonment was an error, arguing that no one with an eye like his would have been drafted into the military. Sartre returned to Paris where he worked with the French resistance to the German occupation, though his duties were mainly writing.

As the Second World War ended, Sartre quickly became a major figure in French intellectual life. He had already published a novel in 1938, *Nausea*, that received fulsome reviews. In 1943 he published *Being and Nothingness*, his major philosophical treatise. Plays and novels that he wrote during the war were published immediately after its end, and Sartre also became the editor of a leading French intellectual and political journal. By 1945 he had sufficient income to quit his teaching job and to work full-time at writing.

Sartre's writings became the chief representative of an intellectual movement known as *existentialism*. Other individuals labelled existentialist are Søren Kierkegaard (1813–55), Friedrich Nietzsche (1844–1900), and Martin Heidegger (1889–1976). Existentialism was not one cohesive set of doctrines, and existentialists differed particularly over the existence of God. Nietzsche and Sartre represented the atheist wing, Kierkegaard the theist. None the less, they did agree on some essential themes: for example, the radical freedom of individuals, the importance of choice and commitment in being an authentic human being, the idea that human life has no meaning over and above what humans give it, and an emphasis on the anguish or dread that comes from the human predicament.

From the mid-1950s on Sartre became more and more involved in politics. He was an active opponent of the French colonial empire, including its attempt to subjugate the Vietnamese. He was an internationally recognized critic of the US War in Vietnam as well as of the Soviet invasion of Hungary in 1956. None the less, from the mid-1950s on he was sympathetic to Marxism, and in 1959 he completed the first part of *The Critique of Dialectical Reason* which attempts to reconcile his existentialist commitment to freedom with the Marxian idea that history is deterministic.

Sartre was as unorthodox in behavior as he was famous for ideas. He was awarded the Nobel Prize for literature in 1964 but declined it; he had done the same thing with the Legion d'Honneur for his military service in 1945. He gave away most of his money to various causes, kept only a very modest apartment, and often slept at friends' apartments rather than his own. He was often involved with women other than de Beauvoir and continued to do so until his death. He experimented with mescaline and amphetamines. He once suffered a serious depression, but announced while riding a bus with friends that he was "tired of being mad" and became and stayed cheerful from that moment on. His philosophy and his life were not separate. The centerpiece of both was freedom. He wrote: "I am the self which I will be."

2   What Is Freedom?

"Freedom" of course has many meanings – it can refer to political liberty or economic rights, for example. Relatedly, it can refer to the absence of coercion or threat from others. Though Sartre had much to say about these issues, his real contributions were his arguments that individual persons control their own decisions and actions – their own lives. He rejected the idea, called *determinism*, that human decisions and actions are *determined* by the individual's past and the laws of nature, that only one choice or action for me now is consistent with the way the world is and with my upbringing, brain processes, and personality and emotions. For Sartre neither nature nor nurture necessitate the way I act; nothing fixes how I behave. This general view is called *anti-determinism*. (Sometimes it is also referred to as indeterminism, the emphasis being on the absence of necessitation in the course of events.)

Determinism and anti-determinism are complex doctrines with different implications. If determinism is true, then no alternatives are up to me, my subjective impression notwithstanding. I may feel like I can dial a number instead of type "w," but under the circumstances I can't dial. I must type "w." If, by contrast, anti-determinism is true, then the best theories that science has to offer will never be able strictly and accurately to predict the future. Some of what happens in the world – whether I type "w," for example – is unknowable until it occurs.

Again: If determinism is true, there is a chain of events leading inevitably to any event. The world and my life within it are entirely "locked." To illustrate by analogy, consider the following case, derived from an example of the philosopher John Locke (1632–1704). Suppose that a person is brought into a room asleep and that the door, the only means out of the room, is bolted shut on the outside. The person awakes, finds the room very agreeable, and thinks she will remain in the room, not knowing she is locked in. The person cannot leave, though she does not recognize this. As far as she is concerned, she is free to leave.

According to determinism, human beings are like the prisoner; and like the prisoner, any feeling we may have of being free does not mean that we are free. Whether we know or like it, the behavior we do perform we must perform. We are locked into it. It is no more up to us how we behave than it is up to the prisoner whether she leaves the room. By contrast, if anti-determinism is true, some events are not inevitable. The world and our lives within it contain "unlocked doors," openings with behavioral opportunities. In one such opening I may dial a number, in another I may type "w."

Does it make any difference whether determinism or anti-determinism is true? Why should it matter to us whether we live in a locked/deterministic or unlocked/anti-deterministic world? An advertisement for a recent book defending determinism boasts as follows: "Shelley wrote an ode to it, Einstein would not abandon it. But it alarmed Immanuel Kant, enraged Samuel Johnson, depressed John Stuart Mill, overcame Freud, and was spurned by Sartre."

There is one big reason why some philosophers, like Sartre, spurn determinism and embrace anti-determinism. Anti-determinism is essential, so they argue, for various things near and dear to the human heart. These include things like moral responsibility or accountability, life-hopes and aspirations, our dignity and individuality as persons, and much else besides. If, for example, persons are morally responsible – genuinely accountable for our actions, so the reasoning goes – anti-determinism must be true. Or if one's life is in a particularly bad or unfortunate way, improving one's situation carries the idea of rising above the tides of necessity, and asserting one's person over the situation. I am not a toy of my circumstances, a leaf in the breeze, a prisoner in a room. Once again, anti-determinism must be true.

We said just now that things near and dear to the human heart may require anti-determinism. Actually, the situation is more complicated than that. Things near and dear may require *libertarianism*, which itself requires but is not completely exhausted by anti-determinism. The point is critical and needs to be explained.

First notice that anti-determinism's denial of necessity – its brand of freedom – is a *negative* thing. Anti-determinism's freedom consists in the absence of something (necessity). Whatever I decide or do now, nothing necessitates it. So we will call the freedom of anti-determinism "negative freedom." However, my subjective impression at the current moment is that *at the moment* not only does nothing stand in the way of my dialing a number or typing "w" – not only does nothing necessitate typing rather than dialing – I am also personally able *to* perform either action. Whether I dial or type is up to me. I therefore seem to have a positive freedom in addition to negative freedom. Positive up-to-me freedom represents the presence of something: the *personal* power or ability to decide and act one way rather than another. Whether I dial or type, it's my say ultimately. As Sartre put the point, "I am indeed already there in the future." It is for the sake of that future, again in Sartre's words, "that I now exert all my strength."

An analogy with two forms of political or legal freedom may help to clarify the difference between the two components of libertarian freedom. Someone has negative freedom, politically, when he has, for example, a legal right not to be interfered with arbitrarily – for example, a right not to be searched without reason by the police. Negative political freedoms are freedoms *from* certain legal constraints and restrictions (e.g. unwarranted search). Positive political freedoms, on the other hand, go beyond freedom from constraint. They involve legal powers or capacities. The right to vote, for example, is a positive freedom. It consists in political entitlement *to* vote. Analogously, libertarian freedom consists in both negative personal freedom (absence of necessitation) and positive personal freedom (ultimate say in decision and action).

What is personal power or ultimate say in decision and action? This is one of the most tricky ideas in the literature of libertarianism and it goes by different names. The libertarian philosopher Robert Kane, for example, calls it "ultimate responsibility" for decision and action; it is also known as "the power of self-determination" and "agent causation." The essential idea is that for the libertarian there is an up-to-me character or feature to free decision and action. This is a positive feature and distinguishable from, although presupposing, the negative one of being unnecessitated. Just because I am negatively free does not mean I am positively free, although I cannot be positively free without being negatively free: I cannot be free *to* without being free *from*.

Consider a skier about to descend down a wintry mountain slope. Imagine that anti-determinism is true and that her descent is negatively free; nothing necessitates whether she takes off down the slope. Indeterminacy is woven into the fabric of her departure; one cannot infer whether she descends until she descends. The point about positive freedom requiring negative freedom but not being exhausted by it can be illustrated with reference to the skier. The libertarian claims that the skier's descent is not her descent – her free deed – unless she somehow produces the descent. The indeterminacy (negative freedom) of the descent means that the descent may not have occurred; it was not inevitable. However, for the action to be hers – something she does – it must be up to her whether she descends; she must be the originator; she must be positively free. Negative freedom leaves room for the descent to be up to her; positive freedom means the descent is up to her.

Libertarianism is the doctrine that persons possess both negative and positive freedom. We are both free *from* necessity (anti-determinism is true, determinism is false) and it is up *to* us how we decide and act. So the question arises: Why should something like moral responsibility hinge on the truth of libertarianism?

Suppose that I am pushed off a cliff. It certainly is not within my power to stop from falling on top of a little child playing below. Suppose I crush the child to death but miraculously survive. I am not morally responsible and cannot be blamed for killing the child. How can that be? Simple: I lacked the personal power not to hit the child. But again: Suppose that I am drinking beer while driving a car and as I guzzle my fifth bottle, I swerve onto the sidewalk and strike an elderly woman waiting for her mail, killing her instantly. I am blameworthy for killing the woman. How can that be? Again simple: it was within my power to avoid killing her. I could have refrained from drinking while driving. Ultimately it was my deed.

The following principle captures the reasoning behind the above two examples:

Moral Responsibility Principle: A person is morally responsible for things that happen just in case it is up to him or her what happens. If he or she possesses libertarian freedom, he or she is morally accountable, otherwise not.

Although (let us suppose) I could not have arranged matters so as not to be pushed off the cliff, I could have arranged matters so as not to swerve while driving and, thus, I am morally responsible for killing the woman but not the child. It was up to me whether to drink and drive. It was not up to me whether to be pushed off the cliff.

If the Moral Responsibility Principle is correct then it is not sufficient for moral responsibility that persons are free from necessity (that anti-determinism is true). It must also be the case that morally responsible agents possess personal power (that what we do is *up to us*). Conversely, if persons don't possess personal power and libertarianism is false, then persons are not morally responsible. We can't be held accountable for what we do – not just for bad things we do, but good actions as well. The former would not incriminate us; the latter would not be to our credit.

Life-hopes? Aspirations? Suppose I have just been thrown into huge debt by ignorant misinvestment and my home has been destroyed by fire. I am tempted to become depressed and embittered: to lose hope for the future. Should I give up? At this point I may feel and say that everything is okay, that I am still in charge of my life. "I can pick myself up. I vow to begin again." You may admire and reinforce my hope. However, the hope makes sense only if libertarianism is true: only if it is up to me whether I collapse under the weight of my misfortune.

Is libertarianism true? Are we free positively? Sartre certainly thought so. Indeed, Sartre was a "radical" or "unrestricted" libertarian. According to radical or unrestricted libertarianism not only is determinism false, but our actions *always* are under our control. Everything we decide and do is up to us.

Radical libertarianism is a bold and immoderate doctrine. Few libertarian philosophers are attracted to it. Is it possible that a compulsive or addict is free? Do these people really have power to refrain from behaving compulsively or addictively? Sartre thought so, but it seems not. It seems that compulsions and addictions necessitate decisions and actions. Part of what it means to call them compulsions and addictions is to admit that their subjects are unfree. Because of such cases and other difficulties with radical libertarianism, most libertarian philosophers claim that persons only *sometimes* are free. Most libertarians embrace "restricted" or "moderate" libertarianism.

According to restricted or moderate libertarianism, in some situations we are free, while in other situations we are unfree. Unfree situations are cases in which our actions are necessitated by one cause or another or cases perhaps in which some *acausal* factor (chance or random occurrence) undermines personal power in decision and action.

We will not explore the contrast between radical and restricted libertarianism. In the rest of this chapter we will look at libertarianism *period* and Sartre's arguments for it. Perhaps people rarely are free; but even if so, then libertarianism is true. Moreover, when talking of freedom, we mean to refer to libertarian freedom; its two ingredients are negative and positive freedom.

3   Sartre's Arguments for Freedom

Sartre offered two basic kinds of argument for the claim that human actions are free from necessity and up to us – for libertarianism. These are arguments based on direct experiences and subjective practices that we all share and arguments based on his analysis of consciousness and the self. The arguments from consciousness are the most complex, but they are also the most interesting and fundamental. The arguments from direct experience are more natural and intuitive, and so we begin with them.

Arguments from direct experience

Sartre held that the facts of experience show us directly that we possess libertarian freedom. Yet he did not think that we learned this through introspection; he denied that we could turn our gaze inward and see our true self making free choices. So he appealed to other kinds of experience, such as the emotional experience of anguish, for example. He claimed that through the experience of anguish we directly perceive our radical freedom: "Anguish," he said, is "the manifestation of freedom."

According to Sartre, anguish differs from fear. Fear is caused by some external event and has a more or less specific object or focus. I fear the snake or the crazed student with the gun. Anguish, however, is directed towards oneself and the situation of acting in the world. We experience anguish because we do not know what we will do, and that is because our future really is open.

Sartre offers numerous interesting examples illustrating his claim. If I am laid off from my job, I will no doubt fear the threat of poverty; a moment later I will experience anguish, anguish over what I am going to do. I realize my future is up to me. If I walk along the edge of a cliff or high building, I also experience anguish. Even if there is a guard rail and I have no fear of slipping or being pushed off, I still may experience anguish and in particular vertigo, which, Sartre suggests, is a kind of anguish. I am uncertain of myself. I perceive that I am free and could throw myself over the edge. Vertigo is the experience of my own freedom.

Other common experiences also show that we are free, according to Sartre. In particular, we are able to question or, more generally, deliberate. Deliberation requires that possibilities be open to me. I cannot truly deliberate about something that I know I cannot do. For example, if I know that I cannot win the Nobel Prize in physics or play for the Chicago Bulls, I cannot deliberate over whether to do so; I could at best imagine or pretend to deliberate over such matters. However, deliberation is something we experience regularly and with certainty; it is a basic fact about human existence. Thus so is our freedom.

What should we make of Sartre's arguments from experience? As for proving we are free in the sense of libertarian (positive, personal power) freedom, they are unconvincing. I may anguish over what to do, but the real cause of my anguish may be environmental or biochemical processes in my brain. Perhaps real deliberation requires freedom, but then the advocate of determinism will deny that we really deliberate. We may *seem* to deliberate, but perhaps that is just another process caused by our nervous system. Even a firm conviction of deliberation may be a subjective illusion. Observe your firm impression that the highway on which you drive is covered with water – knowledge of the relevant optical illusion notwithstanding. Sartre seems to think that it is undeniable both that we deliberate and that we anguish over open possibilities. He seems to think that we perceive these facts directly. Put in these terms, his argument is uncompelling.

The philosopher Carl Hempel, who taught for many years at Princeton University and was as different from Sartre in philosophic outlook as night is to day, once described – no doubt with Locke's prisoner in a room in mind – the unconvincingness of arguments from experience for freedom as follows: "A stubborn feeling of freedom of choice . . . cannot count as evidence . . . for this kind of feeling can surely be deceptive. Indeed I think that the feeling is irrelevant to the question of [libertarianism]" (Hempel 1958).

However, Sartre does make an important point, even if it is no proof of freedom. The examples of anguish, vertigo, and deliberation show just how deep the impression of our freedom goes. In other words, it shows that much of what we believe about ourselves presupposes that we are free in the libertarian sense. We do deliberate; we do experience anguish and vertigo. Echoing Sartre, the philosopher Colin McGinn writes: "All human interaction and self-reflection is suffused with the idea of freedom; there is nothing marginal or exceptional about it. Freedom is a property that we take to be instantiated with enormous frequency" (McGinn 1993). So those who deny that we are free thus have a burden of proof to discharge. They must show that these basic attitudes and experiences are fundamentally misguided or rest on a mistaken assumption. Thus at the very least Sartre's arguments demonstrate that determinists are committed to a drastic reinterpretation of our self-experience.

Arguments from consciousness

Behind Sartre's discussion of anguish and deliberation lurks another more subtle and more fundamental argument for human freedom. This argument builds on claims Sartre makes about the nature of consciousness and the self. Even in its briefest form, it is a complex argument. It may be represented thus:

1 Suppose I type "w." Then *either* (a) the typing was necessitated (it was inescapable at the moment) *or* (b) it was up to me (it was within my power at the moment to type or not to type).
2 If (1a) is true, then something – some event in the world or in my mind perhaps – must have caused me to type without my having any control over that thing.
3 Events in the world and in my mind are rendered meaningful to me only because of my consciousness of them (only because of how I conceive of them).
4 The influence of any event on me depends upon its meaningfulness to me.
5 However, my consciousness – how I conceive of things – is up to me. I control the meaningfulness of things. How I conceive of things is not causally necessitated.
   As Sartre writes: "It is futile to try to invoke pretended *laws* of consciousness."
Therefore,
6 (1b), rather than (1a), is true. My typing "w" was up to me.

For Sartre, being conscious – perceiving and sensing things – involves interpreting the world, representing it to ourselves in certain ways. Consider, for example, the ring of an alarm clock. You hear it ring. Will you get up? According to Sartre, whether you respond depends on how you interpret the alarm. Is it a ring that cannot be ignored, a sign of the obligations you must fulfill? Or is it an annoying bother that is to be ignored? Given you conceive the first, you may get up; given the second, you will not. Or again: suppose that you are a member of the Mafia dispatched to kill a philosophy professor with large gambling debts. You follow the philosophy professor for several days, observe his life and habits. Then comes the moment when you can safely make your move; do you perceive him as a slackard who needs to be eliminated or an absent-minded professor deserving of a break? Will you kill him? If you conceive of him in the first way, you kill him; in the second, you let him go.

Sartre examines many of the things that commonly are said to necessitate human behavior and in each case he argues that their influence depends on conceptions or interpretations by the agent. If we can suppose that these conceptions or interpretations themselves are up to the agent (that the fifth premise above is true), then this means we are free. Whether I get up in response to the alarm is up to me.

Sartre denies that our personality traits, emotions, desires, motives, and so on necessitate our actions. Take something as apparently beyond our control as "fatigue." Sartre argues that fatigue has the influence it does only by means of a prior free interpretative choice on our part. To experience fatigue is to interpret it or conceive of it a certain way, and we interpret it in the light of actions and decisions we make. So two individuals, both equally fatigued, will react quite differently. You may think of yourself as an "athlete," the kind of person who embraces physical challenge; I may think of myself as a "wimp," the kind of person who avoids physical challenge. You interpret the fatigue as something to be overcome or even enjoyed; I give the fatigue a very different meaning. You exert yourself while fatigued; I take a nap. In both cases the fatigue has its influence only via the meaning we each bestow upon it. Fatigue does not necessitate a particular action.

Consider another possible necessitator of action, such as sadness. Sartre does not deny that people become sad. He does deny, however, that they are sad in ways which make their reactions to sadness inevitable. People consciously experience sadness, and this means they take a perspective on it or attribute meaning or significance to it. Whether the sadness is unbearable, how it relates to my life as a whole and to my plans and projects depends on how I interpret it. Again, the meaning that consciousness gives determines its influence.

Sartre notes that we sometimes do think of ourselves as out of control, as fully determined by psychological forces, as a certain kind of person who must do such and such, and so on. He argues that those attitudes are instances of what he calls "bad faith" – instances of trying to deny our freedom by treating ourselves as nothing but a thing like, say, a rock. He holds that bad faith involves making an intellectual error about ourselves, namely, to embrace determinism about ourselves and to try to find patterns in our free acts and then to appeal to those patterns as the necessitating sources of behavior. Sartre denies, however, that these patterns – which people often call "personality traits" – are real causes or entities.

Notice that we frequently try to explain individual behavior by classifying people into types such as aggressive or passive. We then identify more specific qualities that follow from them, such as being outgoing or shy. Finally we get to specific behaviors allegedly explained by reference to personality types and qualities. We think things like: Pierre failed to speak up at the meeting last night because of his shyness which in turn was caused by his passive personality. Sartre holds that these explanations have things exactly backwards. Personality traits and qualities are categories we impose on free actions after the fact. They are useful descriptive fictions. Pierre must reinterpret anew his past acts at each new moment. He may well decide to wallow in the idea that he is a passive person. However, even if he does so, it is because once again he has chosen to do so. If tomorrow he perceives his past personality as an "immature phase" and acts outgoing, he may describe himself in some new category. However, to Sartre the free acts of interpretation and conception are what is real and prior, not the passive or active personality. "I am my acts," Sartre writes, "and they carry in themselves their own justification."

Sartre tells this same story about any and all psychological factors allegedly necessitating my acts. The acts come first, the personality traits are realized only by the processes of acting itself. My "true motives" or "true desires" are only constituted or revealed in the process of choosing. Suppose I am a student struggling in my first philosophy course. My grade thus far is a "D." The term is nearly over. I have 24 hours in which to withdraw from the course without penalty. My fear of a poor grade is intense. It strongly inclines me to drop. Suppose I withdraw from the course. Did the fear necessitate withdrawal? Should I explain my action as caused by the fear? No, not for Sartre, for the question still remains whether I choose to find the fear sufficient reason to withdraw. It was up to me to conceive of fear of a bad grade as sufficient reason for getting out of the course. It need not have been. I had the fear, and it was intense, but whether to decide in terms of it was my ultimate say.

So internal, psychological causes – things in the mind – depend on the meaning we in our consciousness give them for their efficacy. What about the constraints placed on me by the environment, by the world both physical and social? Sartre again does not deny that such constraints exist. He does deny none the less that they are necessitating. Once again he believes that consciousness inserts itself between the environmental factors and their effect. Pierre was put up for adoption immediately after his birth; now grown, he works as a waiter. Pierre can describe himself as an orphan and a waiter, but he is not *just* those things in the way a rock just is a rock. He is conscious of those facts and thus interprets them. Their meaning and influence depend on the choices he makes. They depend on how he weaves them into his life.

Sartre held that our freedom has important consequences for all aspects of our lives. We have already seen that he claimed freedom led to anguish, for freedom is scary. We have also seen that our freedom may lead us to bad faith or, in other words, to adopt ways of living and attitudes that help us deny our freedom. So we try to immerse ourselves into our social position, our past, and so on and pretend that we are nothing but those categories. Doing so is a way of trying to avoid the fact that freedom makes us responsible for our acts.

Critical examination of the argument from consciousness

How strong is Sartre's argument from consciousness? A good way to examine any argument is to identify and evaluate its premises. Since the argument's premises already are identified, and in fact numbered, we will proceed straight to their evaluation.

The central and most crucial premises are the fourth and fifth. Let's begin with the fifth. One problem with Sartre's argument from consciousness centers upon this premise. Sartre assumes that consciousness is free in the positive sense (up to the conscious subject). A lot has been written about whether people's conception of things is up to them. This is a question about the conceptual abilities which persons possess: What is the proper theory of the structure and operation of consciousness? Is it controllable? When a person conceives of a situation a certain way, is this conception causally necessitated or instead up to her? The long answer to this question would take us far afield, but the short answer is that how we conceive of things often is not up to us. Examples? People's faces form a particularly puzzling if necessitating object of conception. They have an infinite variety although they often are inescapably identifiable. You may recognize the face of your mother or lover in a crowd thick with people. Recognizing them is not up to you. It happens immediately and no matter what else you are thinking; even if you try not to recognize them, you will. Something similar is true of speech. Our best theories of speech perception indicate that how we hear words often is completely causally determined. A large experimental literature suggests that causal determination of speech perception may be very extensive.

Certain illnesses and diseases are notoriously riddled with causally determined conceptions. The patient Bernie R. broke down badly when he was released from the hospital and behaved like his drug addiction had returned. So his doctors decided to readmit him. His primary physician, Lawrence L., recognized that Bernie's conception of the world was dictated by his drug problem. He offered the following experiment to prove his point. Bernie was offered a choice between taking a piece of candy for himself or giving it to a child on the ward, though he did not know or even suspect that the candy was candy. Bernie took the candy conceiving of it as a drug. Could he have given it to the child? If what Sartre says in connection with consciousness is correct, he could have given it to the child only if he was conscious of it a certain way (as candy). Could he have conceived of it in that freedom-endowing way? Well, this depends on his addiction. As an addict Bernie could not help but see the candy as a drug. His perception was warped by addiction. Of course, then he could not have given up the candy.

If much in our conception of things is not up to us and consciousness in such cases is unfree, this point is important to the radical or unrestricted libertarian position. It means that Sartrean unrestricted freedom is unfounded. However, if sometimes our consciousness of things is up to us, there is room for restricted freedom.

Forming conceptions or interpretations of things sometimes seems up to us. There is various evidence for and against a conception of things, and it seems and feels to us as if we could adopt any one of a number of different conceptions. In weighing the evidence, mulling it over, we arrive at a sense of which conception is correct, which evidence has more clout. We decide which interpretation to adopt or we may choose to suspend judgment until more evidence has been gathered or analyzed. The phone rings. Is it my friend or the tax collector? Intellectually stepping back I look at the evidence. It's noon and my friend should be phoning. She said she would call at noon. It's a national holiday and very unlikely that the government collects taxes on holidays. So I think: "It's my friend." I answer the phone.

The process of choice among alternative conceptions sometimes seems to rest on free consciousness – on personal judgment of evidence and weight. If so, Sartre's fifth premise is not false but restrictedly true. How we view things is not always up to us but sometimes is. When it is, if Sartre is right, we are free.

What about the fourth premise, that any causal influence on human action must act through conscious processes? If some causes do not work through conscious perception, then perhaps they necessitate actions and strip us of freedom. Why cannot our brain – our nervous system – cause our actions in ways we never perceive? Or perhaps environmental causes influence our brain and behavior without ever entering consciousness.

Sartre has two replies to this challenge. The first consists in distinguishing between action and non-action. Some of our behavior does not qualify as action, the activity of our digestive tract, for example, or the formation of chemicals in our brains; these goings on are behavior *in* us but not *by* us. Actions are behaviors by us, like typing "w" or answering the phone. Non-actions may be causally necessitated by unconscious events, actions cannot. Persons act when purposes, goals, intentions, beliefs, and reasons and so on lie behind their activity. Searching for a beer in the refrigerator is an example of acting. I have a goal (the beer), beliefs (there is beer around somewhere), perceptions (it's in the refrigerator), and so on. Action requires consciousness, non-actions do not. Since actions as such require consciousness, any influence on those actions must work through our conscious awareness. If consciousness is free, those acts are free.

Sartre's distinction between actions and non-actions makes intuitive sense. Yet determinists are unconvinced, for they respond that we never really *act*. Searching for a beer may seem fundamentally different from a behavior like digesting, but that is an illusion due to our incomplete knowledge of the brain. Searching, like digesting, is really just the behavior of the complex physical system that is our body.

Sartre has another, more complicated response to the charge that our brain determines consciousness. Before presenting it let's briefly pause on the notion of the nervous system causing actions.

Human beings are biological organisms, made up of minute parts, including the chemicals in our brain. The following is a type of argument sometimes heard in discussions of freedom:

> The brain causes consciousness; how I conceive of things is necessitated by my neurochemistry. Causation is transitive; if A causes B and B causes C, then A causes C. So, even if my decisions and actions are controlled by my consciousness, since my consciousness (how I conceive of things) is necessitated by my brain, my actions are necessitated by my brain. My actions are not up to me.

We will call this the *brain stemming* problem for libertarian freedom. According to the brain stemming problem, an action such as my typing "w" stems ultimately from my central nervous system – whether we know it or not. Its production may pass through consciousness and for this and other reasons it may qualify as an action (behavior by me), but typing "w" is determined none the less.

In case the nature of the brain stemming problem is unclear, consider the following loose analogy. The authors of this chapter live in Birmingham and we vote in the election of the Alabama governor. We vote because we live in the state because we live in Birmingham (which is a city in the state). Our ability to vote for governor stems from living in Birmingham. Likewise, so the argument goes, consciousness stems from biochemical pathways, long chains of neurochemical processes; and our actions stem from that self-same source. We type "w" because of our neurons; we vote in the gubernatorial election because of our city residence.

Much attention has been paid by friends and foes of libertarianism to the brain stemming problem. The problem goes by different names and it is sometimes difficult to keep score between friends and foes because of the name changes. One such name is the challenge of *neurophysiological determinism*; another is the threat of *the causal closure of physics*; and there are plenty of other names.

Sartre's reply to the brain stemming problem is to deny that consciousness is necessitated by the brain. "Nerves," he says, "don't mean." Consciousness involves a subjective point of view and conceiving and interpreting, but no physical thing (brain) has a subjective view or interprets. So consciousness cannot stem from physical, neurochemical causes. When we act, we act from consciousness and not from the brain.

Sartre's tactic here is simple: to escape the brain stemming problem by denying that the brain produces consciousness. However, potentially lurking behind Sartre's tactic and waiting to be embraced by anyone who endorses it is an immensely controversial thesis about the nature of mind and consciousness called *dualism*. Dualism is the view that humans are psychologically constituted by something non-physical and thus not by the brain. The brain is part of the body only, not part of the person; the person is the mind or conscious mind. Does Sartre's tactic force him to be a dualist? Is dualism a bad thing? We don't have space to explore these questions here, but suffice it to say that many philosophers (as readers of the first chapter may recall) believe that dualism should be rejected. If dualism should be rejected, then libertarianism should not wed itself to dualism.

Dualism may be one way – albeit controversial – to escape from the brain stemming problem. There are others. A second tactic, which bypasses commitment to dualism, offers itself. This is to deny the transitivity of causation. The brain mechanisms responsible for my conception of things are not thereby responsible for whether I type "w" even if my conception – how I see things – is responsible for my typing. Causation is not transitive: A can cause B and B can cause C without A thereby causing C.

Unfortunately, this response to the brain stemming problem is too facile. It is regarded as unappealing in debates about free will or elsewhere to deny that causation is transitive. Why? The short answer is that transitivity appears part of the very idea of causation. Consider a billiards player who wants to get the "8" ball into the corner pocket. He hits the cue ball into the "8" ball which enters the pocket. What caused the "8" ball to enter the pocket? The cue ball? Yes, but ultimately the manner in which it was hit by the player. A (the motion of the player) caused B (the cue ball to strike the "8" ball) which caused C (the "8" ball to enter the corner pocket); hence the player caused the "8" ball to enter the pocket. The transitivity of causation produces causal chains, and explanatorily tracing back from recent links in a chain to earlier links is called causal backtracking. Thus if a person does something because of how he conceives of it and his conception is produced by his brain, then we causally backtrack to the brain as the explanation of the action.

4   Freedom's Finale: Four Alternative Strategies

Many philosophers are reluctant either to embrace dualism or to reject the notion that causation is transitive. So far as they are concerned dualism is incorrect and causation is transitive. So what's left? Should libertarianism be abandoned? Or are there ways in which to defend libertarianism other than with arguments like Sartre's?

In this final section of the chapter we want to outline four alternative strategies that may be adopted in connection with libertarianism. This section is intended to provide the reader with an idea of various alternatives to, as well as within, libertarianism.

First alternative: deterministic abandonment of libertarianism

The first alternative position is to abandon or reject libertarianism by embracing determinism. There are two main ways in which to do this. One is to argue that freedom is compatible with determinism even though libertarianism, of course, is not. This position is called *compatibilism* or *soft determinism*: it is "compatible" and "soft" because determinism, soft determinists claim, is not at odds with freedom. The second is to endorse determinism but argue that freedom is incompatible with determinism. This position is called *hard determinism*: it is "hard" because determinism, hard determinists claim, is at odds with freedom.

Each position has distinctive content and variations. For example, most soft determinists hold that determinism is compatible with both freedom and holding people morally accountable. People are capable of reasoning about their conduct and deciding what to do, in a manner sufficient for us to address them as responsible individuals, liable to praise and blame, even though we live in a "locked" (deterministic) universe. However, some soft determinists argue that the determinist outlook

> leaves no room for moral responsibility – though it leaves adequate space for individual freedom. . . . Freedom [should] be retained and celebrated, while moral responsibility is banished. (Waller 1990)

How can determinism be compatible with freedom? One popular soft determinist way of answering this question goes as follows.

A distinction should be made between whether a decision or choice is free and whether the action or behavior which may stem from the decision or choice is free. Freely deciding to type is one thing; freely typing is another. Determinism is compatible with free action though not with free choice or decision (sometimes also called "free will"). An action is free just when it stems from and comports with

95

a decision; an action is unfree just when it runs contrary to the agent's decision. If, for example, I decide or intend to type but (mistakenly) dial the phone instead, then dialing is unfree; by contrast, if I type, typing is free even though the decision to type is unfree. The crucial soft determinist point is that however precisely we should distinguish between action (overt behavior, bodily movement) and choice, a person whose actions are under control of her decisions is free-in-action even if not free-in-decision or choice.

Then, continue various soft determinists, given the transitivity of causation, this means that a free action should also be classified as determined. Suppose X decides to shake Y's hand and thereby shakes Y's hand. The handshake is a free action. X's decision, however, is determined by complex processes in X's brain; it is the upshot of neurological activity and can be fully explained neuroscientifically. Continues the soft determinist, we should count the decision as unfree and the action as both free (in the sense of stemming from the decision) and unfree (in the sense of stemming from an unfree decision).

One thing to note about the soft determinist answer outlined in the two paragraphs above is that the answer does not make it obvious whether persons are morally responsible for free actions. Much depends on what is involved in being morally responsible. Many soft determinists hold that agents are morally responsible for what they do freely even though their deeds ultimately are necessitated. However, other theorists contend (in a manner similar to libertarians) that it is morally unfair to hold people accountable for actions if decisions or choices are unfree.

Hard determinists, by contrast, are unmoved by debate within soft determinism about whether people are morally responsible and whether freedom of action is sufficient for moral responsibility. For the hard determinist when people do wrong and their victims suffer, wrong-doers are not morally accountable for their misdeeds. Moral accountability or responsibility hinges on libertarian freedom. So long as libertarianism is false, people are not morally responsible. Of course, society may and should punish people's misdeeds. Punishment is useful as a corrective in controlling or altering behavior; but punishment should not be conceived as just moral desert. It should be conceived in terms of its social utility.

The essential hard determinist moral point can be put this way. A dog learning to sit on hearing "sit," for example, is likely to fidget, fret, and fail to sit. Only after a good deal of correction is the response "sit" acquired. To the hard determinist things are no different with people. Society wants and needs to correct misbehavior, but this no more means that miscreants freely behave than teaching a dog to sit means the canine freely sits.

Hard determinists therefore have something in common with libertarians as well as with soft determinists. Like soft determinists they reject anti-determinism; like libertarians they deny that freedom and determinism are compatible and they insist that moral responsibility *per se* requires both negative and positive freedom. Hard determinism and libertarianism are sometimes spoken of as forms of *incompatibilism*.

Taken together, soft and hard determinism have formed historically impressive alternatives to libertarianism. The combined force of the alternatives together with difficulties in libertarianism have led many philosophers to abandon libertarianism entirely.

Sartre, of course, would find either version of the abandonment response to libertarianism completely and totally unacceptable. To Sartre hard determinism is an instance of bad faith, of trying to avoid incrimination for wrong-doing by appealing to the world-view of determinism. Meanwhile the "freedom" of soft determinism is no such thing. Sartre found it difficult to take seriously the idea that someone is free and yet completely causally necessitated at the same time. Only if determinism is false are people really and truly free. As the philosopher Nietzsche once remarked:

> Those who wish to be mediators between two resolute thinkers are marked as mediocre; they lack eyes to see the unparalleled; seeing things as similar and making them the same is the mark of weak eyes.

Sartre would agree. Viewing anti-determinism and determinism as the same in permitting freedom is the mark of weak eyes (i.e. a form of ignorance). Only anti-determinism permits freedom.

Sartre aside, independent difficulties infect both forms of determinism. For one, we have good physical scientific evidence that the world is anti-deterministic: that it ultimately is unpredictable and indeterministic (i.e. there is no 100 percent necessitation). At least at the level of fundamental particles, there are at most only approximate necessities; there are only probabilities or likelihoods things will happen. However, as we will see below, this objection that the world is anti-deterministic may not help the libertarian. The libertarian must specify the sorts or forms of indetermination that help to give persons ultimate say (positive freedom) in their decisions and actions. Is ultimate say consistent with indetermination? One of libertarianism's chief tasks is to provide a plausible account of how a choice, or action, can be both suitably indeterministic and up to me. If a choice or action cannot be both indeterministic and up to me, then libertarianism is false even if determinism also is false.

Soft determinism has a second and more particular problem than the general threat of anti-determinism/indeterminism. It must explain how a choice or action can be both free and determined. Consider the following:

> An uncle rapes his ten-year-old niece and, as a consequence, she suffers life-long emotional disorder. In our questions about him, we ask "Was he free?" The answer seems to hinge on whether he had the power to arrange things so as not to rape the girl: whether raping or not raping was up to him. Is it conceivable that he had such power if determinism is true? If determinism is true, our decisions and actions are necessitated by other events – by our personal histories, for example. The man could have arranged things so as not to rape the girl only if he could have changed those necessitating events. However, persons lack the power to change things in the past. We can't literally backtrack and change our histories. So, if determinism is true, then the man lacked the power to arrange things so as not to rape the girl. Accordingly in committing the rape he was unfree.

To this the soft determinist may counter that there are freedoms (such as freedom of action) other than the freedom of personal power. That's true. But it may be doubted whether these other soft determinist freedoms are sufficient for things like moral responsibility. Consider whether the rapist is morally responsible. Are we really entitled to blame the rapist if his behavior was necessitated? If at the moment he could not have arranged things so as not to rape his niece does he deserve our censure? It may make sense to imprison him (because we want to get him off the streets or make an example of him for others or correct his behavior); but this is not because he *deserves* to be imprisoned. Desert is a matter of justice (not public safety and corrective utility). Punishment seems deserved or just only if people freely choose to behave in wrongful ways – only if what they do is up to them.

Second alternative: a physical basis for libertarianism

Rather than rejecting libertarianism, it is possible to give it a different basis from that found, for example, in Sartre. Some libertarians admit that actions stem from brains; brain activity amplifies up through consciousness and issues in behavior. But then, the alternative continues, the brain is a *causally mixed system*. It contains a mixture of deterministic and indeterministic processes and components. The indeterministic components mean that actions are *unnecessitated,* and for that reason (negatively) free. The deterministic components mean that freedom of action is constrained; not just any action is possible. Only a range of actions, perhaps a very narrow range, is possible.

One way to explain the second alternative is as follows. Suppose (to visit our old friend, the mundane example) I am trying to decide whether to type "w" or to dial a phone number. This effort at decision consists of conscious activity in the brain. Firing patterns there produce other firing patterns, culminating in a sequence of firing patterns on the motor neurons, which, in turn, send electrical impulses down the nerves. Certain patterns result in my typing "w"; certain other patterns would have constituted dialing a phone number. Suppose there are non-necessitated, probabilistic transitions among the patterns mixed in with deterministic processes so that at no point can it be said that typing rather than dialing is inevitable. It may be inevitable that I type or dial, but it is not inevitable that I type and not dial.

Many contemporary libertarians are attracted to the second alternative position. They are drawn to the idea that there is a physical basis for freedom in the brain: to the hypothesis that there are few, if any, fixed necessities in the brain and that somehow the causal mixture of determinacy and indeterminacy insures libertarian freedom. One virtue of such a position is that it avoids commitment to dualism. It is brain-centered. Another is that it permits a kind of anti-deterministic or probabilistic analogue to the transitivity of causation. Free actions ultimately do stem from the brain but not in a manner which undermines freedom. The stemming is not necessitation. However, can a person whose brain is a causally mixed system personally be in control of her decisions and actions and positively free? Does such a person have ultimate say – libertarian freedom? Much depends on what is involved in the system being mixed and how its indeterministic elements are described and where they are located. If, for example, "indeterministic" means "random" or "arbitrary," this seems to undermine freedom rather than help to insure it. Ultimate say, then, rather than requiring indetermination, may be something people fail to have if anti-determinism/indeterminism is true.

Consider: I am trying to decide whether to type "w" or to dial a phone number. The typing will occur only if unbeknownst to me a certain neuron in my cerebral cortex, Neuron #2001, will fire at the moment. Its firing is a random event. If the event occurs I type, otherwise not. Suppose that, as it happens, the neuron fires and I type "w." In that case, did I have personal power to dial a number? Of course it could have happened that I dialed the phone number (had #2001 not fired). So the particular action of typing was not inevitable. But was it my say whether to type or to dial? How can positive freedom – our ultimate say as persons – rest on random events or processes of which we ourselves have neither knowledge nor control? Random occurrences in the brain seem to *weaken* and even perhaps *eliminate* libertarian freedom.

The causally mixed system approach to libertarianism carries an intellectual burden. It must explain how an anti-deterministic process – other perhaps than a random process – can make possible free action and decision. The "free" is not just negative freedom, but under libertarianism also positive freedom. Trying to discharge this burden has occupied much recent work on libertarianism.

Third alternative: the mystery of freedom

In a book with the intimidating title of *The Critique of Pure Reason* the philosopher Immanuel Kant (1724–1804) wrote: "Morality does not . . . require that freedom should be understood, but only that it should not contradict itself." What did Kant mean? Scholars differ, but one interpretation may be paraphrased as follows:

> Human beings are free. But we cannot understand our freedom. Freedom is a mystery to us. Moral accountability demands that we be free – otherwise no negative state of affairs would be anyone's fault, no positive state would be to anyone's credit. However, freedom just is too difficult to grasp with our limited cognitive powers.

The notion that freedom is real but mysterious can appeal to people who have lost patience with attempts to understand it. The relevant notion of mystery is the idea of a profoundly important question or problem that falls outside our intellectual competence to answer or solve – not just our current competence but our competence *period*. Just as birds and fish, say, cannot do calculus, we lack sufficient intellectual powers to figure out how we can be free. As the philosopher Colin McGinn puts it, "we are not gods, cognitively speaking." It may take a god to grasp our freedom.

If gods are needed and freedom is mysterious we are in trouble. Two worries need to be raised about the thesis that freedom, though real, is mysterious. The first worry: how could we discover whether anyone (e.g. the man who raped his niece) was free if we have an *in*ability to understand freedom? If we don't understand freedom, then presumably we cannot know whether someone behaved freely. Having raised this worry, note, we are drawn to a second worry: why would anyone want a power (positive freedom) that he or she cannot understand? After all, what reason is there to think that this is a *good* ability if we cannot comprehend it?

Fourth alternative: the choice of "isms" is ours

Imagine that you are trying to prove that a person at the moment is free. For example, let us return to the typing versus dialing. The act of moving the finger to type is simple and familiar, and you are trying to show that the person who typed could also have dialed a phone number and moved her finger differently – that she had ultimate say at the time of typing. How may you show this? There are several pieces of evidence that may carry weight. For example, if you have seen the person dial a number when at a typing keyboard, and seen this frequently, and in a variety of circumstances – for instances, in which she was under stress or relaxed, or was being observed by her boss, or asked to type, or distracted – you may believe that you have sufficient evidence for saying that she had the power to dial even though she typed. And then suppose you ask her, "Did you think of dialing instead of typing?" She answers, "Of course, but I felt I had a choice and just for the heck of it I typed 'w'." "Typing or dialing may seem like matters of no consequence, but it is a facet of my life over which I have control, and I like to exercise that control whenever possible."

Is this evidence sufficient to establish that the person had personal power – that it was up to her whether to type or to dial? Arguably it is not; the action may have been determined by subtle deterministic processes in the brain or by her personality or emotional condition. But arguably it is; in a way hers is very ordinary evidence. It is also evidence which can be supplemented with other and more extraordinary evidence. Suppose, for example, neuroscientists discover that subtle and complex activity in the brain fails to behave deterministically; it is not predictable or inevitable whether certain neurons will fire, and so on all the way to the muscle movements of typing.

The situation more generally with respect to proving freedom, we may suppose, looks something like this:

> There is evidence that people are free and evidence that people are unfree (determined). The evidence is insufficient either way. The evidence does not make one rather than the other of libertarianism and determinism *the* position to believe.

But then what should we believe? People are free? Decisions and actions are determined?

According to various strictly evidential norms of sound or rational belief advocated by some philosophers, any candidate belief for which there is insufficient evidence should not be believed. In the words of W. K. Clifford: "It is always wrong, everywhere, and for anyone, to believe anything upon insufficient evidence." Hence if evidence for or against freedom is insufficient, we should suspend judgment on whether persons are free.

However, another attitude towards belief is available. "Clifford's exhortation," wrote William James (1842–1910), a famous Harvard philosopher and psychologist, "has to my ears a thoroughly fantastic sound. I myself find it impossible to go along with Clifford." According to less strict norms of rational belief advocated by James and others, when an issue truly is profoundly important to us, as is the issue of freedom, suspending judgment and remaining in belief-limbo is foolish and irrational. In such circumstances we may and should base our beliefs on whichever offers the most overall rewarding and satisfying conception of things. It is necessary at a certain point to pass beyond the evidence and consider the overall advantages and disadvantages of a belief. (Readers of the first chapter will find here an echo of Socrates' attitude towards whether to believe on motivational grounds in life after death.) James added that he is simply unable to endorse determinism, and that libertarianism coheres more satisfyingly with his moral perspective and sense of worth as a person than does determinism; he believes that we as human beings have ultimate say in our decisions and actions and that determinism does not hold sway.

James acknowledges that other philosophers may prefer determinism and even be repulsed by a conception of the world in which persons possess free will. In "The Dilemma of Determinism", James writes:

> A friend . . . once told me that the thought of my universe made him sick, like the sight of the horrible motion of mass maggots in their carrion bed. . . . But I find that every alternative to [belief in free will] is irrational in a deeper way. . . . [It is a] systematic corruption of our moral sanity.

James's message is this. Believing in determinism or free will is an action of a sort, like running or walking; it is something done – albeit a mental deed rather than a bodily movement. Deeds are performed for certain purposes and made reasonable in the light of those purposes. Some purposes are served by believing in determinism; the assumption of determinism, for example, serves the interests of a scientist or psychologist looking for sources of human behavior in natural laws. In the words of the psychologist B. F. Skinner: "If we are to use the methods of science in the field of human affairs, we must assume that behavior is lawful and determined" (Skinner 1953). However, other purposes are served by believing in free will; the assumption of libertarianism, for example, serves the interests of ordinary human interaction, of morally praising, blaming, taking personal credit, and criticizing. If neither belief is decisively favored by the evidence, how should we believe? As determinists? As libertarians/free-willists? To James the purposes of ethics matter more than those of science, and so he endorses libertarianism. In his *Principles of Psychology* he writes of believing that "bad acts cannot be fated, but good ones must be possible in their place." Elsewhere he writes: "Let psychology frankly admit that for her scientific purposes determinism can be claimed, and no one can find fault. . . . [But] ethics makes a counter-claim; and the present writer, for one, has no hesitation in regarding her claim as the stronger, and in assuming that our wills are 'free'."

Actually there are a variety of contrasting purposes, in addition to the two mentioned above, served by endorsing determinism or libertarianism, and James is aware of many of these, though he holds that scientific and ethical purposes are most important. Artistic creativity (for reasons which we do not have space to explore here), for example, may rest on whether persons possess libertarian free-dom; divine omnipotence (for reasons which we also do not have space to explain here) may require determinism. The Jamesian message that the choice between libertarianism and determinism should hinge on purposes served, requires compar-ing and contrasting relevant purposes and trying to decide which carry the most weight. This is a difficult and complex chore. It may even happen that purpose, like evidence, does not tip the balance. For James it does; the claims of morality weigh more heavily than the goals of science or other claims. But undoubtedly some readers will find that they just cannot establish which is more important – ethics or science, artistic creativity or religion, and so on. Perhaps neither evidence nor purpose tips the scale in favor of libertarianism or determinism.

Should our judgment be suspended, endorsing neither libertarianism nor deter-minism, taking what the philosopher John Earman calls "the ostrich tactic"? "Let those," says Earman, "who want to call themselves philosophers bear the risk to their mental health that comes from thinking too much about free will" (Earman 1986). How about not even thinking about the issue and burying our intellectual heads in the sand?

To which James would reply: But if libertarian freedom is possible, its occur-rence and frequency may depend upon believing that one is free. Consider the ostrich. There is no harm to the ostrich in never asking itself whether it can fly, because it can't. It has no wings. But with persons, believing we are free may have a causal bearing on whether we are free. It may help to give us the psychological "wings" we need to decide and act freely. Suspending judgment may be positively harmful; it may somehow cause us to lose our freedom.

To which Sartre would add: The ostrich tactic is, in a word, foul. We *are* free whether we believe it or not. Suspending judgment is bad faith; it does not under-mine freedom. We don't have the freedom to be unfree. So endorse libertarianism and be done with it.

References

Earman, John. 1986. *A Primer on Determinism*. Boston: Reidel.
Hempel, Carl. 1958. Some reflections on "The Case for Determinism." In Sidney Hook (ed.), *Determinism and Freedom in the Age of Modern Science*. New York: Collier Books.
McGinn, Colin. 1993. *Problems in Philosophy: The Limits of Inquiry*. Oxford: Blackwell.

Oaklander, Nathan. 1996. *Existentialist Philosophy: An Introduction*. Englewood Cliffs, NJ: Prentice-Hall.

Skinner, B. F. 1953. *Science and Human Behavior*. New York: The Free Press.

Waller, Bruce. 1990. *Freedom Without Responsibility*. Philadelphia: Temple University Press.

Suggestions for further reading

A good route to Sartre is through studying the existentialist philosophy which he helped to represent. Oaklander's *Existentialist Philosophy* contains selections from Kierkegaard, Nietzsche, and Heidegger as well as Sartre together with useful introductory essays by the editor on each of the philosophers. The most accessible of Sartre's writings for the novice reader are his plays, such as *No Exit* (many editions), novels like *Nausea*, and the essay "Existentialism Is a Humanism" (reprinted in Oaklander).

Determinism is defended in Ted Honderich's *How Free Are You?* (Oxford: Oxford University Press, 1993) and Bruce Waller's *Freedom Without Responsibility*. Determinism as an assumption necessary to a science of human behavior is defended by B. F. Skinner in *Science and Human Behavior*. A good survey for the intellectually ambitious student of the difficulties involved in defining determinism is John Earman's *A Primer on Determinism*.

Libertarianism is defended in Peter van Inwagen's *An Essay on Free Will* (Oxford: Oxford University Press, 1983) and Robert Kane's *The Significance of Free Will* (Oxford: Oxford University Press, 1996). Numerous collections of contemporary essays on freedom are available, including *Free Will*, edited by Gary Watson (Oxford: Oxford University Press, 1982). One of the most readable books on freedom is Daniel Dennett's *Elbow Room: The Varieties of Free Will Worth Wanting* (Cambridge, MA: MIT Press, 1984). James's "The Dilemma of Determinism" is reprinted in his *The Will to Believe and Other Essays* (New York: Dover, 1956).

Introduction to Selected Readings

All of the readings from Sartre come from *Being and Nothingness*, translated by H. H. Barnes (New York: Philosophical Library, 1956). The section entitled "Bad Faith" is Sartre's analysis of our attempt to deny our radical freedom. Sartre's arguments that we directly perceive our own freedom are presented in the section called "Anguish and Vertigo." The other three sections ("Fatigue," "Causes and Consciousness," and "My Past") are versions of Sartre's argument that any causal influences must be given a meaning by consciousness and thus are not determining.

In these readings Sartre uses a few technical terms that have roughly the following meanings:

for itself: human consciousness; contrasted with the *in itself*.

in itself: matter; the basic stuff of the universe aside from consciousness; something uncreated, inert, and eternal.

transcendence: going beyond, taking a perspective on.

nihilation: destruction, elimination; human freedom "nihilates" the causal influence of one's past, social situation, etc.

Turning to the second reading, Pierre Simon de Laplace (1749–1827) was a French astronomer and mathematician, known for his work on the theory of probability and his enthusiasm for Newtonian physics. He defended a brand of determinism according to which the momentary state of the world suffices to uniquely determine the state at any future time. The reading consists of a short excerpt from his *Philosophical Essay on Probability* (1819) in which he argues that human decisions and actions are part of the universe's deterministic system. Only ignorance of the true sources of our action, he says, keeps us believing in indeterminist free will.

Like Sartre, Laplace has stimulated a great deal of attention for the scope of his claims and the bold way in which he makes them. As he sees it, the only alternative to determinism is a universe ruled by randomness or chance – which he finds scientifically unacceptable.

It is worth considering whether Laplace's central conviction – that the more deeply science understands human behavior the more difficult it becomes to maintain belief in free will – can be separated from the Newtonian deterministic world-view which he favored. Would loss of freedom occur if elements in human decision and action were indeterministic? This is the question posed by Daniel Dennett of Tufts University in the third reading selection, "On Giving Libertarians What They Say They Want" which appeared in his book *Brainstorms* (Cambridge, MA: MIT Press, 1981). He offers a suggestion for where in the psychology of human decision-making indeterminism may occur. At first blush Dennett's paper reads like a defense of libertarianism. However, Dennett is not committed to libertarianism. He thinks it important to be clear about the nature of the indeterminism in human decision and action required or wanted by the libertarian. He argues that once an indeterministic element enters into decision-making it can play a causally determined role in decision and action. It turns out, says Dennett, that a certain kind of indeterminism (is this genuine indeterminism?) is compatible with asserting that people decide and act unfreely, even deterministically.

Robert Kane, a philosopher who teaches at the University of Texas, is a libertarian. In the final selection in the chapter, "Free Will: The Elusive Ideal," which appeared in 1994 in the journal *Philosophical Studies*, Kane sets out to do two main things. In the spirit of James he considers the overall advantages of libertarianism: not just evidence for it, but the purposes which embracing libertarianism may serve. Then he attempts to make room for positive freedom/ultimate say (Kane calls this "ultimate responsibility") regarding human decisions or choices by finding a place for indeterminacy at non-random junctures in decision-making. Kane is a restricted libertarian, unlike Sartre who was a radical libertarian. So Kane does not try to establish that each and every decision is free: only that *some* decisions are free. For Kane these are decisions characterized by internal conflict and *indecision* – often psychologically agonizing indecision – in which competing desires, competing considerations, are evenly matched and in which (in a theme reminiscent of Sartre) whether a person finds herself with sufficient reason for deciding one way rather than another depends on whether she chooses or elects, in some sense, to make it a sufficient reason. Kane is concerned, as the chapter urged that libertarians should be concerned, to rebut the charge that indeterminist decisions or choices or actions are merely random and hence not up to the person.

Kane's critics have voiced skepticism about whether freedom should be drawn so narrowly so that indecision has to be present in order for a person to be free. Does this mean that a happy and decisive person – free of internal conflicts – is unfree? However, Kane presents his view modestly. No one, he claims, has yet produced a knock-down defense of libertarianism. A premium has to be placed on understanding the complexity and importance of the issue of human freedom. If a philosopher offers a theory which seems unintuitive in certain respects, fashioning the best theory is a difficult chore and may lie beyond the reach of a single theorist.

Discussion questions

1 What would Sartre say is the cause of B's punching A in the following story? A insults B; A pushes B; A slaps B. Just after the insult, push, and slap, B punches A.
2 According to Laplace, if we knew the laws of nature and the conditions in the universe at any moment, we could predict every future event. So, for example, if we knew the relevant laws and the conditions operating at his birth, we could have predicted that baby Jean-Paul Sartre would grow up to be a famous libertarian philosopher. Do you agree or disagree? Why?
3 Human beings deliberate and make decisions. But if the outcome is already determined, if we could not decide other than we do, are these genuine decisions? Explain.
4 "I know that it was the unannounced quiz on libertarianism (when I had not read the chapter on Sartre) that led me to leave the room – although if I had read the chapter, I would not have left." If that's true, does it mean that the act of leaving was both negatively and positively free?
5 Martin Luther nailed his Ninety-Five Theses on a church door in Wittenberg. He said: "Here I stand, I can do no other." He felt morally obligated to nail the theses. Does that mean he also was unfree in nailing the theses? Answer this question as it would be answered by Sartre. Dennett. Kane.

Readings

Jean-Paul Sartre, *Being and Nothingness* (selections)

Bad Faith

Take the example of a woman who has consented to go out with a particular man for the first time. She knows very well the intentions which the man who is speaking to her cherishes regarding her. She knows also that it will be necessary sooner or later for her to make a decision. But she does not want to realize the urgency; she concerns herself only with what is respectful and discreet in the attitude of her companion. She does not apprehend this conduct as an attempt

Translated by Hazel Barnes (New York: Philosophical Library, 1956).

to achieve what we call "the first approach"; that is, she does not want to see possibilities of temporal development which his conduct presents. She restricts this behavior to what is in the present; she does not wish to read in the phrases which he addresses to her anything other than their explicit meaning. If he says to her, "I find you so attractive!" she disarms this phrase of its sexual background; she attaches to the conversation and to the behavior of the speaker, the immediate meanings, which she imagines as objective qualities. The man who is speaking to her appears to her sincere and respectful as the table is round or square, as the wall coloring is blue or gray. The qualities thus attached to the person she is listening to are in this way fixed in a permanence like that of things, which is no other than the projection of the strict present of the qualities into the temporal flux. This is because she does not quite know what she wants. She is profoundly aware of the desire which she inspires, but the desire cruel and naked would humiliate and horrify her. Yet she would find no charm in a respect which would be only respect. In order to satisfy her, there must be a feeling which is addressed wholly to her *personality* – i.e., to her full freedom – and which would be a recognition of her freedom. But at the same time this feeling must be wholly desire; that is, it must address itself to her body as object. This time then she refuses to apprehend the desire for what it is; she does not even give it a name; she recognizes it only to the extent that it transcends itself toward admiration, esteem, respect and that it is wholly absorbed in the more refined forms which it produces, to the extent of no longer figuring anymore as a sort of warmth and density. But then suppose he takes her hand. This act of her companion risks changing the situation by calling for an immediate decision. To leave the hand there is to consent in herself to flirt, to engage herself. To withdraw it is to break the troubled and unstable harmony which gives the hour its charm. The aim is to postpone the moment of decision as long as possible. We know what happens next; the young woman leaves her hand there, but she *does not notice* that she is leaving it. She does not notice because it happens by chance that she is at this moment all intellect. She draws her companion up to the most lofty regions of sentimental speculation; she speaks of Life, of her life, she shows herself in her essential aspect – a personality, a consciousness. And during this time the divorce of the body from the soul is accomplished; the hand rests inert between the warm hands of her companion – neither consenting nor resisting – a thing.

We shall say that this woman is in bad faith. But we see immediately that she uses various procedures in order to maintain herself in this bad faith. She has disarmed the actions of her companion by reducing them to being only what they are; that is, to existing in the mode of the in–itself. But she permits herself to enjoy his desire, to the extent that she will apprehend it as not being what it is, will recognize its transcendence. Finally while sensing profoundly the presence of her own body – to the point of being aroused, perhaps – she realizes herself as *not being* her own body, and she contemplates it as though from above as a passive object to which events can *happen* but which can neither provoke them nor avoid them because all its possibilities are outside of it. [. . .]

If man is what he is, bad faith is forever impossible and candor ceases to be his ideal and becomes instead his being. But is man what he is? And more generally, how can he *be* what he is when he exists as consciousness of being? If candor or sincerity is a universal value, it is evident that the maxim "one must be what one is" does not serve solely as a regulating principle for judgments and concepts by which I express what I am. It posits not merely an ideal of knowing but an ideal of *being*; it proposes for us an absolute equivalence of being with itself as a prototype of being. In this sense it is necessary that we *make ourselves* what we are. But what *are we* then if we have the constant obligation to make ourselves what we are, if our mode of being is having the obligation to be what we are?

Let us consider this waiter in the café. His movement is quick and forward, a little too precise, a little too rapid. He comes toward the patrons with a step a little too quick. He bends forward a little too eagerly; his voice, his eyes express an interest a little too solicitous for the order of the customer. Finally there he returns, trying to imitate in his walk the inflexible stiffness of some kind of automaton while carrying his tray with the recklessness of a tight-rope-walker by putting it in a perpetually unstable, perpetually broken equilibrium which he perpetually re-establishes by a light movement of the arm and hand. All his behavior seems to us a game. He applies himself to chaining his movements as if they were mechanisms, the one regulating the other; his gestures and even his voice seem to be mechanisms; he gives himself the quickness and pitiless rapidity of things. He is playing, he is amusing himself. But what is he playing? We need not watch long before we can explain it: he is playing at *being* a waiter in a café. There is nothing there to surprise us. The game is a kind of marking out and investigation. The child plays with his body in order to explore it, to take inventory of it; the waiter in the café plays with his condition in order to *realize* it. This obligation is not different from that which is imposed on all tradesmen. Their condition is wholly one of ceremony. The public demands of them that they realize it as a ceremony; there is the dance of the grocer, of the tailor, of the auctioneer, by which they endeavor to persuade their clientele that they are nothing but a grocer, an auctioneer, a tailor. A grocer who dreams is offensive to the buyer, because such a grocer is not wholly a grocer. Society demands that he limit himself to his function as a grocer, just as the soldier at attention makes himself into a soldier-thing with a direct regard which does not see at all, which is no longer meant to see, since it is the rule and not the interest of the moment which determines the point he must fix his eyes on (the sight "fixed at ten paces"). There are indeed many precautions to imprison a man in what he is, as if we lived in perpetual fear that he might escape from it, that he might break away and suddenly elude his condition.

In a parallel situation, from within, the waiter in the café can not be immediately a café waiter in the sense that this inkwell *is* an inkwell, or the glass is a glass. [. . .] I am never any one of my attitudes, any one of my actions. The good speaker is the one who *plays* at speaking, because he can not *be speaking*. The attentive pupil who wishes to *be* attentive, his eyes riveted on the teacher, his ears wide open, so exhausts himself in playing the attentive role that he ends up by no longer hearing anything. Perpetually absent to my body, to my acts, I am despite myself that "divine absence" of which Valéry speaks. I can not say either that I *am* here or that I *am* not here, in the sense that we say "that box of matches *is* on the table"; this would be to confuse my "being-in-the-world" with a "being-in-the-midst-of-the-world." Nor that I *am* standing, nor that I *am* seated; this would be to confuse my body with the idiosyncratic totality of which it is only one of the structures. On all sides I escape being and yet – I am.

But take a mode of being which concerns only myself: I am sad. One might think that surely I am the sadness in the mode of being what I am. What is sadness [. . .] It is the meaning of this dull look with which I view the world, of my bowed shoulders, of my lowered head, of the listlessness in my whole body. But at the very moment when I adopt each of these attitudes, do I not know that I shall not be able to hold on to it? Let a stranger suddenly appear and I will lift up my head, I will assume a lively cheerfulness. What will remain of my sadness except that I obligingly promise it an appointment for later after the departure of the visitor? Moreover is not this sadness itself a *conduct*? Is it not consciousness which affects itself with sadness as a magical recourse against a situation too urgent? And in this case even, should we not say that being sad means first to make oneself sad? That may be, someone will say, but after all doesn't giving oneself the being of sadness mean to *receive* this being? It makes no difference from where I receive it. The fact is that a consciousness which affects itself with sadness is sad precisely for this reason. But it is difficult to comprehend the nature of consciousness; the being-sad is not a ready-made being which I give to myself as I can give this book to my friend. I do not possess the property of *affecting myself with being*. If I make myself sad, I must continue to make myself sad from beginning to end. I can not treat my sadness as an impulse finally achieved and put it on file without re-creating it, nor can I carry it in the manner of an inert body which continues its movement after the initial shock. There is no inertia in consciousness. If I make myself sad, it is because I *am* not sad – the being of the sadness escapes me by and in the very act by which I affect myself with it. [. . .]

The Origin of Negation

Anguish and Vertigo

If our analysis has not led us astray, there ought to exist for the human being, in so far as he is conscious of being, a certain mode of standing opposite his past and his future, as being both this past and this future and as not being them. We shall be able to furnish an immediate reply to this question; it is in anguish that man gets the consciousness of his freedom, or if you prefer, anguish is the mode of being of freedom as consciousness of being; it is in anguish that freedom is, in its being, in question for itself.

Kierkegaard describing anguish in the face of what one lacks characterizes it as anguish in the face of freedom. But Heidegger, whom we know to have been greatly influenced by Kierkegaard, considers anguish instead as the apprehension of nothingness. These two descriptions of anguish do not appear to us contradictory; on the contrary the one implies the other.

First we must acknowledge that Kierkegaard is right; anguish is distinguished from fear in that fear is fear of beings in the world whereas anguish is anguish before myself. Vertigo is anguish to the extent that I am afraid not of falling over the precipice, but of throwing myself over. A situation provokes fear if there is a possibility of my life being changed from without; my being provokes anguish to the extent that I distrust myself and my own reactions in that situation. The artillery preparation which precedes the attack can provoke fear in the soldier who undergoes the bombardment, but anguish is born in him when he tries to foresee the conduct with which he will face the bombardment, when he asks himself if he is going to be able to "hold up." Similarly the recruit who reports for active duty at the beginning of the war can in some instances be afraid of death, but more often he is "afraid of being afraid"; that is, he is filled with anguish before himself. Most of the time dangerous or threatening situations present themselves in facets; they will be apprehended through a feeling of fear or of anguish according to whether we envisage the situation as acting on the man or the man as acting on the situation. The man who has just received a hard blow – for example, losing a great part of his wealth in a crash – can have the fear of threatening poverty. He will experience anguish a moment later when nervously wringing his hands (a symbolic reaction to the action which is imposed but which remains still wholly undetermined), he exclaims to himself; "What am I going to do? But what am I going to do?" In this sense fear and anguish are exclusive of one another since fear is unreflective apprehension of the transcendent and anguish is reflective apprehension of the self; the one is born in the destruction of the other. The normal process in the case which I have just cited is a constant transition from the one to the other. But there exist also situations where anguish appears pure; that is, without ever being preceded or followed by fear. If, for example, I have been raised to a new dignity and charged with a delicate and flattering mission, I can feel anguish at the thought that I will not be capable perhaps of fulfilling it, and yet I will not have the least fear in the world of the consequences of my possible failure.

What is the meaning of anguish in the various examples which I have just given? Let us take up again the example of vertigo. Vertigo announces itself through fear; I am on a narrow path – without a guard rail – which goes along a precipice. The precipice presents itself to me as *to be avoided*; it represents a danger of death. At the same time I conceive of a certain number of causes, originating in universal determinism, which can transform that threat of death into reality: I can slip on a stone and fall into the abyss; the crumbling earth of the path can give way under my steps. Through these various anticipations, I am given to myself as a thing; I am passive in relation to these possibilities; they come to me from without; in so far as I am also an object in the world, subject to gravitation, they are *my* possibilities. At this moment *fear* appears, which in terms of the situation is the apprehension of myself as a destructible transcendent in the midst of transcendents, as an object which does not contain in itself the origin of its future disappearance. My reaction will be of the reflective order; I will pay attention to the stones in the road; I will keep myself as far as possible from the edge of the path. I realize myself as pushing away the threatening situation with all my strength, and I project before myself a certain number of future conducts destined to keep the threats of the world at a distance from me. These conducts are *my* possibilities. I escape fear by the very fact that I am placing myself on a plane where *my own* possibilities are substituted for the transcendent probabilities where human action had no place.

But these conducts, precisely because they are *my* possibilities, do not appear to me as determined by foreign causes. Not only is it not strictly certain that they will be effective; in particular it is not strictly certain that they will be adopted, for they do not have existence sufficient in itself. [. . .] No external cause will remove them. I alone am the permanent source of their non-being, I engage myself in them; in order to cause *my* possibility to appear, I posit the other possibilities so as to nihilate them. This would not produce anguish if I could apprehend myself in my relations with these possibles as a cause producing its effects. In this case the effect defined as my possibility *would be strictly* determined. But then it would cease to be *possible*; it would become simply "about-to-happen." If then I wished to avoid anguish and vertigo, it would be enough if I were to consider the motives (instinct of self-preservation, prior fear, *etc*.), which make me reject the situation envisaged, as *determining* my prior activity in the same way that the presence at a determined point of one given mass determines the courses followed by other masses; it would be necessary, in other words, that I apprehend in myself a strict psychological determinism. But I am in anguish precisely because any conduct on my part is only *possible*, and this means that while constituting a totality of motives *for* pushing away that situation, I at the same moment apprehend these motives as not sufficiently effective. At the very moment when I apprehend my being as *horror* of the precipice, I am conscious of that horror as *not determinant* in relation to my possible conduct. In one sense that horror calls for prudent conduct, and it is in itself a pre-outline of that conduct; in another sense, it posits the final developments of that conduct only as possible, precisely because I do not apprehend it as the *cause* of these final developments but as need, appeal, *etc*. [. . .] If *nothing* compels me to save my life, *nothing* prevents me from precipitating myself into the abyss. The decisive conduct will emanate from a self which I am not yet. Thus the self which I am depends on the self which I am not yet to the exact extent that the self which I am not yet does not depend on the self which I am. Vertigo appears as the apprehension of this dependence. I approach the precipice, and my scrutiny is searching for myself in my very depths. In terms of this moment, I play with my possibilities. My eyes, running over the abyss from top to bottom, imitate the possible fall and realize it symbolically; at the same time suicide, from the fact that it becomes a *possibility* possible for *me*, now causes to appear possible motives for adopting it (suicide would cause anguish to cease). Fortunately these motives in their turn, from the sole fact that they are motives of a possibility, present themselves as ineffective, as non-determinant; they can no more *produce* the suicide than my horror of the fall can *determine me* to avoid it. It is this counter-anguish which generally puts an end to anguish by transmuting it into indecision. Indecision in its turn calls for decision. I abruptly put myself at a distance from the edge of the precipice and resume my way. [. . .]

Being and Doing: Freedom

Causes and consciousness

Generally by cause we mean the reason for the act; that is, the ensemble of rational considerations which justify it. If the government decides on a conversion of Government bonds, it will give the causes for its act: the lessening of the national debt, the rehabilitation of the Treasury. Similarly it is by *causes* that historians are accustomed to explain the acts of ministers or monarchs; they will seek the *causes* for a declaration of war: the occasion is propitious, the attacked country is disorganized because of internal troubles; it is time to put an end to an economic conflict which is in danger of lasting interminably. If Clovis is converted to Catholicism, then inasmuch as so many barbarian kings are Arians, it is because Clovis sees an opportunity of getting into the good graces of the episcopate which is all powerful in Gaul. And so on. One will note here that the cause is characterized as an objective appreciation of the situation. The cause of Clovis' conversion is the political and religious state of Gaul; it is the relative strengths of the episcopate, the great landowners, and the common people. What motivates the conversion of the bonds is the state of the national debt. Nevertheless this objective appreciation can be made only in the light of a pre-supposed end and within the limits of a project of the for-itself toward this end. In order for the power of the episcopate to be revealed to Clovis as the cause of his conversion (that is, in order for him to be able to envisage the objective consequences which this conversion could have) it is necessary first for him to posit as an end the conquest of Gaul. If we suppose that Clovis has other ends, he can find in the situation of the Church causes for his becoming Arian or remaining pagan. It is even possible that in the consideration of the Church he can even find no cause for acting in any way at all; he will then discover nothing in relation to this subject; he will leave the situation of the episcopate in the state of "unrevealed," in a total obscurity. We shall therefore use the term *cause* for the objective apprehension of a determined situation as this situation is revealed in the light of a certain end as being able to serve as the means for attaining this end.

The motive, on the contrary, is generally considered as a subjective fact. It is the ensemble of the desires, emotions, and passions which urge me to accomplish a certain act. The historian looks for motives and takes them into account only as a last resort when the causes are not sufficient to explain the act under consideration. Ferdinand Lot, for example, after having shown that the reasons which are ordinarily given for the conversion of Constantine are insufficient or erroneous, writes:

"Since it is established that Constantine had everything to lose and apparently nothing to gain by embracing Christianity, there is only one conclusion possible – that he yielded to a sudden impulse, pathological or divine as you prefer."[1] Lot is here abandoning the explanation by causes, which seems to him unenlightening, and prefers to it an explanation by motives. The explanation must then be sought in the psychic state – even in the "mental" state – of the historical agent. It follows naturally that the event becomes wholly contingent since another individual with other passions and other desires would have acted differently. In contrast to the historian the psychologist will by preference look for motives; usually he supposes, in fact, that they are "contained in" the state of consciousness which has provoked the action. The ideal rational act would therefore be the one for which the motives would be practically nil and which would be uniquely inspired by an objective appreciation of the situation. The irrational or passionate act will be characterized by the reverse proportion.

It remains for us to explain the relation between causes and motives in the everyday case in which they exist side by side. For example, I can join the Socialist party because I judge that this party serves the interests of justice and of humanity or because I believe that it will become the principal historical force in the years which will follow my joining: these are causes. And at the same time I can have motives: a feeling of pity or charity for certain classes of the oppressed, a feeling of shame at being on the "good side of the barricade," as Gide says, or again an inferiority complex, a desire to shock my relatives, *etc.* What can be meant by the statement that I have joined the Socialist party for these causes *and* these motives? [. . .]

To be sure, the cause is objective; it is the state of contemporary things as it is revealed to a consciousness. It is *objective* that the Roman plebs and aristocracy were corrupted by the time of Constantine or that the Catholic Church is ready to favor a monarch who at the time of Clovis will help it triumph over Arianism. Nevertheless this state of affairs can be revealed only to a for-itself since in general the for-itself is the being by which "there is" a world. Better yet, it can be revealed only to a for-itself which chooses itself in this or that particular way – that is, to a for-itself which has made its own individuality. The for-itself must of necessity have projected itself in this or that way in order to discover the instrumental implications of instrumental-things. Objectively the knife is an instrument made of a blade and a handle. I can grasp it objectively as an instrument to slice with, to cut with. But lacking a hammer, I can just as well grasp the knife as an instrument to hammer with. I can make use of its handle to pound in a nail, and this apprehension is no less *objective*. When Clovis appreciates the aid which the Church can furnish him, it is not certain that a group of prelates or even one particular priest has made any overtures to him, nor even that any member of the clergy has clearly thought of an alliance with a Catholic monarch. The only strictly objective facts, those which any for-itself whatsoever can establish, are the great power of the Church over the people of Gaul and the anxiety of the Church with regard to the

---

[1] Ferdinand Lot. *La fin du monde antique et le début du moyen âge. Renaissance du Livre.* 1927, p. 35.

Arian heresy. In order for these established facts to be organized into a cause for conversion, it is necessary to isolate them from the ensemble – and thereby to nihilate them – and it is necessary to transcend them toward a particular potentiality: the Church's potentiality objectively apprehended by Clovis will be to give its support to a converted king. But this potentiality can be revealed only if the situation is surpassed toward a state of things which does not yet exist – in short, toward a nothingness. In a word the world gives counsel only if one questions it, and one can question it only for a well-determined end.

Therefore the cause, far from determining the action, appears only in and through the project of an action. It is in and through the project of imposing his rule on all of Gaul that the state of the Western Church appears objectively to Clovis as a cause for his conversion. In other words the consciousness which carves out the cause in the ensemble of the world has already its own structure; it has given its own ends to itself, it has projected itself toward its possibles [. . .]

Fatigue

Common opinion does not hold that to be free means only to choose oneself. A choice is said to be free if it is such that it could have been other than what it is. I start out on a hike with friends. At the end of several hours of walking my fatigue increases and finally becomes very painful. At first I resist and then suddenly I let myself go, I give up, I throw my knapsack down on the side of the road and let myself fall down beside it. Someone will reproach me for my act and will mean thereby that I was free – that is, not only was my act not determined by any thing or person, but also I could have succeeded in resisting my fatigue longer, I could have done as my companions did and reached the resting place before relaxing. I shall defend myself by saying that I was *too tired*. Who is right? Or rather is the debate not based on incorrect premises? There is no doubt that I could have done otherwise, but that is not the problem. It ought to be formulated rather like this: could I have done otherwise without perceptibly modifying the organic totality of the projects which I am; or is the fact of resisting my fatigue such that instead of remaining a purely local and accidental modification of my behavior, it could be effected only by means of a radical transformation of my being-in-the-world – a transformation, moreover, which is *possible*? In other words: I could have done otherwise. Agreed. But *at what price*? [. . .] Let us note first that the fatigue by itself could not provoke my decision. [. . .] Here is posited the essential question: my companions are in good health – like me; they have had practically the same training as I so that although it is not possible to *compare* psychic events which occur in different subjectivities, I usually conclude – and witnesses after an objective consideration of our bodies-for-others conclude – that they are for all practical purposes "as fatigued as I am." How does it happen therefore that they suffer their fatigue differently? Someone will say that the difference stems from the fact that I am a "sissy" and that the others are not. But although this evaluation undeniably has a practical bearing on the case and although one could take this into account

113

when there arose a question of deciding whether or not it would be a good idea to take me on another expedition, such an evaluation can not satisfy us here. We have seen that to be ambitious is to project conquering a throne or honors; it is not a *given* which would incite one to conquest; it is this conquest itself. Similarly to be a "sissy" can not be a factual given and is only a name given to the way in which I suffer my fatigue. If therefore I wish to understand under what conditions I can suffer a fatigue as unbearable, it will not help to address oneself to so–called factual givens, which are revealed as being only a choice; it is necessary to attempt to examine this choice itself and to see whether it is not explained within the perspective of a larger choice in which it would be integrated as a secondary structure. If I question one of my companions, he will explain to me that he is fatigued, of course, but that he *loves* his fatigue; he gives himself up to it as to a bath; it appears to him in some way as the privileged instrument for discovering the world which surrounds him, for adapting himself to the rocky roughness of the paths, for discovering the "mountainous" quality of the slopes. In the same way it is this light sunburn on the back of his neck and this slight ringing in his ears which will enable him to realize a direct contact with the sun. Finally the feeling of effort is for him that of fatigue overcome. But as his fatigue is nothing but the passion which he endures so that the dust of the highways, the burning of the sun, the roughness of the roads may exist to the fullest, his effort (*i.e.*, this sweet familiarity with a fatigue which he loves, to which he abandons himself and which nevertheless he himself directs) is given as a way of appropriating the mountain, of suffering it to the end and being victor over it. [. . .] Thus my companion's fatigue is lived in a vaster project of a trusting abandon to nature, of a passion consented to in order that it may exist at full strength, and at the same time the project of sweet mastery and appropriation. It is only in and through this project that the fatigue will be able to be understood and that it will have meaning for him. [. . .]

My past

We have a past. Of course we have been able to establish that this past does not determine our acts as a prior phenomenon determines a consequent phenomenon; we have shown that the past is without force to constitute the present and to sketch out the future. Nevertheless the fact remains that the freedom which escapes toward the future can not give itself any past it likes according to its fancy; there are even more compelling reasons for the fact that it can not produce itself without a past. It has to be its own past, and this past is irremediable. It even seems at first glance that freedom can not modify its past in any way; the past is that which is out of reach and which haunts us at a distance without our even being able to turn back to face it in order to consider it. If the past does not determine our actions, at least it is such that we can not take a new decision except *in terms of it*. If I have been trained at a naval academy, and if I have become an officer in the Navy, at each moment that I assume myself and consider myself, I am engaged; at the very instant when I apprehend myself, I am on watch on the bridge of the ship of which

I am second in command. I can suddenly revolt against this fact, hand in my resignation, decide on suicide. These extreme measures are taken in connection with the past which is mine; if they aim at destroying it, this is because my past exists, and my most radical decisions can succeed only in taking a negative position with respect to my past. But basically this is to recognize the past's immense importance as a backdrop and a point of view. Every action designed to wrench me away from my past must first be conceived in terms of my particular past; that is, the action must before all recognize that it is born out of the particular past which it wishes to destroy. Our acts, says the proverb, follow after us. The past is present and melts insensibly into the present; it is the suit of clothes which I selected six months ago, the house which I have had built, the book which I began last winter, my wife, the promises which I have made to her, my children; all which I *am* I have to be in the mode of having-been. Thus the importance of the past can not be exaggerated [. . .] But we find here the paradox pointed out previously: I can not conceive of myself without a past; better yet, I can no longer *think* anything about myself since I think about what I *am* and since I am in the past; but on the other hand I am the being through whom the past comes to myself and to the world.

Let us examine this paradox more closely. Since freedom is choice, it is change. It is defined by the end which it projects; that is, by the future which it has to be. But precisely because the future is *the not-yet-existing-state of what is*, it can be conceived only within a narrow connection with what is. It is not possible that what is should illuminate what is not yet, for what is is a *lack* and consequently can be known as such only in terms of that which it lacks. The end illuminates what is. But to go looking for the end to-come in order by means of it to make known that-which-is, requires being already beyond what-is in a nihilating withdrawal which makes what-is appear clearly in the state of an isolated-system. What-is, therefore, takes on its meaning only when it is *surpassed* toward the future. There-fore what-is is the past. We see how the past as "that which is to be changed" is indispensable to the choice of the future and how consequently no free surpassing can be effected except in terms of a past, but we can see too how the very *nature* of the past comes to the past from the original choice of a future. In particular the irremediable quality of the past comes from my actual choice of the future; if the past is that in terms of which I conceive and project a new state of things in the future, then the past itself is that which is *left in place*, that which consequently is itself outside all perspective of change. Thus in order for the future to be realizable, it is necessary that the past be irremediable.

It is possible for me not to exist; but if I exist, I can not lack having a past. Such is the form which is assumed here by the "necessity of my contingency." But on the other hand, as we have seen, two existential characteristics in particular qualify the For-itself:

1 Nothing is in consciousness which is not consciousness of being.
2 In my being, my being is in question. This means that nothing comes to me which *is not chosen*.

We have seen, indeed, that a Past which was only Past would collapse in an honorary existence in which it would have lost all connection with the present. In order for us to "have" a past, it is necessary that we maintain it in existence by our very project toward the future; we do not receive our past, but the necessity of our contingency implies that we are not able not to choose it. This is what it means "to have to be one's own past." We see that this necessity, considered here from a purely temporal point of view, is not basically distinct from the primary structure of freedom, which must be the nihilation of the being which it is and which, by this very nihilation, brings it about that *there is* a being which it is.

But while freedom is the choice of an end in terms of the past, conversely the past is what it is only in relation to the end chosen. There is an unchangeable element in the past (*e.g.*, I had whooping cough when I was five years old) and an element which is eminently variable (the meaning of the brute fact in relation to the totality of my being). But since, on the other hand, the meaning of the past fact penetrates it through and through (I can not "recall" my childhood whooping cough outside of a precise project which defines its meaning), it is finally impossible for me to distinguish the unchangeable brute existence from the variable meaning which it includes. To say "I had whooping cough when I was four years old" supposes a thousand projects, in particular the adoption of the calendar as a system of reference for my individual existence (hence the adoption of an original position with regard to the social order) and a confident belief in the accounts which third persons give of my childhood, a belief which certainly goes along with a respect or an affection for my parents, a respect which shapes its meaning for me, *etc.* That brute fact itself *is*, but apart from the witness of others, its date, the technical name of the illness (an ensemble of meanings which depend on my projects) what can it *be*? Thus this brute existence, *although necessarily existent and unchangeable*, stands as the ideal end – beyond reach – of a systematic specification of all the meanings included in a memory. [. . .]

Now the meaning of the past is strictly dependent on my present project. This certainly does not mean that I can make the meaning of my previous acts vary in any way I please; quite the contrary, it means that the fundamental project which I am decides absolutely the meaning which the past which I have to be can have for me and for others. I alone in fact can decide at each moment the *bearing* of the past. I do not decide it by debating it, by deliberating over it, and in each instance evaluating the importance of this or that prior event; but by projecting myself toward my ends, I preserve the past with me, and by action I *decide* its meaning. Who shall decide whether that mystic crisis in my fifteenth year "was" a pure accident of puberty or, on the contrary, the first sign of a future conversion? I myself, according to whether I shall decide – at twenty years of age, at thirty years – to be converted. The project of conversion by a single stroke confers on an adolescent crisis the value of a premonition which I had not taken seriously. Who shall decide whether the period which I spent in prison after a theft was fruitful or deplorable? I – according to whether I give up stealing or become hardened. Who can decide the educational value of a trip, the sincerity of a profession of love, the purity of a past intention, *etc.*? It is I, always I, according to the ends by which I illuminate these past events.

Thus all my past is there pressing, urgent, imperious, but its meanings and the orders which it gives me I choose by the very project of my end. Of course the engagements which I have undertaken weigh upon me. Of course the marriage I made earlier, the house I bought and furnished last year limit my possibilities and dictate my conduct; but precisely because my projects are such I reassume the marriage contract. In other words, precisely because I do not make of it a "marriage contract which is past, surpassed, dead" and because, on the contrary, my projects imply fidelity to the engagements undertaken or the decision to have an "honorable life" as a husband and a father, *etc.*, these projects necessarily come to illuminate the past marriage vow and to confer on it its always actual value. Thus the urgency of the past comes from the future. [. . .]

Pierre Simon de Laplace,
Philosophical Essay on Probability (selection)

All events, even those which because of their small scale do not appear to keep to the great laws of nature, are just as necessary a result of those laws as are the revolutions of the sun. In ignorance of the ties which bind these events to the entire system of the universe, people have made them depend on final causes,[1] or upon chance, depending on whether they happen and recur with regularity, on the one hand, or in an apparently disorderly way, on the other. But these imaginary causes have been gradually pushed out of the way as the boundaries of our knowledge have increased, and they would completely vanish in the face of sound philosophy, which sees in them only the expression of our present ignorance of the true causes.

Present events have a connection with previous ones that is based on the self-evident principle that a thing cannot come into existence without a cause that produces it. This axiom, known under the name of the *principle of sufficient reason*, extends even to actions which people regard as indifferent.[2] The freest will is unable to give birth to them without a determinate motive. Take two situations characterized by exactly similar circumstances: if the will were to act in the first case and refrain from acting in the second, its choice would be an effect without a cause – so it would be, as Leibniz puts it, a case of the 'blind chance' which the Epicureans talk of. Believing in such uncaused events is an illusion of the mind,

Translated by John Cottingham. From *Western Philosophy: An Anthology*, ed. John Cottingham (Oxford: Blackwell, 1996).

[1] Explanations referring to the end state or goal towards which a process or action is apparently directed.

[2] i.e. actions where I seem to have an entirely "open" choice between two options. In traditional terminology, someone was said to possess "liberty of indifference" when entirely free and undetermined as to which of two courses of action to select.

which loses sight of the elusive reasons underlying the will's choice in "indifferent" situations, and convinces itself that the will is self-determined and motiveless.

We must therefore regard the present state of the universe as the effect of its preceding state and as the cause of the one which is to follow. An intelligence which in a single instant could know all the forces which animate the natural world, and the respective situations of all the beings that made it up, could, provided it was vast enough to make an analysis of all the data so supplied, be able to produce a single formula which specified all the movements in the universe from those of the largest bodies in the universe to those of the lightest atom. For such an intelligence, nothing would be "uncertain", and the future, like the past, would be present before its eyes. The human mind, in the perfection which it has been able to give to astronomy, presents a feeble shadow of this intelligence. Its discoveries in mechanics and geometry, added to that of universal gravity, have brought it within reach of including within the same analytical formulae all the past and future states of the world system. By applying the same method to various other objects of its knowledge, it has managed to reduce the observed phenomena to general laws, and to predict the results which must be generated by any given set of circumstances. All the efforts of the human mind in its search for truth tend to bring it continually closer to that vast intelligence we have just imagined; though it will always remain infinitely far removed from it. This onward tendency, peculiar to the human race, is what makes us superior to the animals; it is progress in this area which distinguishes nations and epochs and is their true glory.

Let us recall that in former times, still not so very far away, a heavy rainfall or prolonged drought, a comet trailing a very long tail, eclipses, the aurora borealis, and in general all out of the ordinary phenomena, were regarded as so many signs of celestial anger. Heaven was invoked in order to avert their dire influence. No one prayed to heaven to stop the courses of the planets and the sun; observation had soon made people see the futility of such prayers. But because these unusual phenomena, appearing and disappearing at long intervals, seemed to contravene the order of nature, men supposed that heaven created and altered them at will to punish crimes done on earth. Thus the comet of 1456, with its long tail, spread terror throughout Europe, already appalled by the rapid successes of the Turks, who had just overthrown the Lower Empire. But for us, now that four successive revolutions of the body in question have elapsed, it has aroused a very different interest. The knowledge of the laws of the world–system acquired during the interval had dissipated the fears produced by ignorance of the true relationship of man to the universe; and Halley, having recognized that the appearances of 1531, 1607 and 1682 all related to the same comet, predicted its next return for the end of 1758 or the start of 1759. The learned world impatiently awaited this return, which was destined to confirm one of the greatest discoveries ever made in the sciences, and fulfil the prediction of Seneca when he said, speaking of the revolution of those stars which come from an enormous distance: "The day will come when studies pursued over many centuries will reveal in all clarity things that are now hidden, and posterity will be astonished that we had failed to grasp such clear truths." Clairaut then undertook to analyse the perturbations which the comet had undergone as a result of the action of the two great planets, Jupiter and Saturn; after vast calculations he fixed its next passage at perihelion towards the beginning of April 1759 – which was quickly confirmed by observation. There is no doubt that this regularity which has been demonstrated by astronomy in the movement of the comets also obtains in all other phenomena. The curve described by a simple molecule of air or vapour is determined in just as certain a manner as that of the planetary orbits; there are no differences between the two cases, except those which are a function of our own ignorance.

Daniel Dennett, "On Giving Libertarians What They Say They Want"

Why is the free will problem so persistent? Partly, I suspect, because it is called *the* free will problem. Hilliard, the great card magician, used to fool even his profes- sional colleagues with a trick he called the tuned deck. Twenty times in a row he'd confound the quidnuncs, as he put it, with the same trick, a bit of prestidigitation that resisted all the diagnostic hypotheses of his fellow magicians. The trick, as he eventually revealed, was a masterpiece of subtle misdirection; it consisted entirely of the *name*, "the tuned deck", plus a peculiar but obviously non-functional bit of ritual. It was, you see, *many* tricks, however many different but familiar tricks Hilliard had to perform in order to stay one jump ahead of the solvers. As soon as their experiments and subtle arguments had conclusively eliminated one way of doing the trick, that was the way he would do the trick on future trials. This would have been obvious to his sophisticated onlookers had they not been so intent on finding *the* solution to *the* trick.

The so called free will problem is in fact many not very closely related problems tied together by a name and lots of attendant anxiety. Most people can be brought by reflection to care very much what the truth is on these matters, for each problem poses a threat: to our self-esteem, to our conviction that we are not living deluded lives, to our conviction that we may justifiably trust our grasp of such utterly familiar notions as possibility, opportunity and ability.[1] There is no very good reason to suppose that an acceptable solution to *one* of the problems will be,

---

From Daniel Dennett (ed.), *Brainstorms* (Cambridge, MA: MIT Press, 1981).

[1] An incomplete list of the very different questions composing the free will problem: (1) How can a material thing (a mechanism?) be correctly said to reason, to have reasons, to act on reasons? (2) How can the unique four dimensional non-branching world-worm that comprises all that has happened and will happen admit of a notion of possibilities that are not actualities? What does an *opportunity* look like when the world is viewed *sub specie aeternitatis*? (3) How can a person be an author of decisions, and not merely the locus of causal summation for external influences? (4) How can we make sense of the intuition that an agent can only be responsible if he could have done otherwise? (5) How can we intelligibly describe the relevant mental history of the truly culpable agent – the villain or rational cheat with no excuses? As Socrates asked, can a person knowingly commit evil?

or even point to, an acceptable solution to the others, and we may be misled by residual unallayed worries into rejecting or undervaluing partial solutions, in the misguided hope that we might allay all the doubts with one overarching doctrine or theory. But we don't have any good theories. Since the case for determinism is persuasive and since we all want to believe we have free will, *compatibilism* is the strategic favorite, but we must admit that no compatibilism free of problems while full of the traditional flavors of responsibility has yet been devised.

The alternatives to compatibilism are anything but popular. Both the libertarian and the hard determinist believe that free will and determinism are incompatible. The hard determinist says: "So much the worse for free will." The libertarian says: "So much the worse for determinism," at least with regard to human action. Both alternatives have been roundly and routinely dismissed as at best obscure, at worst incoherent. But alas for the compatibilist, neither view will oblige us by fading away. Their persistence, like Hilliard's success, probably has many explanations. I hope to diagnose just one of them.

In a recent paper, David Wiggins has urged us to look with more sympathy at the program of libertarianism.[2] Wiggins first points out that a familiar argument often presumed to demolish libertarianism begs the question. The first premise of this argument is that every event is either causally determined or random. Then since the libertarian insists that human actions cannot be both free and determined, the libertarian must be supposing that any and all free actions are random. But one would hardly hold oneself responsible for an action that merely happened at random, so libertarianism, far from securing a necessary condition for responsible action, has unwittingly secured a condition that would defeat responsibility altogether. Wiggins points out that the first premise, that every event is either causally determined or random, is not the innocent logical truth it appears to be. The innocent logical truth is that every event is either causally determined or not causally determined. There may be an established sense of the word "random" that is unproblematically synonymous with "not causally determined", but the word "random" in common parlance had further connotations of pointlessness or arbitrariness, and it is these very connotations that ground our acquiescence in the further premise that one would not hold oneself responsible for one's random actions. It may be the case that whatever is random in the sense of being causally undetermined, is random in the sense connoting utter meaninglessness, but that is just what the libertarian wishes to deny. This standard objection to libertarianism, then, assumes what it must prove; it fails to show that undetermined action would be random action, and hence action for which we could not be held responsible.

But is there in fact any reasonable hope that the libertarian can find some defensible ground between the absurdity of "blind chance" on the one hand and on the other what Wiggins calls the cosmic unfairness of the determinist's view of these matters? Wiggins thinks there is. He draws our attention to a speculation of

---

[2] D. Wiggins, "Towards a Reasonable Libertarianism", in T. Honderich, ed., *Essays on Freedom of Action* (London: Routledge & Kegan Paul, 1973).

Russell's: "It might be that without infringing the laws of physics, intelligence could make improbable things happen, as Maxwell's demon would have defeated the second law of thermo-dynamics by opening the trap door to fast-moving particles and closing it to slow-moving particles."[3] Wiggins sees many problems with the speculation, but he does, nevertheless, draw a glimmer of an idea from it.

> For indeterminism maybe all we really need to imagine or conceive is a world in which (a) there is some macroscopic indeterminacy founded in microscopic indeterminacy, and (b) an appreciable number of the free actions or policies or deliberations of individual agents, although they are not even in principle hypothetico-deductively derivable from antecedent conditions, can be such as to persuade us to fit them into meaningful sequences. We need not trace free actions back to volitions construed as little pushes aimed from outside the physical world. What we must find instead are patterns which are coherent and intelligible in the low level terms of practical deliberation, even though they are not amenable to the kind of generalization or necessity which is the stuff of rigorous theory. (p. 52)

The "low level terms of practical deliberation" are, I take it, the familiar terms of intentional or reason-giving explanation. We typically render actions intelligible by citing their reasons, the beliefs and desires of the agent that render the actions at least marginally reasonable under the circumstances. Wiggins is suggesting then that if we could somehow *make sense* of human actions at the level of intentional explanation, then in spite of the fact that those actions might be physically undetermined, they would not be random. Wiggins invites us to take this possibility seriously, but he has little further to say in elaboration or defense of this. He has said enough, however, to suggest to me a number of ways in which we could give libertarians what they seem to want.

Wiggins asks only that human actions be seen to be *intelligible* in the low-level terms of practical deliberation. Surely if human actions were *predictable* in the low-level terms of practical deliberations, they would be intelligible in those terms. So I propose first to demonstrate that there is a way in which human behavior could be strictly undetermined from the physicist's point of view while at the same time accurately predictable from the intentional level. This demonstration, alas, will be very disappointing, for it relies on a cheap trick and what it establishes can be immediately seen to be quite extraneous to the libertarian's interests. But it is a necessary preamble to what I hope will be a more welcome contribution to the libertarian's cause. So let us get the disappointing preamble behind us.

Here is how a bit of human behavior could be undetermined from the physicist's point of view, but quite clearly predictable by the intentionalist. Suppose we were to build an electronic gadget that I will call an answer box. The answer box is designed to record a person's answers to simple questions. It has two buttons, a Yes button, and a No button, and two foot pedals, a Yes pedal, and a No pedal, all

3 Bertrand Russell, *Human Knowledge; Its Scope and Limits* (New York: Simon and Schuster, 1948), Chapter 15, "The Physiology of Sensation and Volition", p. 54.

clearly marked. It also has a little display screen divided in half, and on one side it says "use the buttons" and on the other side it says "use the pedals". We design this bit of apparatus so that only one half of this display screen is illuminated at any one time. Once a minute, a radium randomizer determines, in an entirely undetermined way of course, whether the display screen says "use the buttons" or "use the pedals". I now propose the following experiment. First, we draw up a list of ten very simple questions that have Yes or No answers, questions of the order of difficulty of "Do fish swim?" and "Is Texas bigger than Rhode Island?" We seat a subject at the answer box and announce that a handsome reward will be given to those who correctly follow all the experimental instructions, and a bonus will be given to those who answer all our questions correctly.

Now, can the physicist in principle predict the subject's behavior? Let us suppose the subject is in fact a physically deterministic system, and let us suppose further that the physicist has perfect knowledge of the subject's initial state, all the relevant deterministic laws, and all the interactions within the closed situation of the experimental situation. Still, the unpredictable behavior of the answer box will infect the subject on a macroscopic scale with its own indeterminacy on at least ten occasions during the period the physicist must predict. So the best the physicist can do is issue a multiple disjunctive or multiple conditional prediction. Can the intentionalist do any better? Yes, of course. The intentionalist, having read the instructions given to the subject and having sized up the subject as a person of roughly normal intelligence and motivation, and having seen that all the odd numbered questions have Yes answers and the even numbered questions have No answers, confidently predicts that the subject will behave as follows: "The subject will give Yes answers to questions 1, 3, 5, 7, and 9, and the subject will answer the rest of the questions in the negative". There are no *if's*, *or's* or *maybe's* in those predictions. They are categorical and precise – precise enough for instance to appear in a binding contract or satisfy a court of law.

This is, of course, the cheap trick I warned you about. There is no real difference in the predictive power of the two predictors. The intentionalist for instance is no more in a position to predict whether the subject will move finger or foot than the physicist is, and the physicist may well be able to give predictions that are tantamount to the intentionalist's. The physicist may for instance be able to make this prediction: "When question 6 is presented, if the illuminated sign on the box reads use the pedals, the subject's right foot will move at velocity k until it depresses the No pedal n inches, and if the illuminated sign says use the buttons, the subject's right index finger will trace a trajectory terminating on the No button." Such a prediction is if anything more detailed than the intentionalist's simple prediction of the negative answer to question 6, and it might in fact be more reliable and better grounded as well. But so what? What we are normally interested in, what we are normally interested in *predicting*, moreover, is not the skeletal motion of human beings but their actions, and the intentionalist can predict the actions of the subject (at least insofar as most of us would take any interest in them) without the elaborate rigmarole and calculations of the physicist. The possibility of indeterminacy in the environment of the kind introduced here, and hence the possibility of indeterminacy in the subject's reaction to that environment, is something with regard to which the intentionalistic predictive power is quite neutral. Still, we could not expect the libertarian to be interested in this variety of undetermined human behavior, behavior that is undetermined simply because the behavior of the answer box, something entirely external to the agent, is undetermined.

Suppose then we move something like the answer box inside the agent. It is a commonplace of action theory that virtually all human actions can be accomplished or realized in a wide variety of ways. There are, for instance, indefinitely many ways of insulting your neighbor, or even of asserting that snow is white. And we are often not much interested, nor should we be, in exactly which particular physical motion accomplishes the act we intend. So let us suppose that our nervous system is so constructed and designed that whenever in the implementation of an intention, our control system is faced with two or more options with regard to which we are non-partisan, a purely undetermined tie-breaking "choice" is made. There you are at the supermarket, wanting a can of Campbell's Tomato Soup, and faced with an array of several hundred identical cans of Campbell's Tomato Soup, all roughly equidistant from your hands. What to do? Before you even waste time and energy pondering this trivial problem, let us suppose, a perfectly random factor determines which can your hand reaches out for. This is of course simply a variation on the ancient theme of Buridan's ass, that unfortunate beast who, finding himself hungry, thirsty and equidistant between food and water, perished for lack of the divine nudge that in a human being accomplishes a truly free choice. This has never been a promising vision of the free choice of responsible agents, if only because it seems to secure freedom for such a small and trivial class of our choices. What does it avail me if I am free to choose *this* can of soup, but not free to choose between buying and stealing it? But however unpromising the idea is as a centerpiece for an account of free will, we must not underestimate its possible scope of application. Such trivial choice points seldom obtrude in our conscious deliberation, no doubt, but they are quite possibly ubiquitous nonetheless at an unconscious level. Whenever we choose to perform an action of a certain sort, there are no doubt slight variations in timing, style and skeletal implementation of those actions that are within our power but beneath our concern. For all we know, which variation occurs is *undetermined*. That is, the implementation of any one of our intentional actions may encounter undetermined *choice points* in many places in the causal chain. The resulting behavior would not be distinguishable to our everyday eyes, or from the point of view of our everyday interests, from behavior that was rigidly determined. What we are mainly interested in, as I said before, are actions, not motions, and what we are normally interested in predicting are actions.

It is worth noting that not only can we typically predict actions from the intentional stance without paying heed to possibly undetermined variations of implementation of these actions, but we can even put together chains of intentional predictions that are relatively immune to such variation. In the summer of

1974 many people were confidently predicting that Nixon would resign. [Editors' note: In this paragraph Dennett refers to then US President Richard Nixon and to some of the persons (government officials and news reporters) and circumstances surrounding his impending resignation from the presidency.] As the day and hour approached, the prediction grew more certain and more specific as to time and place; Nixon would resign not just in the near future, but in the next hour, and in the White House and in the presence of television cameramen and so forth. Still, it was not plausible to claim to know just how he would resign, whether he would resign with grace, or dignity, or with an attack on his critics, whether he would enunciate clearly or mumble or tremble. These details were not readily predictable, but most of the further dependent predictions we were interested in making did not hinge on these subtle variations. However Nixon resigned, we could predict that Goldwater would publicly approve of it, Cronkite would report that Goldwater had so approved of it, Sevareid would comment on it, Rodino would terminate the proceedings of the Judiciary Committee, and Gerald Ford would be sworn in as Nixon's successor. Of course some predictions we might have made at the time would have hinged crucially on particular details of the precise manner of Nixon's resignation, and if these details happened to be undetermined both by Nixon's intentions and by any other feature of the moment, then some human actions of perhaps great importance would be infected by the indeterminacy of Nixon's manner at the moment just as our exemplary subject's behavior was infected by the indeterminacy of the answer box. That would not, however, make these actions any the less intelligible to us as actions.

This result is not just what the libertarian is looking for, but it is a useful result nevertheless. It shows that we can indeed install indeterminism in the internal causal chains affecting human behavior *at the macroscopic level* while preserving the intelligibility of practical deliberation that the libertarian requires. We may have good reasons from other quarters for embracing determinism, but we need not fear that macroscopic indeterminism in human behavior would of necessity rob our lives of intelligibility by producing chaos. Thus, philosophers such as Ayer and Hobart,[4] who argue that free will requires determinism, must be wrong. There are *some* ways our world could be macroscopically indeterministic, without that fact remotely threatening the coherence of the intentionalistic conceptual scheme of action description presupposed by claims of moral responsibility.

Still, it seems that all we have done is install indeterminism in a *harmless* place by installing it in an *irrelevant* place. The libertarian would not be relieved to learn that although his decision to murder his neighbor was quite determined, the style and trajectory of the death blow was not. Clearly, what the libertarian has in mind is indeterminism at some earlier point, prior to the ultimate decision or formation of intention, and unless we can provide that, we will not aid the libertarian's cause. But perhaps we can provide that as well.

[4] A. J. Ayer, "Freedom and Necessity", in *Philosophical Essays* (London: Macmillan, 1954); R. B. Hobart, 'Free Will as Involving Determination and Inconceivable Without It", *Mind* (1934).

Let us return then, to Russell's speculation that intelligence might make improbable things happen. Is there any way that something like this could be accomplished? The idea of intelligence exploiting randomness is not unfamiliar. The poet, Paul Valéry, nicely captures the basic idea:

> It takes two to invent anything. The one makes up combinations; the other one chooses, recognizes what he wishes and what is important to him in the mass of the things which the former has imparted to him. What we call genius is much less the work of the first one than the readiness of the second one to grasp the value of what has been laid before him and to choose it.[5]

Here we have the suggestion of an intelligent *selection* from what may be a partially arbitrary or chaotic or random *production*, and what we need is the outline of a model for such a process in human decision-making.

An interesting feature of most important human decision-making is that it is made under time pressure. Even if there are, on occasion, algorithmic decision procedures giving guaranteed optimal solutions to our problems, and even if these decision procedures are in principle available to us, we may not have time or energy to utilize them. We are rushed, but moreover, we are all more or less lazy, even about terribly critical decisions that will affect our lives – our own lives, to say nothing of the lives of others. We invariably settle for a *heuristic* decision procedure; we *satisfice*;[6] we poke around hoping for inspiration; we do our best to think about the problem in a more or less directed way until we must finally stop mulling, summarize our results as best we can, and act. A realistic model of such decision-making just *might* have the following feature: When someone is faced with an important decision, something in him generates a variety of more or less relevant considerations bearing on the decision. Some of these considerations, we may suppose, are determined to be generated, but others may be non-deterministically generated. For instance, Jones, who is finishing her dissertation on Aristotle and the practical syllogism, must decide within a week whether to accept the assistant professorship at the University of Chicago, or the assistant professorship at Swarthmore. She considers the difference in salaries, the probable quality of the students, the quality of her colleagues, the teaching load, the location of the schools, and so forth. Let us suppose that considerations A, B, C, D, E, and F occur to her and that those are the only considerations that occur to her, and that on the basis of those, she decides to accept the job at Swarthmore. She does this *knowing* of course that she could devote more time and energy to this deliberation, could cast about for other relevant considerations, could perhaps dismiss some of A–F as being relatively unimportant and so forth, but being no more meticulous, no more obsessive, than the rest of us about such matters, she settles for the considerations that have occurred to her and makes her decision.

---

[5] Quoted by Jacques Hadamard, in *The Psychology of Invention in the Mathematical Field* (Princeton University Press, 1949), p. 30.

[6] The term is Herbert Simon's. See his *The Sciences of the Artificial* (1969) for a review of the concept.

Let us suppose though, that after sealing her fate with a phone call, consideration G occurs to her, and she says to herself: "If only G had occurred to me before, I would certainly have chosen the University of Chicago instead, but G didn't occur to me." Now it just might be the case that *exactly* which considerations occur to one in such circumstances is to some degree strictly undetermined. If that were the case, then even the intentionalist, knowing everything knowable about Jones' settled beliefs and preferences and desires, might nevertheless be unable to predict her decision, except perhaps conditionally. The intentionalist might be able to argue as follows: "If considerations *A–F* occur to Jones, then she will go Swarthmore," and this would be a prediction that would be grounded on a rational argument based on considerations *A–F* according to which Swarthmore was the best place to go. The intentionalist might go on to add, however, that if consideration G also occurs to Jones (which is strictly unpredictable unless we interfere and draw Jones' attention to G), Jones will choose the University of Chicago instead. Notice that although we are supposing that the decision is in this way strictly unpredictable except conditionally by the intentionalist, whichever choice Jones makes is retrospectively intelligible. There will be a rationale for the decision in either case; in the former case a rational argument in favor of Swarthmore based on *A–F*, and in the latter case, a rational argument in favor of Chicago, based on *A–G*. (There may, of course, be yet another rational argument based on *A–H*, or *I*, or *J*, in favor of Swarthmore, or in favor of going on welfare, or in favor of suicide.) Even if *in principle* we couldn't predict which of many rationales could ultimately be correctly cited in justification or retrospective explanation of the choice made by Jones, we could be confident that there would be some sincere, authentic, and not unintelligible rationale to discover.

The model of decision-making I am proposing has the following feature: when we are faced with an important decision, a consideration-generator whose output is to some degree undetermined produces a series of considerations, some of which may of course be immediately rejected as irrelevant by the agent (consciously or unconsciously). Those considerations that are selected by the agent as having a more than negligible bearing on the decision then figure in a reasoning process, and if the agent is in the main reasonable, those considerations ultimately serve as predictors and explicators of the agent's final decision. What can be said in favor of such a model, bearing in mind that there are many possible substantive variations on the basic theme?

First, I think it captures what Russell was looking for. The intelligent selection, rejection and weighting of the considerations that do occur to the subject is a matter of intelligence making the difference. Intelligence makes the difference here because an intelligent selection and assessment procedure determines which microscopic indeterminacies get amplified, as it were, into important macroscopic determiners of ultimate behavior.

Second, I think it installs indeterminism in the right place for the libertarian, if there is a right place at all. The libertarian could not have wanted to place the indeterminism *at the end* of the agent's assessment and deliberation. It would be insane to hope that after all rational deliberation had terminated with an assessment of the best available course of action, indeterminism would then intervene to flip the coin before action. It is a familiar theme in discussions of free will that the important claim that one could have done otherwise under the circumstances is not plausibly construed as the claim that one could have done otherwise given *exactly* the set of convictions and desires that prevailed at the end of rational deliberation. So if there is to be a crucial undetermined nexus, it had better be prior to the final assessment of the considerations on the stage, which is right where we have located it.

Third, I think that the model is recommended by considerations that have little or nothing to do with the free will problem. It may well turn out to be that from the point of view of biological engineering, it is just more efficient and in the end more rational that decision-making should occur in this way. Time rushes on, and people must act, and there may not be time for a person to canvass all his beliefs, conduct all the investigations and experiments that he would see were relevant, assess every preference in his stock before acting, and it may be that the best way to prevent the inertia of Hamlet from overtaking us is for our decision-making processes to be expedited by a process of partially random generation and test. Even in the rare circumstances where we know there is, say, a decision procedure for determining the optimal solution to a decision problem, it is often more reasonable to proceed swiftly and by heuristic methods, and this strategic principle may in fact be incorporated as a design principle at a fairly fundamental level of cognitive-conative organization.

A fourth observation in favor of the model is that it permits moral education to make a difference, without making all of the difference. A familiar argument against the libertarian is that if our moral decisions were not in fact determined by our moral upbringing, or our moral education, there would be no point in pro-viding such an education for the young. The libertarian who adopted our model could answer that a moral education, while not completely determining the gen-eration of considerations and moral decision-making, can nevertheless have a prior selective effect on the sorts of considerations that will occur. A moral education, like mutual discussion and persuasion generally, could adjust the boundaries and probabilities of the generator without rendering it deterministic.

Fifth – and I think this is perhaps the most important thing to be said in favor of this model – it provides some account of our important intuition that we are the authors of our moral decisions. The unreflective compatibilist is apt to view decision-making on the model of a simple balance or scale on which the pros and cons of action are piled. What gets put on the scale is determined by one's nature and one's nurture, and once all the weights are placed, gravity as it were determines which way the scale will tip, and hence determines which way we will act. On such a view, the agent does not seem in any sense to be the author of the decisions, but at best merely the locus at which the environmental and genetic factors bearing on him interact to produce a decision. It all looks terribly mechan-ical and inevitable, and seems to leave no room for creativity or genius. The model proposed, however, holds out the promise of a distinction between authorship and mere implication in a causal chain.[7]

Consider in this light the difference between completing a lengthy exercise in long division and constructing a proof in, say, Euclidian geometry. There is a sense in which I can be the author of a particular bit of long division, and can take credit if it turns out to be correct, and can take pride in it as well, but there is a stronger sense in which I can claim authorship of a proof in geometry, even if thousands of school children before me have produced the very same proof. There is a sense in which this is something original that I have created. To take pride in one's *computational accuracy* is one thing, and to take pride in one's *inventiveness* is another, and as Valéry claimed, the essence of invention is the intelligent selection from among randomly generated candidates. I think that the sense in which we wish to claim authorship of our moral decisions, and hence claim responsibility for them, requires that we view them as products of intelligent invention, and not merely the results of an assiduous application of formulae. I don't want to overstate this case; certainly many of the decisions we make are so obvious, so black and white, that no one would dream of claiming any special creativity in having made them and yet would still claim complete responsibility for the decisions thus rendered. But if we viewed all our decision-making on those lines, I think our sense of our dignity as moral agents would be considerably impoverished.

Finally, the model I propose points to the multiplicity of decisions that encircle our moral decisions and suggests that in many cases our ultimate decision as to which way to act is less important phenomenologically as a contributor to our sense of free will than the prior decisions affecting our deliberation process itself: the decision, for instance, not to consider any further, to terminate deliberation; or the decision to ignore certain lines of inquiry.

These prior and subsidiary decisions contribute, I think, to our sense of ourselves as responsible free agents, roughly in the following way: I am faced with an important decision to make, and after a certain amount of deliberation, I say to myself: "That's enough. I've considered this matter enough and now I'm going to act," in the full knowledge that I could have considered further, in the full knowledge that the eventualities may prove that I decided in error, but with the acceptance of responsibility in any case.

I have recounted six recommendations for the suggestion that human decision-making involves a non-deterministic generate-and-test procedure. First, it captures whatever is compelling in Russell's hunch. Second, it installs determinism in the only plausible locus for libertarianism (something we have established by a process of elimination). Third, it makes sense from the point of view of strategies of biological engineering. Fourth, it provides a flexible justification of moral education. Fifth, it accounts at least in part for our sense of authorship of our decisions. Sixth, it acknowledges and explains the importance of decisions internal to the deliberation process. It is embarrassing to note, however, that the very feature of

---

[7] Cf. the suggestive discussion of genius in Kant's *Critique of Judgment*, Sections 46, 47.

the model that inspired its promulgation is *apparently* either gratuitous or misdescribed or both, and that is the causal indeterminacy of the generator. We have been supposing, for the sake of the libertarian, that the process that generates considerations for our assessment generates them at least in part by a physically or causally undetermined or random process. But here we seem to be trading on yet another imprecision or ambiguity in the word "random". When a system designer or programmer relies on a "random" generation process, it is not a *physically undetermined* process that is required, but simply a *patternless* process. Computers are typically equipped with a random number generator, but the process that generates the sequence is a perfectly deterministic and determinate process. If it is a good random number generator (and designing one is extraordinarily difficult, it turns out) the sequence will be locally and globally patternless. There will be a complete absence of regularities on which to base predictions about unexamined portions of the sequence.

Isn't it the case that the new improved proposed model for human deliberation can do as well with a random-but-deterministic generation process as with a causally undetermined process? Suppose that to the extent that the considerations that occur to me are unpredictable, they are unpredictable simply because they are fortuitously determined by some arbitrary and irrelevant factors, such as the location of the planets or what I had for breakfast. It appears that this alternative supposition diminishes not one whit the plausibility or utility of the model that I have proposed. Have we in fact given the libertarians what they really want without giving them indeterminism? Perhaps. We have given the libertarians the materials out of which to construct an account of personal authorship of moral decisions, and this is something that the compatibilistic views have never handled well. But something else has emerged as well. Just as the presence or absence of macroscopic indeterminism in the implementation style of intentional actions turned out to be something essentially undetectable from the vantage point of our *Lebenswelt*, a feature with no significant repercussions in the "manifest image", to use Sellars' term, so the rival descriptions of the consideration generator, as random-but-causally-deterministic *versus* random-and-causally-*in*deterministic, will have no clearly testable and contrary implications at the level of micro-neurophysiology, even if we succeed beyond our most optimistic fantasies in mapping deliberation processes onto neural activity.

That fact does not refute libertarianism, or even discredit the motivation behind it, for what it shows once again is that we need not fear that causal indeterminism would make our lives unintelligible. There may not be compelling grounds from *this* quarter for favoring an indeterministic vision of the springs of our action, but if considerations from other quarters favor indeterminism, we can at least be fairly sanguine about the prospects of incorporating indeterminism into our picture of deliberation, even if we cannot yet see what point such an incorporation would have. Wiggins speaks of the cosmic unfairness of determinism, and I do not think the considerations raised here do much to allay our worries about *that*. Even if one embraces the sort of view I have outlined, the deterministic view of the unbranching and inexorable history of the universe can inspire terror or despair, and perhaps the libertarian is right that there is no way to allay these feelings short of a brute denial of determinism. Perhaps such a denial, and only such a denial, would permit us to make sense of the notion that our actual lives are created by us over time out of possibilities that exist in virtue of our earlier decisions; that we trace a path through a branching maze that both defines who we are, and why, to some extent (if we are fortunate enough to maintain against all vicissitudes the integrity of our deliberational machinery) we are *responsible* for being who we are. That prospect deserves an investigation of its own. All I hope to have shown here is that it is a prospect we can and should take seriously.

Robert Kane, "Free Will: The Elusive Ideal"

I

It is no secret that the traditional problem of free will emerged in ancient times with the suspicion that conflicts existed between human freedom and determinism in one or more variant forms of determinism – physical, psychological, theological or fatalistic. If these conflicts between freedom and determinism are not real, the central "free will" problem would be solved – or better, it would be "dissolved," since the worries that generated it would be unfounded. Such a "dissolutionist" strategy regarding free will is a prevalent theme of modern philosophy: the ancient quarrels about free will and determinism can finally be put to rest because there is no genuine conflict between the two. This strategy is old – it had ancient origins in the Stoics – but it took new form in the modern era beginning with Hobbes (as I have argued elsewhere[1]) and had a noble lineage thereafter through Locke, Spinoza, Edwards, Hume, Schopenhauer, Mill and others – down to the twentieth century, when dissolutionism has become the majority view among philosophers.

In its prevalent "modernist" form, dissolutionism leads to "compatibilism" – the view that freedom in every significant sense (free will included) is compatible with determinism. Compatibilism is surely the dominant view on free will among philosophers today (though many ordinary persons continue to regard compatibilism as the "quagmire of evasion" that Kant and James thought it was). [. . .] I am no stranger to these modern dissolutionist views. One of my first philosophical mentors [. . .] was a compatibilist and he had me convinced for a time. Yet, like many others, I continued to wonder if there was not something to the ancient intuitions which led so many to believe that free will was incompatible with determinism, if only we could make more sense of the kind of freedom these intuitions require. Belief is widespread today that an old-fashioned *incompatibilist* free will is essentially mysterious or terminally obscure and that it has no place in the modern scientific picture of human beings emerging in the natural, social and cognitive sciences. Incompatibilist freedom is often misleadingly called "contra-causal freedom," an

From *Philosophical Studies* 75 (1994), 25–60.
[1] Kane, Robert: 1985, *Free Will and Values* (State University of New York Press).

expression that only enhances suspicions of it, as do appeals by its defenders to noumenal selves, transempirical power centers, and notions of agency that cannot be explained in terms of ordinary event causation. By such measures, defenders of incompatibilist freedom (often nowadays called "libertarians") seem to be in full flight from the modern scientific understanding of human beings in order to protect their intuitions.

Deeply troubled by this situation, I set out in 1970 to try some new approach that would put the incompatibilist or libertarian view of freedom into more meaningful dialogue with modern science – physics as well as biology and the cognitive and social sciences with the aim of finding a place for free will in the natural order where we must exercise our freedom. That personal quest is still ongoing and it has turned out to be more than I bargained for. But it did issue in a book on free will and a series of subsequent articles in which my view has evolved in response to objections of other philosophers.[2]

The view of free will I defend is therefore "incompatibilist" or "libertarian" – to use terms now current. [. . .] But my view is unusual even by incompatibilist standards. So, the familiar labels do not tell the whole story. In this paper, I want to explain where and why my view differs from other traditional and contemporary views of freedom and free will, including other incompatibilist or libertarian views. The view presented here is scarcely the last word on the subject and I am less concerned to convince others of its unsullied truth than to show through it that new ways of thinking about the issues are possible. In the vast labyrinth of free will debates, I believe there are whole passages that remain unexplored. A few traditional thinkers opened doors to them, looked down the long darkness, and promptly closed the doors again. I don't know where all these uncharted passages lead, but I want to suggest that we now have to explore them if debates about free will are to move beyond present stalemates.

II

At times in what follows, I paint with a broad brush in order to explain how and why my view differs from others, while homing in at other times on pivotal themes and criticisms. The gaps that remain in this paper will be filled in a new book on free will being written to update my view and answer critics. This paper is something of a prelude to that work.

1 Four Questions

As I see it, there are four questions at the core of traditional free will debates (not the only questions involved, mind you, but the core ones). Roughly stated, they are

---

[2] Kane, Robert: 1985; also 1989, "Two Kinds of Incompatibilism," *Philosophy and Phenomenological Research* 50, pp. 219–254; 1988a, "Libertarianism and Rationality Revisited," *Southern Journal of Philosophy* 26, pp. 441–460; 1988b, "Free Will and Responsibility: Comments on Waller's Review," *Behaviorism* 16, pp. 159–165.

The *Compatibility* Question: Is free will compatible with determinism?

The *Significance* Question: Why do we, or should we, want to possess a free will that is incompatible with determinism? Is it a kind of freedom "worth wanting" (to use Daniel Dennett's useful phrase) and if so, why?

The *Intelligibility* Question: Can we make sense of a freedom or free will that is incompatible with determinism? Is such a freedom coherent or intelligible? Or is it, as many critics claim, essentially mysterious or terminally obscure?

The *Existence* Question: Does such a freedom actually exist in the natural order, and if so, where?

The four questions are intimately related: answers to any one depend on answers to the others. But they can also be fruitfully viewed in pairs. The Compatibility and Significance questions should be treated together, for reasons to be explained in a moment. And the Intelligibility and Existence questions obviously go together. If we cannot say what free will is without obscurity, we don't know what we are looking for when we look for it in the real world.

Imagine that the task for defenders of a traditional incompatibilist free will is to climb to the top of a mountain and get down the other side. The "ascent" of this mountain involves answering the first pair of questions – Compatibility and Significance – in an incompatibilist way; the descent involves answering the second pair of questions – Intelligibility and Existence – for incompatibilist freedom. To get to the top of the mountain, in other words, is to show that there is a significant freedom worth wanting that is incompatible with determinism. In the 1970s and 80s, considerable debate has centered on new arguments for such incompatibility put forward by libertarians like Van Inwagen, Carl Ginet, David Wiggins, James Lamb and others.[3] Such arguments have been controversial – partly because they turn on the interpretation of notoriously difficult terms and expressions like "can," "power," "ability," and "could have done otherwise."

But these new arguments, like all arguments for incompatibilism, are controversial for another reason. Even if successful, they would only get us to the top of the mountain. To get down the other side, one has to show how incompatibilist accounts of freedom can be made intelligible (why they are not essentially incoherent, mysterious or obscure) and how they fit into the natural order. One must, in other words, also address the Intelligibility and Existence questions. Most modern sceptics about libertarian free will believe it *is* incoherent or unintelligible and has no place in the natural order. So they are inclined to believe that abstract arguments for incompatibilism, like those of Van Inwagen, Ginet, et al. *must* be

[3] Van Inwagen, Peter: 1975, "The Incompatibility of Free Will and Determinism," *Philosophical Studies* 27, pp. 185–199; Ginet, Carl: 1967, "Might We Have No Choice?" in K. Lehrer (ed.): *Freedom and Determinism* (Random House, New York), pp. 87–104; Wiggins, David: 1973, "Towards a Reasonable Libertarianism," in T. Honderich (ed.): *Essays on Freedom of Action* (Routledge and Kegan Paul, Boston), pp. 31–62; Lamb, James W.: 1977, "On a Proof of Incompatibilism," *The Philosophical Review* 86, pp. 20–35.

wrong in some way or another, it's just a question of locating the logical or other error in such arguments.

This shows how answers to the "ascent" problem – the Compatibility and Significance questions – depend upon answers to the "descent" problem – the Intelligibility and Existence questions. Abstract arguments for incompatibilism that seem to get us to the top of the mountain are not good enough if we can't get down the other side by making intelligible the incompatibilist freedom these arguments require. The air is cold and thin up there on Incompatibilist Mountain and if one stays up there for any length of time and cannot get down the other side, one's mind becomes clouded in mist and is visited by visions of noumenal selves, non-occurrent causes, transempirical egos and other fantasies.

For such reasons, when I first began to consider free will issues in 1970, my attention was drawn to the descent problem, and in particular, to the pivotal Intelligibility question. It seemed to me that the only way to move beyond current stalemates on free will was to take a new hard look at the Intelligibility question, using it as a springboard for rethinking the other questions, including the Existence question. [...]

2   Multiple Freedoms

One thing made clear by focusing on the Intelligibility question is that "freedom" is a term of many meanings, some of which may designate kinds of freedom that are compatible with determinism, others that are not. This assumption is crucial, I came to believe, for any coherent approach to all four questions, including Compatibility. Nothing but confusion can arise from assuming that we all have a single conception of freedom and then asking whether freedom according to *that* single conception is or is not compatible with determinism (though one often sees the matter put this way in writings on free will).

It follows that the usual textbook formulation of the Compatibility question – "Is freedom compatible with determinism?" – is too simple. If there are different kinds of freedom, the question should be: Is freedom *in every significant sense worth wanting* compatible with determinism?" (This richer question shows in turn how the Compatibility and Significance questions are intertwined.) To answer the expanded question in the negative, incompatibilists do not have to claim that every significant kind of freedom of action or will is incompatible with determinism. Incompatibilists can (and should, I think) concede that there are significant everyday notions of freedom – e.g. freedoms from coercion or compulsion or political oppression – which can be analysed without supposing that determinism is false. To concede this is to allow that, *even if we lived in a determined world*, we could meaningfully distinguish persons who are free from such things as physical restraint, addiction or neurosis, coercion or political oppression, from persons not free from these things; and we could allow that these freedoms would be worth preferring to their opposites even in a determined world.

133

3   Free Will

What incompatibilists *should* claim, as I see it (and what they have often historically claimed), is that there is *at least one* kind of freedom which is not compatible with determinism and it is a *significant kind of freedom worth wanting*. They should not quarrel with compatibilists about whether there are freedoms worth wanting that are compatible with determinism, but rather concede the point and go on to argue that compatibilist freedoms are not the only significant ones. On my view, the additional freedom worth caring about that is not compatible with determinism is what was traditionally called "free will"; and I define it as "the power to be an ultimate creator and sustainer of one's own ends or purposes." Those who defend such a freedom believe that free will in this sense is something worth wanting *over and above* compatibilist freedoms, like freedom from coercion or compulsion or political oppression. This is not to deny the importance of these compatibilist freedoms, but only to suggest that human longings transcend them.

While most contemporary philosophers give lip-service to the "free will" issue, they do not believe it is specifically about free will. They prefer to talk about "free action" rather than free will and about "reasons for action" rather than "acts of will" (or simply "freedom and determinism" rather than "free will and determinism"). My view differs from most other contemporary views in this regard as well. I defend the traditional idea that the free will issue is about "the will" in more than name only. In practice, emphasis on the will means that the locus of indeterminism required by incompatibilist freedom lies primarily in choices, decisions, practical judgments and efforts of will – all of them "acts of will" of one kind or another – which create or sustain the purposes that guide other actions. [. . .]

III

4   Alternative Possibilities

Focusing on free will and the Intelligibility question also led to other differences of approach to the Compatibility question. Most arguments for incompatibilism focus on some version of what Frankfurt has called the principle of "alternative possibilities"[4] – that a free agent must have the power or ability "to do otherwise," or "could have done otherwise." This focus is evident in the most widely discussed recent arguments for incompatibilism mentioned earlier of Van Inwagen, Ginet, Wiggins, Lamb, etc. These arguments are all versions of a general line of thought that Van Inwagen has dubbed the "Consequence Argument":[5] if determinism is true, our acts are consequences of the laws of nature and events in the past. The acts could therefore be otherwise only if the laws of nature or the past were

---

[4] Frankfurt, Harry: 1969, "Alternative Possibilities and Moral Responsibility," *Journal of Philosophy* 66, pp. 829–839.

[5] Van Inwagen, Peter: 1983, *An Essay on Free Will* (Oxford).

different in some way. But we lack the power to make the laws of nature or the past different than they are. So, if determinism is true, we lack the power to do otherwise and are not free.

My intention here is not to review the details of this now familiar Consequence Argument or the vast literature that has grown up around it, including criticisms of different versions of it by Lewis, Slote, Fischer, Watson, Dennett, Gallois, Narveson, Berofsky, Flint, Horgan, Hill, Vihvelin and others.[6] Suffice it to say that the success of the Consequence Argument in any of its forms depends on the interpretation one gives to the agent's power to do otherwise or on whether one accepts the principle of alternative possibilities as a necessary condition for freedom in the first place. It has been amply demonstrated that various compatibilist interpretations of the power or ability to do otherwise will blunt the Consequence Argument. Defenders of the argument, like Van Inwagen and Ginet, admit this. They just don't think that compatibilist interpretations of "power," "ability," or "could have done otherwise" are very plausible or capture our intuitions about the alternative possibilities required by genuine free action.[7]

On this point, current debates about the Consequence Argument seem to have reached a stalemate. While my own intuitions (not surprisingly) side with Van Inwagen and Ginet, it none the less has always seemed to me unsatisfactory to rest the case for incompatibilism entirely on intuitions about problematic terms like "can," "could," "power" and "ability" alone. Intuitions clash all too readily over these terms because (I believe) they are essentially ambivalent. (Their ambivalence is of a piece with the multiple meanings of "free" described in (2) above.) The interesting question, it seemed to me, was *why* compatibilists and incompatibilists had such different and conflicting intuitions about these terms in relation to determinism. To get beyond current stalemates, one has to dig more deeply into the sources of the conflicting intuitions. Attempting to do this, I came to the conclusion that analyzing the power to do otherwise or alternative possibilities *alone* is just *too thin a basis* on which to rest the case for incompatibilism.

---

[6] Lewis, David: 1981, "Are We Free to Break the Laws?" *Theoria* 3, pp. 113–121; Slote, Michael: 1982, "Selective Necessity and Free Will," *Journal of Philosophy* 79, pp. 5–24; Fischer, John Martin: 1983, "Incompatibilism," *Philosophical Studies* 43, pp. 137–147; Watson, Gary: 1987, "Free Action and Free Will," *Mind* 96, pp. 145–172; Dennett, Daniel: 1984, *Elbow Room* (Oxford and MIT); Gallois, Andre: 1977, "Van Inwagen on Incompatibilism and Free Will," *Philosophical Studies* 32, pp. 99–106; Narveson, Jan: 1977, "Compatibilism Defended," *Philosophical Studies* 32, pp. 83–88; Berofsky, Bernard: 1987, *Freedom From Necessity* (Routledge and Kegan Paul, London); Flint, Thomas: 1987, "Compatibilism and the Argument from Unavoidability," *Journal of Philosophy* 84, pp. 423–441; Horgan, Terence: 1985, "Compatibilism and the Consequence Argument," *Philosophical Studies* 47, pp. 339–356; Hill, Christopher: 1992, "Van Inwagen on the Consequence Argument," *Analysis* 52, pp. 49–55; Vihvelin, Kadri: 1988, "The Modal Argument for Incompatibilism," *Philosophical Studies* 53, pp. 227–244. Excellent recent defenses of the Consequence Argument include Ginet, Carl: 1992, *On Action* (Cambridge); Widerker, David: 1987, "On An Argument for Incompatibilism," *Analysis* 47, pp. 37–41; O'Connor, Timothy: 1993, "On the Transfer of Necessity," *Noûs* 27, pp. 204–218. Another recent piece on the argument is Blum, Alex: 1990, "On a Mainstay of Incompatibilism," *Iyyun* 39, pp. 267–279.

[7] Van Inwagen, Peter: 1983; Ginet, Carl: 1992.

5 Ultimate Responsibility

Fortunately, there are other clues to pursue that go beyond alternative possibilities. A careful inspection of the history of debates about free will shows that there were two separable considerations fueling beliefs that freedom is incompatible with determinism. One of these considerations, to be sure, is the "alternative possibilities" condition (call it "AP" hereafter): persons having free will must have the power or ability to do otherwise. But a second and (I believe) more important condition historically fueling incompatibilist intuitions was what I have elsewhere called the condition of "Ultimate Responsibility" or UR:[8] genuinely free agents must have "ultimate" or "buck-stopping" responsibility for their free actions and character. (What this means more exactly will be considered in a moment.)

Beginning in the 1970s, I argued that, while alternative possibilities, or AP, was indeed a necessary condition for some incompatibilist free actions, the real key to incompatibilist intuitions was UR (ultimate responsibility). If you hold AP as a condition for at least some free actions, but reject UR, your intuitions are likely to be compatibilist. But if you hold that AP *and* UR are required for at least some free actions, your intuitions will almost invariably be incompatibilist. I therefore argued that UR lies behind the clash of intuitions between compatibilists and incompatibilists about the meanings of "power," "ability," "could have done otherwise" and related terms and expressions. When these terms and expressions do not require ultimate responsibility (UR) – even if they do require alternate possibilities (AP) – compatibilist interpretations of them are possible. But when they are so interpreted that they require ultimate responsibility (UR), then the power to do otherwise (AP) will be incompatibilist. In the latter case, the Consequence Argument will go through; in the former, it will not. On my view, *"free will" is the historical name that was (properly) given to the kind of freedom that requires UR (as well as AP-for-some-free-actions).* And it is the commitment to UR that makes free will incompatible with determinism. Other kinds of freedom, even if they require AP, may be compatible with determinism.

Despite the historical importance of UR (which I won't try to demonstrate here), it has usually been neglected by philosophers, including contemporary philosophers, in comparison to AP. But in the past few years UR has been getting more attention. A few philosophers, like Galen Strawson and Martha Klein,[9] have also assigned it the central role in free will debates that I believe it has. But Strawson and Klein are not incompatibilists or libertarians. They do not believe that incompatibilist freedom is possible because they do not believe UR can be satisfied. I disagree about that, but I think they are correct in recognizing the importance of UR for traditional intuitions about free will.

---

[8] Kane, Robert: 1989. In earlier writings (Kane: 1985), I called it the "condition of sole or ultimate dominion."

[9] Strawson, Galen: 1986, *Freedom and Belief* (Oxford); Klein, Martha: 1990, *Determinism, Blameworthiness and Deprivation* (Oxford).

IV

6   UR and Sufficient Reason

But what exactly is UR? What does it require? Klein states it this way: "agents should be ultimately responsible for their morally relevant decisions or choices – 'ultimately' in the sense that nothing for which they are not responsible should be the source [or cause] of their decisions or choices."[10] This is the right idea (though it cries out for further clarification). For example, if an agent's present decision issues from the agent's previously formed character and motives, then to be "ultimately" responsible for the present decision, the agent must also be responsible for the character and motives from which it issued. (If this looks to you like it might lead to a regress, then you understand the principle.) If, by contrast, the agent's prior character and motives were wholly formed by factors for which the agent was not responsible – heredity and environment, fate or God, behavioral engineers or social conditioning – the *ultimate* responsibility would not lie with the agent.

While this is the general idea behind ultimate responsibility, it is not easy to give a precise statement of the condition. I have attempted numerous versions since the 1970s, the latest of which is the following:

> UR: An agent is *ultimately responsible* for some (event or state) E's occurring only if (R) the agent is personally responsible for E's occurring in a sense which entails that something the agent willingly did or omitted either was or causally contributed to E's occurrence and there is something the agent could have willingly done or omitted that would have made a difference in whether or not E occurred, and (U) for every X and Y (where X and Y represent occurrences of events and/or states) if the agent is personally responsible for X, and if Y is a sufficient reason (ground or cause or explanation) for X (assuming relevant laws), then the agent must also be personally responsible for Y.

I cannot tie up every loose end of this definition here, but will focus on its key points. R (for "responsibility") is the "base" clause of the definition, U (for "ultimacy") is the recursive clause. R states a minimal necessary (not a sufficient) condition for an agent's being "responsible" for some occurrence according to the definition – roughly, that something the agent willingly (i.e. intentionally and voluntarily[11]) did or omitted had something to do with its being the case. U goes further, requiring for "ultimate" responsibility that the agent also be responsible for anything that is a "sufficient reason" (ground, cause or explanation) for what the agent is responsible for. If antecedent conditions and laws of nature (or prior character and motives) provide a sufficient reason or explanation for an action, then

---

[10] Klein, Martha: 1990, pp. 49, 51.
[11] "Intentionally" in turn means "knowingly" and "purposefully"; and "voluntarily" means "uncoerced" and "non-compulsively."

to be ultimately responsible, the agent must have been responsible (in the sense of R) for at least some of those explaining antecedent conditions, character traits or motives. Something the agent willingly did or omitted must have made a difference in whether or not they were the case. [...]

Roughly stated, UR requires that if an agent is ultimately responsible for an action, the action *cannot have a sufficient reason* (sufficient condition, cause or motive) of any kind *for which the agent is not also responsible*. Compare Aristotle's claim that if a man is responsible for wicked acts issuing from his character, then he must at some time in the past have been responsible for the conditions which made him the way he is. Or consider Plotinus' argument against the Stoics that if the ultimate source or cause (*arche*) of our actions was not in us, but in some conditions none of which were produced by us, we would not be responsible for them.[12] In such manner, UR is meant to capture the familiar notion that we are (to some degree at least) final "authors of our own fate" and "captains of our own souls."

It looks like UR directly implies incompatibilism, but not quite. Rather the satisfaction of UR requires *either* that there be an infinite regress of responsible actions by an agent[13] *or* that some responsible actions of the agent have no sufficient reasons in circumstances beyond the actions themselves (and hence no sufficient causes). If we plausibly assume that the infinite regress option is incoherent (or at least not satisfiable for finite agents), we then have the following argument for incompatibilism: if free will requires UR (ultimate responsibility), and if a freedom requiring UR is both intelligible and satisfiable (thus ruling out infinite regresses), then free will is incompatible with determinism (since some exercises of it cannot have sufficient causes).

The problem is that *both* sides of the disjunction implied by UR could well be unsatisfiable. Infinite regresses of responsible actions or willings seem out of the question. But is the alternative any more plausible? How can there be *responsible* actions – presumably produced and controlled by the agents themselves – that lack sufficient reasons of any kinds in circumstances outside the actions, even in the prior characters and motives of the agents who produce them? Such actions would be undetermined (since they have no sufficient causes), which means that there is an element of chance in their occurrence. And there are well-known problems reconciling chance or indeterminism with the responsibility and control required of genuinely free actions.

With such problems in mind, most contemporary philosophers who have considered the notion of ultimate responsibility in some form or other, like Strawson, Klein, Double, Nagel, Watson, Wolf and others, have done so only to dismiss

---

[12] Aristotle, *Nichomachean Ethics*, Book II, chapter 5, 1114a 13–22, from Ross, W. D. (ed.): 1952, *The Works of Aristotle* (Oxford); Plotinus: 1950, *The Philosophy of Plotinus: Selections from the Enneads* (Appleton-Century Crofts, New York), Ennead 3, Book 1, pp. 60–62. For Aristotle on UR see Sorabji, Richard: 1980, *Necessity, Cause and Blame: Perspective on Aristotle's Theory* (Cornell); and on Plotinus and other ancient writers, see White, Michael: 1985, *Agency and Integrality* (Reidel, Dordrecht).

[13] Responsible actions *or* willed omissions, to be exact.

it as an unsatisfiable condition.[14] The choice that UR seems to provide – either *infinite regresses* or *arbitrary beginnings* – both seem unacceptable. The argument for incompatibilism in terms of UR just given therefore merely highlights the importance of the Intelligibility question. If free will requires UR and *if* a freedom requiring UR is *intelligible* and *satisfiable*, then free will is incompatible with determinism. But is a freedom requiring UR intelligible and satisfiable? If not, UR makes the "ascent" of Incompatibilist Mountain easier only by making the "descent" impossible.

V

7 Significance and Worth

Shifting the focus of free will debate to UR also has an impact on the Significance question as well as on the Compatibility question. Inevitably, the question arises why anyone would *want* a freedom requiring UR, or why it is *worth* wanting? What is so important about ultimate responsibility that it should be required for free will? Standard answers to such questions in the history of philosophy (when ultimate responsibility is recognized at all) have taken the following form. It is said that ultimate responsibility is a prerequisite for other goods that humans highly value. Candidates for these other goods have included (i) "genuine" *creativity*, (ii) *autonomy* (self-legislation) or *self-creation*, (iii) "true" *desert* for one's achievements, (iv) *moral responsibility* in an ultimate sense, (v) being suitable objects of *reactive attitudes* such as admiration, gratitude, resentment and indignation, (vi) genuine *dignity* or *self-worth*, (vii) a true sense of *individuality* or *uniqueness* as a person, (viii) *life-hopes* requiring an *open future*, (ix) genuine (freely given) *love* and *friendship* between persons (or in religious contexts, freely given love toward God), and (x) the ability to say in the fullest sense that one acts *of one's own free will.*[15]

Few people deny the importance of most of the items on this list. But do (i) to (x) really require ultimate responsibility? Critics of incompatibilism say No; and they attempt to give accounts of such things as autonomy, desert, moral responsibility, creativity, dignity, and "of one's own free will," without assuming anything so esoteric as ultimate responsibility or incompatibilist free will. Indeed, some of the best philosophical work by compatibilists since 1970 has been devoted to giving compatibilist analyses of items (i) to (x).[16] Compatibilists further argue that

---

[14] Strawson, Galen: 1986; Klein, Martha: 1990; Double, Richard: 1991, *The Non-reality of Free Will* (Oxford); Nagel, Thomas: 1987, *The View From Nowhere* (Oxford), chapter 7; Watson, Gary: 1987; Wolf, Susan: 1990, *Freedom Within Reason* (Oxford), chapter 3.

[15] Many works discuss one or more of these goods in connection with incompatibilism. Three recent ones of note are Honderich, Ted: 1988, *A Theory of Determinism* Vol. 2 (Oxford); Anglin, W. S.: 1990, *Free Will and the Christian Faith* (Oxford); and Nathan, Nicholas: 1992, *Will and World* (Oxford). Nathan discusses free will in connection with his interesting view of metaphysical questions as involving want–belief conflicts.

[16] Several excellent anthologies collect some of this writing: Watson, Gary (ed.): 1982, *Free Will* (Oxford); Fischer, John Martin (ed.): *Moral Responsibility* (Cornell); Christman, John (ed.): 1989, *The Inner Citadel: Essays on Individual Autonomy* (Oxford). See also, Dworkin, Gerald: 1988, *The Theory and*

incompatibilists are giving themselves away when they insert terms like "genuine" and "true" before "autonomy," "moral responsibility," "creativity," etc. For what incompatibilists mean by "genuine" or "true" autonomy or moral responsibility, etc. is just the kind that requires ultimate responsibility and indeterminism. They are begging the question.

This is another one of those places where free will debates so often end in stalemate. And I think that here, as elsewhere, the only way forward is to dig more deeply into the conflicting intuitions that lie behind the disagreements (another invitation to look into uncharted passages of the labyrinth of free will). In the present context, it means looking more deeply into the question of why ultimate responsibility should be wanted. My recent thoughts on this subject have led in some unusual directions. Unfortunately, I cannot pursue them all here; but I can say something about one line of thought that helps to explain why disagreements about the significance of ultimate responsibility are so deep and intractable.

I think that ultimate responsibility is related to another notion which I have elsewhere called "*objective worth*."[17] To understand what objective worth is, consider a story about one Alan the painter. Alan has been so depressed that a rich friend concocts a scheme to lift his spirits. The friend arranges to have Alan's paintings bought at the local art gallery under assumed names for $10,000 apiece. Alan mistakenly assumes his paintings are being recognized for their artistic merit by knowledgeable critics and collectors and his spirits are lifted. Now let us imagine two possible worlds involving Alan. The first is the one just described in which Alan thinks he is a great artist, and thinks he is being duly recognized as such, but really is not. The other imagined world is a similar one in which Alan has many of the same experiences, including the belief that he is a great artist. But in this second world he really is a great artist and really is being recognized as such; his rich friend is not merely deceiving him to lift his spirits. Finally, let us imagine that in both these worlds Alan dies happily believing he is a great artist, though only in the second world was his belief correct.[18]

Practice of Autonomy (Cambridge); Haworth, Laurence: 1986, *Autonomy* (Yale); Robert Young: 1986, *Personal Autonomy* (St. Martin's); Zimmerman, Michael: 1984, *An Essay on Human Action* (Lang); Slote, Michael: 1980, "Understanding Free Will," *Journal of Philosophy* 77, pp. 136–151; Benson, Paul: 1987, "Freedom and Value," *Journal of Philosophy* 84, pp. 465–487; Bishop, John: 1989, *Natural Agency* (Cambridge); Audi, Robert: 1991, "Responsible Action and Virtuous Character," *Ethics* 101, pp. 304–321; Stampe, Dennis and Gibson, Martha: 1992, "Of One's Own Free Will," *Philosophy and Phenomenological Research* 52, pp. 529–556; Kapitan, Tomis: 1989, "Doxastic Freedom: A Compatibilist Alternative," *American Philosophical Quarterly* 26, pp. 31–41.

[17] In Kane, Robert: 1993, *Through the Moral Maze: Searching for Absolute Values in a Pluralistic World* (Paragon House, New York), chapter 4, which discusses this notion in relation to ethics and value theory.

[18] Philosophers will recognize a connection between this example of Alan and Robert Nozick's well known example of the "experience machine" in his 1974, *Anarchy, State, and Utopia* (Basic Books, New York), p. 18. This is not accidental because Nozick's experience machine is another way of getting at the idea of objective worth. But I use the Alan example here and several others in the above mentioned book to bring out a number of different facets of the idea of objective worth that Nozick does not discuss.

We begin to understand what objective worth is when we ask whether it would make any difference to Alan which of these worlds he lives in. To say that there is an important difference in value in the two worlds for Alan, even though he would not know it and would *feel* equally happy in both, is to say he endorses a notion of *objective* worth. One of the consequences of this notion is that a person's subjective happiness is not the only measure of value. To understand what objective worth means to Alan, we must ask him to imaginatively stand outside the worlds – taking what Nagel calls the "objective" viewpoint – and comparing the two.[19] Of course, we could imagine a third world in which Alan is deceived as in the first, but finds out he is being deceived. And that would be clearly the worst of all three worlds. Yet the fact that the third imagined world is the worst of the three for Alan in no way changes his judgment that the first world where he is deceived (and never knows it) is worse than the second where he is not deceived. And this shows that objective worth means something to Alan, as it would to any of us who would find it demeaning to be told: "Your paintings (or writings or causes or other accomplishments) are really worthless, but, so what, you are having a good time making them (or engaging in them) and that's all that matters."

I want to suggest that the notion of ultimate responsibility is of a piece with the notion of objective worth. If, like Alan, we think that the objective worth of our acts or accomplishments is something valuable over and above the felt satisfaction the acts have or bring, then I suggest we will think that a freedom requiring ultimate responsibility is valuable over and above compatibilist freedoms from coercion, compulsion and oppression. When these compatibilist freedoms are maximally present, there are no constraints or impediments preventing us from having and doing whatever we please. Such freedoms would be enough, if we did not care about more than what pleases us – namely, if we did not care in addition, like Alan, about our "worthiness" or "deservingness" to be pleased. Are our acts or deeds, our accomplishments and we ourselves, objectively worthy of recognition, respect, love or praise, as Alan wished of his paintings? It is this kind of concern for the objective desert of our deeds and characters that leads naturally to a concern about whether those deeds and characters have their ultimate sources in us, rather than in someone or something else (fate or God, genes or environment, social conditioning or behavioral controllers). Do they ultimately rebound to us or not? The answer to this question does not have to do merely with subjective happiness, but with the objective worth of our selves and our lives.[20]

Conversely, if objective worth means little to us, or makes no sense – if we believe that the final perspective Alan or anyone should take is *inside* the worlds, where subjective happiness is all that counts (even if it is based on deception about the objective worth of his deeds or his life) – we are likely to see no point or significance as well in ultimate responsibility and hence in incompatibilist freedom.

[19] Nagel, Thomas: 1987, passim.
[20] I am well aware that this notion of objective worth is problematic. There are weighty questions passed over here about whether such a thing can exist at all and how it would be known – questions I try to address in the work cited in note 17.

For, ultimate responsibility, like objective worth, is not merely about getting what we want, but about being worthy of what we get. This is a great divide on free will; and our standing on one side or the other of it is more a question of attitude or (what I have elsewhere called) "aspiration" than of knowledge. Those for whom objective worth is unimportant or unattainable (who may share the prevalent modern scepticism about "objective" points of view on anything) will naturally wonder what all the fuss is about over ultimate responsibility; while those who think objective worth is important and attainable will wonder how others could be indifferent to issues of ultimate responsibility. Dennett is right in saying that the question is about what kind of free will is "worth wanting." But in answering that question, he and other compatibilists put the emphasis on "wanting," whereas incompatibilists like myself put the emphasis on "worth."

VI

8   Plurality Conditions

Let us turn now to the Intelligibility question. Ultimate responsibility and objective worth may be important to some of us, and so also an incompatibilist free will. But affirming this much gets one only to the top of the mountain. There is now the daunting problem of a descent. Can we make sense of a freedom requiring ultimate responsibility? Is an incompatibilist free will possible? If not, it makes no sense to aspire to it.

For those who believe that incompatibilist freedom is unintelligible, the culprit is the requirement of *indeterminism*. If free choices are undetermined, they must be capable of occurring other than they do, *given exactly the same past circumstances and laws of nature*. There is no easy way around this strong requirement: it is a simple consequence of denying that free choices are determined. But why is such indeterminism a problem? The best way to answer is by example. Suppose you are deliberating between two or more options. Should you vacation in Hawaii or Colorado (or Europe, or wherever)? The matter is important to you and you have been thinking about it for days. You've considered various consequences of each option, imagined contrasting scenarios, consulted brochures and bank accounts, and considered your desires, interests and broader purposes. In the end, you gradually come to believe that Hawaii is the best option, all things considered, and you choose it.

Now if the choice was not determined, then you could have chosen otherwise (say, Colorado), given exactly the same past circumstances (and laws of nature) preceding your actual choice of Hawaii. This means that *exactly the same prior deliberation* through which you came to believe that Hawaii was all things considered the best option may have issued in the choice of Colorado – exactly the same prior thoughts and reasonings, the same imagined scenarios and consequences considered, exactly the same prior beliefs, desires and other motives that led to the choice of Hawaii (not a sliver of difference) would have issued in the choice of

Colorado instead. This is strange to say the least. Even if it *may* have happened, the choice of Colorado would have seemed a fluke or accident, capricious and irrational, given that same prior deliberation which led you in fact to favor Hawaii.

Of course, we can imagine your choosing differently non-capriciously and rationally, *if* something in your past deliberation had been different, if you had had different beliefs or desires, imagined different scenarios, considered other consequences that favored Colorado over Hawaii. This is what compatibilists usually demand – that something relevant to the choice in your past have been different in some way. But compatibilists are not committed to the indeterminist condition, which requires that the alternative choice occur given exactly the same prior circumstances. That condition, say critics of indeterminism, would render free choices "capricious" (or spontaneous or spur-of-the-moment) choices against the grain without having good reasons for them. But if *all* our free choices had to be this way (as Dostoyevsky's "Underground Man" imagined), would that be what we mean by freedom of choice?

To put things in perspective, notice that it is the choosing "otherwise" that causes this problem. It would have been capricious, arbitrary or irrational to choose Colorado, given exactly the same deliberation that led to the choice of Hawaii. But the actual choice of Hawaii need not have been irrational, capricious or arbitrary. Indeed, it is on the assumption that the choice of Hawaii was the reasonable one given the deliberation that the choice of Colorado appeared capricious and irrational. Indeterminism therefore does not rule out *one-way* rationality and non-capriciousness; the problem of indeterminism is with *plural* or *more-than-one-way* rationality and non-capriciousness. What we seem to want in free choice is the power to go more than one way (to choose Hawaii *or* Colorado *or* Europe, or whatever we choose) rationally, intentionally and voluntarily, rather than flukishly, given exactly the same prior deliberation and thought processes. We want, in other words, to satisfy what may be called "plurality conditions" on choice – that our free choices be rational, intentional and voluntarily controlled, *whichever way they go*. [. . .]

VII

9 The Divided Will and Incommensurable Reasons

When we think about free will, therefore, we cannot easily dismiss the plurality conditions (more-than-one-way rationality, intentionality and voluntary control). The problem is that indeterminism causes problems for these conditions. Plurality and indeterminism are both required by ultimate responsibility, as I see it, but they are in conflict with one another. This conflict is pivotal to the debate over Intelligibility.

The first essential step through this thicket is to recognize that free will arises in circumstances where the will of the free agent is deeply divided between conflicting motives. One powerful set of motives is pulling the agent in one direction, while another, different and "incommensurable" (non-comparable) set of motives is pulling the agent in an opposing direction. In recognition of this fact in my earlier book on free will,[21] I made the existence of "incommensurable reason sets" within the mind of the agent a precondition for primordial acts of free will, which I now call "self-forming willings" (or SFWs). These are free acts of the agent that must be *both* undetermined and yet fully rational, intentional and voluntarily controlled. Not all of our free acts have to be "self-forming" in this sense, but *some* acts in our life histories must be so, if we are to say that we were ever "ultimately" responsible for making ourselves into the sorts of persons we are. Self-forming willings are where the buck stops. If the idea of incommensurable reason sets is essential for them, then it is essential for a coherent account of free will.

According to my present thinking, self-forming willings are of at least six kinds.[22] But it is convenient to focus on two important and familiar kinds by way of illustration of their features – moral and prudential choices. Consider a woman on the way to an important sales meeting who witnesses an assault in an alley. Should she stop and call for help or press on to avoid losing a sale crucial to her career? Or, consider an engineer who is a recovering alcoholic trying to salvage his career. Working late at night under great stress he is tempted to have a drink in order to go on. The woman faces a moral conflict, the engineer a prudential one. But in both cases they are torn by competing motives of different and not easily comparable kinds. On the one side, are her moral principles, on the other, her desires for a successful career. On the one side, are his powerful urges to drink and relieve tension, on the other, his desire to kick the booze and turn his life around.

How can we account for their choices one way or the other in these circumstances in a manner that is undetermined, yet plural rational, intentional and voluntarily controlled? In both cases, they must make efforts of will to act morally or prudently against strong temptations to do otherwise. What will explain the success or failure of these efforts? Presumably, their prior character and motives: if strong-willed, they will overcome temptation, if weak-willed, they will succumb. But then one might argue that if prior characters and motives explain the efforts and the choice, UR will require that the agents be responsible for having formed their prior characters and motives by virtue of earlier choices or efforts. A familiar regress would ensue. But this regress might be stopped if sense could be made of the following scenario. The choice in moral and prudential conflict situations terminates an effort (to resist temptation) in one way or another. What is needed is a situation in which the choice is not explained by the prior character and motives alone, or by the prior character and motives plus effort, *even if the prior character and motives can explain the effort.* If such a condition is satisfied, the agent's past character and motives would influence choice either way without determining it. But how can such a condition be satisfied and how would the resulting choice be explained?

The answer is in two parts. The first part consists in saying *how* prior character and motives would explain the effort in cases of moral and prudential choice. They

---

[21] Kane, Robert: 1985, chapter 5.

[22] (1) moral choices or decisions, (2) prudential choices or decisions, (3) practical judgments (about what is good or bad, or what ought to be), (4) changes of intention in action, (5) efforts of will sustaining purposes, and (6) attentional efforts directed at self-control and self modification.

would do so by providing *both* (i) the reasons and dispositions that account for the agent's trying to resist moral or prudential temptation, and (ii) the self-interested reasons or present inclinations that account for why it is *difficult* for the agent to resist temptation. In other words, the complex of past motives and character explains the *conflict* within the agent's will *from both sides*. It explains why the agent makes an effort to resist temptation *and* why it is an *effort*. The inner conflict of will, in other words, is embedded in the prior reasons or motives themselves and it is owing to this fact that prior reasons or motives can explain the conflict and the struggle without necessarily explaining their outcome.

10   Indeterminate Efforts

We now turn to the second part of the answer, which requires that we look at this "effort of will" (to resist moral or prudential temptation) which intervenes between the prior character and motives, on the one hand, and the resulting choice, on the other. Let us suppose that this effort of will which precedes choice is *indeterminate*, thereby making the choice that terminates it *undetermined*. Consider a quantum analogue. Imagine an isolated particle, like an electron, moving toward a thin atomic barrier. Whether or not the particle will penetrate the barrier is undetermined. There is a probability that it will penetrate, but not certainty, because its position and momentum are not both determinate as it moves toward the barrier. Imagine that the choice (to overcome temptation) is like the penetration event. The choice one way or the other is *undetermined* because the process proceeding it and potentially terminating in it (i.e. the effort of will to overcome temptation), is indeterminate.

But this quantum analogy is just that – an analogy. Our efforts of will most likely correspond to complex processes in our brains that are macro-processes involving many neuron firings and connections. How can they be indeterminate? One way to begin thinking about this is to imagine that the neural processes occurring when the efforts are being made are chaotic processes, in the sense of what is nowadays called "chaos theory." In chaotic systems, very minute changes in initial conditions grow exponentially into large differences in final outcome, a phenomenon called "sensitivity to initial conditions." The ubiquity of chaotic systems in nature is now widely recognized; and there is growing interest in the chaotic behavior of the brain at many levels, from the transmission of impulses along individual nerve fibers, to the functioning of neural networks, to the general patterns of brain waves.[23]

But chaotic behavior, though unpredictable, is not necessarily indeterministic. In fact, chaos theory has shown that determinism and predictability need not go hand

[23] See Glass, Leon and Mackey, Michael: 1988, *From Clocks to Chaos: The Rhythms of Life* (Princeton); Scott, George and McMillen, J. Michael (eds.): 1980, *Dissipative Structures and Spatiotemporal Organization Studies in Biomedical Research* (Iowa State); Babloyantz, A. and Destexhe, A. "Strange Attractors in the Human Cortex" in Rensing, L. et al. (eds.): 1985, *Temporal Disorder in Human Oscillatory Systems* (Springer Verlag); Skarda, C. and Freeman, W.: 1987, "How Brains Make Chaos in Order to Make Sense of the World," *Behavioral and Brain Sciences*, pp. 161–195.

in hand. Yet chaos may enter discussions of human freedom in another way if we also bring quantum indeterminacy into the picture, as recently noted by philosophers and scientists, such as James Garson, Jesse Hobbs, Henry Stapp, George P. Scott and Stephen Kellert.[24] As Garson puts it, "Chaotic systems are, by definition, perturbation amplifiers. They can override the general rule that quantum mechanical indeterminacies cancel out at the macro-level. Since chaotic events are exquisitely dependent on the very small, the doings of sub-atomic particles in a very small region of space-time may be reflected in massive differences in global behavior. If we view the brain as a chaotic system that amplifies the non-deterministic sub-atomic events, then chaotic unpredictability is no longer epistemological; it is metaphysical, (or rather physical)" (p. 4). Scott relates this possibility to recent developments in non-equilibrium thermodynamics, arguing that "the action potential waves on the bubble thin membranes of the nerve cells [which] are the most fundamental control activity in human behavior" are non-equilibrium thermodynamic phenomena of the sort that could amplify indeterminate events at the micro-level.[25]

Of special interest are the potential effects of chaotic amplifications on "neural networks." The operation of such networks is holistic in the sense that, as Gordon Globus puts it, "the influence of the whole net" of neurons affects each "individual node [i.e. each neuron] and the influence of the individual node [affects] the whole net."[26] As a consequence, such networks can be sensitive to variations of firings of individual neurons. As Globus says, "Make a few changes in the connection weights [the excitory and inhibitory potentials of neurons] and functionally everything changes [in the neural network] via non-linear interactions . . . the net spontaneously and probabilistically self-organizes." Similarly, the self-organization of the network can affect the firing potentials of its individual nodes. There are reciprocal influences of parts to whole and whole to parts. The flexibility that such reciprocal influences afford in neural networks makes it possible for the brain to respond creatively to an ever changing environment and is one reason for the intense current interest in neural networks.

As a working hypothesis then, imagine that the indeterminate efforts of will involved in moral and prudential choice situations are complex chaotic processes

[24] Garson, James: 1993, "Chaos and Free Will," Unpublished paper delivered to American Philosophical Association, Pacific Division Meeting; Hobbs, Jesse: 1991, "Chaos and Indeterminism," *Canadian Journal of Philosophy* 21, pp. 141–164; Stapp, Henry P.: 1990, "A Quantum Theory of the Mind–Brain Interface," Unpublished presentation to the Conference on Consciousness Within Science, University of California at San Francisco; Scott, George P.: 1991, "Dissipative Structures and the Mind–Body Problem," Scott (ed.) *Time, Rhythms and Chaos in the New Dialogue with Nature* (Iowa State); Kellert, Stephen: 1993, *In the Wake of Chaos* (Chicago).

[25] Scott, George P.: 1991, pp. 266–267. Also see in this connection, Showalter, K., Noyes, R. and Turner, H.: 1979, "Detailed Studies of Trigger Wave Initiation and Detection," *Journal of the American Chemical Society* 101, pp. 746–749.

[26] Globus, Gordon: 1992, "Kane on Incompatibilism: An Exercise in Neurophilosophy," Unpublished paper by a medical psychiatrist/philosopher. Also relevant here is Humberman, P. and Hogg, G.: 1987, "Phase Transitions in Artificial Intelligence Systems," *Artificial Intelligence* 33, pp. 155–172, which shows that chaos exists in neural net models designed to model simple human mental abilities. I am indebted to James Garson for this reference as well as some references of footnote 23.

in the brain involving neural networks that are globally sensitive to quantum indeterminacies at the neuronal level. Persons experience these complex processes phenomenologically as "efforts of will" they are making to resist temptation in moral and prudential situations. The efforts in turn are provoked by competing motives and conflicts within the wills of the persons described in (9). These conflicts create tensions that are reflected in appropriate regions of the brain by movement further from thermodynamic equilibrium which increases the sensitivity to micro-indeterminacies at the neuron level and magnifies these indeterminacies throughout the complex macro-process which, *taken as a whole*, is the effort of will. The agents experience these soul-searching moments as moments of inner struggle and uncertainty about what to do that are reflected in the indeterminacy of their neural processes.

One now adds that when a person does decide in such situations, and the indeterminate effort becomes determinate choice, the person *makes* one set of reasons or motives prevail over the others then and there *by deciding*. It is true that the "strong-will" option (overcoming temptation) and the "weak-willed" one (succumbing to temptation) are not symmetrical, if the agent is trying to overcome temptation. Yet both options are wanted and the agent will settle the issue of which is wanted *more* by deciding. If the business woman and engineer overcome temptation, they will do so by virtue of their efforts. If they fail, it would be because they did not *allow* their efforts to succeed. They chose instead to make their self-interested or present-oriented inclinations prevail.

In such a scenario, the plurality conditions will be satisfied, first, because whichever way they choose, the agents will have reasons (their moral or prudential reasons, on the one hand, or their reasons of self-interest or present satisfaction, on the other); they will have acted for those reasons and they will have made those reasons the predominant ones by choosing for them (plural rationality). Secondly, they will have done all this knowingly and purposefully, whichever way the choice goes (hence plural intentionality). [. . .] Third, such choices can be voluntary, whichever way they go, in the sense of being uncoerced and uncompelled. If the effort of will to overcome temptation in moral or prudential contexts is indeterminate, the outcome either way is not determined. The agent may succeed in overcoming temptation or may fail. But this means that the weak-willed motives (of self-interest or imprudence) are *resistible*, even if the agents should act upon them. And if the motives of self-interest or imprudence are resistible, the weak-willed choice is to that degree not coerced or compulsive. The agents could have succeeded in overcoming temptation, and thus "could have chosen otherwise" in a strong incompatibilist sense of "could." Neither outcome would be determined, but each would be willed by the agent.

VIII

Objection #1: "But if the brain process corresponding to the effort is macro-indeterminate, it remains difficult to see how the outcome could be the agent's doing rather than merely a matter of chance. When neuro-scientists inspect the brain they will find nothing more than an interconnected set of neuron firings in which micro-indeterminacies are not negligible. This process will in turn terminate either in some definite sequence of nerve firings that corresponds to the 'choice' to overcome temptation or in another set of nerve firings corresponding to the 'choice' to succumb to temptation. But why one of these outcomes occurs rather than another will be inexplicable in terms of the preceding process. Probabilities can be assigned, but that's it."[27]

I agree that if the physical descriptions of these events were the only legitimate ones, then free will would look like nothing more than chance or probability. When neuro-scientists described it in physico-chemical terms, all they would get are indeterministic chaotic processes with probabilistic outcomes. In other words, when described from a physical perspective alone, *free will looks like chance*. But the physical description is not the only one to be considered. The indeterministic chaotic process is also, experientially considered, the agent's effort of will – something the agent is *doing*. And the undetermined outcome of the process, one way or the other, is experientially the agent's choice – something the agent does, not something that merely happens to the agent. If we did not add these supervenient descriptions to the physical descriptions, something important would be left out of our picture of the world.[28] Indeed, if we could not add such supervenient descriptions, we could not distinguish mental *actions* from mental happenings generally.[29]

Look at it in another way. Whether we are compatibilists or incompatibilists, most of us experience moral and prudential conflict situations like those of the woman and engineer. And we resolve them one way or another by choosing. Perhaps, sometimes these choices are compulsive; we are overwhelmed by irresist-

---

[27] The objections discussed in this section are a composite of objections made against my view by a number of astute critics, to whom I owe a great debt for helping to provoke refinements in my view. They include Double, Richard, 1991; Waller, Bruce N.: 1988, "Free Will Gone Out of Control: A Critical Study of R. Kane's *Free Will and Values*," *Behaviorism* 16, pp. 149–167; Bernstein, Mark: 1989, Review of *Free Will and Values*, *Noûs* 23, pp. 557–559, and "Kanean Libertarianism" (unpublished manuscript); O'Connor, Timothy: 1992, "Some Puzzles About Free Agency," Ph.D. Dissertation (Cornell), and "Indeterminism and Free Agency: Three Recent Views" (forthcoming in *Philosophy and Phenomenological Research*); Talbott, Thomas: 1986, Review of *Free Will and Values*, *International Philosophical Quarterly* 20, pp. 300–302; Posth, Matthew: 1990, "Freedom and Realism," Ph.D. Dissertation (Northwestern); Tracy, Thomas: 1990, Review of *Free Will and Values*, *Journal of the American Academy of Religion* 22, pp. 389–391; Globus, Gordon: 1992; Williams, Clifford: 1986, Review of *Free Will and Values*, *Canadian Philosophical Reviews* 6, pp. 450–452; Mele, Alfred (a forthcoming book on Self Control and Autonomy). Watson, Gary: 1987 also contains several objections addressed to "teleological intelligibility" views like mine. Constructive criticism has also come from correspondence or discussion with William Hasker, Galen Strawson, Peter Van Inwagen, Randolph Clarke, Robert Audi, George Graham, William Rowe, Max Hocutt, John Post, David Blumenfeld, Jeff Tlumak and Noah Lemos.

[28] Putting this another way, the view I am defending does not require a mind/body dualism of the Cartesian kind, but neither is it compatible with an "eliminative materialism" – one that would simply dispense with "folk psychological" descriptions of human thought and action in favor of merely physio-chemical descriptions of the brain. If all we had were physico-chemical descriptions, then (unless our current physics and chemistry were radically transformed) free will would be written out of the human picture along with consciousness and other familiar mental phenomena.

[29] Two important recent works that argue for this point are O'Shaughnessy, Brian: 1980, *The Will*, 2 vols. (Cambridge) and Ginet, Carl: 1992.

ible desires. But it would be begging too many questions to claim they must always be compulsive. Even many compatibilists want to make room for a distinction between compulsion, on the one hand, and weakness of will, on the other – where we "freely" succumb to temptation (though compatibilists don't think indeterminism is necessarily involved). Now consider such cases of weakness of will. Suppose that future neurologists should inform us that in such cases the efforts of will we are making to overcome temptation correspond to indeterministic chaotic processes in the brain such as I have described. This would certainly give pause to determinists and compatibilists. But should they therefore cease to say that the efforts of will were *their* efforts and the choices resulting from the efforts *their* choice? This would be as absurd, I think, as saying that our perceptions and reasoning processes and their outcomes are not *ours* if they turn out to involve indeterministic chaotic processes in the brain (as well they might, according to some recent suggestions).

Objection #2: "But surely the fact that the efforts are indeterminate takes away, or at least diminishes, our *control* over the resulting choices. By making choice outcomes depend upon indeterministic efforts of will, are you not limiting the power or control that agents have over their free choices, and in particular over those very self-forming choices (SFWs) that are supposed to carry the burden of ultimate responsibility?"

Well, the agents cannot guarantee one outcome rather than the other *beforehand*. But it does not follow that because you cannot guarantee which of a set of outcomes occurs beforehand, that you do not control which of them *occurs*. You have *voluntary control* over a set of options when you can bring about *whichever* one (of them) *you will, when you will* to do so. Since the undetermined choices I described in moral and prudential choice situations are willed by the agents *whatever* way they go *when they are made*, the agents have voluntary control over which of them occurs in this sense, even though they cannot guarantee which one will occur beforehand. (Note that the plurality conditions – which insure more-than-one-way willing – are the key to this result.)

Now if you say that the inability to guarantee an outcome before it occurs is a limitation of voluntary control even if it does not imply the absence of voluntary control, then I grant it. Indeed, I would insist that this limitation is essential for free will. For such antecedent control would mean that our choices or actions were determined by (determinate) prior efforts, character traits, motives and other circumstances. And such "antecedent determinate" control is not compatible with the ultimate control required by ultimate responsibility. The former requires determinism, the latter rules it out. This limitation is therefore one we have to accept as a consequence of free will (at least for SFWs). Rather than hide this, I think incompatibilists should bring it out into the open. Free will is not an unlimited or absolute power. All free choices, including SFWs, are limited by heredity, environment and conditioning. And SFWs are further limited by not being antecedently determinable. But this does not mean we do not have voluntary control over our destinies; it only means that when we engage in self-formation, what we choose is not determined by our *already* formed character and motives.

Objection #3: "I still cannot overcome the feeling that if the effort is indeterminate, the resulting choice is a product of chance and not really in the agent's control. Let me try to put this uneasiness in another way. Do you really escape the charge of *arbitrariness* for choices that terminate indeterminate efforts? The choices may be plural rational in the sense that there are incommensurable reasons for going either way, but isn't the choosing *for* one of these incommensurable sets of reasons rather than another merely arbitrary even if you want to choose by that set more than by any other when you choose?"

I grant that free choices are arbitrary in the sense that they are not fully explicable in terms of the past. But that is because their full meaning and significance do not lie in the past alone. Every free choice, as I argued in a previous work,[30] is the initiation of a "value experiment" whose justification lies in the future. It says in effect: "Let's try this. It's not required by my past, but it is consistent with my past and is one branching pathway my life could now meaningfully take. I'm willing to take responsibility for it one way or the other. It may make me a (morally) better or worse person, a (prudentially) happier or sadder person, but I will know that it was my doing and my own self-making – guided by my past, but not determined by it."

Imagine a writer in the middle of a story whose main character (the story's heroine) is pretty well formed but not completely so. The heroine faces a crisis situation and the writer has not yet drawn her character in the novel in sufficient detail to say exactly how she will react to this situation. The author makes a judgment that she will react one way rather than another and thereby gives greater detail to her character from then on. But the author's judgment was not determined by the heroine's already formed past. For that past was not clear enough in the author's mind to give unique direction. In that sense, the judgment of how she would react in this situation was "arbitrary," but not entirely so. It had input from the character's past and in turn gave input to the character's future. (It is worth noting in this connection that the term "arbitrary" comes from the Latin "arbitrium," which *means* "judgment" – as in "liberum arbitrium voluntatis" or "free judgment of the will," the medieval designation for free will). The point of focusing on the author's narrative "judgment" in this example is, of course, to bring out the fact that free agents are both authors of and characters in their own stories all at once – "making themselves" as they go along out of a past that (if they are truly free) is not so restrictive that it always limits their future pathways to only one.

11   Teleological Intelligibility (TI)

What is required of free choices then is not that they be completely explicable in terms of the past, but that they possess a "teleological intelligibility" or "narrative continuity," which is to say, the choices can be fit into "meaningful sequences," as

---

[30] Kane, Robert: 1985, pp. 92–94.

Wiggins puts it, or fit into a coherent narrative for which the agents themselves are at least partly responsible. For this reason, I have called my theory of free will a "TI" or "teleological intelligibility" theory (borrowing this expression from Gary Watson) and contrasted it with most other libertarian theories which rely on some notion or other of an agent-causation that cannot be accounted for in terms of ordinary notions of event causation (hence "AC" theories).[31] [. . .]

Objection #4: "You claimed to give us an account of incompatibilist free will that avoided mystery and that could be accommodated to modern physical, biological and cognitive science. I can see that you avoid agent-causation, noumenal selves, transempirical egos and other such libertarian strategies that have led to charges of mystery in the past. But with indeterminate efforts of will, are you not substituting a new mystery for the old ones? And is that a gain?"

My view does not eliminate all mystery from free will. What it tries to do is to eliminate mysteries that are created by taking a *distinctively libertarian view of free will* – as opposed to mysteries that confront everyone, no matter what their position of free will. Indeterminate efforts of will are mysterious because they partake of two deep cosmological problems that are problems for everyone not just libertarians. One is the "problem of consciousness": how can sensations, perceptions, thoughts and other conscious experiences be brain processes? Much of the puzzlement that surrounds indeterminate efforts has to do with this general problem of consciousness. How can complex indeterministic processes in the brain be simultaneously experienced as our efforts of will and hence our doings? This is a mystery alright, but consciousness is no more nor less a mystery if the brain processes corresponding to our experienced efforts turn out to be determined rather than undetermined. The problem of how consciously experienced effort is related to brain processes is a problem for everyone, compatibilists and incompatibilists alike.

The other cosmological problem of which free will partakes is the problem of indeterminacy-in-nature, which is pretty mysterious in itself. How can wave/particles, like electrons, have indeterminate trajectories in which their position and momentum cannot both be exact at the same time? How can natural objects have properties like position, momentum or energy that are inexact in reality and not merely inexactly knowable? We know that great scientists, some of whom were in on the founding of quantum theory, like Planck, Einstein and DeBroglie, could not accept the inexact trajectories, the indeterminacy, and other related mysteries of the quantum world. They hoped by way of hidden variables or some entirely new theory to get back to the exactness and determinacy of the classical world. I

[31] Most historical libertarian theories have been agent-cause, or AC, theories of one sort or another; and most contemporary libertarians lean towards some kind of AC theory. (Two exceptions are Carl Ginet (1992) and myself.) William Rowe has done ground-breaking work on the historical roots of AC theories (1987, "Two Concepts of Freedom," *Proceedings of the American Philosophical Association* 62). Several able younger philosophers are attempting to reconstruct and defend AC theories against standard criticisms: e.g. O'Connor, Timothy: 1992, and Clarke, Randolph: 1993, "Towards a Credible Agent-Causal Account of Free Will," *Noûs* 27, pp. 191–203. I wish them well, but I remain convinced along with Ginet that adding non-event causation to libertarian theories merely multiplies problems without explanatory gain.

suggest that we should expect the same resistance and puzzlement over indeterminate efforts when discussing free will as indeterminate trajectories of quantum theory often received. Indeterminate efforts force us to view human action and the life histories of human beings in strange and novel ways, just as indeterminate trajectories and properties force us to view the world of elementary particles in strange and novel ways.[32]

So I agree that indeterminate efforts are mysterious. But their mysteriousness partakes of the twin mysteries of (i) consciousness and (ii) indeterminacy-in-the-nature-of-reality. These are two of the central cosmological problems of the age; and they are problems we all face, no matter what our position on free will. Unlike non-occurrent causes or transempirical power centers, these are not mysteries specifically created by libertarian accounts of free will. Life is full of mysteries, but the mysteries should be created by the world and not by our theories. Moreover, it should not surprise us that "free will" (which Kant regarded as *the* "cosmological" problem) should be intimately related to these two other central cosmological problems.

IX

12   "Of One's Own Free Will"

The title of this final section is the most common phrase in which the expression "free will" still regularly occurs in ordinary discourse. In recent decades, compatibilists have attempted to give accounts of this phrase consistent with determinism. On my "incompatibilist" account of it, agents act "of their own free wills" (in an incompatibilist sense) just in case they are "ultimately responsible" for their actions in the sense of UR.

What is interesting about this interpretation of the phrase "of one's own free will" is that, while it is incompatibilist, it can be satisfied for many actions even when the actions are determined and the agents could not have done otherwise. Dennett cites the case of Luther saying "Here I stand. I cannot do otherwise" when Luther finally broke with Rome.[33] Suppose, says Dennett, that Luther was literally right. He could not then and there have done otherwise because his affirmation was determined by the character and motives he then had. Should this lead us to deny that Luther's act was free and responsible? Dennett says No, thereby arguing that free will and moral responsibility do not require the absence of determinism or even that the agent "could have done otherwise."

---

[32] Amplification of quantum indeterminacy raises special problems here that I haven't the space to discuss. As I argued earlier, the effort of will is related to the indeterministic chaotic brain process taken as a whole. One cannot pry apart its indeterministic parts and deterministic parts and identify either with the effort itself. One therefore does not have effort followed by chance or indeterminism, or indeterminism followed by effort. Rather the effort and the indeterminacy are fused. The effort is indeterminate and the indeterminacy is (a property) of the effort.

[33] Dennett, Daniel: 1984, chapter 6.

As an incompatibilist, I answer as follows. Luther's act *could* have been *free* (performed "of his own free will") and morally *responsible* – indeed "ultimately responsible" – even if it was determined by his character and motives at the time and even if he could not have done otherwise. But this would have been so to the extent that he himself formed his present character and motives by other acts in his past life history (SFWs) that *were* undetermined and with respect to which he *could* have done otherwise rationally, intentionally and voluntarily when he made them. In other words, UR does not require that all acts for which we are ultimately responsible (and hence which are done "of our own free will") must be undetermined. Often we act freely and responsibly (even in an incompatibilist sense) out of a will already formed. What UR requires is that we ourselves formed that will to some degree in the past by acts that were undetermined. This is what allows us to say we are acting out of *our own* free will – a will of our own making – even when our characters and motives determine our actions. (It is also why, in the final analysis, the free will issue is about the will.)

So Dennett may be right about Luther, but wrong about the need for indeterminism and "could have done otherwise." Ultimately responsible acts, or acts done "of our own free will," make up a wider class of actions than the agent's "self-forming" actions (SFWs), which must be undetermined and such that the agent could have done otherwise. But if no actions were self-forming in this way, we would not be *ultimately* responsible for anything we did.[34]

---

[34] I would like to especially thank Mark Bernstein for helpful comments on an earlier draft.

3

Philosophical Theology

Gregory Pence, "Aquinas and the Rationality of Belief in God"

Readings

Thomas Aquinas, "Five Ways to Prove the Existence of God"

William Paley, "The Evidence of Design"

John L. Mackie, "Arguments for Design"

William L. Rowe, "The Cosmological Argument"

Robert Merrihew Adams, "Kierkegaard's Arguments Against Objective Reasoning in Religion"

Fyodor Dostoevsky, "Why Does God Permit Evil?" from *The Brothers Karamazov*

St Thomas Aquinas. Copyright Archivi Alinari/Art Resource,
New York.

GREGORY PENCE

Aquinas and the Rationality of Belief in God

If there were no death of other animals, there would not be life for the lion; if there were no persecution from tyrants, there would be no occasion for the heroic suffering of the martyrs.
Thomas Aquinas, *Summa Theologica*

Can we prove that God exists? One person who believed that we could was the famous philosopher and theologian, St Thomas Aquinas. Aquinas held both that God's existence is provable to the skeptic and also that human reason is a tool for such a proof. This essay uses Aquinas's life and ideas to discuss the reasonableness of belief in God. Its object is neither to use the exact terms of Thomas nor to defend his exact ideas, but to reflect the basic spirit of his philosophical questions in a way that will capture the interest of the modern reader. Along the way, it covers the nature of the concept of God, some traditional proofs of God's existence, objections to these proofs, tensions between faith and reason, and questions of onus of proof in debates between skeptics and believers.

1   Life of Thomas Aquinas

Thomas Aquinas was born near Naples in the thirteenth century, in 1224, and died at age 49. For the preceding 800 years, Augustine had dominated Christian philosophy, and when Aquinas synthesized Aristotelianism and Christianity, his theory ("Thomism") also held sway for centuries. Augustine and Aquinas, two great thinkers of the Christian Church, each created a remarkably long, powerful influence over the thinking of those who came after them. Because of his quiet demeanor and unique appearance, Thomas was known to his fellow students in theology at Paris as "The Dumb Ox." Upon hearing this, his famous teacher and mentor, Peter Abelard, roared back, "This dumb ox will fill the whole world with his bellowing."

Theology differs from philosophy in that the former generally assumes the existence of its object (*theos*, or God), whereas philosophy does not. In the nineteenth century, Pope Leo XII made Thomism virtually the official theology of the Roman Catholic Church. Today, various canons of the Catholic Church require candidates for the priesthood to study Thomistic ideas for several years, and seminary professors are ordered to teach within Thomistic principles.

Thomas received the best, most urbane education of his time, starting at the age of five when he was enrolled in a program of study at a Benedictine abbey, and then, at age 14, entering the University of Naples. While there, he decided to become a Dominican priest and friar, much to the consternation of his family, who had expected him to become a Benedictine monk. At the time, the Dominicans were a new order that espoused evangelical outreach to the masses, partly by begging. In contrast, the Benedictines catered more to tradition and the upper classes, and Benedictine monks generally lived comfortably on huge, Church-owned estates. This is just one instance of many in the history of Western religions of the tension between those who would return believers to a simple, inward life and those who advocate that believers must be led by a sophisticated, modern organization with a hierarchy of leaders.

There is a story, perhaps apocryphal, that when Thomas was on his way from Naples to Paris to take his Dominican vows, he stopped to visit his family, who detained him forcibly for over a year. Convinced that he could not really want to pursue such a life, his brothers tempted him by hiring a young female seductress to enter his chambers late at night. Perhaps his family really wanted him to change Orders. Whatever the case, Thomas resisted, and eventually became a Dominican.

His family's fears appear to have been unfounded. Thomas was never destined to become a simple friar living with the poor among the soup kitchens of his day. His great intellectual gifts were spotted at the University of Paris, which was the greatest university in the world in the thirteenth century for the study of theology. He eventually became a professor of theology there, where he vigorously defended both belief in God and the beliefs of Christianity. Thomas wrote books on almost every subject then known, and as such, qualifies as one of the systematic philosophers of past times whose ideas compose a system or world-view by which to live. His followers are today called "Thomists."

In 1273, while saying Mass in Naples, he experienced a mental aberration, which may have been a mental disturbance caused by brain cancer; it could also have been a mystical vision, which is how Thomas interpreted it. After this event, he ceased writing altogether because, as he said, "I cannot [write], because all that I have written now seems like straw."

Three months later and ill, he obeyed a command from Pope Gregory X to go to a great council to be convened at Lyons. While traveling, he accidentally injured his head, forcing him to seek refuge in a niece's castle nearby, where he died in March of 1274. Forty years later, the process began that shortly thereafter led to awarding sainthood to Thomas. A few decades later, he became a "Doctor of the Church," that is, an official founder of its doctrine.

Despite his short life, Thomas produced a mass of books and works that impresses one today – even more so when we remember that he wrote without aid of computers or typewriters. (His handwriting was almost illegible, but his saving trick was to employ several male secretaries, who transcribed his oral declarations.) By all accounts, he was kind – he even preached sermons to local people. For the most part, however, he was a scholar's scholar and preferred the life of contemplation and writing to that of action or business.

No book of Aquinas is regarded as a "great book" like Plato's *Republic* or Descartes' *Meditations*. His works are suffused with Christian themes and Christian assumptions: he writes as a believer within the family of the Church. His most famous works are *Summa Theologica* ("A Summary of Theology") and *Summa contra Gentiles* ("A Summary against the Gentiles," also known as "The Truth of the Catholic Faith"). Both of these works were written for those first beginning to think about religious questions. The second work is somewhat oddly named, for the "Gentiles" that Thomas has in mind here are those who accepted a naturalistic world-view, that is, a world-view in which God is not needed to explain what occurs.

2   The Concept of God

One of the characteristics of all philosophical reflection is that clear thinking requires that we first become clear about the crucial terms of our discussion. Thomas would certainly agree with this thought; before we begin to think about proofs of God's existence, we need to describe exactly what we mean by the word "God." This task is important because the word "God" may be used to refer to a being identified with both Western religions such as Judaism, Christianity, and Islam, and also to the divine object of Eastern religions such as Hinduism.

In a famous doctrine, Thomas emphasizes that when words such as "just" and "wise" are applied to God, they do not mean the same as when applied to humans. We know what a sad man is and a wise woman, but Thomas says that when we apply these terms to God, we can only do so analogically. As James Ross (1961) points out, in championing this doctrine Thomas is avoiding two problems. First, if "God is wise" means the same as in "The President is wise" then the meaning of the first statement is homocentric (human-centered) and limited, a tenet rejected by contemporaries of Thomas. On the other hand, if "wise" means something totally different when applied to God as when applied to humans, we will understand nothing at all when we hear "God is wise." So Aquinas's doctrine of analogical predication (where words such as "wise," "just," and "good" are predicates applied to God) emerges as a sensible compromise for how we can meaningfully talk and think about God's nature.

But what does it mean to apply a predicate such as "power" analogously to God? Thomas admits that our human knowledge is limited. Man's faculties for knowing, says the Thomistic epistemology (theory of knowledge), are best suited for the natural world, not the immaterial world of God. So we can apply concepts such as power to God, and we do so by subtracting the material aspect of power in the natural world and then, by the principle of proportionality, magnifying that power infinitely to a being in the immaterial world.

Let us describe then some traditional assumptions (including those made by Thomas) about the nature of God. First, God is assumed to be eternal. Nothing existed before him, because God is the cause of everything and created everything, so nothing could exist before God. It is not that there was time during which there was nothing, and then there was God. Rather, there was never a time when God did not exist.

Next, God is assumed to be omnipotent or all-powerful. He created the Earth, the galaxy of the Milky Way, and all the other galaxies of the universe. He can also destroy them, if he wishes. He can turn wine into blood, or make statues weep. He can create organic life out of chemicals. He can create souls out of dust. Finally, for humans what is important is that an omnipotent God can make beings who are by nature mortal into immortal beings. In short, God can do anything.

Third, God is assumed to be omniscient or all-knowing. As Thomas explained in *Summa contra Gentiles* (III), God orders the universe that he created, and governs it according to his reasonable, natural laws. Nothing happens without a purpose, and the purpose of each thing is known by God. God's omniscience extends to the inner minds of humans, and such penetration of our deepest motives has enormous consequences for morality. We may act morally because we secretly want to be liked by others, or because we believe we will be happier doing so, and not because we want to do what is right. God, however, knows exactly why we act as we do, and there is no hiding from his probing eye.

Fourth, and this holds for Jews and Muslims as well as Christians, God is assumed to be good: he is merciful and benevolent to humans. God's goodness is a reflection of his more general attitude to humans, his caring. If God did not care about humans, he would not have created us. He would not have given us an Earth to live on, air to breathe, and plants to eat for food. God cares about whether each human life goes better or worse, and he cares about whether human history is moving toward universal salvation or universal damnation.

Although ordinary believers take it to be completely obvious and uncontroversial that our concept of God includes his benevolent attitude toward humans, this part of God's nature is both important and by no means uncontroversial. For this conception of God is that of *theism*, which assumes a God who is personally involved in the world of humans, who occasionally allows miracles to occur that defy the natural laws of science, who answers the prayers of humans, and who sends emissaries to instruct humans – such as his prophet Moses, his son Jesus, and his Messenger Mohammed.

In contrast, *deism* assumes a conception of a divine being who is not involved in human affairs and who does not intervene with miracles in the natural world. A deistic God is a remote one, who may have created the world and who may judge humans at the Last Judgment, but who otherwise leaves human history alone to run its course. Western religions assume a theistic God, not a deistic one, and we will henceforth assume a theistic concept of God (while being aware that the theologies of most Eastern religions do not make such an assumption).

Aquinas also argues that God is unchanging, immaterial (i.e. totally spiritual), and essentially one thing (i.e. indissoluble into parts). This is knowledge obtained by the so-called "Negative Way" of understanding. These last truths are not very informative, Thomas says, because they just tell us what God is not, not what he is.

3   Arguments for God's Existence

What can human reason know about God? Past philosophers have debated to what extent God's existence can be proved, or his nature known, by reasoning. There are two ways to reason about God: *a priori*, or without any empirical premises about the world, and *a posteriori*, with empirical premises about the world. Thomas discusses both methods, although he believes that only the latter can be used to prove God's existence.

Some people may be skeptical about what reason can prove about God. But let us not be too quick to dismiss reason. After all, it is one of the best tools that the human mind has with which to understand the universe. Even if we come to believe that reason cannot itself prove everything about God, we will have used reason to come to this conclusion.

The Five Ways

Thomas's most famous proofs for the existence of God are called "the Five Ways." All of the arguments of the Five Ways, as well as other arguments for God given elsewhere by Thomas, involve reasoning from a certain, enormously general property of the world to a property of God involving existence. The conclusions of each of the Five Ways are:

1   There must be one ultimate cause of motion.
2   There must be one ultimate cause.
3   There must be one ultimate, common source of all "being" in the universe.
4   The existence of contingent beings implies a being who is necessary.
5   An intelligent being exists who directs the ways the world works.

Later in the history of philosophy, related versions of these conclusions figure in the most famous arguments for the existence of God. Every beginning student in philosophy should be aware of these arguments. Below we will discuss (5) under the Argument from Design and (2) under the First Cause argument, but before we get to these, there is another argument we need to consider.

One famous argument for God's existence that was not one of the Five Ways was first formulated not by Aquinas but by a famous Archbishop of Canterbury named Anselm, who lived (1033–1109) nearly two centuries before Aquinas. This argument is called the Ontological Argument (*ontos*, being) and has several variations. One version of the argument goes like this:

> The concept of God is of a supremely perfect being. (premise 1)
> Existence in reality is a perfection. (premise 2)
> Therefore,
> If people have a concept of God as a supremely perfect being, then they are thinking about a being who exists. (conclusion 1)
> To this first conclusion, we need only add the additional premise that,
> People have a concept of God as a supremely perfect being. (premise 3)
> to get the desired conclusion that,
> Therefore,
> God exists. (conclusion 2)

Support for premise 2 comes from comparing a god who does not exist with one who does. Obviously, existence adds something to God's perfection: God is more perfect existing than not existing. Once we add premise 3, that people actually have the concept of God as a supremely perfect being, it follows that God exists.

Or does it? Isn't this too easy? Whether an argument rationally proves its conclusion depends on two things: whether the premises are true, and whether the conclusion logically follows from its premises. Philosophers and logicians use the words "truth" and "validity" in a special sense different from ordinary language: true premises accurately refer to facts in the world, a valid argument has premises that logically support the conclusion. (Thus validity and truth in these special senses are not synonyms.) Validity is about logical form; truth about the relation of premises to the world. An argument can be valid (have the proper form) and yet have false premises (false content). Furthermore, an argument that has true premises and that is valid is called sound. Ideally, we all use only sound arguments.

For centuries, students of theology and philosophy have studied the soundness of the Ontological Argument, which has other, more complex and subtle versions than the one above. Aquinas himself rejected the Ontological Argument as unsound, so let's see the ways in which the argument can be criticized.

Many wonder how we can know the meaning of premise 1: what does it mean to say that "The concept of God is that of a supremely perfect being?" To say that we can understand a "perfect" God is to imply that we can understand a "less perfect" God, or even an "imperfect" God. Is this correct? Next, even if we can attach some meaning to the claim that the concept of God includes perfection (e.g. by analogical predication), what evidence do we have for this claim? The Bible says a lot of things about the majesty, power, and goodness of God, but rarely speaks of his perfection. Moreover, there are passages in the Bible where God does not seem to act in perfect ways. So premise 1 may be false.

What about premise 2? What does it mean to say that "existence in reality is a perfection"? One thing it cannot mean is some kind of wish-fulfillment by humans: it shouldn't mean that the world is "more perfect for humans" if God exists, but rather, that it is better for God himself to exist. But "better" in what sense? Premise 2 is at best quite unclear.

The most famous kind of attack on this argument is to emphasize that there is the kind of existence that humans and chairs have versus the kind of nebulous "existence" that fantasies, dreams, and thoughts have. Anselm and Aquinas used the phrases *in intellectu* (in the mind or intellect) versus *in re* (in reality) to mark this distinction. While we may have a clear concept of God as a supremely perfect being *in intellectu*, that is not the same as knowing God as a perfect being existing *in re*. Clearly, what most people want to prove is that God exists in the second way. In other words, people want to prove not that the idea of God exists, but that God himself exists.

The problem here can be further clarified in the following way: in a valid argument, all key terms must be used with the same meaning in all the premises and in the conclusion. But if we are switching back and forth between the concept of God and the real existence of God, we are committing a fallacy of ambiguity by using the key term in two different ways. If so, the premises do not entail the conclusion.

Indeed, that seems to be what is going on. Premise 1 is about the concept of God, whereas conclusion 2 is about God himself. The argument is invalid because it goes from premise 1, which discusses a supremely perfect being *in intellectu*, to conclusion 2, where a supremely perfect being is implied to exist *in re*.

Along similar lines, a monk named Gaunilon made his "perfect island" objection to this argument: just because one has the idea of a perfect island, it does not prove that a perfect island exists. Whether or not a particular concept existing *in intellectu* also exists *in re* is always an important question, and one that we cannot just assume or "beg." Begging the question is the mistake in reasoning of assuming to be true what should be proven to be true. To infer that perfection in the idea of God entails a real, existing, perfect God seems to beg this question in the most import-ant way. Why is that? Because, again, many of our ideas do not have a correspond-ing reality as objects, and we ordinarily decide which ones are real by using the test of our senses and experience. Few ideas prove themselves without real experience, but that is just what the Ontological Argument seems to imply.

Of course, supporters of the Ontological Argument argue that it is not a fallacy in the argument that it goes from the idea of God to his reality, because that is exactly what the argument purports to do. This claim seems obvious to them, but not to the skeptic, who will not be convinced by their claim. However, we must remember that the point of a proof is to convince agnostics and skeptics, not to buttress the faith of those already convinced, so the argument does not succeed at what it intends to do.

Overall, the confusion between ideas and things raises enough problems, as well as the problems with premise 1, that the Ontological Argument as stated is put in grave doubt. The Ontological Argument has not proved that "a supremely perfect being exists," but only that "the idea of a supremely perfect being" is a very peculiar idea.

The First Cause Argument

There is also a tendency to overestimate what we can infer by analogy from human experience. Let us look at the famous First Cause Argument for God's existence, which can be constructed like this:

Everything must have a cause or beginning. (premise 1)
The universe must have a cause or beginning. (premise 2)
Therefore,
A cause or beginning of the universe must exist. (conclusion)

Historically, this argument is also called the "Cosmological Argument" for its ideas about the origins of the "cosmos" or universe. Support for the first premise often comes from the assertion that it is absurd to imagine the universe as "just existing" back forever, with no definite beginning.

Let us proceed to evaluate this argument. First, not everyone accepts the truth of premise 1. Whereas everything in the universe might be accepted as having a cause, whether the universe itself has a cause is a different question. Bertrand Russell (1872–1970), a famous English skeptic and atheist, considered it more absurd to believe that the universe was started by God, with nothing existing before God, than to simply believe that the universe always existed.

Second, note that if this argument works, we again have the problem of validity discussed previously because of the changeable meaning of the terms referring to divine objects. To infer that something started the universe is very far from saying that God created it. From the mere fact of a creation of the universe, neither human characteristics can be correctly inferred nor most of God's traditional qualities (as Aristotle also noted). To understand how much is lost, consider this advice: "Pray to the beginning of the universe, it will forgive your sins."

Similarly, even on Thomas's arguments, we cannot infer the traditional God of theism from the somewhat sterile, abstract qualities of necessity, indissolubility, and so on. What Thomas thinks that reason can infer about God from the world is not only not much, it is also not what ordinary believers want in a theology.

For example, Thomas does not think reason can prove that the universe had a beginning in time. Thomas offers persuasive reasons, both for Aristotle's belief that the world existed eternally and for the Christian belief that the world had a beginning in time. But the latter must be accepted on faith, Thomas says, because for all reason understands, the world might have existed from eternity. For any particular beginning point, reason cannot understand why it cannot be asked, "But what existed just before then?" It is this limited nature of reason, he asserts, that reveals the necessity of both faith and use of sources such as the Bible for revealed truth. But to the philosopher, such appeals to faith are not persuasive and can be dangerous because they appear to beg the very question at hand.

The Argument from Design

One of Thomas's arguments, that of Harmony, is essentially the famous Argument from Design. We can summarize this argument in its briefest form this way:

The universe exhibits a purposeful design. (premise 1)
Only a Designer with conscious purposes could explain the existence of a universe with purposeful design. (premise 2)
Therefore,
A purposeful Designer exists. (conclusion)

Does this proof of God's existence work? Remember that the answer depends on whether the argument posits true premises and has a valid form.

The skeptic will first question the meaning of premise 1 that asserts the existence of design or "harmony" in the universe. At the very least, it must be taken to assert that the organization of the material world, that is, the subject studied by physics, chemistry, biology, and geology, reveals the design or plan of an intelligent, rational, superior mind.

The eighteenth-century believer Thomas Paley put this point by his famous argument from analogy: any person who found a fine watch on an uninhabited desert island would be correct in inferring that some skilled intelligence had created such a timepiece. The delicate interconnections of jewels, gears, and springs work together to keep perfect time, and from such a product we can infer a superior intelligence.

Consider woodpeckers. They have no layer of fluid between their brains and craniums, unlike all other vertebrates. This arrangement allows shock waves that are generated from their violent peckings on trees to be harmlessly dissipated through their skulls. If woodpeckers had lots of fluid inside their skulls, like us, the way they get their food would harm them. So it looks like God designed them just right to do what they have to do.

Similarly, Paley argued, when one understands the world around us, one sees the hand of a vastly more skilled, more superior intelligence. Furthermore, Paley argued, even if one had never seen a watch before, or did not understand how the watch worked, one would be justified in inferring superior intelligence. Suppose that one day space voyagers find on a distant star a medical machine that heals any known human disease. Would we not be justified in inferring that superior beings existed and had made such a machine?

The ordinary person often argues in ways similar to Paley. When first seeing the Grand Canyon, a person may exclaim, "There, truly, is the hand of God." In studying ecology and the ozone layer, the college student may marvel at how the earth is such a fragile, complex organism that could be easily destroyed and which obviously has to work just right to sustain human life as we know it. Hence, he or she may reason, God must have created such a wonderful earth for humans to enjoy.

Are these good arguments? Notice first that these arguments reason by analogy. What is important to understand is that, in all analogical reasoning, the strength of the conclusion corresponds to the closeness of fit between the two things compared: the closer the fit, the greater the strength of the conclusion. For example, if one claims that "Government is like running a ship at sea because anyone must be able to take the helm in a storm," then one has weak support because government is not much like piloting a ship. To see this, note that the opposite analogy can also be made, "Government is like a ship at sea in a storm: it needs a strong hand at the helm." The best analogies are made between two very similar things.

So is finding ourselves in a universe with the appearance of design like finding a healing machine on a distant star? The answer will depend on our answers to several questions: does the universe in fact exhibit the design of an omniscient Designer? Second, is such a Designer the only, or most, plausible explanation for the appearance of such a design? Even if the answer to these two questions was positive, how much then could we infer about the nature of the Designer?

Let's first look at the question of whether the universe, and planet Earth, exhibit the kind of design that we see in products such as automobiles, handstitched dresses, and tools. One response is that the world does not appear very well designed for humans at all: there are floods, droughts, plagues of locusts, volcanic eruptions, a deteriorating environment, sexually transmitted diseases, starvation, and earthquakes. Even more generally, the world was created with a scarcity of the basic resources necessary for a decent life of humans: there is a lack of fresh water in the Middle East; of arable land in much of Africa; and in China, millions starve for lack of food. Much of the earth is too cold or too hot for human comfort. If Earth is supposed to be a paradise, should we not fire the architect?

(A biblical believer may retort that once humans had a land of plenty in the Garden of Eden, but Adam's and Eve's sin destroyed this paradise. To this, the skeptic can retort: why create a world where the sins of one couple ruin things for billions upon billions of people who come after? Genesis says that because of Eve's sin, all the billions of women after her must give birth in pain (Genesis 3: 16). Does setting up the world this way show a benevolent design?)

Indeed, it seems that God, if he only wanted to make us happy, could have created the world in a much better way. For one thing, he could have eliminated pain. Surely the absence of pleasure would be enough to motivate most people; they don't need the physical pain of disease and injury to get along. And what about old age and infirmity? Why do humans need to go through these terrible processes? If God loves humans, why not just let us live young and healthy until the day he takes us up to heaven? After all, God could do it, if he chose. So one conclusion about the Argument from Design is that reflection about the state of the world does not reveal the "hand" of a superior craftsman who wanted to design the best possible world for us.

What about premise 2? Is the "hand of God" the only plausible explanation for the appearance of design in our world? The answer to that question is obviously "No." Geological science provides a very lucid description of the creation of the Grand Canyon through millions of years of the erosive effects of the Colorado River after the initial movements of the tectonic plates beneath the earth's crust. Because such an account has been roughly confirmed by scientific predictions and data, it is generally believed by scientists and intelligent laypersons to be the best, most accurate account of this creation. So it is not only not irrational, but in some sense "most rational" to believe that the Grand Canyon was not made by a single act of God in, say, one second.

It is also true that if Earth was like a big watch created by God, it should have been created in a fixed period of time. According to the stories in Genesis, Yahweh took six days to create the Earth and rested on the seventh. In the next books of the Bible, there follows a series of "begats" ("And Serug lived after he begat Nahor two hundred years, and begat . . ."). An eighteenth-century archbishop, James Usher, calculated that, according to these "begats," the earth was created in 4004 BC. If Usher's claim were correct, the geological account would be false.

On the other hand, all our evidence is that the universe took billions of years to evolve to the point where the Earth was created. According to the best estimate from astrophysics and astronomy, the known universe was created about 15 billion years ago in the "big bang," and the planet Earth about 5 billion years ago.

Moreover, evolution explains how humans evolved from primates through billions upon billions of acts of propagation, struggles for survival, mutations, and adaptations. Geology, chemistry, and physics explain much else about how the world was originally created and evolved. And although it takes a rational mind to discover and understand these processes, the processes themselves do not appear to be like the watches Paley describes, that is, artifacts of a purposeful mind who left behind his imprint for humans to discover. Instead, what appears to us as "design" is the result of billions upon billions of lives gradually adapting so that a species may survive in a hostile environment. There is a classic mistake here of getting cause and effect backwards: it is not that God created rivers, plants, and balanced ecosystems so that humans could thrive, but rather, it is only when rivers, plants, and balanced ecosystems emerged in evolution that human beings could survive and increase their numbers.

Take woodpeckers again. In evolution, there were undoubtedly other kinds of birds that did have fluid inside their skulls, and these birds after a while developed head trauma from their hammering. When a mutation occurred that allowed a new kind of bird to hammer without head trauma, it had a competitive advantage. It is the ancestor of our modern woodpecker because it lived longer, got food more easily without harming itself, and bred more progeny, who inherited its new trait.

In the eighteenth century, the skeptic David Hume evaluated the Argument from Design and especially criticized the weakness of the analogical reasoning it employs. Hume asks us to consider our own experience of making things. For example, many humans worked together to build cathedrals or skyscrapers, so why not postulate many gods working together to make a universe? That certainly would be a better analogy than one single designer for anything or everything.

Moreover, when a piece of work has imperfections, we impute those imperfections to the lack of skill of the maker. So if an oak cabinet is delivered and its drawers don't close evenly, we blame the manufacturer. Given the many evils, irrationalities, and misfortunes of humanity and Earth, would not correct analogical reasoning impute only a semi-divine intelligence to the creator of the universe?

Hume also noted that the debate about the Argument from Design is typically couched fallaciously in either–or terms: either the universe was created by the theistic God or it is just random motion. Hume took care to emphasize that if we correctly reason from what we know, there are many, many inferences we can draw between these extremes.

To summarize our discussion of the two premises of the Argument from Design: what appears to be the design or handiwork of a conscious mind is likely something else, so premise 1 loses support. Furthermore, even if we granted that the world exhibits some modest kind of design, there are other explanations possible than that the world was created by God (so premise 2 loses support).

Finally, to repeat a criticism of previous arguments, some forms of the Design Argument are invalid because they move in the premises from a vague, deistic "force" that created the universe to a conclusion about the traditional God of theistic Western religions. So the Argument from Design has serious problems both with its premises and about how "rich" a depiction of a deity it is capable of proving.

A Note on Kant. The German philosopher of the Enlightenment, Immanuel Kant, would later argue that no arguments of this kind can work because the reasoning commits a kind of category error in reasoning from what we know in experience to that which is, by definition, beyond our experience. According to Kant, we have knowledge of causes in this world, but we have no knowledge of what causes a world to exist. Goldfish in an aquarium might "reason" from their experience to conclusions about what caused them to exist, but they would certainly not have the intellectual tools to come to the correct conclusions.

Many of Thomas's special arguments for God's existence fail Kant's test. Aquinas attempts to reason from premises in human experience to things quite beyond, not only human experience, but also beyond any experience (the nature of the creation of the world). If Kant is right, these arguments of Thomas's are fundamentally misconceived.

4   The Problem of Evil

If God is good, omnipotent, and omniscient, why does he allow evil to exist? The famous Problem of Evil is not directly an objection to the existence of God, but rather to the existence of the traditional God of theism (or more precisely, to the way his nature is typically conceived). More specifically, it challenges whether the typical qualities attributed to God are consistent. Thomas answers by saying that "part of His infinite goodness, [is] that He should allow evil to exist, and out of it produce good."

Is this a solution? Let us define a real evil as a very bad thing that lacks a compensating good in the world. On this definition, it is difficult to understand why God allows real evil, if he really cares for us. After all, because he is omnipotent, he certainly has the power to prevent it.

Consider evils such as lethal, congenital defects in babies. One such defect that occurs is the genetic disease Lesch–Nyhan syndrome. This is a rare disorder characterized by severe physical and mental retardation, compulsive biting (of fingers, flesh, and lips), spastic cerebral palsy, and lack of good kidneys for cleaning the blood. Such babies are often born with small teeth, and to prevent their literally eating their own flesh, their arms and heads are tied to wooden splints (hence their slang name, "Jesus babies"). These babies always die, and they die in very painful, awful ways. As their neurological system progressively deteriorates, they writhe and scream as they die over many months.

The existence of such babies is a paradigm of real evil. Why does an all-powerful, good God create such babies? What could possibly justify creating such babies to live only a life of pain before an early death? Is this an example of God's love for humans?

Theodicy ("God's justice") is the field which discusses this problem, after the name of a book by the seventeenth-century philosopher Gottfried Leibniz. One way to understand theodicy is to posit that any solution to the problem of evil must weaken one of these four claims:

1 Real evil exists (the reality-of-evil premise)
2 God is omnipotent (the omnipotence premise)
3 God is benevolent toward humanity (the benevolence premise)
4 God is omniscient (the omniscience premise)

Not all of the above four propositions can be strongly or completely true at the same time. For the four to be compatible, one must be weakened or made "less true" by some modification, as we shall see.

We have already discussed the meaning of God's omnipotence, omniscience, and benevolence, but what does the first premise mean? "Real evil" means a terrible harm to innocent humans, for which there is no compensation by some greater good. The punishment of criminals is not a "real evil" in this sense because criminals are not innocent. The fact that humans sometimes get sick is not necessarily an evil in this sense if sickness in the world is necessary to create some greater good, for example, man's achieving humility or understanding of his finite place in the universe.

For Aquinas, God is essentially good, but there is nothing in the universe that is the opposite of God's goodness, that is, essentially evil. To assert so would be to be guilty of Manicheism or Zoroastrianism, both of which assert the existence of two, equally powerful gods in the universe, a Lord of Light and a Lord of Darkness. For Aquinas and others, these heresies incorrectly imply that God could not smite Satan at any time (because God's power is limited by Satan's equal power). So Aquinas preserves the omnipotence premise by sacrificing the reality-of-evil premise. In other words, he denies the existence of real evil.

Or at least, he does when he's not contradicting himself. For in some passages, Thomas acknowledges the reality of Satan and blames him for the real evils in the world. But that won't work. Why? Because the question always arises as to why God allows the Devil to exist. God can smite Satan instantly and at any time he chooses, so obviously, God has some reason for allowing Satan to continue to exist.

One way to lessen God's responsibility for evil would be to claim that he does not know about it, or that it came about in creation without his knowledge. If a child of two parents does something bad, even though the parents created the child and raised her, the parents may not be responsible for their child's actions if they do not know what she is doing. However, this won't work for God because traditional conceptions of God assume that he is omniscient (all-knowing). Every evil that occurs is known by God.

In his official position on the problem of evil, Thomas holds that evils are not real in the same way that good things are. For Aquinas, evil is like a wound in the body, showing the absence of health, not a thing in itself of substance. Moreover, when we look at the big picture, we must accept that each apparent evil has compensation elsewhere in some greater good. It is just that humans, with their limited understanding, cannot see as far as God and grasp the other good. So ultimately, Aquinas weakens premise 1.

What about this? Is it acceptable? While it may comfort humans to think that a greater good may accompany a present evil, it does not seem to solve the problem. Why? Because God is assumed to be omnipotent, and surely an all-powerful God could have created a world without wars, ignorance, disease, and poverty. In other words, a truly great God could have created a universe where any human could easily understand how each apparent evil had compensation elsewhere in some greater good.

Is it possible that God has already done so? It depends on what is the greatest good for man. The previous discussion, and also the discussion about the Argument from Design, may have committed the meliorist fallacy. Meliorism is the belief that society has an innate tendency to get better, and the "meliorist fallacy" in theodicy is the assumption that the goal of an omnipotent God in creating our world was to make us as happy as possible.

Superficially, and thinking outside a religious tradition, that assumption seems plausible, but within a religious tradition such as Judaism, Islam, or Christianity, it can be challenged. True, God cares about man and is truly benevolent, but should his benevolence take the form of eliminating pain from this earth, doing away with Satan to remove temptations, and allowing each of us to live in a Garden of Eden? This assumes that the meaning of life for each human is to be as happy as possible on earth. To make this assumption is to commit the meliorist fallacy.

Why is that? Because the faith traditions of the West teach that the meaning of life for humans is not to be as happy as possible on earth. Indeed, the meaning of life is not found in this life at all. If one pays careful attention to the original words of Jesus, there is a very clear message that nothing in this world matters at all. The only thing that matters is gaining admission to the coming Kingdom of God.

In other words, let us assume – as many Western religions assert at their core – that the ultimate good for humans is personal salvation. If we grant this premise, then some of the urgency dissipates about the problem of evil (and maybe, too, some of the criticisms of the Argument from Design, because now we can allow that the earth was indeed designed, but not in a way to make us happy).

The previous discussion implicitly assumed that God's benevolence to humans would have egalitarian results, such that all could be saved, but there is much evidence to the contrary in Scripture. True, God could give everyone an equal opportunity to be saved, but true salvation may be only for the elite. And how are the elite to be determined? Only by the most rigorous tests, for the value is great (eternal salvation) and the cost of defeat is high (to be cast out forever into the outer darkness).

There is a story of a man during the fourth century who openly expressed to the Roman ruler his admiration of the Christians for their courage as they were tortured to death before him in the Colosseum. When the ruler said to him, "Fortunately, you're not one of them," he was forced to reply, "Alas, lord, I am a Christian, too." In the face of such a severe test and in such a cruel, arbitrary world, this Christian saint revealed his belief, knowing it meant his almost instant death. (He was put to death in the Colosseum a few days later.)

Irenaeus, the second-century Christian theologian and martyr, also argued that the world is as horrible as it is to test people and to allow the character of the human race to improve (or worsen) over time. Implicitly, his argument was this: only in the face of great evil can great character show itself. Without evil people, there can be no saints.

A Jew who kept his faith in the concentration camp was like the patriarch Abraham, a true "knight of faith." As the modern theologian Elie Wiesel says, the death of six million Jews in the Nazi death camps makes it difficult to believe in a God who cared about those in the camps.

Here the skeptic will demand: is it necessary to have a Hitler and the death of six million Jews in the Final Solution to have a world where believers are tested? Wouldn't a less cruel world be sufficient?

Perhaps, but it is at least possible that our present world is necessary to really test people and that, given such tests, very few people succeed in achieving salvation. Besides, what exactly is the objection here? That there is any test at all? That there is a very tough test, such that only the elite get saved? If so, these objections may reflect more our wishes than any belief about God's indifference.

Irenaeus' argument is ingenious, and it is instructive to consider which premise he weakens. Does he weaken the premise that God is good and cares about us? Perhaps not, for if we assume that a world of evil is the best way to test for who deserves to be saved, then God does care for us in creating such a world. Although the evil appears to be real (the Lesch–Nyhan baby is certainly real), it is not, for it has compensation as a test of salvation for humans, and hence, a world where some humans can reach eternal life. (The parent who makes the saintly choice to care for such a baby is saved.)

On the other hand, one could argue that God does not care for us: why would he create such a cruel world, such stiff tests? Why not make easier tests, with clear questions and immediate feedback? Why not a test where most humans would succeed? These questions assume some form of meliorism and some form of divine, egalitarian benevolence – assumptions Irenaeus would have rejected.

Irenaeus' hypothesis that the character of humanity itself can regress or improve over the millennia also raises a troubling question: suppose that the true test of faith is very strict, for example, when knights of faith had to die for their belief. Over the centuries, suppose that humanity's character has weakened and that we have watered down the tests of faith (such that one can attend a rich church with sports and daycare facilities, belong to a segregated country club, and delude oneself into believing that one is a modern "knight of faith"). Then it would follow that hardly anyone in this generation, perhaps no one at all, will be saved. This line of thought keeps the reality-of-evil premise but severely strains the benevolence premise. Nevertheless, there could be a reply: long ago, God gave to humanity an absolute, definitive standard of how to achieve salvation. Now God created humans and gave them this opportunity for eternal life: what could be more caring? He also gave us free will, not only over their own choices, but over the religious education of our children. If generations of humans have turned away from God and his standard, it is not God's fault, nor does it show that God does not care about his creations.

To summarize our discussion, the problem of evil cannot be easily solved. God cannot be simultaneously and fully both good and omnipotent while real evil exists. However, seen from within faith traditions, the "problem" of evil may not seem as much of a problem as it does to those outside those traditions.

5 Faith and Reason

Not all things about God can be proven. Like Augustine and Hume, Thomas does not think human reason can know everything (Augustine and Hume, however, believe human reason is much more limited than Aquinas does). As mentioned, reason for Thomas cannot prove whether the world had a beginning or is eternal.

Thomas also concluded that one of the most controversial Christian claims cannot be proved by reason, the Doctrine of the Trinity, the belief that God, Jesus, and the Holy Spirit are "three substances in one." For things such as these that are beyond the limits of reason, we must accept other sources such as Scripture or the authority of the Church.

Thomas taught that faith falls midway on a continuum between reason (rational knowledge) and mere opinion. Faith involves more than mere opinion because it involves the intellectual and emotional assent of the person who believes. Faith differs from rational knowledge because the latter is true regardless of one's will, whereas the former requires an act of will to reach the conclusion. Faith, moreover, requires a disposition to believe, a gift that comes from God and in Christianity that is part of what is known as Grace.

It will be instructive here to go forward in time for a contrast. Consider the views on faith and reason of the Danish existentialist philosopher and theologian, Søren Kierkegaard (1813–55), who emphasized that the heart of Christian belief rests on faith and not reason or scientific evidence. Without the mystery of faith, Kierkegaard passionately argued, theism and Christianity would be like scientific facts – facts that are too easy to believe in. For Kierkegaard, a God that could be quickly proved to exist by some simple syllogism would allow intellectual cowards to accept God's existence and not require (in Kierkegaard's famous words) "a leap of faith."

Indeed, for Kierkegaard, modern humans come to a crossroads when thinking about God: if they go down the path of reason and scientific evidence, they may never believe in God or gain access to the subtle mysteries of faith: the more hard-headed, logical, and empirical they become, the less open they will be to the Great Truths. On the other hand, if they "leap" down the path of faith, they may believe in things they cannot justify to those on the other path.

Kierkegaard's modern views have been sketched to show how far he has traveled away from Aquinas. For where Aquinas believed that some beliefs must be taken on faith, he certainly did not think that all the essential beliefs of Christianity must be so accepted, whereas Kierkegaard is dangerously close to the second position. Aquinas believed that there was much work for reason to do in thinking about God, whereas Kierkegaard and his modern followers imply that reason and scientific evidence have very little to do with thinking about God.

Many Christians today assert a strong faith for their belief in God. If they follow Kierkegaard, however, they have forsaken the ancient ideal that belief in God is proven by empirical facts and logic. By divorcing faith from reason and evidence, faith is unanchored in a world of many possible religious beliefs and it may land up in esoteric places – at least, so Aquinas would have thought.

6   Onus of Proof

In debates between believers and skeptics, questions sometimes arise about onus of proof (also called "burden of proof"). This topic concerns who has the duty of proving his position to the other side. After all, it is always easier to criticize than to prove. This point may be what is behind the taunt sometimes heard in debates about God: "Even if I can't prove that God exists, you can't prove that he doesn't." What the previous discussion has shown is that the believer cannot rationally compel the skeptic to believe in God and cannot accuse the skeptic of being irrational for rejecting God's existence. If the believer admits that he only believes as an act of faith, can the skeptic now turn the tables and accuse the believer of being irrational?

First, note that it is not necessary for the skeptic to prove that God does not exist. It is always impossible to prove a negative, especially a negative referring to non-existence. (That skeptic also can't prove that fairies and gremlins don't exist.)

Second, whether the skeptic can charge the believer with irrationality depends on what is meant by "irrational." If "irrational" means that it is contradictory to believe in God, or if it implies believing in something scientifically proven to be false, then the skeptic cannot make his charges stick.

On the other hand, if "irrational" means giving up the normal and best standards of human evaluation, then the skeptic may triumph. The tool of reason and the powers of science are the best standards humans have: when your car doesn't start or your child runs a 104-degree fever, you may try to return things to normal by faith in prayer, but you will be wise to use standards of physics and medical science to solve your problems.

In conclusion, tools of reasoning from logic and science reveal that all arguments for the existence of God fall very short of giving humans the traditional God of theism. This essay has attempted to show how a few elementary kinds of concep-tual analysis (a form of reasoning) can be used to understand the flaws and limita-tions in most attempts to prove the existence of God. Thomas Aquinas was a great thinker who thought deeply about God and who championed many ways to use reason to prove the existence of God. Even Thomas in his time saw that reason had its limits and that the believer must accept some beliefs on faith. What Thomas did not understand is that such an acceptance on faith could be attacked by using standards of reason and evidence, such that eventually, reason and faith would cease to be natural allies in thinking about the existence of God.

References

Ross, James W. 1961. "Analogy as a Rule of Meaning for Religious Language," *Inter-national Philosophical Quarterly* 1.

Suggestions for further reading

Father Frederick C. Copleston's *Aquinas* (Baltimore, MD: Penguin, 1955) defends Aquinas against some of the sharper criticisms of secular, analytic philosophers. Copleston's volume on Aquinas in his multi-volume *History of Philosophy* (New York: Image Books, 1985) discusses Aquinas's place in the history of philosophy and the thought of Thomas in relation to the ancient philosophers and later medieval philosophers. English philosopher Anthony Kenny has done much to bridge the gap between Aquinas and modern philosophers, and almost any of his general books on Aquinas is a good place for a student to begin. For a general overview of the ideas of Aquinas, see Kenny's *Aquinas* (New York: Hill and Wang,

1980). See also his *Aquinas: A Collection of Critical Essays* (New York: Doubleday-Anchor, 1969), especially these sections: logic/metaphysics, theology, philosophy of mind, and moral theology. More recently, and on a specialized topic, see also his *Aquinas on Mind* (New York: Routledge, 1993). Medieval scholars Norman Kretzmann and Eleonore Stump have also helped to revive interest in Thomas, and their *Cambridge Companion to Aquinas* (New York: Cambridge University Press, 1993) is a good place for both students and scholars to find introductory essays on the most important ideas of Thomas. The essays are conveniently written under general headings, such as "ethics," "philosophy of mind," and "biblical commentary and philosophy."

The topic of the rationality of belief in God is one addressed by both ancient, medieval, and modern philosophers. Anthony Kenny's *The God of the Philosophers* (New York: Oxford University Press, 1979) discusses reasonableness of belief in the omniscience and omnipotence of God, and in reference to human free will. He ends by discussing "the God of Reason and the God of Faith." On the Ontological Argument for the existence of God, see Alvin Plantinga, *The Ontological Argument: From St. Anselm to Contemporary Philosophers* (New York: Anchor Books, 1965). Peter Angeles' (ed.) *Critiques of God* (Buffalo, NY: Prometheus, 1976) is a collection of essays critical of belief in God or the usual concepts of God. It includes essays by John Dewey, Bertrand Russell, Sigmund Freud, and Kai Nielsen's "Ethics Without God." The latter article was excerpted from Nielsen's *Ethics Without God* (Buffalo, NY: Prometheus, 1973).

Science is usually thought to undermine belief in God. One distinguished modern philosopher of religion, Richard Swinburne, argues just the opposite in *Is There a God?* (New York: Oxford University Press, 1996). Swinburne argues that modern science provides good evidence for belief in God. Ed L. Miller's *God and Reason: An Invitation to Philosophical Theology* (Englewood Cliffs, NJ: Prentice-Hall, 1995) discusses traditional answers to the question, "Is Belief in God Rational?" Miller is sympathetic to Christian theism. John Mackie's *The Miracle of Theism* (New York: Oxford University Press, 1982) methodically attacks the reasonableness of belief in a theistic God. His chapter on the problem of evil is especially well developed. On the meaning of religious language, see James W. Ross, "Analogy as a Rule of Meaning for Religious Language," *International Philosophical Quarterly*, vol. 1, 1961, which is reprinted in Kenny's collection of essays on Aquinas referred to above.

Introduction to Selected Readings

The selected readings begin with a translation from Thomas Aquinas's famous "Five Ways" of proving the existence of God. The first three of these ways are versions of the Cosmological Argument (discussed by William Rowe: see below). Aquinas argues that: (1) there are things in the world that are changing, but there must be something that does not change; (2) there exist things that are caused by other things, but there must be something whose own existence is uncaused; (3) and there are things in the world that are contingent – that might not have existed – but not everything in the world can be contingent, so something must exist whose existence is not contingent. The short first selection is designed to give the student an impression of how Aquinas actually argued and from what perspective. The remaining essays discuss the more general theme of the rationality of belief in God.

The second selection is by the eighteenth-century writer William Paley. Paley was quite famous for his version of the argument from design, or "teleological argument," for the existence of God, and this argument is reprinted here. Paley argues by analogy that if one were to be walking on an island that appeared to be uninhabited, and one then found a well-made watch, one could rightly infer that some skilled watchmaker had made the particular watch. So humans "find" a world of complicated, interconnected parts, all of which together seem to have the purpose of allowing them to flourish. So, Paley argues, it can be concluded that a Divine "watchmaker" exists and made the world for humans.

The classical treatment of the design argument was by the eighteenth-century Scottish philosopher David Hume in his *Dialogues Concerning Natural Religion*. The third selection, by the late English philosopher John Mackie, begins by summarizing some of Hume's criticisms of this argument. Hume believed that the argument was essentially an argument from analogy, but where (1) the analogy between the things compared is very weak. Moreover, (2) there are alternative explanations for the apparent design of the world; (3) if Divine intelligence caused the world, that does not explain where Divine intelligence itself came from; and (4) if we infer like qualities from like effects, as we usually do in thinking about the world, then the mixture of good and evil effects in the world would lead us to infer that the originating deity is both good and evil. In his more impish moods, Hume has one of his characters speculate that, even assuming design is evident in our world, the best that could be inferred was that the world was created by a semi-intelligent vegetable, or perhaps an infant god on his first attempt at world-making.

The next selection on the Cosmological or First Cause Argument is by contemporary philosopher William L. Rowe, who teaches at Purdue University. Rowe puts the Cosmological Argument in the form of a possibly deductive argument, and then asks whether its premises are true and its form valid. He alerts us to the problem that, in several of its classical forms, the argument's validity may depend on a controversial, suppressed premise. Rowe also nicely illustrates how the classical discussion of this problem in the eighteenth century, by Leibniz and others, depended on the notion of the Principle of Sufficient Reason (PSR). He argues that PSR, when applied to classical versions of this argument, fails to explain at certain key junctures. The most crucial one involves the possibility of an infinite causal series stretching back endlessly into time. Rowe also summarizes an important line of criticism that is called the part/whole fallacy in critical reasoning. Basically, the fallacy is to believe that everything that is true of a part is true of the whole, and vice versa. Just because every event has a cause, or is dependent on something, does not mean that the entire series of causes has a cause or is dependent on something. Rowe ends by revealing a dilemma in one part of the argument. He thinks we are led to a choice between (1) the "brute fact" that every being in the universe is dependent and (2) accepting PSR. This is the basic, useful argumentive strategy in philosophy of setting up two choices, each of which leads to unsatisfactory outcomes. If the argument leads us to such a dilemma, there must be something wrong with the argument.

The next selection is by contemporary philosopher Robert Merrihew Adams of Yale University. Adams here reviews and explains the arguments of the mid-nineteenth-century Danish existentialist, Søren Kierkegaard. Kierkegaard thought we should be suspicious of rational, analytic attempts to prove the existence of God or to know his nature. Both Adams and Kierkegaard argue that some truths cannot be grasped unless the agent is motivated in the first place "to see" the light. Moreover, some such "seeing" may require a "leap of faith" analogous to jumping off a dark ledge and not knowing exactly where one will land. Not every step of a great journey can be seen at the start: some risk is involved in arriving at any worthy destination. So Adams and Kierkegaard attack the very way that most of the discussion of this chapter has taken place. This selection nicely illustrates how discussion of an issue in philosophy over time often evolves to a higher plane: from discussion of an issue to a "meta-discussion" about how the issue was formerly discussed.

The final selection, "Rebellion," from the great nineteenth-century Russian novelist Fyodor Dostoevsky, is from this author's famous *The Brothers Karamazov*. The selection is from two men discussing the evil events that occur in the world, especially the injustices of one person to another, and whether such evil is compatible with a God who is good and caring. In this powerful description of man's inhumanity to man, Dostoevsky argues that it is not.

Discussion questions

1 Explain Thomas Aquinas's idea of analogical predication and its use in describing the qualities of God.
2 What is the Ontological Argument and how can it be criticized?
3 What is the First Cause or Cosmological Argument? What are two ways in which it can be criticized?
4 Explain the different criticisms that can be made of each premise in the Argument from Design.
5 What is theodicy and the Problem of Evil? What is the Test-of-Faith Defense and how does it attempt to solve the Problem of Evil?
6 If everything about the existence of God must be accepted on faith rather than demonstrated by reason, what is given up in putting so much emphasis on faith?

Readings

Thomas Aquinas, "Five Ways to Prove the Existence of God"

First Article

Whether the existence of God is self-evident?

We proceed thus to the First Article: —

Objection 1. It seems that the existence of God is self-evident. For those things are said to be self-evident to us the knowledge of which exists naturally in us, as we can see in regard to first principles. But as Damascene says, "the knowledge of God is naturally implanted in all." Therefore the existence of God is self-evident.

From *The Basic Writings of St. Thomas Aquinas*, ed. Anton C. Pegis (New York and London: Random House and Burns & Oates Ltd, 1945).

Obj. 2. Further, those things are said to be self-evident which are known as soon as the terms are known, which the Philosopher [Aristotle] says is true of the first principles of demonstration. Thus, when the nature of a whole and of a part is known, it is at once recognized that every whole is greater than its part. But as soon as the signification of the name *God* is understood, it is at once seen that God exists. For by this name is signified that thing than which nothing greater can be conceived. But that which exists actually and mentally is greater than that which exists only mentally. Therefore, since as soon as the name *God* is understood it exists mentally, it also follows that it exists actually. Therefore the proposition *God exists* is self-evident.

Obj. 3. Further, the existence of truth is self-evident. For whoever denies the existence of truth grants that truth does not exist: and, if truth does not exist, then the proposition *Truth does not exist* is true: and if there is anything true, there must be truth. But God is truth itself: "I am the way, the truth, and the life" (John, 14:6). Therefore *God exists* is self-evident.

On the contrary, No one can mentally admit the opposite of what is self-evident, as the Philosopher states concerning the first principles of demonstration. But the opposite of the proposition *God is* can be mentally admitted: "The fool said in his heart, There is no God" (Ps. 52:1). Therefore, that God exists is not self-evident.

I answer that, A thing can be self-evident in either of two ways: on the one hand, self-evident in itself, though not to us; on the other, self-evident in itself, and to us. A proposition is self-evident because the predicate is included in the essence of the subject: e.g., *Man is an animal*, for animal is contained in the essence of man. If, therefore, the essence of the predicate and subject be known to all, the proposition will be self-evident to all; as is clear with regard to the first principles of demonstration, the terms of which are certain common notions that no one is ignorant of, such as being and non-being, whole and part, and the like. If, however, there are some to whom the essence of the predicate and subject is unknown, the proposition will be self-evident in itself, but not to those who do not know the meaning of the predicate and subject of the proposition. Therefore, it happens, as Boethius says, that there are some notions of the mind which are common and self-evident only to the learned, as that incorporeal substances are not in space. Therefore I say that this proposition, *God exists*, of itself is self-evident, for the predicate is the same as the subject, because God is His own existence as will be hereafter shown. Now because we do not know the essence of God, the proposition is not self-evident to us, but needs to be demonstrated by things that are more known to us, though less known in their nature – namely, by His effects.

Reply Obj. 1. To know that God exists in a general and confused way is implanted in us by nature, inasmuch as God is man's beatitude. For man naturally desires happiness, and what is naturally desired by man is naturally known by him. This, however, is not to know absolutely that God exists; just as to know that someone is approaching is not the same as to know that Peter is approaching, even though it is Peter who is approaching; for there are many who imagine that man's perfect good, which is happiness, consists in riches, and others in pleasures, and others in something else.

Reply Obj. 2. Perhaps not everyone who hears this name *God* understands it to signify something than which nothing greater can be thought, seeing that some have believed God to be a body. Yet, granted that everyone understands that by this name *God* is signified something than which nothing greater can be thought, nevertheless, it does not therefore follow that he understands that what the name signifies exists actually, but only that it exists mentally. Nor can it be argued that it actually exists, unless it be admitted that there actually exists something than which nothing greater can be thought; and this precisely is not admitted by those who hold that God does not exist.

Reply Obj. 3. The existence of truth in general is self-evident, but the existence of a Primal Truth is not self-evident to us.

Second Article

Whether it can be demonstrated that God exists?

We proceed thus to the Second Article: –

Objection 1. It seems that the existence of God cannot be demonstrated. For it is an article of faith that God exists. But what is of faith cannot be demonstrated, because a demonstration produces scientific knowledge, whereas faith is of the unseen, as is clear from the Apostle (Heb. 11:1). Therefore it cannot be demonstrated that God exists.

Obj. 2. Further, essence is the middle term of demonstration. But we cannot know in what God's essence consists, but solely in what it does not consist, as Damascene says. Therefore we cannot demonstrate that God exists.

Obj. 3. Further, if the existence of God were demonstrated, this could only be from His effects. But His effects are not proportioned to Him, since He is infinite and His effects are finite, and between the finite and infinite there is no proportion. Therefore, since a cause cannot be demonstrated by an effect not proportioned to it, it seems that the existence of God cannot be demonstrated.

On the contrary, The Apostle says: "The invisible things of Him are clearly seen, being understood by the things that are made" (Rom. 1:20). But this would not be unless the existence of God could be demonstrated through the things that are made; for the first thing we must know of anything is whether it exists.

I answer that, Demonstration can be made in two ways: One is through the cause, and is called *propter quid*, and this is to argue from what is prior absolutely. The other is through the effect, and is called a demonstration *quia*; this is to argue from what is prior relatively only to us. When an effect is better known to us than its cause, from the effect we proceed to the knowledge of the cause. And from every effect the existence of its proper cause can be demonstrated, so long as its effects are better known to us; because, since every effect depends upon its cause, if the effect exists, the cause must preexist. Hence the existence of God, insofar as it is not self-evident to us, can be demonstrated from those of His effects which are known to us.

Reply Obj. 1. The existence of God and other like truths about God, which can be known by natural reason, are not articles of faith, but are preambles to the articles; for faith presupposes natural knowledge, even as grace presupposes nature and perfection the perfectible. Nevertheless, there is nothing to prevent a man, who cannot grasp a proof, from accepting, as a matter of faith, something which in itself is capable of being scientifically known and demonstrated.

Reply Obj. 2. When the existence of a cause is demonstrated from an effect, this effect takes the place of the definition of the cause in proving the cause's existence. This is especially the case in regard to God, because, in order to prove the existence of anything, it is necessary to accept as a middle term the meaning of the name, and not its essence, for the question of its essence follows on the question of its existence. Now the names given to God are derived from His effects, as will be later shown. Consequently, in demonstrating the existence of God from His effects, we may take for the middle term the meaning of the name *God*.

Reply Obj. 3. From effects not proportioned to the cause no perfect knowledge of that cause can be obtained. Yet from every effect the existence of the cause can be clearly demonstrated, and so we can demonstrate the existence of God from His effects; though from them we cannot know God perfectly as He is in His essence.

Third Article

Whether God exists?

We proceed thus to the Third Article: –

Objection 1. It seems that God does not exist; because if one of two contraries be infinite, the other would be altogether destroyed. But the name *God* means that He is infinite goodness. If, therefore, God existed, there would be no evil discoverable; but there is evil in the world. Therefore God does not exist.

Obj. 2. Further, it is superfluous to suppose that what can be accounted for by a few principles has been produced by many. But it seems that everything we see in the world can be accounted for by other principles, supposing God did not exist. For all natural things can be reduced to one principle, which is nature; and all voluntary things can be reduced to one principle, which is human reason, or will. Therefore there is no need to suppose God's existence.

On the contrary, It is said in the person of God: "I am Who am" (Exod. 3:14).

I answer that, The existence of God can be proved in five ways.

The first and more manifest way is the argument from motion. It is certain, and evident to our senses, that in the world some things are in motion. Now whatever is moved is moved by another, for nothing can be moved except it is in potentiality to that towards which it is moved; whereas a thing moves inasmuch as it is in act. For motion is nothing else than the reduction of something from potentiality to actuality. But nothing can be reduced from potentiality to actuality, except by something in a state of actuality. Thus that which is actually hot, as fire, makes wood, which is potentially hot, to be actually hot, and thereby moves and changes it. Now it is not possible that the same thing should be at once in actuality and potentiality in the same respect, but only in different respects. For what is actually hot cannot simultaneously be potentially hot; but it is simultaneously potentially cold. It is therefore impossible that in the same respect and in the same way a thing should be both mover and moved, i.e., that it should move itself. Therefore, whatever is moved must be moved by another. If that by which it is moved be itself moved, then this also must needs be moved by another, and that by another again. But this cannot go on to infinity, because then there would be no first mover, and, consequently, no other mover, seeing that subsequent movers move only inasmuch as they are moved by the first mover; as the staff moves only because it is moved by the hand. Therefore it is necessary to arrive at a first mover, moved by no other; and this everyone understands to be God.

The second way is from the nature of efficient cause. In the world of sensible things we find there is an order of efficient causes. There is no case known (neither is it, indeed, possible) in which a thing is found to be the efficient cause of itself; for so it would be prior to itself, which is impossible. Now in efficient causes it is not possible to go on to infinity, because in all efficient causes following in order, the first is the cause of the intermediate cause, and the intermediate is the cause of the ultimate cause, whether the intermediate cause be several, or one only. Now to take away the cause is to take away the effect. Therefore, if there be no first cause among efficient causes, there will be no ultimate, nor any intermediate, cause. But if in efficient causes it is possible to go on to infinity, there will be no first efficient cause, neither will there be an ultimate effect, nor any intermediate efficient causes; all of which is plainly false. Therefore it is necessary to admit a first efficient cause, to which everyone gives the name of God.

The third way is taken from possibility and necessity, and runs thus. We find in nature things that are possible to be and not to be, since they are found to be generated, and to be corrupted, and consequently, it is possible for them to be and not to be. But it is impossible for these always to exist, for that which can not-be at some time is not. Therefore, if everything can not-be, then at one time there was nothing in existence. Now if this were true, even now there would be nothing in existence, because that which does not exist begins to exist only through something already existing. Therefore, if at one time nothing was in existence, it would have been impossible for anything to have begun to exist; and thus even now nothing would be in existence – which is absurd. Therefore, not all beings are merely possible, but there must exist something the existence of which is necessary. But every necessary thing either has its necessity caused by another, or not. Now it is impossible to go on to infinity in necessary things which have their necessity caused by another, as has been already proved in regard to efficient causes. Therefore we cannot but admit the existence of some being having of itself its own necessity, and not receiving it from another, but rather causing in others their necessity. This all men speak of as God.

The fourth way is taken from the gradation to be found in things. Among beings there are some more and some less good, true, noble, and the like. But *more* and *less* are predicated of different things according as they resemble in their different ways something which is the maximum, as a thing is said to be hotter according as it more nearly resembles that which is hottest; so that there is something which is truest, something best, something noblest, and, consequently, something which is most being, for those things that are greatest in truth are greatest in being, as it is written in *Metaphysics* II. Now the maximum in any genus is the cause of all in that genus, as fire, which is the maximum of heat, is the cause of all hot things, as is said in the same book. Therefore there must also be something which is to all beings the cause of their being, goodness, and every other perfection; and this we call God.

The fifth way is taken from the governance of the world. We see that things which lack knowledge, such as natural bodies, act for an end, and this is evident from their acting always, or nearly always, in the same way, so as to obtain the best result. Hence it is plain that they achieve their end, not fortuitously, but designedly. Now whatever lacks knowledge cannot move towards an end, unless it be directed by some being endowed with knowledge and intelligence; as the arrow is directed by the archer. Therefore some intelligent being exists by whom all natural things are directed to their end; and this being we call God.

Reply Obj. 1. As Augustine says: "Since God is the highest good, He would not allow any evil to exist in His works, unless His omnipotence and goodness were such as to bring good even out of evil" (*Enchiridion*, XI). This is part of the infinite goodness of God, that He should allow evil to exist, and out of it produce good.

Reply Obj. 2. Since nature works for a determinate end under the direction of a higher agent, whatever is done by nature must be traced back to God as to its first cause. So likewise whatever is done voluntarily must be traced back to some higher cause other than human reason and will, since these can change and fail; for all things that are changeable and capable of defect must be traced back to an immovable and self-necessary first principle, as has been shown.

William Paley, "The Evidence of Design"

In crossing a heath, suppose I pitched my foot against a *stone*, and were asked how the stone came to be there, I might possibly answer, that, for any thing I knew to the contrary, it had lain there for ever: nor would it perhaps be very easy to show the absurdity of this answer. But suppose I had found a *watch* upon the ground, and it should be enquired how the watch happened to be in that place, I should hardly think of the answer which I had before given, that, for any thing I knew, the watch might have always been there. Yet why should not this answer serve for the watch as well as for the stone? Why is it not as admissible in the second case, as

From his *Natural Theology*, 9th edn (London, 1805).

in the first? For this reason, and for no other, viz. that, when we come to inspect the watch, we perceive (what we could not discover in the stone) that its several parts are framed and put together for a purpose, e.g. that they are so formed and adjusted as to produce motion, and that motion so regulated as to point out the hour of the day; that, if the several parts had been differently shaped from what they are, of a different size from what they are, or placed after any other manner, or in any other order, than that in which they are placed, either no motion at all would have been carried on in the machine, or none which would have answered the use that is now served by it. To reckon up a few of the plainest of these parts, and of their offices, all tending to one result: – We see a cyclindrical box containing a coiled, elastic spring, which, by its endeavour to relax itself, turns round the box. We next observe a flexible chain (artificially wrought for the sake of flexure) communicating the action of the spring from the box to the fusee. We then find a series of wheels, the teeth of which catch in, and apply to, each other, conducting the motion from the fusee to the balance, and from the balance to the pointer; and at the same time, by the size and shape of those wheels, so regulating that motion, as to terminate in causing an index, by an equable and measured progression, to pass over a given space in a given time. We take notice that the wheels are made of brass, in order to keep them from rust; the springs of steel, no other metal being so elastic; that over the face of the watch there is placed a glass, a material employed in no other part of the work, but in the room of which, if there had been any other than a transparent substance, the hour could not be seen without opening the case. This mechanism being observed (it requires indeed an examination of the instrument, and perhaps some previous knowledge of the subject, to perceive and understand it; but being once, as we have said, observed and understood), the inference, we think, is inevitable, that the watch must have had a maker: that there must have existed, at some time and at some place or other, an artificer or artificers who formed it for the purpose which we find it actually to answer; who comprehended its construction, and designed its use.

I

Nor would it, I apprehend, weaken the conclusion, that we had never seen a watch made; that we had never known an artist capable of making one; that we were altogether incapable of executing such a piece of workmanship ourselves, or of understanding in what manner it was performed; all this being no more than what is true of some exquisite remains of ancient art, of some lost arts, and, to the generality of mankind, of the more curious productions of modern manufacture. Does one man in a million know how oval frames are turned? Ignorance of this kind exalts our opinion of the unseen and unknown, artist's skill, if he be unseen and unknown, but raises no doubt in our minds of the existence and agency of such an artist, at some former time, and in some place or other. Nor can I perceive that it varies at all the inference, whether the question arise concerning a human agent, or concerning an agent of a different species, or an agent possessing, in some respects, a different nature.

II

Neither, secondly, would it invalidate our conclusion, that the watch sometimes went wrong, or that it seldom went exactly right. The purpose of the machinery, the design, and the designer, might be evident, and in the case supposed would be evident, in whatever way we accounted for the irregularity of the movement, or whether we could account for it or not. It is not necessary that a machine be perfect, in order to show with what design it was made: still less necessary, where the only question is, whether it were made with any design at all.

III

Nor, thirdly, would it bring any uncertainty into the argument, if there were a few parts of the watch, concerning which we could not discover, or had not yet discovered, in what manner they conduced to the general effect; or even some parts, concerning which we could not ascertain, whether they conduced to that effect in any manner whatever. For, as to the first branch of the case; if, by the loss, or disorder, or decay of the parts in question, the movement of the watch were found in fact to be stopped, or disturbed, or retarded, no doubt would remain in our minds as to the utility or intention of these parts, although we should be unable to investigate the manner according to which, or the connection by which, the ultimate effect depended upon their action, or assistance; and the more complex is the machine, the more likely is this obscurity to arise. Then, as to the second thing supposed, namely, that there were parts which might be spared, without prejudice to the movement of the watch, and that we had proved this by experiment, – these superfluous parts, even if we were completely assured that they were such, would not vacate the reasoning which we had instituted concerning other parts. The indication of contrivance remained, with respect to them, nearly as it was before.

IV

Nor, fourthly, would any man in his senses think the existence of the watch, with its various machinery, accounted for, by being told that it was one out of possible combinations of material forms; that whatever he had found in the place where he found the watch, must have contained some internal configuration or other; and that this configuration might be the structure now exhibited, viz. of the works of a watch, as well as a different structure.

V

Nor, fifthly, would it yield his enquiry more satisfaction to be answered, that there existed in things a principle of order, which had disposed the parts of the watch into their present from and situation. He never knew a watch made by the principle of order; nor can he even form to himself an idea of what is meant by a principle of order, distinct from the intelligence of the watch-maker.

VI

Sixthly, he would be surprised to hear, that the mechanism of the watch was no proof of contrivance, only a motive to induce the mind to think so.

VII

And not less surprised to be informed, that the watch in his hand was nothing more than the result of the laws of *metallic* nature. It is a perversion of language to assign any law, as the efficient, operative cause of any thing. A law presupposes an agent; for it is only the mode, according to which an agent proceeds: it implies a power; for it is the order, according to which that power acts. Without this agent, without this power, which are both distinct from itself, the *law* does nothing; is nothing. The expression, "the law of metallic nature," may sound strange and harsh to a philosophic ear, but it seems quite as justifiable as some others which are more familiar to him, such as "the law of vegetable nature" – "the law of animal nature," or indeed as "the law of nature" in general, when assigned as the cause of phenomena, in exclusion of agency and power; or when it is substituted into the place of these.

VIII

Neither, lastly, would our observer be driven out of his conclusion, or from his confidence in its truth, by being told that he knew nothing at all about the matter. He knows enough for his argument. He knows the utility of the end: he knows the subserviency and adaptation of the means to the end. These points being known, his ignorance of other points, his doubts concerning other points, affect not the certainty of his reasoning. The consciousness of knowing little, need not beget a distrust of that which he does know. . . .

Suppose, in the next place, that the person, who found the watch, should, after some time, discover, that, in addition to all the properties which he had hitherto observed in it, it possessed the unexpected property of producing, in the course of its movement, another watch like itself; (the thing is conceivable;) that it contained within it a mechanism, a system of parts, a mould for instance, or a complex adjustment of lathes, files, and other tools, evidently and separately calculated for this purpose; let us enquire, what effect ought such a discovery to have upon his former conclusion.

I

The first effect would be to increase his admiration of the contrivance, and his conviction of the consummate skill of the contriver. Whether he regarded the object of the contrivance, the distinct apparatus, the intricate, yet in many parts intelligible, mechanism, by which it was carried on, he would perceive, in his new observation, nothing but an additional reason for doing what he had already done; for referring the construction of the watch to design, and to supreme art. If that construction *without* this property, or, which is the same thing, before this property had been noticed, proved intention and art to have been employed about it; still more strong would the proof appear, when he came to the knowledge of this further property, the crown and perfection of all the rest.

II

He would reflect, that though the watch before him were, *in some sense*, the maker of the watch, which was fabricated in the course of its movements, yet it was in a very different sense from that, in which a carpenter, for instance, is the maker of a chair; the author of its contrivance, the cause of the relation of its parts to their use. With respect to these, the first watch was no cause at all to the second: in no such sense as this was it the author of the constitution and order, either of the parts which the new watch contained, or of the parts by the aid and instrumentality of which it was produced. We might possibly say, but with great latitude of expression, that a stream of water ground corn: but no latitude of expression would allow us to say, no stretch of conjecture could lead us to think, that the stream of water built the mill, though it were too ancient for us to know who the builder was. What the stream of water does in the affair is neither more nor less than this: by the application of an unintelligent impulse to a mechanism previously arranged, arranged independently of it, and arranged by intelligence, an effect is produced, viz. the corn is ground. But the effect results from the arrangement. The force of the stream cannot be said to be the cause or author of the effect, still less of the arrangement. Understanding and plan in the formation of the mill were not the less necessary, for any share which the water has in grinding the corn: yet is this share the same, as that which the watch would have contributed to the production of the new watch, upon the supposition assumed in the last section. [. . .]

III

Though it be now no longer probable, that the individual watch which our observer had found, was made immediately by the hand of an artificer, yet doth not this alteration in any wise affect the inference, that an artificer had been originally employed and concerned in the production. The argument from design remains as it was. Marks of design and contrivance are no more accounted for now, than they were before. In the same thing, we may ask for the cause of different properties. We may ask for the cause of the colour of a body, of its hardness, of its heat; and these causes may be all different. We are now asking for the cause of that subserviency to an use, that relation to an end, which we have remarked in the watch before us. No answer is given to this question by telling us that a preceding watch produced it. There cannot be design without a designer; contrivance without a contriver; order without choice; arrangement, without any thing capable of arranging; subserviency and relation to a purpose, without that which could intend a purpose; means suitable to an end, and executing their office in accomplishing that end, without the end ever having been contemplated, or the means accommodated to it. Arrangement, disposition of parts, subserviency of means to an end, relation of instruments to an use, imply the presence of intelligence and mind. No one, therefore, can rationally believe, that the insensible, inanimate watch, from which the watch before us issued, was the proper cause of the mechanism we so much admire in it; could be truly said to have constructed the instrument, disposed its parts, assigned their office, determined their order, action, and mutual dependency, combined their several motions into one result, and that also a result connected with the utilities of other beings. All these properties, therefore, are as much unaccounted for, as they were before.

IV

Nor is any thing gained by running the difficulty further back, i.e. by supposing the watch before us to have been produced from another watch, that from a former, and so on indefinitely. Our going back ever so far brings us no nearer to the least degree of satisfaction upon the subject. Contrivance is still unaccounted for. We still want a contriver. A designing mind is neither supplied by this supposition, nor dispensed with. If the difficulty were diminished the further we went back, by going back indefinitely we might exhaust it. And this is the only case to which this sort of reasoning applies. Where there is a tendency, or, as we increase the number of terms, a continual approach towards a limit, *there*, by supposing the number of terms to be what is called infinite, we may conceive the limit to be attained: but where there is no such tendency, or approach, nothing is effected by lengthening the series. There is no difference as to the point in question, (whatever there may be as to many points), between one series and another; between a series which is finite, and a series which is infinite. A chain, composed of an infinite number of links, can no more support itself, than a chain composed of a finite number of links. And of this we are assured, (though we never *can* have tried the experiment), because, by increasing the number of links, from ten for instance to a hundred, from a hundred to a thousand, &c. we make not the smallest approach, we observe not the smallest tendency, towards self-support. There is no difference in this respect (yet there may be a great difference in several respects), between a chain of a greater or less length, between one chain and another, between one that is finite and one that is infinite. This very much resembles the case before us. The machine, which we are inspecting, demonstrates, by its construction, contrivance and design. Contrivance must have had a contriver, design, a designer; whether the machine immediately proceeded from another machine or not. The circumstance alters not the case. That other machine may, in like manner, have proceeded from a former machine: nor does that alter the case: contrivance must have had a contriver. That former one from one preceding it: no alteration still: a contriver is still necessary. No tendency is perceived, no approach towards a diminution of this necessity. It is the same with any and every succession of these machines; a succession of ten, of a hundred, of a thousand; with one series as with another: a series which is finite, as with a series which is infinite. In whatever other respects they may differ, in this they do not. In all equally, contrivance and design are unaccounted for.

The question is not simply, How came the first watch into existence? which question, it may be pretended, is done away by supposing the series of watches thus produced from one another to have been infinite, and consequently to have had no such *first*, for which it was necessary to provide a cause. This, perhaps, would have been nearly the state of the question, if nothing had been before us but an unorganized, unmechanized, substance, without mark or indication of contrivance. It might be difficult to show that such substance could not have existed from eternity, either in succession (if it were possible, which I think it is not, for unorganized bodies to spring from one another), or by individual perpetuity. But that is not the question now. To suppose it to be so, is to suppose that it made no difference whether we had found a watch or a stone. As it is, the metaphysics of that question have no place; for, in the watch which we are examining, are seen contrivance, design; an end, a purpose; means for the end, adaptation to the purpose. And the question, which irresistibly presses upon our thoughts, is, whence this contrivance and design. The thing required is the intending mind, the adapting hand, the intelligence by which that hand was directed. This question, this demand, is not shaken off, by increasing a number or succession of substances, destitute of these properties; nor the more, by increasing that number to infinity. If it be said, that, upon the supposition of one watch being produced from another in the course of that other's movements, and by means of the mechanism within it, we have a cause for the watch in my hand, viz. the watch from which it proceeded, I deny, that for the design, the contrivance, the suitableness of means to an end, the adaptation of instruments to a use (all which we discover in the watch), we have any cause whatever. It is in vain, therefore, to assign a series of such causes, or to allege that a series may be carried back to infinity; for I do not admit that we have yet any cause at all of the phenomena, still less any series of causes either finite or infinite. Here is contrivance, but no contriver; proofs of design, but no designer.

V

Our observer would further also reflect, that the maker of the watch before him, was, in truth and reality, the maker of every watch produced from it; there being no difference (except that the latter manifests a more exquisite skill) between the making of another watch with his own hands, by the mediation of files, lathes, chisels, &c. and the disposing, fixing, and inserting of these instruments, or of others equivalent to them, in the body of the watch already made, in such a manner, as to form a new watch in the course of the movements which he had given to the old one. It is only working by one set of tools, instead of another.

The conclusion which the *first* examination of the watch, of its works, construction, and movement, suggested, was, that it must have had, for the cause and author of that construction, an artificer, who understood its mechanism, and designed its use. This conclusion is invincible. A *second* examination presents us with a new discovery. The watch is found, in the course of its movement, to produce another watch, similar to itself: and not only so, but we perceive in it a system of organization, separately calculated for that purpose. What effect would this discovery have, or ought it to have, upon our former inference? What, as hath already been said, but to increase, beyond measure, our admiration of the skill, which had been employed in the formation of such a machine? Or shall it, instead of this, all at once turn us round to an opposite conclusion, viz. that no art or skill whatever has been concerned in the business, although all other evidences of art and skill remain as they were, and this last and supreme piece of art be now added to the rest? Can this be maintained without absurdity? Yet this is atheism.

This is atheism: for every indication of contrivance, every manifestation of design, which existed in the watch, exists in the works of nature; with the difference, on the side of nature, of being greater and more, and that in a degree which exceeds all computation. I mean that the contrivances of nature surpass the contrivances of art, in the complexity, subtlety, and curiosity of the mechanism; and still more, if possible, do they go beyond them in number and variety: yet, in a multitude of cases, are not less evidently mechanical, not less evidently contrivances, not less evidently accommodated to their end, or suited to their office, than are the most perfect productions of human ingenuity. . . .

John L. Mackie, "Arguments for Design"

(a)   Hume's Dialogues – Exposition

Perhaps the most popular way of arguing from the world to a god is what is commonly called "the argument from design". However, an argument *from* design to a designer would be trivial: it would not be proper to speak of design unless we were already assuming that there was a designer. The crucial steps are those that lead from certain evidence, from what have been called "marks of design", to the conclusion that something is indeed the product of design. So let us call it the argument to, or for, design.[1]

   This argument flourished particularly in the eighteenth century, when it seemed that (contrary to what Berkeley feared) the progress of natural science was merely revealing richer evidence of the creative activity of God. But the version then current was devastatingly criticized by Hume in his *Dialogues concerning Natural Religion* and (partly following Hume) by Kant. Even more damaging in practice, however, than these philosophical criticisms was the demonstration by Darwin and Wallace in the nineteenth century that one of the most impressive categories of apparent marks of design, the detailed structures of plant and animal bodies and their adaptation to conditions and a way of life, could be explained better by the theory of evolution through natural selection: for example, certain features of the actual geographical distribution of species that were left unexplained by a hypothesis of the special creation of each particular species were readily accounted for by

From *The Miracle of Theism* (Oxford: Oxford University Press, 1982).
   [1] Cf. A. Flew, *God and Philosophy* (Hutchinson, London, 1966), Chapter 3. Hume's *Dialogues Concerning Natural Religion* are edited by N. Kemp Smith (Nelson, Edinburgh, 1947) and by J. V. Price in *David Hume on Religion*, edited by A. W. Colver and J. V. Price (Oxford University Press, 1976). References in the text are to the numbered Parts.

a hypothesis of descent with modification. But, despite these setbacks, the argument for design has never died out, and it has been revived from time to time in new forms. [. . .]

The older form of the argument is well summed up in a speech that Hume puts into the mouth of Cleanthes.

> Look round the world: Contemplate the whole and every part of it: You will find it to be nothing but one great machine, subdivided into an infinite number of lesser machines . . . All these various machines, and even their most minute parts, are adjusted to one another with an accuracy, which ravishes into administration all men, who have ever contemplated them. The curious adapting of means to ends, throughout all nature, resembles exactly, though it much exceeds, the productions of human contrivance; of human design, thought, wisdom, and intelligence. Since therefore the effects resemble each other, we are led to infer, by all the rules of analogy, that the causes also resemble; and that the Author of nature is somewhat similar to the mind of man; though possessed of much larger faculties, proportional to the grandeur of the work, which he has executed. By this argument *a posteriori*, and by this argument alone, we do prove at once the existence of a Deity, and his similarity to human mind and intelligence. (Part II)

What count, then, as marks of design are those features in which natural objects resemble machines made by men: the fitting together of parts and what can be seen as the adaptation of means to ends. (To call it straight out "the adapting of means to ends", rather than just noting that it can be seen as such, would be to jump to the conclusion of the argument for design.) Three kinds of these features particularly impressed eighteenth-century thinkers: the world as a whole, especially the solar system as described by Newton's gravitational theory; the bodies of all sorts of plants and animals, especially certain organs like the eye; and the providential arrangement of things on the surface of the earth, enabling all the different plant and animal species to flourish, and especially the provision of things, including plants and the other animals, for the use of men. Hume's *Dialogues* stress examples of the first two kinds, but say little about the third.

The *Dialogues* are a masterpiece of philosophical literature. One of their most striking features is the way in which Hume plays off against one another his three main characters and, through them, the types of view that they represent. Cleanthes represents natural theology. Relying on the argument for design, he stresses its *a posteriori* and probabilistic character. Since he argues by analogy in a commonsense way, his conclusion is that there is a god who closely resembles human minds; and since he is inferring the attributes of this god from the world that he has designed, Cleanthes takes an optimistic view of the ordinary world in order to be able to infer the goodness of God from the goodness and happiness of his creation. Demea is an equally convinced theist, but he is a hardliner of a much grimmer sort. In so far as he engages in natural theology, he relies on *a priori* arguments, claiming that they give a certainty about God's existence that the design argument cannot give. But his real reliance is on faith: "It is my opinion . . . that each man feels, in a manner, the truth of religion within his own breast". This conviction arises from the miseries and terrors of life, from which we seek relief in religion. Consequently his view of the world is pessimistic in the extreme, but, as we might say, complacently pessimistic. Demea's god is not only infinite but also incomprehensible, and his attributes in no way resemble the human ones from which we borrow terms to describe him. In particular, though we call him good, this does not mean he will act in ways in which men must act to be called good. Philo, the sceptic, allies himself for a while with Demea against Cleanthes, supporting Demea's mysticism only to bring out, in the end, the scepticism latent within it. Similarly he joins with Demea in portraying the utter wretchedness of human (and animal) life in a ceaseless brutal struggle for existence, in preparation for the use of the problem of evil to criticize theism as a whole. But he joins with Cleanthes in criticizing Demea's use of a version of the cosmological argument. He brings many objections against the argument for design, but finally offers Cleanthes a compromise, suggesting that they can agree that there is *some* analogy between the cause of the world and human intelligence, and that any disagreement about the degree of resemblance is merely verbal, because it is indeterminate and so practically meaningless.

Part of Hume's purpose is to bring out the contrasting and inconsistent strains in religious thought which are represented by Cleanthes and Demea. These are often more closely intertwined, so that a single thinker may swing back and forth between them. It is also noteworthy that Cleanthes' views are developed partly by the use of some very characteristically Humean arguments. Nevertheless, there can be no doubt that Hume's own view is represented mainly by Philo, and that the main theme of the *Dialogues* is the criticism of the argument for design. This criticism is stated at considerable length and with a wealth of picturesque detail, but we can perhaps discern five main points. One of these concerns the weakness and remoteness of the analogy between the products of human design and the works of nature, and the resulting vagueness of any conclusion that can be drawn from that analogy. Another consists in the offering of various rival explanatory hypotheses, suggesting that the order (of several sorts) in the natural world, the supposed marks of design, may be due rather to "generation and vegetation" – even a world as a whole may result from something like biological reproduction – or to random rearrangements of particles which are just naturally in constant motion, or to a multiplicity of supernatural beings, or to a world soul, to which the material world belongs like a body, or even (as, he says, the Brahmins assert) to an "infinite spider" that spun the world as a spider spins its web: "Why an orderly system may not be spun from the belly as well as from the brain, it will be difficult for him to give a satisfactory reason" (Part VII). Philo's third point is that even if it were plausible to explain the order in the material world as the product of design by a divine mind, we should thereby be committed to recognizing in that mind itself a complex order as rich as that in the natural world, and therefore as much in need of further explanation: if it is objected that we know how ideas in a mind "fall into order of themselves, and without any *known* cause", it can be replied that the same is true, within our experience, of material (and especially living) things (Part IV).

His fourth point concerns the problem of evil and the inference to the moral qualities of a deity: even if – hard as it seems – one could somehow *reconcile* the occurrence of the evils in the world with the existence of an omnipotent and wholly good god, one could still not hope to *infer* a wholly good god from a manifestly imperfect world. Consequently the supposed moral qualities of the deity, God's perfect goodness, are even more problematic than the intellectual ones (Part V). His fifth point is that whatever one can infer *a posteriori* about the cause of the world from the world itself as we know it, this will be quite useless: we can never argue back to any further conclusions about the ordinary world or our future experience which go beyond the data from which our inference began (Part XII).[2]

These five points come in a natural order, each later one arising out of a concession with regard to those that precede it, as follows:

1   Is the analogy between natural order and artefacts close enough to make theism a good explanation of the former?
2   Even if the answer to 1 is "Yes", various alternative hypotheses, by their availability, weaken the confirmation of the theistic one.
3   Even if the theistic hypothesis would be confirmed (despite 1 and 2) by its ability to explain the order in the world, its status as a satisfactory explanation is challenged by the fact that the divine mind which it postulates would itself be as much in need of explanation (being another case of order) as the order in the world.
4   Even if the theistic hypothesis were well confirmed (despite 1, 2, and 3) by the order in the world, the moral component in it is disproved or disconfirmed by the occurrence of evil, or is, at the very least, unsupported by a world in which there is evil as well as good.
5   Even if the theistic hypothesis survived 1, 2, 3, and 4, and was well confirmed after all, it would still be useless: we could not use it to argue back to otherwise unknown features of the world or of our own lives – for example, to predictions about the course of nature, to the answering of prayer, to the greater happiness of the pious and virtuous as opposed to the irreligious and wicked, or to a life after death containing appropriate punishments, rewards, and compensations.

(b)   *Hume's Dialogues – Discussion*

What are we to say about these five points? [. . .] The first and the fifth depend upon the way in which the design argument and its conclusion are formulated. Hume presents it as an argument from analogy. Houses, watches, and so on are produced by human designers; the world is a bit like a house or a watch or a collection of houses, watches, and the like; therefore it is probably produced by something like a human designer. Thus stated, the initial analogy is indeed pretty

---

[2] This fifth point was also the main thesis of Section 11 of Hume's earlier *Enquiry concerning Human Understanding*.

remote, and any conclusion to which it points is very vague, so that no new inferences about the world or human life could reasonably be drawn from it. Another approach is to take the argument as introducing a god simply as *that which* causes or explains or is responsible for the natural world. There is then no tentative or probabilistic inference, but rather a sheer assumption that there is something that fills this bill; but again, since this entity is introduced and described only in relation to what it is assumed to produce, no new conclusions will follow from the claim that it exists. However, the argument can be recast as the confirming of a hypothesis, and then this hypothesis can be made as determinate and as fruitful of further conclusions as we please. But the more we put into the hypothesis, the further it goes beyond the evidence; so the less well will it be confirmed by that evidence, and the more exposed will it be to the competition of rival hypotheses.

These, however, are general constraints which apply to explanatory scientific hypotheses and theories of whatever sort. And it is simply not true that such hypotheses and theories are useless in this sense. On the contrary, they do support predictions which both give genuine and fairly reliable information and allow the construction of artefacts of new kinds – notably computers, television sets, nuclear weapons, and the other blessings of civilization. But is there some reason to suppose that these constraints are particularly damaging to the theistic hypothesis as an explanation of the "marks of design"? I think there is, because the theistic hypothesis does not *differentially* explain specific phenomena in the way that successful scientific theories do: it does not explain why we have these phenomena rather than others. A scientific hypothesis is often confirmed by its success in explaining exactly what is observed, by tying up what on an alternative view remain as loose ends, and perhaps by predicting further, otherwise unexpected, observations which are then made, or possible constructions which are then successfully carried out. This the theistic hypothesis does not do. It may be objected that there are also general scientific theories which do not determine predictions: Darwin's theory of the origin of species by descent and modification through natural selection would be an example. But Darwin's theory still explains details, such as the various *maladjustments* of structure to function, which its rivals leave unexplained – the webbed feet of upland geese and of frigate birds which do not use them for paddling along on the surface of the water, birds and insects that use their wings for swimming, woodpeckers that never go near a tree, and so on. All these can be understood as results of species moving into new ecological niches, but retaining ancestral features that are no longer used or are put to new, not quite appropriate, uses.[3]

Also, what we call "theories" are sometimes rather general methods of explanation, not propositions which can themselves be true or false, confirmed or disconfirmed. Such a "theory" only provides a framework within which particular explanations of specific phenomena can be constructed, and the question to ask about it is not "Is it true?" but rather "How widely applicable is it?" or "How

---

[3] C. Darwin, *The Origin of Species* (Murray, London, 1900), Chapter VI.

many specific phenomena can be successfully explained by detailed hypotheses within this framework?" This is plainly the status of, for example, sociobiology. Indeed the "theory" of evolution by natural selection can itself operate as such a framework or method. It becomes a theory in the strict sense, a hypothesis that is capable of being true or false, only when it is taken as making the historical claim that all plant and animal species have in fact developed in this way. But the theistic hypothesis does not serve even as such a method for constructing interesting and confirmable specific explanations, which could themselves yield further predictions.

Hume's (or Philo's) second point is developed at great length and with an ingenuity that sometimes lapses into fantasy; this concerns the availability of explanations alternative to that of design. Some of these alternatives are (and are recognized in the *Dialogues* as being) too far-fetched to be taken seriously. But perhaps Hume meant to suggest that the theistic account was no more worthy of being taken seriously than some of its rivals, such as the "infinite spider". However, some of the alternative explanations deserve to be taken very seriously indeed. For example, if the order in the world which is supposed to be a mark of design is located in, say, the regular working of the solar system, then we can point out that if Newton's laws represent ways of working which are natural to objects with mass, we need only find some sequence of events – perhaps, as has been suggested, a near-collision between the sun and some other star – which might leave behind a group of bodies with the appropriate relative motions; from there the thing will run on of its own accord. *Given Newton's laws*, it is really quite easy to make a solar system; certainly no great ingenuity is required. If, as modern astronomy might suggest, the order is located not in the solar system but in the multiplicity of galaxies, then what we naturally look for is a cosmological history that will account for the phenomena; but again it seems likely that the solution will lie in laws, not in ingenuity. If the order is located in plant and animal bodies, then plainly the immediate explanation of this order in the organisms that are around now lies in what Hume called "generation and vegetation", the simple and obvious fact that each individual organism is produced by its parents and then grows. However, this is only an outline explanation; a more adequate immediate explanation would identify and trace the laws and mechanisms and processes of generation and vegetation. If a further explanation is sought, we can now offer the evolutionary one towards which Hume could only make rather fumbling gestures. Evolution by natural selection mimics purposiveness and so can thoroughly explain what Cleanthes calls "the curious adapting of means to ends, throughout all nature". And this is not only *an* alternative hypothesis to that of design, it is clearly the correct one, whereas that of "special creation" is false. As Darwin so convincingly argued, there are many details which his hypothesis explains while that of special creation does not.[4]

This means that since Darwin wrote anyone who wants to use an argument for design must locate elsewhere the order which the designer is postulated to explain.

[4] Op. cit., Chapters XII, XIII, XV.

On the assumption that a full account of the development of life from inorganic materials, and of the gradual evolution of more and more complex organisms, can be given, using as data only the general laws of physics and chemistry and some astronomically understandable initial conditions, this argument for theism will have to take, as the order to be explained, either the atomic and sub-atomic structure of inorganic materials or the basic laws which govern their workings and interactions. Again, after modern developments in cosmology, anyone who wants to use anything like the astronomical variant of the argument must locate the order to be explained in some initial set-up – perhaps somewhere inside the "big bang". This shift, however, is sometimes made in a way that attempts, unfairly, to cancel the necessary concession. It may be said that we still have to explain why there should be materials and laws which are *such that* they can give rise to life and the evolution of complex organisms, or again why there should be an initial cosmological set-up which is *such that* it can generate galaxies containing stars and planetary systems. This is misleading in two ways. On the one hand, it invites us to beg the question by supposing that these future developments are not only causally latent within the initial situation – that is, that it will eventually lead to them or bring them about – but are also already *envisaged* at its formation. On the other hand, it suggests that a *potentiality* for the producing of these developments is part of what still needs to be explained. But this suggestion is unfair. If, as we are supposing, the future developments are accounted for by the initial conditions and materials and laws alone, then it is only for those initial conditions and materials and laws as they are in themselves that any further explanation could reasonably be sought. We must not overload the explanandum by adding to it, even as a potentiality, the developments which we can presume it to have accounted for already.

But it may be argued that there is still something that calls for further explanation. With the various basic materials and physical constants as they contingently are, life and evolution and consciousness are naturally possible; but things might so easily have been different. Is it not remarkable and intrinsically surprising that things happen to be just right for the possibility of these developments? Now someone might say in reply to this objection, "No, we cannot reasonably find it surprising that things should have been such that we could evolve, since if things *had* been otherwise we should not have been here to be surprised". But this is not a good reply, though something like it would be a good reply to a different objection. If there are many thousands of planetary systems throughout the universe, but the conditions are right for the production of life on just one of them, namely ours, we cannot reasonably find it surprising that things should be just right for life *here*; for *here* has been picked out for attention merely in relation to our presence: from a neutral point of view all that is true is that conditions have been right for life far less often than they have been wrong, so their being right once can well be ascribed to chance, and not seen as calling for any further explanation. But the objection we are considering is different. There is only one actual universe, with a unique set of basic materials and physical constants, and it is therefore surprising that the elements of this unique set-up are just right for life when they might easily have been wrong. This is not made less surprising by the fact that if it had not been so, no one would have been here to be surprised. We can properly envisage and consider alternative possibilities which do not include our being there to experience them.[5]

I suspect, however, that this objection also is being presented in a question-begging way. Though some small variation from the actual initial materials and constants would, perhaps, eliminate the possibility of life's having developed as it did, we really have no idea of what other interesting possibilities might have been latent within others of the endless range of possible initial conditions. We are not in a position, therefore, to regard the actual initial materials and constants as a uniquely fruitful set, and as surprising and as specially calling for further explanation on that account.

Once these matters are cleared up, we can see that the shift of topic due to the work of Darwin and his successors greatly diminishes the plausibility of the argument for design. The reciprocal adjustments of structures and functions in myriads of different organisms are indeed so delicate and complicated as to be initially surprising in the extreme, and not merely to invite but to require a search for *some* further explanation; and then the hypothesis of design is at least one to be considered among others. But we find nothing comparable to this in sub-atomic particles or the laws that govern them. Atomic and nuclear physics are, no doubt, intricate enough to be of theoretical as well as practical interest, but we cannot see them as involving reciprocal adjustments which might plausibly be taken as signs of purposiveness.

The shift produced by modern cosmology is less important in this respect, not because any initially surprising reciprocal adjustments have to be postulated in a proposed starting-point of cosmic history, but because none was to be found even in the developed universe. The eighteenth-century thinkers drew quite the wrong conclusion from Newtonian gravitational astronomy. It should, as I have said, have told them not that a solar system is a marvellously coherent machine with mutually assisting and mutually adjusted components (like a watch, only more so), but rather that it is something that, given the gravitational laws, could be botched up with no forethought at all, or that could emerge from a fortuitous concourse of masses. It takes ingenuity to make an orrery, an artificial model of the solar system, precisely because it cannot use the gravitational laws, but no such ingenuity is needed to make a gravitationally governed solar system.

The stock response, however, to the suggestion of alternative, naturalistic, explanations of the supposed marks of design is to say that they only shift the problem further back. If we explain an organism as having arisen by generation and vegetation – and even if we trace these processes in detail – it is said that we still have to explain the parents or ancestors that produced it. If we explain whole species by organic evolution, we still have to explain the primeval organisms from which evolution began. And if we explain these by the action of radiant energy on

[5] Cf. R. Swinburne, *The Existence of God* (Clarendon Press, Oxford, 1974), pp. 137–8.

inorganic mixtures of gases, we still have to explain the atomic structures and the radiation that make this action possible. But, on the one hand, we have seen that in such a shifting back the burden of explanation has grown lighter: there is literally less to explain. And, on the other hand, a similar response is available to the naturalist: if you explain the order in the natural world by a divine plan, you still have to explain the order in the divine mind. As Philo says, "a mental world or universe of ideas requires a cause as much as does a material world or universe of objects". This is what I called his third main point. But there are two different ways in which the theist can try to meet this objection, which bring out two radically different interpretations of the design argument itself.

First, he may say, as Cleanthes does, that he is content with one step in explanation. "Even in common life, if I assign a cause for any event; is it any objection, Philo, that I cannot assign the cause of that cause . . . ? The order and arrangement of nature, the curious adjustment of final causes, the plain use and intention of every part and organ; all these bespeak in the clearest language an intelligent cause or Author . . . You ask me, what is the cause of this cause? I know not; I care not; that concerns not me. I have found a Deity; and here I stop my enquiry" (Part IV). This sounds like a fair reply, but it plays straight into the hands of the naturalist. For, as we have seen, the phenomena to which Cleanthes refers now bespeak in the clearest language not an Author but an evolutionary process. If one step in explanation is enough, this is where we must stop our inquiry.

Alternatively, the theist may say that the divine mind hypothesis terminates the regress of explanation in a way that no naturalistic explanation can. Any naturalistic explanation uses data for which a further explanation is in principle always needed; but a god is self-explanatory. Consequently, however far alternative explanations can be taken, they must lead back to the theistic account in the end, whereas once God has been introduced as a cause, the search for a cause of this cause is out of order. The theist loses every battle but the last.

This is clearly not Cleanthes' view; but this reply is suggested by Philo in one of his temporary alliances with Demea. "To say that all this order in animals and vegetables proceeds ultimately from design is begging the question; nor can that great point be ascertained otherwise than by proving a priori, both that order is, from its own nature, inseparably attached to thought, and that it can never, of itself, or from original unknown principles, belong to matter." And Demea himself stresses that what is needed here is an a priori argument, offering what seems to be a mixture of Leibniz's argument from contingency with the first cause argument (Parts VII, IX).

These two replies, as I said, reflect two different interpretations of the design argument. It may be taken as a genuinely empirical, a posteriori, argument, strictly analogous to the confirmation of a scientific hypothesis or theory. Or it may be taken with a large admixture of a priori principles. As an empirical argument, it needs not only the premiss that certain objects not made by men exhibit a kind of order that is found also in the products of human design; it needs also the premiss that such order is *not* found where there is no designer. But this second premiss is not available as long as we confine ourselves to empirical evidence. As Cleanthes' party constantly reiterates, such order *is* found all over the place where we have as yet no reason to suppose that there is a designer. Paley argued that if we found a watch on the ground we should infer that it had been made by an intelligent being.[6] This is true, because we hardly ever find watches except where the supposition of human manufacture is antecedently plausible – on people's wrists, in their pockets, in jeweller's shops, and so on. But if watches were found as commonly on the seashore as shellfish, or as commonly on dry land as insects, this argument would be undermined. Thus any purely *a posteriori* design argument falls at the first fence: we have no good *empirical* reason for taking the "marks of design" *as* marks of design. "We have . . . experience", Philo concedes, "of ideas, which fall into order of themselves, and without any *known* cause: But . . . we have a much larger experience of matter, which does the same" (Part IV). In fact, the position is even worse for the theist. *Within our experience*, mental structures are always based at least partly on perceptual input: "In all instances which we have ever seen, ideas are copied from real objects, and are ectypal, not archetypal . . . You reverse this order, and give thought the precedence" (Part VIII). The argument for design, therefore, can be sustained only with the help of a supposedly *a priori* double-barrelled principle, that mental order (at least in a god) is self-explanatory, but that all material order not only is not self-explanatory, but is positively improbable and in need of further explanation.

But this double-barrelled principle is recognizable as the core of the cosmological argument. [. . .] There is no reason why mental order as such should be any less in need of further explanation than material order, and the claim that mental order in a god is self-explanatory is just the thesis, central in the cosmological argument, but borrowed there from the ontological one, that God is a necessary being, a being that could not have failed to exist.

Kant, in his criticism of the "physico-theological proof" (his name for the design argument) makes two points which come close to this.[7] He argues that the most that an argument for design could show is that there is an architect of the world, working on pre-existing material; for this is the most that the analogy of human manufacture could indicate. "To prove the contingency of matter itself, we should have to resort to a transcendental argument." He argues also that we cannot reach the notions of absolute totality, absolute unity, and so on by the empirical road. "Accordingly, we then abandon the argument from empirical grounds of proof, and fall back upon the contingency which, in the first steps of the argument, we had inferred from the order and purposiveness of the world. With this contingency as our sole premiss, we then advance, by means of transcendental concepts alone, to the existence of an absolutely necessary being . . . Those who propound the physico-theological argument . . . after advancing some considerable way on the solid ground of nature and experience, and finding themselves just as distant as ever

---

[6] W. Paley, *Natural Theology*, Vol. 6 in *Works* (London, 1805), Chapter I.
[7] *Critique of Pure Reason*, Transcendental Dialectic, Book II, Chapter III, Section 6.

from the object which discloses itself to their reason, they suddenly leave this ground, and pass over into the realm of mere possibilities." Kant thus charges that the design argument has to fall back on the cosmological one, which, he has already claimed, is only a disguised ontological proof. His reason is that the design argument could not take us as far as the theist wants to go. This is a complaint that Hume puts into the mouth of Demea. Kant allows (with some hints of qualification and further objection) that the design argument *could* give us an architect god, though not a creator or a necessary being. But our criticisms show that the argument will not take us even as far as Kant seems to allow without borrowing the *a priori* thesis that there is a vicious metaphysical contingency in all natural things, and, in contrast with this, the "transcendental" concept of a god who is self-explanatory and necessarily existent. It is only with the help of these borrowings that the design argument can introduce the required asymmetry, that any natural explanation uses data which call for further explanation, but that the theistic explanation terminates the regress. Without this asymmetry, the design argument cannot show that there is any need to go beyond the sort of alternative hypothesis that Hume foreshadowed and that Darwin and Wallace supplied, or that there is anything satisfactorily explanatory in the postulation of a supernatural designer. The dependence of the argument for design on ideas that are the core of the cosmological one is greater than Kant himself realized.

William L. Rowe, "The Cosmological Argument"

Since ancient times thoughtful people have sought to justify their religious beliefs. Perhaps the most basic belief for which justification has been sought is the belief that there is a God. The effort to justify belief in the existence of God has generally started either from facts available to believers and nonbelievers alike or from facts, such as the experience of God, normally available only to believers. We shall consider some major attempts to justify belief in God by appealing to facts supposedly available to any rational person, whether religious or not. By starting from such facts theologians and philosophers have developed arguments for the existence of God, arguments which, they have claimed, prove beyond reasonable doubt that there is a God.

Stating the Argument

Arguments for the existence of God are commonly divided into *a posteriori* arguments and *a priori* arguments. An *a posteriori* argument depends on a principle or premise that can be known only by means of our experience of the world. An *a priori* argument, on the other hand, purports to rest on principles all of which can

From *Philosophy of Religion* (Belmont, CA: Wadsworth Publishing Co., 1978), pp. 16–30.

be known independently of our experience of the world, by just reflecting on and understanding them. Of the three major arguments for the existence of God – the Cosmological, the Teleological, and the Ontological – only the last of these is entirely *a priori*. In the Cosmological Argument one starts from some simple fact about the world, such as that it contains things which are caused to exist by other things. In the Teleological Argument a somewhat more complicated fact about the world serves as a starting point, the fact that the world exhibits order and design. In the Ontological Argument, however, one begins simply with a concept of God. In this [article] we shall consider the Cosmological Argument. . . .

Before we state the Cosmological Argument itself, we shall consider some rather general points about the argument. Historically, it can be traced to the writings of the Greek philosophers, Plato and Aristotle, but the major developments in the argument took place in the thirteenth and in the eighteenth centuries. In the thirteenth century, Aquinas put forth five distinct arguments for the existence of God, and of these, the first three are versions of the Cosmological Argument.[1] In the first of these he started from the fact that there are things in the world undergoing change and reasoned to the conclusion that there must be some ulti-mate cause of change that is itself unchanging. In the second he started from the fact that there are things in the world that clearly are caused to exist by other things and reasoned to the conclusion that there must be some ultimate cause of existence whose own existence is itself uncaused. And in the third argument he started from the fact that there are things in the world which need not have existed at all, things which do exist but which we can easily imagine might not, and reasoned to the conclusion that there must be some being that had to be, that exists and could not have failed to exist. Now it might be objected that even if Aquinas' arguments do prove beyond doubt the existence of an unchanging changer, an uncaused cause, and a being that could not have failed to exist, the arguments fail to prove the existence of the theistic God. For the theistic God is supremely good, omnipot-ent, omniscient, and creator of but separate from and independent of the world. How do we know, for example, that the unchanging changer isn't evil or slightly ignorant? The answer to this objection is that the Cosmological Argument has two parts. In the first part the effort is to prove the existence of a special sort of being, for example, a being that could not have failed to exist, or a being that causes change in other things but is itself unchanging. In the second part of the argument the effort is to prove that the special sort of being whose existence has been established in the first part has, and must have, the features – perfect goodness, omnipotence, omniscience, and so on – which go together to make up the theistic idea of God. What this means, then, is that Aquinas' three arguments are different ver-sions of only the first part of the Cosmological Argument. Indeed, in later sections of his *Summa Theologica* Aquinas undertakes to show that the unchanging changer, the uncaused cause of existence, and the being which had to exist are one and the same being and that this single being has all of the attributes of the theistic God.

---

[1] See St. Thomas Aquinas, *Summa Theologica*, 1a. 2, 3.

We noted above that a second major development in the Cosmological Argument took place in the eighteenth century, a development reflected in the writings of the German philosopher, Gottfried Leibniz (1646–1716), and especially in the writings of the English theologian and philosopher, Samuel Clarke (1675–1729). In 1704 Clarke gave a series of lectures, later published under the title *A Demonstration of the Being and Attributes of God*. These lectures constitute, perhaps, the most complete, forceful, and cogent presentation of the Cosmological Argument we possess. The lectures were read by the major skeptical philosopher of the century, David Hume (1711–1776), and in his brilliant attack on the attempt to justify religion in the court of reason, his *Dialogues Concerning Natural Religion*, Hume advanced several penetrating criticisms of Clarke's arguments, criticisms which have persuaded many philosophers in the modern period to reject the Cosmological Argument. In our study of the argument we shall concentrate our attention largely on its eighteenth-century form and try to assess its strengths and weaknesses in the light of the criticisms which Hume and others have advanced against it.

The first part of the eighteenth-century form of the Cosmological Argument seeks to establish the existence of a self-existent being. The second part of the argument attempts to prove that the self-existent being is the theistic God, that is, has the features which we have noted to be basic elements in the theistic idea of God. We shall consider mainly the first part of the argument, for it is against the first part that philosophers from Hume to Russell have advanced very important objections.

In stating the first part of the Cosmological Argument we shall make use of two important concepts, the concept of a *dependent being* and the concept of a *self-existent being*. By "a dependent being" we mean a *being whose existence is accounted for by the causal activity of other things*. Recalling Anselm's division into the three cases: "explained by another," "explained by nothing," and "explained by itself," it's clear that a dependent being is a being whose existence is explained by another. By "a self-existent being" we mean *a being whose existence is accounted for by its own nature*. This idea is an essential element in the theistic concept of God. Again, in terms of Anselm's three cases, a self-existent being is a being whose existence is explained by itself. Armed with these two concepts, the concept of a dependent being and the concept of a self-existent being, we can now state the first part of the Cosmological Argument.

1   Every being (that exists or ever did exist) is either a dependent being or a self-existent being.
2   Not every being can be a dependent being.
Therefore,
3   There exists a self-existent being.

Deductive validity

Before we look critically at each of the premises of this argument, we should note that this argument is, to use an expression from the logician's vocabulary, *deductively valid.* To find out whether an argument is deductively valid we need only ask the question: If its premises were true would its conclusion have to be true? If the answer is yes, the argument is deductively valid. If the answer is no, the argument is deductively invalid. Notice that the question of the validity of an argument is entirely different from the question of whether its premises are in fact true. The following argument is made up entirely of false statements, but it is deductively valid.

1   Babe Ruth is the President of the U.S.
2   The President of the U.S. is from Indiana.
Therefore,
3   Babe Ruth is from Indiana.

The argument is deductively valid because even though its premises are false, if they were true its conclusion would have to be true. Even God, Aquinas would say, cannot bring it about that the premises of this argument are true and yet its conclusion is false, for God's power extends only to what is possible, and it is an absolute impossibility that Babe Ruth be the President, the President be from Indiana, and yet Babe Ruth not be from Indiana.

The Cosmological Argument (that is, its first part) is a deductively valid argument. If its premises are or were true its conclusion would have to be true. It's clear from our example about Babe Ruth, however, that the fact that an argument is deductively valid is insufficient to establish the truth of its conclusion. What else is required? Clearly that we know or have rational grounds for believing that the premises are true. If we know that the Cosmological Argument is deductively valid and can establish that its premises are true, we shall thereby have proved that its conclusion is true. Are, then, the premises of the Cosmological Argument true? To this more difficult question we must now turn.

PSR and the first premise

At first glance the first premise might appear to be an obvious or even trivial truth. But it is neither obvious nor trivial. And if it appears to be obvious or trivial, we must be confusing the idea of a self-existent being with the idea of a being that is not a dependent being. Clearly, it is obviously true that any being is either a dependent being (explained by other things) or it is not a dependent being (not explained by other things). But what our premise says is that any being is either a dependent being (explained by other things) or it is a self-existent being (explained by itself). Consider again Anselm's three cases.

a.   explained by another
b.   explained by nothing
c.   explained by itself

What our first premise asserts is that each being that exists (or ever did exist) is either of sort *a* or of sort *c*. It denies that any being is of sort *b*. And it is this denial that makes the first premise both significant and controversial. The obvious truth we must not confuse it with is the truth that any being is either of sort *a* or not of sort *a*. While this is true it is neither very significant nor controversial.

Earlier we saw that Anselm accepted as a basic principle that whatever exists has an explanation of its existence. Since this basic principle denies that any thing of sort *b* exists or ever did exist, it's clear that Anselm would believe the first premise of our Cosmological Argument. The eighteenth-century proponents of the argument also were convinced of the truth of the basic principle we attributed to Anselm. And because they were convinced of its truth, they readily accepted the first premise of the Cosmological Argument. But by the eighteenth century, Anselm's basic principle had been more fully elaborated and had received a name, "the Principle of Sufficient Reason." Since this principle (PSR, as we shall call it) plays such an important role in justifying the premises of the Cosmological Argument, it will help us to consider it for a moment before we continue our enquiry into the truth or falsity of the premises of the Cosmological Argument.

The Principle of Sufficient Reason (PSR), as it was expressed by both Leibniz and Samuel Clarke, is a very general principle and is best understood as having two parts. In its first part it is simply a restatement of Anselm's principle that there must be an explanation of the *existence* of any being whatever. Thus if we come upon a man in a room, PSR implies that there must be an explanation of the fact that that particular man exists. A moment's reflection, however, reveals that there are many facts about the man other than the mere fact that he exists. There is the fact that the man in question is in the room he's in, rather than somewhere else, the fact that he is in good health, and the fact that he is at the moment thinking of Paris, rather than, say, London. Now the purpose of the second part of PSR is to require an explanation of these facts as well. We may state PSR, therefore, as the principle that *there must be an explanation (a) of the existence of any being, and (b) of any positive fact whatever.* We are now in a position to study the role this very important principle plays in the Cosmological Argument.

Since the proponent of the Cosmological Argument accepts PSR in both its parts, it is clear that he will appeal to its first part, PSRa, as justification for the first premise of the Cosmological Argument. Of course, we can and should enquire into the deeper question of whether the proponent of the argument is rationally justified in accepting PSR itself. But we shall put this question aside for the moment. What we need to see first is whether he is correct in thinking that *if* PSR is true then both of the premises of the Cosmological Argument are true. And what we have just seen is that if only the first part of PSR, that is, PSRa, is true, the first premise of the Cosmological Argument will be true. But what of the second premise of the Argument? For what reasons does the proponent think that it must be true?

The second premise

According to the second premise, not every being that exists can be a dependent being, that is, can have the explanation of its existence in some other being or beings. Presumably, the proponent of the argument thinks there is something fundamentally wrong with the idea that every being that exists is dependent, that each existing being was caused by some other being which in turn was caused by some other being, and so on. But just what does he think is wrong with it? To help us in understanding his thinking, let's simplify things by supposing that there exists only one thing now, A_1, a living thing perhaps, that was brought into existence by something else A_2, which perished shortly after it brought A_1 into existence. Suppose further that A_2 was brought into existence in similar fashion some time ago by A_3, and A_3 by A_4, and so forth back into the past. Each of these beings is a *dependent* being, it owes its existence to the preceding thing in the series. Now if nothing else ever existed but these beings, then what the second premise says would not be true. For if every being that exists or ever did exist is an A and was produced by a preceding A, then every being that exists or ever did exist would be dependent and, accordingly, premise two of the Cosmological Argument would be false. If the proponent of the Cosmological Argument is correct there must, then, be something wrong with the idea that every being that exists or did exist is an A and that they form a causal series, A_1 caused by A_2, A_2 caused by A_3, A_3 caused by A_4, . . . A_n caused by A_{n+1}. How does the proponent of the Cosmological Argument propose to show us that there is something wrong with this view?

A popular but mistaken idea of how the proponent tries to show that something is wrong with the view that every being might be dependent is that he uses the following argument to reject it.

1   There must be a *first being* to start any causal series.
2   If every being were dependent there would be no *first being* to start the causal series.
Therefore,
3   Not every being can be a dependent being.

Although this argument is deductively valid and its second premise is true, its first premise overlooks the distinct possibility that a causal series might be *infinite*, with no first member at all. Thus if we go back to our series of A beings, where each A is dependent, having been produced by the preceding A in the causal series, it's clear that if the series existed it would have no first member, for every A in the series there would be a preceding A which produced it, *ad infinitum*. The first premise of the argument just given assumes that a causal series must stop with a first member somewhere in the distant past. But there seems to be no good reason for making that assumption.

The eighteenth-century proponents of the Cosmological Argument recognized that the causal series of dependent beings could be infinite, without a first member to start the series. They rejected the idea that every being that is or ever was is dependent not because there would then be no first member to the series of dependent beings, but because there would then be no explanation for the fact that there are and have always been dependent beings. To see their reasoning let's return to our simplification of the supposition that the only things that exist or ever did exist are dependent beings. In our simplification of that supposition only one of the dependent beings exists at a time, each one perishing as it produces the next in the series. Perhaps the first thing to note about this supposition is that there is no individual A in the causal series of dependent beings whose existence is unexplained – A_1 is explained by A_2, A_2 by A_3, and A_n by A_{n+1}. So the first part of PSR, PSRa, appears to be satisfied. There is no particular being whose existence lacks an explanation. What, then, is it that lacks an explanation, if every particular A in the causal series of dependent beings has an explanation? It is the *series itself* that lacks an explanation. Or, as I've chosen to express it, *the fact that there are and have always been dependent beings*. For suppose we ask why it is that there are and have always been *A*s in existence. It won't do to say that *A*s have always been producing other *A*s – we can't explain why there have always been *A*s by saying there always have been *A*s. Nor, on the supposition that only *A*s have ever existed, can we explain the fact that there have always been *A*s by appealing to something other than an *A* – for no such thing would have existed. Thus the supposition that the only things that exist or ever existed are dependent things leaves us with a fact for which there can be no explanation; namely, the fact that there are and have always been dependent beings.

Questioning the justification of the second premise

Critics of the Cosmological Argument have raised several important objections against the claim that if every being is dependent the series or collection of those beings would have no explanation. Our understanding of the Cosmological Argument, as well as of its strengths and weaknesses, will be deepened by a careful consideration of these criticisms.

The first criticism is that the proponent of the Cosmological Argument makes the mistake of treating the collection or series of dependent beings as though it were itself a dependent being, and, therefore, requires an explanation of its existence. But, so the objection goes, the collection of dependent beings is not itself a dependent being any more than a collection of stamps is itself a stamp.

A second criticism is that the proponent makes the mistake of inferring that because each member of the collection of dependent beings has a cause the collection itself must have a cause. But, as Bertrand Russell noted, such reasoning is as fallacious as to infer that the human race (that is, the collection of human beings) must have a mother because each member of the collection (each human being) has a mother.

A third criticism is that the proponent of the argument fails to realize that for there to be an explanation of a collection of things is nothing more than for there to be an explanation of each of the things making up the collection. Since in the infinite collection (or series) of dependent beings, each being in the collection does have an explanation – by virtue of having been caused by some preceding member of the collection – the explanation of the collection, so the criticism goes, has already been given. As David Hume remarked, "Did I show you the particular causes of each individual in a collection of twenty particles of matter, I should think it very unreasonable, should you afterwards ask me, what was the cause of the whole twenty. This is sufficiently explained in explaining the cause of the parts."[2]

Finally, even if the proponent of the Cosmological Argument can satisfactorily answer these objections, he must face one last objection to his ingenious attempt to justify premise two of the Cosmological Argument. For someone may agree that if nothing exists but an infinite collection of dependent beings, the infinite collection will have no explanation of its existence, and still refuse to conclude from this that there is something wrong with the idea that every being is a dependent being. Why, he might ask, should we think that everything has to have an explanation? What's wrong with admitting that the fact that there are and have always been dependent beings is a *brute fact*, a fact having no explanation whatever? Why does everything have to have an explanation anyway? We must now see what can be said in response to these several objections.

Responses to criticism

It is certainly a mistake to think that a collection of stamps is itself a stamp, and very likely a mistake to think that the collection of dependent beings is itself a dependent being. But the mere fact that the proponent of the argument thinks that there must be an explanation not only for each member of the collection of dependent beings but for the collection itself is not sufficient grounds for concluding that he must view the collection as itself a dependent being. The collection of human beings, for example, is certainly not itself a human being. Admitting this, however, we might still seek an explanation of why there is a collection of human beings, of why there are such things as human beings at all. So the mere fact that an explanation is demanded for the collection of dependent beings is no proof that the person who demands the explanation must be supposing that the collection itself is just another dependent being.

The second criticism attributes to the proponent of the Cosmological Argument the following bit of reasoning:

1 Every member of the collection of dependent beings has a cause or explanation. Therefore,
2 The collection of dependent beings has a cause or explanation.

As we noted in setting forth this criticism, arguments of this sort are often unreliable. It would be a mistake to conclude that a collection of objects is light in weight simply because each object in the collection is light in weight, for if there were many objects in the collection it might be quite heavy. On the other hand, if

[2] David Hume, *Dialogues Concerning Natural Religion*, Part IX, ed. H. D. Aiken (New York: Hafner Publishing Company, 1948), pp. 59–60.

we know that each marble weighs more than one ounce we could infer validly that the collection of marbles weighs more than an ounce. Fortunately, however, we don't need to decide whether the inference from (1) to (2) is valid or invalid. We need not decide this question because the proponent of the Cosmological Argument need not use this inference to establish that there must be an explanation of the collection of dependent beings. He need not use this inference because he has in PSR a principle from which it follows immediately that the collection of dependent beings has a cause or explanation. For according to PSR every positive fact must have an explanation. If it is a fact that there exists a collection of dependent beings then, according to PSR, that fact too must have an explanation. So it is PSR that the proponent of the Cosmological Argument appeals to in concluding that there must be an explanation of the collection of dependent beings, and not some dubious inference from the premise that each member of the collection has an explanation. It seems, then, that neither of the first two criticisms is strong enough to do any serious damage to the reasoning used to support the second premise of the Cosmological Argument.

The third objection contends that to explain the existence of a collection of things is the same thing as to explain the existence of each of its members. If we consider a collection of dependent beings where each being in the collection is explained by the preceding member which caused it, it's clear that no member of the collection will lack an explanation of its existence. But, so the criticism goes, if we've explained the existence of every member of a collection we've explained the existence of the collection – there's nothing left over to be explained. This forceful criticism, originally advanced by David Hume, has gained considerable support in the modern period. But the criticism rests on an assumption that the proponent of the Cosmological Argument would not accept. The assumption is that to explain the existence of a collection of things it is *sufficient* to explain the existence of every member in the collection. To see what is wrong with this assumption is to understand the basic issue in the reasoning by which the proponent of the Cosmological Argument seeks to establish that not every being can be a dependent being.

In order for there to be an explanation of the existence of the collection of dependent beings, it's clear that the eighteenth-century proponents would require that the following two conditions be satisfied:

C1   There is an explanation of the existence of each of the members of the collection of dependent beings.
C2   There is an explanation of why there are *any* dependent beings.

According to the proponents of the Cosmological Argument if every being that exists or ever did exist is a dependent being – that is, if the whole of reality consists of nothing more than a collection of dependent beings – C1 will be satisfied, but C2 will not be satisfied. And since C2 won't be satisfied there will be no explanation of the collection of dependent beings. The third criticism, therefore, says in effect that if C1 is satisfied C2 will be satisfied, and, since in a collection of dependent beings each member will have an explanation in whatever it was that produced it, C1 will be satisfied. So, therefore, C2 will be satisfied and the collection of dependent beings will have an explanation.

Although the issue is a complicated one, I think it is possible to see that the third criticism rests on a mistake: the mistake of thinking that if C1 is satisfied C2 must also be satisfied. The mistake is a natural one to make for it is easy to imagine circumstances in which if C1 is satisfied C2 also will be satisfied. Suppose, for example, that the whole of reality includes not just a collection of dependent beings but also a self-existent being. Suppose further that instead of each dependent being having been produced by some other dependent being every dependent being was produced by the self-existent being. Finally, let us consider both the possibility that the collection of dependent beings is finite in time and has a first member and the possibility that the collection of dependent beings is infinite in past time, having no first member. Using "G" for the self-existent being, the first possibility may be diagrammed as follows:

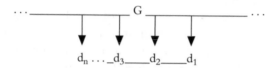

G, we shall say, has always existed and always will. We can think of d_1 as some presently existing dependent being, d_2, d_3, and so forth as dependent beings that existed at some time in the past, and d_n as the first dependent being to exist. The second possibility may be portrayed as follows:

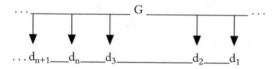

On this diagram there is no first member of the collection of dependent beings. Each member of the infinite collection, however, is explained by reference to the self-existent being G which produced it. Now the interesting point about both these cases is that the explanation that has been provided for the members of the collection of dependent beings carries with it, at least in part, an answer to the question of why there are any dependent beings at all. In both cases we may explain why there are dependent beings by pointing out that there exists a self-existent being that has been engaged in producing them. So once we have learned that the existence of each member of the collection of dependent beings has its existence explained by the fact that G produced it, we have already learned why there are dependent beings.

Someone might object that we haven't really learned why there are dependent beings until we also learn *why* G has been producing them. But, of course, we could also say that we haven't really explained the existence of a particular dependent being, say d_3, until we also learn not just that G produced it but *why* G produced it. The point we need to grasp, however, is that once we admit that every dependent being's existence is explained by G, we must admit that the fact that there are dependent beings has also been explained. So it is not unnatural that someone should think that to explain the existence of the collection of dependent beings is nothing more than to explain the existence of its members. For, as we've seen, to explain the collection's existence is to explain each member's existence and to explain why there are any dependent beings at all. And in the examples we've considered, in doing the one (explaining why each dependent being exists) we've already done the other (explained why there are any dependent beings at all). We must now see, however, that on the supposition that the whole of reality consists *only* of a collection of dependent beings, to give an explanation of each member's existence is not to provide an explanation of why there are dependent beings.

In the examples we've considered we have gone *outside* of the collection of dependent beings in order to explain the members' existence. But if the only beings that exist or ever existed are dependent beings then each dependent being will be explained by some other dependent being, *ad infinitum*. This does not mean that there will be some particular dependent being whose existence is unaccounted for. Each dependent being has an explanation of its existence; namely, in the dependent being which preceded it and produced it. So C1 is satisfied: there is an explanation of the existence of each member of the collection of dependent beings. Turning to C2, however, we can see that it will not be satisfied. We cannot explain why there are (or have ever been) dependent beings by appealing to all the members of the infinite collection of dependent beings. For if the question to be answered is why there are (or have ever been) any dependent beings at all, we cannot answer that question by noting that there always have been dependent beings, each one accounting for the existence of some other dependent being. Thus on the supposition that every being is dependent it seems there will be no explanation of why there are dependent beings. C2 will not be satisfied. Therefore, on the supposition that every being is dependent there will be no explanation of the existence of the collection of dependent beings.

The truth of PSR

We come now to the final criticism of the reasoning supporting the second premise of the Cosmological Argument. According to this criticism, it is admitted that the supposition that every being is dependent implies that there will be a *brute fact* in the universe, a fact, that is, for which there can be no explanation whatever. For there will be no explanation of the fact that dependent beings exist and have always been in existence. It is this brute fact that the proponents of the argument were describing when they pointed out that if every being is dependent the series or collection of dependent beings would lack an explanation of *its* existence. The final criticism asks what is wrong with admitting that the universe contains such a brute, unintelligible fact. In asking this question the critic challenges the fundamental principle, PSR, on which the Cosmological Argument rests. For, as we've seen, the first premise of the argument denies that there exists a being whose existence has no explanation. In support of this premise the proponent appeals to the first part of PSR. The second premise of the argument claims that not every being can be dependent. In support of this premise the proponent appeals to the second part of PSR, the part which states that there must be an explanation of any positive fact whatever.

The proponent reasons that if every being were a dependent being then although the first part of PSR would be satisfied – every being would have an explanation – the second part would be violated, there would be no explanation for the positive fact that there are and have always been dependent beings. For first, since every being is supposed to be dependent, there would be nothing outside of the collection of dependent beings to explain the collection's existence. Second, the fact that each member of the collection has an explanation in some other dependent being is insufficient to explain why there are and have always been dependent beings. And, finally, there is nothing about the collection of dependent beings that would suggest that it is a self-existent collection. Consequently, if every being were dependent, the fact that there are and have always been dependent beings would have no explanation. But this violates the second part of PSR. So the second premise of the Cosmological Argument must be true, not every being can be a dependent being. This conclusion, however, is no better than the principle, PSR, on which it rests. And it is the point of the final criticism to question the truth of PSR. Why, after all, should we accept the idea that every being and every positive fact must have an explanation? Why, in short, should we believe PSR? These are important questions, and any final judgment of the Cosmological Argument depends on how they are answered.

Most of the theologians and philosophers who accept PSR have tried to defend it in either of two ways. Some have held that PSR is (or can be) known *intuitively* to be true. By this they mean that if we fully understand and reflect on what is said by PSR we can see that it must be true. Now, undoubtedly, there are statements which are known intuitively to be true. "Every triangle has exactly three angles" or "No physical object can be in two different places in space at one and the same time" are examples of statements whose truth we can apprehend just by understanding and reflecting on them. The difficulty with the claim that PSR is intuitively true, however, is that a number of very able philosophers fail to apprehend its truth, and some even claim that the principle is false. It is doubtful, therefore, that many of us, if any, know intuitively that PSR is true.

The second way philosophers and theologians who accept PSR have sought to defend it is by claiming that although it is not known to be true, it is, nevertheless, a presupposition of reason, a basic assumption that rational people make, whether or not they reflect sufficiently to become aware of the assumption. It's probably true that there are some assumptions we all make about our world, assumptions which are so basic that most of us are unaware of them. And, I suppose, it might be true that PSR is such an assumption. What bearing would this view of PSR have on the Cosmological Argument? Perhaps the main point to note is that even if PSR is a presupposition we all share, the premises of the Cosmological Argument could still be false. For PSR itself could still be false. The fact, if it is a fact, that all of us *presuppose* that every existing being and every positive fact has an explanation does not imply that no being exists, and no positive fact obtains, without an explanation. Nature is not bound to satisfy our presuppositions. As the American philosopher, William James, once remarked in another connection, "In the great boarding house of nature, the cakes and the butter and the syrup seldom come out so even and leave the plates so clear."

Our study of the first part of the Cosmological Argument has led us to the fundamental principle on which its premises rest, the Principle of Sufficient Reason. Since we do not seem to know that PSR is true we cannot reasonably claim to know that the premises of the Cosmological Argument are true. They might be true. But unless we do know them to be true they cannot *establish* for us the conclusion that there exists a being that has the explanation of its existence within its own nature. If it were shown, however, that even though we do not *know* that PSR is true we all, nevertheless, *presuppose* PSR to be true, then, whether PSR is true or not, to be consistent we should accept the Cosmological Argument. For, as we've seen, its premises imply its conclusion and its premises do seem to follow from PSR. But no one has succeeded in *showing* that PSR is an assumption that most or all of us share. So our final conclusion must be that although the Cosmological Argument might be a *sound* argument (valid with true premises), it does not provide us with good rational grounds for believing that among those beings that exist there is one whose existence is accounted for by its own nature. Having come to this conclusion we may safely put aside the second part of the argument. For even if we succeeded in showing that a self-existent being would have the other attributes of the theistic God, the Cosmological Argument would still not provide us with good rational grounds for belief in God, having failed in its first part to provide us with good rational grounds for believing that there is a self-existent being.

Robert Merrihew Adams, "Kierkegaard's Arguments Against Objective Reasoning in Religion"

It is sometimes held that there is something in the nature of religious faith itself that renders it useless or undesirable to reason objectively in support of such faith, even if the reasoning should happen to have considerable plausibility. Søren Kierkegaard's *Concluding Unscientific Postscript* is probably the document most commonly cited as representative of this view. In the present essay I shall discuss three arguments for the view. I call them the Approximation Argument, the Postponement Argument, and the Passion Argument; and I suggest they can all be found in the *Postscript*. I

From *The Monist* 60 (1977), pp. 48–62.

shall try to show that the Approximation Argument is a bad argument. The other two will not be so easily disposed of, however. I believe they show that Kierkegaard's conclusion, or something like it, does indeed follow from a certain conception of religiousness – a conception which has some appeal, although for reasons which I shall briefly suggest, I am not prepared to accept it.

Kierkegaard uses the word "objective" and its cognates in several senses, most of which need not concern us here. We are interested in the sense in which he uses it when he says, "it is precisely a misunderstanding to seek an objective assurance," and when he speaks of "an objective uncertainty held fast in the appropriation-process of the most passionate inwardness" (pp. 41, 182).[1] Let us say that a piece of reasoning, R, is *objective reasoning* just in case every (or almost every) intelligent, fair-minded, and sufficiently informed person would regard R as showing or tending to show (in the circumstances in which R is used, and to the extent claimed in R) that R's conclusion is true or probably true. Uses of "objective" and "objectively" in other contexts can be understood from their relation to this one; for example, an objective uncertainty is a proposition which cannot be shown by objective reasoning to be certainly true.

1   The Approximation Argument

"Is it possible to base an eternal happiness upon historical knowledge?" is one of the central questions in the *Postscript*, and in the *Philosophical Fragments* to which it is a "postscript." Part of Kierkegaard's answer to the question is that it is not possible to base an eternal happiness on objective reasoning about historical facts.

> For nothing is more readily evident than that the greatest attainable certainty with respect to anything historical is merely an *approximation*. And an approximation, when viewed as a basis for an eternal happiness, is wholly inadequate, since the incommensurability makes a result impossible. (p. 25)

Kierkegaard maintains that it is possible, however, to base an eternal happiness on a belief in historical facts that is independent of objective evidence for them, and that that is what one must do in order to be a Christian. This is the Approximation Argument for the proposition that Christian faith cannot be based on objective reasoning.[2] (It is assumed that some belief about historical facts is an essential part of

---

[1] Søren Kierkegaard, *Concluding Unscientific Postscript*, translated by David F. Swenson; introduction, notes, and completion of translation by Walter Lowrie (Princeton: Princeton University Press, 1941). Page references in parentheses in the body of the present paper are to this work.

[2] The argument is not original with Kierkegaard. It can be found in works of G. E. Lessing and D. F. Strauss that Kierkegaard had read. See especially Thulstrup's quotation and discussion of a passage from Strauss in the commentary portion of Søren Kierkegaard, *Philosophical Fragments*, translated by David F. Swenson, second edition, translation revised by Howard V. Hong, with introduction and commentary by Niels Thulstrup (Princeton: Princeton University Press, 1962), pp. 149–51.

Christian faith, so that if religious faith cannot be based on objective historical reasoning, then Christian faith cannot be based on objective reasoning at all.) Let us examine the argument in detail.

Its first premise is Kierkegaard's claim that "the greatest attainable certainty with respect to anything historical is merely an approximation." I take him to mean that historical evidence, objectively considered, never completely excludes the possibility of error. "It goes without saying," he claims, "that it is impossible in the case of historical problems to reach an objective decision so certain that no doubt could disturb it" (p. 41). For Kierkegaard's purposes it does not matter how small the possibility of error is, so long as it is finitely small (that is, so long as it is not literally infinitesimal). He insists (p. 31) that his Approximation Argument makes no appeal to the supposition that the objective evidence for Christian historical beliefs is weaker than the objective evidence for any other historical belief. The argument turns on a claim about *all* historical evidence. The probability of error in our belief that there was an American Civil War in the nineteenth century, for instance, might be as small as $\frac{1}{10^{2,000,000}}$; that would be a large enough chance of error for Kierkegaard's argument.

It might be disputed, but let us assume for the sake of argument that there is some such finitely small probability of error in the objective grounds for all historical beliefs, as Kierkegaard held. This need not keep us from saying that we "know," and it is "certain," that there was an American Civil War. For such an absurdly small possibility of error is as good as no possibility of error at all, "for all practical intents and purposes," as we might say. Such a possibility of error is too small to be worth worrying about.

But would it be too small to be worth worrying about if we had an *infinite* passionate interest in the question about the Civil War? If we have an infinite passionate interest in something, there is no limit to how important it is to us. (The nature of such an interest will be discussed more fully in section 3 below.) Kierkegaard maintains that in relation to an infinite passionate interest *no* possibility of error is too small to be worth worrying about. "In relation to an eternal happiness, and an infinite passionate interest in its behalf (in which latter alone the former can exist), an iota is of importance, of infinite importance . . ." (p. 28). This is the basis for the second premise of the Approximation Argument, which is Kierkegaard's claim that "an approximation, when viewed as a basis for an eternal happiness, is wholly inadequate" (p. 25). "An approximation is essentially incommensurable with an infinite personal interest in an eternal happiness" (p. 26).

At this point in the argument it is important to have some understanding of Kierkegaard's conception of faith, and the way in which he thinks faith excludes doubt. Faith must be decisive; in fact it seems to consist in a sort of decision-making. "The conclusion of belief is not so much a conclusion as a resolution, and it is for this reason that belief excludes doubt."[3] The decision of faith is a decision

---

[3] Kierkegaard, *Philosophical Fragments*, p. 104; cf. pp. 102–03.

to disregard the possibility of error – to act on what is believed, without hedging one's bets to take account of any possibility of error.

To disregard the possibility of error is not to be unaware of it, or fail to consider it, or lack anxiety about it. Kierkegaard insists that the believer must be keenly *aware* of the risk of error. "If I wish to preserve myself in faith I must constantly be intent upon holding fast the objective uncertainty, so as to remain out upon the deep, over seventy thousand fathoms of water, still preserving my faith" (p. 182).

For Kierkegaard, then, to ask whether faith in a historical fact can be based on objective reasoning is to ask whether objective reasoning can justify one in disregarding the possibility of error which (he thinks) historical evidence always leaves. Here another aspect of Kierkegaard's conception of faith plays its part in the argument. He thinks that in all genuine religious faith the believer is *infinitely* interested in the object of his faith. And he thinks it follows that objective reasoning cannot justify him in disregarding *any* possibility of error about the object of faith, and therefore cannot lead him all the way to religious faith where a historical fact is concerned. The farthest it could lead him is to the conclusion that *if* he had only a certain finite (though very great) interest in the matter, the possibility of error would be too small to be worth worrying about and he would be justified in disregarding it. But faith disregards a possibility of error that *is* worth worrying about, since an infinite interest is involved. Thus faith requires a "leap" beyond the evidence, a leap that cannot be justified by objective reasoning (cf. p. 90).

There is something right in what Kierkegaard is saying here, but his Approximation Argument is a bad argument. He is right in holding that grounds of doubt which may be insignificant for most practical purposes can be extremely troubling for the intensity of a religious concern, and that it may require great decisiveness, or something like courage, to overcome them religiously. But he is mistaken in holding that objective reasoning could not justify one in disregarding any possibility of error about something in which one is infinitely interested.

The mistake, I believe, lies in his overlooking the fact that there are at least two different reasons one might have for disregarding a possibility of error. The first is that the possibility is too small to be worth worrying about. The second is that the risk of not disregarding the possibility of error would be greater than the risk of disregarding it. Of these two reasons only the first is ruled out by the infinite passionate interest.

I will illustrate this point with two examples, one secular and one religious. A certain woman has a very great (though not infinite) interest in her husband's love for her. She rightly judges that the objective evidence available to her renders it 99.9 per cent probable that he loves her truly. The intensity of her interest is sufficient to cause her some *anxiety* over the remaining 1/1,000 chance that he loves her not; for her this chance is not too small to be worth worrying about. (Kierkegaard uses a similar example to support his Approximation Argument; see p. 511.) But she (very reasonably) wants to *disregard* the risk of error, in the sense of not hedging her bets, if he does love her. This desire is at least as strong as her desire not to be deceived if he does not love her. Objective reasoning should therefore suffice to bring her to the conclusion that she ought to disregard the risk of error, since by not disregarding it she would run 999 times as great risk of frustrating one of these desires.

Or suppose you are trying to base your eternal happiness on your relation to Jesus, and therefore have an infinite passionate interest in the question whether he declared Peter and his episcopal successors to be infallible in matters of religious doctrine. You want to be committed to whichever is the true belief on this question, disregarding any possibility of error in it. And suppose, just for the sake of argument, that objective historical evidence renders it 99 per cent probable that Jesus did declare Peter and his successors to be infallible — or 99 per cent probable that he did not — for our present discussion it does not matter which. The one per cent chance of error is enough to make you *anxious*, in view of your infinite interest. But objective reasoning leads to the conclusion that you ought to commit yourself to the more probable opinion, *disregarding* the risk of error, if your strong-est desire in the matter is to be so committed to the true opinion. For the only other way to satisfy this desire would be to commit yourself to the less probable opinion, disregarding the risk of error in it. The first way will be successful if and only if the more probable opinion is true, and the second way if and only if the less probable opinion is true. Surely it is prudent to do what gives you a 99 per cent chance of satisfying your strong desire, in preference to what gives you only a one per cent chance of satisfying it.

In this argument your strong desire to be committed to the true opinion is presupposed. The reasonableness of this desire may depend on a belief for which no probability can be established by purely historical reasoning, such as the belief that Jesus is God. But any difficulties arising from this point are distinct from those urged in the Approximation Argument, which itself presupposes the infinite pas-sionate interest in the historical question.

There is some resemblance between my arguments in these examples and Pas-cal's famous Wager argument. But whereas Pascal's argument turns on weighing an infinite interest against a finite one, mine turn on weighing a large chance of success against a small one. An argument closer to Pascal's will be discussed in section 4 below.

The reader may well have noticed in the foregoing discussion some unclarity about what sort of justification is being demanded and given for religious beliefs about historical facts. There are at least two different types of questions about a proposition which I might try to settle by objective reasoning: (1) Is it probable that the proposition is true? (2) In view of the evidence which I have for and against the proposition, and my interest in the matter, is it prudent for me to have faith in the truth of the proposition, disregarding the possibility of error? Corres-pondingly, we may distinguish two ways in which a belief can be *based on* object-ive reasoning. The proposition believed may be the conclusion of a piece of objective reasoning, and accepted because it is that. We may say that such a belief is *objectively probable*. Or one might hold a belief or maintain a religious faith because of a piece of objective reasoning whose conclusion is that it would be prudent, morally right, or otherwise desirable for one to hold that belief or faith. In this latter case let us say that the belief is *objectively advantageous*. It is clear that historical beliefs can be objectively probable; and in the Approximation Argument, Kierkegaard does not deny Christian historical beliefs can be objectively probable. His thesis is, in effect, that in view of an infinite passionate interest in their subject matter, they cannot be objectively advantageous, and therefore cannot be fully justified objectively, even if they are objectively probable. It is this thesis that I have attempted to refute. I have not been discussing the question whether Christian historical beliefs are objectively probable.

2   The Postponement Argument

The trouble with objective historical reasoning, according to the Approximation Argument, is that it cannot yield complete certainty. But that is not Kierkegaard's only complaint against it as a basis for religious faith. He also objects that objective historical inquiry is never completely finished, so that one who seeks to base his faith on it postpones his religious commitment forever. In the process of historical research "new difficulties arise and are overcome, and new difficulties again arise. Each generation inherits from its predecessor the illusion that the method is quite impeccable, but the learned scholars have not yet succeeded . . . and so forth. . . . The infinite personal passionate interest of the subject . . . vanishes more and more, because the decision is postponed, and postponed as following directly upon the result of the learned inquiry" (p. 28). As soon as we take "an historical document" as "our standard for the determination of Christian truth," we are "involved in a parenthesis whose conclusion is everlastingly prospective" (p. 28) – that is, we are involved in a religious digression which keeps religious commitment forever in the future.[4]

Kierkegaard has such fears about allowing religious faith to rest on *any* empirical reasoning. The danger of postponement of commitment arises not only from the uncertainties of historical scholarship, but also in connection with the design argument for God's existence. In the *Philosophical Fragments* Kierkegaard notes some objections to the attempt to prove God's existence from evidence of "the wisdom in nature, the goodness, the wisdom in the governance of the world," and then says, "even if I began I would never finish, and would in addition have to live constantly in suspense, lest something so terrible should suddenly happen that my bit of proof would be demolished."[5] What we have before us is a quite general sort of objection to the treatment of religious beliefs as empirically testable. On this point many analytical philosophers seem to agree with Kierkegaard. Much discussion

---

[4] Essentially the same argument can be found in a plea, which has had great influence among more recent theologians, for making Christian faith independent of the results of critical historical study of the Bible: Martin Kähler's famous lecture, first delivered in 1892, *Der sogenannte historische Jesus und der geschichtliche biblische Christus* (München: Christus Kaiser Verlag, 1961), p. 50f.

[5] Kierkegaard, *Philosophical Fragments*, p. 52.

in recent analytical philosophy of religion has proceeded from the supposition that religious beliefs are not empirically testable. I think it is far from obvious that that supposition is correct; and it is interesting to consider arguments that may be advanced to support it.

Kierkegaard's statements suggest an argument that I call the Postponement Argument. Its first premise is that one cannot have an authentic religious faith without being totally committed to it. In order to be totally committed to a belief, in the relevant sense, one must be determined not to abandon the belief under any circumstances that one recognizes as epistemically possible.

The second premise is that one cannot yet be totally committed to any belief which one bases on an inquiry in which one recognizes any possibility of a future need to revise the results. Total commitment to any belief so based will necessarily be postponed. I believe that this premise, suitably interpreted, is true. Consider the position of someone who regards himself as committed to a belief on the basis of objective evidence, but who recognizes some possibility that future discoveries will destroy the objective justification of the belief. We must ask how he is disposed to react in the event, however unlikely, that the objective basis of his belief is overthrown. Is he prepared to abandon the belief in that event? If so, he is not totally committed to the belief in the relevant sense. But if he is determined to cling to his belief even if its objective justification is taken away, then he is not basing the belief on the objective justification – or at least he is not basing it solely on the justification.[6]

The conclusion to be drawn from these two premises is that authentic religious faith cannot be based on an inquiry in which one recognizes any possibility of a future need to revise the results. We ought to note that this conclusion embodies two important restrictions on the scope of the argument.

In the first place, we are not given an argument that authentic religious faith cannot *have* an objective justification that is subject to possible future revision. What we are given is an argument that the authentic believer's holding of his religious belief cannot *depend* entirely on such a justification.

In the second place, this conclusion applies only to those who *recognize* some epistemic possibility that the objective results which appear to support their belief may be overturned. I think it would be unreasonable to require, as part of total commitment, a determination with regard to one's response to circumstances that one does not recognize as possible at all. It may be, however, that one does not recognize such a possibility when one ought to.

Kierkegaard needs one further premise in order to arrive at the conclusion that authentic religious faith cannot without error be based on any objective empirical reasoning. This third premise is that in every objective empirical inquiry there is always, objectively considered, some epistemic possibility that the results of the

---

[6] Kierkegaard notes the possibility that in believing in God's existence "I make so bold as to defy all objections, even those that have not yet been made." But in that case he thinks the belief is not really based on the evidence of God's work in the world; "it is not from the works that I make my proof" (*Philosophical Fragments*, p. 52).

inquiry will need to be revised in view of new evidence or new reasoning. I believe Kierkegaard makes this assumption; he certainly makes it with regard to historical inquiry. From this premise it follows that one is in error if in any objective empirical inquiry one does not recognize any possibility of a future need to revise the results. But if one does recognize such a possibility, then according to the conclusion already reached in the Postponement Argument, one cannot base an authentic religious faith on the inquiry.

Some philosophers might attack the third premise of this argument; and certainly it is controversial. But I am more inclined to criticize the first premise. There is undoubtedly something plausible about the claim that authentic religious faith must involve a commitment so complete that the believer is resolved not to abandon his belief under any circumstances that he regards as epistemically possible. If you are willing to abandon your ostensibly religious beliefs for the sake of objective inquiry, mightn't we justly say that objective inquiry is your real religion, the thing to which you are most deeply committed?

There is also something plausible to be said on the other side, however. It has commonly been thought to be an important part of religious ethics that one ought to be humble, teachable, open to correction, new inspiration, and growth of insight, even (and perhaps especially) in important religious beliefs. That view would have to be discarded if we were to concede to Kierkegaard that the heart of commitment in religion is an unconditional determination not to change in one's important religious beliefs. In fact I think there is something radically wrong with this conception of religious commitment. Faith ought not to be thought of as unconditional devotion to a belief. For in the first place the object of religious devotion is not a belief or attitude of one's own, but God. And in the second place it may be doubted that religious devotion to God can or should be completely unconditional. God's love for sinners is sometimes said to be completely unconditional, not being based on any excellence or merit of theirs. But religious devotion to God is generally thought to be based on His goodness and love. It is the part of the strong, not the weak, to love unconditionally. And in relation to God we are weak.

3 The Passion Argument

In Kierkegaard's statements of the Approximation Argument and the Postponement Argument it is assumed that a system of religious beliefs might be objectively probable. It is only for the sake of argument, however, that Kierkegaard allows this assumption. He really holds that religious faith, by its very nature, needs objective *im*probability. "Anything that is almost probable, or probable, or extremely and emphatically probable, is something [one] can almost know, or as good as know, or extremely and emphatically almost *know* – but it is impossible to *believe*" (p. 189). Nor will Kierkegaard countenance the suggestion that religion ought to go beyond belief to some almost-knowledge based on probability. "Faith is the highest passion in a man. There are perhaps many in every generation who do not even reach it, but no one gets further."[7] It would be a betrayal of religion to try to go beyond faith. The suggestion that faith might be replaced by "probabilities and guarantees" is for the believer "a temptation to be resisted with all his strength" (p. 15). The attempt to establish religious beliefs on a foundation of objective probability is therefore no service to religion, but inimical to religion's true interests. The approximation to certainty which might be afforded by objective probability is rejected, not only for the reasons given in the Approximation Argument and Postponement Argument, but also from a deeper motive, "since on the contrary it behooves us to get rid of introductory guarantees of security, proofs from consequences, and the whole mob of public pawnbrokers and guarantors, so as to permit the absurd to stand out in all its clarity – in order that the individual may believe if he wills it; I merely say that it must be strenuous in the highest degree so to believe" (p. 190).

As this last quotation indicates, Kierkegaard thinks that religious belief ought to be based on a strenuous exertion of the will – a passionate striving. His reasons for thinking that objective probability is religiously undesirable have to do with the place of passion in religion, and constitute what I call the Passion Argument. The first premise of the argument is that the most essential and the most valuable feature of religiousness is passion, indeed an infinite passion, a passion of the greatest possible intensity. The second premise is that an infinite passion requires objective improbability. And the conclusion therefore is that that which is most essential and most valuable in religiousness requires objective improbability.

My discussion of this argument will have three parts. (a) First I will try to clarify, very briefly, what it is that is supposed to be objectively improbable. (b) Then we will consider Kierkegaard's reasons for holding that infinite passion requires objective improbability. In so doing we will also gain a clearer understanding of what a Kierkegaardian infinite passion is. (c) Finally I will discuss the first premise of the argument – although issues will arise at that point which I do not pretend to be able to settle by argument.

(a) What are the beliefs whose improbability is needed by religious passion? Kierkegaard will hardly be satisfied with the improbability of just any one belief; it must surely be at least an important belief. On the other hand it would clearly be preposterous to suppose that every belief involved in Christianity must be objectively improbable. (Consider, for example, the belief that the man Jesus did indeed live.) I think that what is demanded in the Passion Argument is the objective improbability of at least one belief which must be true if the goal sought by the religious passion is to be attained.

(b) We can find in the *Postscript* suggestions of several reasons for thinking that an infinite passion needs objective improbability. The two that seem to me most interesting have to do with (i) the risks accepted and (ii) the costs paid in pursuance of a passionate interest.

---

[7] Søren Kierkegaard, *Fear and Trembling*, trans. Walter Lowrie, 2nd edn (Princeton: Princeton University Press, 1970; published in one volume with *The Sickness unto Death*), p. 131. Cf. *Postscript*, p. 31f.

(i) One reason that Kierkegaard has for valuing objective improbability is that it increases the *risk* attaching to the religious life, and risk is so essential for the expression of religious passion that "without risk there is no faith" (p. 182). About the nature of an eternal happiness, the goal of religious striving, Kierkegaard says "there is nothing to be said . . . except that it is the good which is attained by venturing everything absolutely" (p. 382).

> But what then does it mean to venture? A venture is the precise correlative of an uncertainty; when the certainty is there the venture becomes impossible. . . . If what I hope to gain by venturing is itself certain, I do not risk or venture, but make an exchange. . . . No, if I am in truth resolved to venture, in truth resolved to strive for the attainment of the highest good, the uncertainty must be there, and I must have room to move, so to speak. But the largest space I can obtain, where there is room for the most vehement gesture of the passion that embraces the infinite, is uncertainty of knowledge with respect to an eternal happiness, or the certain knowledge that the choice is in the finite sense a piece of madness: now there is room, now you can venture! (pp. 380–82)

How is it that objective improbability provides the largest space for the most vehement gesture of infinite passion? Consider two cases. (A) You plunge into a raging torrent to rescue from drowning someone you love, who is crying for help. (B) You plunge into a raging torrent in a desperate attempt to rescue someone you love, who appears to be unconscious and *may* already have drowned. In both cases you manifest a passionate interest in saving the person, risking your own life in order to do so. But I think Kierkegaard would say there is more passion in the second case than in the first. For in the second case you risk your life in what is, objectively considered, a smaller chance that you will be able to save your loved one. A greater passion is required for a more desperate attempt.

A similar assessment may be made of the following pair of cases. (A′) You stake everything on your faith in the truth of Christianity, knowing that it is objectively 99 per cent probable that Christianity is true. (B′) You stake everything on your faith in the truth of Christianity, knowing that the truth of Christianity is, objectively, possible but so improbable that its probability is, say, as small as $\frac{1}{10^{2,000,000}}$. There is passion in both cases, but Kierkegaard will say that there is more passion in the second case than in the first. For to venture the same stake (namely, everything) on a much smaller chance of success shows greater passion.

Acceptance of risk can thus be seen as a *measure* of the intensity of passion. I believe this provides us with one way of understanding what Kierkegaard means when he calls religious passion "infinite." An *infinite* passionate interest in *x* is an interest so strong that it leads one to make the greatest possible sacrifices in order to obtain *x*, on the smallest possible chance of success. The infinity of the passion is shown in that there is no sacrifice so great one will not make it, and no chance of success so small one will not act on it. A passion which is infinite in this sense requires, by its very nature, a situation of maximum risk for its expression.

It will doubtless be objected that this argument involves a misunderstanding of what a passionate interest is. Such an interest is a disposition. In order to have a great passionate interest it is not necessary actually to make a great sacrifice with a small chance of success; all that is necessary is to have such an intense interest that one *would* do so if an appropriate occasion should arise. It is therefore a mistake to say that there *is* more passion in case (B) than in case (A), or in (B′) than in (A′). More passion is *shown* in (B) than in (A), and in (B′) than in (A′); but an equal passion may exist in cases in which there is no occasion to show it.

This objection may well be correct as regards what we normally mean by "passionate interest." But that is not decisive for the argument. The crucial question is what part dispositions, possibly unactualized, ought to play in religious devotion. And here we must have a digression about the position of the *Postscript* on this question — a position that is complex at best and is not obviously consistent.

In the first place I do not think that Kierkegaard would be prepared to think of passion, or a passionate interest, as primarily a disposition that might remain unactualized. He seems to conceive of passion chiefly as an intensity in which one actually does and feels. "Passion is momentary' (p. 178), although capable of continual repetition. And what is momentary in such a way that it must be repeated rather than protracted is presumably an occurrence rather than a disposition. It agrees with this conception of passion that Kierkegaard idealizes a life of "persistent striving," and says that the religious task is to "exercise" the God–relationship and to give "existential expression" to the religious choice (pp. 110, 364, 367).

All of this supports the view that what Kierkegaard means by "an infinite passionate interest" is a pattern of actual decision-making, in which one continually exercises and expresses one's religiousness by making the greatest possible sacrifices on the smallest possible chance of success. In order to actualize such a pattern of life one needs chances of success that are as small as possible. That is the room that is required for "the most vehement gesture" of infinite passion.

But on the other hand Kierkegaard does allow a dispositional element in the religious life, and even precisely in the making of the greatest possible sacrifices. We might suppose that if we are to make the greatest possible sacrifices in our religious devotion, we must do so by abandoning all worldly interests and devoting all our time and attention to religion. That is what monasticism attempts to do, as Kierkegaard sees it; and (in the *Postscript*, at any rate) he rejects the attempt, contrary to what our argument to this point would have led us to expect of him. He holds that "resignation' (pp. 353, 367) or "renunciation" (pp. 362, 386) of *all* finite ends is precisely the first thing that religiousness requires; but he means a renunciation that is compatible with pursuing and enjoying finite ends (pp. 362–71). This renunciation is the practice of a sort of detachment; Kierkegaard uses the image of a dentist loosening the soft tissues around a tooth, while it is still in place, in preparation for pulling it (p. 367). It is partly a matter of not treating finite things with a desperate seriousness, but with a certain coolness or humor, even while one pursues them (pp. 368, 370).

This coolness is not just a disposition. But the renunciation also has a dispositional aspect. "Now if for any individual an eternal happiness is his highest good, this will mean that all finite satisfactions are volitionally relegated to the status of what may have to be renounced in favor of an eternal happiness" (p. 350). The volitional relegation is not a disposition but an act of choice. The object of this choice, however, appears to be a dispositional state – the state of being such that one *would* forgo any finite satisfaction *if* it *were* religiously necessary or advantageous to do so.

It seems clear that Kierkegaard, in the *Postscript*, is willing to admit a dispositional element at one point in the religious venture, but not at another. It is enough in most cases, he thinks, if one is *prepared* to cease for the sake of religion from pursuing some finite end; but it is not enough that one *would* hold to one's belief in the face of objective improbability. The belief must actually be improbable, although the pursuit of the finite need not actually cease. What is not clear is a reason for this disparity. The following hypothesis, admittedly somewhat speculative as interpretation of the text, is the best explanation I can offer.

The admission of a dispositional element in the religious renunciation of the finite is something to which Kierkegaard seems to be driven by the view that there is no alternative to it except idolatry. For suppose one actually ceases from all worldly pursuits and enters a monastery. In the monastery one would pursue a number of particular ends (such as getting up in the middle of the night to say the offices) which, although religious in a way ("churchy," one might say), are still finite. The absolute *telos* or end of religion is no more to be identified with them than with the ends pursued by an alderman (pp. 362–71). To pretend otherwise would be to make an idolatrous identification of the absolute end with some finite end. An existing person cannot have sacrificed everything by actually having ceased from pursuing *all* finite ends. For as long as he lives and acts he is pursuing some finite end. Therefore his renouncing *everything* finite must be at least partly dispositional.

Kierkegaard does not seem happy with this position. He regards it as of the utmost importance that the religious passion should come to expression. The problem of finding an adequate expression for a passion for an infinite end, in the face of the fact that in every concrete action one will be pursuing some finite end, is treated in the *Postscript* as the central problem of religion (see especially pp. 386–486). If the sacrifice of everything finite must remain largely dispositional, then perhaps it is all the more important to Kierkegaard that the smallness of the chance for which it is sacrificed should be fully actual, so that the infinity of the religious passion may be measured by an actuality in at least one aspect of the religious venture.

(ii) According to Kierkegaard, as I have argued, the intensity of a passion is measured in part by the smallness of the chances of success that one acts on. It can also be measured in part by its *costliness* – that is, by how much one gives up or suffers in acting on those chances. This second measure can also be made the basis of an argument for the claim that an infinite passion requires objective improbability. For the objective improbability of a religious belief, if recognized, increases the costliness of holding it. The risk involved in staking everything on an objectively improbable belief gives rise to an anxiety and mental suffering whose acceptance is itself a sacrifice. It seems to follow that if one is not staking everything on a belief one sees to be objectively improbable, one's passion is not infinite in Kierkegaard's sense, since one's sacrifice could be greater if one did adhere to an improbable belief.

Kierkegaard uses an argument similar to this. For God to give us objective knowledge of Himself, eliminating paradox from it, would be "to lower the price of the God-relationship."

> And even if God could be imagined willing, no man with passion in his heart could desire it. To a maiden genuinely in love it could never occur that she had bought her happiness too dear, but rather that she had not bought it dear enough. And just as the passion of the infinite was itself the truth, so in the case of the highest value it holds true that the price is the value, that a low price means a poor value. . . . (p. 207)

Kierkegaard here appears to hold, first, that an increase in the objective probability of religious belief would reduce its costliness, and second, that the value of a religious life is measured by its cost. I take it his reason for the second of these claims is that passion is the most valuable thing in a religious life and passion is measured by its cost. If we grant Kierkegaard the requisite conception of an infinite passion, we seem once again to have a plausible argument for the view that objective improbability is required for such a passion.

(c) We must therefore consider whether infinite passion, as Kierkegaard conceives of it, ought to be part of the religious ideal of life. Such a passion is a striving, or pattern of decision-making, in which, with the greatest possible intensity of feeling, one continually makes the greatest possible sacrifices on the smallest possible chance of success. This seems to me an impossible ideal. I doubt that any human being could have a passion of this sort, because I doubt that one could make a sacrifice so great that a greater could not be made, or have a (nonzero) chance of success so small that a smaller could not be had.

But even if Kierkegaard's ideal is impossible, one might want to try to approximate it. Intensity of passion might still be measured by the greatness of sacrifices made and the smallness of chances of success acted on, even if we cannot hope for a greatest possible or a smallest possible here. And it could be claimed that the most essential and valuable thing in religiousness is a passion that is very intense (though it cannot be infinite) by this standard – the more intense the better. This claim will not support an argument that objective improbability is absolutely required for religious passion. For a passion could presumably be very intense, involving great sacrifices and risks of some other sort, without an objectively improbable belief. But it could still be argued that objectively improbable religious beliefs enhance the value of the religious life by increasing its sacrifices and diminishing its chances of success, whereas objective probability detracts from the value of religious passion by diminishing its intensity.

The most crucial question about the Passion Argument, then, is whether maximization of sacrifice and risk are so valuable in religion as to make objective improbability a desirable characteristic of religious beliefs. Certainly much religious thought and feeling places a very high value on sacrifice and on passionate intensity. But the doctrine that it is desirable to increase without limit, or to the highest possible degree (if there is one) the cost and risk of a religious life is less plausible (to say the least) than the view that *some* degree of cost and risk may add to the value of a religious life. The former doctrine would set the religious interest at enmity with all other interests, or at least with the best of them. Kierkegaard is surely right in thinking that it would be impossible to live without pursuing some finite ends. But even so it would be possible to exchange the pursuit of better finite ends for the pursuit of worse ones – for example, by exchanging the pursuit of truth, beauty, and satisfying personal relationships for the self-flagellating pursuit of pain. And a way of life would be the costlier for requiring such an exchange. Kierkegaard does not, in the *Postscript*, demand it. But the presuppositions of his Passion Argument seem to imply that such a sacrifice would be religiously desirable. Such a conception of religion is demonic. In a tolerable religious ethics some way must be found to conceive of the religious interest as inclusive rather than exclusive of the best of other interests – including, I think, the interest in having well-grounded beliefs.

4   Pascal's Wager and Kierkegaard's Leap

Ironically, Kierkegaard's views about religious passion suggest a way in which his religious beliefs could be based on objective reasoning – not on reasoning which would show them to be objectively probable, but on reasoning which shows them to be objectively advantageous. Consider the situation of a person whom Kierkegaard would regard as a genuine Christian believer. What would such a person want most of all? He would want above all else to attain the truth through Christianity. That is, he would desire both that Christianity be true and the he himself be related to it as a genuine believer. He would desire that state of affairs (which we may call S) so ardently that he would be willing to sacrifice everything else to obtain it, given only the smallest possible chance of success.

We can therefore construct the following argument, which has an obvious analogy to Pascal's Wager. Let us assume that there is, objectively, some chance, however small, that Christianity is true. This is an assumption which Kierkegaard accepts (p. 31), and I think it is plausible. There are two possibilities, then: either Christianity is true, or it is false. (Others might object to so stark a disjunction, but Kierkegaard will not.) If Christianity is false it is impossible for anyone to obtain S, since S includes the truth of Christianity. It is only if Christianity is true that anything one does will help one or hinder one in obtaining S. And if Christianity is true, one will obtain S just in case one becomes a genuine Christian believer. It seems obvious that one would increase one's chances of becoming a genuine Christian believer by becoming one now (if one can), even if the truth of Christian beliefs is now objectively uncertain or improbable. Hence it would seem to be advantageous for anyone who can to become a genuine Christian believer now, if he wants S so much that he would be willing to sacrifice everything else for the smallest possible chance of obtaining S. Indeed I believe that the argument I have given for this conclusion is a piece of objective reasoning, and that Christian belief is therefore *objectively* advantageous for anyone who wants S as much as a Kierkegaardian genuine Christian must want it.

Of course this argument does not tend at all to show that it is objectively probable that Christianity is true. It only gives a practical, prudential reason for believing, to someone who has a certain desire. Nor does the argument do anything to prove that such an absolutely overriding desire for S is reasonable.[8] It does show, however, that just as Kierkegaard's position has more logical structure than one might at first think, it is more difficult than he probably realized for him to get away entirely from objective justification.

[8] It is worth noting, though, that a similar argument might still provide some less overriding justification of belief to someone who had a strong, but less overriding, desire for S.

Fyodor Dostoevsky, "Why Does God Permit Evil?"

Rebellion

"I must make you one confession," Ivan began. "I could never understand how one can love one's neighbours. It's just one's neighbours, to my mind, that one can't love, though one might love those at a distance. I once read somewhere of John the Merciful, a saint, that when a hungry, frozen beggar came to him, he took him into his bed, held him in his arms, and began breathing into his mouth, which was putrid and loathsome from some awful disease. I am convinced that he did that from 'self-laceration,' from the self-laceration of falsity, for the sake of the charity imposed by duty, as a penance laid on him. For any one to love a man, he must be hidden, for as soon as he shows his face, love is gone."

"Father Zossima has talked of that more than once," observed Alyosha: "he, too, said that the face of a man often hinders many people not practised in love, from loving him. But yet there's a great deal of love in mankind, and almost Christ-like love. I know that myself, Ivan."

"Well, I know nothing of it so far, and can't understand it, and the innumerable mass of mankind are with me there. The question is, whether that's due to men's bad qualities or whether it's inherent in their nature. To my thinking, Christ-like love for men is a miracle impossible on earth. He was God. But we are not gods. Suppose I, for instance, suffer intensely. Another can never know how much I suffer, because he is another and not I. And what's more, a man is rarely ready to admit another's suffering (as though it were a distinction). Why won't he admit it,

From *The Brothers Karamazov*, translated by Constance Garnett (New York: Macmillan, 1923), pp. 215–23.

do you think? Because I smell unpleasant, because I have a stupid face, because I once trod on his foot. Besides there is suffering and suffering; degrading, humiliating suffering such as humbles me – hunger, for instance – my benefactor will perhaps allow me; but when you come to higher suffering – for an idea, for instance – he will very rarely admit that, perhaps because my face strikes him as not at all what he fancies a man should have who suffers for an idea. And so he deprives me instantly of his favour, and not at all from badness of heart. Beggars, especially genteel beggars, ought never to show themselves, but to ask for charity through the newspapers. One can love one's neighbours in the abstract, or even at a distance, but at close quarters it's almost impossible. If it were as on the stage, in the ballet, where if beggars come in, they wear silken rags and tattered lace and beg for alms dancing gracefully, then one might like looking at them. But even then we should not love them. But enough of that. I simply wanted to show you my point of view. I meant to speak of the suffering of mankind generally, but we had better confine ourselves to the sufferings of the children. That reduces the scope of my argument to a tenth of what it would be. Still we'd better keep to the children, though it does weaken my case. But, in the first place, children can be loved even at close quarters, even when they are dirty, even when they are ugly (I fancy, though, children never are ugly). The second reason why I won't speak of grownup people is that, besides being disgusting and unworthy of love, they have a compensation – they've eaten the apple and know good and evil, and they have become 'like god.' They go on eating it still. But the children haven't eaten anything, and are so far innocent. Are you fond of children, Alyosha? I know you are, and you will understand why I prefer to speak of them. If they, too, suffer horribly on earth, they must suffer for their fathers' sins, they must be punished for their fathers, who have eaten the apple; but that reasoning is of the other world and is incomprehensible for the heart of man here on earth. The innocent must not suffer for another's sins, and especially such innocents! You may be surprised at me, Alyosha, but I am awfully fond of children, too. And observe, cruel people, the violent, the rapacious, the Karamazovs are sometimes very fond of children. Children while they are quite little – up to seven, for instance – are so remote from grown-up people; they are different creatures, as it were, of a different species. I knew a criminal in prison who had, in the course of his career as a burglar, murdered whole families, including several children. But when he was in prison, he had a strange affection for them. He spent all his time at his window, watching the children playing in the prison yard. He trained one little boy to come up to his window and made great friends with him. . . . You don't know why I am telling you all this, Alyosha? My head aches and I am sad."

"You speak with a strange air," observed Alyosha uneasily, "as though you were not quite yourself."

"By the way, a Bulgarian I met lately in Moscow," Ivan went on, seeming not to hear his brother's words, "told me about the crimes committed by Turks and Circassians in all parts of Bulgaria through fear of a general rising of the Slavs. They burn villages, murder, outrage women and children, they nail their prisoners by the ears to the fences, leave them so till morning, and in the morning they hang them – all sorts of things you can't imagine. People talk sometimes of bestial cruelty, but that's a great injustice and insult to the beasts; a beast can never be so cruel as a man, so artistically cruel. The tiger only tears and gnaws, that's all he can do. He would never think of nailing people by the ears, even if he were able to do it. These Turks took a pleasure in torturing children, too; cutting the unborn child from the mother's womb, and tossing babies up in the air and catching them on the points of their bayonets before their mother's eyes. Doing it before the mother's eyes was what gave zest to the amusement. Here is another scene that I thought very interesting. Imagine a trembling mother with her baby in her arms, a circle of invading Turks around her. They've planned a diversion; they pet the baby, laugh to make it laugh. They succeed, the baby laughs. At that moment a Turk points a pistol four inches from the baby's face. The baby laughs with glee, holds out its little hands to the pistol, and he pulls the trigger in the baby's face and blows out its brains. Artistic, wasn't it? By the way, Turks are particularly fond of sweet things, they say."

"Brother, what are you driving at?" asked Alyosha.

"I think if the devil doesn't exist, but man has created him, he has created him in his own image and likeness."

"Just as he did God, then?" observed Alyosha.

"'It's wonderful how you can turn words,' as Polonius says in *Hamlet*," laughed Ivan. "You turn my words against me. Well, I am glad. Yours must be a fine God, if man created Him in His image and likeness. You asked just now what I was driving at. You see, I am fond of collecting certain facts, and, would you believe, I even copy anecdotes of a certain sort from newspapers and books, and I've already got a fine collection. The Turks, of course, have gone into it, but they are foreigners. I have specimens from home that are even better than the Turks. You know we prefer beating – rods and scourges – that's our national institution. Nailing ears is unthinkable for us, for we are, after all, Europeans. But the rod and the scourge we have always with us and they cannot be taken from us. Abroad now they scarcely do any beating. Manners are more humane, or laws have been passed, so that they don't dare to flog men now. But they make up for it in another way just as national as ours. And so national that it would be practically impossible among us, though I believe we are being inoculated with it, since the religious movement began in our aristocracy. I have a charming pamphlet, translated from the French, describing how, quite recently, five years ago, a murderer, Richard, was executed – a young man, I believe, of three and twenty, who repented and was converted to the Christian faith at the very scaffold. This Richard was an illegitimate child who was given as a child of six by his parents to some shepherds on the Swiss mountains. They brought him up to work for them. He grew up like a little wild beast among them. The shepherds taught him nothing, and scarcely fed or clothed him, but sent him out at seven to herd the flock in cold and wet, and no one hesitated or scrupled to treat him so. Quite the contrary, they thought they had every right, for Richard had been given to them as a chattel, and they did not even see the necessity of feeding him. Richard himself describes how in those years, like the Prodigal Son in the Gospel, he longed to eat of the mash given to the pigs, which were fattened for sale. But they wouldn't even give him that, and beat him when he stole from the pigs. And that was how he spent all his childhood and his youth, till he grew up and was strong enough to go away and be a thief. The savage began to earn his living as a day labourer in Geneva. He drank what he earned, he lived like a brute, and finished by killing and robbing an old man. He was caught, tried, and condemned to death. They are not sentimentalists there. And in prison he was immediately surrounded by pastors, members of Christian brotherhoods, philanthropic ladies, and the like. They taught him to read and write in prison, and expounded the Gospel to him. They exhorted him, worked upon him, drummed at him incessantly, till at last he solemnly confessed his crime. He was converted. He wrote to the court himself that he was a monster, but that in the end God had vouchsafed him light and shown grace. All Geneva was in excitement about him – all philanthropic and religious Geneva. All the aristo-cratic and well-bred society of the town rushed to the prison, kissed Richard and embraced him; 'You are our brother, you have found grace,' and Richard does nothing but weep with emotion, 'Yes, I've found grace! All my youth and child-hood I was glad of pigs' food, but now even I have found grace. I am dying in the Lord.' 'Yes, Richard, die in the Lord; you have shed blood and must die. Though it's not your fault that you knew not the Lord, when you coveted the pig's food and were beaten for stealing it (which was very wrong of you, for stealing is forbidden); but you've shed blood and you must die.' And on the last day, Richard, perfectly limp, did nothing but cry and repeat every minute: 'This is my happiest day. I am going to the Lord.' 'Yes,' cry the pastors and the judges and philan-thropic ladies. 'This is the happiest day of your life, for you are going to the Lord!' They all walk or drive to the scaffold in procession behind the prison van. At the scaffold they call to Richard: 'Die, brother, die in the Lord, for even thou hast found grace!' And so, covered with his brothers' kisses, Richard is dragged on to the scaffold, and led to the guillotine. And they chopped off his head in brotherly fashion, because he had found grace. Yes, that's characteristic. That pamphlet is translated into Russian by some Russian philanthropists of aristocratic rank and evangelical aspirations, and has been distributed gratis for the enlightenment of the people. The case of Richard is interesting because it's national. Though to us it's absurd to cut off a man's head, because he has become our brother and has found grace, yet we have our own specialty, which is all but worse. Our historical pastime is the direct satisfaction of inflicting pain. There are lines in Nekrassov describing how a peasant lashes a horse on the eyes, 'on its meek eyes,' every one must have seen it. It's peculiarly Russian. He describes how a feeble little nag had foundered under too heavy a load and cannot move. The peasant beats it, beats it savagely, beats it at last not knowing what he is doing in the intoxication of cruelty, thrashes it mercilessly over and over again. 'However weak you are, you must pull, if you die for it.' The nag strains, and then he begins lashing the poor defenceless creature on its weeping, on its 'meek eyes.' The frantic beast tugs and draws the load, trembling all over, gasping for breath, moving sideways, with a sort of unnatural spasmodic action – it's awful in Nekrassov. But that's only a horse, and God has given horses to be beaten. So the Tatars have taught us, and they left us the knout as a remembrance of it. But men, too, can be beaten. A well-educated, cultured gentleman and his wife beat their own child with a birch-rod, a girl of seven. I have an exact account of it. The papa was glad that the birch was covered with twigs. 'It stings more,' said he, and so he began stinging his daughter. I know for a fact there are people who at every blow are worked up to sensuality, to literal sensuality, which increases progressively at every blow they inflict. They beat for a minute, for five minutes, for ten minutes, more often and more savagely. The child screams. At last the child cannot scream, it gasps, 'Daddy! daddy!' By some diabolical unseemly chance the case was brought into court. A counsel is engaged. The Russian people have long called a barrister 'a conscience for hire.' The counsel protests in his client's defence. 'It's such a simple thing,' he says, 'an everyday domestic event. A father corrects his child. To our shame be it said, it is brought into court.' The jury, convinced by him, give a favourable verdict. The public roars with delight that the torturer is acquitted. Ah, pity I wasn't there! I would have proposed to raise a subscription in his honour! . . . Charming pictures.

"But I've still better things about children. I've collected a great, great deal about Russian children, Alyosha. There was a little girl of five who was hated by her father and mother, 'most worthy and respectable people, of good education and breeding.' You see, I must repeat again, it is a peculiar characteristic of many people, this love of torturing children, and children only. To all other types of humanity these torturers behave mildly and benevolently, like cultivated and humane Europeans; but they are very fond of tormenting children, even fond of children themselves in that sense. It's just their defencelessness that tempts the tormentor, just the angelic confidence of the child who has no refuge and no appeal, that sets his vile blood on fire. In every man, of course, a demon lies hidden – the demon of rage, the demon of lustful heat at the screams of the tortured victim, the demon of lawlessness let off the chain, the demon of diseases that follow on vice, gout, kidney disease, and so on.

"This poor child of five was subjected to every possible torture by those culti-vated parents. They beat her, thrashed her, kicked her for no reason till her body was one bruise. Then, they went to greater refinements of cruelty – shut her up all night in the cold and frost in a privy, and because she didn't ask to be taken up at night (as though a child of five sleeping its angelic, sound sleep could be trained to wake and ask), they smeared her face and filled her mouth with excrement, and it was her mother, her mother did this. And that mother could sleep, hearing the poor child's groans! Can you understand why a little creature, who can't even understand what's done to her, should beat her little aching heart with her tiny fist in the dark and the cold, and weep her meek unresentful tears to dear, kind God to protect her? Do you understand that, friend and brother, you pious and humble novice? Do you understand why this infamy must be and is permitted? Without it, I am told, man could not have existed on earth, for he could not have known good and evil. Why should he know that diabolical good and evil when it costs so much? Why, the whole world of knowledge is not worth that child's prayer to 'dear, kind God'! I say nothing of the sufferings of grown-up people, they have eaten the apple, damn them, and the devil take them all! But these little ones! I am making you suffer, Alyosha, you are not yourself. I'll leave off if you like."

"Never mind. I want to suffer too," muttered Alyosha.

"One picture, only one more, because it's so curious, so characteristic, and I have only just read it in some collection of Russian antiquities. I've forgotten the name. I must look it up. It was in the darkest days of serfdom at the beginning of the century, and long live the Liberator of the People! There was in those days a general of aristocratic connections, the owner of great estates, one of those men – somewhat exceptional, I believe, even then – who, retiring from the service into a life of leisure, are convinced that they've earned absolute power over the lives of their subjects. There were such men then. So our general, settled on his property of two thousand souls, lives in pomp, and domineers over his poor neighbours as though they were dependents and buffoons. He has kennels of hundreds of hounds and nearly a hundred dog-boys – all mounted, and in uniform. One day a serf boy, a little child of eight, threw a stone in play and hurt the paw of the general's favourite hound. 'Why is my favourite dog lame?' He is told that the boy threw a stone that hurt the dog's paw. 'So you did it.' The general looked the child up and down. 'Take him.' He was taken – taken from his mother and kept shut up all night. Early that morning the general comes out on horseback, with the hounds, his dependents, dog-boys, and huntsmen, all mounted around him in full hunting parade. The servants are summoned for their edification, and in front of them all stands the mother of the child. The child is brought from the lock-up. It's a gloomy cold, foggy autumn day, a capital day for hunting. The general orders the child to be undressed; the child is stripped naked. He shivers, numb with terror not daring to cry.... 'Make him run,' commands the general. 'Run! run!' shout the dog-boys. The boy runs.... 'At him!' yells the general, and he sets the whole pack of hounds on the child. The hounds catch him, and tear him to pieces before his mother's eyes!... I believe the general was afterwards declared incapable of administering his estates. Well – what did he deserve? To be shot? To be shot for the satisfaction of our moral feelings? Speak, Alyosha!"

"To be shot," murmured Alyosha, lifting his eyes to Ivan with a pale, twisted smile.

"Bravo!" cried Ivan delighted. "If even you say so ... You're a pretty monk! So there is a little devil sitting in your heart, Alyosha Karamazov!"

"What I said was absurd, but——"

"That's just the point, that 'but'!" cried Ivan. "Let me tell you, novice, that the absurd is only too necessary on earth. The world stands on absurdities, and perhaps nothing would have come to pass in it without them. We know what we know!"

"What do you know?"

"I understand nothing," Ivan went on, as though in delirium. "I don't want to understand anything now. I want to stick to the fact. I made up my mind long ago not to understand. If I try to understand anything, I shall be false to the fact and I have determined to stick to the fact."

"Why are you trying me?" Alyosha cried, with sudden distress. "Will you say what you mean at last?"

"Of course, I will; that's what I've been leading up to. You are dear to me, I don't want to let you go, and I won't give you up to your Zossima."

Ivan for a minute was silent, his face became all at once very sad.

"Listen! I took the case of children only to make my case clearer. Of the other tears of humanity with which the earth is soaked from its crust to its centre, I will say nothing. I have narrowed my subject on purpose. I am a bug, and I recognise in all humility that I cannot understand why the world is arranged as it is. Men are themselves to blame, I suppose; they were given paradise, they wanted freedom, and stole fire from heaven, though they knew they would become unhappy, so there is no need to pity them. With my pitiful, earthly, Euclidian understanding, all I know is that there is suffering and that there are none guilty; that cause follows effect, simply and directly; that everything flows and finds its level – but that's only Euclidian nonsense, I know that, and I can't consent to live by it! What comfort is it to me that there are none guilty and that cause follows effect simply and directly, and that I know it – I must have justice, or I will destroy myself. And not justice in some remote infinite time and space, but here on earth, and that I could see myself. I have believed in it. I want to see it, and if I am dead by then, let me rise again, for if it all happens without me, it will be too unfair. Surely I haven't suffered, simply that I, my crimes and my sufferings, may manure the soil of the future harmony for somebody else. I want to see with my own eyes the hind lie down with the lion and the victim rise up and embrace his murderer. I want to be there when every one suddenly understands what it has all been for. All the religions of the world are built on this longing, and I am a believer. But then there are the children, and what am I to do about them? That's a question I can't answer. For the hundredth time I repeat, there are numbers of questions, but I've only taken the children, because in their case what I mean is so unanswerably clear. Listen! If all must suffer to pay for the eternal harmony, what have children to do with it, tell me, please? It's beyond all comprehension why they should suffer, and why they should pay for the harmony. Why should they, too, furnish material to enrich the soil for the harmony of the future? I understand solidarity in sin among men. I understand solidarity in retribution, too; but there can be no such solidarity with children. And if it is really true that they must share responsibility for all their fathers' crimes, such a truth is not of this world and is beyond my comprehension. Some jester will say, perhaps, that the child would have grown up and have sinned, but you see he didn't grow up, he was torn to pieces by the dogs, at eight years old. Oh, Alyosha, I am not blaspheming! I understand, of course, what an upheaval of the universe it will be, when everything in heaven and earth blends in one hymn of praise and everything that lives and has lived cries aloud: 'Thou art just, O Lord, for Thy ways are revealed.' When the mother embraces the fiend who threw her child to the dogs, and all three cry aloud with tears, 'Thou art just, O Lord!'

then, of course, the crown of knowledge will be reached and all will be made clear. But what pulls me up here is that I can't accept that harmony. And while I am on earth, I make haste to take my own measures. You see, Alyosha, perhaps it really may happen that if I live to that moment, or rise again to see it, I, too, perhaps, may cry aloud with the rest, looking at the mother embracing the child's torturer. 'Thou art just, O Lord!' but I don't want to cry aloud then. While there is still time, I hasten to protect myself and so I renounce the higher harmony altogether. It's not worth the tears of that one tortured child who beat itself on the breast with its little fist and prayed in its stinking outhouse, with its unexpiated tears to 'dear, kind God'! It's not worth it, because those tears are unatoned for. They must be atoned for, or there can be no harmony. But how? How are you going to atone for them? Is it possible? By their being avenged? But what do I care for avenging them? What do I care for a hell for oppressors? What good can hell do, since those children have already been tortured? And what becomes of harmony, if there is hell? I want to forgive. I want to embrace. I don't want more suffering. And if the sufferings of children go to swell the sum of sufferings which was necessary to pay for truth, then I protest that the truth is not worth such a price. I don't want the mother to embrace the oppressor who threw her son to the dogs! She dare not forgive him! Let her forgive him for herself, if she will, let her forgive the torturer for the immeasurable suffering of her mother's heart. But the sufferings of her tortured child she has no right to forgive; she dare not forgive the torturer, even if the child were to forgive him! And if that is so, if they dare not forgive, what becomes of harmony? Is there in the whole world a being who would have the right to forgive and could forgive? I don't want harmony. From love for humanity I don't want it. I would rather be left with the unavenged suffering. I would rather remain with my unavenged suffering and unsatisfied indignation, *even if I were wrong*. Besides, too high a price is asked for harmony; it's beyond our means to pay so much to enter on it. And so I hasten to give back my entrance ticket, and if I am an honest man I am bound to give it back as soon as possible. And that I am doing. It's not God that I don't accept, Alyosha, only I most respectfully return Him the ticket."

"That's rebellion," murmured Alyosha, looking down.

"Rebellion? I am sorry you call it that," said Ivan earnestly. "One can hardly live in rebellion, and I want to live. Tell me yourself, I challenge you – answer. Imagine that you are creating a fabric of human destiny with the object of making men happy in the end, giving them peace and rest at last, but that it was essential and inevitable to torture to death only one tiny creature – that baby beating its breast with its fist, for instance – and to found that edifice on its unavenged tears, would you consent to be the architect on those conditions? Tell me, and tell the truth."

"No, I wouldn't consent," said Alyosha softly.

"And can you admit the idea that men for whom you are building it would agree to accept their happiness on the foundation of the unexpiated blood of a little victim? And accepting it would remain happy for ever?"

"No, I can't admit it. Brother," said Alyosha suddenly, with flashing eyes, "you said just now, is there a being in the whole world who would have the right to forgive and could forgive? But there is a Being and He can forgive everything, all and for all, because He gave His innocent blood for all and everything. You have forgotten Him, and on Him is built the edifice, and it is to Him they cry aloud, 'Thou art just, O Lord, for Thy ways are revealed!'"

"Ah! the One without sin and His blood! No, I have not forgotten Him; on the contrary I've been wondering all the time how it was you did not bring Him in before, for usually all arguments on your side put Him in the foreground. . . ."

4

Knowledge and Skepticism

G. Lynn Stephens, "Descartes and the Problem of
Our Knowledge of the External World"

Readings

René Descartes, *Meditations on First Philosophy* (selections)

Bertrand Russell, *The Problems of Philosophy* (selections)

W. V. O. Quine, "Posits and Reality"

Bruce Aune, "Is There a Problem about Knowledge of the External World?"

Frans Hals, *Portrait of Descartes* (Louvre, Paris, France).
Josse/Art Resource, New York.

G. LYNN STEPHENS

Descartes and the Problem of Our Knowledge of the External World

Several persons have urged me to do this, since they knew that I have been practicing a certain method of solving all sorts of difficulties in the sciences. . . . I have therefore considered it my duty to see what I could achieve in this field.
René Descartes, *Meditations on First Philosophy*

I believe that I have two hands. I believe that because I can see them, feel them, hear them clapping. I have reasons of roughly the same sort for believing that I have two feet, that there is a desk in front of me, a telephone on the desk, a tree outside my window, and for a host of other beliefs about the physical objects that make up the world in which I live. Probably a few of those beliefs are false, due to optical illusions, snap judgments, or misinterpretations. But, if I were to begin to have serious doubts about whether any of them are true, my friends would recommend that I seek psychiatric care.

Still, even if I keep my doubts to myself, I might wonder whether I really know that any of these beliefs about the physical world are true. Could the objects that I think I know so well exist only in my mind? Could they be mere figments of my imagination? And if I do know that these things exist outside my mind, exactly how do I know that? And exactly what do I know when I know that some physical object exists? What are these objects?

The area within philosophy that addresses itself to questions about what we know and how we know is called theory of knowledge or epistemology. Philosophers in many different traditions have taken up such questions and the theory of knowledge has a long history. Likewise, philosophers have raised many different sorts of questions about knowledge. However, the "modern" study of epistemo-logy is usually said to have begun with René Descartes' reflections on whether we know and how we know that there is a world outside our own minds. Though contemporary epistemologists for the most part concentrate on less grandiose ques-tions, Descartes' problem of our knowledge of the external world provides a good introduction to the issues in epistemology.

René Descartes (1596–1650) was an eyewitness to one of the great intellectual revolutions in human history. The makers of this revolution, Copernicus, Bruno, Galileo, Kepler, and others, sought to move the Earth. They argued that the Earth is not the fixed, immobile center around which the rest of the universe revolves. It is, they said, a planet (a wanderer, in the original meaning of the term "planet") spinning on its axis as it orbits the Sun. In order to set the Earth in motion, they had to overcome the resistance of authority: the authority of the classical science of Aristotle and Ptolemy, the authority of the Scriptures, and the authority of the Church. They also had to overcome common sense, the authority of our familiar experience of our world.

Try the following experiment. Go out into an open field and stand with your feet firmly planted and your arms relaxed at your sides. Consider what you see, what you hear, what you feel. Does anything in your experience suggest to you that you are now in motion? Do you have any sensation of speed? According to the current version of the theory that Copernicus and Galileo were promoting, you are moving through space at a velocity of 18.51 miles per second as the body on which you are standing orbits the Sun. Further, that body is spinning rapidly. Near the equator the Earth's rotational velocity is over 1,000 miles per hour. Do you feel like you are on a merry-go-round? With sufficient perseverance under favorable viewing conditions you can observe the changes in apparent position first of the sun and then of the moon over twenty-four hours. Does anything that you see tell you that the latter changes are due to the moon's motion, but that in the former case you are the one who is moving?

Ptolemy developed the geocentric picture of the universe into a complex the-oretical model that could be used to make reasonably accurate predictions about the apparent positions of heavenly bodies. But those were details. For Ptolemy, Aristotle, the authors of the Scriptures, the popes – for almost every human being who lived before the Copernican revolution in cosmology, and for many who lived after it – the idea that the Earth is at rest was not a *theory*. It was a plainly observable *fact*: something they could see and feel. So deeply was this "fact" embedded in human experience that even to understand how what Copernicus described was possible required the creation of a new physics and profound revi-sions in the very ideas of motion and rest.

Though Descartes did not live to see the final triumph of Copernican cosmo-logy, he was convinced of its truth, and his mathematical and scientific work made significant contributions to the new physics. But he also found that it raised some disturbing questions. People had been mistaken in one of their most firmly held and apparently best-supported beliefs about their world. Descartes himself had accepted the old cosmology without question in his youth. What else have we gotten wrong? What further errors lie undetected among our beliefs? Will more careful observation and more penetrating reasoning someday show that our new picture of the universe is just as false as our old one? Is there anything of which we can be certain?

Meditations on First Philosophy represents Descartes' answer to this final question. He answers in the affirmative. After a searching examination of his own beliefs, he finds at least four of which he can be certain beyond any possibility of doubt or error. These are:

1   I exist
2   My mind or soul exists
3   God exists
4   Bodies or physical objects exist.

The *Meditations* enjoys a reputation as a revolutionary, epoch-making work. It does in philosophy what the works of Galileo and Kepler did in cosmology: makes a decisive break with previous patterns of thought and turns the whole discipline in a new direction. The *Meditations* marks the beginning of "modern" philosophy.

If one considers the four conclusions listed above this reputation must seem very ill-deserved. None of (1)–(4) would have come as news to any medieval philosopher: none would have aroused even a flicker of dissent. The existence of God and the soul were matters of dogma. The existence of oneself and of physical objects were too obvious to be worth mentioning. It would have been no easy task in Descartes' time to find anyone willing to dispute these conclusions.

But the *Meditations* is not just a list of certainties, and even those who agreed with its conclusions found its arguments surprising. Three features of *Meditations* particularly help to justify its radical reputation. First, Descartes claims to demonstrate the certainty of (1)–(4) relying solely on his own reason. He accepts nothing on faith, takes nobody's word for anything, never appeals to tradition, authority, or popular opinion. Nor does he expect you to take his word for anything. You can work it all out for yourself using your own reason.

Second, while he affirms that we have knowledge of the physical world, he says some surprising things about how such knowledge is possible and about exactly what it amounts to. Our knowledge of physical objects is much more a matter of theorizing or speculation, and much less a matter of perception, than we suppose. Many of our familiar beliefs about objects, such as that they come in different colors, betray a deep confusion on our part. There is much less to our ideas of material objects than we imagine.

Further, the order in which Descartes states his conclusions matters. Our understanding of what we can see and touch seems especially clear when compared to our tenuous grasp of notions like "soul," "mind," or "God." Even if we can attain knowledge of such metaphysical realities, knowledge of concrete physical reality forms the bedrock of our belief system. But, Descartes argues that we can understand nothing more clearly than we understand the mind or God, and that our know-ledge of physical reality depends upon our knowledge of metaphysical reality – not vice versa. Indeed, he maintains that unless we are certain that God exists, we cannot be sure even that we have hands and feet.

Third, it is generally true of the great books in philosophy that they owe their influence more to the problems they pose than to the solutions they offer. In Meditation I Descartes argues that we have reason to doubt whether there is any material world. In the remainder of the *Meditations* he tries to put those doubts to rest, concluding in Meditation VI that the existence of a material world is indeed certain. On the whole, his philosophical successors were intrigued by his problem, but unconvinced by his solution. This led them to devise their own solutions. However, it proved remarkably difficult for any philosopher to solve this problem to the satisfaction of any other philosopher. This gave rise to the suspicion that either Descartes had discovered a genuine but insoluble problem or that there was something wrong with his formulation of the problem. Work on the problem of our knowledge of the external world, as it was later called, became a central focus of philosophical attention. At times, it threatened to become identical with philo-sophy. For that reason, as much as any other, Descartes deserves the title "Founder of Modern Philosophy."

In the main section of this essay, I shall try to help the reader think through Descartes' problem about knowledge of the external world. This requires a fairly detailed discussion of Meditations I and II. I shall provide a much briefer guide to his solution to the problem. In the final section I shall introduce the reader to three more contemporary treatments of our knowledge of the external world, Bertrand Russell's discussion in *The Problems of Philosophy* (1912), Willard Van Orman Quine's essay "Posits and Reality" (1955), and Bruce Aune's *Knowledge, Mind, and Nature* (1967).

There is a great deal more to the *Meditations* than the problem of our knowledge of the external world. Other topics, such as Descartes' account of the distinction between mind and body, and his arguments for the existence of God, are discussed elsewhere in this volume. There are also more questions about knowledge than will arise in my discussion of Descartes' problem. The suggested readings at the end of the chapter provide a starting-point for more extensive exploration of the theory of knowledge.

1 Meditation I: What Can Be Called into Doubt

Meditation I is a demolition job. In it Descartes says, "I will devote myself sin-cerely and without reservation to the general demolition of my opinions" (I.1).[1] Why is this job necessary? He explains that he used to believe many things that he

---

[1] References to the text of the *Meditations* will cite the number of the relevant Meditation (i.e. I to VI), and the number of the relevant paragraph within that Meditation. Thus, "(I.1)" refers to para-graph 1 of Meditation I.

now recognizes as false. This suggests that there may be falsehoods as yet unrecognized among his current beliefs. To detect such false beliefs and prevent himself from being led further astray by drawing conclusions from them, he resolves to call all of his beliefs into question. He will accept them again only if they stand up to this questioning. In this way he can assure that his opinions will be "stable and likely to last" (I.1).

Here is a metaphor for Descartes' project. I own a wooden boat. I discover some rotten beams and planks in my boat and replace them. I wonder: have I found all the rotten ones? Will my boat sink someday because a rotten beam that I have overlooked gives way? I decide to put the boat in dry-dock, disassemble it piece by piece, and carefully examine every board one at a time. I shall then rebuild the boat, reusing only those parts I have found to be sound, and replacing any that prove to be rotten.

But, even if one can understand his motivation, Descartes' plan to eliminate all his mistaken beliefs seems doomed to fail. Suppose that he has accepted some false belief. Presumably, he was satisfied of its truth when he accepted it: otherwise he would never have made it one of his beliefs. Why does he think he can do a better job of detecting its falsehood when he re-examines it? Why won't the same reasons that led him to accept it in the first place lead him to accept it the second time around?

Imagine a thirteenth-century philosopher re-examining his belief that the Earth is at rest. Very likely he would conclude, after a thorough reconsideration, that his belief is true. We know that his belief is false. But, as far as he is concerned, everything – the testimony of the Scriptures and all the recognized authorities, the evidence of his own senses – counts in favor of his belief. Could we expect him to discover his error merely by reviewing the evidence that led him to accept it in the first place?

We face a general problem when we undertake to discover falsehoods among our own beliefs: how can we evaluate them objectively? When we select juries we try to exclude prospective jurors who have already made up their minds about the facts of the case. The rationale for such exclusions is that, having prejudged or taken a position on the case, a juror would find it difficult to give a fair hearing to the evidence presented in court. When we examine our own beliefs, we are considering questions on which we have already made up our minds. To believe something is to be convinced of its truth. Any evaluation we make of it seems bound to be biased in its favor.

So Descartes' project seems a bit pointless. Perhaps a few of our opinions have such a tenuous hold on us that we need only reconsider them to see that they are false. But, the vast majority will sail through their re-examinations with flying colors, whether they are true or not.

The above objection suggests that Descartes intends merely to recall his opinion and ask himself if he still believes it. He might plan to conduct a much more active and thorough evaluation. Consider again our thirteenth-century philosopher: suppose that he were to painstakingly review his evidence that the Earth is at rest,

rechecking the cogency of each argument and evaluating the reliability of his authorities. Suppose he were to make a diligent search for new evidence that bears on the
question. This sort of examination could expose the falsity of his belief. In fact, this
sort of examination did expose the falsity of the belief that the Earth is at rest.

But, what is being proposed here is a lifetime's work – probably several lifetimes.
To thoroughly investigate the truth of a given belief may be a considerable task.
Galileo did not discover that the Earth is moving just by thinking about it. He built
telescopes, devoted long hours to observing the heavens, did complicated calculations.
Nor did he do it all on his own. He made use of the work of many other scientists.
Nothing less would have sufficed to establish the truth of the matter. Presumably
just as much effort would be required to demonstrate conclusively the truth or
falsehood of many of Descartes' beliefs.

And think how many things Descartes must have believed: all his beliefs about
his own past, about history, geography, astronomy, mathematics, art, music, etc.
Even the most cursory investigation of them would take forever.

To deal with the problems raised above Descartes makes two strategic decisions.
First, rather than ask whether an opinion is true, he will ask merely whether there
is any reason to doubt it. To accomplish the general demolition of his opinions,
he says,

> it will not be necessary for me to show that all my opinions are false, which is
> something I could perhaps never manage. Reason now leads me to think that I
> should hold back my assent from opinions which are not completely certain and
> indubitable just as carefully as I do from those which are patently false. So, for the
> purpose of rejecting all my opinions, it will be enough if I find in each of them at
> least some reason for doubt. (I.2)

This decision makes the project of examining all his beliefs more feasible. Presumably, he will find it easier to discover some reason to doubt a belief than to show
that the belief is false. Of course, one might point out that it is harder to show that
a belief is "completely certain and indubitable," than to show that it is probably
true. Descartes realizes that he is setting a high standard. However, given his
concern to discover beliefs that are "likely to last," he feels that it is more important to avoid error than to make sure that he believes whatever is true.

Adopting indubitability as his standard for accepting a belief also helps with the
problem of objectivity. It forces a belief to pass a tougher test than it had to pass
when he first accepted it. Asking whether there is any reason to doubt a belief
encourages him to explore alternatives that he might have dismissed as too implausible or strange to be worth investigating. The more demanding standard counter-
balances "the weight of preconceived opinion" and the "influence of habit" (I.11).
It reduces the chance that a false belief will pass muster merely because he once
accepted it.

Second, he proposes to avoid the endless labor of examining his opinions one at
a time by taking a shortcut. To find reason to doubt his opinions, he observes, "I

need not run through them all individually, which would be an endless task. Once the foundations of a building are undermined, anything built on them collapses of its own accord; so I will go straight for the basic principles on which all my former beliefs rested" (I.2).

His strategy here exploits the interconnectedness of our beliefs. For example, my beliefs that I had breakfast yesterday, that the Civil War ended in 1865, that the Grand Canyon began forming 10 million years ago, and nearly all my other beliefs about past events presuppose that the world has existed for more than thirty seconds. That is, none of those beliefs could be true if nothing existed until thirty seconds ago. So, any reason to doubt that the world is more than half a minute old will also give me reason to doubt all those other beliefs.

Similarly, many distinct beliefs may rest on the same sorts of evidence. For example, I believe many of the things I believe because somebody I trust told me so. I believe that I could talk before my first birthday because my parents told me: that it was 107 in Tucson yesterday because I heard it on the radio, that protons have more mass than neutrinos because I read it in a physics text. If I find reason to doubt that human testimony is ever reliable, then I will have reason to doubt everything I accept based on human testimony.

Taking advantage of the logical and evidential connections among his beliefs, Descartes can raise doubts about vast ranges of beliefs, without having to examine each belief individually. He can bring down the whole structure of his opinions by undermining a few crucial supports.

So, Descartes plans to re-examine all his beliefs by asking whether he has any reason to doubt the "basic principles" on which they rest. What are those basic principles? He starts with this one: "Whatever I have up till now accepted as most true I have acquired either from the senses or through the senses" (I.3). That is, he will ask whether he has any reason to doubt those beliefs he has accepted based on what he sees, or hears, or touches, or tastes, or smells: in short, on what he perceives.

"Beliefs based on perception" includes a wide range of beliefs. I believe that the sky is blue because I see that it is blue: that the telephone is ringing because I hear it ring: that the water is cold because I feel the cold. Other beliefs are not acquired directly from perception, but are based on beliefs that are directly acquired. I believe that a bear passed this way because I see a track in the snow and infer that it was made by a bear. I assume that you are taking a shower because I hear the water running. Descartes will have his demolition project well under way if he finds reason to doubt beliefs "acquired either from the senses or through the senses."

He plants the seeds of doubt by noting in passing that "from time to time I have found that the senses deceive" (I.3). I think that there is water on the road up ahead, but it turns out to be a mirage. The ventriloquist fools me because it sounds like the voice is coming from the dummy. Descartes does not try to make much of such examples, but they serve to remind us that things are not always as they seem. It looked to me as if there was water on the road, but there was no water there.

This does not show that I can perceive water when there is no water there; but it does show that it can seem to me that I am perceiving water when I am not.

Mirages, of course, occur only under special conditions and we learn to detect them. When the car reaches the spot that looked to be under water, I can see clearly that there is no water on the road. I use my senses to discover that things are not as they first appeared to me. So, mirages and other such illusions do not raise any general doubts about my ability to distinguish what I really perceive from what I merely seem to perceive.

Descartes, therefore, moves on to another case that raises more general doubts. I think that I see water ahead on the road down which I am driving my car. I am not seeing water, it is only a mirage and my senses will soon reveal the falsity of my belief. But, what about my belief that I am driving a car? It may seem impossible that I could be wrong about that. I see the hood and the dash. They are no mirage. I hear the motor running and the wind rushing past. I feel the steering wheel clutched in my hands and the pressure of my back against the seat. How could these be illusions?

Well, Descartes might ask (somewhat anachronistically), "Have you ever dreamed that you were driving a car?" Yes. As a matter of fact, I dreamed last night that I was driving to Las Vegas. And, in my dream, it seemed to me that I was seeing the car and the scenery, that I heard the engine, that I felt my hands on the wheel, and all that. So what? I am not dreaming now. I feel wide awake. I see everything clearly. I know that I have my hands on the wheel.

"Last night," Descartes might continue, "when you were dreaming, did you know that it was just a dream? When you seemed to see the scenery and to feel your hands on the wheel, were you thinking that you were just imagining these things; that you were really home, asleep in your bed?" No; it all seemed pretty convincing at the time. In fact, when I woke, before I got my wits about me, I remember wondering whether I was in Las Vegas. "In that case," Descartes replies, "how can you be completely certain that you are not dreaming right now? Perhaps you will awaken in a few minutes to discover that this is all a dream: that you have not been seeing, or hearing, or touching any of these things you now think you perceive. If you consider the matter carefully, you will 'see plainly that there are never any sure signs by means of which being awake can be distinguished from being asleep'" (I.5).

What exactly does Descartes think that he has shown about beliefs acquired from the senses in his discussion of dreaming? That he cannot be certain at any particular time that he really perceives something rather than merely seems to perceive it? That he cannot be certain that he has ever perceived anything, as opposed to merely imagining it? In the former case, I might have reason to doubt that, for example, I am now driving a car, but still be certain that there are such things as cars. The latter option suggests a much more general doubt: a doubt about whether any of the sorts of things I think that I perceive really exist. It is not clear from the text (I.5–8) precisely what beliefs are called into question here. Fortunately, we need not settle this point of interpretation, because he immediately advances another argument designed to raise doubts about whether anything exists to be perceived by the senses.

Descartes thinks that there are some limits on what can be called into question by reflection on dreaming. As he understands dreams, although we do not perceive anything in dreams (at least not by means of our senses), dreams are based on perception.

> Suppose then that I am dreaming, and that these particulars – that my eyes are open, that I am moving my head and stretching out my hands – are not true. Perhaps, indeed, I do not even have such hands or such a body at all. None the less . . . the visions which come in sleep are like paintings, which must have been fashioned in the likeness of things that are real, and hence . . . at least these general kinds of things – eyes, head, hands, and the body as a whole – are things which are not imaginary but are real and exist. . . . Or [if even these] could be imaginary, it must at least be admitted that certain other even simpler and more universal things are real. (I.6)

What he has in mind here is something like this: we can dream of things that are not happening at the moment we are dreaming, and even of things that have never happened, but the contents of our dreams are assembled out of elements that we first experienced in perception. Suppose I dream that I am driving down a solid glass highway in a pickup truck as big as an aircraft carrier with a live dragon as a hood ornament. I have never seen any of these things, but the images of them in my dream will reflect things that I have seen – window panes, ordinary pickups, lizards. I lack the unlimited powers of creativity that would be required for me to dream up something completely from scratch.

If my dreams are composed in this way, then they cannot be a totally misleading guide to reality. Think of all the things I believe during a dream. I am having my driving dream. Some of the things I believe as a result of my dream-experiences are false. I am not in a car; I do not have my hands outstretched. I am not moving. There are no mountains on my left. But, what about my belief that there are cars and mountains, that I have hands? O.K. Maybe I dreamed those up too. I live on a completely smooth planet, in a pre-technological civilization, and I have a body like a slug. But, consider my beliefs about even simpler and more general things: I believe that there are physical objects, that they come in various shapes and colors, that they are distributed in space, etc. Those elements are all part of my dream and they are all true. The details of my dream-world may be false, but it can still accurately represent certain general features of reality (I.7). So, even if I think I am dreaming, I have no reason to doubt my beliefs about the general character of the reality in which I exist.

Whether or not the above reasoning is correct, Descartes rejects its conclusion. The most that it shows is that I could not dream up a totally misleading fantasy world: that the elements from which I assemble my dreams must come from some source outside myself. But, it does not show they come from my perception of external objects. Descartes observes:

And yet firmly rooted in my mind is the long-standing opinion that there is an omnipotent God who made me the kind of creature that I am. How do I know that he has not brought it about that there is no earth, no sky, no extended thing, no shape, no size, no place, while at the same time ensuring that all these things appear to me to exist just as they do now? (I.9)

I could not envision a dream-world lacking all connection to reality. But God can. That's the difference between God and me. God is a creative genius. He does not need to work from a model or take his ideas from any perception of a pre-existing reality. So God would have no trouble imagining a universe full of extended objects of various shapes and sizes standing in various spatial relationships to each other, even though the universe he actually chose to create contains none of that stuff – it is a completely non-physical reality. Call the physical universe that God only imagines "PU" and the non-physical universe he actually created "OU." Now, God knows exactly what sorts of experiences I would have if I existed in PU: that is, he knows how things would look and sound and feel to me if I were perceiving objects in PU by means of certain sense organs. So, God could cause me to have exactly the experiences I would have in PU, but put me in OU. For as long as God kept this up, I would believe all the things I believe now about physical objects (or, all the beliefs I had before I started reading *Meditations*, at least). And all these beliefs, my beliefs about the simple, general features of PU, just as much as my beliefs about the specific particular objects I seem to see right now, would be false.

Once Descartes considers the hypothesis that God might be deceiving him, he is "compelled to admit that there is not one of my former beliefs about which a doubt may not properly be raised" (I.10). He cannot be completely certain of any of those beliefs that he seems to have acquired by sensory perception, because he cannot be certain that he has ever really perceived anything. He must acknowledge the possibility that "the sky, the air, the earth, colors, shapes, sounds, and all external things are merely the delusions of dreams . . . devised to ensnare my judgment" (I.12). Nothing in what he seems to see, to hear, to feel, can assure him that he exists in PU rather than OU. If God is a deceiver anything is possible. The demolition job seems complete.

Before proceeding to Meditation II we need to make sure that we are straight on some points. Descartes does not claim to know that God exists, still less that God is deceiving him. It is just that he cannot rule out these possibilities at present. In fact, if you read all the way to the end of the *Meditations*, you will discover that Descartes does not think that it is possible that God is deceiving him. So he thinks that the argument presented above goes wrong somewhere. (You can figure out from Meditations III, IV, and VI where he thinks it goes wrong.) In Meditation I he plays devil's advocate, making the strongest case he can for a position – skepticism about the external world – that he believes to be untenable in the final analysis. He really does believe, however, that if we had only our perceptual experience to go on we could not rule out the possibility that all our beliefs asserting the existence of a physical reality are false.

I need to make a final point, by the way of a confession. Descartes does not, as I have done, develop his argument in terms of *God* deceiving him. After mentioning that possibility in I.9, he switches to talking about "some malicious demon of the utmost power and cunning" deceiving him (I.10). Given the times in which he lived, Descartes had a healthy fear of saying anything in print that might suggest disrespect for God. They literally burned people at the stake for things like that. But this switch complicates that argument and it reduces the impact of Meditation II where Descartes discovers something that even God could not fool him about. Since times have changed, and since I will not wind up accusing God of deception, leaving the argument in the form presented above involves no risk of fire, earthly or eternal.

2 Meditation II: What Cannot Be Called into Doubt

Descartes' project in Meditation II is partly constructive and partly destructive. He first shows that he does know some things for certain and he shows exactly what it is that he knows. He knows that his own mind exists and that he engages in various mental activities. He then takes a critical look at what he thought he knew about bodies, his own body and the other physical objects he took himself to perceive through his senses. It turns out that he has misunderstood the role of sensory perception in his acquisition of beliefs about bodies. Even if it is possible for him to be certain of the existence of bodies, having knowledge of them cannot be the simple, straightforward affair he previously took it to be.

As Meditation II opens, the world Descartes thought he knew so well lies in ruins. Everything seems to be in doubt. Have any of his beliefs escaped destruction? Can he affirm at least that there must be a God who created him and endowed him with ability to think? No, he concludes: he might be the sole author of his thoughts.

> In that case am not I, at least, something? But I have just said that I have no senses and no body. This is the sticking point: what follows from this? Am I not so bound up with a body and with senses that I cannot exist without them? But I have convinced myself that there is absolutely nothing in the world, no sky, no earth, no minds, no bodies. Does it now follow that I too do not exist? No: if I convinced myself of something then I certainly existed. But there is a deceiver of supreme power and cunning who is deliberately and constantly deceiving me. In that case I too undoubtedly exist, if he is deceiving me; and let him deceive me as much as he can, he will never bring it about that I am nothing so long as I think that I am something. So, after considering everything very thoroughly, I must finally conclude that this proposition, *I am, I exist*, is necessarily true whenever it is put forward by me or conceived in my mind. (II.3)

Even people who know little else about Descartes know that he said "I think, therefore I am"; in Latin, "*Cogito ergo sum*." Though he used these words in other writings (*Discourse on Method*, *Principles of Philosophy*), they do not occur in *Meditations*. However, this famous sentence does seem to sum up his argument here and for that reason the above passage is often referred to as "the Cogito."

Philosophers disagree about the best interpretation of the reasoning by which Descartes arrives at the conclusion that he exists. (See chapter 4 of Feldman's *A Cartesian Introduction to Philosophy*, listed in the Suggested Readings, for an informative discussion of the interpretative issues.) But I think that we can appreciate its force by considering what God would have to do to bring it about that I am deceived when I think I exist. To fix things so that I am deceived when I believe something, for example, that ducks wear boots, God needs to do two things: (1) He needs to make it true that I believe ducks wear boots. Being deceived about something is not the same thing as being ignorant about it. God could arrange it so that I never think about ducks, or so that I never think about my own existence, for that matter. But, that is not deceiving me. To be deceived I have to believe. (2) God has to make it false that ducks wear boots. If what I believe is true, then I am not deceived. To be deceived I have to believe falsely.

Now it would be a snap for God to cause me to be deceived in believing that ducks wear boots. And similarly for most other beliefs. But, if God wants to fix things so that I am deceived when I believe that I exist, then even God has problems. He can easily accomplish the first part of the job: causing me to believe that I exist. But now the second part, making it false that I exist, will be tough to pull off. As Descartes observes, if I have any belief at all, I must exist. In that case, my belief that I exist will be true and God has failed to deceive me. So, maybe God should have started with part (2): fixing things so that "I exist" is false. This is easy for God to do. But now part (1) is the problem. If "I exist" is false, then I do not exist, in which case I cannot have any belief. Once again, God fails to deceive me. There is no way God can arrange things so that I believe that I exist and that belief is false, that is, cause me to falsely believe that I exist. So God cannot cause me to be deceived in believing that I exist: and if God cannot do it, nothing can.

The above argument depends on the principle that, if I believe that I exist, then I must exist. I think that there is no doubt that Descartes appeals to this principle in II.3 and no reasonable doubt that it is true. However, some philosophers wonder whether Descartes can get much help from this principle in Meditation II. To use it to derive the conclusion that he must exist, he needs to first establish that he is certain that he believes that he exists. Russell, in the extract following the selections from the *Meditations*, argues that the doubts raised in Meditation I preclude Descartes from being sure of anything more than that thought, "I exist," occurs. He cannot be sure that he, or anyone else, must be thinking that thought.

At any rate, Descartes finds no reason to doubt his own existence and most philosophers have been willing to grant him that much. However, he himself confesses, "I do not yet have a sufficient understanding of what this 'I' is, that now necessarily exists" (II.4). He believes many things about himself. How many of these can he affirm with certainty? What exactly does he know when he knows that he exists?

To explore these questions he decides to run through some of the things he believes about himself and see which of them are put in doubt by the possibility that God is deceiving him. Had he been asked to say some things about himself, before he embarked on this Meditation, he would have had a ready reply. He would have said first that he had a face, hands, arms, and that whole structure of physical parts that he called his body. He would have gone on to describe the various activities of which he was capable: eating, running, talking and so forth. He would also have mentioned that he could perceive things by means of his senses and that he could think. These latter activities he attributed to his soul, or mind. But, his idea of his soul was rather vague and when he tried to imagine his soul he pictured it as "something tenuous, like a wind or fire," that was somehow contained in his body (II.5). By contrast, he considered himself to understand quite well the nature of his body, since he was able to perceive its qualities very clearly by using his senses.

But, suppose God seeks to deceive him: what can he confidently say of himself now? That he has a body? As he showed in Meditation I, that might be a delusion. That he eats, or runs, or talks? All those activities presuppose the existence of his body. Sense-perception? No: again. "This surely does not occur without a body, and besides, when asleep I have appeared to perceive through the senses many things which I afterwards realized I did not perceive through the senses at all" (II.6).

Finally, he arrives at thinking. Could he be deceived in believing that he thinks? By no means. To be so deceived he would have to believe falsely that he thinks. But, believing, truly or falsely, is just a kind of thinking. So, if he believes that he thinks, then it must be true that he thinks. Here he discovers a completely safe answer to the question, "what am I?" ". . . I am a thing which is real and which truly exists. But what kind of thing? . . . [A] thinking thing" (II.6).

Immediately something further occurs to him. "A thinking thing" is just what he means by the term "mind." He realizes that he is a mind and that at least one mind exists. Of course, he is not certain of the existence of that vaporous stuff contained in the body that he used to imagine when he tried to picture his mind. He cannot be sure that such a tenuous sort of physical thing exists, any more than he can be certain of the existence of nice, solid physical things. He recognizes that that was not what he meant by a mind. He now understands that a mind is just anything that thinks.

Descartes takes care not to say here that he knows he is something non-physical: that he is *only* a mind, and not a body. He does not know, at this point, that he has a body, but he allows that he might be a body. For all he knows, some body, of whose existence he is now uncertain, might "in reality [be] identical with the 'I' of which I am aware" (II.7). So far he knows himself only as a mind – a thinking thing. He takes no position now on the question of whether this thing that thinks is a physical object or not. In Meditation VI, he takes the position that it is not: but that requires further argument. For the present, he leaves open questions about the ultimate nature of mind.

Still, he has learned something about his *idea* of himself. If his idea of himself were the idea of a body, if he could only think of himself as something composed of various physical parts and engaging in various physical activities, then when he found himself doubting the existence of bodies, he would be doubting his own existence. So from the fact that he can be sure of his own existence, while he doubts the existence of any physical object, he can conclude that his idea of himself is not the idea of a body, nor the idea of something that must have a body, or any physical characteristics at all. But, if it is not the idea of something physical, what is there to his idea of himself? It is just the idea of a thing that thinks.

Can he know anything more about himself than merely that he thinks? Yes:

> But what then am I? A thing that thinks. What is that? A thing that doubts, under-stands, affirms, denies, is willing, is unwilling, and also imagines and has sensory perceptions. (II.8)

> This is a considerable list, if everything on it belongs to me. But does it? Is it not one and the same "I" who is now doubting almost everything, who nonetheless understands some things, who affirms that this one thing is true, denies everything else, desires to know more, is unwilling to be deceived, . . . and is aware of many things which apparently come from the senses? Are not all these things just as true as the fact that I exist, even if I am asleep . . . , and even if he who created me is doing all he can to deceive me? . . . The fact that it is I who am doubting and understanding and willing is so evident that I see no way of making it any clearer. (II.9)

The term "thinking" covers a wide range of mental activities for Descartes. It includes not just intellectual activities such as reasoning, but desiring, willing, even sensory experience. He regards it as certain that he engages in all those sorts of activities. Not even God could trick him into believing that he doubts, affirms, or desires when he does not.

But much remains unclear about what he means to say in the passage quoted above and about whether he has presented a strong case for claims he makes there. Obviously he thinks that he knows some things for certain about his own mind. Does he think he knows everything about it? Presumably God could deceive him about his past thoughts. God could make him seem to remember that he denied the existence of bodies yesterday, though he had no such thought yesterday. So is he certain of what he is thinking only while he is thinking it? Could things happen in his mind without his being aware of them? How can he be so sure that God could not fool him into thinking that he understands when he does not understand, or that he is willing when he is not willing? Saying that all this "is so evident that I see no way of making it any clearer" does not sound like much of an answer.

Nevertheless, many philosophers have been willing to grant that, at least in some cases, people cannot be mistaken about what is going on in their own minds. I cannot be deceived when I believe that I am in pain, or believe that I am thinking about my mother, or believe that I want some ice cream. The reasons other philosophers have given for thinking that I can be mistaken about such things are too complicated to get into in this essay.

Rather than continue the discussion of these general issues, let us look at a particular entry in Descartes' list of things that he knows for certain. In II.8 he says that he is a thing that "has sensory perceptions." Has he forgotten that he said in II.6 that he could not be sure that he has sense perceptions? "Sense-perception? This surely does not occur without a body, and besides, when asleep I have appeared to perceive through the senses many things which I afterwards realized I did not perceive through the senses at all." He has not forgotten; rather he wants to reconsider what he means by "sensory perception." Look at his discussion at the end of II.9.

> Lastly, it is also the same "I" who has sensory perceptions, or is aware of bodily things as it were through the senses. For example, I am now seeing light, hearing a noise, feeling heat. But I am asleep, so all this is false. Yet I certainly *seem* to see, to hear, and to be warmed. This cannot be false; what is called "having a sensory perception" is strictly just this, and in this restricted sense of the term it is simply thinking.

So I can be certain that I seem to see, but not that I see. And Descartes now wants to restrict the term "sensory perception" to seeming to see, seeming to hear, etc., whereas in II.6 the term apparently referred to seeing or hearing rather than to seeming to see or hear. But what is the difference between seeing and seeming to see, and why can I be wrong about whether I see, but not about whether I seem to see?

Seeing is something that I cannot do unless I have a body. I see with my eyes. Furthermore, what I see is always a body or some sort of physical thing. When I am seeing something, for example, my hand, light is being reflected from my hand into my eyes. Seeing involves a physical interaction between a visual sense organ and some object. But this is not all there is to seeing. When I see I am also "aware of bodily things." Light being reflected from my hand into my eyes is a purely physical affair. But, my being aware of my hand is something that involves my soul or mind. So seeing is neither purely physical, nor purely mental: it is an activity that requires both body and soul.

Seeming to see, on the other hand, is purely mental. It is just a kind of thinking. I can be seeming to see my hand, even if I am asleep with my eyes closed, and even if I have no hand. So, the possibility that there are no physical objects raises no doubts in me about whether I seem to see, because all that has to be true in order for me to seem to see is that various thoughts or experiences occur in my mind.

But, I cannot be certain that I see, unless I am certain that I have eyes, or some sort of visual sense organs, and that some physical object exists to be seen. So doubts about the existence of physical objects lead to doubts about whether I see.

Is there no connection between seeing and seeming to see? Why do I call a particular kind of thinking "seeming to *see?*" Perhaps because when I seem to see I tend to believe that I am seeing: as in dreams where my seeming to see my hand leads me to believe, falsely, that I am seeing my hand. Why should there be this connection between seeming to see and believing that you see? Here is one explanation: because seeming to see is just the mental part of seeing. What happens when I see is that the physical interaction of my eyes and an object causes me to seem to see that object. Seeing is just an instance of seeming to see that is caused in me in the right way. So, whenever I see I also seem to see: but not vice versa. I could be caused to seem to see in lots of ways. Only some of them are the "right" way for seeing. Thus, in dreams I am somehow caused to seem to see objects, though my eyes are closed and there are no objects there to be seen. Or, God could cause me to seem to see my hand, even though I have no eyes and no hand. In order to know for certain that I am seeing my hand, then, it is not enough for me to know that I seem to see my hand. I have to know that my seeming to see is being caused in the right way. I have to be sure of the physical part of seeing as well as of the mental part.

The same holds for other sorts of sensory perception. Hearing, touch, taste, and smell all involve a mental part and a physical part. The mental part of hearing a bell ring is seeming to hear a bell ring. The mental part of smelling a dead fish is seeming to smell a dead fish. Let us call all these seemings "sensations." When we hear or smell, etc., we are having a particular sort of sensation that is being caused by the stimulation of a sense organ – ear, skin, nose – by a physical object. We can be sure that we are having the sensation, without knowing what is causing us to have it. Thus, doubts about the existence of physical objects lead to doubts about whether we hear, or touch, or smell, without raising doubts about whether we have sensations of noise, or warmth, or rotten odors.

Even after considering all the above, Descartes finds it difficult to shake the feeling that he understands bodily things better than he understands his mind. He has a firm grasp of the various kinds of thinking, but not of the thing that does the thinking. He has no doubts about the existence of his mind, but he cannot imagine or picture it. But he finds it easy to imagine bodies: to picture their colors, shapes, and other properties. He may not know for sure that bodies exist, but he feels that he knows what sorts of things they would be if they did exist (II.10).

To counteract this tendency, he performs a thought-experiment. Suppose that I take a piece of wax and examine it closely. It has a yellowish color, a rectangular shape, and is about so big. It is hard and cool to the touch. The odor of flowers and the taste of honey still linger in it. It is fresh from the honeycomb. Now, I place it in a pan and hold the pan over a fire. After a short time I find in the pan a puddle of hot, clear liquid. The odor of flowers has been replaced by a paraffiny smell: there is no sweetness in the taste. I ask myself, "Is this thing in the pan now the same piece of wax I placed there a few minutes ago?" Everyone would agree that it is. Then I reflect:

> So what was it in the wax that I understood with such distinctness? Evidently none of the features which I arrived at by means of the senses; for whatever came under taste, smell, sight, touch or hearing has now altered – yet the wax remains. (II.11)

Descartes' point here is something like the point he made earlier about his idea of himself. Before he carefully considered the matter, he supposed that his idea of himself was the idea of something with a face and hands and other bodily parts: something that eats and moves. But he found that he could strip himself of all these attributes while remaining sure of his own existence. He concluded, therefore, that his idea of himself was not the idea of something with these bodily characteristics. In his thought-experiment, he began by thinking of the piece of wax as something with a definite color, shape, texture, taste, odor. But he comes to realize that all these characteristics of the wax can change, while the same piece of wax remains. What, then, is his idea of the wax? What kind of thing is it that remains the same through all these changes? He concludes that his idea of the wax was simply the idea of a body that could exhibit to him a whole range of diverse qualities. As he conceives it, the wax is not the yellowish color, the rectangular shape, the sweet taste that he perceived through his senses. Rather, it is something that exists, as it were, beneath those qualities and can exist without them.

But how could he know anything of this body? All his senses show him a color, a shape, a taste, an odor. He answers that "the true nature of this piece of wax is perceived by the mind alone" (II.12).

> But what is this wax which is perceived by the mind alone? It is of course the same wax which I see, which I touch, which I picture in my imagination, in short the same wax which I thought it to be from the start. And yet, and here is the point, the perception I have of it is a case not of vision or touch or imagination – nor has it ever been, despite previous appearances – but of purely mental scrutiny . . . (II.12)

His point can be put a bit more clearly. Originally, I thought I knew that the wax was there because I saw that it was there, I felt it there with my hands, I smelled that it was there. But, I now understand that what I should say is not that I saw that the wax was there, but that I judged or inferred that it was there based on what I saw. All that my senses revealed to me were particular qualities of color, shape, taste, and so forth. I made the judgment that the appearance of such qualities to me indicated the presence of some body, some physical thing. This judgment represents a speculative leap beyond what appeared to my senses. It embodies a theory about the causes of such appearances. My idea of the wax is part of that theory, not something found in what appears to my senses.

But all this is what we ought say, not what we ordinarily do say. Descartes notes:

> We say that we see the wax itself, if it is there before us, not that we judge it to be there from its color or shape; and this might lead me to conclude without more ado that knowledge of the wax comes from what the eye sees, and not from the scrutiny of the mind alone. (II.13)

However, he also notes that we are not ordinarily very careful to distinguish what we actually see from what we infer based on what we see. He continues:

> But then if I look out of the window and see men crossing the square . . . I normally say that I see the men themselves, just as I say that I see the wax. Yet do I see any more than hats and coats which could conceal automatons? I *judge* that they are men. And so something which I thought I was seeing with my eyes is in fact grasped solely by the faculty of judgement which is in my mind. (II.13)

Strictly speaking, I *see* a hat and a coat and I judge that there is a human being underneath. But, if I want to understand the role of sense perception in knowledge of bodies, Descartes says that I must speak even more strictly. I *see* colorful shapes and I judge that they are hats and coats. Or, better yet, what I am aware of when I say that I see a hat or a piece of wax are colorful shapes and I judge that their presence indicates the presence of an appropriate physical object.

Descartes seems to be suggesting here that the wax is hiding behind its own qualities like a person underneath a hat and coat. But, the hat and coat are not part of the person. A person can walk around without any clothes. However, we never find the wax without some qualities on. Surely, the color of the wax, its odor, its texture is somehow part of the wax. True, the color and other qualities can change while the wax remains, but whatever color or other quality it has at a given time is part of the wax at that time. So when I see the color of the wax I am seeing the wax. I do not see a yellowish shape and judge that there is wax underneath: I see that the wax is yellowish.

Descartes rejects the premise on which the above reasoning rests. Looking ahead to Meditation VI and back at our discussion of seeing and seeming to see, we can work out his view. He denies that the colors, shapes, textures, odors of which I am aware when I perceive the wax through my senses are parts of the wax. Actually these qualities belong to my sensations: they are part of my seeming to see the wax, not things I see in the wax. What is in the wax is just some property that causes me to seem to see it as yellowish.

What property of the wax causes yellowish sensations in me? That is not a question that can be settled just by thinking about my idea of the wax. It requires scientific investigation. In the case of colors, the properties in objects that cause us to seem to see them as colored are now known to be complex and various. They have to do with how the atomic structure of the object affects its tendencies to absorb or reflect photons of various energies or wave lengths. For sensations of warmth and cold it is a little easier to specify the relevant property in the object: it is, roughly, the intensity of the vibratory motion of the molecules composing the object (at least for relatively solid objects). Of course, I do not even seem to see these features of objects; nevertheless, these are the things *in* the objects that cause me to seem to see them as yellowish, to seem to feel them as warm, and so on. The color or warmth I seem to perceive occurs in me – in my mind or my thoughts – not in the object. So what sense perception reveals, strictly speaking, is not the object and its properties, but various features of my own sensations – which I judge to be caused by the action of the object on my sense organs.

It is now time to take stock of what Descartes thinks he has established in Meditation II:

1   The idea of a physical object or body is just the idea of something existing outside my mind and having various properties that, acting on my sense organs under appropriate conditions, cause me to have various sensations.
2   I can no more imagine or picture what bodies are in themselves than I can imagine or picture my mind itself: the images I form of bodies depict only how they appear to me, not how they are in themselves.
3   The existence of bodies is something inferred or postulated by my mind, not something seen, or heard, or felt through my senses.
4   My belief that I perceive bodies depends on my belief that my sensations, which are the only things of which I am strictly aware when I think I perceive, are sometimes caused by the action of a body on my sense organs.
5   But, since I cannot rule out the possibility that my sensations are always caused by something other than bodies, for example, by a deceiving God, I cannot be certain that I ever perceive bodies and, hence, I cannot be certain that bodies exist.
6   I am certain that I exist, but contrary to what I once supposed, this is not knowledge of the existence of any physical object: I am known to myself only as a thinking thing, a mind.
7   Thus, I am certain of my own existence, the existence of a mind, even while I am uncertain that any body exists.
8   Further, since I arrive at my beliefs about bodies based, in part, on my awareness of my own thinking, I can only have knowledge of bodies if I first know that I think.

Reflecting on all of the above, Descartes realizes how confused he was when he used to suppose that what he knew best and understood most clearly were the bodies he perceived through his senses. Now he appreciates that it is his own mind whose existence and activities he knows most certainly and comprehends most clearly, and that if he can attain any certain knowledge of bodies, he must build such knowledge on the foundation provided by his knowledge of his own mind.

3   The Problem of Our Knowledge of the External World

Descartes' reflections on knowledge of mind and knowledge of the physical world in Meditation II struck a responsive chord among his philosophical successors. It seemed to them that he was right to maintain that, when we set out to obtain knowledge of the physical world, ultimately, all we have to go on is our awareness of what is happening in our own minds. Obviously, we can be aware of objects only if they make some impact on our thoughts, our conscious experience. But, all that directly registers in us as a result of such impacts are changes in the character of our own sensations. Of course, we firmly believe that some of these changes in how things seem to us result from the action of physical objects on our sense organs. But it does seem hard to deny that whatever is going on in our minds at any given time *could* be going on just as it is even if there were no bodies and no sense organs. God could be fooling us. So, how can we ever know that any of our sensations are caused by bodies? And, if we cannot know that, how could we know that bodies exist, that there is any world outside our minds?

It is somewhat surprising, at first blush, that philosophers started worrying about this problem at the time when scientists were beginning to make great strides in understanding the nature and operations of the physical world. Just when scientists were figuring out the structure of and the laws governing the physical universe, philosophers began wondering whether it even existed. This is particularly puzzling since the scientists and the philosophers were often the same people, as in the case of Descartes. In fact, however, the emerging scientific account of the nature of physical reality seemed to make the problem of our knowledge of bodies all the more compelling.

As both Russell and Quine emphasize in the selections at the end of this chapter, the story about physical objects told by the natural sciences made them out to be very different than they appear to us. Descartes' wax, and even comparatively more solid tables and desks, are conceived in physics as swarms of molecules – things too small for us to see. Those molecules themselves are composed of still smaller atoms and atoms of smaller, more elementary particles. Solid objects turn out to be mostly empty space. With the advent of quantum physics, objects got stranger still. We cannot describe what matter is like at the atomic level in the familiar terms we use to talk about physical objects. At that level, things behave as if they were both point-like particles and waves in some medium. They have no position unless they are measured and before they are measured they seem to be in lots of different places at the same time.

Reading physics books makes it very tempting to say that the world of solid, colorful, flavorful objects that have definite, stable shapes and positions is only a world that we seem to see. It exists only in our thoughts and experiences. The world that exists outside our minds, on the other hand, is a world whose features can be precisely described only in the abstract language of mathematics. It has little in common with the world we seem to see and touch.

Nevertheless, the evidence for the existence of this quantum reality seems to come down to various things happening in that world we seem to see, that world in our own thoughts. To be justified in believing that objects, whatever their nature, exist outside our minds, we have to be justified in believing that, on some occasions at least, our sensations are caused by such objects. Descartes believed he could prove that we are justified in affirming this latter belief.

In the briefest sketch, his solution to the problem goes as follows. He argues that reason can guarantee the truth of our belief in the existence of a physical world outside our minds. First, we need to prove the existence of God. In Meditation III he argues that, from the mere fact that we have an idea of God, something he thinks we know merely by our awareness of our own thoughts, we can conclude that an infinitely perfect being, God, must exist. Our understanding of what it means to be infinitely perfect assures us that God cannot deceive us. Meditation IV shows that, since God is no deceiver, we can be certain that any beliefs at which we arrive by the *proper* use of the intellectual faculties God has given us must be true. Finally, by a complicated argument in Meditation VI, he establishes that we arrive at our belief that certain of our sensations are caused by physical objects and, hence, at our belief in the existence of physical objects, by the proper use of our God-given faculties. If we were wrong about this it would be God's fault, not ours: but God can never be at fault.

Later philosophers found fault with just about every move in this argument: with Descartes' proof of God's existence; with his assumption that a perfect being would not deceive us; with his assertion that our belief in the existence of external objects arises from a proper use of our intellectual faculties.

Descartes' critics – and most of the philosophers who came after him were critics – divide into two camps. One camp accepts his basic account of our epistemological predicament. We do face the problem of having to infer from our sensations, of which we are directly aware, the existence of an external world, of which we cannot be directly aware. Critics of this sort reject Descartes' solution, but accept his problem. Usually they have offered their own solutions. But some, notably the eighteenth-century Scottish philosopher David Hume, have argued that the problem is insoluble and have embraced skepticism.

Critics in the second camp deny that Descartes has presented us with a genuine problem. These philosophers try to identify some confusion or error in his formulation of the problem and, thereby, to show that we need no solution to it. Many different arguments of this general sort are possible. The most popular one has been the argument that we need not show how we can be justified in believing that external objects exist without directly perceiving them, because we do perceive external objects directly. Descartes goes wrong when he asserts that it is our own sensations rather than external objects and their qualities of which we are aware in perception.

The former sort of criticism dominated discussions of knowledge of the external world in the three centuries after Descartes' death. The latter has been most prominent during the second half of the twentieth century. The reader can explore these issues in the selections from the writings of Russell, Quine, and Aune reprinted in this chapter.

Suggestions for further reading

Fred Feldman's *A Cartesian Introduction to Philosophy* (New York: McGraw-Hill, 1980) and Georges Dicker's *Descartes: An Analytical and Historical Introduction* (Oxford: Oxford University Press, 1993) make *Meditations* accessible to beginning students of philosophy. Their approaches are complementary, Feldman focusing more on understanding the general issues raised in *Meditations* and Dicker on explaining the text. Dicker provides a useful bibliography of works on Descartes by contemporary philosophers. John Cottingham's *Descartes* (Oxford: Blackwell, 1986) does a particularly fine job of explaining Descartes' views in their historical context.

Bruce Aune provides an up-to-date account of the problem of our knowledge of the external world in *Knowledge of the External World* (New York: Routledge, 1991). This is probably the best place to start for students interested in exploring the problem. It introduces the main positions regarding knowledge of external reality and directs the reader to the works of the philosophers who have defended them.

There is a vast literature devoted to epistemology or theory of knowledge. Most of the issues discussed in that literature arise, in some form, in connection with the problem of our knowledge of the external world. However, concern with that problem is not the only perspective from which to approach questions about what we know and how we know it: for many such questions it is not the best perspective. For that reason, I recommend three books in epistemology that do not make that problem their central focus. Taken together these works offer a fairly thorough survey of the sorts of questions and the approaches to answering them that dominate contemporary epistemology. Laurence BonJour's *The Structure of Empirical Knowledge* (Cambridge, MA: Harvard University Press, 1985) explores the question of whether our knowledge of the world rests on a foundation. Descartes supposed that certain of our beliefs are justified for us directly, independent of their relations to other beliefs, and that the rest of our knowledge is built up by inference from these basic, or fundamental, beliefs. This foundationalist picture exercised a powerful influence on philosophical thinking about knowledge well into the twentieth century and still has considerable appeal. BonJour argues that it has led us into a dead end and that we need a different, coherentist picture of the structure of knowledge.

Richard Foley accepts many of BonJour's objections to foundationalism in his *The Theory of Epistemic Rationality* (Cambridge, MA: Harvard University Press, 1987). However, he argues that a modified form of foundationalism still provides the best account of what makes it rational for us to believe something. His book is especially useful for its discussion of the various standpoints from which we can assess the rationality of particular beliefs.

Alvin Goldman's *Epistemology and Cognition* (Cambridge, MA: Harvard University Press, 1986) discusses philosophical questions about knowledge in the context of biological and psychological research on cognition. Recall that Quine emphasizes that philosophy operates within our scientific investigation of the world rather than standing above or outside it. Goldman's book surveys some of the most important scientific work on perception, memory, problem solving, and belief formation. He argues that traditional philosophical concerns about rationality and justification must be pursued with an eye toward this work.

Introduction to Selected Readings

The readings begin with Descartes' *Meditations on First Philosophy* (1641). Meditations I, II, and VI are presented in their entirety, along with those sections of Meditations III and IV that are needed for Descartes' solution to the problem of our knowledge of the external world.

The next three readings provide a sample of more recent discussions of the problem. The first of these comes from the writings of the Cambridge philosopher and mathematician Bertrand Russell (1872–1970), one of the giants of twentieth-century philosophy. In this selection from his *The Problems of Philosophy* (1912) Russell endorses and expands on Descartes' account of the problem of our knowledge of the external world and offers his own solution.

Russell dispenses with any appeal to God. Rather than seek a theological guarantee, he argues that we are justified in supposing that physical objects exist because the hypothesis that some of our sensations are caused by the action of physical objects on our sense organs provides the simplest and most plausible explanation of what we know goes on in our minds. He agrees with Descartes that we are immediately aware only of our own sensations ("sense data" in his terminology). But, he maintains that the best way to make sense of why we have the sensations we have and when we have them is to suppose that some of those sensations are caused by bodies.

He does not insist, however, that this is the only possible explanation. He acknowledges that we cannot be absolutely certain that our hypothesis is true. But we can know that it is better than any competing hypothesis, such as the hypothesis that God is deceiving us, that we have examined. Of course, we cannot be sure that a better hypothesis will never come along. He argues, however, that certainty is not to be had with regard to the existence of an external world. We cannot be as sure of the existence of external objects as we are of what goes on in our own minds.

"Posits and Reality" (1955) by Willard Van Orman Quine, a contemporary American philosopher, now professor emeritus at Harvard University, represents a greater departure from Descartes' understanding of the problem. Quine also thinks that we have no better reason for accepting the hypothesis that physical objects exist than that this hypothesis provides the best available explanation of what we seem to see, seem to hear, and so forth. And he agrees with Russell that this is reason enough to accept it until something better comes along. But Quine argues further that this is the same sort of reason we have for believing in the existence of sensations. Sensations, like physical objects, are "posits." We postulate their existence in order to explain how we come to know what we know about physical objects. We have no better reason to believe in these postulated mental occurrences than that the hypothesis that they exist helps us to make sense of how we get around in our world. And the same goes for molecules, atoms, and all the exotic objects postulated by physics.

It may sound like Quine is building a house of cards. We posit physical objects to explain our sensations and posit sensations to explain how we know about objects. But he insists that bodies, sensations, and even atoms and molecules are all parts of one picture of reality. From within that picture we can raise and answer questions about what we know and how we know it, but we cannot step outside that picture and determine how well it matches some external reality. By working from the inside we can alter the picture by investigating particular questions using the best methods we have available. Over time we may change the picture radically. But, we can only work on it piecemeal. We cannot tear it down and start over from scratch.

In contrast to the metaphor of putting our ship in dry-dock and completely disassembling it, Quine offers an alternative metaphor. We have to fix our ship while it is afloat. We can make lots of alterations from the inside. Given enough time we can radically alter its configuration. But, we cannot abandon ship.

Bruce Aune, currently professor of philosophy at the University of Massachusetts at Amherst, addresses the recent tendency to dismiss Descartes' problem in the fourth and final reading, excerpted from the introductory chapter of his book *Knowledge, Mind, and Nature* (1967). Aune explains how objections to the Cartesian account of perception and the nature of physical objects have led many contemporary philosophers to deny that Descartes has discovered any real problem in Meditations I and II. These philosophers insist that we perceive physical objects directly, and that the colors and other qualities of which we are aware in perception belong to physical objects themselves rather than to our experiences of them.

Aune argues that these critics fail to provide a plausible alternative to the basic Cartesian account of perception. He further argues that their views on the nature of objects conflict with the most reasonable interpretation of what contemporary science tells us about the physical world. Accordingly, he maintains, they have not shown us how to get around Descartes' problem. He acknowledges, however, that accepting the Cartesian account of perception seems to push us toward a radical skepticism that precludes, not only knowledge of external objects, but also knowledge of other minds and even knowledge of the self. Thus, Descartes' problem appears to be more threatening than Descartes realized.

The material reprinted here covers only Aune's statement of the problem. He devotes the rest of his book to a detailed argument that the basic Cartesian account of perception does not lead to such disastrous consequences. Like Russell and Quine, Aune believes that we can be justifiably confident of the existence of an external world, even if it turns out to be a different sort of world from the one depicted in our prereflective judgments about physical objects.

Discussion questions

1   What problems do we encounter when we try to discover falsehoods among our own beliefs? How does Descartes' "method of doubt" handle these problems?

2   Descartes says that I can be deceived in thinking that I *see* my hands, but that I cannot be deceived when I think that I *seem to see* my hands. What is the difference between seeing and seeming to see? Why can I be wrong about one but not the other?

3   How does Descartes' discussion of the block of wax show that I know about the wax by "mental scrutiny" rather than merely by means of my senses?

4   In what ways is the supposition that the whole of life is a dream a less simple account of the facts of our experience than the common-sense hypothesis that there really are objects independent of us?

5   Quine argues that sense data, common-sense bodies, and atoms are all in the same boat: all are equally fundamental and equally theoretical. In what way is each fundamental and theoretical?

6   Aune suggests that an atomistic conception of physical objects threatens to push us down a slippery slope into utter skepticism. By what stages do we descend from atomism to this disaster? Why isn't direct realism a promising strategy for avoiding this disaster?

Readings

René Descartes, *Meditations on First Philosophy*

Meditations on First Philosophy

In which are demonstrated the existence of God and the distinction between the human soul and the body

First Meditation

What can be called into doubt

Some years ago I was struck by the large number of falsehoods that I had accepted as true in my childhood, and by the highly doubtful nature of the whole edifice that I had subsequently based on them. I realized that it was necessary, once in the course of my life, to demolish everything completely and start again right from the foundations if I wanted to establish anything at all in the sciences that was stable and likely to last. But the task looked an enormous one, and I began to wait until I should reach a mature enough age to ensure that no subsequent time of life would be more suitable for tackling such inquiries. This led me to put the project off for so long that I would now be to blame if by pondering over it any further I wasted the time still left for carrying it out. So today I have expressly rid my mind of all worries and arranged for myself a clear stretch of free time. I am here quite alone, and at last I will devote myself sincerely and without reservation to the general demolition of my opinions.

But to accomplish this, it will not be necessary for me to show that all my opinions are false, which is something I could perhaps never manage. Reason now leads me to think that I should hold back my assent from opinions which are not completely certain and indubitable just as carefully as I do from those which are patently false. So, for the purpose of rejecting all my opinions, it will be enough if I find in each of them at least some reason for doubt. And to do this I will not need to run through them all individually, which would be an endless task. Once the foundations of a building are undermined, anything built on them collapses of its own accord; so I will go straight for the basic principles on which all my former beliefs rested.

From *The Philosophical Writings of Descartes*, vol. 2; translated by John Cottingham, Robert Stoothoff, and Dugald Murdoch (Cambridge: Cambridge University Press, 1984).

Whatever I have up till now accepted as most true I have acquired either from the senses or through the senses. But from time to time I have found that the senses deceive, and it is prudent never to trust completely those who have deceived us even once.

Yet although the senses occasionally deceive us with respect to objects which are very small or in the distance, there are many other beliefs about which doubt is quite impossible, even though they are derived from the senses – for example, that I am here, sitting by the fire, wearing a winter dressing-gown, holding this piece of paper in my hands, and so on. Again, how could it be denied that these hands or this whole body are mine? Unless perhaps I were to liken myself to madmen, whose brains are so damaged by the persistent vapours of melancholia that they firmly maintain they are kings when they are paupers, or say they are dressed in purple when they are naked, or that their heads are made of earthenware, or that they are pumpkins, or made of glass. But such people are insane, and I would be thought equally mad if I took anything from them as a model for myself.

A brilliant piece of reasoning! As if I were not a man who sleeps at night, and regularly has all the same experiences while asleep as madmen do when awake – indeed sometimes even more improbable ones. How often, asleep at night, am I convinced of just such familiar events – that I am here in my dressing-gown, sitting by the fire – when in fact I am lying undressed in bed! Yet at the moment my eyes are certainly wide awake when I look at this piece of paper; I shake my head and it is not asleep; as I stretch out and feel my hand I do so deliberately, and I know what I am doing. All this would not happen with such distinctness to someone asleep. Indeed! As if I did not remember other occasions when I have been tricked by exactly similar thoughts while asleep! As I think about this more carefully, I see plainly that there are never any sure signs by means of which being awake can be distinguished from being asleep. The result is that I begin to feel dazed, and this very feeling only reinforces the notion that I may be asleep.

Suppose then that I am dreaming, and that these particulars – that my eyes are open, that I am moving my head and stretching out my hands – are not true. Perhaps, indeed, I do not even have such hands or such a body at all. Nonetheless, it must surely be admitted that the visions which come in sleep are like paintings, which must have been fashioned in the likeness of things that are real, and hence that at least these general kinds of things – eyes, head, hands and the body as a whole – are things which are not imaginary but are real and exist. For even when painters try to create sirens and satyrs with the most extraordinary bodies, they cannot give them natures which are new in all respects; they simply jumble up the limbs of different animals. Or if perhaps they manage to think up something so new that nothing remotely similar has ever been seen before – something which is therefore completely fictitious and unreal – at least the colours used in the composition must be real. By similar reasoning, although these general kinds of things – eyes, head, hands and so on – could be imaginary, it must at least be admitted that certain other even simpler and more universal things are real. These are as it were the real colours from which we form all the images of things, whether true or false, that occur in our thought.

This class appears to include corporeal nature in general, and its extension; the shape of extended things; the quantity, or size and number of these things; the place in which they may exist, the time through which they may endure, and so on.

So a reasonable conclusion from this might be that physics, astronomy, medicine, and all other disciplines which depend on the study of composite things, are doubtful; while arithmetic, geometry and other subjects of this kind, which deal only with the simplest and most general things, regardless of whether they really exist in nature or not, contain something certain and indubitable. For whether I am awake or asleep, two and three added together are five, and a square has no more than four sides. It seems impossible that such transparent truths should incur any suspicion of being false.

And yet firmly rooted in my mind is the long-standing opinion that there is an omnipotent God who made me the kind of creature that I am. How do I know that he has not brought it about that there is no earth, no sky, no extended thing, no shape, no size, no place, while at the same time ensuring that all these things appear to me to exist just as they do now? What is more, since I sometimes believe that others go astray in cases where they think they have the most perfect knowledge, may I not similarly go wrong every time I add two and three or count the sides of a square, or in some even simpler matter, if that is imaginable? But perhaps God would not have allowed me to be deceived in this way, since he is said to be supremely good. But if it were inconsistent with his goodness to have created me such that I am deceived all the time, it would seem equally foreign to his goodness to allow me to be deceived even occasionally; yet this last assertion cannot be made.

Perhaps there may be some who would prefer to deny the existence of so powerful a God rather than believe that everything else is uncertain. Let us not argue with them, but grant them that everything said about God is a fiction. According to their supposition, then, I have arrived at my present state by fate or chance or a continuous chain of events, or by some other means; yet since deception and error seem to be imperfections, the less powerful they make my original cause, the more likely it is that I am so imperfect as to be deceived all the time. I have no answer to these arguments, but am finally compelled to admit that there is not one of my former beliefs about which a doubt may not properly be raised; and this is not a flippant or ill-considered conclusion, but is based on powerful and well thought-out reasons. So in future I must withhold my assent from these former beliefs just as carefully as I would from obvious falsehoods, if I want to discover any certainty.

But it is not enough merely to have noticed this; I must make an effort to remember it. My habitual opinions keep coming back, and, despite my wishes, they capture my belief, which is as it were bound over to them as a result of long occupation and the law of custom. I shall never get out of the habit of confidently assenting to these opinions, so long as I suppose them to be what in fact they are, namely highly probable opinions – opinions which, despite the fact that they are in a sense doubtful, as has just been shown, it is still much more reasonable to believe than to deny. In view of this, I think it will be a good plan to turn my will in completely the opposite direction and deceive myself, by pretending for a time that these former opinions are utterly false and imaginary. I shall do this until the weight of preconceived opinion is counter-balanced and the distorting influence of habit no longer prevents my judgement from perceiving things correctly. In the meantime, I know that no danger or error will result from my plan, and that I cannot possibly go too far in my distrustful attitude. This is because the task now in hand does not involve action but merely the acquisition of knowledge.

I will suppose therefore that not God, who is supremely good and the source of truth, but rather some malicious demon of the utmost power and cunning has employed all his energies in order to deceive me. I shall think that the sky, the air, the earth, colours, shapes, sounds and all external things are merely the delusions of dreams which he has devised to ensnare my judgement. I shall consider myself as not having hands or eyes, or flesh, or blood or senses, but as falsely believing that I have all these things. I shall stubbornly and firmly persist in this meditation; and, even if it is not in my power to know any truth, I shall at least do what is in my power, that is, resolutely guard against assenting to any falsehoods, so that the deceiver, however powerful and cunning he may be, will be unable to impose on me in the slightest degree. But this is an arduous undertaking, and a kind of laziness brings me back to normal life. I am like a prisoner who is enjoying an imaginary freedom while asleep; as he begins to suspect that he is asleep, he dreads being woken up, and goes along with the pleasant illusion as long as he can. In the same way, I happily slide back into my old opinions and dread being shaken out of them, for fear that my peaceful sleep may be followed by hard labour when I wake, and that I shall have to toil not in the light, but amid the inextricable darkness of the problems I have now raised.

Second Meditation

The nature of the human mind, and how it is better known than the body

So serious are the doubts into which I have been thrown as a result of yesterday's meditation that I can neither put them out of my mind nor see any way of resolving them. It feels as if I have fallen unexpectedly into a deep whirlpool which tumbles me around so that I can neither stand on the bottom nor swim up to the top. Nevertheless I will make an effort and once more attempt the same path which I started on yesterday. Anything which admits of the slightest doubt I will set aside just as if I had found it to be wholly false; and I will proceed in this way until I recognize something certain, or, if nothing else, until I at least recognize for certain that there is no certainty. Archimedes used to demand just one firm and immovable point in order to shift the entire earth; so I too can hope for great things if I manage to find just one thing, however slight, that is certain and unshakeable.

I will suppose then, that everything I see is spurious. I will believe that my memory tells me lies, and that none of the things that it reports ever happened.

I have no senses. Body, shape, extension, movement and place are chimeras. So what remains true? Perhaps just the one fact that nothing is certain.

Yet apart from everything I have just listed, how do I know that there is not something else which does not allow even the slightest occasion for doubt? Is there not a God, or whatever I may call him, who puts into me the thoughts I am now having? But why do I think this, since I myself may perhaps be the author of these thoughts? In that case am not I, at least, something? But I have just said that I have no senses and no body. This is the sticking point: what follows from this? Am I not so bound up with a body and with senses that I cannot exist without them? But I have convinced myself that there is absolutely nothing in the world, no sky, no earth, no minds, no bodies. Does it now follow that I too do not exist? No: if I convinced myself of something then I certainly existed. But there is a deceiver of supreme power and cunning who is deliberately and constantly deceiving me. In that case I too undoubtedly exist, if he is deceiving me; and let him deceive me as much as he can, he will never bring it about that I am nothing so long as I think that I am something. So after considering everything very thoroughly, I must finally conclude that this proposition, *I am, I exist*, is necessarily true whenever it is put forward by me or conceived in my mind.

But I do not yet have a sufficient understanding of what this "I" is, that now necessarily exists. So I must be on my guard against carelessly taking something else to be this "I", and so making a mistake in the very item of knowledge that I maintain is the most certain and evident of all. I will therefore go back and meditate on what I originally believed myself to be, before I embarked on this present train of thought. I will then subtract anything capable of being weakened, even minimally, by the arguments now introduced, so that what is left at the end may be exactly and only what is certain and unshakeable.

What then did I formerly think I was? A man. But what is a man? Shall I say "a rational animal"? No; for then I should have to inquire what an animal is, what rationality is, and in this way one question would lead me down the slope to other harder ones, and I do not now have the time to waste on subtleties of this kind. Instead I propose to concentrate on what came into my thoughts spontaneously and quite naturally whenever I used to consider what I was. Well, the first thought to come to mind was that I had a face, hands, arms and the whole mechanical structure of limbs which can be seen in a corpse, and which I called the body. The next thought was that I was nourished, that I moved about, and that I engaged in sense-perception and thinking; and these actions I attributed to the soul. But as to the nature of this soul, either I did not think about this or else I imagined it to be something tenuous, like a wind or fire or ether, which permeated my more solid parts. As to the body, however, I had no doubts about it, but thought I knew its nature distinctly. If I had tried to describe the mental conception I had of it, I would have expressed it as follows: by a body I understand whatever has a determinable shape and a definable location and can occupy a space in such a way as to exclude any other body; it can be perceived by touch, sight, hearing, taste or smell, and can be moved in various ways, not by itself but by whatever else comes into contact with it. For, according to my judgement, the power of self-movement, like the power of sensation or of thought, was quite foreign to the nature of a body; indeed, it was a source of wonder to me that certain bodies were found to contain faculties of this kind.

But what shall I now say that I am, when I am supposing that there is some supremely powerful and, if it is permissible to say so, malicious deceiver, who is deliberately trying to trick me in every way he can? Can I now assert that I possess even the most insignificant of all the attributes which I have just said belong to the nature of a body? I scrutinize them, think about them, go over them again, but nothing suggests itself; it is tiresome and pointless to go through the list once more. But what about the attributes I assigned to the soul? Nutrition or movement? Since now I do not have a body, these are mere fabrications. Sense-perception? This surely does not occur without a body, and besides, when asleep I have appeared to perceive through the senses many things which I afterwards realized I did not perceive through the senses at all. Thinking? At last I have discovered it – thought; this alone is inseparable from me. I am, I exist – that is certain. But for how long? For as long as I am thinking. For it could be that were I totally to cease from thinking, I should totally cease to exist. At present I am not admitting anything except what is necessarily true. I am, then, in the strict sense only a thing that thinks; that is, I am a mind, or intelligence, or intellect, or reason – words whose meaning I have been ignorant of until now. But for all that I am a thing which is real and which truly exists. But what kind of a thing? As I have just said – a thinking thing.

What else am I? I will use my imagination. I am not that structure of limbs which is called a human body. I am not even some thin vapour which permeates the limbs – a wind, fire, air, breath, or whatever I depict in my imagination; for these are things which I have supposed to be nothing. Let this supposition stand; for all that I am still something. And yet may it not perhaps be the case that these very things which I am supposing to be nothing, because they are unknown to me, are in reality identical with the "I" of which I am aware? I do not know, and for the moment I shall not argue the point, since I can make judgements only about things which are known to me. I know that I exist; the question is, what is this "I" that I know? If the "I" is understood strictly as we have been taking it, then it is quite certain that knowledge of it does not depend on things of whose existence I am as yet unaware; so it cannot depend on any of the things which I invent in my imagination. And this very word "invent" shows me my mistake. It would indeed be a case of fictitious invention if I used my imagination to establish that I was something or other; for imagining is simply contemplating the shape or image of a corporeal thing. Yet now I know for certain both that I exist and at the same time that all such images and, in general, everything relating to the nature of body, could be mere dreams ⟨and chimeras⟩. Once this point has been grasped, to say "I will use my imagination to get to know more distinctly what I am" would seem to be as silly as saying "I am now awake, and see some truth; but since my vision is not yet clear enough, I will deliberately fall asleep so that my dreams may provide a truer and clearer representation." I thus realize that none of the things that the imagination enables me to grasp is at all relevant to this knowledge of myself which I possess, and that the mind must therefore be most carefully diverted from such things if it is to perceive its own nature as distinctly as possible.

But what then am I? A thing that thinks. What is that? A thing that doubts, understands, affirms, denies, is willing, is unwilling, and also imagines and has sensory perceptions.

This is a considerable list, if everything on it belongs to me. But does it? Is it not one and the same "I" who is now doubting almost everything, who nonetheless understands some things, who affirms that this one thing is true, denies everything else, desires to know more, is unwilling to be deceived, imagines many things even involuntarily, and is aware of many things which apparently come from the senses? Are not all these things just as true as the fact that I exist, even if I am asleep all the time, and even if he who created me is doing all he can to deceive me? Which of all these activities is distinct from my thinking? Which of them can be said to be separate from myself? The fact that it is I who am doubting and understanding and willing is so evident that I see no way of making it any clearer. But it is also the case that the "I" who imagines is the same "I". For even if, as I have supposed, none of the objects of imagination are real, the power of imagination is something which really exists and is part of my thinking. Lastly, it is also the same "I" who has sensory perceptions, or is aware of bodily things as it were through the senses. For example, I am now seeing light, hearing a noise, feeling heat. But I am asleep, so all this is false. Yet I certainly *seem* to see, to hear, and to be warmed. This cannot be false; what is called "having a sensory perception" is strictly just this, and in this restricted sense of the term it is simply thinking.

From all this I am beginning to have a rather better understanding of what I am. But it still appears – and I cannot stop thinking this – that the corporeal things of which images are formed in my thought, and which the senses investigate, are known with much more distinctness than this puzzling "I" which cannot be pictured in the imagination. And yet it is surely surprising that I should have a more distinct grasp of things which I realize are doubtful, unknown and foreign to me, than I have of that which is true and known – my own self. But I see what it is: my mind enjoys wandering off and will not yet submit to being restrained within the bounds of truth. Very well then; just this once let us give it a completely free rein, so that after a while, when it is time to tighten the reins, it may more readily submit to being curbed.

Let us consider the things which people commonly think they understand most distinctly of all; that is, the bodies which we touch and see. I do not mean bodies in general – for general perceptions are apt to be somewhat more confused – but one particular body. Let us take, for example, this piece of wax. It has just been taken from the honeycomb; it has not yet quite lost the taste of the honey; it retains some of the scent of the flowers from which it was gathered; its colour, shape and size are plain to see; it is hard, cold and can be handled without difficulty; if you rap it with your knuckle it makes a sound. In short, it has everything which appears necessary to enable a body to be known as distinctly as possible. But even as I speak, I put the wax by the fire, and look: the residual taste is eliminated, the smell goes away, the colour changes, the shape is lost, the size increases; it becomes liquid and hot; you can hardly touch it, and if you strike it, it no longer makes a sound. But does the same wax remain? It must be admitted that it does; no one denies it, no one thinks otherwise. So what was it in the wax that I understood with such distinctness? Evidently none of the features which I arrived at by means of the senses; for whatever came under taste, smell, sight, touch or hearing has now altered – yet the wax remains.

Perhaps the answer lies in the thought which now comes to my mind; namely, the wax was not after all the sweetness of the honey, or the fragrance of the flowers, or the whiteness, or the shape, or the sound, but was rather a body which presented itself to me in these various forms a little while ago, but which now exhibits different ones. But what exactly is it that I am now imagining? Let us concentrate, take away everything which does not belong to the wax, and see what is left: merely something extended, flexible and changeable. But what is meant here by "flexible" and "changeable"? Is it what I picture in my imagination: that this piece of wax is capable of changing from a round shape to a square shape, or from a square shape to a triangular shape? Not at all; for I can grasp that the wax is capable of countless changes of this kind, yet I am unable to run through this immeasurable number of changes in my imagination, from which it follows that it is not the faculty of imagination that gives me my grasp of the wax as flexible and changeable. And what is meant by "extended"? Is the extension of the wax also unknown? For it increases if the wax melts, increases again if it boils, and is greater still if the heat is increased. I would not be making a correct judgement about the nature of wax unless I believed it capable of being extended in many more different ways than I will ever encompass in my imagination. I must therefore admit that the nature of this piece of wax is in no way revealed by my imagination, but is perceived by the mind alone. (I am speaking of this particular piece of wax; the point is even clearer with regard to wax in general.) But what is this wax which is perceived by the mind alone? It is of course the same wax which I see, which I touch, which I picture in my imagination, in short the same wax which I thought it to be from the start. And yet, and here is the point, the perception I have of it is a case not of vision or touch or imagination – nor has it ever been, despite previous appearances – but of purely mental scrutiny; and this can be imperfect and confused, as it was before, or clear and distinct as it is now, depending on how carefully I concentrate on what the wax consists in.

But as I reach this conclusion I am amazed at how ⟨weak and⟩ prone to error my mind is. For although I am thinking about these matters within myself, silently and without speaking, nonetheless the actual words bring me up short, and I am almost tricked by ordinary ways of talking. We say that we see the wax itself, if it is there before us, not that we judge it to be there from its colour or shape; and this might lead me to conclude without more ado that knowledge of the wax comes from what the eye sees, and not from the scrutiny of the mind alone. But then if

I look out of the window and see men crossing the square, as I just happen to have done, I normally say that I see the men themselves, just as I say that I see the wax. Yet do I see any more than hats and coats which could conceal automatons? I *judge* that they are men. And so something which I thought I was seeing with my eyes is in fact grasped solely by the faculty of judgement which is in my mind.

However, one who wants to achieve knowledge above the ordinary level should feel ashamed at having taken ordinary ways of talking as a basis for doubt. So let us proceed, and consider on which occasion my perception of the nature of the wax was more perfect and evident. Was it when I first looked at it, and believed I knew it by my external senses, or at least by what they call the "common" sense – that is, the power of imagination? Or is my knowledge more perfect now, after a more careful investigation of the nature of the wax and of the means by which it is known? Any doubt on this issue would clearly be foolish; for what distinctness was there in my earlier perception? Was there anything in it which an animal could not possess? But when I distinguish the wax from its outward forms – take the clothes off, as it were, and consider it naked – then although my judgement may still contain errors, at least my perception now requires a human mind.

But what am I to say about this mind, or about myself? (So far, remember, I am not admitting that there is anything else in me except a mind.) What, I ask, is this "I" which seems to perceive the wax so distinctly? Surely my awareness of my own self is not merely much truer and more certain than my awareness of the wax, but also much more distinct and evident. For if I judge that the wax exists from the fact that I see it, clearly this same fact entails much more evidently that I myself also exist. It is possible that what I see is not really the wax; it is possible that I do not even have eyes with which to see anything. But when I see, or think I see (I am not here distinguishing the two), it is simply not possible that I who am now thinking am not something. By the same token, if I judge that the wax exists from the fact that I touch it, the same result follows, namely that I exist. If I judge that it exists from the fact that I imagine it, or for any other reason, exactly the same thing follows. And the result that I have grasped in the case of the wax may be applied to everything else located outside me. Moreover, if my perception of the wax seemed more distinct after it was established not just by sight or touch but by many other considerations, it must be admitted that I now know myself even more distinctly. This is because every consideration whatsoever which contributes to my perception of the wax, or of any other body, cannot but establish even more effectively the nature of my own mind. But besides this, there is so much else in the mind itself which can serve to make my knowledge of it more distinct, that it scarcely seems worth going through the contributions made by considering bodily things.

I see that without any effort I have now finally got back to where I wanted. I now know that even bodies are not strictly perceived by the senses or the faculty of imagination but by the intellect alone, and that this perception derives not from their being touched or seen but from their being understood; and in view of this I know plainly that I can achieve an easier and more evident perception of my own mind than of anything else. But since the habit of holding on to old opinions cannot be set aside so quickly, I should like to stop here and meditate for some time on this new knowledge I have gained, so as to fix it more deeply in my memory.

Third Meditation

The existence of God

I will now shut my eyes, stop my ears, and withdraw all my senses. I will eliminate from my thoughts all images of bodily things, or rather, since this is hardly possible, I will regard all such images as vacuous, false and worthless. I will converse with myself and scrutinize myself more deeply; and in this way I will attempt to achieve, little by little, a more intimate knowledge of myself. I am a thing that thinks: that is, a thing that doubts, affirms, denies, understands a few things, is ignorant of many things, is willing, is unwilling, and also which imagines and has sensory perceptions; for as I have noted before, even though the objects of my sensory experience and imagination may have no existence outside me, nonetheless the modes of thinking which I refer to as cases of sensory perception and imagination, in so far as they are simply modes of thinking, do exist within me – of that I am certain.

In this brief list I have gone through everything I truly know, or at least everything I have so far discovered that I know. Now I will cast around more carefully to see whether there may be other things within me which I have not yet noticed. I am certain that I am a thinking thing. Do I not therefore also know what is required for my being certain about anything? In this first item of knowledge there is simply a clear and distinct perception of what I am asserting; this would not be enough to make me certain of the truth of the matter if it could ever turn out that something which I perceived with such clarity and distinctness was false. So I now seem to be able to lay it down as a general rule that whatever I perceive very clearly and distinctly is true.

Yet I previously accepted as wholly certain and evident many things which I afterwards realized were doubtful. What were these? The earth, sky, stars, and everything else that I apprehended with the senses. But what was it about them that I perceived clearly? Just that the ideas, or thoughts, of such things appeared before my mind. Yet even now I am not denying that these ideas occur within me. But there was something else which I used to assert, and which through habitual belief I thought I perceived clearly, although I did not in fact do so. This was that there were things outside me which were the sources of my ideas and which resembled them in all respects. Here was my mistake; or at any rate, if my judgement was true, it was not thanks to the strength of my perception.

But what about when I was considering something very simple and straightforward in arithmetic or geometry, for example that two and three added together make five, and so on? Did I not see at least these things clearly enough to affirm their truth? Indeed, the only reason for my later judgement that they were open to doubt was that it occurred to me that perhaps some God could have given me a nature such that I was deceived even in matters which seemed most evident. And whenever my preconceived belief in the supreme power of God comes to mind, I cannot but admit that it would be easy for him, if he so desired, to bring it about that I go wrong even in those matters which I think I see utterly clearly with my mind's eye. Yet when I turn to the things themselves which I think I perceive very clearly, I am so convinced by them that I spontaneously declare: let whoever can do so deceive me, he will never bring it about that I am nothing, so long as I continue to think I am something; or make it true at some future time that I have never existed, since it is now true that I exist; or bring it about that two and three added together are more or less than five, or anything of this kind in which I see a manifest contradiction. And since I have no cause to think that there is a deceiving God, and I do not yet even know for sure whether there is a God at all, any reason for doubt which depends simply on this supposition is a very slight and, so to speak, metaphysical one. But in order to remove even this slight reason for doubt, as soon as the opportunity arises I must examine whether there is a God, and, if there is, whether he can be a deceiver. For if I do not know this, it seems that I can never be quite certain about anything else.

First, however, considerations of order appear to dictate that I now classify my thoughts into definite kinds, and ask which of them can properly be said to be the bearers of truth and falsity. Some of my thoughts are as it were the images of things, and it is only in these cases that the term "idea" is strictly appropriate – for example, when I think of a man, or a chimera, or the sky, or an angel, or God. Other thoughts have various additional forms: thus when I will, or am afraid, or affirm, or deny, there is always a particular thing which I take as the object of my thought, but my thought includes something more than the likeness of that thing. Some thoughts in this category are called volitions or emotions, while others are called judgements.

Now as far as ideas are concerned, provided they are considered solely in themselves and I do not refer them to anything else, they cannot strictly speaking be false; for whether it is a goat or a chimera that I am imagining, it is just as true that I imagine the former as the latter. As for the will and the emotions, here too one need not worry about falsity; for even if the things which I may desire are wicked or even non-existent, that does not make it any less true that I desire them. Thus the only remaining thoughts where I must be on my guard against making a mistake are judgements. And the chief and most common mistake which is to be found here consists in my judging that the ideas which are in me resemble, or conform to, things located outside me. Of course, if I considered just the ideas themselves simply as modes of my thought, without referring them to anything else, they could scarcely give me any material for error.

Among my ideas, some appear to be innate, some to be adventitious, and others to have been invented by me. My understanding of what a thing is, what truth is, and what thought is, seems to derive simply from my own nature. But my hearing a noise, as I do now, or seeing the sun, or feeling the fire, comes from things which are located outside me, or so I have hitherto judged. Lastly, sirens, hippogriffs and the like are my own invention. But perhaps all my ideas may be thought of as adventitious, or they may all be innate, or all made up; for as yet I have not clearly perceived their true origin.

But the chief question at this point concerns the ideas which I take to be derived from things existing outside me: what is my reason for thinking that they resemble these things? Nature has apparently taught me to think this. But in addition I know by experience that these ideas do not depend on my will, and hence that they do not depend simply on me. Frequently I notice them even when I do not want to: now, for example, I feel the heat whether I want to or not, and this is why I think that this sensation or idea of heat comes to me from something other than myself, namely the heat of the fire by which I am sitting. And the most obvious judgement for me to make is that the thing in question transmits to me its own likeness rather than something else.

I will now see if these arguments are strong enough. When I say "Nature taught me to think this", all I mean is that a spontaneous impulse leads me to believe it, not that its truth has been revealed to me by some natural light. There is a big difference here. Whatever is revealed to me by the natural light – for example that from the fact that I am doubting it follows that I exist, and so on – cannot in any way be open to doubt. This is because there cannot be another faculty both as trustworthy as the natural light and also capable of showing me that such things are not true. But as for my natural impulses, I have often judged in the past that they were pushing me in the wrong direction when it was a question of choosing the good, and I do not see why I should place any greater confidence in them in other matters.

Then again, although these ideas do not depend on my will, it does not follow that they must come from things located outside me. Just as the impulses which I was speaking of a moment ago seem opposed to my will even though they are within me, so there may be some other faculty not yet fully known to me, which produces these ideas without any assistance from external things; this is, after all, just how I have always thought ideas are produced in me when I am dreaming.

And finally, even if these ideas did come from things other than myself, it would not follow that they must resemble those things. Indeed, I think I have often discovered a great disparity ⟨between an object and its idea⟩ in many cases. For example, there are two different ideas of the sun which I find within me. One of them, which is acquired as it were from the senses and which is a prime example of an idea which I reckon to come from an external source, makes the sun appear very small. The other idea is based on astronomical reasoning, that is, it is derived from certain notions which are innate in me (or else it is constructed by me in some other way), and this idea shows the sun to be several times larger than the earth. Obviously both these ideas cannot resemble the sun which exists outside me; and reason persuades me that the idea which seems to have emanated most directly from the sun itself has in fact no resemblance to it at all.

All these considerations are enough to establish that it is not reliable judgement but merely some blind impulse that has made me believe up till now that there exist things distinct from myself which transmit to me ideas or images of themselves through the sense organs or in some other way.

But it now occurs to me that there is another way of investigating whether some of the things of which I possess ideas exist outside me. In so far as the ideas are ⟨considered⟩ simply ⟨as⟩ modes of thought, there is no recognizable inequality among them: they all appear to come from within me in the same fashion. But in so far as different ideas ⟨are considered as images which⟩ represent different things, it is clear that they differ widely. Undoubtedly, the ideas which represent substances to me amount to something more and, so to speak, contain within themselves more objective reality than the ideas which merely represent modes or accidents. Again, the idea that gives me my understanding of a supreme God, eternal, infinite, ⟨immutable,⟩ omniscient, omnipotent and the creator of all things that exist apart from him, certainly has in it more objective reality than the ideas that represent finite substances.

Now it is manifest by the natural light that there must be at least as much ⟨reality⟩ in the efficient and total cause as in the effect of that cause. For where, I ask, could the effect get its reality from, if not from the cause? And how could the cause give it to the effect unless it possessed it? It follows from this both that something cannot arise from nothing, and also that what is more perfect – that is, contains in itself more reality – cannot arise from what is less perfect. And this is transparently true not only in the case of effects which possess ⟨what the philosophers call⟩ actual or formal reality, but also in the case of ideas, where one is considering only ⟨what they call⟩ objective reality. A stone, for example, which previously did not exist, cannot begin to exist unless it is produced by something which contains, either formally or eminently everything to be found in the stone; similarly, heat cannot be produced in an object which was not previously hot, except by something of at least the same order ⟨degree or kind⟩ of perfection as heat, and so on. But it is also true that the *idea* of heat, or of a stone, cannot exist in me unless it is put there by some cause which contains at least as much reality as I conceive to be in the heat or in the stone. For although this cause does not transfer any of its actual or formal reality to my idea, it should not on that account be supposed that it must be less real. The nature of an idea is such that of itself it requires no formal reality except what it derives from my thought, of which it is a mode. But in order for a given idea to contain such and such objective reality, it must surely derive it from some cause which contains at least as much formal reality as there is objective reality in the idea. For if we suppose that an idea contains something which was not in its cause, it must have got this from nothing; yet the mode of being by which a thing exists objectively ⟨or representatively⟩ in the intellect by way of an idea, imperfect though it may be, is certainly not nothing, and so it cannot come from nothing.

And although the reality which I am considering in my ideas is merely objective reality, I must not on that account suppose that the same reality need not exist formally in the causes of my ideas, but that it is enough for it to be present in them objectively. For just as the objective mode of being belongs to ideas by their very nature, so the formal mode of being belongs to the causes of ideas – or at least the first and most important ones – by *their* very nature. And although one idea may perhaps originate from another, there cannot be an infinite regress here; eventually one must reach a primary idea, the cause of which will be like an archetype which contains formally ⟨and in fact⟩ all the reality ⟨or perfection⟩ which is present only objectively ⟨or representatively⟩ in the idea. So it is clear to me, by the natural light, that the ideas in me are like ⟨pictures, or⟩ images which can easily fall short of the perfection of the things from which they are taken, but which cannot contain anything greater or more perfect.

The longer and more carefully I examine all these points, the more clearly and distinctly I recognize their truth. But what is my conclusion to be? If the objective reality of any of my ideas turns out to be so great that I am sure the same reality does not reside in me, either formally or eminently, and hence that I myself cannot be its cause, it will necessarily follow that I am not alone in the world, but that some other thing which is the cause of this idea also exists. But if no such idea is to be found in me, I shall have no argument to convince me of the existence of anything apart from myself. For despite a most careful and comprehensive survey, this is the only argument I have so far been able to find.

Among my ideas, apart from the idea which gives me a representation of myself, which cannot present any difficulty in this context, there are ideas which variously represent God, corporeal and inanimate things, angels, animals and finally other men like myself.

As far as concerns the ideas which represent other men, or animals, or angels, I have no difficulty in understanding that they could be put together from the ideas I have of myself, of corporeal things and of God, even if the world contained no men besides me, no animals and no angels.

As to my ideas of corporeal things, I can see nothing in them which is so great ⟨or excellent⟩ as to make it seem impossible that it originated in myself. For if I scrutinize them thoroughly and examine them one by one, in the way in which I examined the idea of the wax yesterday, I notice that the things which I perceive clearly and distinctly in them are very few in number. The list comprises size, or extension in length, breadth and depth; shape, which is a function of the boundaries of this extension; position, which is a relation between various items possessing shape; and motion, or change in position; to these may be added substance, duration and number. But as for all the rest, including light and colours, sounds, smells, tastes, heat and cold and the other tactile qualities, I think of these only in a very confused and obscure way, to the extent that I do not even know whether they are true or false, that is, whether the ideas I have of them are ideas of real things or of non-things. For although, as I have noted before, falsity in the strict sense, or formal falsity, can occur only in judgements, there is another kind of falsity, material falsity, which occurs in ideas, when they represent non-things as things. For example, the ideas which I have of heat and cold contain so little clarity and distinctness that they do not enable me to tell whether cold is merely the absence of heat or vice versa, or whether both of them are real qualities, or neither is. And since there can be no ideas which are not as it were of things, if it is true that cold is nothing but the absence of heat, the idea which represents it to me as something real and positive deserves to be called false; and the same goes for other ideas of this kind.

Such ideas obviously do not require me to posit a source distinct from myself. For on the one hand, if they are false, that is, represent non-things, I know by the natural light that they arise from nothing – that is, they are in me only because of a deficiency and lack of perfection in my nature. If on the other hand they are true, then since the reality which they represent is so extremely slight that I cannot even distinguish it from a non-thing, I do not see why they cannot originate from myself.

With regard to the clear and distinct elements in my ideas of corporeal things, it appears that I could have borrowed some of these from my idea of myself, namely substance, duration, number and anything else of this kind. For example, I think that a stone is a substance, or is a thing capable of existing independently, and I also think that I am a substance. Admittedly I conceive of myself as a thing that thinks and is not extended, whereas I conceive of the stone as a thing that is extended and does not think, so that the two conceptions differ enormously; but they seem to agree with respect to the classification "substance". Again, I perceive that I now exist, and remember that I have existed for some time; moreover, I have various thoughts which I can count; it is in these ways that I acquire the ideas of duration and number which I can then transfer to other things. As for all the other elements which make up the ideas of corporeal things, namely extension, shape, position and movement, these are not formally contained in me, since I am nothing but a thinking thing; but since they are merely modes of a substance, and I am a substance, it seems possible that they are contained in me eminently.

So there remains only the idea of God; and I must consider whether there is anything in the idea which could not have originated in myself. By the word "God" I understand a substance that is infinite, ⟨eternal, immutable,⟩ independent, supremely intelligent, supremely powerful, and which created both myself and everything else (if anything else there be) that exists. All these attributes are such that, the more carefully I concentrate on them, the less possible it seems that they could have originated from me alone. So from what has been said it must be concluded that God necessarily exists. [. . .]

Fourth Meditation

Truth and falsity

During these past few days I have accustomed myself to leading my mind away from the senses; and I have taken careful note of the fact that there is very little about corporeal things that is truly perceived, whereas much more is known about the human mind, and still more about God. The result is that I now have no difficulty in turning my mind away from imaginable things and towards things which are objects of the intellect alone and are totally separate from matter. And indeed the idea I have of the human mind, in so far as it is a thinking thing, which is not extended in length, breadth or height and has no other bodily characteristics, is much more distinct than the idea of any corporeal thing. And when I consider the fact that I have doubts, or that I am a thing that is incomplete and dependent, then there arises in me a clear and distinct idea of a being who is independent and complete, that is, an idea of God. And from the mere fact that there is such an idea within me, or that I who possess this idea exist, I clearly infer that God also exists, and that every single moment of my entire existence depends on him. So clear is this conclusion that I am confident that the human intellect cannot know anything that is more evident or more certain. And now, from this contemplation of the true God, in whom all the treasures of wisdom and the sciences lie hidden, I think I can see a way forward to the knowledge of other things.

To begin with, I recognize that it is impossible that God should ever deceive me. For in every case of trickery or deception some imperfection is to be found; and although the ability to deceive appears to be an indication of cleverness or power, the will to deceive is undoubtedly evidence of malice or weakness, and so cannot apply to God.

Next, I know by experience that there is in me a faculty of judgement which, like everything else which is in me, I certainly received from God. And since God does not wish to deceive me, he surely did not give me the kind of faculty which would ever enable me to go wrong while using it correctly.

There would be no further doubt on this issue were it not that what I have just said appears to imply that I am incapable of ever going wrong. For if everything that is in me comes from God, and he did not endow me with a faculty for making mistakes, it appears that I can never go wrong. And certainly, so long as I think only of God, and turn my whole attention to him, I can find no cause of error or falsity. But when I turn back to myself, I know by experience that I am prone to countless errors. On looking for the cause of these errors, I find that I possess not only a real and positive idea of God, or a being who is supremely perfect, but also what may be described as a negative idea of nothingness, or of that which is farthest removed from all perfection. I realize that I am, as it were, something intermediate between God and nothingness, or between supreme being and non-being: my nature is such that in so far as I was created by the supreme being, there is nothing in me to enable me to go wrong or lead me astray; but in so far as I participate in nothingness or non-being, that is, in so far as I am not myself the supreme being and am lacking in countless respects, it is no wonder that I make mistakes. I understand, then, that error as such is not something real which depends on God, but merely a defect. Hence my going wrong does not require me to have a faculty specially bestowed on me by God; it simply happens as a result of the fact that the faculty of true judgement which I have from God is in my case not infinite.

But this is still not entirely satisfactory. For error is not a pure negation, but rather a privation or lack of some knowledge which somehow should be in me. And when I concentrate on the nature of God, it seems impossible that he should have placed in me a faculty which is not perfect of its kind, or which lacks some perfection which it ought to have. The more skilled the craftsman the more perfect the work produced by him; if this is so, how can anything produced by the supreme creator of all things not be complete and perfect in all respects? There is, moreover, no doubt that God could have given me a nature such that I was never mistaken; again, there is no doubt that he always wills what is best. Is it then better that I should make mistakes than that I should not do so?

As I reflect on these matters more attentively, it occurs to me first of all that it is no cause for surprise if I do not understand the reasons for some of God's actions; and there is no call to doubt his existence if I happen to find that there are other instances where I do not grasp why or how certain things were made by him. For since I now know that my own nature is very weak and limited, whereas the nature of God is immense, incomprehensible and infinite, I also know without more ado that he is capable of countless things whose causes are beyond my knowledge. And for this reason alone I consider the customary search for final causes to be totally useless in physics; there is considerable rashness in thinking myself capable of investigating the ⟨impenetrable⟩ purposes of God.

It also occurs to me that whenever we are inquiring whether the works of God are perfect, we ought to look at the whole universe, not just at one created thing on its own. For what would perhaps rightly appear very imperfect if it existed on its own is quite perfect when its function as a part of the universe is considered. It is true that, since my decision to doubt everything, it is so far only myself and God whose existence I have been able to know with certainty; but after considering the immense power of God, I cannot deny that many other things have been made by him, or at least could have been made, and hence that I may have a place in the universal scheme of things.

Next, when I look more closely at myself and inquire into the nature of my errors (for these are the only evidence of some imperfection in me), I notice that they depend on two concurrent causes, namely on the faculty of knowledge which is in me, and on the faculty of choice or freedom of the will; that is, they depend on both the intellect and the will simultaneously. Now all that the intellect does is to enable me to perceive the ideas which are subjects for possible judgements; and when regarded strictly in this light, it turns out to contain no error in the proper sense of that term. For although countless things may exist without there being any corresponding ideas in me, it should not, strictly speaking, be said that I am deprived of these ideas, but merely that I lack them, in a negative sense. This is because I cannot produce any reason to prove that God ought to have given me a greater faculty of knowledge than he did; and no matter how skilled I understand a craftsman to be, this does not make me think he ought to have put into every one of his works all the perfections which he is able to put into some of them. Besides, I cannot complain that the will or freedom of choice which I received from God is not sufficiently extensive or perfect, since I know by experience that it is not restricted in any way. Indeed, I think it is very noteworthy that there is nothing else in me which is so perfect and so great that the possibility of a further increase in its perfection or greatness is beyond my understanding. If, for example, I consider the faculty of understanding, I immediately recognize that in my case it is extremely slight and very finite, and I at once form the idea of an understanding which is much greater – indeed supremely great and infinite; and from the very fact that I can form an idea of it, I perceive that it belongs to the nature of God. Similarly, if I examine the faculties of memory or imagination, or any others, I discover that in my case each one of these faculties is weak and limited, while in the case of God it is immeasurable. It is only the will, or freedom of choice, which I experience within me to be so great that the idea of any greater faculty is beyond my grasp; so much so that it is above all in virtue of the will that I understand myself to bear in some way the image and likeness of God. For although God's will is incomparably greater than mine, both in virtue of the knowledge and power that accompany it and make it more firm and efficacious, and also in virtue of its object, in that it ranges over a greater number of items, nevertheless it does not seem any greater than mine when considered as will in the essential and strict sense. This is because the will simply consists in our ability to do or not do something (that is, to affirm or deny, to pursue or avoid); or rather, it consists simply in the fact that when the intellect puts something forward for affirmation or denial or for pursuit or avoidance, our inclinations are such that we do not feel we are determined by any external force. In order to be free, there is no need for me to be inclined both ways; on the contrary, the more I incline in one direction – either because I clearly understand that reasons of truth and goodness point that way, or because of a divinely produced disposition of my inmost thoughts – the freer is my choice. Neither divine grace nor natural knowledge ever diminishes freedom; on the contrary, they increase and strengthen it. But the indifference I feel when there is no reason pushing me in one direction rather than another is the lowest grade of freedom; it is evidence not of any perfection of freedom, but rather of a defect in knowledge or a kind of negation. For if I always saw clearly what was true and good, I should never have to deliberate about the right judgement or choice; in that case, although I should be wholly free, it would be impossible for me ever to be in a state of indifference.

From these considerations I perceive that the power of willing which I received from God is not, when considered in itself, the cause of my mistakes; for it is both extremely ample and also perfect of its kind. Nor is my power of understanding to blame; for since my understanding comes from God, everything that I understand I undoubtedly understand correctly, and any error here is impossible. So what then is the source of my mistakes? It must be simply this: the scope of the will is wider than that of the intellect; but instead of restricting it within the same limits, I extend its use to matters which I do not understand. Since the will is indifferent in such cases, it easily turns aside from what is true and good, and this is the source of my error and sin.

For example, during these past few days I have been asking whether anything in the world exists, and I have realized that from the very fact of my raising this question it follows quite evidently that I exist. I could not but judge that something which I understood so clearly was true; but this was not because I was compelled so to judge by any external force, but because a great light in the intellect was followed by a great inclination in the will, and thus the spontaneity and freedom of my belief was all the greater in proportion to my lack of indifference. But now, besides the knowledge that I exist, in so far as I am a thinking thing, an idea of corporeal nature comes into my mind; and I happen to be in doubt as to whether the thinking nature which is in me, or rather which I am, is distinct from this corporeal nature or identical with it. I am making the further supposition that my intellect has not yet come upon any persuasive reason in favour of one alternative rather than the other. This obviously implies that I am indifferent as to whether I should assert or deny either alternative, or indeed refrain from making any judgement on the matter.

What is more, this indifference does not merely apply to cases where the intellect is wholly ignorant, but extends in general to every case where the intellect does not have sufficiently clear knowledge at the time when the will deliberates. For although probable conjectures may pull me in one direction, the mere knowledge that they are simply conjectures, and not certain and indubitable reasons, is itself quite enough to push my assent the other way. My experience in the last few days confirms this: the mere fact that I found that all my previous beliefs were in some sense open to doubt was enough to turn my absolutely confident belief in their truth into the supposition that they were wholly false.

If, however, I simply refrain from making a judgement in cases where I do not perceive the truth with sufficient clarity and distinctness, then it is clear that I am behaving correctly and avoiding error. But if in such cases I either affirm or deny, then I am not using my free will correctly. If I go for the alternative which is false, then obviously I shall be in error; if I take the other side, then it is by pure chance that I arrive at the truth, and I shall still be at fault since it is clear by the natural light that the perception of the intellect should always precede the determination of the will. In this incorrect use of free will may be found the privation which constitutes the essence of error. The privation, I say, lies in the operation of the will in so far as it proceeds from me, but not in the faculty of will which I received from God, nor even in its operation, in so far as it depends on him. [. . .]

Sixth Meditation

The existence of material things, and the real distinction between mind and body

It remains for me to examine whether material things exist. And at least I now know they are capable of existing, in so far as they are the subject-matter of pure mathematics, since I perceive them clearly and distinctly. For there is no doubt that God is capable of creating everything that I am capable of perceiving in this manner; and I have never judged that something could not be made by him except on the grounds that there would be a contradiction in my perceiving it distinctly. The conclusion that material things exist is also suggested by the faculty of imagination, which I am aware of using when I turn my mind to material things. For when I give more attentive consideration to what imagination is, it seems to be nothing else but an application of the cognitive faculty to a body which is intimately present to it, and which therefore exists.

To make this clear, I will first examine the difference between imagination and pure understanding. When I imagine a triangle, for example, I do not merely understand that it is a figure bounded by three lines, but at the same time I also see the three lines with my mind's eye as if they were present before me; and this is what I call imagining. But if I want to think of a chiliagon, although I understand that it is a figure consisting of a thousand sides just as well as I understand the triangle to be a three-sided figure, I do not in the same way imagine the thousand sides or see them as if they were present before me. It is true that since I am in the habit of imagining something whenever I think of a corporeal thing, I may construct in my mind a confused representation of some figure; but it is clear that this is not a chiliagon. For it differs in no way from the representation I should form if I were thinking of a myriagon, or any figure with very many sides. Moreover, such a representation is useless for recognizing the properties which distinguish a chiliagon from other polygons. But suppose I am dealing with a pentagon: I can of course understand the figure of a pentagon, just as I can the figure of a chiliagon, without the help of the imagination; but I can also imagine a pentagon, by applying my mind's eye to its five sides and the area contained within them. And in doing this I notice quite clearly that imagination requires a peculiar effort of mind which is not required for understanding; this additional effort of mind clearly shows the difference between imagination and pure understanding.

Besides this, I consider that this power of imagining which is in me, differing as it does from the power of understanding, is not a necessary constituent of my own essence, that is, of the essence of my mind. For if I lacked it, I should undoubtedly remain the same individual as I now am; from which it seems to follow that it depends on something distinct from myself. And I can easily understand that, if there does exist some body to which the mind is so joined that it can apply itself to contemplate it, as it were, whenever it pleases, then it may possibly be this very body that enables me to imagine corporeal things. So the difference between this mode of thinking and pure understanding may simply be this: when the mind understands, it in some way turns towards itself and inspects one of the ideas which are within it; but when it imagines, it turns towards the body and looks at something in the body which conforms to an idea understood by the mind or perceived by the senses. I can, as I say, easily understand that this is how imagination comes about, if the body exists; and since there is no other equally suitable way of explaining imagination that comes to mind, I can make a probable conjecture that the body exists. But this is only a probability; and despite a careful and comprehensive investigation, I do not yet see how the distinct idea of corporeal nature which I find in my imagination can provide any basis for a necessary inference that some body exists.

But besides that corporeal nature which is the subject-matter of pure mathematics, there is much else that I habitually imagine, such as colours, sounds, tastes, pain and so on – though not so distinctly. Now I perceive these things much better by means of the senses, which is how, with the assistance of memory, they appear to have reached the imagination. So in order to deal with them more fully, I must pay equal attention to the senses, and see whether the things which are perceived by means of that mode of thinking which I call "sensory perception" provide me with any sure argument for the existence of corporeal things.

To begin with, I will go back over all the things which I previously took to be perceived by the senses, and reckoned to be true; and I will go over my reasons for thinking this. Next, I will set out my reasons for subsequently calling these things into doubt. And finally I will consider what I should now believe about them.

First of all then, I perceived by my senses that I had a head, hands, feet and other limbs making up the body which I regarded as part of myself, or perhaps even as my whole self. I also perceived by my senses that this body was situated among many other bodies which could affect it in various favourable or unfavourable ways; and I gauged the favourable effects by a sensation of pleasure, and the unfavourable ones by a sensation of pain. In addition to pain and pleasure, I also had sensations within me of hunger, thirst, and other such appetites, and also of physical propensities towards cheerfulness, sadness, anger and similar emotions. And outside me, besides the extension, shapes and movements of bodies, I also had sensations of their hardness and heat, and of the other tactile qualities. In addition, I had sensations of light, colours, smells, tastes and sounds, the variety of which enabled me to distinguish the sky, the earth, the seas, and all other bodies, one from another. Considering the ideas of all these qualities which presented themselves to my thought, although the ideas were, strictly speaking, the only immediate objects of my sensory awareness, it was not unreasonable for me to think that the items which I was perceiving through the senses were things quite distinct from my thought, namely bodies which produced the ideas. For my experience was that these ideas came to me quite without my consent, so that I could not have sensory awareness of any object, even if I wanted to, unless it was present to my sense organs; and I could not avoid having sensory awareness of it when it was present. And since the ideas perceived by the senses were much more lively and vivid and even, in their own way, more distinct than any of those which I deliberately formed through meditating or which I found impressed on my memory, it seemed impossible that they should have come from within me; so the only alternative was that they came from other things. Since the sole source of my knowledge of these things was the ideas themselves, the supposition that the things resembled the ideas was bound to occur to me. In addition, I remembered that the use of my senses had come first, while the use of my reason came only later; and I saw that the ideas which I formed myself were less vivid than those which I perceived with the senses and were, for the most part, made up of elements of sensory ideas. In this way I easily convinced myself that I had nothing at all in the intellect which I had not previously had in sensation. As for the body which by some special right I called "mine", my belief that this body, more than any other, belonged to me had some justification. For I could never be separated from it, as I could from other bodies; and I felt all my appetites and emotions in, and on account of, this body; and finally, I was aware of pain and pleasurable ticklings in parts of this body, but not in other bodies external to it. But why should that curious sensation of pain give rise to a particular distress of mind; or why should a certain kind of delight follow on a tickling sensation? Again, why should that curious tugging in the stomach which I call hunger tell me that I should eat, or a dryness of the throat tell me to drink, and so on? I was not able to give any explanation of all this, except that nature taught me so. For there is absolutely no connection (at least that I can understand) between the tugging sensation and the decision to take food, or between the sensation of something causing pain and the mental apprehension of distress that arises from that sensation. These and other judgements that I made concerning sensory objects, I was apparently taught to make by nature; for I had already made up my mind that this was how things were, before working out any arguments to prove it.

Later on, however, I had many experiences which gradually undermined all the faith I had had in the senses. Sometimes towers which had looked round from a distance appeared square from close up; and enormous statues standing on their pediments did not seem large when observed from the ground. In these and countless other such cases, I found that the judgements of the external senses were mistaken. And this applied not just to the external senses but to the internal senses as well. For what can be more internal than pain? And yet I had heard that those who had had a leg or an arm amputated sometimes still seemed to feel pain inter-mittently in the missing part of the body. So even in my own case it was appar-ently not quite certain that a particular limb was hurting, even if I felt pain in it. To these reasons for doubting, I recently added two very general ones. The first was that every sensory experience I have ever thought I was having while awake I can also think of myself as sometimes having while asleep; and since I do not believe that what I seem to perceive in sleep comes from things located outside me, I did not see why I should be any more inclined to believe this of what I think I perceive while awake. The second reason for doubt was that since I did not know the author of my being (or at least was pretending not to), I saw nothing to rule out the possibility that my natural constitution made me prone to error even in matters which seemed to me most true. As for the reasons for my previous confident belief in the truth of the things perceived by the senses, I had no trouble in refuting them. For since I apparently had natural impulses towards many things which reason told me to avoid, I reckoned that a great deal of confidence should not be placed in what I was taught by nature. And despite the fact that the perceptions of the senses were not dependent on my will, I did not think that I should on that account infer that they proceeded from things distinct from myself, since I might perhaps have a faculty not yet known to me which produced them.

But now, when I am beginning to achieve a better knowledge of myself and the author of my being, although I do not think I should heedlessly accept everything I seem to have acquired from the senses, neither do I think that everything should be called into doubt.

First, I know that everything which I clearly and distinctly understand is capable of being created by God so as to correspond exactly with my understanding of it. Hence the fact that I can clearly and distinctly understand one thing apart from another is enough to make me certain that the two things are distinct, since they are capable of being separated, at least by God. The question of what kind of power is required to bring about such a separation does not affect the judgement that the two things are distinct. Thus, simply by knowing that I exist and seeing at the same time that absolutely nothing else belongs to my nature or essence except that I am a thinking thing, I can infer correctly that my essence consists solely in the fact that I am a thinking thing. It is true that I may have (or, to anticipate, that I certainly have) a body that is very closely joined to me. But nevertheless, on the one hand I have a clear and distinct idea of myself, in so far as I am simply a thinking, non-extended thing; and on the other hand I have a distinct idea of body, in so far as this is simply an extended, non-thinking thing. And accordingly, it is certain that I am really distinct from my body, and can exist without it.

Besides this, I find in myself faculties for certain special modes of thinking, namely imagination and sensory perception. Now I can clearly and distinctly understand myself as a whole without these faculties; but I cannot, conversely, understand these faculties without me, that is, without an intellectual substance to inhere in. This is because there is an intellectual act included in their essential definition; and hence I perceive that the distinction between them and myself corresponds to the distinction between the modes of a thing and the thing itself. Of course I also recognize that there are other faculties (like those of changing position, of taking on various shapes, and so on) which, like sensory perception and imagination, cannot be understood apart from some substance for them to inhere in, and hence cannot exist without it. But it is clear that these other faculties, if they exist, must be in a corporeal or extended substance and not an intellectual one; for the clear and distinct conception of them includes extension, but does not include any intellectual act whatsoever. Now there is in me a passive faculty of sensory perception, that is, a faculty for receiving and recognizing the ideas of sensible objects; but I could not make use of it unless there was also an active faculty, either in me or in something else, which produced or brought about these ideas. But this faculty cannot be in me, since clearly it presupposes no intellectual act on my part, and the ideas in question are produced without my cooperation and often even against my will. So the only alternative is that it is in another substance distinct from me — a substance which contains either formally or eminently all the reality which exists objectively in the ideas produced by this faculty (as I have just noted). This substance is either a body, that is, a corporeal nature, in which case it will contain formally ⟨and in fact⟩ everything which is to be found objectively ⟨or representatively⟩ in the ideas; or else it is God, or some creature more noble than a body, in which case it will contain eminently whatever is to be found in the ideas. But since God is not a deceiver, it is quite clear that he does not transmit the ideas to me either directly from himself, or indirectly, via some creature which contains the objective reality of the ideas not formally but only eminently. For God has given me no faculty at all for recognizing any such source for these ideas; on the contrary, he has given me a great propensity to believe that they are produced by corporeal things. So I do not see how God could be understood to be anything but a deceiver if the ideas were transmitted from a source other than corporeal things. It follows that corporeal things exist. They may not all exist in a way that exactly corresponds with my sensory grasp of them, for in many cases the grasp of the senses is very obscure and confused. But at least they possess all the properties which I clearly and distinctly understand, that is, all those which, viewed in general terms, are comprised within the subject-matter of pure mathematics.

What of the other aspects of corporeal things which are either particular (for example that the sun is of such and such a size or shape), or less clearly understood, such as light or sound or pain, and so on? Despite the high degree of doubt and uncertainty involved here, the very fact that God is not a deceiver, and the consequent impossibility of there being any falsity in my opinions which cannot be corrected by some other faculty supplied by God, offers me a sure hope that I can attain the truth even in these matters. Indeed, there is no doubt that everything that I am taught by nature contains some truth. For if nature is considered in its general aspect, then I understand by the term nothing other than God himself, or the ordered system of created things established by God. And by my own nature in particular I understand nothing other than the totality of things bestowed on me by God.

There is nothing that my own nature teaches me more vividly than that I have a body, and that when I feel pain there is something wrong with the body, and that when I am hungry or thirsty the body needs food and drink, and so on. So I should not doubt that there is some truth in this.

Nature also teaches me, by these sensations of pain, hunger, thirst and so on, that I am not merely present in my body as a sailor is present in a ship, but that I am very closely joined and, as it were, intermingled with it, so that I and the body form a unit. If this were not so, I, who am nothing but a thinking thing, would not feel pain when the body was hurt, but would perceive the damage purely by the intellect, just as a sailor perceives by sight if anything in his ship is broken. Similarly, when the body needed food or drink, I should have an explicit understanding of the fact, instead of having confused sensations of hunger and thirst. For these sensations of hunger, thirst, pain and so on are nothing but confused modes of thinking which arise from the union and, as it were, intermingling of the mind with the body.

I am also taught by nature that various other bodies exist in the vicinity of my body, and that some of these are to be sought out and others avoided. And from the fact that I perceive by my senses a great variety of colours, sounds, smells and tastes, as well as differences in heat, hardness and the like, I am correct in inferring that the bodies which are the source of these various sensory perceptions possess differences corresponding to them, though perhaps not resembling them. Also, the fact that some of the perceptions are agreeable to me while others are disagreeable makes it quite certain that my body, or rather my whole self, in so far as I am a combination of body and mind, can be affected by the various beneficial or harmful bodies which surround it.

There are, however, many other things which I may appear to have been taught by nature, but which in reality I acquired not from nature but from a habit of making ill-considered judgements; and it is therefore quite possible that these are false. Cases in point are the belief that any space in which nothing is occurring to stimulate my senses must be empty; or that the heat in a body is something exactly resembling the idea of heat which is in me; or that when a body is white or green, the selfsame whiteness or greenness which I perceive through my senses is present in the body; or that in a body which is bitter or sweet there is the selfsame taste which I experience, and so on; or, finally, that stars and towers and other distant bodies have the same size and shape which they present to my senses, and other examples of this kind. But to make sure that my perceptions in this matter are sufficiently distinct, I must more accurately define exactly what I mean when I say that I am taught something by nature. In this context I am taking nature to be something more limited than the totality of things bestowed on me by God. For this includes many things that belong to the mind alone – for example my perception that what is done cannot be undone, and all other things that are known by the natural light; but at this stage I am not speaking of these matters. It also includes much that relates to the body alone, like the tendency to move in a downward direction, and so on; but I am not speaking of these matters either. My sole concern here is with what God has bestowed on me as a combination of mind and body. My nature, then, in this limited sense, does indeed teach me to avoid what induces a feeling of pain and to seek out what induces feelings of pleasure, and so on. But it does not appear to teach us to draw any conclusions from these sensory perceptions about things located outside us without waiting until the intellect has examined the matter. For knowledge of the truth about such things seems to belong to the mind alone, not to the combination of mind and body. Hence, although a star has no greater effect on my eye than the flame of a small light, that does not mean that there is any real or positive inclination in me to believe that the star is no bigger than the light; I have simply made this judgement from childhood onwards without any rational basis. Similarly, although I feel heat when I go near a fire and feel pain when I go too near, there is no convincing argument for supposing that there is something in the fire which resembles the heat, any more than for supposing that there is something which resembles the pain. There is simply reason to suppose that there is something in the fire, whatever it may eventually turn out to be, which produces in us the feelings of heat or pain. And likewise, even though there is nothing in any given space that stimulates the senses, it does not follow that there is no body there. In these cases and many others I see that I have been in the habit of misusing the order of nature. For the proper purpose of the sensory perceptions given me by nature is simply to inform the mind of what is beneficial or harmful for the composite of which the mind is a part; and to this extent they are sufficiently clear and distinct. But I misuse them by treating them as reliable touchstones for immediate judgements about the essential nature of the bodies located outside us; yet this is an area where they provide only very obscure information.

I have already looked in sufficient detail at how, notwithstanding the goodness of God, it may happen that my judgements are false. But a further problem now comes to mind regarding those very things which nature presents to me as objects which I should seek out or avoid, and also regarding the internal sensations, where I seem to have detected errors – e.g. when someone is tricked by the pleasant taste of some food into eating the poison concealed inside it. Yet in this case, what the man's nature urges him to go for is simply what is responsible for the pleasant taste, and not the poison, which his nature knows nothing about. The only inference that can be drawn from this is that his nature is not omniscient. And this is not surprising, since man is a limited thing, and so it is only fitting that his perfection should be limited.

And yet it is not unusual for us to go wrong even in cases where nature does urge us towards something. Those who are ill, for example, may desire food or drink that will shortly afterwards turn out to be bad for them. Perhaps it may be said that they go wrong because their nature is disordered, but this does not remove the difficulty. A sick man is no less one of God's creatures than a healthy one, and it seems no less a contradiction to suppose that he has received from God a nature which deceives him. Yet a clock constructed with wheels and weights observes all the laws of its nature just as closely when it is badly made and tells the wrong time as when it completely fulfils the wishes of the clockmaker. In the same way, I might consider the body of a man as a kind of machine equipped with and made up of bones, nerves, muscles, veins, blood and skin in such a way that, even if there were no mind in it, it would still perform all the same movements as it now does in those cases where movement is not under the control of the will or, consequently, of the mind. I can easily see that if such a body suffers from dropsy, for example, and is affected by the dryness of the throat which normally produces in the mind the sensation of thirst, the resulting condition of the nerves and other parts will dispose the body to take a drink, with the result that the disease will be aggravated. Yet this is just as natural as the body's being stimulated by a similar dryness of the throat to take a drink when there is no such illness and the drink is beneficial. Admittedly, when I consider the purpose of the clock, I may say that it is departing from its nature when it does not tell the right time; and similarly when I consider the mechanism of the human body, I may think that, in relation to the movements which normally occur in it, it too is deviating from its nature if the throat is dry at a time when drinking is not beneficial to its continued health. But I am well aware that "nature" as I have just used it has a very different significance from "nature" in the other sense. As I have just used it, "nature" is simply a label which depends on my thought; it is quite extraneous to the things to which it is applied, and depends simply on my comparison between the idea of a sick man and a badly-made clock, and the idea of a healthy man and a well-made clock. But by "nature" in the other sense I understand something which is really to be found in the things themselves; in this sense, therefore, the term contains something of the truth.

When we say, then, with respect to the body suffering from dropsy, that it has a disordered nature because it has a dry throat and yet does not need drink, the term "nature" is here used merely as an extraneous label. However, with respect to the composite, that is, the mind united with this body, what is involved is not a mere label, but a true error of nature, namely that it is thirsty at a time when drink is going to cause it harm. It thus remains to inquire how it is that the goodness of God does not prevent nature, in this sense, from deceiving us.

The first observation I make at this point is that there is a great difference between the mind and the body, inasmuch as the body is by its very nature always divisible, while the mind is utterly indivisible. For when I consider the mind, or myself in so far as I am merely a thinking thing, I am unable to distinguish any parts within myself; I understand myself to be something quite single and complete. Although the whole mind seems to be united to the whole body, I recognize that if a foot or arm or any other part of the body is cut off, nothing has thereby been taken away from the mind. As for the faculties of willing, of understanding, of sensory perception and so on, these cannot be termed parts of the mind, since it is one and the same mind that wills, and understands and has sensory perceptions. By contrast, there is no corporeal or extended thing that I can think of which in my thought I cannot easily divide into parts; and this very fact makes me understand that it is divisible. This one argument would be enough to show me that the mind is completely different from the body, even if I did not already know as much from other considerations.

My next observation is that the mind is not immediately affected by all parts of the body, but only by the brain, or perhaps just by one small part of the brain, namely the part which is said to contain the "common" sense. Every time this part of the brain is in a given state, it presents the same signals to the mind, even though the other parts of the body may be in a different condition at the time. This is established by countless observations, which there is no need to review here.

I observe, in addition, that the nature of the body is such that whenever any part of it is moved by another part which is some distance away, it can always be moved in the same fashion by any of the parts which lie in between, even if the more distant part does nothing. For example, in a cord ABCD, if one end D is pulled so that the other end A moves, the exact same movement could have been brought about if one of the intermediate points B or C had been pulled, and D had not moved at all. In similar fashion, when I feel a pain in my foot, physiology tells me that this happens by means of nerves distributed throughout the foot, and that these nerves are like cords which go from the foot right up to the brain. When the nerves are pulled in the foot, they in turn pull on inner parts of the brain to which they are attached, and produce a certain motion in them; and nature has laid it down that this motion should produce in the mind a sensation of pain, as occurring in the foot. But since these nerves, in passing from the foot to the brain, must pass through the calf, the thigh, the lumbar region, the back and the neck, it can happen that, even if it is not the part in the foot but one of the intermediate parts which is being pulled, the same motion will occur in the brain as occurs when the foot is hurt, and so it will necessarily come about that the mind feels the same sensation of pain. And we must suppose the same thing happens with regard to any other sensation.

My final observation is that any given movement occurring in the part of the brain that immediately affects the mind produces just one corresponding sensation; and hence the best system that could be devised is that it should produce the one sensation which, of all possible sensations, is most especially and most frequently conducive to the preservation of the healthy man. And experience shows that the sensations which nature has given us are all of this kind; and so there is absolutely nothing to be found in them that does not bear witness to the power and goodness of God. For example, when the nerves in the foot are set in motion in a violent and unusual manner, this motion, by way of the spinal cord, reaches the inner parts of the brain, and there gives the mind its signal for having a certain sensation, namely the sensation of a pain as occurring in the foot. This stimulates the mind to do its best to get rid of the cause of the pain, which it takes to be harmful to the foot. It is true that God could have made the nature of man such that this particular motion in the brain indicated something else to the mind; it might, for example, have made the mind aware of the actual motion occurring in the brain, or in the foot, or in any of the intermediate regions; or it might have indicated something else entirely. But there is nothing else which would have been so conducive to the continued well-being of the body. In the same way, when we need drink, there arises a certain dryness in the throat; this sets in motion the nerves of the throat, which in turn move the inner parts of the brain. This motion produces in the mind a sensation of thirst, because the most useful thing for us to know about the whole business is that we need drink in order to stay healthy. And so it is in the other cases.

It is quite clear from all this that, notwithstanding the immense goodness of God, the nature of man as a combination of mind and body is such that it is bound to mislead him from time to time. For there may be some occurrence, not in the foot but in one of the other areas through which the nerves travel in their route from the foot to the brain, or even in the brain itself; and if this cause produces the same motion which is generally produced by injury to the foot, then pain will be felt as if it were in the foot. This deception of the senses is natural, because a given motion in the brain must always produce the same sensation in the mind; and the origin of the motion in question is much more often going to be something which is hurting the foot, rather than something existing elsewhere. So it is reasonable that this motion should always indicate to the mind a pain in the foot rather than in any other part of the body. Again, dryness of the throat may sometimes arise not, as it normally does, from the fact that a drink is necessary to the health of the body, but from some quite opposite cause, as happens in the case of the man with dropsy. Yet it is much better that it should mislead on this occasion than that it should always mislead when the body is in good health. And the same goes for the other cases.

This consideration is the greatest help to me, not only for noticing all the errors to which my nature is liable, but also for enabling me to correct or avoid them without difficulty. For I know that in matters regarding the well-being of the body, all my senses report the truth much more frequently than not. Also, I can almost always make use of more than one sense to investigate the same thing; and in addition, I can use both my memory, which connects present experiences with preceding ones, and my intellect, which has by now examined all the causes of error. Accordingly, I should not have any further fears about the falsity of what my senses tell me every day; on the contrary, the exaggerated doubts of the last few days should be dismissed as laughable. This applies especially to the principal reason for doubt, namely my inability to distinguish between being asleep and being awake. For I now notice that there is a vast difference between the two, in that dreams are never linked by memory with all the other actions of life as waking experiences are. If, while I am awake, anyone were suddenly to appear to me and then disappear immediately, as happens in sleep, so that I could not see where he had come from or where he had gone to, it would not be unreasonable for me to judge that he was a ghost, or a vision created in my brain, rather than a real man. But when I distinctly see where things come from and where and when they come to me, and when I can connect my perceptions of them with the whole of the rest of my life without a break, then I am quite certain that when I encounter these things I am not asleep but awake. And I ought not to have even the slightest doubt of their reality if, after calling upon all the senses as well as my memory and my intellect in order to check them, I receive no conflicting reports from any of these sources. For from the fact that God is not a deceiver it follows that in cases like these I am completely free from error. But since the pressure of things to be done does not always allow us to stop and make such a meticulous check, it must be admitted that in this human life we are often liable to make mistakes about particular things, and we must acknowledge the weakness of our nature.

Bertrand Russell, *The Problems of Philosophy* (selections)

I   Appearance and Reality

Is there any knowledge in the world which is so certain that no reasonable man could doubt it? This question, which at first sight might not seem difficult, is really

From *The Problems of Philosophy* (Oxford: Oxford University Press, 1959), chapters I–III.

one of the most difficult that can be asked. When we have realized the obstacles in the way of a straightforward and confident answer, we shall be well launched on the study of philosophy – for philosophy is merely the attempt to answer such ultimate questions, not carelessly and dogmatically, as we do in ordinary life and even in the sciences, but critically, after exploring all that makes such questions puzzling, and after realizing all the vagueness and confusion that underlie our ordinary ideas.

In daily life, we assume as certain many things which, on a closer scrutiny, are found to be so full of apparent contradictions that only a great amount of thought enables us to know what it is that we really may believe. In the search for certainty, it is natural to begin with our present experiences, and in some sense, no doubt, knowledge is to be derived from them. But any statement as to what it is that our immediate experiences make us know is very likely to be wrong. It seems to me that I am now sitting in a chair, at a table of a certain shape, on which I see sheets of paper with writing or print. By turning my head I see out of the window buildings and clouds and the sun. I believe that the sun is about ninety-three million miles from the earth; that it is a hot globe many times bigger than the earth; that, owing to the earth's rotation, it rises every morning, and will continue to do so for an indefinite time in the future. I believe that, if any other normal person comes into my room, he will see the same chairs and tables and books and papers as I see, and that the table which I see is the same as the table which I feel pressing against my arm. All this seems to be so evident as to be hardly worth stating, except in answer to a man who doubts whether I know anything. Yet all this may be reasonably doubted, and all of it requires much careful discussion before we can be sure that we have stated it in a form that is wholly true.

To make our difficulties plain, let us concentrate attention on the table. To the eye it is oblong, brown and shiny, to the touch it is smooth and cool and hard; when I tap it, it gives out a wooden sound. Any one else who sees and feels and hears the table will agree with this description, so that it might seem as if no difficulty would arise; but as soon as we try to be more precise our troubles begin. Although I believe that the table is "really" of the same colour all over, the parts that reflect the light look much brighter than the other parts, and some parts look white because of reflected light. I know that, if I move, the parts that reflect the light will be different, so that the apparent distribution of colours on the table will change. It follows that if several people are looking at the table at the same moment, no two of them will see exactly the same distribution of colours, because no two can see it from exactly the same point of view, and any change in the point of view makes some change in the way the light is reflected.

For most practical purposes these differences are unimportant, but to the painter they are all-important: the painter has to unlearn the habit of thinking that things seem to have the colour which common sense says they "really" have, and to learn the habit of seeing things as they appear. Here we have already the beginning of one of the distinctions that cause most trouble in philosophy – the distinction between "appearance" and "reality", between what things seem to be and what they are. The painter wants to know what things seem to be, the practical man and the philosopher want to know what they are; but the philosopher's wish to know this is stronger than the practical man's, and is more troubled by knowledge as to the difficulties of answering the question.

To return to the table. It is evident from what we have found, that there is no colour which pre-eminently appears to be *the* colour of the table, or even of any one particular part of the table – it appears to be of different colours from different points of view, and there is no reason for regarding some of these as more really its colour than others. And we know that even from a given point of view the colour will seem different by artificial light, or to a colour-blind man, or to a man wearing blue spectacles, while in the dark there will be no colour at all, though to touch and hearing the table will be unchanged. This colour is not something which is inherent in the table, but something depending upon the table and the spectator and the way the light falls on the table. When, in ordinary life, we speak of *the* colour of the table, we only mean the sort of colour which it will seem to have to a normal spectator from an ordinary point of view under usual conditions of light. But the other colours which appear under other conditions have just as good a right to be considered real; and therefore, to avoid favouritism, we are compelled to deny that, in itself, the table has any one particular colour.

The same thing applies to the texture. With the naked eye one can see the grain, but otherwise the table looks smooth and even. If we looked at it through a microscope, we should see roughnesses and hills and valleys, and all sorts of differences that are imperceptible to the naked eye. Which of these is the "real" table? We are naturally tempted to say that what we see through the microscope is more real, but that in turn would be changed by a still more powerful microscope. If, then, we cannot trust what we see with the naked eye, why should we trust what we see through a microscope? Thus, again, the confidence in our senses with which we began deserts us.

The *shape* of the table is no better. We are all in the habit of judging as to the "real" shapes of things, and we do this so unreflectingly that we come to think we actually see the real shapes. But, in fact, as we all have to learn if we try to draw, a given thing looks different in shape from every different point of view. If our table is "really" rectangular, it will look, from almost all points of view, as if it had two acute angles and two obtuse angles. If opposite sides are parallel, they will look as if they converged to a point away from the spectator; if they are of equal length, they will look as if the nearer side were longer. All these things are not commonly noticed in looking at a table, because experience has taught us to construct the "real" shape from the apparent shape, and the "real" shape is what interests us as practical men. But the "real" shape is not what we see; it is something inferred from what we see. And what we see is constantly changing in shape as we move about the room; so that here again the senses seem not to give us the truth about the table itself, but only about the appearance of the table.

Similar difficulties arise when we consider the sense of touch. It is true that the table always gives us a sensation of hardness, and we feel that it resists pressure. But the sensation we obtain depends upon how hard we press the table and also upon what part of the body we press with; thus the various sensations due to various pressures or various parts of the body cannot be supposed to reveal *directly* any definite property of the table, but at most to be *signs* of some property which perhaps *causes* all the sensations, but is not actually apparent in any of them. And the same applies still more obviously to the sounds which can be elicited by rapping the table.

Thus it becomes evident that the real table, if there is one, is not the same as what we immediately experience by sight or touch or hearing. The real table, if there is one, is not *immediately* known to us at all, but must be an inference from what is immediately known. Hence, two very difficult questions at once arise; namely, (1) Is there a real table at all? (2) If so, what sort of object can it be?

It will help us in considering these questions to have a few simple terms of which the meaning is definite and clear. Let us give the name of "sense-data" to the things that are immediately known in sensation: such things as colours, sounds, smells, hardnesses, roughnesses, and so on. We shall give the name "sensation" to the experience of being immediately aware of these things. Thus, whenever we see a colour, we have a sensation *of* the colour, but the colour itself is a sense-datum, not a sensation. The colour is that *of* which we are immediately aware, and the awareness itself is the sensation. It is plain that if we are to know anything about the table, it must be by means of the sense-data – brown colour, oblong shape, smoothness, etc. – which we associate with the table; but, for the reasons which have been given, we cannot say that the table *is* the sense-data, or even that the sense-data are directly properties of the table. Thus a problem arises as to the relation of the sense-data to the real table, supposing there is such a thing.

The real table, if it exists, we will call a "physical object". Thus we have to consider the relation of sense-data to physical objects. The collection of all phys-ical objects is called "matter". Thus our two questions may be re-stated as follows: (1) Is there any such thing as matter? (2) If so, what is its nature?

The philosopher who first brought prominently forward the reasons for regard-ing the immediate objects of our senses as not existing independently of us was Bishop Berkeley (1685–1753). His *Three Dialogues between Hylas and Philonous, in Opposition to Sceptics and Atheists*, undertake to prove that there is no such thing as matter at all, and that the world consists of nothing but minds and their ideas. Hylas has hitherto believed in matter, but he is no match for Philonous, who mercilessly drives him into contradictions and paradoxes, and makes his own denial of matter seem, in the end, as if it were almost common sense. The arguments employed are of very different value: some are important and sound, others are confused or quibbling. But Berkeley retains the merit of having shown that the existence of matter is capable of being denied without absurdity, and that if there are any things that exist independently of us they cannot be the immediate objects of our sensations.

There are two different questions involved when we ask whether matter exists, and it is important to keep them clear. We commonly mean by "matter" something which is opposed to "mind", something which we think of as occupying space and as radically incapable of any sort of thought or consciousness. It is chiefly in this sense that Berkeley denies matter; that is to say, he does not deny that the sense-data which we commonly take as signs of the existence of the table are really signs of the existence of *something* independent of us, but he does deny that this something is non-mental, that it is neither mind nor ideas entertained by some mind. He admits that there must be something which continues to exist when we go out of the room or shut our eyes, and that what we call seeing the table does really give us reason for believing in something which persists even when we are not seeing it. But he thinks that this something cannot be radically different in nature from what we see, and cannot be independent of seeing altogether, though it must be independent of *our* seeing. He is thus led to regard the "real" table as an idea in the mind of God. Such an idea has the required permanence and independence of ourselves, without being – as matter would otherwise be – something quite unknowable, in the sense that we can only infer it, and can never be directly and immediately aware of it.

Other philosophers since Berkeley have also held that, although the table does not depend for its existence upon being seen by me, it does depend upon being seen (or otherwise apprehended in sensation) by *some* mind – not necessarily the mind of God, but more often the whole collective mind of the universe. This they hold, as Berkeley does, chiefly because they think there can be nothing real – or at any rate nothing known to be real – except minds and their thoughts and feelings. We might state the argument by which they support their view in some such way as this: "Whatever can be thought of is an idea in the mind of the person thinking of it; therefore nothing can be thought of except ideas in minds; therefore anything else is inconceivable, and what is inconceivable cannot exist."

Such an argument, in my opinion, is fallacious; and of course those who advance it do not put it so shortly or so crudely. But whether valid or not, the argument has been very widely advanced in one form or another; and very many philosophers, perhaps a majority, have held that there is nothing real except minds and their ideas. Such philosophers are called "idealists". When they come to explaining matter, they either say, like Berkeley, that matter is really nothing but a collection of ideas, or they say, like Leibniz (1646–1716), that what appears as matter is really a collection of more or less rudimentary minds.

But these philosophers, though they deny matter as opposed to mind, nevertheless, in another sense, admit matter. It will be remembered that we asked two questions; namely, (1) Is there a real table at all? (2) If so, what sort of object can it be? Now both Berkeley and Leibniz admit that there is a real table, but Berkeley says it is certain ideas in the mind of God, and Leibniz says it is a colony of souls. Thus both of them answer our first question in the affirmative, and only diverge from the views of ordinary mortals in their answer to our second question. In fact, almost all philosophers seem to be agreed that there is a real table: they almost all agree that, however much our sense-data – colour, shape, smoothness, etc. – may depend upon us, yet their occurrence is a sign of something existing independently of us, something differing, perhaps, completely from our sense-data, and yet to be regarded as causing those sense-data whenever we are in a suitable relation to the real table.

Now obviously this point in which the philosophers are agreed – the view that there *is* a real table, whatever its nature may be – is vitally important, and it will be worth while to consider what reasons there are for accepting this view before we go on to the further question as to the nature of the real table. Our next chapter, therefore, will be concerned with the reasons for supposing that there is a real table at all.

Before we go farther it will be well to consider for a moment what it is that we have discovered so far. It has appeared that, if we take any common object of the sort that is supposed to be known by the senses, what the senses *immediately* tell us is not the truth about the object as it is apart from us, but only the truth about certain sense-data which, so far as we can see, depend upon the relations between us and the object. Thus what we directly see and feel is merely "appearance", which we believe to be a sign of some "reality" behind. But if the reality is not what appears, have we any means of knowing whether there is any reality at all? And if so, have we any means of finding out what it is like?

Such questions are bewildering, and it is difficult to know that even the strangest hypotheses may not be true. Thus our familiar table, which has roused but the slightest thoughts in us hitherto, has become a problem full of surprising possibilities. The one thing we know about it is that it is not what it seems. Beyond this modest result, so far, we have the most complete liberty of conjecture. Leibniz tells us it is a community of souls: Berkeley tells us it is an idea in the mind of God; sober science, scarcely less wonderful, tells us it is a vast collection of electric charges in violent motion.

Among these surprising possibilities, doubt suggests that perhaps there is no table at all. Philosophy, if it cannot *answer* so many questions as we could wish, has at least the power of *asking* questions which increase the interest of the world, and show the strangeness and wonder lying just below the surface even in the commonest things of daily life.

II   The Existence of Matter

In this chapter we have to ask ourselves whether, in any sense at all, there is such a thing as matter. Is there a table which has a certain intrinsic nature, and continues to exist when I am not looking, or is the table merely a product of my imagination, a dream-table in a very prolonged dream? This question is of the greatest import- ance. For if we cannot be sure of the independent existence of objects, we cannot be sure of the independent existence of other people's bodies, and therefore still less of other people's minds, since we have no grounds for believing in their minds except such as are derived from observing their bodies. Thus if we cannot be sure of the independent existence of objects, we shall be left alone in a desert – it may be that the whole outer world is nothing but a dream, and that we alone exist. This is an uncomfortable possibility; but although it cannot be strictly *proved* to be false, there is not the slightest reason to suppose that it is true. In this chapter we have to see why this is the case.

Before we embark upon doubtful matters, let us try to find some more or less fixed point from which to start. Although we are doubting the physical existence of the table, we are not doubting the existence of the sense-data which made us think there was a table; we are not doubting that, while we look, a certain colour and shape appear to us, and while we press, a certain sensation of hardness is experienced by us. All this, which is psychological, we are not calling in question. In fact, whatever else may be doubtful, some at least of our immediate experiences seem absolutely certain.

Descartes (1596–1650), the founder of modern philosophy, invented a method which may still be used with profit – the method of systematic doubt. He determined that he would believe nothing which he did not see quite clearly and distinctly to be true. Whatever he could bring himself to doubt, he would doubt, until he saw reason for not doubting it. By applying this method he gradually became convinced that the only existence of which he could be *quite* certain was his own. He imagined a deceitful demon, who presented unreal things to his senses in a perpetual phantasmagoria; it might be very improbable that such a demon existed, but still it was possible, and therefore doubt concerning things perceived by the senses was possible.

But doubt concerning his own existence was not possible, for if he did not exist, no demon could deceive him. If he doubted, he must exist; if he had any experiences whatever, he must exist. Thus his own existence was an absolute certainty to him. "I think, therefore I am," he said (*Cogito, ergo sum*); and on the basis of this certainty he set to work to build up again the world of knowledge which his doubt had laid in ruins. By inventing the method of doubt, and by showing that subjective things are the most certain, Descartes performed a great service to philosophy, and one which makes him still useful to all students of the subject.

But some care is needed in using Descartes' argument. "*I* think, therefore *I* am" says rather more than is strictly certain. It might seem as though we were quite sure of being the same person to-day as we were yesterday, and this is no doubt true in some sense. But the real Self is as hard to arrive at as the real table, and does not seem to have that absolute, convincing certainty that belongs to particular experiences. When I look at my table and see a certain brown colour, what is quite certain at once is not "*I* am seeing a brown colour", but rather, "a brown colour is being seen". This of course involves something (or somebody) which (or who) sees the brown colour; but it does not of itself involve that more or less permanent person whom we call "I". So far as immediate certainty goes, it might be that the something which sees the brown colour is quite momentary, and not the same as the something which has some different experience the next moment.

Thus it is our particular thoughts and feelings that have primitive certainty. And this applies to dreams and hallucinations as well as to normal perceptions: when we dream or see a ghost, we certainly do have the sensations we think we have, but for various reasons it is held that no physical object corresponds to these sensations. Thus the certainty of our knowledge of our own experiences does not have to be limited in any way to allow for exceptional cases. Here, therefore, we have, for what it is worth, a solid basis from which to begin our pursuit of knowledge.

The problem we have to consider is this: Granted that we are certain of our own sense-data, have we any reason for regarding them as signs of the existence of something else, which we can call the physical object? When we have enumerated all the sense-data which we should naturally regard as connected with the table, have we said all there is to say about the table, or is there still something else – something not a sense-datum, something which persists when we go out of the room? Common sense unhesitatingly answers that there is. What can be bought and sold and pushed about and have a cloth laid on it, and so on, cannot be a *mere* collection of sense-data. If the cloth completely hides the table, we shall derive no sense-data from the table, and therefore, if the table were merely sense-data, it would have ceased to exist, and the cloth would be suspended in empty air, resting, by a miracle, in the place where the table formerly was. This seems plainly absurd; but whoever wishes to become a philosopher must learn not to be frightened by absurdities.

One great reason why it is felt that we must secure a physical object in addition to the sense-data, is that we want the *same* object for different people. When ten people are sitting round a dinner-table, it seems preposterous to maintain that they are not seeing the same tablecloth, the same knives and forks and spoons and glasses. But the sense-data are private to each separate person; what is immediately present to the sight of one is not immediately present to the sight of another: they all see things from slightly different points of view, and therefore see them slightly differently. Thus, if there are to be public neutral objects, which can be in some sense known to many different people, there must be something over and above the private and particular sense-data which appear to various people. What reason, then, have we for believing that there are such public neutral objects?

The first answer that naturally occurs to one is that, although different people may see the table slightly differently, still they all see more or less similar things when they look at the table, and the variations in what they see follow the laws of perspective and reflection of light, so that it is easy to arrive at a permanent object underlying all the different people's sense-data. I bought my table from the former occupant of my room; I could not buy *his* sense-data, which died when he went away, but I could and did buy the confident expectation of more or less similar sense-data. Thus it is the fact that different people have similar sense-data, and that one person in a given place at different times has similar sense-data, which makes us suppose that over and above the sense-data there is a permanent public object which underlies or causes the sense-data of various people at various times.

Now in so far as the above considerations depend upon supposing that there are other people besides ourselves, they beg the very question at issue. Other people are represented to me by certain sense-data, such as the sight of them or the sound of their voices, and if I had no reason to believe that there were physical objects independent of my sense-data, I should have no reason to believe that other people exist except as part of my dream. Thus, when we are trying to show that there must be objects independent of our own sense-data, we cannot appeal to the testimony of other people, since this testimony itself consists of sense-data, and does not reveal other people's experiences unless our own sense-data are signs of things existing independently of us. We must therefore, if possible, find, in our own purely private experiences, characteristics which show, or tend to show, that there are in the world things other than ourselves and our private experiences.

In one sense it must be admitted that we can never *prove* the existence of things other than ourselves and our experiences. No logical absurdity results from the hypothesis that the world consists of myself and my thoughts and feelings and sensations, and that everything else is mere fancy. In dreams a very complicated world may seem to be present, and yet on waking we find it was a delusion; that is to say, we find that the sense-data in the dream do not appear to have corresponded with such physical objects as we should naturally infer from our sense-data. (It is true that, when the physical world is assumed, it is possible to find physical causes for the sense-data in dreams: a door banging, for instance, may cause us to dream of a naval engagement. But although, in this case, there is a physical *cause* for the sense-data, there is not a physical object *corresponding* to the sense-data in the way in which an actual naval battle would correspond.) There is no logical impossibility in the supposition that the whole of life is a dream, in which we ourselves create all the objects that come before us. But although this is not logically impossible, there is no reason whatever to suppose that it is true; and it is, in fact, a less simple hypothesis, viewed as a means of accounting for the facts of our own life, than the common-sense hypothesis that there really àre objects independent of us, whose action on us causes our sensations.

The way in which simplicity comes in from supposing that there really are physical objects is easily seen. If the cat appears at one moment in one part of the room, and at another in another part, it is natural to suppose that it has moved from the one to the other, passing over a series of intermediate positions. But if it is merely a set of sense-data, it cannot have ever been in any place where I did not see it; thus we shall have to suppose that it did not exist at all while I was not looking, but suddenly sprang into being in a new place. If the cat exists whether I see it or not, we can understand from our own experience how it gets hungry between one meal and the next; but if it does not exist when I am not seeing it, it seems odd that appetite should grow during non-existence as fast as during existence. And if the cat consists only of sense-data, it cannot be *hungry*, since no hunger but my own can be a sense-datum to me. Thus the behaviour of the sense-data which represent the cat to me, though it seems quite natural when regarded as an expression of hunger, becomes utterly inexplicable when regarded as mere movements and changes of patches of colour, which are as incapable of hunger as a triangle is of playing football.

But the difficulty in the case of the cat is nothing compared to the difficulty in the case of human beings. When human beings speak – that is, when we hear certain noises which we associate with ideas, and simultaneously see certain motions of lips and expressions of face – it is very difficult to suppose that what we hear is not the expression of a thought, as we know it would be if we emitted the same sounds. Of course similar things happen in dreams, where we are mistaken as to the existence of other people. But dreams are more or less suggested by what we call waking life, and are capable of being more or less accounted for on scientific principles if we assume that there really is a physical world. Thus every principle of simplicity urges us to adopt the natural view, that there really are objects other than ourselves and our sense-data which have an existence not dependent upon our perceiving them.

Of course it is not by argument that we originally come by our belief in an independent external world. We find this belief ready in ourselves as soon as we begin to reflect: it is what may be called an *instinctive* belief. We should never have been led to question this belief but for the fact that, at any rate in the case of sight, it seems as if the sense-datum itself were instinctively believed to be the independent object, whereas argument shows that the object cannot be identical with the sense-datum. This discovery, however – which is not at all paradoxical in the case of taste and smell and sound, and only slightly so in the case of touch – leaves undiminished our instinctive belief that there *are* objects *corresponding* to our sense-data. Since this belief does not lead to any difficulties, but on the contrary tends to simplify and systematize our account of our experiences, there seems no good reason for rejecting it. We may therefore admit – though with a slight doubt derived from dreams – that the external world does really exist, and is not wholly dependent for its existence upon our continuing to perceive it.

The argument which has led us to this conclusion is doubtless less strong than we could wish, but it is typical of many philosophical arguments, and it is therefore worth while to consider briefly its general character and validity. All knowledge, we find, must be built up upon our instinctive beliefs, and if these are rejected, nothing is left. But among our instinctive beliefs some are much stronger than others, while many have, by habit and association, become entangled with other beliefs, not really instinctive, but falsely supposed to be part of what is believed instinctively.

Philosophy should show us the hierarchy of our instinctive beliefs, beginning with those we hold most strongly, and presenting each as much isolated and as free from irrelevant additions as possible. It should take care to show that, in the form in which they are finally set forth, our instinctive beliefs do not clash, but form a harmonious system. There can never be any reason for rejecting one instinctive belief except that it clashes with others; thus, if they are found to harmonize, the whole system becomes worthy of acceptance.

It is of course *possible* that all or any of our beliefs may be mistaken, and therefore all ought to be held with at least some slight element of doubt. But we cannot have *reason* to reject a belief except on the ground of some other belief. Hence, by organizing our instinctive beliefs and their consequences, by considering which among them is most possible, if necessary, to modify or abandon, we can arrive, on the basis of accepting as our sole data what we instinctively believe, at an orderly systematic organization of our knowledge, in which, though the *possibility* of error remains, its likelihood is diminished by the interrelation of the parts and by the critical scrutiny which has preceded acquiescence.

This function, at least, philosophy can perform. Most philosophers, rightly or wrongly, believe that philosophy can do much more than this – that it can give us knowledge, not otherwise attainable, concerning the universe as a whole, and concerning the nature of ultimate reality. Whether this be the case or not, the more modest function we have spoken of can certainly be performed by philosophy, and certainly suffices, for those who have once begun to doubt the adequacy of common sense, to justify the arduous and difficult labours that philosophical problems involve.

III   The Nature of Matter

In the preceding chapter we agreed, though without being able to find demonstrative reasons, that it is rational to believe that our sense-data – for example, those which we regard as associated with my table – are really signs of the existence of something independent of us and our perceptions. That is to say, over and above the sensations of colour, hardness, noise, and so on, which make up the appearance of the table to me, I assume that there is something else, *of* which these things are appearances. The colour ceases to exist if I shut my eyes, the sensation of hardness ceases to exist if I remove my arm from contact with the table, the sound ceases to exist if I cease to rap the table with my knuckles. But I do not believe that when all these things cease the table ceases. On the contrary, I believe that it is because the table exists continuously that all these sense-data will reappear when I open my eyes, replace my arm, and begin again to rap with my knuckles. The question we have to consider in this chapter is: What is the nature of this real table, which persists independently of my perception of it?

To this question physical science gives an answer, somewhat incomplete it is true, and in part still very hypothetical, but yet deserving of respect so far as it goes. Physical science, more or less unconsciously, has drifted into the view that all natural phenomena ought to be reduced to motions. Light and heat and sound are all due to wave-motions, which travel from the body emitting them to the person who sees light or feels heat or hears sound. That which has the wave-motion is either aether or "gross matter", but in either case is what the philosopher would call matter. The only properties which science assigns to it are position in space, and the power of motion according to the laws of motion. Science does not deny that it *may* have other properties; but if so, such other properties are not useful to the man of science, and in no way assist him in explaining the phenomena.

It is sometimes said that "light *is* a form of wave-motion", but this is misleading, for the light which we immediately see, which we know directly by means of our senses, is *not* a form of wave-motion, but something quite different – something which we all know if we are not blind, though we cannot describe it so as to convey our knowledge to a man who is blind. A wave-motion, on the contrary, could quite well be described to a blind man, since he can acquire a knowledge of space by the sense of touch; and he can experience a wave-motion by a sea voyage almost as well as we can. But this, which a blind man can understand, is not what we mean by *light*: we mean by *light* just that which a blind man can never understand, and which we can never describe to him.

Now this something, which all of us who are not blind know, is not, according to science, really to be found in the outer world: it is something caused by the action of certain waves upon the eyes and nerves and brain of the person who sees the light. When it is said that light *is* waves, what is really meant is that waves are the physical cause of our sensations of light. But light itself, the thing which seeing people experience and blind people do not, is not supposed by science to form any part of the world that is independent of us and our senses. And very similar remarks would apply to other kinds of sensations.

It is not only colours and sounds and so on that are absent from the scientific world of matter, but also *space* as we get it through sight or touch. It is essential to science that its matter should be in *a* space, but the space in which it is cannot be exactly the space we see or feel. To begin with, space as we see it is not the same as space as we get it by the sense of touch; it is only by experience in infancy that we learn how to touch things we see, or how to get a sight of things which we feel touching us. But the space of science is neutral as between touch and sight; thus it cannot be either the space of touch or the space of sight.

Again, different people see the same object as of different shapes, according to their point of view. A circular coin, for example, though we should always *judge* it to be circular, will *look* oval unless we are straight in front of it. When we judge that it *is* circular, we are judging that it has a real shape which is not its apparent shape, but belongs to it intrinsically apart from its appearance. But this real shape, which is what concerns science, must be in a real space, not the same as anybody's *apparent* space. The real space is public, the apparent space is private to the percipient. In different people's *private* spaces the same object seems to have different shapes; thus the real space, in which it has its real shape, must be different from the private spaces. The space of science, therefore, though *connected* with the spaces we see and feel, is not identical with them, and the manner of its connexion requires investigation.

We agreed provisionally that physical objects cannot be quite like our sense-data, but may be regarded as *causing* our sensations. These physical objects are in the space of science, which we may call "physical" space. It is important to notice that, if our sensations are to be caused by physical objects, there must be a physical space containing these objects and our sense-organs and nerves and brain. We get a sensation of touch from an object when we are in contact with it; that is to say, when some part of our body occupies a place in physical space quite close to the space occupied by the object. We see an object (roughly speaking) when no opaque body is between the object and our eyes in physical space. Similarly, we only hear or smell or taste an object when we are sufficiently near to it, or when it touches the tongue, or has some suitable position in physical space relatively to our body. We cannot begin to state what different sensations we shall derive from a given object under different circumstances unless we regard the object and our body as both in one physical space, for it is mainly the relative positions of the object and our body that determine what sensations we shall derive from the object.

Now our sense-data are situated in our private spaces, either the space of sight or the space of touch or such vaguer spaces as other senses may give us. If, as science and common sense assume, there is one public all-embracing physical space in which physical objects are, the relative positions of physical objects in physical space must more or less correspond to the relative positions of sense-data in our private spaces. There is no difficulty in supposing this to be the case. If we see on a road one house nearer to us than another, our other senses will bear out the view that it is nearer; for example, it will be reached sooner if we walk along the road. Other people will agree that the house which looks nearer to us is nearer; the ordnance map will take the same view; and thus everything points to a spatial relation between the houses corresponding to the relation between the sense-data which we see when we look at the houses. Thus we may assume that there is a physical space in which physical objects have spatial relations corresponding to those which the corresponding sense-data have in our private spaces. It is this physical space which is dealt with in geometry and assumed in physics and astronomy.

Assuming that there is physical space, and that it does thus correspond to private spaces, what can we know about it? We can know *only* what is required in order to secure the correspondence. That is to say, we can know nothing of what it is like in itself, but we can know the sort of arrangement of physical objects which results from their spatial relations. We can know, for example, that the earth and moon and sun are in one straight line during an eclipse, though we cannot know what a physical straight line is in itself, as we know the look of a straight line in our visual space. Thus we come to know much more about the *relations* of distances in physical space than about the distances themselves; we may know that one distance is greater than another, or that it is along the same straight line as the other, but we cannot have that immediate acquaintance with physical distances that we have with distances in our private spaces, or with colours or sounds or other sense-data. We can know all those things about physical space which a man born blind might know through other people about the space of sight; but the kind of things which a man born blind could never know about the space of sight we also cannot know about physical space. We can know the properties of the relations required to preserve the correspondence with sense-data, but we cannot know the nature of the terms between which the relations hold.

With regard to time, our *feeling* of duration or of the lapse of time is notoriously an unsafe guide as to the time that has elapsed by the clock. Times when we are bored or suffering pain pass slowly, times when we are agreeably occupied pass quickly, and times when we are sleeping pass almost as if they did not exist. Thus, in so far as time is constituted by duration, there is the same necessity for distinguishing a public and a private time as there was in the case of space. But in so far as time consists in an *order* of before and after, there is no need to make such a distinction; the time-order which events seem to have is, so far as we can see, the same as the time-order which they do have. At any rate no reason can be given for supposing that the two orders are not the same. The same is usually true of space: if a regiment of men are marching along a road, the *shape* of the regiment will look different from different points of view, but the men will appear arranged in the same *order* from all points of view. Hence we regard the *order* as true also in physical space, whereas the shape is only supposed to correspond to the physical space so far as is required for the preservation of the order.

In saying that the time-order which events *seem to have* is the same as the time-order which they *really have*, it is necessary to guard against a possible misunderstanding. It must not be supposed that the various states of different physical objects have the same time-order as the sense-data which constitute the perceptions of those objects. Considered as physical objects, the thunder and lightning are simultaneous; that is to say, the lightning is simultaneous with the disturbance of the air in the place where the disturbance begins, namely, where the lightning is. But the sense-datum which we call hearing the thunder does not take place until the disturbance of the air has travelled as far as to where we are. Similarly, it takes about eight minutes for the sun's light to reach us; thus, when we see the sun we are seeing the sun of eight minutes ago. So far as our sense-data afford evidence as to the physical sun they afford evidence as to the physical sun of eight minutes ago; if the physical sun had ceased to exist within the last eight minutes, that would make no difference to the sense-data which we call "seeing the sun". This affords a fresh illustration of the necessity of distinguishing between sense-data and physical objects.

What we have found as regards space is much the same as what we find in relation to the correspondence of the sense-data with their physical counterparts. If one object looks blue and another red, we may reasonably presume that there is some corresponding difference between the physical objects; if two objects both look blue, we may presume a corresponding similarity. But we cannot hope to be acquainted directly with the quality in the physical object which makes it look blue or red. Science tells us that this quality is a certain sort of wave-motion, and this sounds familiar, because we think of wave-motions in the space we see. But the wave-motions must really be in physical space, with which we have no direct acquaintance; thus the real wave-motions have not that familiarity which we might have supposed them to have. And what holds for colours is closely similar to what holds for other sense-data. Thus we find that, although the *relations* of physical objects have all sorts of knowable properties, derived from their correspondence with the relations of sense-data, the physical objects themselves remain unknown in their intrinsic nature, so far at least as can be discovered by means of the senses. The question remains whether there is any other method of discovering the intrinsic nature of physical objects.

The most natural, though not ultimately the most defensible, hypothesis to adopt in the first instance, at any rate as regards visual sense-data, would be that, though physical objects cannot, for the reasons we have been considering, be *exactly* like sense-data, yet they may be more or less like. According to this view, physical objects will, for example, really have colours, and we might, by good luck, see an object as of the colour it really is. The colour which an object seems to have at any given moment will in general be very similar, though not quite the same, from many different points of view; we might thus suppose the "real" colour to be a sort of medium colour, intermediate between the various shades which appear from the different points of view.

Such a theory is perhaps not capable of being definitely refuted, but it can be shown to be groundless. To begin with, it is plain that the colour we see depends only upon the nature of the light-waves that strike the eye, and is therefore modified by the medium intervening between us and the object, as well as by the manner in which light is reflected from the object in the direction of the eye. The intervening air alters colours unless it is perfectly clear, and any strong reflection will alter them completely. Thus the colour we see is a result of the ray as it reaches the eye, and not simply a property of the object from which the ray comes. Hence, also, provided certain waves reach the eye, we shall see a certain colour, whether the object from which the waves start has any colour or not. Thus it is quite gratuitous to suppose that physical objects have colours, and therefore there is no justification for making such a supposition. Exactly similar arguments will apply to other sense-data.

It remains to ask whether there are any general philosophical arguments enabling us to say that, if matter is real, it *must* be of such and such a nature. As explained above, very many philosophers, perhaps most, have held that whatever is real must be in some sense mental, or at any rate that whatever we can know anything about must be in some sense mental. Such philosophers are called "idealists". Idealists tell us that what appears as matter is really something mental; namely, either (as Leibniz held) more or less rudimentary minds, or (as Berkeley contended) ideas in the minds which, as we should commonly say, "perceive" the matter. Thus idealists deny the existence of matter as something intrinsically different from mind, though they do not deny that our sense-data are signs of something which exists independently of our private sensations.

Willard Van Orman Quine, "Posits and Reality"

I   Subvisible Particles

According to physics my desk is, for all its seeming fixity and solidity, a swarm of vibrating molecules. The desk as we sense it is comparable to a distant haystack in which we cannot distinguish the individual stalks; comparable also to a wheel in

From *The Ways of Paradox and Other Essays*, rev. edn, ed. W. V. O. Quine (Cambridge, MA: Harvard University Press, 1976).

which, because of its rapid rotation, we cannot distinguish the individual spokes. Comparable, but with a difference. By approaching the haystack we can distinguish the stalks, and by retarding the wheel we can distinguish the spokes. On the other hand no glimpse is to be had of the separate molecules of the desk; they are, we are told, too small.

Lacking such experience, what evidence can the physicist muster for his doctrine of molecules? His answer is that there is a convergence of indirect evidence, drawn from such varied phenomena as expansion, heat conduction, capillary attraction, and surface tension. The point is that these miscellaneous phenomena can, if we assume the molecular theory, be marshaled under the familiar laws of motion. The fancifulness of thus assuming a substructure of moving particles of imperceptible size is offset by a gain in naturalness and scope on the part of the aggregate laws of physics. The molecular theory is felt, moreover, to gain corroboration progressively as the physicist's predictions of future observations turn out to be fulfilled, and as the theory proves to invite extensions covering additional classes of phenomena.

The benefits thus credited to the molecular doctrine may be divided into five. One is simplicity: empirical laws concerning seemingly dissimilar phenomena are integrated into a compact and unitary theory. Another is familiarity of principle: the already familiar laws of motion are made to serve where independent laws would otherwise have been needed. A third is scope: the resulting unitary theory implies a wider array of testable consequences than any likely accumulation of separate laws would have implied. A fourth is fecundity: successful further extensions of theory are expedited. The fifth goes without saying: such testable consequences of the theory as have been tested have turned out well, aside from such sparse exceptions as may in good conscience be chalked up to unexplained interferences.

Simplicity, the first of the listed benefits, is a vague business. We may be fairly sure of this much: theories are more or less simple, more or less unitary, only relative to one or another given vocabulary or conceptual apparatus. Simplicity is, if not quite subjective, at any rate parochial. Yet simplicity contributes to scope, as follows. An empirical theory, typically, generalizes or extrapolates from sample data, and thus covers more phenomena than have been checked. Simplicity, by our lights, is what guides our extrapolation. Hence the simpler the theory, on the whole, the wider this unchecked coverage.

As for the fourth benefit, fecundity, obviously it is a consequence of the first two, simplicity and familiarity, for these two traits are the best conditions for effective thinking.

Not all the listed benefits are generally attributable to accepted scientific theories, though all are to be prized when available. Thus the benefit of familiarity of principle may, as in quantum theory and relativity theory, be renounced, its loss being regretted but outweighed.

But to get back. In its manifest content the molecular doctrine bears directly on unobservable reality, affirming a structure of minute swarming particles. On the other hand any defense of it has to do rather with its indirect bearing on observable reality. The doctrine has this indirect bearing by being the core of an integrated physical theory which implies truths about expansion, conduction, and so on. The benefits which we have been surveying are benefits which the molecular doctrine, as core, brings to the physics of these latter observable phenomena.

Suppose now we were to excise that core but retain the surrounding ring of derivative laws, thus not disturbing the observable consequences. The retained laws could be viewed thenceforward as autonomous empirical laws, innocent of any molecular commitment. Granted, this combination of empirical laws would never have been achieved without the unifying aid of a molecular doctrine at the center; note the recent remarks on scope. But we might still delete the molecular doctrine once it has thus served its heuristic purpose.

This reflection strengthens a natural suspicion: that the benefits conferred by the molecular doctrine give the physicist good reason to prize it, but afford no evidence of its truth. Though the doctrine succeed to perfection in its indirect bearing on observable reality, the question of its truth has to do rather with its direct claim on unobservable reality. Might the molecular doctrine not be ever so useful in organizing and extending our knowledge of the behavior of observable things, and yet be factually false?

One may question, on closer consideration, whether this is really an intelligible possibility. Let us reflect upon our words and how we learned them.

II Posits and Analogies

Words are human artifacts, meaningless save as our associating them with experience endows them with meaning. The word "swarm" is initially meaningful to us through association with such experiences as that of a hovering swarm of gnats, or a swarm of dust motes in a shaft of sunlight. When we extend the word to desks and the like, we are engaged in drawing an analogy between swarms ordinarily so-called, on the one hand, and desks, etc., on the other. The word "molecule" is then given meaning derivatively: having conceived of desks analogically as swarms, we imagine molecules as the things the desks are swarms of.

The purported question of fact, the question whether the familiar objects around us are really swarms of subvisible particles in vibration, now begins to waver and dissolve. If the words involved here make sense only by analogy, then the only question of fact is the question how good an analogy there is between the behavior of a desk or the like and the behavior, e.g., of a swarm of gnats. What had seemed a direct bearing of the molecular doctrine upon reality has now dwindled to an analogy.

Even this analogical content, moreover, is incidental, variable, and at length dispensable. In particular the analogy between the swarming of the molecules of a solid and the swarming of gnats is only moderately faithful; a supplementary aid to appreciating the dynamics of the molecules of a solid is found in the analogy of a stack of bedsprings. In another and more recondite part of physics, the theory of light, the tenuousness of analogy is notorious: the analogy of particles is useful up to a point and the analogy of waves is useful up to a point, but neither suffices to the exclusion of the other. Faithful analogies are an aid to the physicist's early progress in an unaccustomed medium, but, like water-wings, they are an aid which he learns to get along without.

In §I we contrasted a direct and an indirect bearing of the molecular doctrine upon reality. But the direct bearing has not withstood scrutiny. Where there had at first seemed to be an undecidable question of unobservable fact, we now find mere analogy at most and not necessarily that. So the only way in which we now find the molecular doctrine genuinely to bear upon reality is the indirect way, via implications in observable phenomena.

The effect of this conclusion upon the status of molecules is that they lose even the dignity of inferred or hypothetical entities which may or may not really be there. The very sentences which seem to propound them and treat of them are gibberish by themselves, and indirectly significant only as contributory clauses of an inclusive system which does also treat of the real. The molecular physicist is, like all of us, concerned with commonplace reality, and merely finds that he can simplify his laws by positing an esoteric supplement to the exoteric universe. He can devise simpler laws for this enriched universe, this "sesquiverse" of his own decree, than he has been able to devise for its real or original portion alone.

In §I we imagined deleting the molecular doctrine from the midst of the derivative body of physical theory. From our present vantage point, however, we see that operation as insignificant; there is no substantive doctrine of molecules to delete. The sentences which seem to propound molecules are just devices for organizing the significant sentences of physical theory. No matter if physics makes molecules or other insensible particles seem more fundamental than the objects of common sense; the particles are posited for the sake of a simple physics.

The tendency of our own reflections has been, conversely, to belittle molecules and their ilk, leaving common-sense bodies supreme. Still, it may now be protested, this invidious contrast is unwarranted. What are given in sensation are variformed and varicolored visual patches, varitextured and varitemperatured tactual feels, and an assortment of tones, tastes, smells, and other odds and ends; desks are no more to be found among these data than molecules. If we have evidence for the existence of the bodies of common sense, we have it only in the way in which we may be said to have evidence for the existence of molecules. The positing of either sort of body is good science insofar merely as it helps us formulate our laws – laws whose ultimate evidence lies in the sense data of the past, and whose ultimate vindication lies in anticipation of sense data of the future. The positing of molecules differs from the positing of the bodies of common sense mainly in degree of sophistication. In whatever sense the molecules in my desk are unreal and a figment of the imagination of the scientist, in that sense the desk itself is unreal and a figment of the imagination of the race.

This double verdict of unreality leaves us nothing, evidently, but the raw sense data themselves. It leaves each of us, indeed, nothing but his own sense data; for the assumption of there being other persons has no better support than has the assumption of there being any other sorts of external objects. It leaves each of us in the position of solipsism, according to which there is nobody else in the world, nor indeed any world but the pageant of one's own sense data.

III   Restitution

Surely now we have been caught up in a wrong line of reasoning. Not only is the conclusion bizarre; it vitiates the very considerations that lead to it. We cannot properly represent man as inventing a myth of physical objects to fit past and present sense data, for past ones are lost except to memory; and memory, far from being a straightforward register of past sense data, usually depends on past posits of physical objects. The positing of physical objects must be seen not as an *ex post facto* systematization of data, but as a move prior to which no appreciable data would be available to systematize.

Something went wrong with our standard of reality. We became doubtful of the reality of molecules because the physicist's statement that there are molecules took on the aspect of a mere technical convenience in smoothing the laws of physics. Next we noted that common-sense bodies are epistemologically much on a par with the molecules, and inferred the unreality of the common-sense bodies them-selves. Here our bemusement becomes visible. Unless we change meanings in midstream, the familiar bodies around us are as real as can be; and it smacks of a contradiction in terms to conclude otherwise. Having noted that man has no evid-ence for the existence of bodies beyond the fact that their assumption helps him organize experience, we should have done well, instead of disclaiming evidence for the existence of bodies, to conclude: such, then, at bottom, is what evidence is, both for ordinary bodies and for molecules.

This point about evidence does not upset the evidential priority of sense data. On the contrary, the point about evidence is precisely that the testimony of the senses *does* (contrary to Berkeley's notion) count as evidence for bodies, such being (as Samuel Johnson perceived) just the sort of thing that evidence is. We can continue to recognize, as in §II, that molecules and even the gross bodies of common sense are simply posited in the course of organizing our responses to stimulation; but a moral to draw from our reconsideration of the terms "reality" and "evidence" is that posits are not *ipso facto* unreal. The benefits of the molecular doctrine which so impressed us in §I, and the manifest benefits of the aboriginal posit of ordinary bodies, are the best evidence of reality we can ask (pending, of course, evidence of the same sort for some alternative ontology).

Sense data are posits too. They are posits of psychological theory, but not, on that account, unreal. The sense datum may be construed as a hypothetical com-ponent of subjective experience standing in closest possible correspondence to the experimentally measurable conditions of physical stimulation of the end organs. In seeking to isolate sense data we engage in empirical psychology, associating physical stimuli with human resources. I shall not guess how useful the positing of sense data may be for psychological theory, or more specifically for a psychologically grounded theory of evidence, nor what detailed traits may profitably be postulated concerning them. In our flight from the fictitious to the real, in any event, we have come full circle.

Sense data, if they are to be posited at all, are fundamental in one respect; the small particles of physics are fundamental in a second respect, and common-sense bodies in a third. Sense data are *evidentially* fundamental: every man is beholden to his senses for every hint of bodies. The physical particles are *naturally* fundamental, in this kind of way: laws of behavior of those particles afford, so far as we know, the simplest formulation of a general theory of what happens. Common-sense bodies, finally, are *conceptually* fundamental: it is by reference to them that the very notions of reality and evidence are acquired, and that the concepts which have to do with physical particles or even with sense data tend to be framed and phrased. But these three types of priority must not be viewed as somehow determining three competing, self-sufficient conceptual schemes. Our one serious conceptual scheme is the inclusive, evolving one of science, which we inherit and, in our several small ways, help to improve.

IV   Working from Within

It is by thinking within this unitary conceptual scheme itself, thinking about the processes of the physical world, that we come to appreciate that the world can be evidenced only through stimulation of our senses. It is by thinking within the same conceptual scheme that we come to appreciate that language, being a social art, is learned primarily with reference to intersubjectively conspicuous objects, and hence that such objects are bound to be central conceptually. Both of these *aperçus* are part of the scientific understanding of the scientific enterprise; not prior to it. Insofar as they help the scientist to proceed more knowingly about his business, science is using its findings to improve its own techniques. Epistemology, on this view, is not logically prior somehow to common sense or to the refined common sense which is science; it is part rather of the overall scientific enterprise, an enterprise which Neurath has likened to that of rebuilding a ship while staying afloat in it.

Epistemology, so conceived, continues to probe the sensory evidence for discourse about the world; but it no longer seeks to relate such discourse somehow to an imaginary and impossible sense-datum language. Rather it faces the fact that society teaches us our physicalistic language by training us to associate various physicalistic sentences directly, in multifarious ways, with irritations of our sensory surfaces, and by training us also to associate various such sentences with one another.

The complex totality of such associations is a fluctuating field of force. Some sentences about bodies are, for one person or for many, firmly conditioned one by one to sensory stimulation of specifiable sorts. Roughly specifiable sequences of nerve hits can confirm us in statements about having had breakfast, or there being a brick house on Elm Street, beyond the power of secondary associations with other sentences to add or detract. But there is in this respect a grading-off from one example to another. Many sentences even about common-sense bodies rest wholly on indirect evidence; witness the statement that one of the pennies now in my pocket was in my pocket last week. Conversely, sentences even about electrons are sometimes directly conditioned to sensory stimulation, e.g. via the cloud chamber. The status of a given sentence, in point of direct or indirect connection with the senses, can change as one's experience accumulates; thus a man's first confrontation with a cloud chamber may forge a direct sensory link to some sentences which hitherto bore, for him, only the most indirect sensory relevance. Moreover the sensory relevance of sentences will differ widely from person to person; uniformity comes only where the pressure for communication comes.

Statements about bodies, common-sense or recondite, thus commonly make little or no empirical sense except as bits of a collectively significant containing system. Various statements can surely be supplanted by their negations, without conflict with any possible sensory contingency, provided that we revise other portions of our science in compensatory ways. Science is empirically underdetermined: there is slack. What can be said about the hypothetical particles of physics is underdetermined by what can be said about sensible bodies, and what can be said about these is underdetermined by the stimulation of our surfaces. An inkling of this circumstance has doubtless fostered the tendency to look upon the hypothetical particles of physics as more of a fiction than sensible bodies, and these as more of a fiction than sense data. But the tendency is a perverse one, for it ascribes full reality only to a domain of objects for which there is no autonomous system of discourse at all.

Better simply to explore, realistically, the less-than-rigid connections that obtain between sensory stimulus and physical doctrine, without viewing this want of rigidity as impugning the physical doctrine. Benefits of the sort recounted in §I are what count for the molecular doctrine or any, and we can hope for no surer touchstone of reality. We can hope to improve our physics by seeking the same sorts of benefits in fuller measure, and we may even facilitate such endeavors by better understanding the degrees of freedom that prevail between stimulatory evidence and physical doctrine. But as a medium for such epistemological inquiry we can choose no better than the selfsame world theory which we are trying to improve, this being the best available at the time.

Bruce Aune, "Is There a Problem About Knowledge of the External World?"

1   Sense Data and Recent Philosophy

One of the oldest contentions of critical philosophy is that our knowledge of the world around us is based on the data of sensory experience. Although this contention

From *Knowledge, Mind, and Nature* (New York: Random House, 1967).

seems to be entirely obvious and unproblematic, it has actually been a notorious source of philosophical puzzlement. This puzzlement grows naturally from the observation that the data of sense are not always entirely reliable. We sometimes seem to see, smell, or hear things that are simply not there. Historically, the favored explanation of this phenomenon is that what we immediately perceive, in sensation, is not the outer world itself but rather certain effects that the world produces in our consciousness. A red object normally produces a distinctive sensation in a standard observer, but sometimes this sort of sensation may be produced when no red object is present. This may happen either because of something unusual in the perceiver, such as too many martinis, or because of something unusual about the conditions under which the perception occurs, such as the presence of a peculiar reddish light.

Once it is granted that the immediate objects of perception are sensations, or sense data, rather than the public objects that are said to produce them, the question naturally arises as to how we can be sure that these public objects have the qualities we take them to have. If we do not immediately perceive them, how indeed can we be sure that they exist at all? Attempts to answer these questions have led to the remarkable variety of philosophical positions distinctive of the period since the Renaissance. Some philosophers, such as Descartes, have argued that the goodness of God assures us that, under certain conditions at least, our claims about the world must be true. Others, like Berkeley, have argued that it is an illusion to suppose that there even is a public world of the sort described by Descartes. The world that actually exists must rather be understood as some kind of construct out of sensory experiences. As this idea was later expressed, to speak of public objects is to speak of systems of actual and possible sense data. Other philosophers have frankly embraced a form of skepticism, arguing that if there is an outer public world, we really cannot know anything about it. We may assume, as a matter of custom, that such a world exists, but there is no rational way of proving that it does.

Any idea leading to such peculiar claims about the world is bound to come under sharp attack sooner or later, and this has happened in recent years. In opposition to the idea that the immediate data of sense are essentially subjective, the trend has been to defend a view that might be called "direct realism." As its name implies, those accepting this view are inclined to argue that public reality is actually open to direct inspection. We know that a common world exists, and we know what it is like, because we directly perceive it. The old idea that we really perceive only our own sensory experiences is simply false, springing from a hasty and seriously confused analysis of the concepts involved in assessing perceptual claims. [. . .] It may be granted, of course, that there are sensory *experiences* – experiences of seeing, or seeming to see, something red – but these experiences are not a kind of object standing between us and the world. If I am experiencing, or seeing, something red, the thing that is red is not my experience, it is *what* I experience – and this may be a fire-engine. Similarly, when I seem to see something red, my experience of seeming-to-see is not red; in fact, in this case no red thing may be present at all. On this view there is thus no commitment to any object of perception other than the objects that constitute our common world. [. . .]

This often militant insistence that sensory experiences are not themselves objects of perception led, however, to a certain paradox when coupled with the traditional assumption that our basic means of gaining knowledge is by perception. This paradox concerns the possibility of knowing anything at all about sensory experiences. If we cannot directly perceive them, why should we think that they actually exist? In the past twenty years it has become fashionable in certain quarters to answer this question by interpreting sensory experiences, and indeed mental states generally, as constructs out of behavior. This approach gains plausibility from the common assumption that the language of everyday life, the accepted touchstone of good philosophical sense, is essentially a public one, whose intersubjective character can be preserved only by the requirement that the claims formulated in its terms be intersubjectively confirmable. Since the activities of human beings open to public scrutiny are in principle limited mainly to overt behavior – the faces they make, the sounds they utter – it becomes natural to argue that talk about sensory and mental phenomena must be construed as highly abbreviated talk about complicated patterns of behavior. [. . .]

This kind of behaviorism may seem to be about as bizarre a position as any defended by traditional philosophers. Yet it cannot be denied that it carries with it certain theoretical rewards that might, for certain thinkers, prove almost irresistible. [. . .] We are obviously no longer threatened by solipsism or by a form of skepticism regarding the external world, and we are immediately able to provide quick and easy solutions to such age-old problems as Other Minds and the Relation between Body and Mind. This being so, it is entirely understandable that philosophers concerned mainly with abstract, theoretical problems might actually become convinced that behaviorism is a highly liberating position to defend.

2   An Alternative Basis for Sense Data

Although a good share of the detailed analysis supporting the recent revolt against sense data is extremely subtle and persuasive, its general strategy is unlikely to be convincing to a hard-headed defender of traditional empiricism. Not only does the emphasis on how *we* speak and on the logic of *our* language have an unmistakable air of circularity when brought to bear against a philosopher for whom solipsism is a living issue, but the behavioristic tendency of the approach does patent injustice to the myriad phenomena of subjective experience, the enormous variety of which is catalogued in the endless annals of phenomenology and introspective psychology. Moreover, the new approach to sense data fails to appreciate some of the major considerations that have led empiricists to insist upon such entities. These considerations have little to do with the analysis of language. [. . .] Their source is rather a speculative, scientific one, and they remain alive for anyone who takes seriously a micro-theory of matter.

Recent historical studies have demonstrated the remarkable extent to which the epistemological problems of modern empiricism were a natural development from the "corpuscularian philosophy" of the seventeenth century.[1] This philosophy revived the speculative ideas of the atomists of ancient Greece, and it is illuminating to consider these ideas in their original form. For familiar reasons, the ancient atomists thought that the world must be composed of tiny particles jostling together in empty space. These tiny objects were considered to be colorless. If they had color individually, it would be difficult to understand how their mere movement, as in the churning of the surf, should bring about a change in the color one sees. Epicurus apparently thought that while individual atoms were colorless, the groups they composed were not. Color, for him, is something that clings to skins or membranes, filmy arrays of atoms that are shed from the surfaces of weighty aggregates and interact with the subtle atoms of the human mind. Color is not therefore a subjective phenomenon for Epicurus: it really exists "out there" on atomic aggregates and on their skins, which permeate the ambient air. Disregarding his theory of perception, one might characterize his view by saying that, according to him, color is an emergent property of groups of atoms, a feature that exists independently of actual and even potential perceivers: a thoroughly objective phenomenon.

Leucippus and Democritus, on the other hand, although they taught before Epicurus, evidently had what scientists would call a more up-to-date theory. Relying on the obvious fact that the colors a man sees depend in part on the condition of his body, they apparently decided that colors and other sensible qualities are really aspects of the perceiver. One does of course think of physical objects as having color, not just of one's sense impressions of these objects as having it. But this fact has always been readily accommodated by the atomist: physical color, as opposed to phenomenal color, is just the power or disposition of an object to produce certain sense impressions in a sentient being. Thus, while physical objects, rainbows, and the like are properly said to have color, this means no more than that these public things have certain dispositions: the sensuous, colorful part of the world is really subjective, a feature, in some sense, of sentient beings.

It is well known by now that the relativity-of-perception arguments cannot themselves show that the sensuous part of the world is really subjective.[2] But these arguments are not necessary to the modern atomist. For him, the Epicurean idea of colors as emergent properties of atom clusters may be rejected on two grounds: first, that we have no good reason, theoretical or otherwise, to think that colors *are* emergent properties of atom clusters; and second, that we have good theoretical reasons for thinking that perceivers are not in intimate contact with the objects they claim to see. This latter conviction is justified by a complex psychophysical theory according to which the colors a man sees are the result of the bombardment of his retinas by radiation and of highly complicated changes in his nervous system.

[1] See esp. Maurice Mandelbaum, *Philosophy, Science, and Sense Perception* (Baltimore: Johns Hopkins University Press, 1964), and R. Harré, *Matter and Method* (London: Macmillan, 1964).

[2] On this see, e.g., J. L. Austin, *Sense and Sensibilia*, G. Warnock, ed. (Oxford: Clarendon Press, 1962), Ch. 3.

Visual fire does not accordingly flow from a man's eyes, coalesce around an object, and return with a carbon copy. Vision is the result of stray radiation.

The atomist's theory, or a modern version of it, is naturally tempting to anyone who takes theoretical science seriously and interprets it in a straightforward way. And, for many scientifically minded thinkers, science ought to be taken seriously and interpreted in a straightforward way, since it is the peculiar task of science to tell us what our world is like, how it is put together – and to be straightforward about it. If in line with this attitude we too are moved to accept physical theory as giving us the best available picture of reality, writ both large and small, then the idea of sense impressions or sense data should strike us as both legitimate and extremely important. [. . .]

3   Does Direct Realism Clash with Scientific Theory?

Can one be a direct realist of the contemporary variety and also accept physical theory at its face value? This question is awkward to answer because contemporary realists tend not to develop their views in a systematic way. In light, however, of the foregoing discussion of atomism, we might approach this question by asking whether a direct realist could consistently accept the dispositional analysis of color that seems to be demanded by scientific theory. If he could not accept this analysis, or something like it, the presumption would be that he could not accept the theory that prompts it. [. . .]

Actually, it is hardly necessary to provide complex arguments showing that the dispositional analysis is unacceptable to a direct realist. If a man really is a *direct* realist, then he is committed to the view that one can directly perceive public objects and directly perceive that they have this or that quality. And surely one of the most striking qualities of public things is their color. As Berkeley pointed out, you cannot actually see something that is totally colorless; it would be invisible. Dispositions, however, cannot be directly perceived; you can *infer* that something has a certain disposition by seeing what it does in certain circumstances, but you cannot see the disposition or "power" itself – any more than you can *see* the disposition of an unlit match to light *if* scratched.

To make this obvious point about direct realism is to recall the familiar claim of realists that color predicates are ostensively definable.[3] One is said to learn the meaning of basic color words by associating them with the colors that things can be directly seen to have. Color words such as "red" are thus commonly regarded as conceptually primitive, and not capable of any illuminating *verbal* definition. To know what redness is you really have to experience it; and if you are not color-blind you can expect to have this experience if you look at any fire-engine. The redness of a fire-engine, like the redness of a barn, is essentially a simple quality, which you can directly see but never explain to a blind man.

[3] See e.g., Martin Lean, *Sense Perception and Matter* (London: Routledge & Kegan Paul, 1953), pp. 17ff.

The foregoing remarks make it appear that the direct realist is firmly committed to something like an Epicurean view of color. As already seen, however, a view of this sort seems far out of line with the claims of physical theory. Not only does this theory evidently rule out the idea that a system of colorless particles could be totally enveloped in a sensuous redness, but it implies that all of the *sensible* qualities apparent in perception are in some sense subjective, belonging to perceivers rather than to bare, molecular reality. If physical theory is accepted at face-value, it then appears that the realist's view will have to be rejected as scientifically untenable.

In an effort to save direct realism and therefore common sense from this kind of objection, a number of escapes have been suggested. One of the most common explanations is that science and common sense ought not to be viewed as competing.[4] Ordinary discourse concerning colors and sounds involves a conceptual system distinct from that of theoretical science. These two conceptual systems actually represent alternative ways of viewing reality. Each is adequate in its own right, each has its own practical utility and its own criteria of application. But an attempt to unite them into a single view of the existing world involves some kind of category mistake. "Red," as a term of ordinary language, is incapable of informative verbal definition; yet it does have a legitimate application, and it is possible to correct people who misapply it. Physical theory, on the other hand, is utterly independent of ordinary language; it has its own criteria of application, its own standard of adequacy. Because it represents a distinct way of viewing reality, it cannot possibly be inconsistent with ordinary language. In fact, there are no logical relations whatever between such assertions as "That is red" and "That is a collection of largely FeO_2 molecules." [. . .]

However, the idea that the language of theory is *not* conceptually independent of ordinary discourse does seem extremely plausible. [. . .] After all, we normally employ physical theory in order to state just what physical conditions must obtain in order that such common things as rainbows can actually be seen. In fact, most of the explanations we are normally prepared to give of even the most humdrum occurrences involve both theoretical and ordinary conceptions. Take, for instance, the familiar example of the oar half-immersed in water. Who could explain its peculiar bent appearance without *some* reference to theoretical principles? Or again, who could explain why a man wearing a black suit in the tropics is likely to be uncomfortable, if reference to scientific theories were inadmissible or improper in such ordinary cases? Plainly, the yoking together of both ordinary and theoretical notions is as common as anything could possibly be; and the contention that these notions belong to utterly different conceptual schemes, each scheme having no logical connection with the other, *seems* as extravagant and far from fact as any contention of traditional philosophy.

Another explanation for possible conflict between theory and common sense is that we are far too literal-minded about the claims of contemporary physical theory. The standard manner of expositing this theory is actually very misleading,

---

[4] See Gilbert Ryle, *Dilemmas* (Cambridge, Eng.: Cambridge University Press, 1954), Ch. 5.

at least from a philosophical point of view; and like other misleading forms of exposition, it needs careful interpretation. In addition to the straightforward approach already considered, two alternative interpretations have been worked out by philosophers of science, and either one of these can quickly nullify the paradox in point.

Consider, first, the *operationalist* interpretation of theoretical concepts.[5] According to this view, alleged talk about theoretical entities is really just a shorthand way of talking about observable phenomena, the sort of thing that is adequately describable in the language of everyday life. Electrons, for example, are not really concrete or even highly tenuous objects; they are best understood as "logical constructions." We get into difficulty talking about them only because we fail to realize this. The term "electron" admittedly seems to refer to a unitary existing entity, but actually it is a kind of portmanteau word, which allows us to speak in a highly abbreviated way about a large class of observable phenomena, such as tracks in the Wilson cloud chamber, observable deflections in electrometers, and so on.

Another relevant interpretation is that of the *instrumentalist*.[6] In his view theoretical statements are not really statements; they do not, that is, speak about anything at all, not even classes of observable phenomena. They are rather calculating devices, tools of prediction. As tools, however, they are more like barometers than actual statements: we use them for the job of predicting observations, not for stating what we take to be basic truths about reality. The actual nature of reality is something that we know well enough by observation. We can simply see that reality is made up of shoes, ships, sealing wax; and any suggestion that it might be quite different from what our eyes and ears disclose can be nothing but irresponsible sophistry. What can we do but call a spade a spade? And what more can we reasonably demand of science than that it give us devices, tools, that will allow us to predict whether a given spade is sturdy enough for digging up the garden?

These two views, operationalism and instrumentalism, though to my mind completely wrong-headed, have nevertheless been associated with distinguished names, and have naturally proved attractive to direct realists eager to vindicate the claims of common sense and to defend the primacy of ordinary language. It is clear, however, that both views rest uneasy with a literal interpretation of the scientific method, and they obviously involve the idea that the nature of reality is to be discovered mainly by observation, not by the indirect confirmation of often highly rarefied theories. According to these philosophies of science, if an electron is not the kind of thing that could conceivably be *observed* by the senses, then we mislead ourselves and others if we speak of electrons as included among the furniture of the world. The concept of such a thing must rather be regarded as a "logical construction" out of observables, or else as a mere calculating device, aiding prediction but lacking all objective reference.

[5] On this see Ernest Nagel, *The Structure of Science* (New York: Harcourt, Brace and World, 1961), pp. 120–121, and Arthur Pap, *An Introduction to the Philosophy of Science* (New York: Free Press of Glencoe, 1962), Ch. 3.

[6] See Nagel, *The Structure of Science*, pp. 129–140.

It is crucial to note that anyone who seriously accepts these assumptions is also committed to defend some form of philosophical behaviorism. As indicated at the beginning of this chapter, mental states are by no means *publicly* observable. Hence, philosophers with instrumentalist or operationalist leanings must regard even such expressions as "stinging pain" and "mild headache" as mere calculating devices, nonreferential expressions that merely allow us to predict observable behavior, or else as a kind of shorthand which enables us to refer to a wide variety of behavior in an extremely economical way. In either case their interpretation of these terms is bound to be highly unconvincing.

In general, it does not take much imagination to see that in an age of electron microscopes, Wilson cloud chambers, and worry about radioactive fallout, the general contentions of the operationalist or the instrumentalist are very hard to take seriously – all the more so when they imply that sinus or migraine headaches are either nothing at all (instrumentalism) or merely patterns of observable behavior (operationalism). One would surely think that the inner, occurrent, episodic character of a sinus headache is vastly more obvious than the cogency of any principle that would commit one to deny this.

4   A Problem of Perception

Since at least one of these doubtful construals of the molecular theory of matter seems necessary for a thoroughgoing defense of direct realism, the latter must be regarded as having at least a strong *prima facie* implausibility when the entire range of our knowledge is taken into account. On the other hand, the atomist's theory discussed earlier has special troubles of its own. Not only does it face a very serious difficulty in providing a sound dispositional analysis of sensible qualities such as color, but it appears to put one on a slippery slope that leads to all the puzzles of traditional epistemology.

The path of this slope can be sketched as follows. According to physical theory, the objects of our world do not really have the qualities they appear to have. Sensuous purples cannot strictly enclose the extremities of jostling micro-particles. This means that we do not see these objects as they actually are. Perception is rather concerned with the subjective appearance of things, not with the things themselves. Knowledge of the true nature of the world is thus a wholly theoretical affair; it is attained only by inference. But inference gives knowledge only if there is a secure basis for inference. This secure basis obviously cannot be purely theoretical, for theoretical matters are just the ones to be known by inference. Since matters of fact cannot be known *a priori*, the basis in question must be that of sense experience.

But how can sense experience provide a basis for claims about what is purely theoretical, that is, not directly observable? We cannot, after all, *observe* a correlation between what is observable and what is not. In fact, our experiential data might be as they are even if no external world existed. Lacking any experience of a correlation between our experiences and their alleged physical causes, we thus have no real assurance, and absolutely no right to assume, that there *is* an unobservable world lying behind those experiences. Hence we land in skepticism.

Skepticism is not, however, the worst consequence of this line of thought. Since our words can have referential meaning only if they are defined in terms of what we can experience, it appears that it is actually senseless to speak of a world of empirical objects from which we are, in principle, denied perceptual access. Berkeley made this last point very clearly when he argued that by "extension," as by "color," we mean something that can be perceived. Thus, by hypothesis, the alleged atomic world, as something distinct from the appearances we are said to perceive, cannot literally be extended or colored – in fact, none of our descriptive words can literally apply to it. This being so, any attempt to *say* something about such a world must be incoherent; indeed the very idea of such a world makes no sense at all.

But not only can we never directly observe and meaningfully describe the alleged world of the atomist; we can never even observe and describe the *selves* of such a world: we can observe and describe only the *appearances* of such selves. Hence even the idea of a scientific self is empty. This result is even worse than ordinary solipsism, for no self is strictly observable at all, not even a phenomenal one. As Hume put it in a famous passage:

> . . . when I enter most intimately into what I call *myself*, I always stumble on some perception or other. . . . I can never catch *myself* at any time without a perception, and never can observe anything but the perception. . . . The mind is a kind of theatre, where several perceptions successively make their appearance. . . . [But] the comparison of the theatre must not mislead us. They are the successive perceptions only, that constitute the mind; nor have we the most distant notion of the place, where these scenes are represented, or of the materials, of which it is composed.[7]

Although the preceding remarks are not entirely spelled out, they at least approximate the usual sketch of the slippery slope from atomism, classically conceived, to solipsism and utter intellectual disaster. This outcome is not perhaps forced on the atomist, for he might be able to refute one or more of the premises that define the slope's hideous shape. Still, as the philosophical infighting of two centuries makes abundantly clear, a mistake in the argument is very difficult to isolate and defend convincingly against all comers. So we seem to have a genuine problem. On the one hand, contemporary realism about perceptual objects, for all its sophistication and subtlety on matters of linguistic detail, apparently has crucial shortcomings. Not only does it lead, or give strong indications of leading, to such absurdities as philosophical behaviorism, but it evidently commits one to highly questionable

---

[7] David Hume, *A Treatise of Human Nature*, L. A. Selby-Bigge, ed. (Oxford: Clarendon Press, 1888), I, iv, 6.

interpretations of scientific theory. On the other hand, an attempt to do full justice to scientific theory in the way outlined above, which is the natural approach to take, apparently leads to disaster.

Since both contemporary realism and traditional, atomistic empiricism seem to involve fundamental difficulties, a thorough reappraisal of both would appear to be an obvious first step in working out an adequate philosophy of mind and nature. [. . .]

5

The Scientific Method

Harold Kincaid, "Mill and the Nature of Science"

Readings

John Stuart Mill, *A System of Logic* (selections)

Carl Hempel, "Scientific Inquiry: Invention and Test"

Karl Popper, "Philosophy of Science: A Personal Report"

Thomas Kuhn, *The Structure of Scientific Revolutions* (selections)

J. J. C. Smart, "Physics and Reality"

John Stuart Mill. Culver Pictures, Inc.

HAROLD KINCAID

Mill and the Nature of Science

An hypothesis being a mere supposition, there are no other limits to hypotheses than those of the human imagination . . . Accordingly, most thinkers of any degree of sobriety allow, that an hypothesis of this kind is not to be received as probably true because it accounts for all the known phenomena.

John Stuart Mill, *A System of Logic*

Modern science tells us some very strange things about the universe. For example, cosmologists claim that there is good scientific evidence that the universe began in a Big Bang. At the moment of the Big Bang, all the matter of the universe was concentrated into an infinitely small point, one that had an infinite density and an infinite temperature. That point then expanded to be the universe we know today. Scientists say equally weird things about the subatomic particles making up matter. Electrons, for example, supposedly have no definite location when unobserved. They are in a state of "superposition" or are "probability waves" – they are both at some particular spot and not at it in some sense. Many more such fantastic claims are commonplace in modern science.

As strange as these claims may seem, scientists still assert them with a straight face. They do so because these are not mere speculations. They are the products of our best science, the result of enormous work and careful experimental manipulation of nature. Moreover, much modern technology from lasers to computer chips employs these results with great success. So not only do these strange ideas have strong experimental support, they have led to useful results.

So we have a puzzle. Science urges us to believe some very bizarre things, things that are sometimes so bizarre it is not even clear we can understand them. Yet science seems our best shot at knowing the world. So should we take what science says seriously? After all, humankind has been spinning tales about the universe for centuries. Many of them are unbelievable myths – for example, that humans are reincarnated as animals after death. So what distinguishes these fantastic myths from the fantastic stories that science tells?

This chapter focuses on such questions. Two issues will be fundamental. The first issue is *realism*: should we take science literally? Should we believe that current science is approximately true – that it tells us the way the world really is? The second issue is about *method*: what methods, procedures, and practices make scientific stories believable? What is the nature of scientific investigation that separates science from mythology, religion, and pseudoscience? In what follows we look at various answers to these questions and the arguments given in their support. More specifically, we shall look at the arguments of those – called *scientific realists* – who claim that we have good reason to think the fantastic stories of current science are indeed true. We also shall look at various accounts of the scientific method including *inductivism, the method of hypotheses*, and *falsificationism*. These doctrines try to specify the rules governing successful scientific inquiry.

We begin our discussion of these issues with the ideas of John Stuart Mill (1806–73). Mill is perhaps the first philosopher to discuss at length both the issues of scientific realism and scientific method; his views are unorthodox and yet carefully argued. They provide essential background for more contemporary thought about these topics.

1 John Stuart Mill and Scientific Reasoning

John Stuart Mill was born in London in 1806. He had a unique father, and even more unique upbringing. His father, James Mill, was an important historian and social critic in his own right. He was part of a philosophical circle that developed the doctrine of utilitarianism, a doctrine thought to be quite radical when first advocated. James Mill also wrote a three-volume *History of India* that became the standard historical work on India, which was a British colony at the time.

Though Mill was educated by his father at home, he nevertheless received an excellent education. James taught his son ancient Greek when he was three, and Latin at eight. By age 14 Mill had done extensive work in logic and mathematics. Large parts of Mill's time were spent studying at the same table his father used to write his history of India, and young John's life was much like a constant oral examination. In his early twenties Mill suffered a severe bout of depression, which he attributed to this overly intellectual childhood.

Mill did not marry until late in life. However, he had a deep if platonic relationship for twenty years with Harriet Taylor, who was married at the time. After the death of her husband, she and Mill married.

For many years Mill worked for the East India Company which managed most of Britain's trade with India. He rose to a relatively high position but left when the East India Company lost its concession with the government.

Mill was quite well known in his own lifetime. He was elected to Parliament. More importantly, he was probably the leading British intellectual of the nineteenth century. His writings covered a range of topics from logic and philosophy of science to ethics to economics. And he was highly influential in all these areas. His *Principles of Political Economy* (1848) has an important place in the history of economic thought. His *On Liberty* (1861) is probably the most famous defense of freedom of speech. In *Utilitarianism* (1859) he developed that doctrine in ways that went much beyond the ideas of his father and Jeremy Bentham, the other founding father of utilitarianism in ethics. Mill wrote an early "feminist" classic, *The Subjection of Women* (1861), an ardent defense of equality for women. Finally, his *System of Logic* (1843) is one of the first sophisticated attempts to analyze and interpret the practices of modern science.

Much of Mill's writings focus on science and how it works. For our purposes, most interesting are his discussion of two things: the nature of scientific method, and scientific realism. We begin with the former.

By "scientific method" Mill had in mind something more than some rough rules of thumb or platitudes about science such as "test your assumptions" or "collect data." Mill, like many philosophers of science since, had hopes of identifying the *logic* of scientific reasoning. Logic is the study of valid or good rules of inference. Consider the following inference: if I drink a gallon of whiskey, then I will get a hangover. I just drank a gallon of whiskey. Therefore, I will get a hangover. This inference instantiates a rule of good reasoning known as modus ponens. Modus ponens says that from the truth of these two statements

1   if A, then B
2   A

we can infer

3   B

Such rules of logic are supposed to have a special character – they are supposed to be *universal*. Modus ponens holds regardless of time, place, and subject matter. No matter what you are reasoning about or who is doing the reasoning, modus ponens gives correct inferences.

Mill wanted to find something similar that described scientific reasoning. In other words, he wanted to find the general rules of good scientific reasoning – the rules that allow us to infer the most reasonable hypothesis from our data and observations. He thought those rules should be a kind of logic in that they would be universal, holding for all good science at all times and all subject matters.

According to Mill, scientific reasoning – and ultimately all reasoning – has two components. The first component is the evidence given directly to us by the senses. Mill takes this evidence to be facts of consciousness or, in effect, how things seem to us. Thus I am aware of being in pain, or of heat, or of seeing a red visual field. Mill thought that all reasoning began from such facts; they are not inferences but things we experience directly. The view that all knowledge ultimately derives from sense experience is called *empiricism*, and Mill was one of its most consistent advocates. This view contrasts sharply with that of Descartes, for example, who denied that all knowledge comes from experience (see chapter 4).

The second component of scientific reasoning concerns the rules for drawing conclusions about things beyond what we directly experience. Mill claimed that all such reasoning was *inductive*, and Mill's view of scientific method is correspondingly called *inductivism*. A good way to understand inductive inferences is to contrast them to their opposite, namely, *deductive* inferences. Deductive inferences are ones where the premises or initial facts one begins with guarantee the truth of the conclusion you infer. For example, if I know that all professors are perverts and that Jones is a professor, then I can infer with certainty that Jones is a pervert. In short, I can deduce that fact from the information I started with. Inductive inferences, on the other hand, do not guarantee the truth of their conclusions. Instead, they give us some reason to believe the conclusion true. So if every professor you have had so far in your college career has had a beard, that would give you some reason to believe most professors have a beard. But your experience does not guarantee you are right. After all, it may be that you have only had humanities professors where beards are much more common than, say, in business professors.

So *inductive inferences are those in which the information contained in the conclusions go beyond the information in the premises.* Here are some sample inductive inferences:

A magazine poll of 20,000 individuals found that a majority of them get no exercise. Therefore a majority of Americans get no exercise.

Newton's laws of motion have accurately described the motion of all bodies observed so far. Therefore Newton's laws will describe the motion of bodies observed in the future.

All AIDS patients have the HIV virus. Therefore HIV causes AIDS.

Each of these inferences infers beyond the facts they start with; each conclusion could turn out false even if the starting facts are true. So, Mill thought that all scientific reasoning was inductive reasoning. It began with the certainties of direct experience and then built up knowledge by generalizing from that experience. Put this way, Mill's view may sound like an obvious platitude without much content. It is not, for two reasons: first, for Mill, inductive reasoning does *not* allow the apparently common practice of first proposing a hypothesis and then concluding it is true because it fits with what we observe; and second, Mill thought he could describe the general rules that guided inductive inferences. In other words, Mill thought he had uncovered the method that scientists implicitly follow in discovering scientific laws and hypotheses. Looking at these two claims will give you a much better feel for Mill's inductivism.

Richard Feynman, the Nobel Prize winning physicist, described the scientific method in this way: "In general we look for a new law by the following process. We guess it. Then we compute the consequences of the guess to see what would be implied if this law that we guess is right. Then we compare the result of the computation with nature . . . to see if it works" (Feynman 1965: 156). *Mill denied that such reasoning was legitimate.* The mere fact that some speculation fits with observed facts is no reason at all to believe it, on Mill's view. Only hypotheses that have been inductively derived from observations are reasonable to believe. We must begin with the data and then derive generalizations from them.

Why did Mill reject the practice – what he called "the method of hypotheses" – that Feynman thought so obvious? Mill's main concern is this: more than one hypothesis can fit the data. So if we guess a hypothesis that turns out to predict correctly, that does not mean there are not other, incompatible hypotheses that also predict correctly. Unless we can rule out competing explanations, we have no particular reason to believe the particular hypothesis we have hit upon. A doctor, for example, who identifies a diagnosis that fits your symptoms has not finished his or her job until other diagnoses have been ruled out.

Mill considered and rejected two rationales for Feynman's approach. Sometimes it seems we have only one hypothesis; there are no competing hypotheses – no alternative explanations of what we observe are conceivable. In such situations isn't it reasonable to believe the hypothesis that does fit the facts? Mill thought not. Just because we cannot conceive alternative explanations for some phenomena does not mean they do not exist; our inability to imagine other possibilities may just reflect our limited capacities, our prejudices, our ignorance. Indeed, the history of human thought is full of cases where what was judged inconceivable at one time was later shown to be true.

Another common defense of the method of hypotheses might be called the "coincidence argument." This argument claims that if a hypothesis fits a series of different facts, then it is too much of a coincidence to think it is not true. Perhaps fitting with a single fact is little reason to believe a claim, but if the hypothesis fits many different facts, then we ought to believe it. How else can we explain its successful predictions other than by its truth? Mill was not moved by this reasoning. He granted that if a hypothesis successfully predicts many different facts, then something is going on. In other words, there must be some explanation for the hypothesis' correct implications. However, the explanation need not be that the hypothesis is *true*. We can draw that conclusion only if we can show that no other hypothesis is consistent with the same range of facts.

Consider the following example: eighteenth-century scientists explained the process of combustion – as happens, for example, when wood burns – by appealing to something they called "phlogiston." When combustion occurred, phlogiston was given off by the burning substance until it was depleted. At that point, the combustion stopped. So the phlogiston hypothesis explained what was going on in combustion and why it stopped. The phlogiston hypothesis also explained another fact. If you place a small animal in a closed container with a fire, the animal eventually dies, even if it is shielded from the heat. The reason? Animals cannot survive by breathing phlogiston, and thus when the phlogiston fills the container, they expire.

Of course, we know today that there is no such thing as phlogiston. Combustion removes oxygen from the container, and that is why the combustion is extinguished and the animal killed. Mill draws the obvious moral from cases like these: the consistency of a hypothesis with even a broad range of facts does not show it reasonable to believe, for there may still be competing explanations.

These arguments are in some ways similar to Descartes' skeptical reasoning discussed in chapter 4. The dream argument, for example, points out that when I seem to experience something, I may not be able to infer that what I am experiencing is really there. Dreams or an evil genius out to fool me are possible competing hypotheses. Descartes' moral, then, is similar to Mill's: to have knowledge we must rule out competing explanations. Mill does, however, provide rather different reasons for worry about competing explanations for our experience, namely, the history of science.

Mill thought that these considerations showed that scientific reasoning must always be inductive – it must always start from the data and move only to hypotheses that can be generalized on the basis of the data. Moreover, Mill thought that he could identify the basic rules or methods for making such inductive generalizations. The methods are intuitive and powerful, and it will thus be worth looking at several of them to get a better feel for Mill's inductivism.

One method Mill called the *method of difference*. It is a way of taking a set of observations and inferring what caused what. The key idea is that we look for a difference that holds only when the effect to be explained is present. Look at the following schema:

Conditions	Effect
A B C	present
A C D	present
A B D	absent

We observe various combinations of conditions and notice whether the effect of interest is present or absent. From the information in our table, the method of difference tells us to infer that C is the cause of the effect, for C seems to make the difference. When it is present, the effect is seen; when it is not, no effect is observed.

Another of Mill's methods works from the other direction and is called the *method of agreement*. Here we look at observations for what is the *same* to infer causes. If only one factor is present in all cases when the effect is present, then we can infer that factor is the cause. The schema looks like this:

Conditions	Effect
A B C	present
A C D	present
A B D	present

A is the only condition common to the various appearances of the effect, so we infer A is the cause.

Mill hoped that these two methods and others like them provided a logic of science, one that avoided the guessing and speculation of the method of hypotheses. The methods of agreement and difference should work regardless of the subject matter or historical moment, and they seemingly do not involve guessing at hypotheses; instead, they generalize from observations.

So far we have been looking at Mill's account of scientific method or, in other words, his attempt to explain the unique features that separate science from other activities. His answer is that careful adherence to the inductive method as embodied, for example, in the methods of agreement and difference does the trick. We have yet to look, however, at what Mill said about the other big question raised at the beginning of this chapter. That question was one about scientific realism – of whether we should take the weird things modern science says at face value and as probably true. I thus turn next to what Mill had to say on this issue. It largely follows from what he believed about scientific method, and so our discussion can be briefer.

The term "scientific realism" has several related but different connotations among philosophers. But in its most vigorous form it claims that we know that current science is on the right track. Modern, mature science describes the way the world really is, at least in its basic outlines. Mill rejected this claim. That doesn't mean he claimed to know that modern science is false; rather, his thesis is the more limited one that we do not have compelling evidence to think it is true.

Thus Mill rejected scientific realism. He has a variety of reasons for doing so, some of which would take us too far into the technical details of his philosophy. However, his main motivation we have already seen. Mill thought scientific realism relied essentially on the method of hypotheses. As we shall see later, Mill was and remains right about this – many scientific realists defend their view on the grounds that it makes good sense of the facts about science. The hypothesis that current science is largely true, they claim, makes good sense of its experimental success, its progress, its wide scope, and its ability to produce technically useful applications. Such reasoning involves accepting a hypothesis – in this case a hypothesis about science – on the grounds that it fits with the facts.

Of course we know what Mill thought of such reasoning. The mere fact that a hypothesis fits with the facts is little reason to believe it. Yet if scientific realism is defended on the grounds that it fits with the facts about science, we are using the method of hypotheses to defend scientific realism. We saw above, however, that Mill rejected the method of hypotheses. So it is not surprising that he rejects a scientific realism based on it. Again, Mill is not claiming to know that modern science is false. He simply denies that we know it is true or approximately true. The only way to know that would be to rule out all competing explanations for science's success other than its truth. Mill denied we could do that, in large part because he thought that ultimately our only evidence about anything is the way things seem to us. While we can speculate about what causes the world of our

327

experience, we cannot have real knowledge that goes beyond our experience. It takes careful inductions to get knowledge, but we can only hypothesize about things we can never observe.

It is interesting to note that in some ways Descartes would agree with Mill here. As we saw in chapter 4, Descartes thought he could *prove* the existence of God. He would not have been satisfied with merely postulating God as the best explanation he could think of for various facts about the world. However, Mill denied that proof beyond experience was possible; Descartes thought that it was.

Mill's arguments have, of course, not gone unchallenged. In the remainder of this chapter we shall look in detail at criticisms of Mill. Those criticisms take two basic forms: they either deny that inductivism captures the scientific method or they assert that scientific realism can be defended against Mill's doubts. In the process we shall survey some important recent developments in the philosophy of science.

A first doubt about Mill's inductivism is that his methods do not do what they are supposed to. According to Mill, the methods of agreement and difference are reliable ways to produce causal generalizations from observations. They allegedly avoid the need for prior, unsupported hypotheses that is characteristic of the method of hypotheses. But do they? Consider the following example: I am trying to determine the cause of hangovers. I carefully observe the conditions present prior to having a hangover. Here is the schema I observe:

Condition	Effect
drinking water and vodka	hangover
drinking water and whiskey	hangover
drinking water and rum	hangover

By the method of agreement, I conclude that drinking water causes hangovers!

What has gone wrong here? Obviously if we redescribe the conditions, we can get closer to the right answer. Instead of drinking water and some specific alcohol, we can describe the conditions in each case as drinking water and alcohol. Then the method of agreement favors neither condition as a cause.

The most obvious moral is that Mill failed to give us rules of inductive inference that are always reliable. Yet there is a larger moral lurking here as well: it is impossible to generalize from observations without the aid of prior hypotheses. If we believe that vodka, whiskey, and rum have the same basic nature, then we will describe the conditions preceding hangovers differently than if we think they are very different substances. Similarly, calling the symptoms a "hangover" also depends on a prior hypothesis, namely, that these symptoms are caused by something consumed rather than a virus, for example. So categorizing the data itself commits us to various assumptions about the world. Moreover, I did a great many things before having the hangover besides drink liquids. I wore black socks, developed photographs in my darkroom, went scuba diving, and what not. In focusing on just the things that I drank, I am again making the assumption or hypothesis that these other conditions are not relevant to hangovers.

Of course, Mill would want our assumptions to be based on prior inductions from experience. But the moral here is that he wants the impossible – because hypotheses and assumptions are built in from the ground up. In the process of selecting and describing data we are making assumptions and relying on hypotheses. So a purely inductive method is impossible.

This conclusion also raises doubts about another part of Mill's philosophy. Earlier we said that he was an empiricist, for he claimed that all knowledge is derived from sense experience. He also thought that sense experience – our visual, tactile, etc., experiences – were "directly given." In other words, we know our experiences without inference and thus, Mill thought, without error. However, the claim I made above that hypotheses are involved at all stages in science should also raise serious doubts about this idea of the "given." How the world seems to us is arguably partly a function of what we already believe.

Thus Mill seems to have been wrong when he claimed that good science proceeds purely inductively. No doubt generalizing from experience is essential to science, and Mill was quite right to suggest that practices like the method of agreement are central to good science. Yet he claimed much more for these methods than they can deliver, namely, a reliable way of generalizing from data that depends on no merely postulated hypotheses.

2   Karl Popper and Falsificationism

These criticisms of Mill's inductivism are widely accepted. However, some philosophers after Mill have thought that his goal – identifying the logic of scientific reasoning – was nevertheless a crucial one, and they proposed alternative accounts of scientific reasoning. One very influential such account comes from Sir Karl Popper (1902–95). Popper shared Mill's suspicions about the method of hypotheses; he too worried that showing a hypothesis compatible with some set of data does little to support it. Consider again how the method of hypotheses seems to work. I propose a hypothesis and then determine what the hypothesis would predict about some specific situation. For example, my car will not start, and I hypothesize that it is out of gas. My reasoning seems to be:

1   If a car is out of gas, it will not start
2   My car will not start
3   Thus my car is out of gas

Yet this kind of reasoning is clearly a fallacy. If you do not see why, consider this parallel case:

1   If you live in Alabama, you live in the USA
2   You live in the USA
3   Therefore you live in Alabama

The problem is that there are many different places to live in the USA, and likewise the problem is that a lack of gas is not the only possible explanation for why my car does not start. It could be an electrical problem or, who knows, maybe monkeys have escaped from the circus in town and stuck bananas down my gas tank.

Popper noticed, however, that another related kind of reasoning avoids these problems. Consider this reasoning:

1 If you live in Alabama, then you live in the USA
2 You do not live in the USA
3 Therefore you do not live in Alabama

This form of reasoning is valid. In the case of my car, it would take this form:

1 If a car is out of gas, then it will not start
2 My car starts
3 Therefore it cannot be out of gas

What does this have to do with scientific method? Well, it suggested to Popper the idea that although scientific hypotheses cannot be conclusively proven, they can be conclusively *disproven*. Popper thus advocated the view that the essence of science lies in trying to falsify hypotheses. Falsifying hypotheses seems to follow the second schema of reasoning described above. For example, consider the hypothesis that infection with the HIV virus causes AIDS. That hypothesis entails that people with AIDS should show up positive on a test for HIV antibodies which the body produces in response to infection. So it would only take one confirmed case of someone with AIDS with no positive antibody test to conclude that HIV is not the cause or the sole cause of AIDS.

Popper's account of the scientific process is called *falsificationism*, for obvious reasons. Two key ideas in falsificationism are that (1) the essence of scientific method is the attempt to falsify hypotheses, and (2) the difference between science and pseudoscience is that science is falsifiable and pseudoscience is not. Scientists attempt to falsify hypotheses when they perform what Popper calls "stringent tests." Imagine the following two tests of Newton's laws of motion. First test: since Newton proposed that bodies exert a force of gravitation proportional to their mass, we derive the prediction that objects dropped on the Earth will fall downward. We find the prediction holds. Second test: given the masses and orbits of the planets in our solar system, if Newton's laws are true there should be a planet previously unknown beyond Uranus at such and such a distance. Astronomers search for the planet and find what we now call Neptune. The first test is not stringent, because it predicts very little – any downward motion means a successful test. In short, the odds of the test turning out negative are small. The second test is very stringent, for it claims that something quite precise will be seen, something that we have prior reason to think false. To Popper the essence of good scientific method is the search for such stringent tests.

Falsifiability is a somewhat different notion. A hypothesis is *falsifiable* if it is logically incompatible with some observation or data. In other words, a hypothesis is unfalsifiable if there is no possible observation that could conflict with it. Popper thought that Marxism and Freudian psychology were unfalsifiable in this sense and thus not real sciences. Here is the kind of thing he had in mind: Marxists claim that the state – the government – exists to serve the interests of the ruling class, which Marx took to be the wealthy. Yet when critics of Marxism point out that the state often helps those not in the "ruling class" such as labor unions, the poor, and so on, Marxists come up with excuses. They say, for example, that these are measures to keep the population docile so that the basic system can continue. So these things really do promote the interests of the ruling class.

Popper thought there was something deeply suspicious about these moves. He diagnosed the problem as a lack of falsifiability – nothing would or could show Marxism wrong and thus Marxism was pseudoscience.

Obviously stringent tests and falsifiability are important to science. Yet it is doubtful that they have the central role Popper thought. Popper rejected the method of hypotheses and inductivism because they do not produce determinate results; successful predictions from one hypothesis or inductions from one set of data do not rule out other competing explanations equally consistent with the facts. He advocated falsificationism as an alternative that avoided those uncertainties. It takes only one case to falsify a hypothesis, Popper claimed; rejecting falsified hypotheses represents a valid form of inference. So the process of falsification provides a certainty that the method of hypotheses does not. However, we have good reason to think that falsification is no more certain nor different in its logic than the method of hypotheses.

The basic problem is that hypotheses are seldom tested alone. To test a scientific theory, we have to set up the appropriate experimental conditions. Establishing those conditions requires us to know many other things about the world. So to test the hypothesis that HIV causes AIDS, we have to know about antibodies, the biochemistry that goes into testing for antibodies, and so on. This idea that testing a hypothesis involves much more than just the hypothesis at issue is called the "holism of testing." Because testing is holistic, failed tests are not decisive and clear-cut in the way Popper claimed. If someone who apparently has AIDS shows up negative on an HIV test, I have several alternatives. I could reject HIV as the cause of AIDS, but that hypothesis has much evidence going for it. I could alternatively ask if I had made a mistake somewhere in my test. Perhaps my understanding of the biochemistry involved is wrong; perhaps antibodies don't form in the same way with HIV as with other viruses; perhaps my test is not sensitive enough.

How do I decide what to do? Once again I have to rely on prior hypotheses and inductive inferences. My HIV antibody tests have sometimes been wrong in the past, so maybe they are again. The hypothesized mechanism of action of HIV is indeed quite unusual, so perhaps we should not always expect to see antibodies in the usual numbers that our tests can detect. And so on. So it is no simple and obvious matter whether we should reject the hypothesis at issue if a prediction fails to come true. Falsification seems no more certain than other elements of scientific testing.

What about Popper's ideas about the difference between science and pseudo-science? Again, things are not nearly so clear-cut as Popper suggested. Marxism may be a fuzzy doctrine, but it is not completely untestable. Take the idea mentioned earlier that the state serves the interests of the ruling class. If we specify criteria for being in the upper class, and we identify various important social institutions and key roles within them, then a test of sorts is possible. We can ask whether those key individuals fall into the upper class as we defined it. Of course, this is not a conclusive test, but few single scientific tests are, as we saw above.

Popper's distinction may make more sense, however, if we apply it to *people*. Pseudoscientists are those such as astrologers who would never give up their pet theories no matter what the evidence showed.

3   Thomas Kuhn and Changing Paradigms in Science

Neither Mill nor Popper seems to have successfully identified the scientific method. I want to look now at another critic of Mill, this time one who doubts there is any scientific method at all. The critic I have in mind is Thomas Kuhn (1922–96), whose *Structure of Scientific Revolutions* has been enormously influential, inside philosophy and out. Despite the differences between Mill and Popper, they shared two central assumptions: that there is a logic of science – some universal rules or methods for producing reasonable results – and that science has advanced over time by applying those rules over and over again to objective data, thereby increasing our knowledge. Kuhn denies both these assumptions. He argues that if you look at how real science is done (and Kuhn's training included a PhD in physics) and at the real history of science, things look very different. There is no universal scientific method, and science does not grow by increasing our knowledge but by overthrowing previous world-views.

Kuhn is best known for his claim that all science is dominated by "paradigms." A scientific paradigm is the basic framework that guides the work of a specific scientific tradition. The paradigm involves the dominant scientific theory, but it also includes standards for what is good science, a specific set of categories for describing the world, and assumptions about what questions need to be answered and how. The day-to-day activity of the scientist consists in fleshing out or extending this general paradigm to new areas or with new detail. Such activity Kuhn calls "puzzle-solving," for the rules are set out in advance by the dominant paradigm and a failure to produce good results is a failure in the scientist or puzzle-solver. In short, basic paradigms are not rejected when the data do not fit them. Note how different this picture is from Popper's.

Kuhn does not deny that science changes due to experiments and data collection. Yet major scientific developments involve dropping one paradigm for another. Since each paradigm has different standards for what is good science and different ways of categorizing the world, changes are not driven by applying one scientific method to objective data. They are instead much more like political revolutions, where one group ousts another and institutes an entirely new order.

An example may help make these ideas a bit clearer. In the Middle Ages the dominant paradigm for physics and astronomy was the Ptolemaic–Aristotelian system. It placed the Earth at the center of the universe. It assumed that any orbit of a planet could only be circular, for the circle was the most perfect figure and God created a perfect universe. It assumed that motion on the Earth and motion of the heavens were very different things and required different explanations. The key question about terrestrial motion for the Ptolemaic–Aristotelian system was what kept objects in motion. A "resting" object was in its natural state, and thus physics ought to explain what kept something in motion. The Ptolemaic–Aristotelian system also had specific ideas about what counted as good evidence: consistency with the divine revelations in the Bible and with common sense were paramount.

Of course the Ptolemaic system was eventually replaced with a very different world-view, one established by Copernicus and Newton. In the new paradigm, nothing was special about the Earth and it was removed from the center of the universe. Nothing was special about circular motions, and planets were given elliptical orbits. Consistency with divine revelation and common sense took a back seat. Observations aided by instruments and experiments as well as mathematical precision became decisive standards. The questions to be answered also changed. Newton's first law says that bodies in motion will stay in motion unless some force acts upon them. So the question to be answered is not why bodies move but why they change their motion. The new paradigm likewise assumed that motions in the heavens and motions on Earth were subject to the same principles.

Kuhn argued that the change from the Ptolemaic to the Copernican system did not result simply from applying the scientific method to the data. The two paradigms differed radically on what they took the data to be, how it was described, what needed to be explained, and what good science is. Moreover, for simple predictive purposes, the Ptolemaic system was in fact more accurate – if you wanted to know where the stars would be tomorrow, it was a better tool. Though Kuhn himself did not like to put it this way, his view seems to suggest that scientific change is not a rational but a sociological process.

You can see now how Kuhn challenges the assumptions common to both Mill and Popper. They believed that there was a universal scientific method and that it drove scientific change. Kuhn thinks science at different times is dominated by different paradigms. That means science at different times has very different ideas about good method. Even when scientists from different paradigms appeal to seemingly common scientific virtues such as empirical accuracy, they have entirely different senses of what that involves. There is no universal scientific method. Nor did Kuhn think that objective data are available to decide disputes between paradigms. Different paradigms will produce different descriptions and interpretations of the data; they will also have different standards about which data are relevant or important.

4 Scientific Realism

We will raise some criticism of Kuhn a bit later. However, I want to turn now to discuss Mill's second big thesis about science. We have been looking at critiques of and alternatives to his picture of scientific method. Yet Mill's anti-realism – his view that we do not know that our best science is approximately correct – is equally controversial. Once again, of course, the issues are complicated.

Recall Mill's main attack on scientific realism: postulating the truth of science to explain facts about science is using the method of hypotheses. But the method of hypotheses is illegitimate; thus, so too is scientific realism. However, we argued above that Mill's attack on the method of hypotheses was somewhat misguided. A purely inductive approach that depends on no postulated hypotheses is impossible. Mill thought we could have reliable scientific knowledge about our experiences because that knowledge was inductive. So either he must conclude that we cannot even know how things seem or he must allow that postulating hypotheses about things beyond our experience can be justifiable. In short, there is no fundamental divide between the directly observed and the merely postulated. Claims about scientific realism are not fundamentally flawed simply because they hypothesize about what goes on beyond our experience.

One way to see the point here is to consider what Mill had to say about geology and cosmology, for example. These are disciplines that talk about events distant in time and space. The explosion of a supernova many millions of light years away is one example. The processes that formed the early Earth are another. They are so distant that we will never observe them, though perhaps they would be observable if we could manage to get ourselves there. Mill thought inferences about these kind of events legitimate and not subject to the doubts he had about the method of hypotheses. Yet are they not in a real sense unobservable as well? So why should we treat them any differently than we treat hypothesized entities in the here and now that we cannot directly observe? Mill struggled with this problem. From our perspective it illustrates the point just made that there is nothing in principle wrong with scientific realism simply because it hypothesizes about what cannot be observed.

Mill is not completely done for, however. Even if we inevitably hypothesize and postulate, not all hypothesizing is legitimate. Mill is right to worry about the process of accepting hypotheses on the grounds that they fit the facts. Unless competing accounts can be ruled out, fitting the facts is weak evidence. So while scientific realism is not illegitimate simply because it hypothesizes, it will only be plausible if it is the *best* explanation for the facts about science – and that means better than any alternative explanation for those facts.

Contemporary scientific realists think they can make their case. They believe the best explanation for the facts about modern science must be that modern science truly tells us the way the world is. What facts do they have in mind? At least the following:

Modern science has been able to produce ever more precise predictions about the world that are confirmed by observation.

Modern science is able to explain many diverse, complicated phenomena by appeal to a few fundamental laws.

Modern science allows us to manipulate nature successfully in a host of ways, including making complex machinery, going to the moon, etc.

Realists ask what explains these facts. They argue that only the truth of scientific realism – only the assumption that current science is more or less correct – will do the job. Modern science is able to provide more and more accurate predictions because it is on the right track; only if your theories had the basic structure of reality right would they be refinable in this way. If the fundamental laws of science were not right, it would be an amazing coincidence that they are able to explain such diverse phenomena. And how could modern science not be right, given that we can use it to build computers, rockets, and the like?

What should we think of this argument? Mill no doubt would still be suspicious. Earlier we saw that he was unconvinced by coincidence arguments for the method of hypotheses. Coincidence arguments are ones that go: "this postulated hypothesis must be true, because it would be an amazing coincidence if it fit as many facts as it does and yet was false." Mill replied that such coincidences do indeed need to be explained, but the truth of the hypothesis is not the only possible explanation. False theories can have multiple correct predictions. This point remains valid, even if Mill's inductivism is misconceived.

So the argument for scientific realism cannot rest with simply pointing to the various facts about science that it explains. Scientific realists must rule out competing explanations for the success of modern science. What would those competing explanations be? Well, we have already seen one – Kuhn's account of science. He argued that scientific success depends on paradigms. Scientists accept the theories they do for largely sociological reasons; change from one scientific theory to another is not forced by the evidence. Modern science produces ever more precise predictions only because scientists ignore areas where a paradigm cannot be refined and concentrate on those areas where it can. Science manages to explain many diverse phenomena with simple laws only because it has a dominant paradigm that narrows the focus of the scientists to just those phenomena that it can explain. Thus if Kuhn's account is right, we have a clear alternative to scientific realism: science succeeds not because it has things right but because social processes assure that we will agree that it has succeeded.

Kuhn's general sociological approach is one that is now very trendy. Many commentators on science have pushed it even further, claiming that all science is a "social construction" with no more claim on the truth than any set of beliefs in society. Scientists come to the beliefs they do by processes of negotiation, rhetoric, and the usual ways anybody comes to believe things. There is no such thing as absolute truth; the only legitimate notion of truth is a relative one: the "truth" is always the truth that has been constructed or agreed upon by some community.

There are, however, deep problems with this sort of relativism. The most glaring problem results when we ask whether these sociological approaches apply to themselves. Is Kuhn's account of science itself just one possible paradigm? Is the belief that science is a social construction itself a social construction? If the answer is no, then we have to ask why it is that scientists cannot get truth but historians and sociologists of science can. If the answer is yes, then we can ask why we should believe their views. If sociologists of science are just using rhetoric to convince us, if their views have no more going for them than any other set of beliefs, then it hardly seems they are reasonable ones to have. In short, these sociological approaches seem self-refuting.

A second related problem comes from the stories Kuhn and others tell about how science works. It is not so clear that they do a good job of describing real scientific practice. In the case of Kuhn, there are doubts about the history he uses to support his view. His description of the shift from the Ptolemaic to the Copernican world-view greatly simplifies a long historical process. Kuhn compares world-views that are many centuries apart without looking in detail at the piecemeal process that led to the rejection of one and the adoption of another. That makes the shift between them look radical indeed. Yet the process that convinced people to change their minds over those centuries may have involved many small, reasonable changes in belief.

To see the problem, consider an analogy from the moral and political realm. Current views about the races and the sexes in Western societies differ enormously from views dominant a century ago when women and non-Caucasians were thought inherently inferior and slavery and discrimination perfectly morally acceptable. If we compare these views to those we hold today, it will seems as if we simply have radically different moral beliefs, ones so different that the two sides might hardly seem able to communicate. However, the real historical process over that 100-year period was not one where people suddenly adopted a very different set of moral beliefs. Instead, attitudes about minorities and women changed slowly and haltingly, often as the result of public debate, education, and changing experiences. Arguments and reason did play a role – the process looks irrational only if we ignore those intervening steps. Similar piecemeal processes may well have gone on in the change from medieval science to modern science.

So there are doubts about the sociological competitors to scientific realism. Where does that leave us? Social constructivism is not the only alternative to scientific realism. Remember that the latter says that we know, have good reason to believe, etc., that modern science is largely right or true. A third alternative is to grant that modern science has lots of evidence – it does – but deny that this shows us it must be right. Just as we may grant that juries can rationally weigh the evidence and yet still ask whether they have reached the correct verdict, so too with science. One reason we may doubt that reasonable juries make the right decision is our past experience; reasonable juries carefully weighing the evidence have made mistakes before. We can make a similar argument about science. This argument is sometimes called *the pessimistic induction*. Here is a simple example of it: Newton was real smart. Einstein showed that Newton was wrong. So Einstein may be wrong too. More seriously, the pessimistic induction generalizes from our past experience with science. We know that there have been scientific theories in the past that had great predictive success in a variety of domains, were far superior to their competitors, and were used to make great technical achievements. They had, in short, all the virtues that are supposed to indicate that a theory must be true according to scientific realists. Yet past scientific theories with these traits were eventually shown to be wrong. Newton's laws, Einstein showed, hold only under a restricted range of conditions; as general laws, they are false. There are arguably numerous such examples where successful scientific theories are later overthrown and shown to be inaccurate pictures of reality. Thus we cannot take current success to show that current science is largely right.

As always in philosophy, the argument does not end here. Scientific realists can try to deny the pessimistic induction in various ways – for example, by arguing that Newton was not wrong but rather just "approximately right." None the less, the pessimistic induction is certainly an argument Mill would have liked, for it generalizes from experience in the way Mill thought crucial to good science.

References

Feynman, Richard. 1965. *The Character of Physical Law* (Cambridge, MA: MIT Press).

Suggestions for further reading

Alan Ryan's *John Stuart Mill* (Atlantic Highlands: Humanities Press, 1987) and John Skorupski's *John Stuart Mill* (London: Routledge, 1989) are general surveys of Mill's thought that include discussions of his views on epistemology and philosophy of science. Good general surveys of issues about scientific method and realism can be found in Anthony O'Hear's *Introduction to the Philosophy of Science* (Oxford: Oxford University Press, 1989), Edwin Hung's *The Nature of Science: Problems and Perspectives* (Mountain View, CA: Wadsworth, 1997), Arthur Zucker's *Introduction to the Philosophy of Science* (Englewood Cliffs, NJ: Prentice-Hall, 1966), and Wesley Salmon et al., *Introduction to the Philosophy of Science* (Englewood Cliffs, NJ: Prentice-Hall, 1992). David Oldroyd provides a historical introduction to the philosophy of science in his *The Arch of Knowledge* (New York: Methuen, 1986). A classical discussion of scientific method is Wesley Salmon's *The Foundations of Scientific Inference* (University of Pittsburgh Press, 1967). A more recent discussion of scientific method using ideas from the probability calculus is Colin Howson and Peter Urbach's *Scientific Reasoning: The Bayesian Approach* (LaSalle, IL: Open Court, 1993). A useful collection of articles on scientific realism is *Scientific Realism* edited by Jarrett Leplin (Berkeley, CA: University of California Press, 1984). For a sophisticated and detailed defense of realism, see Philip Kitcher, *The Advancement of Science* (Oxford: Oxford University Press, 1993). For defense of a view that tries to avoid the pitfalls of both realism and anti-realism about science, see

Arthur Fine's *The Shaky Game* (Chicago: University of Chicago Press, 1986). A collection of essays on Thomas Kuhn's work can be found in *World Changes: Thomas Kuhn and the Nature of Science*, edited by Paul Horwich (Cambridge, MA: MIT Press, 1993).

Introduction to Selected Readings

The selections from Mill come from his *System of Logic*. They discuss briefly his notion of inductivism, the methods of agreement and difference, and his criticisms of the method of hypotheses. For Mill, good science begins with what is given directly to the senses and then generalizes by inductive inference to new truths. Mill hoped to find some general set of rules that describe how such reasoning works, and the methods of agreement and difference are part of his attempt to describe those rules. His comments on the method of hypotheses are brief, but he argues persuasively that the mere fact that some belief or hypothesis fits with what we have observed is very little reason to believe it is true.

The selection from Carl Hempel does several things. It gives a nice example of scientific reasoning (Semmelweis's work on childbed fever), one that could easily be described in terms of Mill's methods. It also criticizes inductivism along the lines discussed in this essay: it is impossible to approach the data without making prior assumptions, *contra* the inductivist's claim to the contrary. What facts we collect, how we describe them, how we categorize them, and how we generalize from them all require prior assumptions about how the world works. Hempel's alternative to inductivism is his version of the method of hypotheses. His selection describes how that method is supposed to work.

The selection from Karl Popper outlines his reasons for thinking that the essence of science is falsification. He lays out his arguments for the claim that although hypotheses can never be conclusively confirmed, they can be conclusively disconfirmed. Popper also makes the argument that Marxism and Freudian theory are pseudoscientific, for they are not falsifiable.

Kuhn's claims that science is guided by "paradigms" and that there is no single scientific method are represented in the selections from *The Structure of Scientific Revolutions*. There Kuhn discusses the idea of "normal" science and compares scientific change to political revolutions. Kuhn's claims that science is guided by paradigms and that scientific change is a sociological process have been enormously influential, both in how people think about science as well as in other disciplines where the notion of a paradigm has also been applied. Kuhn paid close attention to the actual day-to-day activities of scientists, and for many people this was a refreshing change from the search for an abstract logic of science as is found in Mill, Hempel, and Popper.

The piece by J. J. C. Smart comes from his *Our Place in the Universe* and provides a clear version of the coincidence argument for scientific realism. Smart is a long-standing defender of that view. For Smart, we have knowledge of unobservable things like atomic particles, knowledge that is on a par with our knowledge of everyday physical objects. Many different pieces of evidence make sense if these unobservable entities are real – we can provide a simple explanation for diverse phenomena by postulating them. Smart asserts that it would be an amazing coincidence if all the phenomena we observe appeared as if they were caused by subatomic particles and yet such particles did not exist. Smart also argues against Kuhn's claim that scientific change involves a complete change of paradigms. Smart thinks that much knowledge is preserved, even when science undergoes drastic change in theories.

Discussion questions

1   Why does Mill think that the method of hypotheses is inadequate?
2   Explain Popper's criticism of Marxism and Freudian psychology.
3   Explain Hempel's criticisms of what he calls "the narrow inductivist conception of scientific inquiry."
4   Explain what Kuhn means by "normal science" and why he calls it puzzle-solving.
5   What is Smart's argument for the reality of unobservable entities?

Readings

John Stuart Mill, selections from *A System of Logic*

Introduction

Logic is concerned with inferences, not with intuitive truths. [. . .] Truths are known to us in two ways: some are known directly, and of themselves; some through the medium of other truths. The former are the subject of Intuition, or Consciousness; the latter, of Inference. The truths known by intuition are the original premises from which all others are inferred. Our assent to the conclusion being grounded on the truth of the premises, we never could arrive at any knowledge by reasoning, unless something could be known antecedently to all reasoning.

Examples of truths known to us by immediate consciousness, are our own bodily sensations and mental feelings. I know directly, and of my own knowledge, that I was vexed yesterday, or that I am hungry to-day. Examples of truths which we know only by way of inference, are occurrences which took place while we were absent, the events recorded in history, or the theorems of mathematics. The two former we infer from the testimony adduced, or from the traces of those past occurrences which still exist; the latter, from the premises laid down in books of geometry, under the title of definitions and axioms. Whatever we are capable of knowing must belong to the one class or to the other; must be in the number of the primitive data, or of the conclusions which can be drawn from these.

With the original data, or ultimate premises of our knowledge; with their number or nature, the mode in which they are obtained, or the tests by which they may be distinguished; logic, in a direct way at least, has, in the sense in which I conceive the science, nothing to do. These questions are partly not a subject of science at all, partly that of a very different science.

Whatever is known to us by consciousness, is known beyond possibility of question. What one sees or feels, whether bodily or mentally, one cannot but be

From *Collected Works of John Stuart Mill*, ed. J. M. Robson (Toronto: University of Toronto Press).

sure that one sees or feels. No science is required for the purpose of establishing such truths; no rules of art can render our knowledge of them more certain than it is in itself. There is no logic for this portion of our knowledge. [. . .]

The province of logic must be restricted to that portion of our knowledge which consists of inferences from truths previously known; whether those anteced- ent data be general propositions, or particular observations and perceptions. Logic is not the science of Belief, but the science of Proof, or Evidence. In so far as belief professes to be founded on proof, the office of logic is to supply a test for ascertain- ing whether or not the belief is well grounded. With the claims which any pro- position has to belief on the evidence of consciousness, that is, without evidence in the proper sense of the word, logic has nothing to do. [. . .]

Preliminary Observations on Induction in General

Importance of an inductive logic. The portion of the present inquiry upon which we are now about to enter, may be considered as the principal, both from its surpass- ing in intricacy all the other branches, and because it relates to a process which has been shown in the preceding Book to be that in which the investigation of nature essentially consists. We have found that all Inference, consequently all Proof, and all discovery of truths not self-evident, consists of inductions, and the interpretation of inductions: that all our knowledge, not intuitive, comes to us exclusively from that source. What Induction is, therefore, and what conditions render it legitimate, cannot but be deemed the main question of the science of logic – the question which includes all others. It is, however, one which professed writers on logic have almost entirely passed over. The generalities of the subject have not been altogether neglected by metaphysicians; but, for want of sufficient acquaintance with the processes by which science has actually succeeded in establishing general truths, their analysis of the inductive operation, even when unexceptionable as to correct- ness, has not been specific enough to be made the foundation of practical rules, which might be for induction itself what the rules of the syllogism are for the interpretation of induction: while those by whom physical science has been carried to its present state of improvement – and who, to arrive at a complete theory of the process, needed only to generalize, and adapt to all varieties of problems, the methods which they themselves employed in their habitual pursuits – never until very lately made any serious attempt to philosophize on the subject, nor regarded the mode in which they arrived at their conclusions as deserving of study, inde- pendently of the conclusions themselves. [. . .]

Of Inductions Improperly So Called

Inductions distinguished from verbal transformations. Induction, then, is that operation of the mind, by which we infer that what we know to be true in a particular case or cases, will be true in all cases which resemble the former in certain assignable respects. In other words, Induction is the process by which we conclude that what is true of certain individuals of a class is true of the whole class, or that what is true at certain times will be true in similar circumstances at all times. [. . .]

Of the Four Methods of Experimental Inquiry

Method of Agreement. The simplest and most obvious modes of singling out from among the circumstances which precede or follow a phenomenon, those with which it is really connected by an invariable law, are two in number. One is, by comparing together different instances in which the phenomenon occurs. The other is, by comparing instances in which the phenomenon does occur, with instances in other respects similar in which it does not. These two methods may be respectively denominated, the Method of Agreement, and the Method of Difference.

In illustrating these methods, it will be necessary to bear in mind the twofold character of inquiries into the laws of phenomena; which may be either inquiries into the cause of a given effect, or into the effects or properties of a given cause. We shall consider the methods in their application to either order of investigation, and shall draw our examples equally from both.

We shall denote antecedents by the large letters of the alphabet, and the consequents corresponding to them by the small. Let A, then, be an agent or cause, and let the object of our inquiry be to ascertain what are the effects of this cause. If we can either find, or produce, the agent A in such varieties of circumstances, that the different cases have no circumstance in common except A; then whatever effect we find to be produced in all our trials, is indicated as the effect of A. Suppose, for example, that A is tried along with B and C, and that the effect is *a b c*; and suppose that A is next tried with D and E, but without B and C, and that the effect is *a d e*. Then we may reason thus: *b* and *c* are not effects of A, for they were not produced by it in the second experiment; nor are *d* and *e*, for they were not produced in the first. Whatever is really the effect of A must have been produced in both instances; now this condition is fulfilled by no circumstance except *a*. The phenomenon *a* cannot have been the effect of B or C, since it was produced where they were not; nor of D or E; since it was produced where they were not. Therefore it is the effect of A.

For example, let the antecedent A be the contact of an alkaline substance and an oil. This combination being tried under several varieties of circumstances, resembling each other in nothing else, the results agree in the production of a greasy and detersive or saponaceous substance: it is therefore concluded that the combination of an oil and an alkali causes the production of a soap. It is thus we inquire, by the Method of Agreement, into the effect of a given cause. [. . .]

First Canon

If two or more instances of the phenomenon under investigation have only one circumstance in common, the circumstance in which alone all the instances agree, is the cause (or effect) of the given phenomenon.

Quitting for the present the Method of Agreement, to which we shall almost immediately return, we proceed to a still more potent instrument of the investigation of nature, the Method of Difference.

Method of Difference. In the Method of Agreement, we endeavoured to obtain instances which agreed in the given circumstance but differed in every other: in the present method we require, on the contrary, two instances resembling one another in every other respect, but differing in the presence or absence of the phenomenon we wish to study. If our object be to discover the effects of an agent A, we must procure A in some set of ascertained circumstances, as A B C, and having noted the effects produced, compare them with the effect of the remaining circumstances B C, when A is absent. If the effect of A B C is *a b c*, and the effect of B C, *b c*, it is evident that the effect of A is *a*. So again, if we begin at the other end, and desire to investigate the cause of an effect *a*, we must select an instance, as *a b c*, in which the effect occurs, and in which the antecedents were A B C, and we must look out for another instance in which the remaining circumstances, *b c*, occur without *a*. If the antecedents, in that instance, are B C, we know that the cause of *a* must be A: either A alone, or A in conjunction with some of the other circumstances present.

It is scarcely necessary to give examples of a logical process to which we owe almost all the inductive conclusions we draw in daily life. When a man is shot through the heart, it is by this method we know that it was the gunshot which killed him: for he was in the fulness of life immediately before, all circumstances being the same, except the wound.

The axioms implied in this method are evidently the following. Whatever antecedent cannot be excluded without preventing the phenomenon, is the cause, or a condition, of that phenomenon: Whatever consequent can be excluded, with no other difference in the antecedents than the absence of a particular one, is the effect of that one. Instead of comparing different instances of a phenomenon, to discover in what they agree, this method compares an instance of its occurrence with an instance of its non-occurrence, to discover in what they differ. The canon which is the regulating principle of the Method of Difference may be expressed as follows:

Second Canon

If an instance in which the phenomenon under investigation occurs, and an instance in which it does not occur, have every circumstance in common save one, that one occurring only in the former; the circumstance in which alone the two instances differ, is the effect, or the cause, or an indispensable part of the cause, of the phenomenon. [. . .]

Of the Limits to the Explanation of Laws of Nature

The proper use of scientific hypotheses. An hypothesis is any supposition which we make (either without actual evidence, or on evidence avowedly insufficient) in order to endeavour to deduce from it conclusions in accordance with facts which are known to be real; under the idea that if the conclusions to which the hypothesis leads are known truths, the hypothesis itself either must be, or at least is likely to be, true. If the hypothesis relates to the cause, or mode of production of a phenomenon, it will serve, if admitted, to explain such facts as are found capable of being deduced from it. And this explanation is the purpose of many, if not most, hypotheses. Since explaining, in the scientific sense, means resolving an uniformity which is not a law of causation, into the laws of causation from which it results, or a complex law of causation into simpler and more general ones from which it is capable of being deductively inferred; if there do not exist any known laws which fulfil this requirement, we may feign or imagine some which would fulfil it; and this is making an hypothesis.

An hypothesis being a mere supposition, there are no other limits to hypotheses than those of the human imagination; we may, if we please, imagine, by way of accounting for an effect, some cause of a kind utterly unknown, and acting according to a law altogether fictitious. [. . .]

Accordingly, most thinkers of any degree of sobriety allow, that an hypothesis of this kind is not to be received as probably true because it accounts for all the known phenomena; since this is a condition sometimes fulfilled tolerably well by two conflicting hypotheses; while there are probably many others which are equally possible, but which, for want of anything analogous in our experience, our minds are unfitted to conceive. But it seems to be thought that an hypothesis of the sort in question is entitled to a more favourable reception, if, besides accounting for all the facts previously known, it has led to the anticipation and prediction of others which experience afterwards verified [. . .] Such predictions and their fulfilment are, indeed, well calculated to impress the uninformed, whose faith in science rests solely on similar coincidences between its prophecies and what comes to pass. But it is strange that any considerable stress should be laid upon such a coincidence by persons of scientific attainments. [. . .]

But it is not, I conceive, a valid reason for accepting any given hypothesis, that we are unable to imagine any other which will account for the facts. There is no necessity for supposing that the true explanation must be one which, with only our present experience, we could imagine. Among the natural agents with which we are acquainted, the vibrations of an elastic fluid may be the only one whose laws bear a close resemblance to those of light; but we cannot tell that there does not exist an unknown cause, other than an elastic ether diffused through space, yet producing effects identical in some respects with those which would result from the undulations of such an ether. To assume that no such cause can exist, appears to me an extreme case of assumption without evidence. And at the risk of being charged with want of modesty, I cannot help expressing astonishment that a philosopher of Dr. Whewell's abilities and attainments should have written an elaborate treatise on the philosophy of induction, in which he recognises absolutely no mode of induction except that of trying hypothesis after hypothesis until one is found which fits the phenomena; which one, when found, is to be assumed as true, with no other reservation than that if on re-examination it should appear to assume more than is needful for explaining the phenomena, the superfluous part of the assumption should be cut off. And this without the slightest distinction between the cases in which it may be known beforehand that two different hypotheses cannot lead to the same result, and those in which, for aught we can ever know, the range of suppositions, all equally consistent with the phenomena, may be infinite.

Nevertheless, I do not agree with M. Comte in condemning those who employ themselves in working out into detail the application of these hypotheses to the explanation of ascertained facts; provided they bear in mind that the utmost they can prove is, not that the hypothesis *is*, but that it *may* be true. [. . .]

Some inquiries apparently hypothetical are really inductive. It is necessary, before quitting the subject of hypotheses, to guard against the appearance of reflecting upon the scientific value of several branches of physical inquiry, which, though only in their infancy, I hold to be strictly inductive. There is a great difference between inventing agencies to account for classes of phenomena, and endeavouring, in conformity with known laws, to conjecture what former collocations of known agents may have given birth to individual facts still in existence. The latter is the legitimate operation of inferring from an observed effect, the existence, in time past, of a cause similar to that by which we know it to be produced in all cases in which we have actual experience of its origin. This, for example, is the scope of the inquiries of geology; and they are no more illogical or visionary than judicial inquiries, which also aim at discovering a past event by inference from those of its effects which still subsist. As we can ascertain whether a man was murdered or died a natural death, from the indications exhibited by the corpse, the presence or absence of signs of struggling on the ground or on the adjacent objects, the marks of blood, the footsteps of the supposed murderers, and so on, proceeding throughout on uniformities ascertained by a perfect induction without any mixture of hypothesis; so if we find, on and beneath the surface of our planet, masses exactly similar to deposits from water, or to results of the cooling of matter melted by fire, we may justly conclude that such has been their origin; and if the effects, though similar in kind, are on a far larger scale than any which are now produced, we may rationally, and without hypothesis, conclude either that the causes existed formerly with greater intensity, or that they have operated during an enormous length of time. Further than this no geologist of authority has, since the rise of the present enlightened school of geological speculation, attempted to go. [. . .]

Carl Hempel, "Scientific Inquiry: Invention and Test"

A Case History as an Example

As a simple illustration of some important aspects of scientific inquiry let us consider Semmelweis' work on childbed fever. Ignaz Semmelweis, a physician of Hungarian birth, did this work during the years from 1844 to 1848 at the Vienna General Hospital. As a member of the medical staff of the First Maternity Division in the hospital, Semmelweis was distressed to find that a large proportion of the women who were delivered of their babies in that division contracted a serious and often fatal illness known as puerperal fever or childbed fever. In 1844, as many as 260 out of 3,157 mothers in the First Division, or 8.2 per cent, died of the disease; for 1845, the death rate was 6.8 per cent, and for 1846, it was 11.4 per cent. These figures were all the more alarming because in the adjacent Second Maternity Division of the same hospital, which accommodated almost as many women as the First, the death toll from childbed fever was much lower: 2.3, 2.0, and 2.7 per cent for the same years. In a book that he wrote later on the causation and the prevention of childbed fever, Semmelweis describes his efforts to resolve the dreadful puzzle.

He began by considering various explanations that were current at the time; some of these he rejected out of hand as incompatible with well-established facts; others he subjected to specific tests.

One widely accepted view attributed the ravages of puerperal fever to "epidemic influences", which were vaguely described as "atmospheric-cosmic-telluric changes" spreading over whole districts and causing childbed fever in women in confinement. But how, Semmelweis reasons, could such influences have plagued the First Division for years and yet spared the Second? And how could this view be reconciled with the fact that while the fever was raging in the hospital, hardly a case occurred in the city of Vienna or in its surroundings: a genuine epidemic, such as cholera, would not be so selective. Finally, Semmelweis notes that some of the women admitted to the First Division, living far from the hospital, had been overcome by labor on their way and had given birth in the street: yet despite these adverse conditions, the death rate from childbed fever among these cases of "street birth" was lower than the average for the First Division.

On another view, overcrowding was a cause of mortality in the First Division. But Semmelweis points out that in fact the crowding was heavier in the Second Division, partly as a result of the desperate efforts of patients to avoid assignment to the notorious First Division. He also rejects two similar conjectures that were current, by noting that there were no differences between the two Divisions in regard to diet or general care of the patients.

In 1846, a commission that had been appointed to investigate the matter attributed the prevalence of illness in the First Division to injuries resulting from rough

From *Philosophy of Natural Science* (Englewood Cliffs, NJ: Prentice-Hall, 1966), pp. 3–15, 17–18.

examination by the medical students, all of whom received their obstetrical training in the First Division. Semmelweis notes in refutation of this view that (a) the injuries resulting naturally from the process of birth are much more extensive than those that might be caused by rough examination; (b) the midwives who received their training in the Second Division examined their patients in much the same manner but without the same ill effects; (c) when, in response to the commission's report, the number of medical students was halved and their examinations of the women were reduced to a minimum, the mortality, after a brief decline, rose to higher levels than ever before.

Various psychological explanations were attempted. One of them noted that the First Division was so arranged that a priest bearing the last sacrament to a dying woman had to pass through five wards before reaching the sickroom beyond: the appearance of the priest, preceded by an attendant ringing a bell, was held to have a terrifying and debilitating effect upon the patients in the wards and thus to make them more likely victims of childbed fever. In the Second Division, this adverse factor was absent, since the priest had direct access to the sickroom. Semmelweis decided to test this conjecture. He persuaded the priest to come by a roundabout route and without ringing of the bell, in order to reach the sick chamber silently and unobserved. But the mortality in the First Division did not decrease.

A new idea was suggested to Semmelweis by the observation that in the First Division the women were delivered lying on their backs; in the Second Division, on their sides. Though he thought it unlikely, he decided "like a drowning man clutching at a straw", to test whether this difference in procedure was significant. He introduced the use of the lateral position in the First Division, but again, the mortality remained unaffected.

At last, early in 1847, an accident gave Semmelweis the decisive clue for his solution of the problem. A colleague of his, Kolletschka, received a puncture wound in the finger, from the scalpel of a student with whom he was performing an autopsy, and died after an agonizing illness during which he displayed the same symptoms that Semmelweis had observed in the victims of childbed fever. Although the role of micro-organisms in such infections had not yet been recognized at the time, Semmelweis realized that "cadaveric matter" which the student's scalpel had introduced into Kolletschka's blood stream had caused his colleague's fatal illness. And the similarities between the course of Kolletschka's disease and that of the women in his clinic led Semmelweis to the conclusion that his patients had died of the same kind of blood poisoning: he, his colleagues, and the medical students had been the carriers of the infectious material, for he and his associates used to come to the wards directly from performing dissections in the autopsy room, and examine the women in labor after only superficially washing their hands, which often retained a characteristic foul odor.

Again, Semmelweis put his idea to a test. He reasoned that if he were right, then childbed fever could be prevented by chemically destroying the infectious material adhering to the hands. He therefore issued an order requiring all medical students to wash their hands in a solution of chlorinated lime before making an examination.

The mortality from childbed fever promptly began to decrease, and for the year 1848 it fell to 1.27 per cent in the First Division, compared to 1.33 in the Second.

In further support of his idea, or of his *hypothesis*, as we will also say, Semmelweis notes that it accounts for the fact that the mortality in the Second Division consistently was so much lower: the patients there were attended by midwives, whose training did not include anatomical instruction by dissection of cadavers.

The hypothesis also explained the lower mortality among "street births": women who arrived with babies in arms were rarely examined after admission and thus had a better chance of escaping infection.

Similarly, the hypothesis accounted for the fact that the victims of childbed fever among the newborn babies were all among those whose mothers had contracted the disease during labor; for then the infection could be transmitted to the baby before birth, through the common bloodstream of mother and child, whereas this was impossible when the mother remained healthy.

Further clinical experiences soon led Semmelweis to broaden his hypothesis. On one occasion, for example, he and his associates, having carefully disinfected their hands, examined first a woman in labor who was suffering from a festering cervical cancer; then they proceeded to examine twelve other women in the same room, after only routine washing without renewed disinfection. Eleven of the twelve patients died of puerperal fever. Semmelweis concluded that childbed fever can be caused not only by cadaveric material, but also by "putrid matter derived from living organisms."

Basic Steps in Testing a Hypothesis

We have seen how, in his search for the cause of childbed fever, Semmelweis examined various hypotheses that had been suggested as possible answers. How such hypotheses are arrived at in the first place is an intriguing question which we will consider later. First, however, let us examine how a hypothesis, once proposed, is tested.

Sometimes, the procedure is quite direct. Consider the conjectures that differences in crowding, or in diet, or in general care account for the difference in mortality between the two divisions. As Semmelweis points out, these conflict with readily observable facts. There are no such differences between the divisions; the hypotheses are therefore rejected as false.

But usually the test will be less simple and straightforward. Take the hypothesis attributing the high mortality in the First Division to the dread evoked by the appearance of the priest with his attendant. The intensity of that dread, and especially its effect upon childbed fever, are not as directly ascertainable as are differences in crowding or in diet, and Semmelweis uses an indirect method of testing. He asks himself: Are there any readily observable effects that should occur if the hypothesis were true? And he reasons: *If* the hypothesis were true, *then* an appropriate change in the priest's procedure should be followed by a decline in fatalities.

He checks this implication by a simple experiment and finds it false, and he therefore rejects the hypothesis.

Similarly, to test his conjecture about the position of the women during delivery, he reasons: *If* this conjecture should be true, *then* adoption of the lateral position in the First Division will reduce the mortality. Again, the implication is shown false by his experiment, and the conjecture is discarded.

In the last two cases, the test is based on an argument to the effect that *if* the contemplated hypothesis, say *H*, is true, *then* certain observable events (e.g., decline in mortality) should occur under specified circumstances (e.g., if the priest refrains from walking through the wards, or if the women are delivered in lateral position); or briefly, if *H* is true, then so is *I*, where *I* is a statement describing the observable occurrences to be expected. For convenience, let us say that *I* is inferred from, or implied by, *H*; and let us call *I* a *test implication of the hypothesis H*. (We will later give a more accurate description of the relation between *I* and *H*.)

In our last two examples, experiments show the test implication to be false, and the hypothesis is accordingly rejected. The reasoning that leads to the rejection may be schematized as follows:

> If *H* is true, then so is *I*.
>
> 2*a*] But (as the evidence shows) *I* is not true.
> _____
>
> *H* is not true.

Any argument of this form, called *modus tollens* in logic, is deductively valid; that is, if its premisses (the sentences above the horizontal line) are true, then its conclusion (the sentence below the horizontal line) is unfailingly true as well. Hence, if the premisses of (2*a*) are properly established, the hypothesis *H* that is being tested must indeed be rejected.

Next, let us consider the case where observation or experiment bears out the test implication *I*. From his hypothesis that childbed fever is blood poisoning produced by cadaveric matter, Semmelweis infers that suitable antiseptic measures will reduce fatalities from the disease. This time, experiment shows the test implication to be true. But this favorable outcome does not conclusively prove the hypothesis true, for the underlying argument would have the form

> If *H* is true, then so is *I*.
>
> 2*b*] (As the evidence shows) *I* is true.
> _____
>
> *H* is true.

And this mode of reasoning, which is referred to as the *fallacy of affirming the consequent*, is deductively invalid, that is, its conclusion may be false even if its premisses are true. This is in fact illustrated by Semmelweis' own experience. The initial version of his account of childbed fever as a form of blood poisoning presented infection with cadaveric matter essentially as the one and only source of the disease; and he was right in reasoning that if this hypothesis should be true, then destruction of cadaveric particles by antiseptic washing should reduce the mortality. Furthermore, his experiment did show the test implication to be true. Hence, in this case, the premisses of (2b) were both true. Yet, his hypothesis was false, for as he later discovered, putrid material from living organisms, too, could produce childbed fever.

Thus, the favorable outcome of a test, i.e., the fact that a test implication inferred from a hypothesis is found to be true, does not prove the hypothesis to be true. Even if many implications of a hypothesis have been borne out by careful tests, the hypothesis may still be false. The following argument still commits the fallacy of affirming the consequent:

> If H is true, then so are $I_1, I_2, \ldots, I_n$.
>
> 2c] (As the evidence shows) $I_1, I_2, \ldots, I_n$ are all true.
> _____
>
> H is true.

This, too, can be illustrated by reference to Semmelweis' final hypothesis in its first version. As we noted earlier, his hypothesis also yields the test implications that among cases of street births admitted to the First Division, mortality from puerperal fever should be below the average for the Division, and that infants of mothers who escape the illness do not contract childbed fever; and these implications, too, were borne out by the evidence – even though the first version of the final hypothesis was false.

But the observation that a favorable outcome of however many tests does not afford conclusive proof for a hypothesis should not lead us to think that if we have subjected a hypothesis to a number of tests and all of them have had a favorable outcome, we are no better off than if we had not tested the hypothesis at all. For each of our tests might conceivably have had an unfavorable outcome and might have led to the rejection of the hypothesis. A set of favorable results obtained by testing different test implications, $I_1, I_2, \ldots, I_n$, of a hypothesis, shows that as far as these particular implications are concerned, the hypothesis has been borne out; and while this result does not afford a complete proof of the hypothesis, it provides at least some support, some partial corroboration or confirmation for it. The extent of this support will depend on various aspects of the hypothesis and of the test data.

Let us now consider another example, which will also bring to our attention some further aspects of scientific inquiry.

As was known at Galileo's time, and probably much earlier, a simple suction pump, which draws water from a well by means of a piston that can be raised in the pump barrel, will lift water no higher than about 34 feet above the surface of the well. Galileo was intrigued by this limitation and suggested an explanation for it, which was, however, unsound. After Galileo's death, his pupil Torricelli advanced a new answer. He argued that the earth is surrounded by a sea of air, which, by reason of its weight exerts pressure upon the surface below, and that this pressure upon the surface of the well forces water up the pump barrel when the piston is raised. The maximum length of 34 feet for the water column in the barrel thus reflects simply the total pressure of the atmosphere upon the surface of the well.

It is evidently impossible to determine by direct inspection or observation whether this account is correct, and Torricelli tested it indirectly. He reasoned that *if* his conjecture were true, *then* the pressure of the atmosphere should also be capable of supporting a proportionately shorter column of mercury; indeed, since the specific gravity of mercury is about 14 times that of water, the length of the mercury column should be about 34/14 feet, or slightly less than 2½ feet. He checked this test implication by means of an ingeniously simple device, which was, in effect, the mercury barometer. The well of water is replaced by an open vessel containing mercury; the barrel of the suction pump is replaced by a glass tube sealed off at one end. The tube is completely filled with mercury and closed by placing the thumb tightly over the open end. It is then inverted, the open end is submerged in the mercury well, and the thumb is withdrawn; whereupon the mercury column in the tube drops until its length is about 30 inches – just as predicted by Torricelli's hypothesis.

A further test implication of that hypothesis was noted by Pascal, who reasoned that if the mercury in Torricelli's barometer is counterbalanced by the pressure of the air above the open mercury well, then its length should decrease with increasing altitude, since the weight of the air overhead becomes smaller. At Pascal's request, this implication was checked by his brother-in-law, Périer, who measured the length of the mercury column in the Torricelli barometer at the foot of the Puy-de-Dôme, a mountain some 4,800 feet high, and then carefully carried the apparatus to the top and repeated the measurement there while a control barometer was left at the bottom under the supervision of an assistant. Périer found the mercury column at the top of the mountain more than three inches shorter than at the bottom, whereas the length of the column in the control barometer had remained unchanged throughout the day.

The Role of Induction in Scientific Inquiry

We have considered some scientific investigations in which a problem was tackled by proposing tentative answers in the form of hypotheses that were then tested by deriving from them suitable test implications and checking these by observation or experiment.

But how are suitable hypotheses arrived at in the first place? It is sometimes held that they are inferred from antecedently collected data by means of a procedure called *inductive inference*, as contradistinguished from deductive inference, from which it differs in important respects.

In a deductively valid argument, the conclusion is related to the premises in such a way that if the premises are true then the conclusion cannot fail to be true as well. This requirement is satisfied, for example, by any argument of the following general form:

If *p*, then *q*.
It is not the case that *q*.

It is not the case that *p*.

Brief reflection shows that no matter what particular statements may stand at the places marked by the letters "*p*" and "*q*", the conclusion will certainly be true if the premises are. In fact, our schema represents the argument form called *modus tollens*, to which we referred earlier.

Another type of deductively valid inference is illustrated by this example:

Any sodium salt, when put into the flame of a Bunsen burner, turns the flame yellow.
This piece of rock salt is a sodium salt.

This piece of rock salt, when put into the flame of a Bunsen burner, will turn the flame yellow.

Arguments of the latter kind are often said to lead from the general (here, the premiss about all sodium salts) to the particular (a conclusion about the particular piece of rock salt). Inductive inferences, by contrast, are sometimes described as leading from premises about particular cases to a conclusion that has the character of a general law or principle. For example, from premises to the effect that each of the particular samples of various sodium salts that have so far been subjected to the Bunsen flame test did turn the flame yellow, inductive inference supposedly leads to the general conclusion that all sodium salts, when put into the flame of a Bunsen burner, turn the flame yellow. But in this case, the truth of the premises obviously does *not* guarantee the truth of the conclusion; for even if it is the case that all samples of sodium salts examined so far did turn the Bunsen flame yellow, it remains quite possible that new kinds of sodium salt might yet be found that do not conform to this generalization. Indeed, even some kinds of sodium salt that have already been tested with positive result might conceivably fail to satisfy the generalization under special physical conditions (such as very strong magnetic fields or the like) in which they have not yet been examined. For this reason, the premises of an inductive inference are often said to imply the conclusion only with more or less high probability, whereas the premises of a deductive inference imply the conclusion with certainty.

The idea that in scientific inquiry, inductive inference from antecedently collected data leads to appropriate general principles is clearly embodied in the following account of how a scientist would ideally proceed:

If we try to imagine how a mind of superhuman power and reach, but normal so far as the logical processes of its thought are concerned, ... would use the scientific method, the process would be as follows: First, all facts would be observed and recorded, *without selection* or *a priori* guess as to their relative importance. Secondly, the observed and recorded facts would be analyzed, compared, and classified, *without hypothesis or postulates* other than those necessarily involved in the logic of thought.

Third, from this analysis of the facts generalizations would be inductively drawn as to the relations, classificatory or causal, between them. Fourth, further research would be deductive as well as inductive, employing inferences from previously established generalizations.[1]

This passage distinguishes four stages in an ideal scientific inquiry: (1) observation and recording of all facts, (2) analysis and classification of these facts, (3) inductive derivation of generalizations from them, and (4) further testing of the generalizations. The first two of these stages are specifically assumed not to make use of any guesses or hypotheses as to how the observed facts might be interconnected; this restriction seems to have been imposed in the belief that such preconceived ideas would introduce a bias and would jeopardize the scientific objectivity of the investigation.

But the view expressed in the quoted passage — I will call it *the narrow inductivist conception of scientific inquiry* — is untenable, for several reasons. A brief survey of these can serve to amplify and to supplement our earlier remarks on scientific procedure.

First, a scientific investigation as here envisaged could never get off the ground. Even its first phase could never be carried out, for a collection of *all* the facts would have to await the end of the world, so to speak; and even all the facts *up to now* cannot be collected, since there are an infinite number and variety of them. Are we to examine, for example, all the grains of sand in all the deserts and on all the beaches, and are we to record their shapes, their weights, their chemical composition, their distances from each other, their constantly changing temperature, and their equally changing distance from the center of the moon? Are we to record the floating thoughts that cross our minds in the tedious process? The shapes of the clouds overhead, the changing color of the sky? The construction and the trade name of our writing equipment? Our own life histories and those of our fellow investigators? All these, and untold other things, are, after all, among "all the facts up to now".

Perhaps, then, all that should be required in the first phase is that all the *relevant* facts be collected. But relevant to what? Though the author does not mention this, let us suppose that the inquiry is concerned with a specified *problem*. Should we not then begin by collecting all the facts — or better, all available data — relevant to that problem? This notion still makes no clear sense. Semmelweis sought to solve one specific problem, yet he collected quite different kinds of data at different stages of his inquiry. And rightly so; for what particular sorts of data it is reasonable to collect is not determined by the problem under study, but by a tentative answer to it that the investigator entertains in the form of a conjecture or hypothesis. Given the conjecture that mortality from childbed fever was increased by the terrifying appearance of the priest and his attendant with the death bell, it was relevant to collect data on the consequences of having the priest change his routine; but it would have been totally irrelevant to check what would happen if doctors and

---

[1] A. B. Wolfe, "Functional Economics," in *The Trend of Economics*, ed. R. G. Tugwell (New York: Alfred A. Knopf, Inc., 1924), p. 450 (italics are quoted).

students disinfected their hands before examining their patients. With respect to Semmelweis' eventual contamination hypothesis, data of the latter kind were clearly relevant, and those of the former kind totally irrelevant.

Empirical "facts" or findings, therefore, can be qualified as logically relevant or irrelevant only in reference to a given hypothesis, but not in reference to a given problem.

Suppose now that a hypothesis H has been advanced as a tentative answer to a research problem: what kinds of data would be relevant to H? Our earlier examples suggest an answer: A finding is relevant to H if either its occurrence or its non-occurrence can be inferred from H. Take Torricelli's hypothesis, for example. As we saw, Pascal inferred from it that the mercury column in a barometer should grow shorter if the barometer were carried up a mountain. Therefore, any finding to the effect that this did indeed happen in a particular case is relevant to the hypotheses; but so would be the finding that the length of the mercury column had remained unchanged or that it had decreased and then increased during the ascent, for such findings would refute Pascal's test implication and would thus disconfirm Torricelli's hypothesis. Data of the former kind may be called positively, or favorably, relevant to the hypothesis; those of the latter kind negatively, or unfavorably, relevant.

In sum, the maxim that data should be gathered without guidance by antecedent hypotheses about the connections among the facts under study is self-defeating, and it is certainly not followed in scientific inquiry. On the contrary, tentative hypotheses are needed to give direction to a scientific investigation. Such hypotheses determine, among other things, what data should be collected at a given point in a scientific investigation.

It is of interest of note that social scientists trying to check a hypothesis by reference to the vast store of facts recorded by the U.S. Bureau of the Census, or by other data-gathering organizations, sometimes find to their disappointment that the values of some variable that plays a central role in the hypothesis have nowhere been systematically recorded. This remark is not, of course, intended as a criticism of data gathering: those engaged in the process no doubt try to select facts that might prove relevant to future hypotheses; the observation is simply meant to illustrate the impossibility of collecting "all the relevant data" without knowledge of the hypotheses to which the data are to have relevance.

The second stage envisaged in our quoted passage is open to similar criticism. A set of empirical "facts" can be analyzed and classified in many different ways, most of which will be unilluminating for the purposes of a given inquiry. Semmelweis could have classified the women in the maternity wards according to criteria such as age, place of residence, marital status, dietary habits, and so forth; but information on these would have provided no clue to a patient's prospects of becoming a victim of childbed fever. What Semmelweis sought were criteria that would be significantly connected with those prospects; and for this purpose, as he eventually found, it was illuminating to single out those women who were attended by medical personnel with contaminated hands; for it was with this characteristic, or with the corresponding class of patients, that high mortality from childbed fever was associated.

Thus, if a particular way of analyzing and classifying empirical findings is to lead to an explanation of the phenomena concerned, then it must be based on hypotheses about how those phenomena are connected; without such hypotheses, analysis and classification are blind.

Our critical reflections on the first two stages of inquiry as envisaged in the quoted passage also undercut the notion that hypotheses are introduced only in the third stage, by inductive inference from antecedently collected data. But some further remarks on the subject should be added here.

Induction is sometimes conceived as a method that leads, by means of mechanically applicable rules, from observed facts to corresponding general principles. In this case, the rules of inductive inference would provide effective canons of scientific discovery; induction would be a mechanical procedure analogous to the familiar routine for the multiplication of integers, which leads, in a finite number of predetermined and mechanically performable steps, to the corresponding product. Actually, however, no such general and mechanical induction procedure is available at present; otherwise, the much studied problem of the causation of cancer, for example, would hardly have remained unsolved to this day. Nor can the discovery of such a procedure ever be expected. For – to mention one reason – scientific hypotheses and theories are usually couched in terms that do not occur at all in the description of the empirical findings on which they rest, and which they serve to explain. For example, theories about the atomic and subatomic structure of matter contain terms such as "atom", "electron", "proton", "neutron", "psi-function", etc.; yet they are based on laboratory findings about the spectra of various gases, tracks in cloud and bubble chambers, quantitative aspects of chemical reactions, and so forth – all of which can be described without the use of those "theoretical terms". Induction rules of the kind here envisaged would therefore have to provide a mechanical routine for constructing, on the basis of the given data, a hypothesis or theory stated in terms of some quite novel concepts, which are nowhere used in the description of the data themselves. Surely, no general mechanical rule of procedure can be expected to achieve this. Could there be a general rule, for example, which, when applied to the data available to Galileo concerning the limited effectiveness of suction pumps, would, by a mechanical routine, produce a hypothesis based on the concept of a sea of air?

To be sure, mechanical procedures for inductively "inferring" a hypothesis on the basis of given data may be specifiable for situations of special, and relatively simple, kinds. For example, if the length of a copper rod has been measured at several different temperatures, the resulting pairs of associated values for temperature and length may be represented by points in a plane coordinate system, and a curve may be drawn through them in accordance with some particular rule of curve fitting. The curve then graphically represents a general quantitative hypothesis that expresses the length of the rod as a specific function of its temperature. But note that this hypothesis contains no novel terms; it is expressible in terms of the concepts of temperature and length, which are used also in describing the data. Moreover, the choice of "associated" values of temperature and length as data already presupposes a guiding hypothesis; namely, that with each value of the temperature, exactly one value of the length of the copper rod is associated, so that its length is indeed a function of its temperature alone. The mechanical curve-fitting routine then serves only to select a particular function as the appropriate one. This point is important; for suppose that instead of a copper rod, we examine a body of nitrogen gas enclosed in a cylindrical container with a movable piston as a lid, and that we measure its volume at several different temperatures. If we were to use this procedure in an effort to obtain from our data a *general* hypothesis representing the volume of the gas as a function of its temperature, we would fail, because the volume of a gas is a function both of its temperature and of the pressure exerted upon it, so that at the same temperature, the given gas may assume different volumes.

Thus, even in these simple cases, the mechanical procedures for the construction of a hypothesis do only part of the job, for they presuppose an antecedent, less specific hypothesis (i.e., that a certain physical variable is a function of one single other variable), which is not obtainable by the same procedure.

There are, then, no generally applicable "rules of induction", by which hypotheses or theories can be mechanically derived or inferred from empirical data. The transition from data to theory requires creative imagination. Scientific hypotheses and theories are not *derived* from observed facts, but *invented* in order to account for them. They constitute guesses at the connections that might obtain between the phenomena under study, at uniformities and patterns that might underlie their occurrence. [. . .]

Scientific knowledge, as we have seen, is not arrived at by applying some inductive inference procedure to antecedently collected data, but rather by what is often called "the method of hypothesis", i.e. by inventing hypotheses as tentative answers to a problem under study, and then subjecting these to empirical test. It will be part of such test to see whether the hypothesis is borne out by whatever relevant findings may have been gathered before its formulation; an acceptable hypothesis will have to fit the available relevant data. Another part of the test will consist in deriving new test implications from the hypothesis and checking these by suitable observations or experiments. As we noted earlier, even extensive testing with entirely favorable results does not establish a hypothesis conclusively, but provides only more or less strong support for it. [. . .]

Karl Popper, "Philosophy of Science: A Personal Report"

Mr. Turnbull had predicted evil consequences, both in the House and out of it, and was now doing the best in his power to bring about the verification of his own prophecies. (Anthony Trollope)

From *British Philosophy in Mid-Century: A Cambridge Symposium*, ed. C. M. Mace (London: George Allen and Unwin, 1957), pp. 155–63, 171–2, 178–9, 183.

When I received the list of participants in this course and realized that I had been asked to speak to philosophical colleagues, I came to the conclusion, after some hesitation and consultation, that you would probably prefer me to speak about those problems which interest me most, and about those developments with which I am most intimately acquainted. I therefore decided to do what I have never done before: to give you a report about my own work in the field of the philosophy of science, since the autumn of 1919 when I first began to grapple with the problem, "*When should a theory be ranked as scientific?*" or, "*Is there a criterion of the scientific character or status of a theory?*"

The problem which troubled me at the time was neither, When is a theory true? nor, When is a theory acceptable? My problem was different. *I wished to distinguish between science and pseudo-science*; knowing very well that science often errs, and that pseudo-science may happen to stumble upon the truth.

I knew, of course, what was the most widely accepted answer to my problem: that science is distinguished from pseudo-science – or from "metaphysics" – by its *empirical method*; that it is essentially inductive, proceeding from observation and experiment. But this did not satisfy me. On the contrary, I often formulated my problem as one of distinguishing between a genuinely empirical method and a non-empirical or even a pseudo-empirical one; i.e. a method which does in fact appeal to observation and experiment but does not come up to scientific standards. Astrology, with its stupendous mass of empirical evidence based on observed horoscopes and biographies, is a case in point.

But this was not the example which led me to my problem; and it may perhaps interest you if I briefly describe the atmosphere in which my problem arose. Following the collapse of the Austrian Empire, there had been a revolution in Austria; the air was full of revolutionary slogans, ideas, and new and often wild theories. Among the theories which interested me, Einstein's theory of relativity was no doubt by far the most important. Three others were Marx's theory of history, Freud's psycho-analysis, and Alfred Adler's so-called "individual psychology".

There was a lot of popular nonsense talked about these theories, and especially about relativity (as still happens even today) but I was fortunate in those who introduced me to the study of this theory. We all – the little circle of students to which I belonged – were thrilled with the result of the eclipse observation which in 1919 brought the first important confirmation of Einstein's theory of gravitation. It was a great experience for us – one which had a lasting influence on my intellectual development.

The three other theories I have mentioned were also widely discussed among students at that time. I myself happened to come into personal contact with Alfred Adler, and even to co-operate with him in his social work among the children and young people in the working-class districts of Vienna where he had established social guidance clinics.

It was during the summer of 1919 that I began to feel more and more dissatisfied with these three theories – the Marxist theory of history, psycho-analysis, and individual psychology – and dubious about their claims to scientific status. One might say that my problem first took the form, "What is wrong with Marxism, psycho-analysis, and individual psychology? Why are they so different from mathematical physics and especially from the theory of relativity?"

In order to appreciate this contrast, I might mention that few of us at the time would have said that they believed in the *truth* of Einstein's theory of gravitation. This shows that it was not any doubt of the *truth* of these other three theories which bothered me: it was a different thing. Yet neither was it that I merely felt mathematical physics to be more exact than the sociological or psychological type of theory. Thus what worried me was neither the problem of truth, at that stage at least, nor the problem of exactness or of measurability. It was rather that I felt that these other three theories posed as sciences while in fact they were of the character of primitive myths rather than of science; that they resembled astrology rather than astronomy.

I found that those of my friends who were admirers of Marx, Freud, and Adler, were strongly impressed by a number of points shared by these theories, and especially by their apparent *explanatory power*. These theories appeared to be able to explain practically everything that happened, within the fields to which they referred. Their study had the effect of an intellectual conversion or revelation – of opening your eyes to the truth hidden from those not yet initiated. Once your eyes were thus opened, you saw confirming instances everywhere: the world was full of *verifications* of the theory. Whatever happened always confirmed it. Thus its truth appeared obvious; and unbelievers were, clearly, people who did not want to see the truth – either because it was against their class interest, or because of their repressions which were still "unanalysed", and crying aloud for treatment.

The most characteristic element in the situation seemed to me the incessant stream of confirmations, of observations which "verified" the theories in question; and this was the point constantly emphasized by their adherents. A Marxist could not open a newspaper without finding on every page confirming evidence for his interpretation of history – not only in the news, but also in the way it was presented (revealing the class bias of the paper), and especially, of course, in what the paper did *not* say. The Freudian analysts emphasized that their theories were daily, nay, hourly, verified by their "clinical observations". And as to Adler, I was much impressed by a personal experience. Once, in 1919, I reported to him a case which to me did not seem particularly Adlerian, but which he found no difficulty whatever in analysing in terms of his theory of inferiority feelings, although he had not even seen the child. Slightly shocked, I asked him how he could be so sure about all this. "Because of my thousandfold experience", he replied; whereupon I could not help saying: "And with this new case, I suppose, your experience is now even thousand-and-one-fold."

What I had in mind was that his previous observations may not have been much sounder than this new one; that each had been interpreted in the light of "previous experience", and, at the same time, counted as additional confirmation. What, I asked myself, did it confirm? No more than the possibility of interpreting a case in the light of the theory. But this meant very little, I reflected, since every conceivable case could be interpreted in the light of Adler's theory, or equally of Freud's. To illustrate this, take two very different cases of human behaviour – one, let us say, of a man who pushes a child into the water with the intention of drowning it; and another, of a man who sacrifices his life in an attempt to save the child. Each of these two cases can be explained with equal ease in Freudian as well as in Adlerian terms. According to Freud, the first man suffered from repression (say, of some component of his Oedipus complex), while the second had achieved sublimation. According to Adler, the first man suffered from feelings of inferiority (producing, perhaps, the need to prove to himself that he dared to commit a crime, etc.), and so did the second man (whose need was to prove to himself that he dared to rescue the child). I could not think of any conceivable instance of human behaviour which could not be interpreted in terms of either theory. It was precisely this fact – that they always fitted, that they were always confirmed – which, in the eyes of their admirers, constituted the strongest arguments in favour of these theories. It began to dawn on me that this apparent strength was in fact their greatest weakness.

With Einstein's theory, the situation was strikingly different. Take one typical instance – Einstein's prediction, just then confirmed by the findings of Eddington's expedition. Einstein's gravitational theory had led to the result that light was attracted by heavy bodies (such as the sun) very much as material bodies were attracted. It could be calculated that, as a consequence, light from a distant fixed star whose apparent position was close to the sun would reach the earth from such a direction that the star would seem to be slightly shifted away from the sun; or in other words, that stars close to the sun would look as if they had moved a little away from the sun, and from one another. This is a thing which cannot normally be observed since normally such stars are invisible, owing to the sun's overwhelming brightness; but during an eclipse, it is possible to take photographs showing such stars. If the same constellation is photographed without the sun, one can measure the distances on the two photographs, and check the predicted effect.

Now the impressive thing about this case is the *risk* involved in a prediction of this kind. If observation shows that the predicted effect is definitely absent, then the theory is simply refuted. The theory is *incompatible with certain possible results of observation* – in fact, with results which, before Einstein, everybody would have expected. This is a vastly different situation from the one I have previously described when it turned out that the theories in question were compatible with the most divergent human behaviour, so that it was practically impossible to describe human behaviour which could not be interpreted as being in agreement with these theories.

These considerations led me, in the winter of 1919–20, to conclusions which I may now reformulate as follows.

(1) It is easy to obtain confirmations, or verifications, for nearly every theory – if we look for confirmations.

(2) Confirmations should count only if they are the result of *risky predictions*; that is to say, if, unenlightened by the theory in question, we should have expected an

event which was incompatible with the theory – an event which, had it happened, would have refuted the theory.

(3) Every "good" scientific theory is one which forbids certain things to happen; the more a theory forbids, the better it is.

(4) A theory which is not refutable by any conceivable event is non-scientific. Irrefutability is not a virtue of a theory (as people often think) but a vice.

(5) Every genuine *test* of a theory is an attempt to falsify it, or to refute it. Testability is falsifiability; but there are degrees of testability: some theories are more testable, more exposed to refutation, than others; they take, as it were, greater risks.

(6) Confirming evidence does not count *except when it is the result of a genuine test of the theory*; and this means that it can be presented as an unsuccessful but serious attempt to falsify the theory.

(7) Some genuinely testable theories, when found to be false, are still upheld by their admirers – for example, by introducing *ad hoc* some auxiliary assumption, or by re-interpreting the theory *ad hoc* in such a way that it escapes refutation. Such a procedure is always possible, but it rescues the theory from refutation only at the price of destroying or at least lowering its scientific status. (I later described such a rescuing operation as a "*conventionalist twist*", or as a "*conventionalist stratagem*".)

One can sum up all this by saying that *falsifiability, or refutability, is a criterion of the scientific status of a theory.*

I may perhaps exemplify this with the help of the various theories so far mentioned. Einstein's theory of gravitation clearly satisfies the criterion of falsifiability. Even if our measuring instruments at the time did not allow us to pronounce the result of the test with complete assurance, there was clearly a possibility of refuting the theory.

Astrology did not pass the test. Clearly, astrologers were impressed, and misled, by what they believed to be confirming evidence – so much so that they were quite unimpressed by any unfavourable evidence. Moreover, by making their interpretations and prophecies sufficiently vague, they were able to explain away anything that might have been a refutation of the theory, had the theory and the prophecies been more precise. In order to escape falsification, they destroyed the testability of their theory. It is a typical soothsayer's trick to predict things so vaguely that the predictions can hardly fail; that they become irrefutable.

The Marxist theory of history, in spite of the serious efforts of some of its founders and followers, ultimately adopted this soothsaying practice. In some of its earlier formulations (for example in Marx's analysis of the character of the "coming social revolution"), their predictions were testable, but in fact falsified.[1] Yet instead of recognizing this, the followers of Marx re-interpreted both the theory and the evidence to make them agree. In this way they rescued the theory from refutation; but they did so at the price of adopting a device which made it irrefutable. They thus gave a "conventionalist twist" to the theory; and by this stratagem, they destroyed its much advertised claim to scientific status.

[1] See, for example, my *Open Society and Its Enemies* (London, 1945), chapter 15, section iii, and notes 13–14.

The two psycho-analytic theories were in a different class. They were simply non-testable, irrefutable. There was no conceivable human behaviour which could contradict them. This does not mean that Freud and Adler were not seeing certain things correctly; I personally do not doubt that much of what they say is of considerable importance, and may well play its part one day in a psychological science which is testable. But it does mean that the "clinical observations" which analysts naively believe to confirm their theory[2] cannot do this any more than the daily confirmations which astrologers find in their practice. And as for Freud's epic of the Egos, the Super Egos, and the Ids, no substantially stronger claim to scientific status can be made for it than for Homer's collected stories from the Olympus. These theories describe some facts, but in the manner of myths. They contain most interesting psychological suggestions, but not in a testable form.

At the same time, I realized that such myths may be developed, and become testable; that, historically speaking, all (or nearly all) scientific theories originate from myths, and that a myth may contain important anticipations of scientific theories. Examples are Empedocles' theory of evolution by trial and error, or Parmenides' myth of the unchanging block universe in which nothing ever happens and which, if we add another dimension, becomes Einstein's block universe (in which too, nothing ever happens, since everything is, four-dimensionally speaking, determined and laid down from the beginning). I thus felt that, if a theory is found to be non-scientific, or "metaphysical" (as we might say), it is not thereby found to be unimportant, or insignificant, or "meaningless", or "nonsensical".[3] But it cannot claim to be backed by empirical evidence in the scientific sense – although it may easily be, in some genetic sense, the "result of observation".

---

[2] "Clinical observations", like all other observations, are *interpretations in the light of theories*; and for this reason alone, they are apt to seem to support those theories in the light of which they were interpreted. But real support can be obtained only by observations undertaken as tests (by "attempted refutations"); and for this purpose, *criteria of refutation* have to be laid down beforehand: it must be agreed which observable situations, if actually observed, mean that the theory is refuted. But what kind of clinical responses would refute, to the satisfaction of the analyst, not merely a particular analytic diagnosis but psycho-analysis itself? And have such criteria ever been discussed, or agreed upon by analysts? Is there not, on the contrary, a whole family of analytic concepts, such as "ambivalence" (I do not suggest that there is no such thing as ambivalence), which would make it difficult, if not impossible, to agree upon such criteria? Moreover, how much headway has been made in investigating the question of the extent to which the (conscious or unconscious) expectations and theories held by the analyst influence the "clinical responses" of the patient? (I say nothing about the conscious attempts to influence the patient by proposing interpretations to him, etc.) Years ago, I introduced the term "*Oedipus effect*" to describe the influence of a theory, or expectation, or prediction, *upon the event which it predicts* or describes: it will be remembered that the causal chain leading to Oedipus' parricide was started by the oracle's prediction of this event. This is a characteristic and recurrent theme of such myths, but one which seems to have failed to attract the interest of the analysts; perhaps not quite accidentally.

[3] The case of astrology, nowadays a typical pseudo-science, may illustrate this point. It was attacked by Aristotelians and other rationalists, down to Newton's day, for the wrong reason – for its now accepted assertion that the planets had an "influence" upon terrestrial ("sublunar") events. In fact, Newton's theory of gravity, and especially the lunar theory of the tides, was an offspring of astrological lore, and it thus comes from the same stable as, for example, the theory that "influenza" epidemics are due to an astral "influence".

(There were a great many other theories of this pre-scientific or pseudo-scientific character, some of them, unfortunately, as influential as the Marxist interpretation of history; for example, the racialist interpretation of history – another of those impressive and all-explanatory theories which act like revelations upon weak minds.)

Thus the problem which I tried to solve by proposing the criterion of falsifiability was neither a problem of meaningfulness or significance, nor a problem of truth or acceptability. It was the problem of drawing a line (as well as this can be done) between the statements, or systems of statements, of the empirical sciences, and all other statements – whether they are of a religious or of a metaphysical character, or simply pseudo-scientific. Years later – it must have been in 1928 or 1929 – I called this first problem of mine the *"problem of demarcation"*. The criterion of falsifiability is a solution of this problem of demarcation, for it says that, in order to be ranked as scientific, statements or systems of statements must be capable of conflicting with possible, or conceivable, observations. [. . .]

The belief that science proceeds from observation to theory is still so widely and so firmly held that my denial of it is often met with incredulity. It has even been suspected of being insincere – a denial of what nobody in his senses can doubt.

But in fact, the belief that we can start with pure observations only, without anything in the nature of a theory, is absurd; as may be illustrated by the story of the man who dedicated his life to natural science: wrote down everything he could observe: and bequeathed his priceless collection of observations to the Royal Society, to be used as inductive evidence. This story should show us that though beetles may profitably be collected, observations may not.

I once tried to bring home the same point to a group of physics students in Vienna, twenty-five years ago, by beginning a lecture with the following instructions: "Take pencil and paper; carefully observe, and write down what you have observed!" They asked, of course, *what* I wanted them to observe. Clearly, the instruction "observe!" is absurd. (It is not even proper English.) Observation is always selective. It needs a chosen object, a definite task, an interest, a point of view, a problem. And its description presupposes a descriptive language, with property words; it presupposes similarity, and classification, which, again, presupposes interests, points of view, and problems. "A hungry animal", writes Katz,[4] "divides the environment into edible and inedible things. An animal in flight sees roads to escape and hiding places . . . Generally speaking, objects change . . . according to the needs of the animal." We may add that objects can be classified, and can become similar or dissimilar, *only* in this way – by being related to needs and interests. This rule applies not only to animals but also to scientists. For the animal, a point of view is provided by its needs, the task of the moment, and its expectations; for the scientist, by his theoretical interests, the special problems under investigation, and the theories which he accepts as a kind of background: his frame of reference, his "horizon of expectations". [. . .]

---

[4] D. Katz, *Animals and Men*, ch. 7.

Nevertheless, the rôle of logical argument, of deductive logical reasoning, remains all-important for the critical approach; not because it allows us to prove our theories, or to infer them from observation statements, but because only by purely deductive reasoning is it possible for us to discover what our theories imply, and thus to criticize them effectively. Criticism, I said, is an attempt to find the weak spots of a theory, and these, as a rule, can be found only in the more remote logical consequences which can be derived from it. It is here that pure logical reasoning plays its important part in science.

Hume was right in stressing that our theories cannot be validly inferred from what we can know to be true – neither from observations nor from anything else. He concluded from this that our belief in them was irrational. If "belief" means here our inability to doubt the constancy of our natural laws, then Hume is again right: this kind of dogmatic belief has, one might say, a physiological rather than a rational basis. If, however, the term "belief" is taken to cover our critical acceptance of scientific theories – a tentative acceptance combined with eagerness to revise the theory if we succeed in designing a test which it cannot pass – then Hume was wrong. In such an acceptance of theories there is nothing irrational. There is not even anything irrational in relying, for practical purposes, upon well tested theories, for no more rational course of action is open to us.

Assume that we have deliberately made it our task to live in this unknown world of ours; to adjust ourselves to it as well as we can; to take advantage of the opportunities we can find in it; and to explain it, *if* this is possible (we need not assume that it is), and as far as it is possible, with the help of laws and explanatory theories. *If we have made this our task, then there is no more rational procedure than the method of trial and error – of conjecture and refutation*: of boldly proposing theories; of trying our best to show that these are erroneous; and of accepting them tentatively if our critical efforts are unsuccessful. [. . .]

As long as a theory stands up to the severest tests we can design, it is accepted; if it does not, it is rejected. But it is never inferred, in any sense, from the empirical evidence. There is neither a psychological nor a logical induction. *Only the falsity of the theory can be inferred from empirical evidence, and this inference is a purely deductive one.*

Hume showed that it is not possible to infer a theory from observation statements; but this does not affect the possibility of refuting a theory by observation statements. The full appreciation of this possibility makes the relation between theories and observations perfectly clear. [. . .]

Thomas Kuhn, "Scientific Revolutions"

The Route to Normal Science

In this essay, "normal science" means research firmly based upon one or more past scientific achievements, achievements that some particular scientific community

Selections from *The Structure of Scientific Revolutions*, 2nd edn (Chicago: University of Chicago Press, 1970), pp. 10–20, 35–41, 92–5, 103, 109–11, 128–9.

acknowledges for a time as supplying the foundation for its further practice. Today such achievements are recounted, though seldom in their original form, by science textbooks, elementary and advanced. These textbooks expound the body of accepted theory, illustrate many or all of its successful applications, and compare these applications with exemplary observations and experiments. Before such books became popular early in the nineteenth century (and until even more recently in the newly matured sciences), many of the famous classics of science fulfilled a similar function. Aristotle's *Physica*, Ptolemy's *Almagest*, Newton's *Principia* and *Opticks*, Franklin's *Electricity*, Lavoisier's *Chemistry*, and Lyell's *Geology* – these and many other works served for a time implicitly to define the legitimate problems and methods of a research field for succeeding generations of practitioners. They were able to do so because they shared two essential characteristics. Their achievement was sufficiently unprecedented to attract an enduring group of adherents away from competing modes of scientific activity. Simultaneously, it was sufficiently open-ended to leave all sorts of problems for the redefined group of practitioners to resolve.

Achievements that share these two characteristics I shall henceforth refer to as "paradigms," a term that relates closely to "normal science." By choosing it, I mean to suggest that some accepted examples of actual scientific practice – examples which include law, theory, application, and instrumentation together – provide models from which spring particular coherent traditions of scientific research. These are the traditions which the historian describes under such rubrics as "Ptolemaic astronomy" (or "Copernican"), "Aristotelian dynamics" (or "Newtonian"), "corpuscular optics" (or "wave optics"), and so on. The study of paradigms, including many that are far more specialized than those named illustratively above, is what mainly prepares the student for membership in the particular scientific community with which he will later practice. Because he there joins men who learned the bases of their field from the same concrete models, his subsequent practice will seldom evoke overt disagreement over fundamentals. Men whose research is based on shared paradigms are committed to the same rules and standards for scientific practice. That commitment and the apparent consensus it produces are prerequisites for normal science, i.e., for the genesis and continuation of a particular research tradition.

Because in this essay the concept of a paradigm will often substitute for a variety of familiar notions, more will need to be said about the reasons for its introduction. Why is the concrete scientific achievement, as a locus of professional commitment, prior to the various concepts, laws, theories, and points of view that may be abstracted from it? In what sense is the shared paradigm a fundamental unit for the student of scientific development, a unit that cannot be fully reduced to logically atomic components which might function in its stead? Answers to these questions and to others like them will prove basic to an understanding both of normal science and of the associated concept of paradigms. That more abstract discussion will depend, however, upon a previous exposure to examples of normal science or of paradigms in operation. In particular, both these related concepts will be clarified by noting that there can be a sort of scientific research without paradigms, or at least without any so unequivocal and so binding as the ones named above. Acquisition of a paradigm and of the more esoteric type of research it permits is a sign of maturity in the development of any given scientific field.

If the historian traces the scientific knowledge of any selected group of related phenomena backward in time, he is likely to encounter some minor variant of a pattern here illustrated from the history of physical optics. Today's physics textbooks tell the student that light is photons, i.e., quantum-mechanical entities that exhibit some characteristics of waves and some of particles. Research proceeds accordingly, or rather according to the more elaborate and mathematical characterization from which this usual verbalization is derived. That characterization of light is, however, scarcely half a century old. Before it was developed by Planck, Einstein, and others early in this century, physics texts taught that light was transverse wave motion, a conception rooted in a paradigm that derived ultimately from the optical writings of Young and Fresnel in the early nineteenth century. Nor was the wave theory the first to be embraced by almost all practitioners of optical science. During the eighteenth century the paradigm for this field was provided by Newton's *Opticks*, which taught that light was material corpuscles. At that time physicists sought evidence, as the early wave theorists had not, of the pressure exerted by light particles impinging on solid bodies.[1]

These transformations of the paradigms of physical optics are scientific revolutions, and the successive transition from one paradigm to another via revolution is the usual developmental pattern of mature science. It is not, however, the pattern characteristic of the period before Newton's work, and that is the contrast that concerns us here. No period between remote antiquity and the end of the seventeenth century exhibited a single generally accepted view about the nature of light. Instead there were a number of competing schools and subschools, most of them espousing one variant or another of Epicurean, Aristotelian, or Platonic theory. One group took light to be particles emanating from material bodies; for another it was a modification of the medium that intervened between the body and the eye; still another explained light in terms of an interaction of the medium with an emanation from the eye; and there were other combinations and modifications besides. Each of the corresponding schools derived strength from its relation to some particular metaphysic, and each emphasized, as paradigmatic observations, the particular cluster of optical phenomena that its own theory could do most to explain. Other observations were dealt with by *ad hoc* elaborations, or they remained as outstanding problems for further research.[2]

At various times all these schools made significant contributions to the body of concepts, phenomena, and techniques from which Newton drew the first nearly uniformly accepted paradigm for physical optics. Any definition of the scientist that

---

[1] Joseph Priestley, *The History and Present State of Discoveries Relating to Vision, Light, and Colours* (London, 1772), pp. 385–90.

[2] Vasco Ronchi, *Histoire de la lumière*, trans. Jean Taton (Paris, 1956), chaps. i–iv.

excludes at least the more creative members of these various schools will exclude their modern successors as well. Those men were scientists. Yet anyone examining a survey of physical optics before Newton may well conclude that, though the field's practitioners were scientists, the net result of their activity was something less than science. Being able to take no common body of belief for granted, each writer on physical optics felt forced to build his field anew from its foundations. In doing so, his choice of supporting observation and experiment was relatively free, for there was no standard set of methods or of phenomena that every optical writer felt forced to employ and explain. Under these circumstances, the dialogue of the resulting books was often directed as much to the members of other schools as it was to nature. That pattern is not unfamiliar in a number of creative fields today, nor is it incompatible with significant discovery and invention. It is not, however, the pattern of development that physical optics acquired after Newton and that other natural sciences make familiar today.

The history of electrical research in the first half of the eighteenth century provides a more concrete and better known example of the way a science develops before it acquires its first universally received paradigm. During that period there were almost as many views about the nature of electricity as there were important electrical experimenters, men like Hauksbee, Gray, Desaguliers, Du Fay, Nollett, Watson, Franklin, and others. All their numerous concepts of electricity had something in common – they were partially derived from one or another version of the mechanico-corpuscular philosophy that guided all scientific research of the day. In addition, all were components of real scientific theories, of theories that had been drawn in part from experiment and observation and that partially determined the choice and interpretation of additional problems undertaken in research. Yet though all the experiments were electrical and though most of the experimenters read each other's works, their theories had no more than a family resemblance.[3]

One early group of theories, following seventeenth-century practice, regarded attraction and frictional generation as the fundamental electrical phenomena. This group tended to treat repulsion as a secondary effect due to some sort of mechanical rebounding and also to postpone for as long as possible both discussion and systematic research on Gray's newly discovered effect, electrical conduction. Other "electricians" (the term is their own) took attraction and repulsion to be equally elementary manifestations of electricity and modified their theories and research accordingly. (Actually, this group is remarkably small – even Franklin's theory never quite accounted for the mutual repulsion of two negatively charged bodies.) But they had as much difficulty as the first group in accounting simultaneously for any but the simplest conduction effects. Those effects, however, provided the starting point for still a third group, one which tended to speak of electricity as a "fluid" that could run through conductors rather than as an "effluvium" that

---

[3] Duane Roller and Duane H. D. Roller, *The Development of the Concept of Electric Charge: Electricity from the Greeks to Coulomb* ("Harvard Case Histories in Experimental Science," Case 8; Cambridge, Mass., 1954); and I. B. Cohen, *Franklin and Newton: An Inquiry into Speculative Newtonian Experimental Science and Franklin's Work in Electricity as an Example Thereof* (Philadelphia, 1956), chaps. vii–xii.

emanated from non–conductors. This group, in its turn, had difficulty reconciling its theory with a number of attractive and repulsive effects. Only through the work of Franklin and his immediate successors did a theory arise that could account with something like equal facility for very nearly all these effects and that therefore could and did provide a subsequent generation of "electricians" with a common paradigm for its research.

Excluding those fields, like mathematics and astronomy, in which the first firm paradigms date from prehistory and also those, like biochemistry, that arose by division and recombination of specialties already matured, the situations outlined above are historically typical. Though it involves my continuing to employ the unfortunate simplification that tags an extended historical episode with a single and somewhat arbitrarily chosen name (e.g., Newton or Franklin), I suggest that similar fundamental disagreements characterized, for example, the study of motion before Aristotle and of statics before Archimedes, the study of heat before Black, of chemistry before Boyle and Boerhaave, and of historical geology before Hutton. In parts of biology – the study of heredity, for example – the first universally received paradigms are still more recent; and it remains an open question what parts of social science have yet acquired such paradigms at all. History suggests that the road to a firm research consensus is extraordinarily arduous.

History also suggests, however, some reasons for the difficulties encountered on that road. In the absence of a paradigm or some candidate for paradigm, all of the facts that could possibly pertain to the development of a given science are likely to seem equally relevant. As a result, early fact-gathering is a far more nearly random activity than the one that subsequent scientific development makes familiar. Furthermore, in the absence of a reason for seeking some particular form of more recondite information, early fact-gathering is usually restricted to the wealth of data that lie ready to hand. The resulting pool of facts contains those accessible to casual observation and experiment together with some of the more esoteric data retrievable from established crafts like medicine, calendar making, and metallurgy. Because the crafts are one readily accessible source of facts that could not have been casually discovered, technology has often played a vital role in the emergence of new sciences.

But though this sort of fact-collecting has been essential to the origin of many significant sciences, anyone who examines, for example, Pliny's encyclopedic writings or the Baconian natural histories of the seventeenth century will discover that it produces a morass. One somehow hesitates to call the literature that results scientific. The Baconian "histories" of heat, color, wind, mining, and so on, are filled with information, some of it recondite. But they juxtapose facts that will later prove revealing (e.g., heating by mixture) with others (e.g., the warmth of dung heaps) that will for some time remain too complex to be integrated with theory at all.[4] In addition, since any description must be partial, the typical natural history

---

[4] Compare the sketch for a natural history of heat in Bacon's *Novum Organum*, Vol. VIII of *The Works of Francis Bacon*, ed. J. Spedding, R. L. Ellis, and D. D. Heath (New York, 1869), pp. 179–203.

often omits from its immensely circumstantial accounts just those details that later scientists will find sources of important illumination. Almost none of the early "histories" of electricity, for example, mention that chaff, attracted to a rubbed glass rod, bounces off again. That effect seemed mechanical, not electrical.[5] More-over, since the casual fact-gatherer seldom possesses the time or the tools to be critical, the natural histories often juxtapose descriptions like the above with others, say, heating by antiperistasis (or by cooling), that we are now quite unable to confirm.[6] Only very occasionally, as in the cases of ancient statics, dynamics, and geometrical optics, do facts collected with so little guidance from pre-established theory speak with sufficient clarity to permit the emergence of a first paradigm.

This is the situation that creates the schools characteristic of the early stages of a science's development. No natural history can be interpreted in the absence of at least some implicit body of intertwined theoretical and methodological belief that permits selection, evaluation, and criticism. If that body of belief is not already implicit in the collection of facts – in which case more than "mere facts" are at hand – it must be externally supplied, perhaps by a current metaphysic, by another science, or by personal and historical accident. No wonder, then, that in the early stages of the development of any science different men confronting the same range of phenomena, but not usually all the same particular phenomena, describe and interpret them in different ways. What is surprising, and perhaps also unique in its degree to the fields we call science, is that such initial divergences should ever largely disappear.

For they do disappear to a very considerable extent and then apparently once and for all. Furthermore, their disappearance is usually caused by the triumph of one of the pre-paradigm schools, which, because of its own characteristic beliefs and preconceptions, emphasized only some special part of the too sizable and inchoate pool of information. Those electricians who thought electricity a fluid and therefore gave particular emphasis to conduction provide an excellent case in point. Led by this belief, which could scarcely cope with the known multi-plicity of attractive and repulsive effects, several of them conceived the idea of bottling the electrical fluid. The immediate fruit of their efforts was the Leyden jar, a device which might never have been discovered by a man exploring nature casually or at random, but which was in fact independently developed by at least two investigators in the early 1740's.[7] Almost from the start of his electrical researches, Franklin was particularly concerned to explain that strange and, in the event, particularly revealing piece of special apparatus. His success in doing so provided the most effective of the arguments that made his theory a paradigm, though one that was still unable to account for quite all the known cases of

[5] Roller and Roller, *op. cit.*, pp. 14, 22, 28, 43. Only after the work recorded in the last of these citations do repulsive effects gain general recognition as unequivocally electrical.

[6] Bacon, *op. cit.*, pp. 235, 337, says, "Water slightly warm is more easily frozen than quite cold." For a partial account of the earlier history of this strange observation, see Marshall Clagett, *Giovanni Marliani and Late Medieval Physics* (New York, 1941), chap. iv.

[7] Roller and Roller, *op. cit.*, pp. 51–54.

electrical repulsion.[8] To be accepted as a paradigm, a theory must seem better than its competitors, but it need not, and in fact never does, explain all the facts with which it can be confronted.

What the fluid theory of electricity did for the subgroup that held it, the Franklinian paradigm later did for the entire group of electricians. It suggested which experiments would be worth performing and which, because directed to secondary or to overly complex manifestations of electricity, would not. Only the paradigm did the job far more effectively, partly because the end of interschool debate ended the constant reiteration of fundamentals and partly because the confidence that they were on the right track encouraged scientists to undertake more precise, esoteric, and consuming sorts of work.[9] Freed from the concern with any and all electrical phenomena, the united group of electricians could pursue selected phenomena in far more detail, designing much special equipment for the task and employing it more stubbornly and systematically than electricians had ever done before. Both fact collection and theory articulation became highly directed activities. The effectiveness and efficiency of electrical research increased accordingly, providing evidence for a societal version of Francis Bacon's acute methodological dictum: "Truth emerges more readily from error than from confusion."[10]

We shall be examining the nature of this highly directed or paradigm-based research later, but must first note briefly how the emergence of a paradigm affects the structure of the group that practices the field. When, in the development of a natural science, an individual or group first produces a synthesis able to attract most of the next generation's practitioners, the older schools gradually disappear. In part their disappearance is caused by their members' conversion to the new paradigm. But there are always some men who cling to one or another of the older views, and they are simply read out of the profession, which thereafter ignores their work. The new paradigm implies a new and more rigid definition of the field. Those unwilling or unable to accommodate their work to it must proceed in isolation or attach themselves to some other group.[11] Historically, they have often simply stayed

[8] The troublesome case was the mutual repulsion of negatively charged bodies, for which see Cohen, *op. cit.*, pp. 491–94, 531–43.

[9] It should be noted that the acceptance of Franklin's theory did not end quite all debate. In 1759 Robert Symmer proposed a two-fluid version of that theory, and for many years thereafter electricians were divided about whether electricity was a single fluid or two. But the debates on this subject only confirm what has been said above about the manner in which a universally recognized achievement unites the profession. Electricians, though they continued divided on this point, rapidly concluded that no experimental tests could distinguish the two versions of the theory and that they were therefore equivalent. After that, both schools could and did exploit all the benefits that the Franklinian theory provided (*ibid.*, pp. 543–46, 548–54).

[10] Bacon, *op. cit.*, p. 210.

[11] The history of electricity provides an excellent example which could be duplicated from the careers of Priestley, Kelvin, and others. Franklin reports that Nollet, who at mid-century was the most influential of the Continental electricians, "lived to see himself the last of his Sect, except Mr. B. – his Eleve and immediate Disciple" (Max Farrand [ed.], *Benjamin Franklin's Memoirs* [Berkeley, Calif., 1949], pp. 384–86). More interesting, however, is the endurance of whole schools in increasing isolation from professional science. Consider, for example, the case of astrology, which was once an

in the departments of philosophy from which so many of the special sciences have been spawned. As these indications hint, it is sometimes just its reception of a paradigm that transforms a group previously interested merely in the study of nature into a profession or, at least, a discipline. In the sciences (though not in fields like medicine, technology, and law, of which the principal *raison d'être* is an external social need), the formation of specialized journals, the foundation of specialists' societies, and the claim for a special place in the curriculum have usually been associated with a group's first reception of a single paradigm. At least this was the case between the time, a century and a half ago, when the institutional pattern of scientific specialization first developed and the very recent time when the paraphernalia of specialization acquired a prestige of their own.

The more rigid definition of the scientific group has other consequences. When the individual scientist can take a paradigm for granted, he need no longer, in his major works, attempt to build his field anew, starting from first principles and justifying the use of each concept introduced. That can be left to the writer of textbooks. Given a textbook, however, the creative scientist can begin his research where it leaves off and thus concentrate exclusively upon the subtlest and most esoteric aspects of the natural phenomena that concern his group. And as he does this, his research communiqués will begin to change in ways whose evolution has been too little studied but whose modern end products are obvious to all and oppressive to many. No longer will his researches usually be embodied in books addressed, like Franklin's *Experiments . . . on Electricity* or Darwin's *Origin of Species*, to anyone who might be interested in the subject matter of the field. Instead they will usually appear as brief articles addressed only to professional colleagues, the men whose knowledge of a shared paradigm can be assumed and who prove to be the only ones able to read the papers addressed to them. [. . .]

Normal Science as Puzzle-solving

Perhaps the most striking feature of the normal research problems we have encountered is how little they aim to produce major novelties, conceptual or phenomenal. Sometimes, as in a wave-length measurement, everything but the most esoteric detail of the result is known in advance, and the typical latitude of expectation is only somewhat wider. Coulomb's measurements need not, perhaps, have fitted an inverse square law; the men who worked on heating by compression were often prepared for any one of several results. Yet even in cases like these the range of anticipated, and thus of assimilable, results is always small compared with the

---

integral part of astronomy. Or consider the continuation in the late eighteenth and early nineteenth centuries of a previously respected tradition of "romantic" chemistry. This is the tradition discussed by Charles C. Gillispie in "The *Encyclopédie* and the Jacobin Philosophy of Science: A Study in Ideas and Consequences," *Critical Problems in the History of Science*, ed. Marshall Clagett (Madison, Wis., 1959), pp. 255–89; and "The Formation of Lamarck's Evolutionary Theory," *Archives internationales d'histoire des sciences*, XXXVII (1956), 323–38.

range that imagination can conceive. And the project whose outcome does not fall in that narrower range is usually just a research failure, one which reflects not on nature but on the scientist.

In the eighteenth century, for example, little attention was paid to the experiments that measured electrical attraction with devices like the pan balance. Because they yielded neither consistent nor simple results, they could not be used to articulate the paradigm from which they derived. Therefore, they remained *mere* facts, unrelated and unrelatable to the continuing progress of electrical research. Only in retrospect, possessed of a subsequent paradigm, can we see what characteristics of electrical phenomena they display. Coulomb and his contemporaries, of course, also possessed this later paradigm or one that, when applied to the problem of attraction, yielded the same expectations. That is why Coulomb was able to design apparatus that gave a result assimilable by paradigm articulation. But it is also why that result surprised no one and why several of Coulomb's contemporaries had been able to predict it in advance. Even the project whose goal is paradigm articulation does not aim at the *unexpected* novelty.

But if the aim of normal science is not major substantive novelties – if failure to come near the anticipated result is usually failure as a scientist – then why are these problems undertaken at all? Part of the answer has already been developed. To scientists, at least, the results gained in normal research are significant because they add to the scope and precision with which the paradigm can be applied. That answer, however, cannot account for the enthusiasm and devotion that scientists display for the problems of normal research. No one devotes years to, say, the development of a better spectrometer or the production of an improved solution to the problem of vibrating strings simply because of the importance of the information that will be obtained. The data to be gained by computing ephemerides or by further measurements with an existing instrument are often just as significant, but those activities are regularly spurned by scientists because they are so largely repetitions of procedures that have been carried through before. That rejection provides a clue to the fascination of the normal research problem. Though its outcome can be anticipated, often in detail so great that what remains to be known is itself uninteresting, the way to achieve that outcome remains very much in doubt. Bringing a normal research problem to a conclusion is achieving the anticipated in a new way, and it requires the solution of all sorts of complex instrumental, conceptual, and mathematical puzzles. The man who succeeds proves himself an expert puzzle-solver, and the challenge of the puzzle is an important part of what usually drives him on.

The terms "puzzle" and "puzzle-solver" highlight several of the themes that have become increasingly prominent in the preceding pages. Puzzles are, in the entirely standard meaning here employed, that special category of problems that can serve to test ingenuity or skill in solution. Dictionary illustrations are "jigsaw puzzle" and "crossword puzzle," and it is the characteristics that these share with the problems of normal science that we now need to isolate. One of them has just been mentioned. It is no criterion of goodness in a puzzle that its outcome be intrinsically interesting or important. On the contrary, the really pressing problems, e.g., a cure for cancer or the design of a lasting peace, are often not puzzles at all, largely because they may not have any solution. Consider the jigsaw puzzle whose pieces are selected at random from each of two different puzzle boxes. Since that problem is likely to defy (though it might not) even the most ingenious of men, it cannot serve as a test of skill in solution. In any usual sense it is not a puzzle at all. Though intrinsic value is no criterion for a puzzle, the assured existence of a solution is.

We have already seen, however, that one of the things a scientific community acquires with a paradigm is a criterion for choosing problems that, while the paradigm is taken for granted, can be assumed to have solutions. To a great extent these are the only problems that the community will admit as scientific or encourage its members to undertake. Other problems, including many that had previously been standard, are rejected as metaphysical, as the concern of another discipline, or sometimes as just too problematic to be worth the time. A paradigm can, for that matter, even insulate the community from those socially important problems that are not reducible to the puzzle form, because they cannot be stated in terms of the conceptual and instrumental tools the paradigm supplies. Such problems can be a distraction, a lesson brilliantly illustrated by several facets of seventeenth-century Baconianism and by some of the contemporary social sciences. One of the reasons why normal science seems to progress so rapidly is that its practitioners concentrate on problems that only their own lack of ingenuity should keep them from solving.

If, however, the problems of normal science are puzzles in this sense, we need no longer ask why scientists attack them with such passion and devotion. A man may be attracted to science for all sorts of reasons. Among them are the desire to be useful, the excitement of exploring new territory, the hope of finding order, and the drive to test established knowledge. These motives and others besides also help to determine the particular problems that will later engage him. Furthermore, though the result is occasional frustration, there is good reason why motives like these should first attract him and then lead him on.[12] The scientific enterprise as a whole does from time to time prove useful, open up new territory, display order, and test long-accepted belief. Nevertheless, *the individual* engaged on a normal research problem *is almost never doing any one of these things*. Once engaged, his motivation is of a rather different sort. What then challenges him is the conviction that, if only he is skilful enough, he will succeed in solving a puzzle that no one before has solved or solved so well. Many of the greatest scientific minds have devoted all of their professional attention to demanding puzzles of this sort. On most occasions any particular field of specialization offers nothing else to do, a fact that makes it no less fascinating to the proper sort of addict.

[12] The frustrations induced by the conflict between the individual's role and the over-all pattern of scientific development can, however, occasionally be quite serious. On this subject, see Lawrence S. Kubie, "Some Unsolved Problems of the Scientific Career," *American Scientist*, XLI (1953), 596–613; and XLII (1954), 104–12.

Turn now to another, more difficult, and more revealing aspect of the parallelism between puzzles and the problems of normal science. If it is to classify as a puzzle, a problem must be characterized by more than an assured solution. There must also be rules that limit both the nature of acceptable solutions and the steps by which they are to be obtained. To solve a jigsaw puzzle is not, for example, merely "to make a picture." Either a child or a contemporary artist could do that by scattering selected pieces, as abstract shapes, upon some neutral ground. The picture thus produced might be far better, and would certainly be more original, than the one from which the puzzle had been made. Nevertheless, such a picture would not be a solution. To achieve that all the pieces must be used, their plain sides must be turned down, and they must be interlocked without forcing until no holes remain. Those are among the rules that govern jigsaw-puzzle solutions. Similar restrictions upon the admissible solutions of crossword puzzles, riddles, chess problems, and so on, are readily discovered.

If we can accept a considerably broadened use of the term "rule" – one that will occasionally equate it with "established viewpoint" or with "preconception" – then the problems accessible within a given research tradition display something much like this set of puzzle characteristics. The man who builds an instrument to determine optical wave lengths must not be satisfied with a piece of equipment that merely attributes particular numbers to particular spectral lines. He is not just an explorer or measurer. On the contrary, he must show, by analyzing his apparatus in terms of the established body of optical theory, that the numbers his instrument produces are the ones that enter theory as wave lengths. If some residual vagueness in the theory or some unanalyzed component of his apparatus prevents his completing that demonstration, his colleagues may well conclude that he has measured nothing at all. For example, the electron-scattering maxima that were later diagnosed as indices of electron wave length had no apparent significance when first observed and recorded. Before they became measures of anything, they had to be related to a theory that predicted the wave-like behavior of matter in motion. And even after that relation was pointed out, the apparatus had to be redesigned so that the experimental results might be correlated unequivocally with theory.[13] Until those conditions had been satisfied, no problem had been solved.

Similar sorts of restrictions bound the admissible solutions to theoretical problems. Throughout the eighteenth century those scientists who tried to derive the observed motion of the moon from Newton's laws of motion and gravitation consistently failed to do so. As a result, some of them suggested replacing the inverse square law with a law that deviated from it at small distances. To do that, however, would have been to change the paradigm, to define a new puzzle, and not to solve the old one. In the event, scientists preserved the rules until, in 1750, one of them discovered how they could successfully be applied.[14] Only a change in the rules of the game could have provided an alternative.

[13] For a brief account of the evolution of these experiments, see page 4 of C. J. Davisson's lecture in *Les prix Nobel en 1937* (Stockholm, 1938).

[14] W. Whewell, *History of the Inductive Sciences* (rev. ed.; London, 1847), II, 101–5, 220–22.

The study of normal-scientific traditions discloses many additional rules, and these provide much information about the commitments that scientists derive from their paradigms. What can we say are the main categories into which these rules fall?[15] The most obvious and probably the most binding is exemplified by the sorts of generalizations we have just noted. These are explicit statements of scientific law and about scientific concepts and theories. While they continue to be honored, such statements help to set puzzles and to limit acceptable solutions. Newton's Laws, for example, performed those functions during the eighteenth and nineteenth centuries. As long as they did so, quantity-of-matter was a fundamental ontological category for physical scientists, and the forces that act between bits of matter were a dominant topic for research.[16] In chemistry the laws of fixed and definite proportions had, for a long time, an exactly similar force – setting the problem of atomic weights, bounding the admissible results of chemical analyses, and informing chemists what atoms and molecules, compounds and mixtures were. Maxwell's equations and the laws of statistical thermo-dynamics have the same hold and function today.

Rules like these are, however, neither the only nor even the most interesting variety displayed by historical study. At a level lower or more concrete than that of laws and theories, there is, for example, a multitude of commitments to preferred types of instrumentation and to the ways in which accepted instruments may legitimately be employed. Changing attitudes toward the role of fire in chemical analyses played a vital part in the development of chemistry in the seventeenth century.[17] Helmholtz, in the nineteenth, encountered strong resistance from physiologists to the notion that physical experimentation could illuminate their field.[18] And in this century the curious history of chemical chromatography again illustrates the endurance of instrumental commitments that, as much as laws and theory, provide scientists with rules of the game.[19] When we analyze the discovery of X-rays, we shall find reasons for commitments of this sort.

Less local and temporary, though still not unchanging characteristics of science, are the higher level, quasi-metaphysical commitments that historical study so regularly displays. After about 1630, for example, and particularly after the appearance of Descartes's immensely influential scientific writings, most physical scientists assumed that the universe was composed of microscopic corpuscles and that all natural phenomena could be explained in terms of corpuscular shape, size, motion, and interaction. That nest of commitments proved to be both metaphysical and methodological. As metaphysical, it told scientists what sorts of entities the universe

---

[15] I owe this question to W. O. Hagstrom, whose work in the sociology of science sometimes overlaps my own.

[16] For these aspects of Newtonianism, see Cohen, *op. cit.*, chap. vii, esp. pp. 255–57, 275–77.

[17] H. Metzger, *Les doctrines chimiques en France du début du XVII*ᵉ *siècle à la fin du XVIII*ᵉ *siècle* (Paris, 1923), pp. 359–61; Marie Boas, *Robert Boyle and Seventeenth-Century Chemistry* (Cambridge, 1958), pp. 112–15.

[18] Leo Königsberger, *Hermann von Helmholtz*, trans. Francis A. Welby (Oxford, 1906), pp. 65–66.

[19] James E. Meinhard, "Chromatography: A Perspective," *Science*, CX (1949), 387–92.

did and did not contain: there was only shaped matter in motion. As methodological, it told them what ultimate laws and fundamental explanations must be like: laws must specify corpuscular motion and interaction, and explanation must reduce any given natural phenomenon to corpuscular action under these laws. More important still, the corpuscular conception of the universe told scientists what many of their research problems should be. [. . .]

The Nature and Necessity of Scientific Revolutions

[We now] consider the problems that provide this essay with its title. What are scientific revolutions, and what is their function in scientific development? Much of the answer to these questions has been anticipated in earlier sections. In particular, the preceding discussion has indicated that scientific revolutions are here taken to be those non–cumulative developmental episodes in which an older paradigm is replaced in whole or in part by an incompatible new one. There is more to be said, however, and an essential part of it can be introduced by asking one further question. Why should a change of paradigm be called a revolution? In the face of the vast and essential differences between political and scientific development, what parallelism can justify the metaphor that finds revolutions in both?

One aspect of the parallelism must already be apparent. Political revolutions are inaugurated by a growing sense, often restricted to a segment of the political community, that existing institutions have ceased adequately to meet the problems posed by an environment that they have in part created. In much the same way, scientific revolutions are inaugurated by a growing sense, again often restricted to a narrow subdivision of the scientific community, that an existing paradigm has ceased to function adequately in the exploration of an aspect of nature to which that paradigm itself had previously led the way. In both political and scientific development the sense of malfunction that can lead to crisis is prerequisite to revolution. Furthermore, though it admittedly strains the metaphor, that parallelism holds not only for the major paradigm changes, like those attributable to Copernicus and Lavoisier, but also for the far smaller ones associated with the assimilation of a new sort of phenomenon, like oxygen or X–rays. Scientific revolutions need seem revolutionary only to those whose paradigms are affected by them. To outsiders they may, like the Balkan revolutions of the early twentieth century, seem normal parts of the developmental process. Astronomers, for example, could accept X–rays as a mere addition to knowledge, for their paradigms were unaffected by the existence of the new radiation. But for men like Kelvin, Crookes, and Roentgen, whose research dealt with radiation theory or with cathode ray tubes, the emergence of X–rays necessarily violated one paradigm as it created another. That is why these rays could be discovered only through something's first going wrong with normal research.

This genetic aspect of the parallel between political and scientific development should no longer be open to doubt. The parallel has, however, a second and more profound aspect upon which the significance of the first depends. Political revolutions aim to change political institutions in ways that those institutions themselves prohibit. Their success therefore necessitates the partial relinquishment of one set of institutions in favor of another, and in the interim, society is not fully governed by institutions at all. Initially it is crisis alone that attenuates the role of political institutions as we have already seen it attenuate the role of paradigms. In increasing numbers individuals become increasingly estranged from political life and behave more and more eccentrically within it. Then, as the crisis deepens, many of these individuals commit themselves to some concrete proposal for the reconstruction of society in a new institutional framework. At that point the society is divided into competing camps or parties, one seeking to defend the old institutional constellation, the others seeking to institute some new one. And, once that polarization has occurred, *political recourse fails*. Because they differ about the institutional matrix within which political change is to be achieved and evaluated, because they acknowledge no supra-institutional framework for the adjudication of revolutionary difference, the parties to a revolutionary conflict must finally resort to the techniques of mass persuasion, often including force. Though revolutions have had a vital role in the evolution of political institutions, that role depends upon their being partially extrapolitical or extrainstitutional events.

The remainder of this essay aims to demonstrate that the historical study of paradigm change reveals very similar characteristics in the evolution of the sciences. Like the choice between competing political institutions, that between competing paradigms proves to be a choice between incompatible modes of community life. Because it has that character, the choice is not and cannot be determined merely by the evaluative procedures characteristic of normal science, for these depend in part upon a particular paradigm, and that paradigm is at issue. When paradigms enter, as they must, into a debate about paradigm choice, their role is necessarily circular. Each group uses its own paradigm to argue in that paradigm's defense.

The resulting circularity does not, of course, make the arguments wrong or even ineffectual. The man who premises a paradigm when arguing in its defense can none the less provide a clear exhibit of what scientific practice will be like for those who adopt the new view of nature. That exhibit can be immensely persuasive, often compellingly so. Yet, whatever its force, the status of the circular argument is only that of persuasion. It cannot be made logically or even probabilistically compelling for those who refuse to step into the circle. The premises and values shared by the two parties to a debate over paradigms are not sufficiently extensive for that. As in political revolutions, so in paradigm choice – there is no standard higher than the assent of the relevant community. To discover how scientific revolutions are effected, we shall therefore have to examine not only the impact of nature and of logic, but also the techniques of persuasive argumentation effective within the quite special groups that constitute the community of scientists.

To discover why this issue of paradigm choice can never be unequivocally settled by logic and experiment alone, we must shortly examine the nature of the differences that separate the proponents of a traditional paradigm from their revolutionary successors. We have, however, already noted numerous examples of such differences, and no one will doubt that history can supply many others. What is more likely to be doubted than their existence − and what must therefore be considered first − is that such examples provide essential information about the nature of science. Granting that paradigm rejection has been a historic fact, does it illuminate more than human credulity and confusion? Are there intrinsic reasons why the assimilation of either a new sort of phenomenon or a new scientific theory must demand the rejection of an older paradigm? [. . .]

Let us, therefore, now take it for granted that the differences between successive paradigms are both necessary and irreconcilable. Can we then say more explicitly what sorts of differences these are? The most apparent type has already been illustrated repeatedly. Successive paradigms tell us different things about the population of the universe and about that population's behavior. They differ, that is, about such questions as the existence of subatomic particles, the materiality of light, and the conservation of heat or of energy. These are the substantive differences between successive paradigms, and they require no further illustration. But paradigms differ in more than substance, for they are directed not only to nature but also back upon the science that produced them. They are the source of the methods, problem-field, and standards of solution accepted by any mature scientific community at any given time. As a result, the reception of a new paradigm often necessitates a redefinition of the corresponding science. Some old problems may be relegated to another science or declared entirely "unscientific." Others that were previously non-existent or trivial may, with a new paradigm, become the very archetypes of significant scientific achievement. And as the problems change, so, often, does the standard that distinguishes a real scientific solution from a mere metaphysical speculation, word game, or mathematical play. The normal-scientific tradition that emerges from a scientific revolution is not only incompatible but often actually incommensurable with that which has gone before. [. . .]

Previously, we had principally examined the paradigm's role as a vehicle for scientific theory. In that role it functions by telling the scientist about the entities that nature does and does not contain and about the ways in which those entities behave. That information provides a map whose details are elucidated by mature scientific research. And since nature is too complex and varied to be explored at random, that map is as essential as observation and experiment to science's continuing development. Through the theories they embody, paradigms prove to be constitutive of the research activity. They are also, however, constitutive of science in other respects, and that is now the point. In particular, our most recent examples show that paradigms provide scientists not only with a map but also with some of the directions essential for map-making. In learning a paradigm the scientist acquires theory, methods, and standards together, usually in an inextricable mixture. Therefore, when paradigms change, there are usually significant shifts in the criteria determining the legitimacy both of problems and of proposed solutions.

That observation [. . .] provides our first explicit indication of why the choice between competing paradigms regularly raises questions that cannot be resolved by the criteria of normal science. To the extent, as significant as it is incomplete, that two scientific schools disagree about what is a problem and what a solution, they will inevitably talk through each other when debating the relative merits of their respective paradigms. In the partially circular arguments that regularly result, each paradigm will be shown to satisfy more or less the criteria that it dictates for itself and to fall short of a few of those dictated by its opponent. There are other reasons, too, for the incompleteness of logical contact that consistently characterizes paradigm debates. For example, since no paradigm ever solves all the problems it defines and since no two paradigms leave all the same problems unsolved, paradigm debates always involve the question: Which problems is it more significant to have solved? Like the issue of competing standards, that question of values can be answered only in terms of criteria that lie outside of normal science altogether, and it is that recourse to external criteria that most obviously makes paradigm debates revolutionary. Something even more fundamental than standards and values is, however, also at stake. I have so far argued only that paradigms are constitutive of science. Now I wish to display a sense in which they are constitutive of nature as well.

Revolutions as Changes of World View

Examining the record of past research from the vantage of contemporary historiography, the historian of science may be tempted to exclaim that when paradigms change, the world itself changes with them. Led by a new paradigm, scientists adopt new instruments and look in new places. Even more important, during revolutions scientists see new and different things when looking with familiar instruments in places they have looked before. It is rather as if the professional community had been suddenly transported to another planet where familiar objects are seen in a different light and are joined by unfamiliar ones as well. Of course, nothing of quite that sort does occur: there is no geographical transplantation; outside the laboratory everyday affairs usually continue as before. Nevertheless, paradigm changes do cause scientists to see the world of their research-engagement differently. In so far as their only recourse to that world is through what they see and do, we may want to say that after a revolution scientists are responding to a different world. [. . .]

All of this may seem more reasonable if we again remember that neither scientists nor laymen learn to see the world piecemeal or item by item. Except when all the conceptual and manipulative categories are prepared in advance – e.g., for the discovery of an additional transuranic element or for catching sight of a new house – both scientists and laymen sort out whole areas together from the flux of experience. The child who transfers the word "mama" from all humans to all females and then to his mother is not just learning what "mama" means or who his mother is. Simultaneously he is learning some of the differences between males and females as well as something about the ways in which all but one female will behave toward him. His reactions, expectations, and beliefs – indeed, much of his perceived world – change accordingly. By the same token, the Copernicans who denied its traditional title "planet" to the sun were not only learning what "planet" meant or what the sun was. Instead, they were changing the meaning of "planet" so that it could continue to make useful distinctions in a world where all celestial bodies, not just the sun, were seen differently from the way they had been seen before. The same point could be made about any of our earlier examples. To see oxygen instead of dephlogisticated air, the condenser instead of the Leyden jar, or the pendulum instead of constrained fall, was only one part of an integrated shift in the scientist's vision of a great many related chemical, electrical, or dynamical phenomena. Paradigms determine large areas of experience at the same time. [. . .]

J. J. C. Smart, "Physics and Reality"

Physics and Common Sense

In his popular book *The Nature of the Physical World* Sir Arthur Eddington propounded a memorable paradox. He spoke of the table on which he was writing, and rather playfully distinguished two tables: the common sense table and the table as known to science. The common sense table is brown, solid and inert, while the scientific table is made up of particles such as electrons and protons, of which colour cannot be meaningfully predicated, and in rapid motion and separated by empty space, so that their combined bulk amounts to a tiny proportion of the bulk of the table itself. Which is the real table, or are both real?

Some philosophers and scientists plump for the common sense table. They want to say that physics is just a dodge for predicting occurrences among those things that we can see or feel with our ordinary senses. Some, such as Ernst Mach, even went further and said that talk of common sense objects (e.g. tables) is itself just a dodge for predicting regularities among our sense experiences. That is, they combine scepticism about Eddington's scientific table with a scepticism about ordinary common sense objects, or else, what does not seem to me to be ontologically very different, they claim that statements about common sense objects can at least approximately be translated into sentences about sense experiences. This is the philosophical doctrine called "phenomenalism" and in essence it goes back to the great eighteenth-century philosopher Bishop Berkeley. [. . .] Other philosophers, of whom I am one, would accept the reality of both the common sense table and the scientific table: the scientific table just is the common sense table. What is different is our mode of describing it, much as when one and the same person might be described either as the professor of anatomy or as the dean of the medical faculty. [. . .]

From *Our Place in the Universe* (Oxford: Blackwell, 1989), pp. 49–56, 60–1, 63–5.

Reality and Truth

What about those philosophers and scientists who, as I remarked near the beginning of this chapter, plump exclusively for the reality of the common sense table, that is, who think of talk about electrons, neutrinos, curved space–time and so on as merely a useful dodge for predicting what can be observed at the macroscopic level in the laboratory, or with instruments or by means of telescopes? Their espousal of such a philosophy was partly due to an extreme of empiricist thought, which though a healthy reaction to *a priori* metaphysics, like most reactions went too far. Even Newton said that he did not make hypotheses, and yet of course he in fact made wonderful and beautiful hypotheses. Partly it has in recent times come from reflection on the apparently paradoxical nature of quantum mechanics. In the case of some scientists it also comes from unnecessary suspicion of perfectly good English words like "true" and "real". These are sometimes put by scientists in shudder quotation marks, and are thought of as horrid mushy words in contrast to sensible words such as "geodesic" or "neutrino" that are used by scientists. [. . .]

Realism and Anti-Realism

Those scientists who do not have unnecessary qualms about "true" and "real" and who are not seduced by extreme empiricist or "positivist" philosophy will mostly assume that in their theories they are talking about real things and are not merely using a dodge for making predictions about observations in the laboratory or in the observatory. Consider, for example, theories about what happened in the first few moments after the "big bang" from which the universe is supposed to have originated. I conjecture that most cosmologists think of this as real history, no less than conjectures about dinosaurs, or even about the battle of Waterloo. Now can such an implicit attitude be justified philosophically?

We shall be concerned with arguments for the reality of what we may call the "theoretical entities" of science. The terminology is slightly misleading because one and the same thing may be a theoretical entity in one context and an observational entity in another context. Thus there is a sense in which a murder may be a theoretical entity for Sherlock Holmes but an object of perception and memory for the criminal. We know about electrons, neutrinos, curved space–time and so on more in the way that Sherlock Holmes knows about the murder than in the way that the criminal does or an eyewitness would. We cannot directly perceive these entities. We know about them from galvanometer readings, spectrometer photographs, bubble chamber tracks, observations of the position of Mercury, and so on. But then we cannot directly perceive dinosaurs though we could have done so if we had lived at an appropriate place and time. Sherlock Holmes was not able to perceive the murder, though he could have done so if he had been appropriately placed. The difference with the so-called "theoretical entities" of physics is that there are physical reasons why we could not directly perceive them. For example, physicists know about neutrinos because the postulation of them provides a plausible explanation of some features of certain bubble chamber tracks. It all fits in with a web of belief (to use a metaphor favoured by W. V. Quine) about electric charges, conservation of momentum and of energy, and various other things. Because of their lack of charge, neutrinos do not leave bubble chamber or cloud chamber tracks, but the neutrino was postulated to balance up the momenta of other particles which did show themselves by such tracks. The reasoning is holistic, and depends on the best way either of preserving the web of belief or of reconstructing it without wholly destroying it as a philosophical sceptic would wish to do. (A thoroughgoing philosophical scepticism never succeeds, because without a web of belief of some sort we would be dead.) I have given the example of the neutrino, because the evidence for its existence is very indirect, but of course the evidence for even those particles that do leave bubble chamber tracks is indirect too, though to a lesser degree.

Now a scientific anti-realist might say that all the evidence shows is that the world is just *as if* there were electrons, neutrinos, etc. The postulation of them, according to the anti-realist, is a sort of fairy story which is not to be believed: it is there just so that we can put some order into our observations and predict fresh observations. My reaction to this is to express incredulity. Is it not implausible that things should be merely "as if", at least on a holistic scale? Certainly there are isolated analogies that legitimately enable us to talk in terms of "as if". We can of course say such a thing as that an inductor and a capacitor in series oscillate electrically just as if the oscillations were mechanical and the inductor was a heavy mass and the capacitor a spring. Certainly there are these isolated analogies that enable us to talk merely of "as if". Nevertheless it is most unplausible that the laboratory phenomena taken as a whole, or at any rate over a wide scope, are just *as if* there were the theoretical entities. Would not rejection of full-blooded realism about the theoretical entities be as bad as if Sherlock Holmes were to say that the footprint on the rose bed, the blood in the library, the disappearance of the butler, etc., was just *as if* there had been a murder? Admittedly Sherlock Holmes may ultimately come to grip the murderer by the collar, and we cannot do anything like this with electrons, neutrinos or curved space-time. The realist can counter this objection by saying that there are theoretical reasons why we cannot grip the theoretical entities (metaphorically) by the collar, and so can accept one part of the analogy while reasonably rejecting another part of it. Our knowledge of the physics and physiology of perception explains why we cannot perceive individual atoms or electrons.

Suppose that Sherlock Holmes comes to the conclusion that the butler was the murderer. He does so because this is overwhelmingly the simplest hypothesis to explain the facts. Critics of so-called "circumstantial evidence" are in effect complaining that there could be other hypotheses that would be consistent with the evidence. Obviously the circumstantiality of evidence is a matter of degree – the less plausible the other hypotheses the less the circumstantiality. Even the best evidence (short of direct perception) is circumstantial to some degree. Even if blood were found on the butler's hands, and shown by laboratory tests (not available in Sherlock Holmes's day) to be the victim's blood, and if the butler signed a detailed confession, a fantastic and unplausible but self-consistent hypothesis could be proposed that would be consistent with the butler's innocence. Readers of the Sherlock Holmes stories may remember that Holmes talked of "deducing" the identity of the criminal. This, however, was loose talk that if taken literally would suggest that Holmes's ability to theorize about logic was greatly inferior to his ability to apply scientific method. [. . .]

My argument for the reality of the unobservable entities postulated by theoretical physics is that it is too much to believe that the complex and messy regularities – or non-regularities – on the observational level are just *as if* the theoretical entities exist. Postulation of the theoretical entities gives a simpler and aesthetically more satisfying picture of the world. Taking simplicity and aesthetic satisfyingness as characteristic of a good explanation, the argument could be subsumed under the notion of "argument to the best explanation". In the same way, Sherlock Holmes believed that the butler was the murderer because this gave the only simple explanation of the observed evidence. Any other proposed explanation would strike him and the police as complicated and far-fetched – in short, improbable. [. . .]

This consideration shows that an essential premiss for my argument is that the universe is simple. I do not know how to justify this, and I am afraid that I need to accept the advantage of theft over honest toil (to use an expression of Bertrand Russell's in another context) and put this up as a postulate. Note that I am talking of *ontological* simplicity. Neither realists nor anti-realists would deny the *pragmatic* advantages of simple theories. [. . .] The necessity for an ontological appeal to simplicity is what worries me most in defending realism. Let me now mention some other difficulties for realism.

The first difficulty comes from the fact that theories get overturned and replaced by others. So will not electrons one day go the way of the Ptolemaic celestial spheres or the phlogiston of eighteenth-century theorizing about combustion or the ether of nineteenth-century electrodynamics? I have for long thought that philosophers of science have greatly exaggerated this problem. Many of them have pursued philosophy of science in close connection with the history of science. Contemporary and recent historians of science have understandably been keen to oppose the old idea of the progress of science as an infallible brick by brick cumulation. They have stressed the creativity and imaginativeness of theory construction. Laudable though this is, I think that these historians of science have gone too much to the other extreme. For example, exciting discoveries in nuclear field theory have little or no effect on the quantum theory of atomic spectra, and the latter has practically no effect on protein chemistry. And so on. Science has been in modern times much more cumulative than historians of science, such as Kuhn, may tempt us to think, notwithstanding the many good insights of these historians. The existence of conceptual revolution is not completely antithetical to the existence of cumulation.

No matter what strange new things the physicists of the next generation will tell us about electrons, will they ever reject the thesis that a hydrogen atom has one proton and one electron, or that the sea, rivers and lakes on planet Earth are largely constituted of H_2O molecules? J. J. Thomson had a different, because classical, concept of the electron from that of Born or Dirac. Nevertheless, there are still many sentences containing the word "electron" which all three of these scientists would accept and which are still accepted. Looking back on the theory used by Thomson, from the vantage-point of present quantum theory, we can surely say that the predicate ". . . is an electron" as used by Thomson is true of the very same objects of which the predicate ". . . is an electron" in quantum mechanics is true. We can also see that many of Thomson's assertions about these objects (e.g. about the ratio of charge to mass, which he was the first to measure) are either true or else at least approximately true. In a mature science, such as has existed from the late nineteenth century, there is no reason to suppose that for the most part the things we assert to exist now will not continue to be asserted to exist, and that our present theories will not be regarded as at least an approximation to the truth. If this is agreed we have drawn the teeth of the objection from theory change. If it had been the case that all or most theories would later be shown to be not even approximately true then at any stage we would indeed have no reason to believe in the reality of entities postulated at that stage. I also suspect that the sorts of examples of theory change used by historians of science to oppose the cumulative picture of science are often very untypical of mature science.

6

The Nature of Morality

James Rachels, "Nietzsche and the Objectivity of Morals"

Readings

Friedrich Nietzsche, *Beyond Good and Evil*, and *On the Genealogy of Morals* (selections)

David Hume, "Morality, Sentiment, and Reason" (selections from *A Treatise of Human Nature* and *An Inquiry Concerning the Principles of Morals*)

A. J. Ayer, "A Defense of Emotivism"

Renford Bambrough, "A Proof of the Objectivity of Morals"

Ronald Dworkin, "The Concept of a Moral Position"

Friedrich Nietzsche. Culver Pictures, Inc.

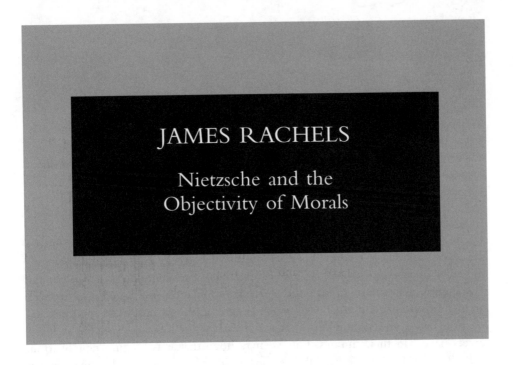

I understand the philosopher as a terrible explosive, endangering everything.
Friedrich Nietzsche, *Ecce Homo*

1   Nietzsche's Rejection of Traditional Morality

Few philosophers are as infuriating as Friedrich Nietzsche. Today he enjoys great popularity. His haunted-looking face adorns tee-shirts and coffee mugs, and his writings can be found in any shopping-mall bookstore. Yet for a half-century after his death in 1900, Nietzsche was a disreputable figure who seemed destined to be remembered as one of the pre-eminent villains of modern thought. It is not hard to understand why. His views were often outrageous, and he expressed himself in angry, belligerent prose. The combination could be stunning.

What he wrote about women, for example, seemed to flow from some deep personal bitterness:

> What is truth to woman? From the beginning, nothing has been more alien, repugnant, and hostile to woman than truth – her great art is the lie, her highest concern is mere appearance and beauty. (BG 232)

And if women care nothing about truth, why do some of them pursue scholarly careers? Nietzsche's explanation is that "When a woman has scholarly inclinations, there is usually something wrong with her sexually" (BG 144). Even the worst misogynists will usually concede women something – if they are no good as intellectuals, perhaps they are at least fit to be cooks. But Nietzsche does not even leave them that:

> Stupidity in the kitchen; woman as cook: the gruesome thoughtlessness to which the feeding of the family and of the master of the house is abandoned! Woman does not understand what food means – and wants to be cook. (BG 234)

As if this weren't bad enough, there was an even more serious charge against Nietzsche. He was taken as a prophet by the Nazis, and it is easy to see why. Read superficially, his writings seemed to blame the Jews for the worst turns of history and to call for a new race of supermen to dominate the world. Hitler's apologists quoted with relish such lines as "The young stock-exchange Jew is altogether the most disgusting invention of mankind" (HA 475). Hitler himself visited the Nietzsche Archive in Weimar and was photographed contemplating a bust of the philosopher. Near the end of the Second World War Bertrand Russell wrote: "[Nietzsche's] followers have had their innings, but we may hope that it is coming rapidly to an end" (HP 773). Considering all this, one might well wonder why Nietzsche is regarded today as a great moral philosopher.

How Nietzsche got such a bad reputation

Nietzsche's remarks about women can hardly be defended. But he was neither an anti-Semite nor a nationalist, and it was only by distorting his thought that the Nazis could claim him. Nietzsche was particularly unfortunate in the events that made their distortions possible.

Nietzsche was born in 1844 in Rücken, Germany. His father, a Lutheran pastor, died when Friedrich was four years old, leaving the boy to be raised in a household consisting of five women – his mother, his sister, his grandmother, and two maiden aunts. Some commentators have linked Nietzsche's later misogyny to this circumstance. Be that as it may, Nietzsche was a brilliant student and became a university professor in Basel, Switzerland when he was only 25 years old. After one year in the job, however, he volunteered as a medical orderly in the Franco-Prussian war, and when he returned to Basel a few months later his health was ruined. For a time, he was enthusiastic about the music of Richard Wagner. He became friends with the celebrated composer, but eventually Nietzsche broke off the relationship, at least in part because he was disgusted with the mindless nationalism and anti-Semitism of the Wagner clique. At the age of 35, he quit teaching to devote himself completely to writing. During the next decade he produced a book a year. Then in 1889, when Nietzsche was 45, everything went tragically wrong. He went insane, and eleven years later he was dead. Although it is not certain what was wrong with him, syphilis is a strong possibility.

At the time he went insane, Nietzsche did not have much of a reputation. Although he had published a number of books, they were not widely read. But his reputation grew during the next decade, and by the time he died he had become famous. Mercifully, Nietzsche never knew the kind of reputation he was to acquire: he would become known as the champion of doctrines that, in fact, he detested. This was largely due to his sister Elisabeth.

When Nietzsche had been a part of the Wagner circle, Elisabeth had also become involved with it. It was a glamorous crowd, and she loved the excitement. In 1885 she married a fringe member of the group, a professional anti-Semitic agitator named Bernhard Förster, and together they embarked on a monument-ally harebrained adventure: they set out to found a racially pure, Aryan colony in the jungles of South America. They raised enough money to take fourteen families to Paraguay, where they founded "Neuva Germania" – New Germany – in an isolated spot 150 miles up-river from Asunción. Things went badly from the beginning. The land was unsuitable for farming, the climate was stifling, there were insects everywhere, and the Europeans had no idea how to manage living in the jungle. Förster committed suicide. Elisabeth's way out of the mess was provided by her brother's collapse: she could return to Germany to take care of Friedrich, leaving the hapless settlers to fend for themselves.

Back in Germany, Elisabeth turned out to have a genius for promoting her brother, or herself, which came to the same thing. She arranged for publication of cheap editions of Nietzsche's books. She collected and edited his unpublished papers. She established the "Nietzsche Archive." She wrote a three-volume bio-graphy of her brother, featuring herself as his dearest friend. In short, she set her-self up as the chief guardian of the Nietzsche heritage. As Nietzsche's reputation grew, she became an important person in German cultural life. Three times she was nominated for the Nobel Prize in literature (although there is no reason to think the Nobel Committee took the nomination seriously). She cultivated the friendship of Mussolini and Hitler, encouraging them to believe that her brother's thinking went along with theirs. On the occasion of one meeting between the two leaders, she sent them a telegram declaring that "the spirit of Nietzsche hovers over this meeting of the two greatest statesmen of Europe" (MF 194). When Elisabeth died in 1935, the leading figures of the Third Reich, including the Führer himself, attended her funeral.

Some of Nietzsche's ideas, such as his notion of the *Übermensch*, may have possessed a natural appeal for the Nazis. But Nietzsche was no anti-Semite, and he could be made to appear so only by taking his words out of context. The remark about the "young stock-exchange Jew," for example, is a half-sentence from a passage in which Nietzsche is praising the Jews and condemning bigotry. It is worth quoting this passage at length because it shows what a vast gulf separated the real Nietzsche from the hate-mongers:

> [T]he whole problem of the Jews exists only in nation-states, for here their energy and higher intelligence, their accumulated capital of spirit and will, gathered from generation to generation through a long schooling in suffering, must become so preponderant as to arouse mass envy and hatred. In almost all contemporary nations,

therefore – in direct proportion to the degree to which they act up nationalistically – the literary obscenity is spreading of leading the Jews to slaughter as scapegoats of every conceivable public and internal misfortune. . . . Unpleasant, even dangerous qualities can be found in every nation and every individual: it is cruel to demand that the Jew be an exception. In him, these qualities may even be dangerous and revolting to an unusual degree; and perhaps the young stock-exchange Jew is altogether the most disgusting invention of mankind. In spite of that, I should like to know how much one must forgive a people in a total accounting when they have had the most painful history of all peoples . . . [I]n the darkest times of the Middle Ages, when the Asiatic cloud masses had gathered heavily over Europe, it was Jewish free-thinkers, scholars, and physicians who clung to the banner of enlightenment and spiritual independence in the face of the harshest personal pressures and defended Europe against Asia. We owe it to their exertions, not least of all, that a more natural, more rational, and certainly unmythical explanation of the world was eventually able to triumph again, and that the bond of culture which now links us with the enlightenment of Greco-Roman antiquity remained unbroken. (HA 475)

Anti-Semites, Nietzsche says, are "people whose nature is still feeble and uncertain," who could "easily be wiped out" by the Jews, "the strongest, toughest, and purest race at present living in Europe" (BG 251). The anti-Semites "are all men of *ressentiment*, physiologically unfortunate and worm-eaten." Nietzsche said of those who went to Paraguay with Elisabeth, "I am so happy that they voluntarily exile themselves from Europe" (YN 219).

The attack on "slave morality"

Why did Nietzsche take such pains to denounce anti-Semitism? Partly it was because hatred of the Jews was a potent force in Europe at that time, and so it was important, on general grounds, to declare where one stood. But Nietzsche had a more specific reason to distance himself from the anti-Semites. In his writings he sometimes said harsh things about historical Judaism, and he did not want these remarks to be misunderstood.

Nietzsche believed that the Western moral tradition was rotten to the core, and this tradition, in his view, originated with the ancient Israelites. The Israelites were an enslaved people. As a result, they developed an ethic tailored to the needs of slaves:

Suppose the violated, oppressed, suffering, unfree, who are uncertain of themselves and weary, moralize: what will their moral valuations have in common? . . . [T]hose qualities are brought out and flooded with light which serve to ease existence for those who suffer: here pity, the complaisant and obliging hand, the warm heart, patience, industry, humility, and friendliness are honored – for here these are the most useful qualities and almost the only means for enduring the pressure of existence. (BG 260)

Nietzsche says of the Jews: "They mark the beginning of the slave rebellion in morals" (BG 195). But if the Jews originated this way of thinking, the Christians took it over, and Nietzsche is no less harsh in his comments about them: "Christianity," he said, is "a form of mortal hostility to reality as yet unsurpassed" (AC 27). The Christians proclaimed that the meek shall inherit the earth; they preached humility and self-denial; they regarded pride as a sin. Nietzsche saw this as the dominant ethic of Western culture, and he hated it.

Slave morality glorifies the wrong kind of man, but that is not the whole problem. At a deeper level, it is the mark of an unhealthy mind, a mind in which hatred and resentment have taken control.

> They walk among us as embodied reproaches, as warnings to us – as if health, well-constitutedness, strength, pride, and the sense of power were in themselves necessarily vicious things for which one must pay some day, and pay bitterly: how ready they themselves are at bottom to *make* one pay; how they crave to be *hangmen*. There is among them an abundance of the vengeful disguised as judges, who constantly bear the word "justice" in their mouths like poisonous spittle . . . Nor is there lacking among them that most disgusting species of the vain, the mendacious failures whose aim is to appear as "beautiful souls" and who bring to market their deformed sensuality, wrapped up in verses and other swaddling clothes, as "purity of heart": the species of moral masturbaters and "self-gratifiers." (GM 3.14)

And eventually the sickness spreads:

> Undoubtedly if they succeeded in poisoning the consciences of the fortunate with their own misery, with all misery, so that one day the fortunate began to be ashamed of their good fortune and perhaps said one to another: "it is disgraceful to be fortunate: there is too much misery!" (GM 3.14)

And thus the ethic of "compassion" is born.

Nietzsche contrasts slave morality with an outlook that idealizes a different sort of person. "The noble type of man" is the opposite of the slave. He is strong rather than weak, proud rather than humble, and self-affirming rather than self-denying. He is "the ideal of the most high-spirited, alive, and world-affirming human being" (BG 56). A man endowed with such qualities will live his life boldly, making his own rules, confident of himself and of his own value. "The herd," Nietzsche said, will envy and despise such self-sufficient men. Incapable of looking beyond traditional values, they will call such men "immoral." But that does not matter; the new man will not care what the herd thinks. He will have only contempt for their morality, which is at bottom nothing more than an expression of their fear and resentment of his superiority.

Nietzsche referred to such men as *Übermenschen*; and it was this notion that the Nazis cited to support their idea of an Aryan "superman." One of the most striking things about this superior man is that he creates his own values:

> The noble type of man experiences *itself* as determining values; it does not need approval; it judges, "what is harmful to me is harmful in itself"; it knows itself to be that which first accords honor to things; it is *value-creating*. (BG 260)

How can someone create his own values? It is possible because the noble man realizes something important about morality: not only does he realize that the old morality is a sham; even more importantly, he realizes that there is nothing about the nature of the world that requires him to accept any pre-determined moral code. He knows, as Nietzsche put it, that "There are no moral facts" (TI 7.1).

2   Are There Any Moral Facts?

Ethics, in Nietzsche's view, is a deeply problematic subject. The problem is not merely that we sometimes make mistakes in our moral thinking, or that we need to adopt a different moral outlook than the one we have customarily chosen. Nietzsche's diagnosis was more radical than that. He insisted that no moral outlook, regardless of its content, has any basis in reality. The world does not contain anything that could make moral judgments true or false. "There are no moral phenomena at all," he wrote, "but only moral interpretations of phenomena" (BG 108).

This would not be so disturbing if there were a God to issue instructions about how we should live – then, even in the absence of "moral phenomena," the divine commandments could still form the basis of ethics. But the difficulty for ethics is deepened because, on Nietzsche's view, there is no God – or, in his more colorful phrase, "God is dead" (GS 125). Indeed, those who believe in God suffer from the same delusion as those who believe in objective morality:

> Moral judgement has this in common with religious judgement, that it believes in realities which do not exist. . . . Moral judgement belongs, as does religious judgement, to a level of ignorance at which even the concept of the real, the distinction between the real and the imaginary, is lacking . . . To this extent moral judgement is never to be taken literally: as such it never contains anything but nonsense. (TI 7.1)

Thus, Nietzsche considered himself to have been announcing a crisis in Western history: we have reached a point at which ethics has lost its foundations, and it is not clear how – or if – those foundations can be rebuilt.

The relation between ethics and our overall view of what the world is like

Nietzsche was not the first to be troubled about ethics or to be skeptical about "moral facts." Philosophers have been worried about these problems since the beginning of the seventeenth century. To see why, we must understand the difference modern science has made to our way of understanding the world. Before the rise of modern science, people could reasonably believe that their moral judgments were warranted by the facts of nature. Their view of what the world was like supported such a belief. But from the point of view of modern science, the world looks very different. The world as described by Galileo, Newton, and Darwin has no place for "facts" about right and wrong.

The Aristotelian world-view The Greeks developed a way of understanding the world that dominated Western thinking for over 1,700 years. They conceived the world to be an orderly system in which everything has its proper place and function. A central feature of this conception was the idea that everything in nature exists for a purpose.

Aristotle incorporated this idea into his system of thought around 350 BC when he said that, in order to understand anything, four questions must be asked: What is it? What is it made of? How did it come to exist? And what is it for? (The answers might be: this is a knife, it is made of metal, it was made by a craftsman, and it is used for cutting.) Aristotle assumed that the last question – What is it for? – could sensibly be asked of anything whatever. "Nature," he said, "belongs to the class of causes which act for the sake of something" (BW 249).

It seems obvious that artifacts such as knives have purposes, because we have a purpose in mind when we make them. But what about natural objects that we do not make? Do they have purposes too? Aristotle thought so. One of his examples was that we have teeth so that we can chew. Such biological examples are quite persuasive; the parts of our bodies do seem, intuitively, to have particular purposes – eyes are for seeing, the heart is for pumping blood, and so on. But Aristotle's thesis was not limited to organic beings. According to him, everything in nature has a purpose. He also thought, to take a different sort of example, that rain falls so that plants can grow. As odd as it may seem to a modern reader, Aristotle was perfectly serious about this. He considered other alternatives, such as that the rain falls "of necessity" and that this helps the plants only by "coincidence," and rejected them. He even considered a hypothesis strikingly like Darwinian natural selection:

> Wherever then all the parts [of plants and animals] came about just what they would have been if they had come to be for an end, such things survived, being organized spontaneously in a fitting way; whereas those which grew otherwise perished and continue to perish, as Empedocles says his "man-faced ox-progeny" did. (BW 249)

But Aristotle rejects this, too. His considered view was that plants and animals are what they are, and that the rain falls as it does, "because it is better so."

The world, therefore, is an orderly, rational system, with each thing having its own proper place and serving its own special purpose. There is a neat hierarchy: the rain exists for the sake of the plants, the plants exist for the sake of the animals, and the animals exist – of course – for the sake of people, whose well-being is the point of the whole arrangement.

> [W]e must believe, first that plants exist for the sake of animals, second that all other animals exist for the sake of man, tame animals for the use he can make of them as well as for the food they provide; and as for wild animals, most though not all of these can be used for food or are useful in other ways; clothing and instruments can be made out of them. If then we are right in believing that nature makes nothing without some end in view, nothing to no purpose, it must be that nature has made all things specifically for the sake of man. (AP 40)

391

It was a stunningly anthropocentric view. Aristotle may be forgiven, however, when we consider that virtually every important thinker in our history has entertained some such thought. Humans are a remarkably vain species.

The Christian thinkers who came later found this view of the world to be perfectly congenial. There was only one thing missing: God needed to be added to make the picture complete. (Aristotle had denied that God was a necessary part of the picture. For him, the world-view we have outlined was not religious; it was simply a description of how things are.) Thus the Christian thinkers said that the rain falls to help the plants because that is what the Creator intended, and the animals are for human use because that is what God made them for. Values and purposes were, therefore, conceived to be a fundamental part of the nature of things, because the world was believed to have been created according to a divine plan.

The implication of the Aristotelian world-view for ethics   This view of the world had a number of consequences for ethics. On the most general level, it affirmed the supreme value of human life and it explained why humans are entitled to do whatever they please with the rest of nature. The basic moral arrangement – human beings, whose lives are sacred, dominating a world made for their benefit – was enshrined as The Natural Order of Things.

At a more detailed level, a corollary of this outlook was that the "laws of nature" specify how things ought to be as well as describing how things are. In turn, knowing how things ought to be enables us to evaluate states-of-affairs as objectively good or bad. Things are as they ought to be when they are serving their natural purposes; when they do not or cannot serve those purposes, things have gone wrong. Thus, teeth that have decayed and cannot be used for chewing are defective; and drought, which deprives plants of the rain they need, is a natural, objective evil.

There are also implications for human action: moral rules are now viewed as one type of law of nature. The key idea here is that some forms of human behavior are "natural," while others are not; and "unnatural" acts are said to be wrong. Beneficence, for example, is natural for us because God has made us as social creatures. We want and need the friendship of other people and we have natural affections for them; hence, behaving brutishly toward them is unnatural. Or to take a different sort of example, the purpose of the sex organs is procreation. Thus any use of them for other purposes is "contrary to nature" – and that is why the Christian Church has traditionally regarded any form of sexual activity that does not result in procreation, such as masturbation, gay sex, or the use of contraceptives, as impermissible.

This combination of ideas, together with others like them, formed the core of an ethical outlook known as natural-law ethics. The theory of natural law was adumbrated most fully by St Thomas Aquinas (1224–74), who lived at a time when the Aristotelian world-view was unchallenged. St Thomas was the foremost thinker among traditional Catholic theologians. Today natural-law theory still has adherents inside the Catholic Church, but few outside. The reason is that the Aristotelian world-view, on which natural-law ethics depended, has been replaced by the outlook of modern science.

The world-view of modern science   The Aristotelian world-view began to break up in the sixteenth century when it was discovered that the earth orbits the sun, rather than the other way around. This was an alarming development, because the earth's being at the center of things was an important symbol of mankind's central place in the divine plan. The Church responded by declaring the Copernican cosmology to be heresy and persecuting those who taught it, forcing some to recant and putting others to death.

But the heliocentric solar system was by no means the most subversive aspect of the emerging new science. Galileo, Newton, and others developed ways of understanding natural phenomena that made no use of evaluative notions. On their way of thinking, the rain has no purpose. It does not fall in order to help the plants grow. Instead, it falls as a result of physical causes. Is it, then, a mere coincidence that there happen to be plants growing beneath the rain to benefit from it? The Aristotelians and the Christians had found this too far-fetched to believe: how can the wonderful arrangement of nature, with each part supplementing and benefiting the other, be mere coincidence? But the modern thinkers eventually found a way to explain the whole set-up: the plants are there because they have evolved, by natural selection, in the rainy climate. Natural selection produces an orderly arrangement which appears to have been designed, but, as Darwin emphasized, that is only an illusion. To explain nature there is no need to assume teleological principles, neither Aristotle's "final causes" nor the Christians' God. This was by far the more insidious feature of the new science.

This style of explanation – appealing only to physical laws devoid of any evaluative content – was developed in such great and persuasive detail, in connection with so many natural phenomena, that educated people universally gravitated to it. With its superior predictive and explanatory power, this way of thinking transformed people's view of what the world is like. But part of the transformation, inseparable from the rest, was an altered view of the nature of ethics. Right and wrong could no longer be deduced from the nature of things in themselves, for on the new view the natural world does not, in and of itself, manifest value and purpose. The inhabitants of the world may have needs and desires that generate values special to them, but that is all. The world apart from those inhabitants knows and cares nothing for their values, and it has no values of its own. A hundred and fifty years before Nietzsche declared that "There are no moral facts," the Scottish philosopher David Hume had come to the same conclusion. Hume summed up the moral implications of the new world-view when he wrote:

> Take any action allow'd to be vicious: Wilful murder, for instance. Examine it in all lights, and see if you can find that matter of fact, or real existence, which you call *vice*. In whichever way you take it, you find only certain passions, motives, volitions and thoughts. There is no other matter of fact in the case. (TH 468)

To the old idea that "nature has made all things for the sake of man," Hume replied: "The life of a man is of no greater importance to the universe than that of an oyster" (EM 590).

3   Nietzsche's Perspectivism

We have been considering one possible basis for denying that there are moral facts, namely, the appeal to the world-view of modern science. But Nietzsche's rejection of moral facts was based on a much more radical idea. His skepticism about moral facts was part of a larger skepticism about all facts, including those of science.

> Against positivism, which halts at phenomena – "There are only facts" – I would say: No, facts is precisely what there is not, only interpretations. We cannot establish any fact "in itself": perhaps it is folly to want to do such a thing. (WP 481)

It is a mistake, he thought, to believe that we can know what the world is "really" like. We view the world from a limited perspective and interpret it according to our needs and desires. That is all we can do. To demand more – to demand that we see things as they really are, independent of any interpretation, is like asking that we see with "an eye turned in no particular direction." "There is *only* a perspective seeing," says Nietzsche, "*only* a perspective 'knowing'" (GM 3.12). "It is our needs that interpret the world; our drives and their For and Against" (WP 481).

All our knowing is human knowing. We are one particular species, occupying one particular position in the universe, and we inevitably interpret things from our own limited point of view. But it is easy to forget this. We commonly assume the world simply is the way it appears to us. We call the view from our own vantage-point "knowledge," as though our standpoint has some special, privileged status. Nietzsche writes:

> In some remote corner of the universe, poured out and glittering in innumerable solar systems, there once was a star on which clever animals invented knowledge. That was the haughtiest and most mendacious minute of "world history" – and yet only a minute. After nature had drawn a few breaths the star grew cold, and the clever animals had to die.
>
> One might invent such a fable and still not have illustrated sufficiently how wretched, how shadowy and flighty, how aimless and arbitrary, the human intellect appears in nature. . . . Only its owner gives it such importance, as if the world pivoted around it. But if we could communicate with the mosquito, then we would learn that it floats through the air with the same self-importance, feeling within itself the flying center of the world. (TL 42)

Nietzsche was reacting against a cluster of ideas that has become known as modernity. Modernity is an outlook that embraces the world-view of modern science, but it includes more than just science. It includes such conceptions as these:

- that the world consists of facts that exist independently of human beliefs and desires;
- that human beings have capacities of reason and perception that enable them to discover what those facts are;
- that there is one objectively correct way of understanding what the world is like, and human reason is capable of attaining such an understanding;
- that there is one logic, one scientific method, one set of rational principles that are independent of historical and cultural context; and
- that rational thought will show us the one correct way we should live and how an enlightened society should be structured and governed.

If you reject all this and look for an alternative – especially an alternative that involves some form of relativism – then you are post-modern. Accepting Nietzsche's perspectivism is one way of being post-modern. Some commentators believe that Nietzsche's primary importance is that he was an early and trenchant critic of modernity. Today one often hears this opinion in literary circles, where being "post-modern" is equated with being in the know.

A limited objectivity

The idea that "there are no facts, only interpretations" is disturbing, as Nietzsche knew it would be. What, exactly, are its implications? There are two obvious questions that need to be addressed:

1   Does this mean we are free to believe whatever we like, because any interpretation of the world is as good as any other? And,
2   Does this mean that objectivity is impossible – that we can never achieve an objective understanding of what the world is like?

Let us consider these one at a time.

1. Are we free to interpret the world in any way we choose?   Nietzsche does not think so. Not all interpretations are equal; some are better than others. In this respect, interpreting the world is like interpreting a work of art. There are no "facts" about what a work of art really means – there may be many legitimate ways to view a work of art, and many different meanings that may legitimately be attached to it. In fact, the richer the artwork, the greater are the possibilities for alternative interpretation. Moreover, our interpretations of an artwork will inevitably be colored by our particular backgrounds and experience. But this does not mean that there aren't better and worse interpretations. Obviously, some interpretations of art can still be insightful, while others are silly.

The same is true of interpreting the world: even though there is no single "correct" way of viewing the world, some viewings are reasonable while others are preposterous. Christianity is Nietzsche's favorite example of a preposterous interpretation. Christianity, he says, is nothing but a blatant projection of how some people would like for things to be. Christians have the astonishing arrogance to imagine that the entire universe was made for their benefit. They have persuaded themselves that they were created in the image of God, who loves them above all others and who made the world as a home for them. They believe in addition that they will never perish, because God will keep them eternally in heaven. The self-aggrandizement and wish-fulfillment of such a view are evident. Therefore, even though he rejects "facts" and insists that all knowledge is a matter of interpretation, Nietzsche does not hesitate to denounce "the falseness and mendaciousness of all Christian interpretations of the world" (WP 1).

This, however, only raises a further question. What makes one interpretation better than another? It is difficult to give a general answer, because there are a variety of ways in which an interpretation might be assessed. Christianity, on Nietzsche's view, involves crude projections of human wishes and assumes the existence of a divine being when there is no good reason to think such a being actually exists. The world-view of science, on the other hand, does not involve such blatant wish-fulfillment and does not assume the existence of supernatural beings. Unlike Christianity, science is not a "lie." Rather than being mendacious, science merely abstracts and oversimplifies. But science is also an interpretation motivated by our needs – in particular, our need for order and our need to control and exploit events. If we understand that science is essentially a tool we have developed to serve these needs, we will understand both its strength and its limitations. Its strength is that it serves these needs very well. Its limitations are its perspectival character and its essential connection with these needs – which means that it is not, and could not be, a source of "absolute truth" about the way things are. Unlike Christianity, science can be embraced, for what it is, by reasonable people.

Other interpretations might have different sorts of virtues and vices. The important thing is to cultivate what Nietzsche calls an "intellectual conscience," the habit of critically assessing rival interpretations and seeing them for what they are. Nietzsche laments that most people lack such a conscience:

> The great majority of people does not consider it contemptible to believe this or that and to live accordingly, without first having given themselves an account of the final and most certain reasons pro and con, and without even troubling themselves about such reasons afterward: the most gifted men and noblest women still belong to this "great majority." (GS 2)

2. Is objectivity possible? Even if every set of beliefs expresses some particular interpretation of the world, it is still possible, on Nietzsche's view, to achieve a kind of objectivity. There are at least three things one can do to accomplish this.

The first step toward being objective is simply to realize that the world cannot be comprehended within a single point of view. We will continue to form beliefs and act on them – we can hardly do otherwise, if we go on living as human beings

– but we will be appropriately modest in what we claim for our outlook. We will not make the mistake of identifying "truth" with any one point of view.

The second step is the cultivation of an intellectual conscience. We can learn to "give ourselves an account of the reasons pro and con" before crediting any particular interpretation of the world; and when we adopt an interpretation, we can do so without having any illusions about its nature and purpose.

Finally, we can learn to look at things from different perspectives and take them all into account when we form our conceptions. Objectivity, says Nietzsche, may be understood as

> the ability *to control* one's Pro and Con and to dispose of them, so that one knows how to employ a *variety* of perspectives and affective interpretations in the service of knowledge . . . the more affects we allow to speak about one thing, the more eyes, different eyes, we can use to observe one thing, the more complete will our "concept" of this thing, our "objectivity," be. (GM 3.12)

Our understanding of morality can especially benefit from this sort of approach. The more we can control our emotions and examine morals from a variety of perspectives, "the more complete will our 'objectivity' be."

Moralities

Rather than speaking of "morality," which suggests a single universal system of right and wrong, Nietzsche often prefers to focus on "moralities," using a term that emphasizes the multitude of outlooks that actually exist. But although they may differ in important ways, all moralities have certain things in common. They are all rival perspectives invented by humans to serve human purposes. At the most general level, they are social products, that arise within communities, and their function is to protect the community and to ensure its preservation. Moral values are, in Nietzsche's words,

> always expressions of the needs of a community and herd: whatever benefits it most – and second most, and third most – that is also considered the first standard of value of all individuals. . . . The conditions for the preservation of different communities were very different; hence there were very different moralities. (GS 116)

Like all interpretations, rival moralities may be subjected to the scrutiny of the "intellectual conscience." We can ask about any particular morality:

- What is its historical origin?
- Whose interests does it serve?
- What motivates people to accept it? What deep human needs and drives give it life?
- What are its psychological effects on the people who live under its sway? What sort of people do they become?

Although Nietzsche repeatedly says that there are "many moralities," the only one he discusses at length is the slave morality of Western culture – an understandable choice, perhaps, considering that this is the morality of Nietzsche's own culture (and ours). As we have seen, slave morality originated with the Jews, whose experience of bondage led them to develop an ethic that glorified such traits as humility, obedience, and self-denial. What deep human feelings are being expressed here? Nietzsche's answer is fear – fear of failure, fear of being hurt, fear of one's own insufficiencies, and above all else, fear of people superior to oneself. Superior people are, after all, stronger and more capable, and so they pose a threat. They can win the competition for life's goods, and in furthering their own interests they can hurt those more vulnerable than themselves. So, to be safe, one needs some way of controlling them and neutralizing their great natural advantage. A code of conduct that limits what they may do accomplishes this. "Fear," Nietzsche says, "is the mother of morals" (BG 201).

Slave morality also emphasizes such values as pity and compassion, and we may profitably ask whose interests are served by such an ethic. Who benefits from an ethic that requires us to take pity on those worse off than ourselves, to share what we have with others, to feed the hungry? In short, who benefits from an ethic of self-sacrificial altruism? The answer, plainly, is that such an ethic serves the interests of the weak and the poor. It is not the strong, self-sufficient man who benefits from charity – on the contrary, an ethic that requires self-sacrificial altruism imposes burdens on him to benefit someone else. Indeed, so long as slave morality prevails in a society it will be hard for strong, self-sufficient people to arise and flourish – slave morality is not an ethic designed with their needs in mind.

All this, Nietzsche thinks, provides the "intellectual conscience" with ample grounds for rejecting slave morality. There is, then, a limited sense in which ethics can be objective. The old distinction between "objective" and "subjective" morality becomes, in Nietzsche's hands, the distinction between views that survive scrutiny by the intellectual conscience and those that do not. If we can look into the origins of an ethical view, examine its psychological and social functions, consider from various perspectives its effects on different types of people, with different interests – if we can do all this, and still find it agreeable to adopt this outlook, or some modified part of it, then it has all the objective validity that such a perspective could ever have. (Conversely, if no moral view survives this kind of scrutiny – that is a possibility Nietzsche took very seriously – then it might turn out that morality must be rejected altogether.) This may not be "objective" in the robust sense of corresponding to "moral facts," but it is a very long way from believing whatever we choose.

4   Morality Without Illusions

If there are no moral facts and no God, what becomes of morality? This had been one of the primary questions of philosophy from the seventeenth century on. And many thinkers had concurred with Nietzsche's general answer: ethics, they said, must be understood as a purely human phenomenon – as the product of human needs, interests, and desires – and nothing else.

Thomas Hobbes, the foremost English philosopher of the seventeenth century, suggested one way in which ethics might be understood in purely human terms. Hobbes assumed that "good" and "bad" are just names we give to things we like and dislike. Thus, when we like different things, we may disagree about what is good or bad. However, Hobbes said, in our fundamental psychological makeup we are all very much alike. We are all basically self-interested creatures who want to live and to live as well as possible. This is the key to understanding ethics. Ethics arises when people realize what they must do to live well.

The Social Contract

Hobbes was the first important modern thinker to provide a secular, naturalistic basis for ethics. He pointed out that each of us is enormously better off living in a mutually cooperative society than we would be if we tried to make it on our own. The benefits of social living go far beyond companionship: social cooperation makes possible schools, hospitals, and highways; houses with electricity and central heating; airplanes and telephones; newspapers and books: movies, opera, and football; science and agriculture. Without social cooperation we would lose all of this. Therefore, it is to the advantage of each of us to do whatever is necessary to establish and maintain a cooperative society.

But it turns out that a mutually cooperative society can exist only if we adopt certain rules of behavior – rules that require telling the truth, keeping our promises, respecting one another's lives and property, and so on:

- Without the presumption that people will tell the truth, there would be no reason for people to pay any attention to what other people say. Communication would be impossible. And without communication among its members, society would collapse.
- Without the requirement that people keep their promises, there could be no division of labor – workers could not count on getting paid, retailers could not rely on their agreements with suppliers, and so on – and the economy would collapse. There could be no business, no building, no agriculture, no medicine.
- Without assurances against assault, murder, and theft, no one could feel secure; everyone would have to be constantly on guard against everyone else, and social cooperation would be impossible.

Thus, to obtain the benefits of social living, we must strike a bargain with one another, with each of us agreeing to obey these rules, provided others do likewise. (We must also establish mechanisms for enforcing these rules – such as legal sanctions and other, less formal methods of enforcement – so that we can count on one another to obey them.) This "social contract" is the basis of morality. Indeed, morality can be defined as nothing more or less than the set of rules that rational people will agree to obey, for their mutual benefit, provided that other people will obey them as well.

This way of understanding morality has a number of appealing features. First, it takes the mystery out of ethics and makes it a practical, down-to-earth business. Living morally is not a matter of blind obedience to the mysterious dictates of a supernatural being; nor is it a matter of fidelity to lofty but pointless abstract rules. Instead, it is a matter of doing what it takes to make social living possible.

Second, this theory makes it clear how morality can be rational and objective even if there are no moral facts. It is not merely a matter of opinion that the rule against murder must be a part of any workable social scheme; or that rational people, to secure their own welfare, must agree to adopt such a rule. Nor is it merely a matter of opinion that rules requiring truthfulness and promise-keeping are needed for people to flourish in a social setting. Even if there are no moral facts, the reasoning that leads to such conclusions is perfectly objective. In this sense, Hobbes did "want to supply a rational foundation for morality," as Nietzsche put it – but he did not simply "accept morality as 'given'," as Nietzsche charges. Instead he accepted the same limitations as Nietzsche – no God and no moral facts – and worked within those limits to construct a positive account of moral obligation.

Third, the Social Contract Theory explains why we should care about ethics. If there is no God to punish us, why should we bother to do what is "right," especially when it is not to our advantage? The answer is that it is to our advantage to live in a society where people behave morally – thus, it is rational for us to accept moral restrictions on our conduct as part of a bargain we make with other people. We benefit directly from the ethical conduct of others, and our own compliance with the moral rules is the price we pay to secure their compliance.

Fourth, the Social Contract approach gives us a sensible and mature way of determining what our ethical duties really are. When "morality" is mentioned, the first thing that pops into many people's minds is an attempt to restrict their sex lives. It is unfortunate that "morals" has come to have such a connotation. The whole purpose of having a system of morality, according to Social Contract Theory, is to make it possible for people to live their individual lives in a setting of social cooperation – its purpose is not to tell people what kinds of lives they should live (except in so far as it is necessary to restrict conduct in the interests of maintaining social cooperation). Therefore, an ethic based on the Social Contract would have little interest in what people do in their bedrooms.

Finally, we may note again that Social Contract Theory assumes relatively little about human nature. It treats human beings as self-interested creatures and does not assume that they are naturally altruistic, even to the slightest degree. One of the theory's charms is that it can reach the conclusion that we ought, often, to behave altruistically, without assuming that we are naturally altruistic. We want to live as well as possible, and moral obligations are created as we band together with other people to form the cooperative societies that are necessary for us to achieve this fundamentally self-interested goal.

Altruism and self-interest   Are people essentially self-interested? Although the Social
Contract Theory continues to attract supporters, not many philosophers and psychologists today would accept Hobbes's egoistic view of human nature. It seems
evident that humans have at least some altruistic feelings, if only for their family
and friends. We have evolved as social creatures just as surely as we have evolved
as creatures with legs – thus, caring for our kin and members of our local group is
as natural for us as walking.

If humans do have some degree of natural altruism, does this have any significance for morals? David Hume thought so. Hume agreed with Hobbes that our
moral opinions are expressions of our feelings. In 1740, when he invited his readers
to consider "wilful murder" and see if they could find that "matter of fact" called
"vice," Hume concluded that:

> You never can find it, till you turn your reflexion into your own breast, and find a
> sentiment of disapprobation, which arises in you, towards this action. Here is a matter
> of fact; but 'tis the object of feeling . . . It lies in yourself, not in the object. So that
> when you pronounce any action or character to be vicious, you mean nothing, but
> that from the constitution of your nature you have a feeling or sentiment of blame
> from the contemplation of it. (TH 468–9)

And what, exactly, is "the constitution of our nature?" Of course, it is part of our
nature to care about ourselves and our own welfare. But Hume added that we also
have "social sentiments" – feelings that connect us with other people and make us
concerned about their welfare. That is why, Hume said, we measure right and
wrong by "the true interests of mankind":

> In all determinations of morality, this circumstance of public utility is ever principally
> in view; and wherever disputes arise, either in philosophy or common life, concern-
> ing the bounds of duty, the question cannot, by any means, be decided with greater
> certainty than by ascertaining, on any side, the true interests of mankind. (IP 12–13)

This view came to be known as Utilitarianism. In modern moral philosophy it is
the chief alternative to the theory of the Social Contract.

Utilitarianism

Utilitarians hold that there is one principle that sums up all our moral duties. The
ultimate moral principle is that we should always do whatever will produce the
greatest possible balance of happiness over unhappiness for everyone who will be
affected by our action. This "principle of utility" is deceptively simple. It is actually
a combination of three ideas: first, in determining what to do, we should be guided
by the expected consequences of our actions – we should do whatever will have
the best consequences. Second, in determining which consequences are best, we
should give the greatest possible weight to the happiness or unhappiness that would
be caused – we should do whatever will cause the most happiness or the least

unhappiness. And finally, the principle of utility assumes that each individual's happiness is equally as important as anyone else's.

Although Hume proposed this theory, two other philosophers elaborated it in greater detail. Jeremy Bentham, an Englishman whose life spanned the eighteenth and nineteenth centuries, was the leader of a group of philosophical radicals who aimed to reform the laws of Britain along Utilitarian lines. They were remarkably successful in advancing such causes as prison reform and restrictions on the use of child labor. John Stuart Mill, the son of one of Bentham's original followers, gave the theory its most popular and influential defense in his book *Utilitarianism*, published in 1861.

The Utilitarian movement attracted critics from the outset. It was an easy target because it ignored conventional religious notions. The point of morality, according to the Utilitarians, had nothing to do with obedience to God or gaining credit in Heaven. Rather, the point was just to make life in this world as comfortable and happy as possible. So some critics condemned Utilitarianism as a godless doctrine. To this Mill replied:

> [T]he question depends upon what idea we have formed of the moral character of the Deity. If it be a true belief that God desires, above all things, the happiness of his creatures, and that this was his purpose in their creation, utility is not only not a godless doctrine, but more profoundly religious than any other. (MU 28)

Utilitarianism was also an easy target because it was (and still is) a subversive theory, in that it turned many traditional moral ideas upside-down. Bentham argued, for example, that the purpose of the criminal justice system cannot be understood in the traditional way as "paying back" miscreants for their wicked deeds – that only piles misery upon misery. Instead, the social response to crime should be threefold: to identify and deal with the causes of criminal behavior; where possible, to reform individual lawbreakers and make them into productive citizens; and to "punish" people only in so far as it is necessary to deter others from committing similar crimes. (Today, of course, these are familiar ideas, but only because the Utilitarians' victory was so sweeping.) Or, to take a different example: by insisting that everyone's happiness is equally important, the Utilitarians offended various elitist notions of group superiority. According to the Utilitarian standard, neither race, sex, nor social class makes a difference to one's moral status. Mill himself wrote a book on *The Subjection of Women* which became a classic of the nineteenth-century suffragist movement.

Finally, Utilitarianism was controversial because it had no use for "absolute" moral rules. The Utilitarians regarded the traditional rules – against killing, lying, breaking one's promises, and so on – as "rules of thumb," useful because following them will generally be for the best. But they are not absolute – whenever breaking such a rule will have better results for everyone concerned, the rule should be broken. The rule against killing, for example, might be suspended in the case of voluntary euthanasia for someone dying of a painful illness. Moreover, the Utilitarians regarded some traditional rules as dubious, even as rules-of-thumb. For example, Christian moralists had traditionally said that masturbation is evil; but from the point of view of the Principle of Utility, it appears to be perfectly harmless. A more serious matter is the traditional religious condemnation of homosexuality, which has resulted in misery for countless people. Utilitarianism implies that if an activity makes people happy, without anyone being harmed, it cannot be wrong.

But it is one thing to describe a moral view; it is another thing to justify it. Utilitarianism says that our moral duty is to "promote the general happiness." Why should we do that? This is the key question. As Mill puts it,

> I feel that I am bound not to rob or murder, betray or deceive; but why am I bound to promote the general happiness? If my own happiness lies in something else, why may I not give that the preference? (MU 34)

Aside from the "external sanctions" of law and public opinion, Mill thinks there is only one possible reason for accepting this or any other moral standard. The "internal sanction" of morality must always be "a feeling in our minds," regardless of what sort of ethic this feeling endorses:

> The ultimate sanction, therefore, of all morality (external motives apart) being a subjective feeling in our own minds, I see nothing embarrassing to those whose standard is utility in the question, What is the sanction of that particular standard? We may answer, the same as all other moral standards – the conscientious feelings of mankind. Undoubtedly this sanction has no binding efficacy on those who do not possess the feelings it appeals to; but neither will these persons be more obedient to any other moral principle than the utilitarian one. (MU 37)

The kind of morality we accept will, therefore, depend on the nature of our feelings: if human beings have "social feelings," then Mill says that utilitarian morality will be the natural standard for them.

> The firm foundation [of utilitarian morality] is that of the social feelings of mankind – the desire to be in unity with our fellow creatures, which is already a powerful principle in human nature, and happily one of those which tend to become stronger, even without express inculcation, from the influences of advancing civilization. (MU 40)

Impartiality

Utilitarianism, as we have seen, has implications that are at odds with traditional morality. Much the same could be said about Social Contract Theory. In most of the practical matters that have been mentioned – punishment, racial discrimination, women's rights, euthanasia, homosexuality – the two theories have similar implications. But there is one matter on which they differ dramatically. Utilitarians believe that we have a very extensive moral duty to help other people. Social Contract Theorists deny this.

Suppose, for example, you are thinking of spending $1,000 for a new living room carpet. Should you do this? What are the alternatives? One alternative is to give the money to an agency such as the United Nations Children's Fund. Each year between 10 and 20 million third-world children die of easily preventable diseases, because there isn't enough money to provide the vitamin-A capsules, antibiotics, and oral rehydration treatments they need. By giving the money to UNICEF, and making do a while longer with your old carpet, you could provide much-needed medical care for dozens of children. From the point of view of utility — seeking the best overall outcome for everyone concerned — there is no doubt you should give the money to UNICEF. Obviously, the medicine will help the kids a lot more than the new rug will help you.

But from the point of view of the Social Contract, things look very different. If morality rests on an agreement between people — remember, an agreement they enter into to promote their own interests — what would the agreement say about helping other people? Certainly, we would want the contract to impose a duty not to harm other people, even strangers. Each of us would obviously benefit from that. And it might be in our best interests to accept a mutual obligation to provide aid to others when it is easy and convenient to do so. But would rational people accept a general duty to provide virtually unlimited aid to strangers, even at great cost to themselves? From the standpoint of self-interest, that sounds crazy. Jan Narveson, a contract theorist who teaches philosophy at the University of Waterloo in Canada, writes:

> [M]orals, if they are to be rational, must amount to agreements among people — people of all kinds, each pursuing his or her own interests, which are various and do not necessarily include much concern for others and their interests. But people have minds, and apply information gleaned from observing the world around them to the task of promoting their interests, and they have a broad repertoire of powers including some that can make them exceedingly dangerous, as well as others that can make them very helpful. This gives us reason to agree with each other that we will refrain from harming others in the pursuit of our interests, to respect each other's property and grant extensive civil rights, but not necessarily to go very far out of our way to be very helpful to those we don't know and may not particularly care for. (MM 130–1)

> It is reasonable, then, to arrive at a general understanding that we shall be ready to help when help is urgent and when giving it is not very onerous to us. But a general understanding that we shall help everyone as if they were our spouses or dearest friends is quite another matter. (MM 146)

Unlike many philosophers who prefer to keep things abstract, Narveson is good about spelling out the implications of his view in a way that leaves no room for misunderstanding:

> What about parting with the means for making your sweet little daughter's birthday party a memorable one, in order to keep a dozen strangers alive on the other side of

the world? Is this something you are morally required to do? Indeed not. She may well matter to you more than they. This illustrates again the fact that people do not "count equally" for most of us. Normal people care more about some people than others, and build their very lives around those carings. (MM 145)

Which view is correct? Do we have a moral duty to provide extensive aid to strangers, or not? Both views appeal ultimately to our emotions. A striking feature of Narveson's contractarian argument is its appeal to the fact that we care more for some people than others. This is certainly true: as he says, we care more for our own children than for "strangers on the other side of the world." But does this really mean that I may choose some trivial benefit for my children over the very lives of the strangers? Suppose there were two buttons on my desk at this moment: by pressing button A, I can provide my son with a nice party; by pressing B, I can save the lives of a dozen strangers. Is it really all right for me to press A, just because I "care more" for my son? Mill agrees that the issue must be decided on the basis of feelings (how else could it be?), but for him it is not these small-scale personal feelings that have the final say. Instead, it is one's "conscientious feelings" – the feelings that prevail after everything has been thought through – that finally determine one's obligations. Mill assumes that we cannot, when we are thoughtful and reflective, approve of ourselves pushing button A.

However, some contemporary Utilitarians have argued that the matter need not be left to the vicissitudes of individual feeling. It may be true, they say, that we all care more for ourselves, our family, and our friends than we care for strangers. But we have rational capacities as well as feelings, and if we think objectively about the matter, we will realize that other people are no different. Others, even strangers, also care about themselves, their families, and their friends, in the same way that we do. Their needs and interests are comparable to our own. In fact, there is nothing of this general sort that makes anyone different from anyone else – and if we are in all relevant respects similar to one another, then there is no justification for anyone taking his or her own interests to be more important. Peter Singer, a utilitarian philosopher at the University of Melbourne in Australia, writes:

> Reason makes it possible for us to see ourselves in this way . . . I am able to see that I am just one being among others, with interests and desires like others. I have a personal perspective on the world, from which my interests are at the front and centre of the stage, the interests of my family and friends are close behind, and the interests of strangers are pushed to the back and sides. But reason enables me to see that others have similarly subjective perspectives, and that from "the point of view of the universe" my perspective is no more privileged than theirs. Thus my ability to reason shows me the possibility of detaching myself from my own perspective, and shows me what the universe might look like if I had no personal perspective. (HL 229)

So, from an objective viewpoint, each of us must acknowledge that our own perspective – our own particular set of needs, interests, likes, and dislikes – is only one among many and has no special status. This thought is not unlike Nietzsche's idea that each of us looks at things from a particular perspective and in order to think objectively we must realize this and consider how things look from other perspectives as well. As Nietzsche put it, "the more affects we allow to speak about one thing, the more eyes, different eyes, we can use to observe one thing, the more complete will our 'concept' of this thing, our 'objectivity,' be" (GM 3.12). But the Utilitarians draw a very un-Nietzschean conclusion from this: namely, that from a moral point of view, everyone counts equally.

5 Nietzsche's Noble Man

Near the end of his career Nietzsche described his moral philosophy as a form of naturalism. "I might designate the tendency of these reflections," he said, "as moralistic naturalism: my task is to translate the apparently emancipated and denatured moral values back into their nature – i.e., into their natural 'immorality'." By a "denatured" ethics he meant an ethic that associates morality with "the antithesis of life, with 'God' – also as the revelation of a higher world which here and there looks down upon us through them." A naturalistic ethics, on the other hand, would see morality as having "the aim of enhancing life" (WP 298–9).

Considering this, we might expect Nietzsche to find Utilitarianism congenial. But when he speaks of morality's "enhancing life" Nietzsche does not mean enhancing the lives of everyone alike. On his view, not everyone's life is worthy of being enhanced. Rather, he meant enhancing the life of a particular kind of person – his noble man. Utilitarianism would require the noble man to make sacrifices to benefit the less worthy; thus it is a variation of the slave morality that Nietzsche rejects. After his initial description of slave morality as an ethic of "the obliging hand, the warm heart," Nietzsche adds: "Slave morality is essentially a morality of utility" (BG 260).

Equally, remembering Nietzsche's remarks about morality being a social product, we might expect him to be sympathetic to the idea of a Social Contract. But neither will he have any part of this conception. In *Beyond Good and Evil* he gives a clear statement of the basic idea of the Social Contract and rejects it emphatically:

> Refraining mutually from injury, violence, and exploitation and placing one's will on a par with that of someone else – this may become, in a certain rough sense, good manners among individuals if the appropriate conditions are present (namely, if these men are actually similar in strength and value standards and belong together in *one* body). But as soon as this principle is extended [to include everyone], and possibly even accepted as the *fundamental principle of society*, it immediately proves to be what it really is – a will to the *denial* of life, a principle of disintegration and decay. (BG 259)

The problem, once again, is Nietzsche's conviction that not all human beings are equally worthy of respect. Who will be included in the Social Contract? So long as the noble man is dealing with men similar to himself, all is well. Then the contract amounts to little more than "good manners" between them. But when "the herd" is allowed into the arrangement, there is trouble. The "noble man" does not belong in "one body" with "the cowardly, the petty . . . those who humble themselves, the doglike people who allow themselves to be maltreated, the begging flatterers, above all the liars . . ." For him, "the exalted, proud states of the soul are experienced as conferring distinction and determining the order of rank. The noble human being separates from himself those in whom the opposite of such exalted, proud states finds expression: he despises them" (BG 260). To lower himself to a position of "equality" with them, subjecting himself to a contract in which all are equal partners, is beneath him – his life will "disintegrate and decay" in such a degrading arrangement.

The noble man's virtues

If he rejects these options, what does Nietzsche offer in their place? What positive understanding of morality does he finally endorse? How, when all is said and done, does Nietzsche think we ought to live?

In keeping with his "amoralism," Nietzsche never says we ought to live one way rather than another – he had nothing but contempt for that sort of pious pronouncement. (Besides, the noble man creates his own values; he does not take instructions from anyone, not even Nietzsche.) Yet Nietzsche says enough to make it clear what sort of people he thinks are worthy of respect and what sort of ethical theory would be appropriate to describing them.

Nietzsche's ethical theory – in so far as we may shoe-horn his various remarks into the confines of a conventional theory – is a type of Virtue Theory. Virtue Theory is an approach to ethics that begins by describing the traits of character (the "virtues") that make a person admirable. This was the approach taken by Socrates, Plato, and Aristotle; indeed, in the ancient world this way of understanding morality was more or less taken for granted. The virtues were regarded as fundamental, and the notion of right action came into play only derivatively, as the notion of what a virtuous person would do. Modern theories such as Social Contract Theory and Utilitarianism take things the other way around: they take the notion of right action as primary, concentrating on the nature and justification of the rules that determine what we should do. The two approaches lead to strikingly different pictures of the moral life. Nietzsche was clear in his preference for the former: "It is obvious," he said, "that moral designations were everywhere first applied to *human beings* and only later, derivatively, to actions" (BG 260).

Nietzsche's description of the "noble man" may be understood in this context, as an account of the qualities of character that make a person admirable. What sort of person would that be? And should we agree that Nietzsche's noble man really is admirable?

Pride and self-direction   As we have already observed, Nietzsche sometimes presents the noble man as the antithesis of the "slave" of traditional ethics – rather than being humble, obedient, and self-denying, the noble man is proud, self-directing, and self-affirming. This is probably the most attractive aspect of Nietzsche's description of him. The reader is apt to think that Nietzsche is on to something important: should we embrace the "slave morality" of humility and obedience or should we choose instead a life of pride and self-direction? When the options are put like this, the answer may seem obvious. Certainly, as Nietzsche describes the alternatives, pride and self-direction seem like easy winners. But a little thought shows that things are not so simple. The truth probably lies somewhere in between the extremes that Nietzsche presents.

First, it is too simple to say that we should be proud rather than humble (or, for that matter, the other way around). Pride is justified in some circumstances but not in others. Modesty is appropriate when we reflect on our limitations and on the difference between what we could accomplish and what we actually have accomplished. Modesty is also called for when we think about the greater achievements of others. Pride, on the other hand, is justified when we have done our best and the result has been of value. In general, our attitude toward ourselves should reflect the truth. This isn't very exciting – it certainly isn't as exciting as Nietzsche's bold declarations – but it does seem to be correct. As for humility, if we mean by this a habitual groveling self-deprecation, then Nietzsche was certainly right.

Similarly, while self-direction is no doubt a great good, there are obviously times when a wise person will take his cue from others. It is easy to think of examples: we follow instructions when working at a job under another person's direction, when submitting to the authority of a police officer or a judge, or when we are ignorant about a situation and we have available the advice of someone who is more knowledgeable and experienced. As Aristotle observed, it is a matter of practical wisdom to recognize when it is best to defer to someone else. If Nietzsche's criticism of the traditional virtue of obedience seems to hit the mark, it may be only because some traditional moralists got the nature of this virtue wrong. But Nietzsche's alternative is not altogether satisfactory either. There is a difference between confident self-direction and arrogance, and Nietzsche's flamboyant way of writing often blurs that difference. One is a virtue; the other is not.

We may also note that although Nietzsche predicted he would be condemned by "the herd," most people today would find at least part of his view quite congenial. Many of the "traditional" virtues that he criticized so harshly were in fact the monkish virtues of medieval Europe. While the priest's vows of "poverty, chastity, and obedience" remain familiar, they no longer express an ideal that many people would willingly embrace. They belong, at best, to a very particular way of life, and today even priests sometimes rebel against them.

Egoism Nietzsche does not describe the noble man merely as proud and self-directing. If that were all there were to him, the noble man could be a pretty ordinary kind of person, with a conventional moral outlook. He could even be a Utilitarian. After all, a proud, self-directing man could devote his life to helping the poor: when he "creates his own values," he could choose the values of kindness and compassion.

But Nietzsche rejects this possibility. The noble man, he says, disdains "compassionate feelings and a 'warm heart'" (BG 260). He may sometimes help the poor – although he certainly would not devote his life to them – but not because he cares anything about their welfare. Instead, he may help them as a way of displaying his own power:

> [T]he noble human being, too, helps the unfortunate, but not, or almost not, from pity, but prompted more by an urge begotten by excess of power. The noble human being honors himself as one who is powerful . . . (BG 260)

What Nietzsche says here is strongly reminiscent of Hobbes's definition of charity: "There can be no greater argument to a man, of his own power," said Hobbes, "than to find himself able not only to accomplish his own desires, but also to assist other men in theirs: and this is that conception wherein consisteth charity" (HN 221). Like Hobbes's everyman, Nietzsche's noble man may sometimes seem selfless, but in reality his motive is "self-glorification" (BG 260). Thus Nietzsche sides with those who believe "altruism" is just a myth. "Selfless" and "unegoistic" actions, he says, are "all unreal, imaginary" (WP 786).

The noble man is therefore amoral in two senses. First, he knows that there are no moral facts and that "moralities" are only devices by which the herd attempts to control and limit him. He finds this knowledge deeply liberating. He is freed to assert his own will, rejecting all constraints except those he chooses to impose on himself. And second, when he chooses which constraints to impose on himself, "compassionate feelings and a 'warm heart'" are permitted no influence. The noble man does not pretend otherwise. He says, without qualm, "What is harmful to me is harmful in itself" (BG 260).

It is a nice question whether the noble man simply has a different morality than other people or rejects morality altogether. The noble man has his standards – he admires some things and detests others; he behaves in some ways and considers other forms of behavior beneath him. We might call this his morality. (Writing about himself, Nietzsche once declared that, rather than lacking a morality, he had "a more severe morality than anybody" (DL 102).) Nevertheless, if we conceive of morality in the usual way, as a set of constraints limiting what one may do in the pursuit of self-interest, it might be more perspicuous to say that the noble man rejects morality altogether. This description of him seems even more apt when we consider some further aspects of the noble man's character.

The dark side of Nietzsche's noble man   Nietzsche does what we should expect a great philosopher to do: he identifies and challenges assumptions that others unthinkingly take for granted. There is something enormously appealing about his iconoclastic spirit. Yet at the same time there is a side to Nietzsche's thought that is deeply troubling. He seriously believed that there is an "order of rank" among people, and that superior people are free to use "inferior" people as means to their own ends. This was not a racial or nationalist doctrine – he did not identify the noble men with Aryans or Germans or anything like that. Nevertheless, in describing the character of his noble man, Nietzsche permits him options that no other major moral philosopher would countenance. No one but Nietzsche could have written that:

> The essential characteristic of a good and healthy aristocracy, however, is that it . . . accepts with a good conscience the sacrifice of untold human beings who, for its sake, must be reduced and lowered to incomplete human beings, to slaves, to instruments. The fundamental faith simply has to be that society must not exist for society's sake but only as the foundation and scaffolding on which a choice type of being is able to raise itself to its higher task and to a higher state of being . . . (BG 258)

When we read such words, we may naturally assume that they are not to be taken at face value, and we may search for an interpretation that removes the sting. There is, in fact, a serious point here, with which one might have some sympathy. One might think of the "choice type of being" as Beethoven or Newton or Churchill – men whose creative achievements set them apart. It is not hard to understand the special value of such individuals and to see the point of making special provisions for them. Thus, if we want to maximize the best things in a culture, we must create conditions in which such people can flourish; and that will be a very different sort of project than seeking to promote everyone's welfare equally. This, one might think, is the real and defensible point of Nietzsche's elitism.

But Nietzsche's harsh words can be softened only up to a point. He mentions "sympathy, the kind, helping hand, the warm heart, patience, diligence, and friendliness" only to sneer at them. We must, he says, "resist all sentimental weakness" and realize that "life itself is *essentially* appropriation, injury, overpowering of what is alien and weaker; suppression, hardness, imposition of one's own forms, incorporation, and at least, at its mildest, exploitation" – and so, he insists, it is pointless to object to such things (BG 259). He is too insistent, too explicit, and goes on at too great a length to permit a reading that would make him into some sort of misunderstood nice-guy.

Thus, Nietzsche's call for a "new kind of man," expressed in such compelling prose – "Behold, I teach you the overman. The overman is the meaning of the earth. Let your will say: the overman shall be the meaning of the earth!" (TZ 1.3) – which seemed at first to be the most exciting and interesting part of his moral philosophy, turns out on closer inspection to be, at the same time, its most disappointing aspect. Perhaps an even harsher appraisal might be justified. One does not have to be a profound thinker to realize that there is not enough sympathy, kindness, and helpfulness in the world, and that injury, suppression, and exploitation are great evils. If that is right, then even though Nietzsche was no Nazi, and even though he might be admired for fifteen volumes of brilliant writing, he was, in the end, a philosophical villain after all.

References

Most of Nietzsche's writings are divided into sections, and for ease of reference it is customary to refer to section numbers rather than to page numbers of particular editions. I have used the following editions, giving page numbers only when there are no section numbers available. The citation for the quotation at the beginning of the essay ("I understand the philosopher as a terrible explosive . . .") would be (EH 5.3), meaning the third section of the fifth part of Nietzsche's *Ecce Homo*.

Nietzsche's works

TL   "On Truth and Lie in an Extra-Moral Sense." Written in 1873. Translated by Walter Kaufmann, in Kaufmann, ed., *The Portable Nietzsche*. New York: Viking Press, 1954.

HA   *Human, All-Too-Human*. First published in 1878. Translated by Walter Kaufmann, in Kaufmann, ed., *The Portable Nietzsche*. New York: Viking Press, 1954.

GS   *The Gay Science*. First published in 1882. Translated by Walter Kaufmann. New York: Vintage Books, 1974.

DL   Draft of a Letter to Paul Ree. 1882. Translated by Walter Kaufmann, in Kaufmann, ed., *The Portable Nietzsche*. New York: Viking Press, 1954.

TZ   *Thus Spoke Zarathustra*. First published in 1883. Translated by Walter Kaufmann, in Kaufmann, ed., *The Portable Nietzsche*. New York: Viking Press, 1954.

WP   *The Will to Power*. Notes written 1883–8. Translated by Walter Kaufmann. New York: Random House, 1967.

BG   *Beyond Good and Evil*. First published in 1886. Translated by Walter Kaufmann. New York: Vintage Books, 1966.

GM   *On the Genealogy of Morals*. First published in 1887. Translated by Walter Kaufmann and R. J. Hollingdale. New York: Vintage Books, 1967.

EH   *Ecce Homo*. Written in 1888. Translated by Walter Kaufmann, in Kaufmann, ed., *Basic Writings of Nietzsche*. New York: The Modern Library, 1966.

AC   *The Anti-Christ*. In *Twilight of the Idols and The Anti-Christ*. Written in 1888. Translated by R. J. Hollingdale. Harmondsworth: Penguin Books, 1968.

TI   *Twilight of the Idols*. In *Twilight of the Idols and The Anti-Christ*. Written in 1888. Translated by R. J. Hollingdale. Harmondsworth: Penguin Books, 1968.

Other works cited

BW   Aristotle. *The Basic Works of Aristotle*, edited by Richard McKeon. New York: Random House, 1941.

AP   ——— . *The Politics*. Translated by T. A. Sinclair. Harmondsworth: Penguin Books, 1962.

HN   Hobbes, Thomas. "Human Nature." First published in 1650. Included in *Body, Man, and Citizen: Selections from Thomas Hobbes*, edited by Richard S. Peters. New York: Collier Books, 1962.

TH   Hume, David. *A Treatise of Human Nature*. Oxford: Oxford University Press, 1888; originally published in 1739–40.

EM   ——— . *Essays Moral Political and Literary*. Oxford: Oxford University Press, 1963; originally published in 1741–2.

IP   ——— . *An Inquiry Concerning the Principles of Morals*. Indianapolis: Bobbs-Merrill, 1957; originally published in 1752.

MF   Macintyre, Ben. *Forgotten Fatherland: The Search for Elisabeth Nietzsche.* New York: Farrar Straus Giroux, 1992; paperback published by HarperCollins.

MU   Mill, John Stuart. *Utilitarianism.* Indianapolis: Bobbs-Merrill, 1967; originally published in 1861.

MM   Narveson, Jan. *Moral Matters.* Peterborough, Ontario: Broadview Press, 1993.

HP   Russell, Bertrand. *A History of Western Philosophy.* New York: Simon and Schuster, 1945.

HL   Singer, Peter. *How Are We to Live?* Amherst, New York: Prometheus Books, 1995.

YN   Yovel, Yirmiyahu. "Nietzsche, the Jews, and Ressentiment." In *Nietzsche, Genealogy, Morality,* edited by Richard Schacht (Berkeley: University of California Press, 1994), 214–36.

Suggestions for further reading

In Nietzsche's writings, a good place to begin is *On the Genealogy of Morals,* translated by Walter Kaufmann and R. J. Hollingdale (New York: Vintage Books, 1967). *Beyond Good and Evil,* translated by Kaufmann (New York: Vintage Books, 1966), is also recommended. Kaufmann's collection *The Portable Nietzsche* (New York: Viking Press, 1954) is useful as an introduction to Nietzsche's writings.

Walter Kaufmann was a leading interpreter as well as translator of Nietzsche. His *Nietzsche: Philosopher, Psychologist, Antichrist* (Princeton: Princeton University Press, 1950; paperback published by Meridian Books) was largely responsible for the rehabilitation of Nietzsche's reputation. Although it no longer represents the best of Nietzsche scholarship, it is still worth reading. Arthur C. Danto's *Nietzsche as Philosopher* (New York: Macmillan, 1965) was the book that got philosophers in the English-speaking world to start taking Nietzsche seriously. Many good books about Nietzsche have been published in more recent years: Richard Schacht's *Nietzsche* (London: Routledge & Kegan Paul, 1983) is one example. For a shorter introduction, try Michael Tanner's *Nietzsche* (Oxford: Oxford University Press, 1994).

Three good anthologies of articles by various writers are: *Reading Nietzsche,* edited by Robert C. Solomon and Kathleen M. Higgins (New York: Oxford University Press, 1988); *Nietzsche, Genealogy, Morality,* edited by Richard Schacht (Berkeley: University of California Press, 1994); and *The Cambridge Companion to Nietzsche,* edited by Bernd Magnus and Kathleen M. Higgins (Cambridge: Cambridge University Press, 1996).

In 1990 the journalist Ben Macintyre had the bright idea to go to Paraguay to see if anything remains today of the colony founded by Elisabeth and Bernhard Förster. The story of his journey and what he found, together with an account of Elisabeth's life, are in his fascinating book *Forgotten Fatherland: The Search for Elisabeth Nietzsche* (New York: Farrar Straus Giroux, 1992; paperback published by HarperCollins).

For further information about various theories and issues in moral philosophy, see James Rachels, *The Elements of Moral Philosophy,* second edition (New York: Random House, 1998).

Introduction to Selected Readings

Like Nietzsche, the great Scottish philosopher David Hume (1711–76) denied that there are "moral facts." There are facts about the way things are, Hume said, but not facts about how things ought to be. Unlike Nietzsche, however, Hume offers a straightforward and easy-to-understand picture of how moral judgment works: our rational faculties inform us about the way things are. Then, as we reflect on what we know, we find sentiments arising within us: we like some things, and dislike others; we want some things to happen, and we want other things not to happen. We make our choices on that basis. For Hume, it is important to notice that without the sentiments, we could make no choices. "Reason alone" provides no guidance for action, and that is why reason alone cannot be the source of morality.

In Hume's day the idea that morality comes from "sentiment, not reason" was considered scandalous, and this was among the reasons he was never able to secure the position he wanted as a university professor. (A prominent clergyman complained to Hume's publisher: "You have often told me of this man's moral virtues. He may have many, for aught I know; but let me observe to you, there are vices of the mind as well as the body: and I think a wickeder mind, and more obstinately bent on public mischief, I never knew.") So instead Hume worked at a variety of jobs, including university librarian in his native Edinburgh and first secretary of the British Embassy in Paris, where he was a favorite of the French intellectuals. He was admired for his writings on science, politics, history, religion, and psychology, as well as ethics.

In the twentieth century Hume's writings have been held in such high regard that it has been common for philosophers to define their own views by comparing them to his. The essays by Ayer, Bambrough, and Dworkin are all, in one way or another, responses to Hume's and Nietzsche's view that there are no "facts" in ethics.

A. J. Ayer (1910–89), a distinguished British philosopher who wrote twenty books on philosophical topics (including one on Hume), argues that Hume was essentially right. Ayer was a leading representative of a philosophical view called emotivism. According to emotivism, moral judgments do not state facts. Instead, they serve a pair of related purposes: they express our emotions (saying "Abortion is morally unacceptable" is like exclaiming: "Abortion – bah!"); and they are used to influence people's behavior (saying "Abortion is murder" is like urging people not to have abortions). Emotivism was probably the purest form of ethical subjectivism that will ever be devised.

Today, however, ethical subjectivism is a minority view among serious students of philosophy. The essay by Renford Bambrough and Ronald Dworkin provide some indication of why this is so. Bambrough attacks ethical subjectivism head-on and defends the common-sense view that some moral propositions are true, no matter what anyone thinks or how anyone feels. We know, for example, that a child about to undergo surgery should be given an anesthetic. Anyone who denies this, Bambrough says, is simply wrong. His strategy is to discredit subjectivism by showing that the arguments for it – including Hume's arguments – are flawed. Once the fallacies in those arguments are exposed, subjectivism loses its appeal.

Ronald Dworkin adopts a different sort of strategy. If a moral judgment is nothing more than an expression of how we feel, then any old prejudice could count as a moral judgment. But, as Dworkin points out, this is not true. There is a difference between spouting off a prejudice and taking a moral position. Dworkin, a professor of jurisprudence at both Oxford University and New York University Law School, explains that having a moral view means having a position that is based on rationally defensible principles. The selection reprinted here is taken from a longer article by Dworkin in which he is considering, among other things, whether there should be laws disadvantageous to homosexuals. Many people think that, as a matter of fundamental morality, there is something wrong with gay sex. This provides a good example for thinking about the difference between a principled moral position and a mere prejudice.

Discussion questions

1   Nietzsche says there is no objective basis for ethics, in part because there is no God. This suggests that if God exists and creates right and wrong, then there would be an objective basis for ethics. A question that has frequently been asked is whether God has reasons for making something right or wrong. If so, it is argued, then there is an objective basis for ethics outside of God; if not, then God's choices are arbitrary and there is still no objective basis for ethics. Is this line of thought correct?

2   In Aristotle's world-view there are purposes in nature, and things that promote natural purposes are right or good and the opposite are wrong or bad. Does this mean it is *morally* wrong to fail to take care of your teeth if that would prevent their being used for chewing? In other words, which values and purposes, on Aristotle's world-view, are *moral* values and purposes?

3   Identify different notions of subjectivity and objectivity discussed in the chapter.

4   Some people refuse to vote because they think it is irrational – it is a waste of their time (and thus against their interests) and will make no difference. A similar line of thought has been argued against the Social Contract Theory of morality. The theory says it is rational for everyone to accept moral restrictions on their conduct. Is it?

5   Utilitarian moral thought has been very attractive to many people because it focuses on making life better for people. Yet there have been many important objections raised against it. The text mentions two. Some others are that it would require an increase in population on the ground that there would be more happiness in the world; that it would make it all right to punish an innocent person in order to prevent a riot; that it might permit very great inequality; that it would be incompatible with individual rights. How might a utilitarian respond to some of these charges?

6   Though rejecting modernity, Nietzsche is not a relativist. What is relativism? Should the rejection of the idea of objective truth lead one to embrace relativism?

Readings

Friedrich Nietzsche, selections from
Beyond Good and Evil and *On the Genealogy of Morals*

From *Beyond Good and Evil*

Refraining mutually from injury, violence, and exploitation and placing one's will on a par with that of someone else – this may become, in a certain rough sense,

From *Beyond Good and Evil*, translated by Walter Kaufmann (New York: Vintage Books, 1966), pp. 203–9, and *On the Genealogy of Morals*, translated by Walter Kaufmann and R. J. Hollingdale (New York: Vintage Books, 1967), pp. 118–25.

good manners among individuals if the appropriate conditions are present (namely, if these men are actually similar in strength and value standards and belong together in *one* body). But as soon as this principle is extended, and possibly even accepted as the *fundamental principle of society*, it immediately proves to be what it really is – a will to the *denial* of life, a principle of disintegration and decay.

Here we must beware of superficiality and get to the bottom of the matter, resisting all sentimental weakness: life itself is *essentially* appropriation, injury, over-powering of what is alien and weaker; suppression, hardness, imposition of one's own forms, incorporation and at least, at its mildest, exploitation – but why should one always use those words in which a slanderous intent has been imprinted for ages?

Even the body within which individuals treat each other as equals, as suggested before – and this happens in every healthy aristocracy – if it is a living and not a dying body, has to do to other bodies what the individuals within it refrain from doing to each other: it will have to be an incarnate will to power, it will strive to grow, spread, seize, become predominant – not from any morality or immorality but because it is *living* and because life simply *is* will to power. But there is no point on which the ordinary consciousness of Europeans resists instruction as on this: everywhere people are now raving, even under scientific disguises, about coming conditions of society in which "the exploitative aspect" will be removed – which sounds to me as if they promised to invent a way of life that would dispense with all organic functions. "Exploitation" does not belong to a corrupt or imperfect and primitive society: it belongs to the *essence* of what lives, as a basic organic function; it is a consequence of the will to power, which is after all the will of life.

If this should be an innovation as a theory – as a reality it is the *primordial fact* of all history: people ought to be honest with themselves at least that far.

Wandering through the many subtler and coarser moralities which have so far been prevalent on earth, or still are prevalent, I found that certain features recurred regularly together and were closely associated – until I finally discovered two basic types and one basic difference.

There are *master morality* and *slave morality* – I add immediately that in all the higher and more mixed cultures there also appear attempts at mediation between these two moralities, and yet more often the interpenetration and mutual misunder-standing of both, and at times they occur directly alongside each other – even in the same human being, within a *single* soul. The moral discrimination of values has originated either among a ruling group whose consciousness of its difference from the ruled group was accompanied by delight – or among the ruled, the slaves and dependents of every degree.

In the first case, when the ruling group determines what is "good," the exalted, proud states of the soul are experienced as conferring distinction and determining the order of rank. The noble human being separates from himself those in whom the opposite of such exalted, proud states finds expression: he despises them. It should be noted immediately that in this first type of morality the opposition of "good" and "*bad*" means approximately the same as "noble" and "contemptible." (The opposition of "good" and "*evil*" has a different origin.) One feels contempt for the cowardly, the anxious, the petty, those intent on narrow utility; also for the suspicious with their unfree glances, those who humble themselves, the doglike people who allow themselves to be maltreated, the begging flatterers, above all the liars: it is part of the fundamental faith of all aristocrats that the common people lie. "We truthful ones" – thus the nobility of ancient Greece referred to itself.

It is obvious that moral designations were everywhere first applied to *human beings* and only later, derivatively, to actions. Therefore it is a gross mistake when historians of morality start from such questions as: why was the compassionate act praised? The noble type of man experiences *itself* as determining values; it does not need approval; it judges, "what is harmful to me is harmful in itself"; it knows itself to be that which first accords honor to things; it is *value-creating*. Everything it knows as part of itself it honors: such a morality is self-glorification. In the foreground there is the feeling of fullness, of power that seeks to overflow, the happiness of high tension, the consciousness of wealth that would give and bestow: the noble human being, too, helps the unfortunate, but not, or almost not, from pity, but prompted more by an urge begotten by excess of power. The noble human being honors himself as one who is powerful, also as one who has power over himself, who knows how to speak and be silent, who delights in being severe and hard with himself and respects all severity and hardness. "A hard heart Wotan put into my breast," says an old Scandinavian saga: a fitting poetic expression, seeing that it comes from the soul of a proud Viking. Such a type of man is actually proud of the fact that he is *not* made for pity, and the hero of the saga therefore adds as a warning: "If the heart is not hard in youth it will never harden." Noble and courageous human beings who think that way are furthest removed from that morality which finds the distinction of morality precisely in pity, or in acting for others, or in *désintéressement*; faith in oneself, pride in oneself, a fundamental hostility and irony against "selflessness" belong just as definitely to noble morality as does a slight disdain and caution regarding compassionate feelings and a "warm heart."

It is the powerful who *understand* how to honor; this is their art, their realm of invention. The profound reverence for age and tradition – all law rests on this double reverence – the faith and prejudice in favor of ancestors and disfavor of those yet to come are typical of the morality of the powerful; and when the men of "modern ideas," conversely, believe almost instinctively in "progress" and "the future" and more and more lack respect for age, this in itself would sufficiently betray the ignoble origin of these "ideas."

A morality of the ruling group, however, is most alien and embarrassing to the present taste in the severity of its principle that one has duties only to one's peers; that against beings of a lower rank, against everything alien, one may behave as one pleases or "as the heart desires," and in any case "beyond good and evil" – here pity and like feelings may find their place. The capacity for, and the duty of, long gratitude and long revenge – both only among one's peers – refinement in repaying, the sophisticated concept of friendship, a certain necessity for having enemies (as it were, as drainage ditches for the affects of envy, quarrelsomeness, exuberance – at bottom, in order to be capable of being good *friends*): all these are typical characteristics of noble morality which, as suggested, is not the morality of "modern ideas" and therefore is hard to empathize with today, also hard to dig up and uncover.

It is different with the second type of morality, *slave morality*. Suppose the violated, oppressed, suffering, unfree, who are uncertain of themselves and weary, moralize: what will their moral valuations have in common? Probably, a pessimistic suspicion about the whole condition of man will find expression, perhaps a condemnation of man along with his condition. The slave's eye is not favorable to the virtues of the powerful: he is skeptical and suspicious, *subtly* suspicious, of all the "good" that is honored there – he would like to persuade himself that even their happiness is not genuine. Conversely, those qualities are brought out and flooded with light which serve to ease existence for those who suffer: here pity, the complaisant and obliging hand, the warm heart, patience, industry, humility, and friendliness are honored – for here these are the most useful qualities and almost the only means for enduring the pressure of existence. Slave morality is essentially a morality of utility.

Here is the place for the origin of that famous opposition of "good" and "evil": into evil one's feelings project power and dangerousness, a certain terribleness, subtlety, and strength that does not permit contempt to develop. According to slave morality, those who are "evil" thus inspire fear; according to master morality it is precisely those who are "good" that inspire, and wish to inspire, fear, while the "bad" are felt to be contemptible.

The opposition reaches its climax when, as a logical consequence of slave morality, a touch of disdain is associated also with the "good" of this morality – this may be slight and benevolent – because the good human being has to be *undangerous* in the slaves' way of thinking: he is good-natured, easy to deceive, a little stupid perhaps, *un bonhomme*. Wherever slave morality becomes preponderant, language tends to bring the words "good" and "stupid" closer together.

One last fundamental difference: the longing for *freedom*, the instinct for happiness and the subtleties of the feeling of freedom belong just as necessarily to slave morality and morals as artful and enthusiastic reverence and devotion are the regular symptom of an aristocratic way of thinking and evaluating.

This makes plain why love *as passion* – which is our European specialty – simply must be of noble origin: as is well known, its invention must be credited to the Provençal knight-poets, those magnificent and inventive human beings of the "*gai saber*" to whom Europe owes so many things and almost owes itself.

Among the things that may be hardest to understand for a noble human being is vanity: he will be tempted to deny it, where another type of human being could not find it more palpable. The problem for him is to imagine people who seek to create a good opinion of themselves which they do not have of themselves – and thus also do not "deserve" – and who nevertheless end up *believing* this good opinion themselves. This strikes him half as such bad taste and lack of self-respect, and half as so baroquely irrational, that he would like to consider vanity as exceptional, and in most cases when it is spoken of he doubts it.

He will say, for example: "I may be mistaken about my value and nevertheless demand that my value, exactly as I define it, should be acknowledged by others as well – but this is no vanity (but conceit or, more frequently, what is called 'humility' or 'modesty')." Or: "For many reasons I may take pleasure in the good opinion of others: perhaps because I honor and love them and all their pleasures give me pleasure; perhaps also because their good opinion confirms and strengthens my faith in my own good opinion; perhaps because the good opinion of others, even in cases where I do not share it, is still useful to me or promises to become so – but all that is not vanity."

The noble human being must force himself, with the aid of history, to recognize that, since time immemorial, in all somehow dependent social strata the common man *was* only what he was *considered*: not at all used to positing values himself, he also attached no other value to himself than his masters attached to him (it is the characteristic *right of masters* to create values).

It may be understood as the consequence of an immense atavism that even now the ordinary man still always *waits* for an opinion about himself and then instinctively submits to that – but by no means only a "good" opinion; also a bad and unfair one (consider, for example, the great majority of the self-estimates and self-underestimates that believing women accept from their father-confessors, and believing Christians quite generally from their church).

In accordance with the slowly arising democratic order of things (and its cause, the intermarriage of masters and slaves), the originally noble and rare urge to ascribe value to oneself on one's own and to "think well" of oneself will actually be encouraged and spread more and more now; but it is always opposed by an older, ampler, and more deeply ingrained propensity – and in the phenomenon of "vanity" this older propensity masters the younger one. The vain person is delighted by *every* good opinion he hears of himself (quite apart from all considerations of its utility, and also apart from truth or falsehood), just as every bad opinion of him pains him: for he submits to both, he *feels* subjected to them in accordance with that oldest instinct of submission that breaks out in him.

It is "the slave" in the blood of the vain person, a residue of the slave's craftiness – and how much "slave" is still residual in woman, for example! – that seeks to *seduce* him to good opinions about himself; it is also the slave who afterwards immediately prostrates himself before these opinions as if he had not called them forth.

And to say it once more: vanity is an atavism.

From *On the Genealogy of Morals*

Suppose such an incarnate will to contradiction and antinaturalness is induced to *philosophize*: upon what will it vent its innermost contrariness? Upon what is felt most certainly to be real and actual: it will look for error precisely where the instinct of life most unconditionally posits truth. It will, for example, like the ascetics of the Vedanta philosophy, downgrade physicality to an illusion; likewise pain, multiplicity, the entire conceptual antithesis "subject" and "object" – errors, nothing but errors! To renounce belief in one's ego, to deny one's own "reality" – what a triumph! not merely over the senses, over appearance, but a much higher kind of triumph, a violation and cruelty against *reason* – a voluptuous pleasure that reaches its height when the ascetic self-contempt and self-mockery of reason declares: "*there is* a realm of truth and being, but reason is *excluded* from it!"

(Incidentally, even in the Kantian concept of the "intelligible character of things" something remains of this lascivious ascetic discord that loves to turn reason against reason: for "intelligible character" signifies in Kant that things are so constituted that the intellect comprehends just enough of them to know that for the intellect they are – *utterly incomprehensible.*)

But precisely because we seek knowledge, let us not be ungrateful to such resolute reversals of accustomed perspectives and valuations with which the spirit has, with apparent mischievousness and futility, raged against itself for so long: to see differently in this way for once, to *want* to see differently, is no small discipline and preparation of the intellect for its future "objectivity" – the latter understood not as "contemplation without interest" (which is a nonsensical absurdity), but as the ability *to control* one's Pro and Con and to dispose of them, so that one knows how to employ a *variety* of perspectives and affective interpretations in the service of knowledge.

Henceforth, my dear philosophers, let us be on guard against the dangerous old conceptual fiction that posited a "pure, will-less, painless, timeless knowing subject"; let us guard against the snares of such contradictory concepts as "pure reason," "absolute spirituality," "knowledge in itself": these always demand that we should think of an eye that is completely unthinkable, an eye turned in no particular direction, in which the active and interpreting forces, through which alone seeing becomes seeing *something*, are supposed to be lacking; these always demand of the eye an absurdity and a nonsense. There is *only* a perspective seeing, *only* a perspective "knowing"; and the *more* affects we allow to speak about one thing, the *more* eyes, different eyes, we can use to observe one thing, the more complete will our "concept" of this thing, our "objectivity," be. But to eliminate the will altogether, to suspend each and every affect, supposing we were capable of this – what would that mean but to *castrate* the intellect?

But let us return to our problem. It will be immediately obvious that such a self-contradiction as the ascetic appears to represent, "life *against* life," is, physiologically considered and not merely psychologically, a simple absurdity. It can only be *apparent*; it must be a kind of provisional formulation, an interpretation and psycho-logical misunderstanding of something whose real nature could not for a long time be understood or described *as it really was* – a mere word inserted into an old *gap* in human knowledge. Let us replace it with a brief formulation of the facts of the matter: *the ascetic ideal springs from the protective instinct of a degenerating life* which tries by all means to sustain itself and to fight for its existence; it indicates a partial physiological obstruction and exhaustion against which the deepest instincts of life, which have remained intact, continually struggle with new expedients and devices. The ascetic ideal is such an expedient; the case is therefore the opposite of what those who reverence this ideal believe: life wrestles in it and through it with death and *against* death; the ascetic ideal is an artifice for the *preservation* of life.

That this ideal acquired such power and ruled over men as imperiously as we find it in history, especially wherever the civilization and taming of man has been carried through, expresses a great fact: the *sickliness* of the type of man we have had hitherto, or at least of the tamed man, and the physiological struggle of man against death (more precisely: against disgust with life, against exhaustion, against the desire for the "end"). The ascetic priest is the incarnate desire to be different, to be in a different place, and indeed this desire at its greatest extreme, its distinctive fervor and passion; but precisely this power of his desire is the chain that holds him captive so that he becomes a tool for the creation of more favorable conditions for being here and being man – it is precisely this *power* that enables him to persuade to existence the whole herd of the ill-constituted, disgruntled, underprivileged, unfortunate, and all who suffer of themselves, by instinctively going before them as their shepherd. You will see my point: this ascetic priest, this apparent enemy of life, this *denier* – precisely he is among the greatest *conserving* and yes-creating forces of life.

Where does it come from, this sickliness? For man is more sick, uncertain, changeable, indeterminate than any other animal, there is no doubt of that – he is *the* sick animal: how has that come about? Certainly he has also dared more, done more new things, braved more and challenged fate more than all the other animals put together: he, the great experimenter with himself, discontented and insatiable, wrestling with animals, nature, and gods for ultimate dominion – he, still unvanquished, eternally directed toward the future, whose own restless energies never leave him in peace, so that his future digs like a spur into the flesh of every present – how should such a courageous and richly endowed animal not also be the most imperiled, the most chronically and profoundly sick of all sick animals?

Man has often had enough; there are actual epidemics of having had enough (as around 1348, at the time of the dance of death); but even this nausea, this weariness, this disgust with himself – all this bursts from him with such violence that it at once becomes a new fetter. The No he says to life brings to light, as if by magic, an abundance of tender Yeses; even when he *wounds* himself, this master of destruction, of self-destruction – the very wound itself afterward compels him *to live*.

The more normal sickliness becomes among men – and we cannot deny its normality – the higher should be the honor accorded the rare cases of great power of soul and body, man's *lucky hits*; the more we should protect the well-constituted from the worst kind of air, the air of the sickroom. It this done?

The sick represent the greatest danger for the healthy; it is *not* the strongest but the weakest who spell disaster for the strong. It this known?

Broadly speaking, it is not fear of man that we should desire to see diminished; for this fear compels the strong to be strong, and occasionally terrible – it *maintains* the well-constituted type of man. What is to be feared, what has a more calamitous effect than any other calamity, is that man should inspire not profound fear but profound *nausea*; also not great fear but great *pity*. Suppose these two were one day to unite, they would inevitably beget one of the uncanniest monsters: the "last will" of man, his will to nothingness, nihilism. And indeed a great deal points to this union. Whoever can smell not only with his nose but also with his eyes and ears, scents almost everywhere he goes today something like the air of madhouses and hospitals – I am speaking, of course, of the cultural domain, of every kind of "Europe" on this earth. The *sick* are man's greatest danger; *not* the evil, *not* the "beasts of prey." Those who are failures from the start, downtrodden, crushed – it is they, the *weakest*, who must undermine life among men, who call into question and poison most dangerously our trust in life, in man, and in ourselves. Where does one not encounter that veiled glance which burdens one with a profound sadness, that inward-turned glance of the born failure which betrays how such a man speaks to himself – that glance which is a sigh! "If only I were someone else," sighs this glance: "but there is no hope of that. I am who I am: how could I ever get free of myself? And yet – I *am sick of myself!*"

It is on such soil, on swampy ground, that every weed, every poisonous plant grows, always so small, so hidden, so false, so saccharine. Here the worms of vengefulness and rancor swarm; here the air stinks of secrets and concealment; here the web of the most malicious of all conspiracies is being spun constantly – the conspiracy of the suffering against the well-constituted and victorious, here the aspect of the victorious is *hatred*. And what mendaciousness is employed to disguise that this hatred is hatred! What a display of grand words and postures, what an art of "honest" calumny! These failures: what noble eloquence flows from their lips! How much sugary, slimy, humble submissiveness swims in their eyes! What do they really want? At least to *represent* justice, love, wisdom, superiority – that is the ambition of the "lowest," the sick. And how skillful such an ambition makes them! Admire above all the forger's skill with which the stamp of virtue, even the ring, the golden-sounding ring of virtue, is here counterfeited. They monopolize virtue, these weak, hopelessly sick people, there is no doubt of it: "we alone are the good and just," they say, "we alone are *homines bonae voluntatis.*" They walk among us as embodied reproaches, as warnings to us – as if health, well-constitutedness, strength, pride, and the sense of power were in themselves necessarily vicious things for which one must pay some day, and pay bitterly: how ready they themselves are at bottom to *make* one pay; how they crave to be *hangmen*. There is among them an abundance of the vengeful disguised as judges, who constantly bear the word "justice" in their mouths like poisonous spittle, always with pursed lips, always ready to spit upon all who are not discontented but go their way in good spirits. Nor is there lacking among them that most disgusting species of the vain, the mendacious failures whose aim is to appear as "beautiful souls" and who bring to market their deformed sensuality, wrapped up in verses and other swaddling clothes, as "purity of heart": the species of moral masturbaters and "self-gratifiers." The will of the weak to represent *some* form of superiority, their instinct for devious paths to tyranny over the healthy – where can it not be discovered, this will to power of the weakest!

The sick woman especially: no one can excel her in the wiles to dominate, oppress, and tyrannize. The sick woman spares nothing, living or dead; she will dig up the most deeply buried things (the Bogos say: "woman is a hyena").

Examine the background of every family, every organization, every common-wealth: everywhere the struggle of the sick against the healthy – a silent struggle as a rule, with petty poisons, with pinpricks, with sly long-suffering expressions, but occasionally also with that invalid's Phariseeism of *loud* gestures that likes best to pose as "noble indignation." This hoarse, indignant barking of sick dogs, this rabid mendaciousness and rage of "noble" Pharisees, penetrates even the hallowed halls of science (I again remind readers who have ears for such things of that Berlin apostle of revenge, Eugen Dühring, who employs moral mumbo-jumbo more indecently and repulsively than anyone else in Germany today: Dühring, the foremost moral bigmouth today – unexcelled even among his own ilk, the anti-Semites).

They are all men of *ressentiment*, physiologically unfortunate and worm-eaten, a whole tremulous realm of subterranean revenge, inexhaustible and insatiable in outbursts against the fortunate and happy and in masquerades of revenge and pre-texts for revenge: when would they achieve the ultimate, subtlest, sublimest triumph of revenge? Undoubtedly if they succeeded in *poisoning the consciences* of the fortun-ate with their own misery, with all misery, so that one day the fortunate began to be ashamed of their good fortune and perhaps said one to another: "it is disgraceful to be fortunate: *there is too much misery!*"

But no greater or more calamitous misunderstanding is possible than for the happy, well-constituted, powerful in soul and body, to begin to doubt their *right to happiness* in this fashion. Away with this "inverted world"! Away with this shame-ful emasculation of feeling! That the sick should *not* make the healthy sick – and this is what such an emasculation would involve – should surely be our supreme concern on earth; but this requires above all that the healthy should be *segregated* from the sick, guarded even from the sight of the sick, that they may not confound themselves with the sick. Or is it their task, perhaps, to be nurses or physicians?

But no worse misunderstanding and denial of *their* task can be imagined: the higher *ought* not to degrade itself to the status of an instrument of the lower, the pathos of distance *ought* to keep their tasks eternally separate! Their right to exist, the privilege of the full-toned bell over the false and cracked, is a thousand times greater: they alone are our *warranty* for the future, they alone are *liable* for the future of man. The sick can never have the ability or obligation to do what *they* can do, what *they* ought to do: but if they are to be able to do what *they* alone ought to do, how can they at the same time be physicians, consolers, and "saviors" of the sick?

And therefore let us have fresh air! fresh air! and keep clear of the madhouses and hospitals of culture! And therefore let us have good company, *our* company! Or solitude, if it must be! But away from the sickening fumes of inner corruption and the hidden rot of disease! . . . So that we may, at least for a while yet, guard ourselves, my friends, against the two worst contagions that may be reserved just for us — against the *great nausea at man!* against *great pity for man!*

David Hume, "Morality, Sentiment, and Reason"

Moral Distinctions not Deriv'd from Reason

Those who affirm that virtue is nothing but a conformity to reason; that there are eternal fitnesses and unfitnesses of things, which are the same to every rational being that considers them; that the immutable measures of right and wrong impose an obligation, not only on human creatures, but also on the Deity himself: All these systems concur in the opinion, that morality, like truth, is discern'd merely by ideas, and by their juxtaposition and comparison. In order, therefore, to judge of these systems, we need only consider, whether it be possible, from reason alone, to distinguish betwixt moral good and evil, or whether there must concur some other principles to enable us to make that distinction.

If morality had naturally no influence on human passions and actions, 'twere in vain to take such pains to inculcate it; and nothing wou'd be more fruitless than that multitude of rules and precepts, with which all moralists abound. Philosophy is commonly divided into *speculative* and *practical*; and as morality is always comprehended under the latter division, 'tis supposed to influence our passions and actions, and to go beyond the calm and indolent judgments of the understanding. And this is confirm'd by common experience, which informs us, that men are often govern'd by their duties, and are deter'd from some actions by the opinion of injustice, and impell'd to others by that of obligation.

Since morals, therefore, have an influence on the actions and affections, it follows, that they cannot be deriv'd from reason; and that because reason alone, as we have already prov'd, can never have any such influence. Morals excite passions, and produce or prevent actions. Reason of itself is utterly impotent in this particular. The rules of morality, therefore, are not conclusions of our reason.

No one, I believe, will deny the justness of this inference; nor is there any other means of evading it, than by denying that principle, on which it is founded. As long as it is allow'd, that reason has no influence on our passions and actions, 'tis in vain to pretend, that morality is discover'd only by a deduction of reason. An active principle can never be founded on an inactive; and if reason be inactive in itself, it must remain so in all its shapes and appearances, whether it exerts itself in natural or moral subjects, whether it considers the powers of external bodies, or the actions of rational beings.

It would be tedious to repeat all the arguments, by which I have prov'd that reason is perfectly inert, and can never either prevent or produce any action or

From *A Treatise of Human Nature* (1740) and *An Inquiry Concerning the Principles of Morals* (1751).

affection. 'Twill be easy to recollect what has been said upon that subject. I shall only recall on this occasion one of these arguments, which I shall endeavour to render still more conclusive, and more applicable to the present subject.

Reason is the discovery of truth or falsehood. Truth or falsehood consists in an agreement or disagreement either to the *real* relations of ideas, or to *real* existence and matter of fact. Whatever, therefore, is not susceptible of this agreement or disagreement, is incapable of being true or false, and can never be an object of our reason. Now 'tis evident our passions, volitions, and actions, are not susceptible of any such agreement or disagreement; being original facts and realities, compleat in themselves, and implying no reference to other passions, volitions, and actions. 'Tis impossible, therefore, they can be pronounced either true or false, and be either contrary or conformable to reason.

This argument is of double advantage to our present purpose. For it proves *directly*, that actions do not derive their merit from a conformity to reason, nor their blame from a contrariety to it; and it proves the same truth more *indirectly*, by shewing us, that as reason can never immediately prevent or produce any action by contradicting or approving of it, it cannot be the source of moral good and evil, which are found to have that influence. Actions may be laudable or blameable; but they cannot be reasonable or unreasonable: Laudable or blameable, therefore, are not the same with reasonable or unreasonable. The merit and demerit of actions frequently contradict, and sometimes control our natural propensities. But reason has no such influence. Moral distinctions, therefore, are not the offspring of reason. Reason is wholly inactive, and can never be the source of so active a principle as conscience, or a sense of morals.

. . . Take any action allow'd to be vicious: Wilful murder, for instance. Examine it in all lights, and see if you can find that matter of fact, or real existence, which you call *vice*. In which ever way you take it, you find only certain passions, motives, volitions and thoughts. There is no other matter of fact in the case. The vice entirely escapes you, as long as you consider the object. You never can find it, till you turn your reflexion into your own breast, and find a sentiment of disapprobation, which arises in you, towards this action. Here is a matter of fact; but 'tis the object of feeling, not of reason. It lies in yourself, not in the object. So that when you pronounce any action or character to be vicious, you mean nothing, but that from the constitution of your nature you have a feeling or sentiment of blame from the contemplation of it. Vice and virtue, therefore, may be compar'd to sounds, colours, heat and cold, which, according to modern philosophy, are not qualities in objects, but perceptions in the mind: And this discovery in morals, like that other in physics, is to be regarded as a considerable advancement of the speculative sciences; tho', like that too, it has little or no influence on practice. Nothing can be more real, or concern us more, than our own sentiments of pleasure and uneasiness; and if these be favourable to virtue, and unfavourable to vice, no more can be requisite to the regulation of our conduct and behaviour.

I cannot forbear adding to these reasonings an observation, which may, perhaps, be found of some importance. In every system of morality, which I have hitherto met with, I have always remark'd, that the author proceeds for some time in the ordinary way of reasoning, and establishes the being of a God, or makes observations concerning human affairs; when of a sudden I am surpriz'd to find, that instead of the usual copulations of propositions, *is*, and *is not*, I meet with no proposition that is not connected with an *ought*, or an *ought not*. This change is imperceptible; but is, however, of the last consequence. For as this *ought*, or *ought not*, expresses some new relation or affirmation, 'tis necessary that it shou'd be observ'd and explain'd; and at the same time that a reason should be given, for what seems altogether inconceivable, how this new relation can be a deduction from others, which are entirely different from it. But as authors do not commonly use this precaution, I shall presume to recommend it to the readers; and am persuaded, that this small attention wou'd subvert all the vulgar systems of morality, and let us see, that the distinction of vice and virtue is not founded merely on the relations of objects, nor is perceiv'd by reason.

Of the General Principles of Morals

There has been a controversy started of late, much better worth examination, concerning the general foundation of Morals; whether they be derived from Reason or from Sentiment; whether we attain the knowledge of them by a chain of argument and induction or by an immediate feeling and finer internal sense; whether, like all sound judgment of truth and falsehood, they should be the same to every rational intelligent being; or whether, like the perception of beauty and deformity, they be founded entirely on the particular fabric and constitution of the human species.

The ancient philosophers, though they often affirm that virtue is nothing but conformity to reason, yet in general seem to consider morals as deriving their existence from taste and sentiment. On the other hand, our modern enquirers, though they also talk much of the beauty of virtue and deformity of vice, yet have commonly endeavoured to account for these distinctions by metaphysical reasonings, and by deductions from the most abstract principles of the understanding. Such confusion reigned in these subjects that an opposition of the greatest consequence could prevail between one system and another, and even in the parts of almost each individual system; and yet nobody, till very lately, was ever sensible of it. The elegant Lord Shaftesbury, who first gave occasion to remark this distinction, and who in general adhered to the principles of the ancients, is not himself entirely free from the same confusion.

It must be acknowledged that both sides of the question are susceptible of specious arguments. Moral distinctions, it may be said, are discernible by pure *reason*; else, whence the many disputes that reign in common life, as well as in philosophy, with regard to this subject: the long chain of proofs often produced on both sides, the examples cited, the authorities appealed to, the analogies employed, the fallacies detected, the inferences drawn, and the several conclusions adjusted to their proper principles. Truth is disputable, not taste; what exists in the nature of things is the standard of our judgment; what each man feels within himself is the standard of sentiment. Propositions in geometry may be proved, systems in physics may be controverted; but the harmony of verse, the tenderness of passion, the brilliancy of wit, must give immediate pleasure. No man reasons concerning another's beauty, but frequently concerning the justice or injustice of his actions. In every criminal trial the first object of the prisoner is to disprove the facts alleged and deny the actions imputed to him; the second, to prove that, even if these actions were real, they might be justified as innocent and lawful. It is confessedly by deductions of the understanding that the first point is ascertained: how can we suppose that a different faculty of the mind is employed in fixing the other?

On the other hand, those who would resolve all moral determinations into *sentiment* may endeavour to show that it is impossible to reason ever to draw conclusions of this nature. To virtue, say they, it belongs to be *amiable,* and vice *odious.* This forms their very nature or essence. But can reason or argumentation distribute these different epithets to any subjects, and pronounce beforehand that this must produce love, and that hatred? Or what other reason can we ever assign for these affections but the original fabric and formation of the human mind, which is naturally adapted to receive them?

The end of all moral speculations is to teach us our duty; and by proper representations of the deformity of vice and beauty of virtue, beget correspondent habits, and engage us to avoid the one and embrace the other. But is this ever to be expected from inferences and conclusions of the understanding, which of them- selves have no hold of the affections or set in motion the active powers of men? They discover truths; but where the truths which they discover are indifferent and beget no desire or aversion, they can have no influence on conduct and behaviour. What is honourable, what is fair, what is becoming, what is noble, what is gener- ous, takes possession of the heart and animates us to embrace and maintain it. What is intelligible, what is evident, what is probable, what is true, procures only the cool assent of the understanding and, gratifying a speculative curiosity, puts an end to our researches.

Extinguish all the warm feelings and prepossessions in favour of virtue, and all disgust or aversion to vice; render men totally indifferent towards these distinctions, and morality is no longer a practical study, not has any tendency to regulate our lives and actions.

These arguments on each side – and many more might be produced – are so plausible that I am apt to suspect they may, the one as well as the other, be solid and satisfactory, and that *reason* and *sentiment* concur in almost all moral determinations and conclusions. The final sentence, it is probable, which pronounces characters and actions amiable or odious, praiseworthy or blamable; that which stamps on them the mark of honour or infamy, approbation or censure; that which renders morality an active principle and constitutes virtue our happiness, and vice our misery – it is probable, I say, that this final sentence depends on some internal sense or feeling which nature has made universal in the whole species. For what else can have an influence of this nature? But in order to pave the way for such a sentiment, and give a proper discernment of its object, it is often necessary, we find, that much reasoning should precede, that nice distinctions be made, just conclusions drawn, distant comparisons formed, complicated relations examined, and general facts fixed and ascertained. Some species of beauty, especially the natural kinds, on their first appearance command our affection and approbation; and where they fail of this effect, it is impossible for any reasoning to redress their influence, or adapt them better to our taste and sentiment. But in many orders of beauty, particularly those of the finer arts, it is requisite to employ much reasoning in order to feel the proper sentiment; and a false relish may frequently be corrected by argument and reflection. There are just grounds to conclude that moral beauty partakes much of this latter species, and demands the assistance of our intellectual faculties in order to give it a suitable influence on the human mind.

A. J. Ayer, "A Defense of Emotivism"

The distinctions that I wish to make can best be brought out by an example. Suppose that someone has committed a murder. Then part of the story consists of what we may call the police court details; where and when and how the killing was effected; the identity of the murderer and of his victim; the relationship in which they stood to one another. Next there are the questions of motive: The murderer may have been suffering from jealousy, or he may have been anxious to obtain money; he may have been avenging a private injury, or pursuing some political end. These questions of motive are, on one level, a matter of the agent's reflections before the act; and these may very well take the form of moral judgements. Thus he may tell himself that his victim is a bad man and that the world would be better for his removal, or, in a different case, that it is his duty to rid his country of a tyrant, or, like Raskolnikov in *Crime and Punishment*, that he is a superior being who has in these circumstances the right to kill. A psychoanalyst who examines the case may, however, tell a different story. He may say that the political assassin is really revenging himself upon his father, or that the man who persuades himself that he is a social benefactor is really exhibiting a lust for power, or, in a case like that of Raskolnikov, that the murderer does not really believe that he has the right to kill.

All these are statements of fact; not indeed that the man has, or has not, the right to kill, but that this is what he tells himself. They are verified or confuted, as the case may be, by observation. It is a matter of fact, in my usage of the term, that the victim was killed at such and such a place and at such and such a time and in such and such a manner. It is also a matter of fact that the murderer had certain conscious motives. To himself they are known primarily by introspection; to others

From A. J. Ayer, *Philosophical Essays* (New York and London: St Martin's Press and Macmillan, 1954), pp. 233–9, 245–9.

by various features of his overt behaviour, including what he says. As regards his unconscious motives the only criterion is his overt behaviour. It can indeed plausibly be argued that to talk about the unconscious is always equivalent to talking about overt behaviour, though often in a very complicated way. Now there seems to me to be a very good sense in which to tell a story of this kind, that this is what the man did and that these were his reasons for doing it, is to give a complete description of the facts. Or rather, since one can never be in a position to say that any such description is complete, what will be missing from it will be further information of the same type; what we obtain when this information is added is a more elaborate account of the circumstances of the action, and of its antecedents and consequences. But now suppose that instead of developing the story in this circumstantial way, one applies an ethical predicate to it. Suppose that instead of asking what it was that really happened, or what the agent's motives really were, we ask whether he was justified in acting as he did. Did he have the right to kill? Is it true that he had the right? Is it a fact that he acted rightly? It does not matter in this connection what answer we give. The question for moral philosophy is not whether a certain action is right or wrong, but what is implied by saying that it is right, or saying that it is wrong. Suppose then that we say that the man acted rightly. The point that I wish to make is that in saying this we are not elaborating or modifying our description of the situation in the way that we should be elaborating it if we gave further police court details, or in the way that we should be modifying it if we showed that the agent's motives were different from what they had been thought to be. To say that his motives were good, or that they were bad, is not to say what they were. To say that the man acted rightly, or that he acted wrongly, is not to say what he did. And when one has said what he did, when one has described the situation in the way that I have outlined, then to add that he was justified, or alternatively that he was not, is not to say any more about what he did; it does not add a further detail to the story. It is for this reason that these ethical predicates are not factual; they do not describe any features of the situation to which they are applied. But they do, someone may object, they describe its ethical features. But what are these ethical features? And how are they related to the other features of the situation, to what we may provisionally call its "natural" features? Let us consider this.

To begin with, it is, or should be, clear that the connection is not logical. Let us assume that two observers agree about all the circumstances of the case, including the agent's motives, but that they disagree in their evaluation of it. Then neither of them is contradicting himself. Otherwise the use of the ethical term would add nothing to the circumstantial description; it would serve merely as a repetition, or partial repetition, of it. But neither, as I hope to show, is the connection factual. There is nothing that counts as observing the *designata* of the ethical predicates, apart from observing the natural features of the situation. But what alternative is left? Certainly it can be said that the ethical features in some way depend upon the natural. We can and do give reasons for our moral judgements, just as we do for our aesthetic judgements, where the same argument applies. We fasten on motives, point to consequences, ask what would happen if everyone were to behave in such a way, and so forth. But the question is: In what way do these reasons support the judgements? Not in a logical sense. Ethical argument is not formal demonstration. And not in a scientific sense either. For then the goodness or badness of the situation, the rightness or wrongness of the action, would have to be something apart from the situation, something independently verifiable, for which the facts adduced as the reasons for the moral judgement were evidence. But in these moral cases the two coincide. There is no procedure of examining the value of the facts, as distinct from examining the facts themselves. We may say that we have evidence for our moral judgements, but we cannot distinguish between pointing to the evidence itself and pointing to that for which it is supposed to be evidence. Which means that in the scientific sense it is not evidence at all.

My own answer to this question is that what are accounted reasons for our moral judgements are reasons only in the sense that they determine attitudes. One attempts to influence another person morally by calling his attention to certain natural features of the situation, which are such as will be likely to evoke from him the desired response. Or again one may give reasons to oneself as a means of settling on an attitude or, more importantly, as a means of coming to some practical decision. Of course there are many cases in which one applies an ethical term without there being any question of one's having to act oneself, or even to persuade others to act, in any present situation. Moral judgements passed upon the behaviour of historical or fictitious characters provide obvious examples. But an action or a situation is morally evaluated always as an action or a situation of a certain kind. What is approved or disapproved is something repeatable. In saying that Brutus or Raskolnikov acted rightly, I am giving myself and others leave to imitate them should similar circumstances arise. I show myself to be favourably disposed in either case towards actions of that type. Similarly, in saying that they acted wrongly, I express a resolution not to imitate them, and endeavour also to discourage others. It may be thought that the mere use of the dyslogistic word "wrongly" is not much of a discouragement, although it does have some emotive force. But that is where the reasons come in. I discourage others or at any rate hope to discourage them, by telling them why I think the action wrong; and here the argument may take various forms. One method is to appeal to some moral principle, as, for example, that human life is sacred, and show that it applies to the given case. It is assumed that the principle is one that already has some influence upon those to whom the argument is addressed. Alternatively, one may try to establish certain facts, as, for example, that the act in question caused, or was such as would be likely to cause, a great deal of unhappiness; and here it is assumed that the consideration of these facts will modify the hearer's attitude. It is assumed that he regards the increase of human misery as something undesirable, something if possible to be avoided. As for the moral judgement itself, it may be regarded as expressing the attitude which the reasons given for it are calculated to evoke. To say, as I once did, that these moral judgements are merely expressive of certain feelings, feelings of approval or disapproval, is an oversimplification. The fact is

rather that what may be described as moral attitudes consist in certain patterns of behaviour, and that the expression of a moral judgement is an element in the pattern. The moral judgement expresses the attitude in the sense that it contributes to defining it. Why people respond favourably to certain facts and unfavourably to others is a question for the sociologist, into which I do not here propose to enter. I should imagine that the utilitarians had gone some way towards answering this question, although theirs is almost certainly not the whole answer. But my concern at present is only to analyse the use of ethical terms, not scientifically to explain it.
[. . .]

I hope that I have gone some way towards making clear what the theory which I am advocating is. Let me now say what it is not. In the first place, I am not saying that morals are trivial or unimportant, or that people ought not to bother with them. For this would itself be a judgement of value, which I have not made and do not wish to make. And even if I did wish to make it it would have no logical connection with my theory. For the theory is entirely on the level of analysis; it is an attempt to show what people are doing when they make moral judgements; it is not a set of suggestions as to what moral judgements they are to make. And this is true of all moral philosophy, as I understand it. All moral theories, intuitionist, naturalistic, objectivist, emotive, and the rest, in so far as they are philosophical theories, are neutral as regards actual conduct. To speak technically, they belong to the field of metaethics, not ethics proper. That is why it is silly, as well as presumptuous, for any one type of philosopher to pose as the champion of virtue. And it is also one reason why many people find moral philosophy an unsatisfying subject. For they mistakenly look to the moral philosopher for guidance.

Again, when I say that moral judgements are emotive rather than descriptive, that they are persuasive expressions of attitudes and not statements of fact, and consequently that they cannot be either true or false, or at least that it would make for clarity if the categories of truth and falsehood were not applied to them, I am not saying that nothing is good or bad, right or wrong, or that it does not matter what we do. For once more such a statement would itself be the expression of a moral attitude. This attitude is not entailed by the theory, nor do I in fact adopt it. It would indeed be a difficult position to maintain. It would exclude even egotism as a policy, for the decision to consult nothing but one's own pleasure is itself a value judgement. What it requires is that one should live without any policy at all. This may or may not be feasible. My point is simply that I am not recommending it. Neither, in expounding my metaethical theory, am I recommending the opposite. It is indeed to be expected that a moral philosopher, even in my sense of the term, will have his moral standards and that he will sometimes make moral judgements; but these moral judgements cannot be a logical consequence of his philosophy. To analyse moral judgements is not itself to moralize.

Finally, I am not saying that anything that anybody thinks right is right; that putting people into concentration camps is preferable to allowing them free speech if somebody happens to think so, and that the contrary is also preferable if somebody thinks that it is. If my theory did entail this, it would be contradictory; for two different courses of action cannot each be preferable to the other. But it does not entail anything of the sort. On my analysis, to say that something which somebody thinks right really is right is to range oneself on his side, to adhere to that particular standpoint, and certainly I do not adhere to every standpoint whatsoever. I adhere to some, and not to others, like everybody else who has any moral views at all. It is, indeed, true that in a case where one person A approves of X, and another person B approves of not-X, A may correctly express his attitude towards X by saying that it is good, or right, and that B may correctly use the same term to express his attitude towards not-X. But there is no contradiction here. There would be a contradiction if from the fact that A was using words honestly and correctly when he said that X was good, and that B was using words honestly and correctly when he said that not-X was good, it followed that both X and not-X were good, or that X was both good and bad. But this does not follow, inasmuch as the conclusion that X is good, or that not-X is good, itself expresses the attitude of a third party, the speaker, who is by no means bound to agree with both A and B. In this example, indeed, he cannot consistently agree with both, though he may disagree with both if he regards both X and not-X as ethically neutral, or as contraries rather than contradictories in respect of value. It is easy to miss this point, which is essential for the understanding of our position. To say that anything is right if someone thinks so is unobjectionable if it means no more than that anyone is entitled to use the word "right" to refer to something of which he morally approves. But this is not the way in which it is ordinarily taken. It is ordinarily taken as the enunciation of a moral principle. As a moral principle it does appear contradictory; it is at least doubtful whether to say of a man that he commits himself morally both to X and not-X is to describe a possible attitude. But it may perhaps be construed as a principle of universal moral tolerance. As such, it may appeal to some; it does not, in fact, to me. But the important point is that it is not entailed by the theory, which is neutral as regards all moral principles. And here I may repeat that in saying that it is neutral as regards all moral principles I am not saying that it recommends them all alike, nor that it condemns them all alike. It is not that sort of theory. No philosophical theory is.

But even if there is no logical connection between this metaethical theory and any particular type of conduct, may there not be a psychological connection? Does not the promulgation of such a theory encourage moral laxity? Has not its effect been to destroy people's confidence in accepted moral standards? And will not the result of this be that something mischievous will take their place? Such charges have, indeed, been made, but I do not know upon what evidence. The question how people's conduct is actually affected by their acceptance of a metaethical theory is one for empirical investigation; and in this case, so far as I know, no serious investigation has yet been carried out. My own observations, for what they are worth, do not suggest that those who accept the "positivist" analysis of moral judgements conduct themselves very differently as a class from those who reject it; and, indeed, I doubt if the study of moral philosophy does, in general, have any very marked effect upon people's conduct. The way to test the point would be to convert a sufficiently large number of people from one metaethical view to another and make careful observations of their behaviour before and after their conversions. Assuming that their behaviour changed in some significant way, it would then have to be decided by further experiment whether this was due to the change in their philosophical beliefs or to some other factor. If it could be shown, as I believe it could not, that the general acceptance of the sort of analysis of moral judgements that I have been putting forward would have unhappy social consequences, the conclusion drawn by illiberal persons might be that the doctrine ought to be kept secret. For my part I think that I should dispute this conclusion on moral grounds, but this is a question which I am not now concerned to argue. What I have tried to show is not that the theory I am defending is expedient, but that it is true.

Renford Bambrough, "A Proof of the Objectivity of Morals"

My proof that we have moral knowledge consists essentially in saying, "We know that this child, who is about to undergo what would otherwise be painful surgery, should be given an anaesthetic before the operation. Therefore we know at least one moral proposition to be true." I argue that no proposition that could plausibly be alleged as a reason in favour of doubting the truth of the proposition that the child should be given an anaesthetic can possibly be more certainly true than that proposition itself. If a philosopher produces an argument against my claim to *know* that the child should be given an anaesthetic, I can therefore be sure in advance that *either* at least one of the premises of his argument is false, *or* there is a mistake in the reasoning by which he purports to derive from his premises the conclusion that I do not know that the child should be given an anaesthetic. [. . .]

Those who reject the common sense account of moral knowledge, like those who reject the common sense account of our knowledge of the external world, do of course offer arguments in favour of their rejection. [. . .] It will be impossible in a small space to give a full treatment of any one argument, and it will also be impossible to refer to all the arguments that have been offered by moral philosophers who are consciously or unconsciously in conflict with common sense. I shall refer briefly to the most familiar and most plausible arguments, and I shall give to each of them the outline of what I believe to be an adequate answer in defence of the common sense account.

"Moral disagreement is more widespread, more radical and more persistent than disagreement about matters of fact."

I have two main comments to make on this suggestion: the first is that it is almost certainly untrue, and the second is that it is quite certainly irrelevant.

The objection loses much of its plausibility as soon as we insist on comparing the comparable. We are usually invited to contrast our admirably close agreement that

From *American Journal of Jurisprudence* (1969).

there is a glass of water on the table with the depth, vigour and tenacity of our disagreements about capital punishment, abortion, birth control and nuclear disarmament. But this is a game that may be played by two or more players. A sufficient reply in kind is to contrast our general agreement that this child should have an anaesthetic with the strength and warmth of the disagreements between cosmologists and radio astronomers about the interpretation of certain radio-astronomical observations. If the moral sceptic then reminds us of Christian Science we can offer him in exchange the Flat Earth Society.

But this is a side issue. Even if it is true that moral disagreement is more acute and more persistent than other forms of disagreement, it does not follow that moral knowledge is impossible. However long and violent a dispute may be, and however few or many heads may be counted on this side or on that, it remains possible that one party to the dispute is right and the others wrong. Galileo was right when he contradicted the Cardinals: and so was Wilberforce when he rebuked the slave owners.

There is a more direct and decisive way of showing the irrelevance of the argument from persistent disagreement. The question of whether a given type of enquiry is objective is the question whether it is *logically capable* of reaching knowledge, and is therefore an *a priori*, logical question. The question of how much agreement or disagreement there is between those who actually engage in that enquiry is a question of psychological or sociological fact. It follows that the question about the actual extent of agreement or disagreement has no bearing on the question of the objectivity of the enquiry. If this were not so, the objectivity of every enquiry might wax and wane through the centuries as men became more or less disputatious or more or less proficient in the arts of persuasion.

"Our moral opinions are conditioned by our environment and upbringing."

It is under this heading that we are reminded of the variegated customs and beliefs of Hottentots, Eskimos, Polynesians and American Indians, which do indeed differ widely from each other and from our own. But this objection is really a special case of the general argument from disagreement, and it can be answered on the same lines. The beliefs of the Hottentots and the Polynesians about straightforwardly factual matters differs widely from our own, but that does not tempt us to say that science is subjective.

It is true that most of those who are born and bred in the stately homes of England have a different outlook on life from that of the Welsh miner or the Highland crofter, but it is also true that all these classes of people differ widely in their factual beliefs, and not least in their factual beliefs about themselves and each other.

Let us consider some of the moral sceptic's favourite examples, which are often presented as though they settled the issue beyond further argument.

(1) Herodotus reports that within the Persian Empire there were some tribes who buried their dead and some who burned them. Each group thought that the other's practice was barbarous. But (a) they agreed that respect must be shown to the dead; (b) they lived under very different climatic conditions; (c) we can now

see that they were guilty of moral myopia in setting such store by what happened, for good or bad reasons, to be their own particular practice. Moral progress in this field has consisted in coming to recognize that burying-versus-burning is not an issue on which it is necessary for the whole of mankind to have a single, fixed, universal standpoint, regardless of variations of conditions in time and place.

(2) Some societies practise polygamous marriage. Others favour monogamy. Here again there need be no absolute and unvarying rule. In societies where women heavily outnumber men, institutions may be appropriate which would be out of place in societies where the numbers of men and women are roughly equal. The moralist who insists that monogamy is right regardless of circumstances, is like the inhabitant of the northern hemisphere who insists that it is always and everywhere cold at Christmas, or the inhabitant of the southern hemisphere who cannot believe that it is ever or anywhere cold at Christmas.

(3) Some societies do not disapprove of what we condemn as "stealing." In such societies, anybody may take from anybody else's house anything he may need or want. This case serves further to illustrate that circumstances objectively alter cases, the relative is not only compatible with, but actually required by, the objective and rational determination of questions of right and wrong. I can maintain with all possible force that Bill Sykes is a rogue, and that prudence requires me to lock all my doors and windows against him, without being committed to holding that if an Eskimo takes whalemeat from the unlocked igloo of another Eskimo, then one of them is a knave and the other a fool. It is not that we disapprove of stealing and that the Eskimos do not, but that their circumstances differ so much from ours as to call for new consideration and a different judgment, which may be that in their situation stealing is innocent, or that in their situation there is no private property and therefore no possibility of *stealing* at all.

(4) Some tribes leave their elderly and useless members to die in the forest. Others, including our own, provide old age pensions and geriatric hospitals. But we should have to reconsider our arrangements if we found that the care of the aged involved for us the consequences that it might involve for a nomadic and pastoral people: general starvation because the old could not keep pace with the necessary movement to new pastures, children and domestic animals a prey to wild beasts, a life burdensome to all and destined to end with the extinction of the tribe.

"When I say that something is good or bad or right or wrong I commit myself, and reveal something of my attitudes and feelings."

This is quite true, but it is equally and analogously true that when I say that something is true or false, or even that something is red or round, I also commit myself and reveal something of my *beliefs*. Some emotivist and imperativist philosophers have sometimes failed to draw a clear enough distinction between what is said or meant by a particular form of expression and what is implied or suggested by it, and even those who have distinguished clearly and correctly between meaning and implication in the case of moral propositions have often failed to see that exactly the same distinction can be drawn in the case of nonmoral propositions. If I say "this is good" and then add "but I do not approve of it," I certainly behave oddly enough to owe you an explanation, but I behave equally oddly and owe you a comparable explanation if I say "that is true, but I don't believe it." If it is held that I contradict myself in the first case, it must be allowed that I contradict myself in the second case. If it is claimed that I do not contradict myself in the second case, then it must be allowed that I do not contradict myself in the first case. If this point can be used as an argument against the objectivity of morals, then it can also be used as an argument against the objectivity of science, logic, and of every other branch of enquiry.

The parallel between *approve* and *believe* and between *good* and *true* is so close that it provides a useful test of the paradoxes of subjectivism and emotivism. The emotivist puts the cart before the horse in trying to explain goodness in terms of approval, just as he would if he tried to explain truth in terms of belief. Belief cannot be explained without introducing the notion of truth, and approval cannot be explained without introducing the notion of goodness. To believe is (roughly) to hold to be true, and to approve is (equally roughly) to hold to be good. Hence it is as unsatisfactory to try to reduce goodness to approval, or to approval plus some other component, as it would be to try to reduce truth to belief, or to belief plus some other component.

If we are to give a correct account of the logical character of morality we must preserve the distinction between appearance and reality, between seeming and really being, that we clearly and admittedly have to preserve if we are to give a correct account of truth and belief. Just as we do and must hope that what we believe (what seems to us to be true) is and will be in fact true, so we must hope that what we approve (what seems to us to be good) is and will be in fact good.

I can say of another "He thinks it is raining, but it is not," and of myself, "I thought it was raining but it was not." I can also say of another "He thinks it is good, but it is not," and of myself "I thought it was good, but it was not."

"After every circumstance, every relation is known, the understanding has no further room to operate, nor any object on which it could employ itself."

This sentence from the first Appendix to Hume's *Enquiry Concerning the Principles of Morals* is the moral sceptic's favourite quotation, and he uses it for several purposes, including some that are alien to Hume's intentions. Sometimes it is no more than a flourish added to the argument from disagreement. Sometimes it is used in support of the claim that there comes a point in every moral dispute when further reasoning is not so much ineffective as impossible in principle. In either case the answer is once again a firm *tu quoque*. In any sense in which it is true that there may or must come a point in moral enquiry beyond which no further reasoning is possible, it is in that same sense equally true that there may or must be a point in any enquiry at which the reasoning has to stop. Nothing can be proved to a man who will accept nothing that has not been proved. Moore recognized that his proof of an external world uses premises which have not themselves been proved. Not even in pure mathematics, that paradigm of strict security of reasoning, can we *force* a man to accept our premises or our modes of inference; and therefore we cannot force him to accept our conclusions. Once again the moral sceptic counts as a reason for doubting the objectivity of morals a feature of moral enquiry which is exactly paralleled in other departments of enquiry where he does *not* count it as a reason for scepticism. If he is to be consistent, he must either withdraw his argument against the objectivity of morals or subscribe also to an analogous argument against the objectivity of mathematics, physics, history, and every other branch of enquiry.

But of course such an argument gives no support to a sceptical conclusion about any of these enquiries. However conclusive a mode of reasoning may be, and however accurately we may use it, it always remains possible that we shall fail to convince a man who disagrees with us. There may come a point in a moral dispute when it is wiser to agree to differ than to persist with fruitless efforts to convince an opponent. But this by itself is no more a reason for doubting the truth of our premises and the validity of our arguments than the teacher's failure to convince a pupil of the validity of a proof of Pythagoras' theorem is a reason for doubting the validity of the proof and the truth of the theorem. It is notorious that even an expert physicist may fail to convince a member of the Flat Earth Society that the earth is not flat, but we nevertheless *know* that the earth is not flat. Lewis Carroll's tortoise ingeniously resisted the best efforts of Achilles to convince him of the validity of a simple deductive argument, but of course the argument *is* valid.

"A dispute which is purely moral is inconclusive in principle. The specifically moral element in moral disputes is one which cannot be resolved by investigation and reflection."

This objection brings into the open an assumption that is made at least implicitly by most of those who use Hume's remark as a subjective weapon: the assumption that whatever is a logical or factual dispute, or a mixture of logic and factual disputes, is necessarily *not* a moral dispute; that nothing is a moral dispute unless it is *purely* moral in the sense that it is a dispute between parties who agree on *all* the relevant factual and logical questions. But the *purely moral* dispute envisaged by this assumption is a pure fiction. The search for the "specifically moral elements" in moral disputes is a wild goose chase, and is the result of the initial confusion of supposing that no feature of moral reasoning is *really* a feature of moral reasoning, or is *characteristic* of moral reasoning, unless it is peculiar to moral reasoning. It is as if one insisted that a ginger cake could be fully characterized, and could only be characterized, by saying that there is ginger in it. It is true that ginger is the peculiar ingredient of a ginger cake as contrasted with other cakes, but no cake can be made entirely of ginger, and the ingredients that are combined with ginger to make ginger cakes are the same as those that are combined with chocolate, lemon, orange or vanilla to make other kinds of cakes; and ginger itself, when combined with other ingredients and treated in other ways, goes into the making of ginger puddings, ginger biscuits and ginger beer.

To the question "What is the place of reason in ethics?" why should we not answer: "The place of reason in ethics is exactly what it is in other enquiries, to enable us to find out the relevant facts and to make our judgments mutually consistent, to expose factual errors and detect logical inconsistencies"? This might seem to imply that there are some moral judgments which will serve as starting points for any moral enquiry, and will not themselves be proved, as others may be proved by being derived from them or disproved by being shown to be incompatible with them, and also to imply that we cannot engage in moral argument with a man with whom we agree on *no* moral question. In so far as these implications are correct they apply to all enquiry and not only to moral enquiry, and they do not, when correctly construed, constitute any objection to the rationality and objectivity of morality or of any other mode of enquiry. [. . .]

"*There are recognized methods for settling factual and logical disputes, but there are no recognized methods for settling moral disputes.*"

This is either false, or true but irrelevant, according to how it is understood. Too often those who make this complaint are arguing in a circle, since they will count nothing as a recognized method of argument unless it is a recognized method of logical or scientific argument. If we adopt this interpretation, then it is true that there is no recognized method of moral argument, but the lack of such methods does not affect the claim that morality is objective. One department of enquiry has not been shown to be no true department of enquiry when all that has been shown is that it cannot be carried on by exactly the methods that are appropriate to some other department of enquiry. We know without the help of the sceptic that morality is not identical with logic or science.

But in its most straightforward sense the claim is simply false. There *are* recognized methods of moral argument. Whenever we say "How would you like it if somebody did this to you?" or "How would it be if we all acted like this?" we are arguing according to recognized and established methods, and are in fact appealing to the consistency-requirement to which I have already referred. It is true that such appeals are often ineffective, but it is also true that well-founded logical or scientific arguments often fail to convince those to whom they are addressed. If the present objection is pursued beyond this point it turns into the argument from radical disagreement.

Now the moral sceptic is even more inclined to exaggerate the amount of disagreement that there is about methods of moral argument than he is inclined to exaggerate the amount of disagreement of moral belief as such. One reason for this is that he concentrates his attention on the admittedly striking and important fact that there is an enormous amount of immoral *conduct*. But most of those who *behave* immorally appeal to the very same methods of moral argument as those who condemn their immoral conduct. Hitler broke many promises, but he did not explicitly hold that promisebreaking as such and in general was justified. When others broke their promises to him he complained with the same force and in the same terms as those with whom he himself had failed to keep faith. And whenever he broke a promise he tried to *justify* his breach by claiming that other obligations overrode the duty to keep the promise. He did not simply deny that it was his duty to keep promises. He thus entered into the very process of argument by which it is possible to condemn so many of his own actions. He was *inconsistent* in requiring of other nations and their leaders standards of conduct to which he himself did not conform, and in failing to produce *convincing reasons* for his own departures from the agreed standards.

Ronald Dworkin, "The Concept of a Moral Position"

We might start with the fact that terms like "moral position" and "moral conviction" function in our conventional morality as terms of justification and criticism, as well as of description. It is true that we sometimes speak of a group's "morals," or "morality," or "moral beliefs," or "moral positions" or "moral convictions," in what might be called an anthropological sense, meaning to refer to whatever attitudes the group displays about the propriety of human conduct, qualities or goals. We say, in this sense, that the morality of Nazi Germany was based on prejudice, or was irrational. But we also use some of these terms, particularly "moral position" and "moral conviction," in a discriminatory sense, to contrast the positions they describe with prejudices, rationalizations, matters of personal aversion or taste, arbitrary stands, and the like. One use – perhaps the most characteristic use – of this discriminatory sense is to offer a limited but important sort of justification for an act, when the moral issues surrounding that act are unclear or in dispute.

Suppose I tell you that I propose to vote against a man running for a public office of trust because I know him to be a homosexual and because I believe that homosexuality is profoundly immoral. If you disagree that homosexuality is immoral, you may accuse me of being about to cast my vote unfairly, acting on prejudice or out of a personal repugnance which is irrelevant to the moral issue. I might then try to convert you to my position on homosexuality, but if I fail in this I shall still want to convince you of what you and I will both take to be a separate point – that my vote was based upon *a* moral position, in the discriminatory sense, even though one which differs from yours. I shall want to persuade you of this, because if I do I am entitled to expect that you will alter your opinion of me and of what I am about to do. Your judgment of my character will be different – you might still think me eccentric (or puritanical or unsophisticated) but these are types of character and not faults of character. Your judgment of my act will also be different, in this respect. You will admit that so long as I hold my moral position, I have a moral right to vote against the homosexual, because I have a right (indeed a duty) to vote my own convictions. You would not admit such a right (or duty) if you were still persuaded that I was acting out of a prejudice or a personal taste.

I am entitled to expect that your opinion will change in these ways, because these distinctions are a part of the conventional morality you and I share, and which forms the background for our discussion. They enforce the difference between positions we must respect, although we think them wrong, and positions we need not respect because they offend some ground rule of moral reasoning. A great deal of debate about moral issues (in real life, although not in philosophy texts) consists of arguments that some position falls on one or the other side of this crucial line.

It is this feature of conventional morality that animates Lord Devlin's argument that society has the right to follow its own lights. We must therefore examine that

From "Lord Devlin and the Enforcement of Morals," *The Yale Law Journal*, vol. 75, no. 5 (April 1966), pp. 986–1005.

discriminatory concept of a moral position more closely, and we can do so by pursuing our imaginary conversation. What must I do to convince you that my position is a moral position?

(a) I must produce some reasons for it. This is not to say that I have to articulate a moral principle I am following or a general moral theory to which I subscribe. Very few people can do either, and the ability to hold a moral position is not limited to those who can.

My reason need not be a principle or theory at all. It must only point out some aspect or feature of homosexuality which moves me to regard it as immoral: the fact that the Bible forbids it, for example, or that one who practices homosexuality becomes unfit for marriage and parenthood. Of course, any such reason would presuppose my acceptance of some general principle or theory, but I need not be able to state what it is, or realize that I am relying upon it.

Not every reason I might give will do, however. Some will be excluded by general criteria stipulating sorts of reasons which do not count. We might take note of four of the most important such criteria:

(i) If I tell you that homosexuals are morally inferior because they do not have heterosexual desires, and so are not "real men," you would reject that reason as showing one type of prejudice. Prejudices, in general, are postures of judgment that take into account considerations our conventions exclude. In a structured context, like a trial or a contest, the ground rules exclude all but certain considerations, and a prejudice is a basis of judgment which violates these rules. Our conventions stipulate some ground rules of moral judgment which obtain even apart from such special contexts, the most important of which is that a man must not be held morally inferior on the basis of some physical, racial or other characteristic he cannot help having. Thus a man whose moral judgments about Jews, or Negroes, or Southerners, or women, or effeminate men are based on his belief that any member of these classes automatically deserves less respect, without regard to anything he himself has done, is said to be prejudiced against that group.

(ii) If I base my view about homosexuals on a personal emotional reaction ("they make me sick") you would reject that reason as well. We distinguish moral positions from emotional reactions, not because moral positions are supposed to be unemotional or dispassionate – quite the reverse is true – but because the moral position is supposed to justify the emotional reaction, and not vice versa. If a man is unable to produce such reasons, we do not deny the fact of his emotional involvement, which may have important social or political consequences, but we do not take this involvement as demonstrating his moral conviction. Indeed, it is just this sort of position – a severe emotional reaction to a practice or a situation for which one cannot account – that we tend to describe, in lay terms, as a phobia or an obsession.

(iii) If I base my position on a proposition of fact ("homosexual acts are physically debilitating") which is not only false, but is so implausible that it challenges the minimal standards of evidence and argument I generally accept and impose upon others, then you would regard my belief, even though sincere, as a form of rationalization, and disqualify my reason on that ground. (Rationalization is a complex concept, and also includes, as we shall see, the production of reasons which suggest general theories I do not accept.)

(iv) If I can argue for my own position only by citing the beliefs of others ("everyone knows homosexuality is a sin") you will conclude that I am parroting and not relying on a moral conviction of my own. With the possible (though complex) exception of a deity, there is no moral authority to which I can appeal and so automatically make my position a moral one. I must have my own reasons, though of course I may have been taught these reasons by others.

No doubt many readers will disagree with these thumbnail sketches of prejudice, mere emotional reaction, rationalization and parroting. Some may have their own theories of what these are. I want to emphasize now only that these are distinct concepts, whatever the details of the differences might be, and that they have a role in deciding whether to treat another's position as a moral conviction. They are not merely epithets to be pasted on positions we strongly dislike.

(b) Suppose I do produce a reason which is not disqualified on one of these (or on similar) grounds. That reason will presuppose some general moral principle or theory, even though I may not be able to state that principle or theory, and do not have it in mind when I speak. If I offer, as my reason, the fact that the Bible forbids homosexual acts, or that homosexual acts make it less likely that the actor will marry and raise children, I suggest that I accept the theory my reason presupposes, and you will not be satisfied that my position is a moral one if you believe that I do not. It may be a question of my sincerity — do I in fact believe that the injunctions of the Bible are morally binding as such, or that all men have a duty to procreate? Sincerity is not, however, the only issue, for consistency is also in point. I may believe that I accept one of these general positions, and be wrong, because my other beliefs, and my own conduct on other occasions, may be inconsistent with it. I may reject certain Biblical injunctions, or I may hold that men have a right to remain bachelors if they please or use contraceptives all their lives.

Of course, my general moral positions may have qualifications and exceptions. The difference between an exception and an inconsistency is that the former can be supported by reasons which presuppose other moral positions I can properly claim to hold. Suppose I condemn all homosexuals on Biblical authority, but not all fornicators. What reasons can I offer for the distinction? If I can produce none which supports it, I cannot claim to accept the general position about Biblical authority. If I do produce a reason which seems to support the distinction, the same sorts of question may be asked about that reason as were asked about my original reply. What general position does the reason for my exception presuppose? Can I sincerely claim to accept that further general position? Suppose my reason, for example, is that fornication is now very common and has been sanctioned by custom. Do I really believe that what is immoral becomes moral when it becomes popular? If not, and if I can produce no other reason for the distinction, I cannot claim to accept the general position that what the Bible condemns is immoral. Of course, I may be persuaded, when this is pointed out, to change my views on fornication. But you would be alert to the question of whether this is a genuine change of heart, or only a performance for the sake of the argument.

In principle there is no limit to these ramifications of my original claim, though of course, no actual argument is likely to pursue very many of them.

(c) But do I really have to have a reason to make my position a matter of moral conviction? Most men think that acts which cause unnecessary suffering, or break a serious promise with no excuse, are immoral, and yet they could give no reason for these beliefs? They feel that no reason is necessary, because they take it as axiomatic or self-evident that these are immoral acts. It seems contrary to common sense to deny that a position held in this way can be a moral position.

Yet there is an important difference between believing that one's position is self-evident and just not having a reason for one's position. The former presupposes a positive belief that no further reason is necessary, that the immorality of the act in question does not depend upon its social effects, or its effects on the character of the actor, or its proscription by a deity, or anything else, but follows from the nature of the act itself. The claim that a particular position is axiomatic, in other words, does supply a reason of a special sort, namely that the act is immoral in and of itself, and this special reason, like the others we considered, may be inconsistent with more general theories I hold.

The moral arguments we make presuppose not only moral principles, but also more abstract positions about moral reasoning. In particular, they presuppose positions about what kinds of acts can be immoral in and of themselves. When I criticize your moral opinions, or attempt to justify my own disregard of traditional moral rules I think are silly, I will proceed by denying that the act in question has any of the several features that can make an act immoral – that it involves no breach of an undertaking or duty, for example, harms no one including the actor, is not proscribed by any organized religion, and is not illegal. I proceed in this way because I assume that the ultimate grounds of immorality are limited to some such small set of very general standards. I may assert this assumption directly or it may emerge from the pattern of my argument. In either event, I will enforce it by calling positions which can claim no support from any of these ultimate standards *arbitrary*, as I should certainly do if you said that photography was immoral, for instance, or swimming. Even if I cannot articulate this underlying assumption, I shall still apply it, and since the ultimate criteria I recognize are among the most abstract of my moral standards, they will not vary much from those my neighbors recognize and apply. Although many who despise homosexuals are unable to say why, few would claim affirmatively that one needs no reason, for this would make their position, on their own standards, an arbitrary one.

(d) This anatomy of our argument could be continued, but it is already long enough to justify some conclusions. If the issue between us is whether my views on homosexuality amount to a moral position, and hence whether I am entitled to vote against a homosexual on that ground, I cannot settle the issue by reporting my feelings. You will want to consider the reasons I can produce to support my belief, and whether my other views and behavior are consistent with the theories these reasons presuppose. You will have, of course, to apply your own understanding, which may differ in detail from mine, of what a prejudice or a rationalization is, for example, and of when one view is inconsistent with another. You and I may end in disagreement over whether my position is a moral one, partly because of such differences in understanding, and partly because one is less likely to recognize these illegitimate grounds in himself than in others.

We must avoid the skeptical fallacy of passing from these facts to the conclusion that there is no such thing as a prejudice or a rationalization or an inconsistency, or that these terms mean merely that the one who uses them strongly dislikes the positions he describes this way. That would be like arguing that because different people have different understandings of what jealousy is, and can in good faith disagree about whether one of them is jealous, there is no such thing as jealousy, and one who says another is jealous merely means he dislikes him very much.

Theodore M. Benditt, "Locke: The Individual,
the Public, the State"

Readings

Plato, *The Republic* (selections)

Thomas Hobbes, *Leviathan* (selections)

John Locke, *Second Treatise on Civil Government* (selections)

John Stuart Mill, *On Liberty* (selections)

George Dargo, *Law in the New Republic* (selections)

Charles A. Reich, "The New Property" (selections)

Michael Sandel, "Morality and the Liberal Ideal"

Iris Marion Young, "Impartiality and the Civic Public" (selections)

John Locke. Culver Pictures, Inc.

THEODORE M. BENDITT

Locke: The Individual, the Public, the State

The great and chief *end, therefore, of men's uniting into commonwealths, and putting themselves under government,* is the preservation of their property. . . . *The* supreme power cannot take *from any man any part of his* property *without . . . his own consent,* i.e., *without the consent of the majority.*

John Locke, *Second Treatise on Civil Government*

1 Authoritarians with a Difference

Plato

In *The Republic*, one of the great works of political thought, the Greek philosopher Plato considers some of the problems of human social organization – namely, how society can be organized so as to realize justice and promote well-being and happiness. Plato was born in 428 BC to an aristocratic family many of whose members were involved in Athenian public life, on the anti-democratic side. When he was young Athens was defeated by Sparta, a defeat which Plato attributed to democracy; later his teacher Socrates was put to death by Athenian democracy. According to some commentators, Plato admired the (possibly mythical) constitution of Sparta, to which his own utopian ideas bear a resemblance.

Plato's political philosophy begins with the idea that by paying attention to nature and the natural order we can understand how things ought to be (see chapter 6 for a discussion of this notion as applied to morality). The state, as Plato sees it, is a natural institution reflecting the structure of human nature. The human soul, he believes, is composed of three parts – reason, spirit, and appetite. A person functions well, and is well and happy, when these are in harmony, each fulfilling its proper role and not overbalancing the others. People have these characteristics to different degrees and thus are naturally divided into social classes. Those people in whom appetite predominates are the majority; they are the ones who engage in the trades that supply the material needs of society. Those in whom spirit predominates are the auxiliaries, who protect the society from aggression. The leaders are those in whom reason predominates. But while they are naturally selected for leadership, they are not naturally prepared. They must undergo a rigorous program of education, the details of which are explained by Plato in *The Republic*. The pinnacle of the educational process is the achievement of genuine knowledge (as opposed to mere belief), which enables the guardians to ascertain what is good and worthy and thus makes them capable of ruling effectively over others. For this reason the leaders are referred to as "philosopher-kings." Finally, just as a person functions well and is happy when the three aspects of the soul are in harmony, so also a society functions well and its people are happy, and justice is achieved, when they are doing their appropriate jobs and the three classes function harmoniously: ". . . everyone must pursue one occupation . . . , that for which his nature best fitted him. . . . [J]ustice is to perform one's own task and not to meddle with that of others" (433a).

How will people be kept in their places and, more importantly, accept their situations, since voluntary acceptance is essential to smooth functioning? On the one hand, Plato does allow for movement between classes – a worker who is especially capable, or an auxiliary who is not, might be educated for another class. But for the rest, people are to be educated to accept their stations in life, their education being reinforced by a "noble fiction," a "necessary untruth" (414c), about people having either gold, or silver, or iron or bronze in their constitutions, making them suited by nature for certain roles in society.

When we ask why certain people ought to have authority (and for Plato it is absolute authority) over others, Plato has two sorts of answers. One answer is that it is natural. Each thing (and person) should do what it is by nature suited for, and some people are better suited for rule. But Plato's other answer is the more important. Ruling, or leadership in general, is a talent that some people have and others do not, and among those having it, some possess it to a greater degree than others. Further, leadership ability can be improved by education and experience. Given this, Plato offers us a dilemma. Either those with the most talent and training are the leaders, in which case government is authoritarian, or those with less talent and training are the rulers, in which case we have poor government. Take your pick!

Government in Plato's state is for the people – the purpose of the state is to promote the well-being and happiness of the whole, not merely of a part, of the citizenry. This might mean providing for the sick or the aged, or promoting agriculture, or regulating trade, or educating people. At the same time, though, people must be shaped for a life in society – it is the role of the state to decide what the well-being and happiness of people are and to develop a citizenry that will find them in the state. Accordingly, the guardians, in order to promote a stable society, will enforce a private religion and a public morality and will raise children with the official myths about gold, silver, and brass as part of the human constitution. Further, since children imitate what they are exposed to, they should not be exposed to a wide variety of experiences, for this could lead to bad as well as good behavior. This is true particularly of exposure to music, literature, and poetry. The result of this carefully controlled educational process, according to Plato, will be the good of the whole society and also the good of the individual.

One of the most likely objections to Plato's state is that we do not want others, however capable, to have absolute authority over us; it is simply too dangerous. Power, we know, tends to be corrupting. Plato is alert to this problem, and his answer reveals the extreme and utopian nature of his vision. Power corrupts because people find its exercise gratifying and because they use it to promote their own interests, often at the expense of others'. Plato's solution is to take away any reason a guardian might have to abuse power. The guardians own no property, so they cannot gain materially by their positions. They live communally. Their children are raised communally and not by their parents, so there is no motive to try to gain advantages for one's offspring. There are no exclusive sexual relationships and sex is rationed. In Plato's state leadership is not something a person would want for its "perks" – it is a difficult duty performed for the good of all. Does this take the sting out of absolute authority? Perhaps. Some of us might find it acceptable *if* we had great confidence that the leaders focused entirely on the best for all of us, were not able to exploit their positions for their own advantage, and had greater ability than others to make good decisions. But no one would have such confidence.

Below is a summary of some of the basic questions of political philosophy, and Plato's answers. Later we will look at Hobbes's and Locke's answers to the same questions.

What is the origin of the state?	The state is a natural, historically evolving, entity.
What is the justification of the state?	It is in accord with the natural order.
Who should rule?	The wisest should rule.
What is the role of the state?	To promote welfare and protect against threats.
What limitations are there on the state?	None with respect to the governed; the rulers can't have private families or property.
What is justice in the state?	The harmonious functioning of the three classes.
Is there a right to disobey or revolt?	Not in the ideal state, but yes in an actual, less than ideal state.

Hobbes

Thomas Hobbes (1588–1679) lived during a turbulent period of English history which saw a great struggle between the monarchy and Parliament. Educated at Oxford, Hobbes interacted with some of the most influential minds in Europe – Francis Bacon, René Descartes, and Galileo. His earliest publication was a translation of Thucydides' history of the war between Athens and Sparta, in which Thucydides blames Athens' defeat on its democratic system. Hobbes likewise saw democracy as a system that breeds divergent opinion and thus political insecurity, the antidote to which is absolute power.

The political writings Hobbes produced during the 1640s and 1650s reflect the danger and uncertainty of the period. The monarchy and Parliament were independent bases of power that came into conflict with one another. Religious difference was part of the conflict, but the substance of the dispute was not Hobbes's concern – it was not particular interpretations of the Bible, but the very existence of debate, of some people putting their private view of things ahead of settled, publicly accepted views and laws, that undermined public order.

Hobbes's political philosophy is an argument for why people should accept a *single, unlimited, absolute, sovereign* authority. The argument is simple. Hobbes asks us to think about what kinds of beings we are and to work out, in our minds, what our situation would be if we lived together without a single, unlimited, absolute, sovereign authority to obey and to fear. To help us work this out, Hobbes describes a condition he calls the state of nature, which is simply a situation in which there are no rules or rulers. In such a condition there is (in Hobbes's opinion) no morality limiting anyone's behavior, and in fact everyone has a "right to all things." Human beings are thoroughly self-interested; they want whatever will improve their lives, and with no rules and no enforcers, there is nothing to prevent their taking what they can from others. Further, since people are roughly equal in strength, no one is strong enough to have the assurance that she or he will not be a victim of others. Such a condition is what Hobbes calls a state of war, in which people must be on guard at all times, must spend most of their time and energy worrying about security, and therefore must, as much as possible, avoid other people. Common projects would be out of the question, since they rely on trust. Food and survival would be the major concerns, and no one would have time or energy for the things that, for most of us, make life worth living. In a ringing phrase, Hobbes describes life in the state of nature as "solitary, poor, nasty, brutish, and short."

How is this to be avoided? First of all, Hobbes notes, we all have the desire for peace, and secondly we all have the capacity of reason. Reason shows us how peace can be achieved; it tells us that each of us must agree with everyone else to renounce our right to all things, to establish some one individual or group of individuals as absolute sovereign, and to obey the dictates of the sovereign. This is the social contract we enter into on the condition that all others enter into it, and it is necessary (and rational) for all of us to do so if we are to avoid the horrors of the state of nature.

Reduced to its barest essentials, Hobbes's argument is that we all want, more than anything, to stay alive, and the only way to assure this, given that we must live with others, is for all of us, collectively, to establish an absolute authority who creates rules and enforces them. One question we might ask is why the authority must have absolute power. Why not allow the sovereign to have only limited authority – the right to make and enforce rules with regard to some, but not all, things? Or perhaps divided authority, wherein different agencies have jurisdiction over different affairs of life? Hobbes's answer is that if sovereignty is not single and undivided, the situation is unstable – there is always the potential for conflict and thus for civil war (i.e. for a return to the state of nature). The great legal philosopher John Austin, writing more than a century later, offered a conceptual argument against limited or divided authority. Laws, he said, are commands of the sovereign. The only way, therefore, that there could be legal limitations on the lawgiver would be for that individual to be the recipient of a command of the sovereign – in which case the lawgiver cannot be sovereign after all. Thus, as a logical matter, sovereignty cannot be limited. Indeed, it follows that the sovereign must, literally, be outside the law, and all law must emanate from someone who is not bound by law. Hobbes himself made this a feature of the Social Contract. When people come together to enter into the Social Contract, the sovereign is not party to the contract. The people do not enter into an agreement with the sovereign – if they did, that would limit the sovereign by imposing duties on it. Rather, the people agree with one another to cede all power to the sovereign, who is thereby obligated to nothing.

Are there, then, no limitations on the sovereign? And if none, does it make sense for people to agree to obey such a ruler? There are no formal or legal limitations on Hobbes's sovereign, as we have seen above. There are, though, some practical limitations. For one thing, people in the state of nature, as part of their right to all things, have the right, which they retain on entering the Social Contract, to preserve their lives. Thus, they may resist anything, even if in accordance with law, that threatens their lives, for anything that threatens a person's life re-creates the state of nature as far as he is concerned, and then anything goes. Another practical limitation is that the sovereign is mortal and accordingly is at personal risk if people are treated badly. The sovereign thus has good reason to promote the interests of the citizenry. But, of course, Hobbes's sovereign has the authority to do otherwise, so why would people establish such a position? The heart of Hobbes's answer is that however badly we are treated by the sovereign, we are still better off than being in the state of nature, which is the only realistic alternative to establishing a sovereign with absolute authority. This was the lesson of the English civil wars.

Plato and Hobbes have come up with similar results – a rationale for absolute authority. Yet there are considerable differences. Whereas Plato thinks that people's duty to obey the law derives from the natural order of things, and also from the duties we owe the state for having nurtured us and made us who we are (analogous to the duties we owe our parents), Hobbes takes the view that the state is a human artifact and that we have no obligations but those we freely and voluntarily undertake. In a more modern phrase, government, according to Hobbes, rests on the consent of the governed. Another important difference concerns the role of government. Whereas for Plato the purpose of government is to shape us as individuals and to promote our well-being and happiness, for Hobbes the purpose of government is to protect us and to create a framework of order within which we are free (that is, as free as the sovereign chooses to leave us) to pursue our own ends, our own forms of life. This seems to be Hobbes's idea of *good* government, even if no one can claim, against the sovereign, a right to it. As we shall see, this is a major point from which John Locke dissents. Before getting to Locke, though, let us look at Hobbes's answers to the basic questions of political philosophy.

What is the origin of the state?	The state is a conventional, man-made, entity.
What is the justification of the state?	It rests on voluntary commitment – a contract.
Who should rule?	The strongest – whoever can keep order.
What is the role of the state?	To prevent strife, maintain order.
What limitations are there on the state?	Can't threaten people's lives.
What is justice in the state?	Obeying the law.
Is there a right to disobey or revolt?	Only if the ruler threatens life or is unable to protect.

2   Locke: Intellectual Forebear of the US Constitution

John Locke

Like Hobbes, John Locke (1632–1704) lived through a period of political unrest in which, owing to the political fortunes of his patron, he was forced on two occasions to flee England. He was living in the Netherlands when, in 1688, James II was deposed and William of Orange, who had been advised by Locke, was installed as King of England. Early the following year Locke returned to England accompanying the princess of Orange, who later became Queen Mary. In 1690 Locke published his *Two Treatises of Government*, which, though regarded as justifying the Glorious Revolution of 1688, were completed several years earlier. The *Second Treatise* was influential with such figures as Thomas Jefferson, Thomas Paine, Baron de Montesquieu, and Jean-Jacques Rousseau, and the Constitution of the United States resonates with its ideas.

Whereas Hobbes was concerned primarily with security, holding that citizens can demand nothing of government other than the establishment and enforcement of rules, Locke, writing thirty or forty years later, believed that the English monarchy was overstepping its traditional areas of authority and interfering with people's liberty and property. Locke's methodology is similar to Hobbes's – he adopts the strategy of a hypothetical state of nature and asks us to think through its implications for government. Conclusions similar to Hobbes's follow: the state is an artifactual and alterable institution, and people's obligations to obey it rest on voluntary commitment to a widespread social contract. Like Hobbes, Locke sees the role of government as minimal. However, he sees the starting-points of the argument differently and so comes to some significantly different conclusions.

For one thing, Locke gives us a different picture of human motivation. Whereas Hobbes believes people are so thoroughly self-interested that they cannot co-exist in the state of nature, Locke thinks people are benevolent to a substantial degree, such that they can work together on cooperative projects in the state of nature. The other very important difference, for Locke, is that there are natural rights and moral obligations in the state of nature – most importantly the rights to life, liberty, and property – and that knowledge of rights and obligations is readily available to anyone who will "consult reason." What, then, is problematic about life in the state of nature? Why would people want to escape it? Why would they want to enter into a contract to establish a government that will, by its very nature, limit their liberty?

The difficulty is this. In the state of nature each person has the right to punish those violating the natural law and to seek reparation for injury, but the attempt to do this leads to conflict. A person might be mistaken about whether someone else has violated the natural law and so might punish an innocent person, which is likely to provoke retaliation. And since the natural law is not written anywhere, but depends on people's own understandings, there can be different ideas about what it says. Even with the best of intentions people are prone to take a view of rights and obligations that is favorable to themselves. Finally, a person might simply lack the power to punish a violation of natural law. These difficulties make the state of nature inadequate, and so, according to Locke, people, wanting peace, establish a government to create settled rules, ascertain violations of them, and punish offenders. "And thus all private judgment of every particular member being excluded, the community comes to be umpire . . ." (Locke, §87).

The type of government we have is determined, according to Locke, by who has the legislative power, and he holds that the political community created by the Social Contract is a democracy, ruled by the majority. Most of us are so imbued with the majority principle that we would think it unnecessary to give arguments for it. Locke, though, actually gives arguments – which, in point of fact, are not very satisfactory. He seems almost to think that a group or community literally cannot move itself to do something unless a majority of its members choose to move in that direction. At another point he says simply that there is a natural right to live under legislation approved by the majority.

Whatever the merit of these arguments, Locke, and we, are committed to the majority principle. Locke's main concern is controlling the power of government *vis-à-vis* the individual, and he offers a number of devices to protect people from the abuse of power. The rulers must govern by standing laws; there must be known, authorized judges; legislative power may not be delegated; taxation is permitted only with consent (of the majority); property may not be taken without consent (of the majority); separation of legislature and executive, while not required, is best.

Most important, Locke argues that natural law and natural rights set limits to government. In establishing government people do not give up their rights to life, liberty, and property. These carry over into the state; government is thereby limited, having only the powers delegated to it. Further, a piece of legislation that is contrary to natural law is not valid. Finally, the people retain the right to revolution: "... the legislative being only a fiduciary power to act for certain ends, there remains still in the people a supreme power to remove or alter the legislative, when they find the legislative act contrary to the trust reposed in them" (§149). No doubt this was regarded by eighteenth-century American colonists as justifying their revolution.

Property rights are very important in Locke's political philosophy, for they limit what government can do. Furthermore, they protect people against government in another way, since people who have their own sources of livelihood are better able to resist various official pressures. How exactly does a person acquire rights to property? Usually we acquire something, including real estate, by buying it from someone else. Obviously, though, there has to be a first owner of a piece of property, so the question is how something that was originally unowned becomes someone's property in the first place. This is the problem of *initial acquisition*. Locke says that God put things here for us to use and that originally they were ours in common. A person can, however, remove something from the common and make it his own property by mixing his labor with it. Everyone, he argues, has "a property" in his own person and in his labor; when a person by his labor changes something that is unowned from its natural state, he has mixed his labor with it and it thereby becomes his property.

As intuitive and attractive as this idea may seem, critics have pointed out that it is not clear exactly how mixing one's labor with something makes it his property. One suggestion is that when something that is owned (such as one's labor) becomes so entwined or intermingled with something previously unowned that they cannot be distinguished or separated, ownership expands to encompass the whole. But to this the contemporary philosopher Robert Nozick has retorted:

[W]hy isn't mixing what I own with what I don't own a way of losing what I own rather than a way of gaining what I don't? If I own a can of tomato juice and spill it in the sea so that its molecules ... mingle evenly throughout the sea, do I thereby come to own the sea, or have I foolishly dissipated my tomato juice? (Nozick 1974: 174–5)

Another possibility is this: mixing one's labor with something makes it more valuable – indeed, the entire value may be due to the labor spent to make the item useful. If value is created, then surely it belongs to she or he who has created it, and certainly it would be unjust to let others have the benefits of another's efforts. This is a plausible argument and is particularly persuasive with regard to artifacts. But Locke means his argument to apply also, indeed especially, to real property – tilling the soil and raising crops gives the farmer a right to the property he has worked. Critics, however, have wondered how the farmer's mixing his labor with the top few inches of soil can give him property rights in subterranean minerals, or the right to farm the property (and exclude others from doing so) the following year. Why shouldn't someone else have the opportunity to mix labor with the soil the next year to grow crops for himself?

While it is not an answer to the question, we might think that farmer #2 should find some unused land for himself rather than challenging farmer #1's claim. This is a thought we might reasonably have so long as other land of decent quality is available. But eventually the land will run out – there will not be land remaining that is, in Locke's phrase, "enough and as good." What then? At some point, Locke says, private appropriation must cease and the remaining land must be left in common for all to use. It would be wrong, he believes, for the entire earth to be private property, leaving segments of the population with nothing. Prior to the extensive privatization of property everyone had something of value – the right to use the earth in common with others; if it is all privatized, those who have none are made much worse off; therefore, Locke concludes, privatization may not proceed to such lengths.

Once more, let us summarize a set of answers to the basic questions of political philosophy.

What is the origin of the state?	The state is a conventional, man-made, entity.
What is the justification of the state?	It rests on voluntary commitment – a contract.
Who should rule?	Those chosen by the majority.
What is the role of the state?	To provide security and protect life, liberty, and property.
What limitations are there on the state?	Can't violate natural law.
What is justice in the state?	Obeying valid law (i.e. respecting natural rights).
Is there a right to disobey or revolt?	Yes, if natural rights are violated.

Protecting individuals and minorities in a democracy

Locke's idea of government has been called the night-watchman state. Its job is to protect people from external aggression and from internal violence, theft, and fraud. Taxation is necessary to support legitimate (but limited) governmental functions, though taxes must be approved by a majority in the legislature. Beyond these, government has little role to play in our lives; people have a large area of freedom from governmental interference, defined by the rights to life, liberty, and property, to make their own choices about how to live and to make private arrangements with others for that purpose. Locke was quite concerned about the possibility of governmental tyranny, particularly by the executive. The primary focus of his political philosophy is to prevent this, and his solution is to put government in the hands of the people, who certainly would not threaten their own rights.

As things evolved in the practice of democracy, however, a serious issue, which Locke never considered, emerged – threats to the rights of one part of the citizenry by another part. The threat of tyranny comes not only from, say, a monarch putting its wishes ahead of the rights of the citizenry, but from one part of the people (a majority) putting its wishes or beliefs ahead of the rights of others (of course, the majority tells itself it is not violating others' rights – and though this may sometimes be so, sometimes it is not). If, then, democracy protects us against the tyranny of a powerful executive, what protects us (as individuals and minorities) against the tyranny of the majority? There are interesting devices that help give us this protection. Each of them holds the hope of extending Locke's ideas in ways that are compatible with his core principles. In a later section of this chapter we will see if they really do so.

The "extensive republic"   In the debate leading up to the adoption of the US Constitution, James Madison, one of the principal authors of *The Federalist Papers*, was quite concerned about the problem of faction. In a democracy everyone expects to be in the minority on some votes but in the majority on others: win some, lose some. But when the population divides into factions, some people can lose regularly, and on important matters. This is especially likely to occur when the divisions are based on race, religion, or economic status; in such cases a permanent minority can emerge whose rights may well be threatened. How might the threat of faction be minimized? Madison's answer is ingenious and was influential in the establishment of the American republic. The threat occurs when a majority has a common passion or interest and finds it easy to act in concert. This is most likely to occur when the population is small. It might be helpful to think of the people in a small town with common interests opposed to the interests of a few; the point is not that the majority is wrong, but that it might be and that it can easily get its way. Madison's solution is a governmental structure that makes it difficult for those with the common passion or interest to act together on it. What he proposes is an "extensive republic," that is, a large political unit and a central government in addition to state and local governments. In an extensive republic there is a wider variety of passions and interests, and thus less likelihood that there will be a majority with the same interests or opinions, and if there is such a majority, it is less likely that its members will discover one another and be able to act in concert (this may be brought into question by modern methods of communication). Furthermore, he argues, in a republic the views of the people are filtered through leaders, and the larger the republic, the better the selection of leaders. Madison's argument for the security of people's rights parallels his observation that the best protection of religious freedom is for there to be a multiplicity of sects; the greater the variety of religious belief, the less likely that any sect will be suppressed. Likewise, the more interests there are among the people, the less likely that any will be systematically suppressed.

Judicial review In a democracy, the majority rules. But in a limited democracy, even a majority may not do certain things if they would infringe individual rights. In a democracy those who favor a given action are very unlikely to say to themselves "I know this infringes some people's rights, but we have the power and we can do it." Rather, they are unlikely to think they are violating anyone's rights – but, of course, those who are adversely affected may see things differently. How shall such a conflict be settled in a democracy? By majority vote? After all, every legislator is sworn to uphold the Constitution, and if there is a disagreement about how the Constitution should be interpreted, how else should this be settled than by a vote? It is easy to see, though, that rights may not be very secure, and may fail to impose an effective limit on government, if the very majority that wants to achieve some end has the prerogative of deciding whether it is complying with the Constitution.

This issue was presented in the famous Supreme Court case of *Marbury v. Madison* in 1803. The facts of the case are thoroughly Byzantine and give an insight into the political machinations of the earliest days of the American republic. In deciding the case, Chief Justice John Marshall held that the Supreme Court has the final authority to determine whether an act of Congress is in accordance with the Constitution. He argued, quite simply, that courts have the obligation to interpret the law, and the Constitution is part of the law (though this seems obvious to us, there are democracies in which the constitution is not part of the law in the sense that the regular courts have the authority to interpret it). Therefore, he said, for a judge to fail to determine whether a statute accords with the Constitution would be to fail to treat the Constitution as part of the law and, accordingly, to fulfill the obligation of a judge. Although the case did not present an issue of individual rights *vis-à-vis* the government, judicial review thus became established, to be widely used in later years where, in the opinion of the justices, government had overreached itself in violation of constitutionally protected rights of individuals.

It has often been noted that judicial review is an ironic tool of democracy, since it is inherently undemocratic. At least one of the main underlying ideas of democracy is that people disagree about important matters and that the only fair and peaceful way to proceed is to cast votes and accede to the majority will. That is what the

Social Contract is all about. And yet on some of the most important controversies we entrust the decision to a group of individuals who are not elected and who are, deliberately, insulated as much as possible from public opinion and accountability. The reader should consider for herself or himself which approach is the better guarantor of individual rights – and also the extent to which individual rights should be protected from majority goals.

An answer to the foregoing does not fully determine the matter, for if we choose judicial review, we must still decide what sort of decision procedure judges should use. One candidate, prominent in recent discussions, is the idea of judicial deference – deferring to the legislature as the democratic arm of government (as contrasted with the judiciary). Given what has been said above, it is apparent that such a policy only raises anew the arguments over the entire matter of judicial review. There are, though, a number of other approaches, variously lumped under the phrases "judicial restraint" and "judicial activism," that have been embraced by various jurists: literal interpretation; intention of the framers; developing an interpretive theory that, though not explicitly stated in the document, reconciles its parts and thus can be said to be implicit in the document; and others, none of which will be discussed here. For about half a century there has been an approach to Constitutional interpretation that applies different levels of judicial "scrutiny" to different sorts of issues: where laws have been passed that allegedly infringe certain civil rights (primarily those explicitly mentioned in the Constitution), the courts apply the test of "strict" scrutiny, requiring that there be a compelling state interest to justify the infringement, whereas, when the rights in question are so-called economic rights, the courts are more inclined to apply a reduced level of scrutiny – that is, they are more inclined to defer to the legislatures. These are important matters, very much part of the recent political discussion in the United States, but cannot be pursued further in this book.

The harm principle   There is an important distinction in Locke's philosophy between the public and the private: there is a limited area of public concern and a considerable private area of freedom defined by individual rights. Within the private realm is found the economy; business, manufacturing, agriculture, and all of the other things having to do with people earning their livelihoods are matters of private concern. Relations between husbands and wives and between parents and children are largely matters of private concern, as are lifestyle choices. For what, we might ask, is freedom for if not to make our own choices about what is good or worthwhile in life, rather than to have other people's ideas forced upon us? Tyranny is found not only in autocratic rule. Perhaps the word "tyranny" is too strong when it is not the whim of an autocrat that controls us, but it can be oppressive none the less to have to live according to the standards of the majority, however heartfelt our neighbors' demands and however right they think they are. The phrase "tyranny of the majority" has been coined for such a state of affairs. But exactly how much freedom *should* we have? How large is the zone of privacy? To what extent should public standards control our behavior?

Though Locke never adequately addressed these important questions, others did, most notably John Stuart Mill in his influential *On Liberty* (1859). Mill tries to mark the boundary between the individual and society by "one very simple principle,"

> that the sole end for which mankind are warranted, individually or collectively, in interfering with the liberty of action of any of their number is self-protection. That the only purpose for which power can be rightfully exercised over any member of a civilized community, against his will, is to prevent harm to others. His own good, either physical or moral, is not a sufficient warrant. He cannot rightfully be compelled to do or forbear because it will be better for him to do so, because it will make him happier, because, in the opinion of others, to do so would be wise or even right. These are good reasons for remonstrating with him, or reasoning with him, or persuading him, or entreating him, but not for compelling him or visiting him with any evil in case he do otherwise. . . . The only part of the conduct of anyone for which he is amenable to society is that which concerns others. In the part which merely concerns himself, his independence is, of right, absolute. Over himself, over his own body and mind, the individual is sovereign. (Mill 1859: 68–9)

Mill thus tries to define two areas of protected liberty. First, people have very broad liberties of conscience, thought, speech, and expression that operate as limitations on governmental power. Second, people have a general liberty of action: freedom, quite independent of what people do with it, is valuable and may be limited only when there is adequate reason to do so. It is important to note that Mill's view is not that x or y or z is important, in consequence of which people must be free to do x or y or z. Rather, he believes that freedom itself is a substantial value, so that no matter what a person wants to do, she or he is not to be interfered with unless others will be harmed thereby. Thus are the interests of minorities, even minorities of one, to be protected from majorities.

Contracts Contracts are interesting devices for keeping other people, including government, out of private matters. There is a popular impression that areas of law such as torts, contracts, and property are merely technical (that is, non-political) aspects of law and that the politics of law shows up only in criminal and constitutional law. In fact, though, all areas of law reflect moral and political viewpoints. Contract law, perhaps surprisingly, embodies an important element of Locke's political philosophy. Contracts are entered into by private individuals in the exercise of their freedom. People commit themselves to various terms, are morally and legally bound because they have given their words or signed agreements, and can be sued if they fail to fulfill them. If you have made a bad bargain, you are nevertheless obligated to fulfill your agreement; if you don't read the fine print, you have nevertheless agreed and are obligated; if you have been presented with a "take it or leave it" form to sign, and you sign, you are obligated however unfavorable the terms. The contract will not be reviewed for fairness, for that would make the judgment of other people (such as judges and juries), rather than the commitment of the parties, the basis for enforcement. It would, in effect, change the agreement and undermine the idea that free people make their own private arrangements with the role of government being limited to enforcement. Here is a device, then, for protecting the prerogatives of individuals against the interference of a possibly disapproving majority.

Contracts have sometimes been thought of as "private legislation." If legislation by a public body in a democracy represents the power of the majority over the minority whereby some people are subject to the opinions of others about what is right or best, then contracts are areas in which private individuals make a law unto themselves – they, not others, decide what their futures shall be, provided, of course, that public agencies do not have the power to modify or defeat the agreement.

3   Issues Within the Tradition

Locke's principles constitute the framework of government in the United States. There are issues, however, where the principles do not provide clear guidance, or where their implications seem to many people to be at odds with other social values. Questions frequently arise about what should happen when the exercise of individual rights adversely affects the public. In other cases issues arise as to whose standards – the individual's or the public's – should prevail. This section of the chapter is called "Issues Within the Tradition," implying that the issues do not call into question the basic principles, but question their completeness or adequacy.

Natural property rights

The idea of natural property rights has not found favor with everyone. Some difficulties with the idea were discussed earlier. Another problem has to do with the relation between the initial acquisition of property and property rights that people have at present. The theory is that at some earlier time someone does something that puts the stamp of ownership on previously unowned land. The owner may dispose of it as she or he wishes – it can be left to an heir or given or sold to someone else. Each successive owner does the same, right up to the present time, so that present holdings (for the most part) are justified on natural rights grounds. If property is acquired improperly, there are legal processes for correcting things; if uncorrected, there will be holdings that are not justified on natural rights grounds (though we might not know which they are). Thus, the idea of natural property rights is compelling only if there is property whose ownership is based on an initial acquisition and a series of legitimate subsequent transactions. The problem, however, is that there might not be a spot of land on the face of the planet the ownership of which can be traced through a legitimate set of transfers from an unproblematic initial appropriation. If this is the case then the property rights that the framers of the Constitution were protecting were simply the set of property

458

rights that happened to exist in the newly established United States. This does not mean, of course, that there are no property rights at all; it means that a different rationale for property is needed.

Another problem that has been raised with Locke's argument for natural property rights has to do with what property is – that is, with what a person actually acquires when she or he gets some property. Though we normally think of property as a thing (your desk, my house, the ground on which it sits, are pieces of property), it is now widely held that property is not a thing but a *bundle of rights*, including the right to use, alienate (sell), bequeath, manage, have the income from, use as security, destroy, and others. The basic question is not "what is property?" but "what is ownership? what does it mean to *own* something?" Why does this matter? It matters because the rights mentioned above are separable; a person might have some of the rights associated with property but not others – I might, for example, have the right to occupy a piece of land, or to the income it produces, but not the right to sell it or leave it to my heirs. Furthermore, the various property-related rights can be held by different individuals, even with respect to the same object or piece of land. Given this, the question for Locke, and for the natural property rights idea, is exactly which rights a person who mixes his labor with something, gets. Why is it the full bundle of rights, the most extensive set of rights, with respect to something, as Locke thought, rather than some valuable but limited group of rights?

Extending property rights

Let us suppose, for the sake of argument, that the case for natural property rights is doubtful. There is still, though, an argument in favor of property rights. Property rights *protect* us. "As a practical matter, he who controls my economic destiny controls much more of my life as well" (Scalia 1985: 704). This applies both to individual and to governmental attempts to control us – it is easier to resist pressures if we have an independent source of livelihood, which is what property gives us. However, with the decline of real property as the dominant form of wealth, it plays a protective role for fewer people than it once did. Most people work for someone else; their incomes, job security, and professional status, their certifications, degrees, licenses, and memberships in various associations, and even such things as welfare and other so-called entitlements are the most important underpinnings of people and their essential interests. Justice Scalia's point about the importance of not being subject to the control of others can apply to intangible property and to all of the items mentioned above. A similar observation was made a number of years ago by Charles Reich in his important article "The New Property":

> Political rights presuppose that individuals and private groups have the will and the means to act independently. But so long as individuals are motivated largely by self-interest, their well-being must first be independent. Civil liberties must have a basis in property, or bills of rights will not preserve them. (Reich 1964: 771)

Reich argues that licenses, degrees, and even entitlements should be regarded as forms of property (he calls it "new" property) and that some of the protections afforded to traditional property be afforded to new property. Our courts have now widely recognized that people can have property rights in these things. The recognition has taken the form of extending due process ("No person shall be . . . deprived of life, liberty, or property, without due process of law. . . .") protections to such things as welfare benefits, medical licenses, government contracts, public employment, and membership in some private organizations.

What would Locke think of this? It's hard to say, for it goes beyond the notions Locke had in mind. In some ways it is in keeping with Lockean themes of independence and protection of the individual from the state. On the other hand traditionalists (conservatives) about property might think it distorts the very idea of property rights.

Regulation of property

There are ever-increasing ways in which the exercise of real property rights can adversely affect other individuals, the economy or character of a region, or the country at large. As illustration, consider some important property issues in the history of the United States. From the early days of the republic issues related to property were never completely clear or settled. Particularly important for the growth of the country was property rights with respect to waterways – the respective rights of the owner of the land along the river and the public. Around the year 1670 Matthew Hale, Lord Chief Justice of England, wrote a tract entitled *De Portibus Maris*, which was first published in 1787. In the United States Hale's treatise was quickly recognized as stating the established law on the matter. In 1805 New York's Chancellor Kent, expounding Hale's views, said that freshwater rivers generally belong "of common right" to riparian owners, but none the less

> may be under the servitude of the public interest, and may be of common or public use for the carriage of boats, etc., and in that sense may be regarded as common highways by water. . . . [Such navigable streams], as well in the parts where they are of private as of public property, are public rivers *juris publici*. . . . They are called public rivers, not in reference to the property of the river, but to the public use. . . . The Hudson at Stillwater is capable of being held and enjoyed as private property, but it is, notwithstanding, to be deemed a public highway for public uses. (Scheiber 1971: 336)

Throughout the nineteenth century, courts struggled with the issue of which rivers are entirely private property and which are burdened with rights of the public and for what purposes, and, of course, which public uses would require compensation. The essential point, though, is that from very early days it was recognized that property rights needed to be reconciled with public needs, that the need for security of property had to contend with social and economic change and the need to put property to new uses for the good of the public. Thus the Supreme Court of Iowa held in 1856 that the Mississippi River was a public highway and therefore that private rights had to absorb public uses; the United States Supreme Court adopted the same view in 1877. Extending some of these principles to other areas the Supreme Court came to hold that in eminent domain cases property could be transferred to other private owners where a public use was involved and that the police power could be used to regulate private property used for public purposes. Thus, railroads came to be regarded as improved highways and indispensable to the public interest, and in *Munn v. Illinois* in 1877 the Court held that grain elevators and public warehouses could be regulated under the police power as businesses affected with a public interest. In another case decided the same year the Court said that "the public authorities ought to have entire control of the great passage-ways of commerce and navigation, to be exercised for the public advantage and convenience."

What would Locke think of the idea that private property rights may be modi-fied to accommodate public needs? On the face of it Locke would seem to be with those who argued forcefully that private property precludes such regulation, and for a long time after *Munn* the regulation of property was systematically diminished (until 1934, when the Supreme Court reinstated the *Munn*-like idea that if there is adequate reason, an industry is "subject to control for the public good"). Though some would reject it, and though there is often great controversy in particular cases, it is fair to say that it is widely believed that the exercise of property rights can have profoundly adverse effects on the well-being of the public, that the welfare of the public cannot be held hostage to private rights, and that at least sometimes property can be required to carry the burden of important public interests – even without compensation. At the present time in the United States, however, there is a political reaction to attempts by government to regulate prop-erty – critics regard many regulations as "takings" that require compensation. Courts are thus still called upon to establish lines between public and private by distinguishing legitimate regulations from takings.

The harm principle

John Stuart Mill, as we saw earlier, takes seriously the idea of a right to liberty and tries to give it a clear delineation. But critics have raised questions about the concept of harm, for everything depends on how clear we are about this. Physical damage and infringements of property rights are obvious cases of harm, and if harm were restricted to these it would be clear that a public that respected people's rights could not pass laws enforcing the public morality – laws, for example, against homosexuality and prostitution. But, it has been argued, things like these cause *moral* harm to those involved and *psychic* harm to others, which justifies the major-ity in prohibiting such behaviors if it so desires. If these are genuine categories of harm, then Mill's principle fails, for virtually everything will be amenable to pub-licly determined standards and the area of privacy will be almost non-existent.

Defenders of liberty are skeptical about moral harm, seeing no difference between believing that someone's behavior is morally wrong and the claim that she or he is harmed by it, for, unlike other sorts of harm, it is not independently detectable. When it comes to other sorts of harm, a person can be expected to acknowledge that the harm has occurred and to regret the behavior producing it. But this is not what we typically find with respect to so-called moral harm.

Consider next psychic harm. The idea is that many people are very offended by certain conduct. Perhaps the offense is worse if people (have to) see the conduct, such as sexual activity in public or advertisements for nude dancing. But offense is also taken when the behavior at issue is completely private, for people can be outraged simply by the knowledge that certain things are taking place, including homosexual acts by consenting adults in private. Taking up the argument for Mill, the legal philosopher H. L. A. Hart argues that

> To punish people for causing this form of distress [the distress which is inseparable from the bare knowledge that others are acting in ways you think wrong] would be tantamount to punishing them simply because others object to what they do; and the only liberty that could coexist with this . . . is liberty to do those things to which no one seriously objects. (Hart 1966: 47)

This is a powerful argument. And yet, if psychic distress is not allowed as a basis for prohibiting certain behavior, what shall we say about laws regulating what can be done with the bodies of the recently deceased? What is the basis for prohibiting a teaching hospital from keeping a body for dissection in anatomy classes (assuming the person, when alive, made no provision for disposition of the body) unless it is the sensibilities of the family – that is, distress caused by knowledge of what is happening to the body? Or the basis for prohibiting people from embalming deceased members of their families and putting them on display, or shrinking their heads and selling them as curiosities? But how different are these from distress at the knowledge that others are using drugs or engaging in what is seen as deviant sex? Or from concern about "playing God" when it comes to DNA research that produces new life forms?

This discussion does not aim to reach a conclusion about the enforcement of morals or about so-called victimless crimes. The goal has been to indicate some of the considerations bearing on liberty, on the extent to which we believe, with Locke and with Mill, in a right to liberty and in an extensive zone of freedom from the majority's ideas about how to live. The goal has also been to update Locke and Mill – to show that the contemporary debate resonates with ideas that have had an important role in shaping our society and politics.

Public inroads into private agreements

Contract law, as it has developed over time, does not completely square with the idea that contracts are purely private arrangements. In some cases legislatures, with the approval of the courts, have removed certain things from the realm of private agreements. Since the latter part of the nineteenth century in the United States and Europe, for example, laws have been passed governing terms of employment (hours, wages, working conditions, and the right to join a union) and the safety of food and drugs. Such laws can be viewed as limitations on the freedom of contract, affirming public standards of fairness and safety in place of private agreements. In other cases the courts have injected public standards into private agreements, in effect modifying private arrangements. For example, some contracts are extremely one-sided; the superior bargaining position of one party enables that person to exact terms that would strike most of us as unfair, and the weaker party, perhaps out of desperation, agrees to the terms. Frequently contracts of this sort are declared to be "unconscionable" and are not enforced. As another example, courts have sometimes, in effect, added provisions to contracts by declaring that one party must be understood to have, implicitly, warranted something, when there was no explicit agreement on the matter.

From the standpoint of the public/private distinction – the balance between the rights of individuals to a zone within which to make their own choices and the prerogative of the public to impose its (that is, the majority's) ideas of how people should behave – there is great similarity between issues relating to so-called victimless crimes and issues relating to what might be called victimless contracts. What is significant is that in each case we have found that we do not want to adhere strictly to the kind of public/private distinction that Locke's philosophy suggests. We like freedom, but we seem to want public standards to prevail sometimes.

Social justice: the welfare state

Social justice is regarded as an important – some would say the most important – social goal and responsibility of government, yet Locke devotes little attention to it. Concerned as he is with governmental infringements of people's rights to liberty and property, he has nothing to say about, for example, the relief of poverty. Justice according to Locke, we may suppose, is achieved if everyone has what she or he is entitled to as a matter of natural right (and as a matter of law – which comes to the same thing for Locke, who believes that laws that do not accord with natural rights are not valid). Taxation for the relief of poverty, though, conflicts with individual liberty. Robert Nozick makes the point by asking:

> if it would be illegitimate for a tax system to seize some of a man's leisure (forced labor) for the purpose of serving the needy, how can it be legitimate for a tax system to seize some of a man's goods for that purpose? (Nozick 1974: 170)

Most of us, however, though regarding liberty as important, believe that other values are important also, and that sometimes the one predominates and sometimes another. Indeed, some of the classical proponents of the free market, including Adam Smith, held such views.

One such value is equality of opportunity underwritten by government and, where necessary, by taxation, as in the case of universal, tax-supported education. Social justice is also thought by many to require progressive income taxation and welfare programs for the injured, disabled, and poor. For most people the contemporary debate is about the extent of welfare, not the principle.

Some critics of the liberty-trumps-everything philosophy argue that the notion of liberty itself points the way toward greater public involvement in a variety of social ills. First, there is the belief of some opponents of welfare that taxation infringes freedom whereas voluntary transactions, as in the market, do not. Critics reject this picture – a poor person who has to accept a low-paying, dangerous job simply to stay alive and feed her children is, they believe, coerced. There is power outside of government as well as within it, and just as it is the business of government to prevent officials from abusing their power, so also, according to these critics, it is the business of government to prevent private abuses of power.

Second, it has been argued that the great leaps in the development of the welfare state have been, in part, motivated by an effort to promote freedom – in a special sense of that term. The concept of freedom in Locke's philosophy is what is called "negative" freedom – the notion of being free from coercion, that is, from attempts to prevent us doing what we want to do. What has been advanced as a supplement to this idea is called "positive" freedom – the idea that even if no one is hindering me from doing something, I am not really free to do it if I lack the means, the resources, to do it. What point is there, it is asked, in saying that I am free to purchase food or clothes if I am poor and have no means of doing so? Therefore, making people free requires seeing that they have some resources. Of course, no one needs to be made completely free in this sense (that is, able to afford everything); what is required is that people's freedom be increased and made more equal to others' freedom.

John Rawls, one of the most influential political philosophers of the twentieth century, defends the idea of social justice in a different way. Society, he believes, is an enterprise in which people participate for mutual advantage. The terms of participation are fair, according to Rawls, only if they would be agreed upon by everyone in circumstances in which no one knew what her or his own prospects in life were (in Rawls's terminology, only if the principles governing society were selected from behind a "veil of ignorance"). Under these circumstances, he argues, the social principles we would endorse are ones under which the worst-off members of society would be helped by the others through taxation or other devices.

Issues surrounding social justice are discussed in more detail and from different perspectives (including Rawls's and Karl Marx's) in chapter 8.

4 Attacks on the Tradition

There are contemporary political philosophers who have doubts about Locke's basic principles – about the whole idea of individual rights to life, liberty, and property. Criticism has especially been aimed at the following implications of Locke's principles:

1   Neutrality with regard to conceptions of the good life. People have different ideas about what is good or worthwhile in life, about what happiness is, and about how they want to live. The idea of governmental neutrality about conceptions of the good life is that government must treat everyone with equal concern and respect, which means not favoring one person's ideas about how to live over another's.
2   A distinction between the public and the private. There are areas of people's lives that are off-limits to government and within which people may make their own choices regarding how to live. The private realm of life includes the family and religion; it is the realm of feeling and thought and emotion; it is the realm of personal choice; it is the place where one seeks respite from the public confrontations of life.
3   Protection against group coercion. The general idea here is that part of government's job is to protect us from the attempts of others, including otherwise praiseworthy social institutions, to control us. There are many non-governmental organizations to which people belong, such as churches, unions, clubs, schools, fraternal societies, and the like, that claim our allegiance. Freedom of association protects people's participation in these groups and organizations – government can't stop our involvement in such groups. But government still protects people's rights against some group demands, and it insists that the organizations be voluntary, which means that an individual must have a right to get out of the group.

We will look at two contemporary criticisms of Locke's basic principles. One is communitarianism, the name suggesting a focus on the community rather than the individual, and the other is a branch of feminist thought that has something in common with communitarianism.

Communitarianism

There have always been varieties of communitarian thought, which in recent years has seen a resurgence of interest in the United States and elsewhere. The case for communitarianism stems from perceived consequences of the tradition outlined above, including crime, apathy, declining moral values, and rootlessness. The failures are blamed on the family, schools, neighborhoods, religious and ethnic groups, and other structures within society that are responsible for promoting moral values, building character, and instilling the virtues of citizenship. As one observer sees it, problems have been brought on by "the four mobilities" – geographic mobility (people move frequently), social mobility (the lives of many are not similar to their parents'), marital mobility (separation, divorce, remarriage), and political mobility (especially the weakening of local political organization). These are said to be consequences of a political orientation that emphasizes the individual and her or his rights and insists on a realm of life that is private, for this weakens people's sense of being involved with, and concerned about, other people and the community at large. People are not as self- or inner-directed as the Lockean tradition seems to assume; most people find their cues for proper behavior outside, not within, themselves. Furthermore, people need to belong; belonging to something larger than ourselves allows us to feel that we have a place and are valued. Indeed, it gives most of us a sense of our identity, of who we are. In the language of some of the writings, our "selves" are not "thin" – we do not think of ourselves as beings who are abstracted from our social contexts; rather, our selves are "thick," constituted by our attachments to others. What we *are* is a matter of our connections and involvements. The self is said to be "embedded" or "situated," and a political philosophy that starts from any other premise is mistaken.

While some communitarians are content to seek improvements within the existing political framework of individual rights, others say an entirely new politics is needed, one that reflects our social nature by favoring social institutions and the common good more than does the Lockean tradition. A politics of the common good, it has been suggested, would more readily permit a municipality to ban pornographic bookstores as offensive to its way of life and values, or to regulate plant closings in order to protect against sudden disruptive change. The important thing in these examples is the notion that the common good is more important than individual rights.

It is hard to see exactly what sort of political institutions go along with a commitment to the common good. Would electoral institutions as we know them be compatible with communitarianism? How about the basic civil rights? Unfortunately, modern communitarians have not answered these questions. One critic, though, suggests that we look at the writings of Benjamin Rush, a physician who signed the Declaration of Independence. Rush rejected the idea of broad education for Americans on the ground that they were too diverse already; he favored the adoption of the Bible as a school book. He explicitly opposed the religious toleration advanced by Thomas Jefferson and opposed Jefferson's idea that a person is entitled to live for himself, saying "Our country includes family, friends and property, and should be preferred to them all. Let our pupil be taught that he does not belong to himself, but that he is public property."

Clearly communitarian thought is not just one thing, and it is hard to tell whether it must embrace Rush-like ideas. But it is clear that at least some versions of it are quite contrary to the political tradition outlined in this chapter. This might be a good moment to reflect also on some of Plato's ideas, discussed at the beginning of the chapter, which focus on harmony and suggest that the role of government is to promote virtue and a common conception of the good life.

Feminism

Feminism too is not one thing, and some versions involve the rejection of parts of our political tradition. Every version of feminism holds that in virtually all human societies women have been dominated, disadvantaged, and oppressed by men and that this sorry state of affairs needs to be corrected. One important branch of feminist thought holds that there are no significant differences between males and females. There are differences, to be sure, but none of them justify differential treatment in education or in political and economic status. Our social and political ideals are fine; the problem is that too many men think they apply only to themselves. Men have denied full human and social status to women (and to minorities); being dominant in society, men have defined full social status in male (and also in white) terms and have defined women (and minorities) as Other. Recognizing the inaccuracy of these conceptions and the equality of all people is the first step toward achieving the public realization that our society has not been living up to its principles. This was the goal of the first feminists in our society; it remains the goal of many feminists today.

Another, more recent, branch of feminist thought, however, believes that males and females are different in ways that count (though there is some dispute as to whether the differences are genetic or culturally produced – that is, produced by the roles men have given women). This branch of feminism holds that there is a female way of perceiving and thinking about the world, and a female moral outlook emphasizing caring and connection with others. These contrast with the male approach to the world, which is analytical, abstractly rational, competitive, controlling, and has a moral outlook based on rights and impersonal justice.

One of the most significant works advancing this point of view is Carol Gilligan's *In a Different Voice* (1982), which offers empirical support for the differences. Males and females, Gilligan says, tend to come at problems from different perspectives, the males responding to hierarchy and the females to relationships among people; males tend to resort to abstract principles whereas females respond more to circumstances. Despite this, she observes, theories of human development emphasize the former and ignore the latter – in other words, they define human development in male terms and omit the different moral and intellectual development of females. Likewise, Gilligan says, where males tend to see the social world as confrontational, females tend to see it as involving connections; males tend to see the need to give way because of others, whereas females tend to think in terms of what others expect of them.

What political prescriptions follow from these ideas? Iris Marion Young, in a selection included in this text, believes that "contemporary emancipatory politics" should "break with modernism."

> After two centuries of faith that the ideal of equality and fraternity included women has still not brought emancipation for women, contemporary feminists have begun to question the faith itself. Recent feminist analyses . . . increasingly argue that ideals of liberalism and contract theory, such as formal equality and universal rationality, are deeply marred by masculine biases about what it means to be human and the nature of society. . . . [T]here is little hope of laundering some of its ideals to make it possible to include women. (Young 1987: 58)

Since important female characteristics are largely excluded from our (male-biased) moral outlook, it is argued, our politics too has a male bias, which results in the exclusion of women from the public (political) realm and permits their domination by men in the private realm. What is needed, Young believes, is a redefinition of the public and the private, making public issues out of matters regarded by the tradition as private – this is at least one meaning of the feminist slogan "the personal is political." In this respect Young's approach has similarities to communitarian thought.

References

Plato. 1974. *The Republic.* Translated by G. M. A. Grube. Indianapolis: Hackett Publishing Co.

Locke, John. [1690] 1960. *Two Treatises of Government.* Edited by Peter Laslett. New York: New American Library.

Nozick, Robert. 1974. *Anarchy, State, and Utopia.* New York: Basic Books.

Mill, John Stuart. [1859] 1974. *On Liberty.* New York: Penguin.

Scalia, Antonin. 1985. Economic affairs as human affairs. *The Cato Journal* 4: 703–9.

Reich, Charles A. 1964. The new property. *Yale Law Journal* 73: 733–87.

Scheiber, Harry N. 1971. The road to *Munn*: eminent domain and the concept of public purpose in the state courts. In Donald Fleming and Bernard Bailyn (eds), *Law in American History.* Boston and Toronto: Little, Brown & Co.

Hart, H. L. A. 1966. *Law, Liberty, and Morality.* New York: Vintage Books.

Gilligan, Carol. 1982. *In a Different Voice.* Cambridge, MA: Harvard University Press.

Young, Iris Marion. 1987. Impartiality and the civic public. In Seyla Benhabib and Drucilla Cornell (eds), *Feminism as Critique,* pp. 57–76. Minneapolis: University of Minnesota Press.

Suggestions for further reading

There is an extensive secondary literature on John Locke's political philosophy, including his philosophy of property. He is represented in virtually all histories of philosophy and general readers in political philosophy. For a biography see Maurice Cranston's *John Locke: A Biography* (London: Longman, 1957). A brief overview of Locke's overall philosophy is contained in J. D. Mabbott's *John Locke* (Cambridge, MA: Schenkman, 1973); a good recent collection of essays on the full range of Locke's philosophy is *The Cambridge Companion to Locke* (Cambridge: Cambridge University Press, 1994) edited by Vere Chappell. There is a collection of essays on Locke's political ideas entitled *Life, Liberty, and Property,* edited by Gordon J. Schochet (Belmont, CA: Wadsworth, 1971). Robert Nozick's *Anarchy, State, and Utopia* (New York: Basic Books, 1974) contains an excellent discussion of Locke's political ideas, including his philosophy of property. Selections from *Anarchy, State, and Utopia,* including Nozick's discussion of Locke, are reprinted in chapter 8 of this book.

There are a number of good treatments of Locke's political ideas. A. John Simmons's *The Lockean Theory of Rights* (Princeton: Princeton University Press, 1992) is a study of Locke's theory of natural moral rights and their role in his conception of political obligation and the authority of government. Two books on Locke on property are James Tully's *A Discourse on Property: John Locke and His Adversaries* (Cambridge: Cambridge University Press, 1980) and Gopal Sreenivasan's *The Limits of Lockean Rights of Property* (New York: Oxford University

Press, 1995), which maintain that Locke's defense of private property supports egalitarianism in the ownership of property. Two books take up Locke's influence on the founding of the American political system: *The Unvarnished Doctrine: Locke, Liberalism, and the American Revolution* (Durham, NC: Duke University Press, 1990) by Steven M. Dworetz, and Jerome Huyler's *Locke in America: The Moral Philosophy of the Founding Era* (1995). Finally, John Marshall, in *John Locke: Resistance, Religion and Responsibility* (Cambridge: Cambridge University Press, 1994), offers a reinterpretation of Locke's moral, social, and religious thought.

The best contemporary discussion of Social Contract Theory is John Rawls's *A Theory of Justice* (Cambridge, MA: Harvard University Press, 1971), in which Rawls offers a new contract theory. Selections from this work are also reprinted here in chapter 8. Nozick's *Anarchy, State, and Utopia* (1974) is a rebuttal that defends Lockean ideas. There is a substantial literature on Mill's harm principle including a well-known debate between Lord Patrick Devlin (*The Enforcement of Morals*; London: Oxford University Press, 1965) and H. L. A. Hart (*Law, Liberty, and Morality*; New York: Vintage Books, 1966). *The Federalist Papers* (New York: New American Library, 1961) contains excellent discussions of the way government should be structured to protect the citizenry from those in power. There is a substantial literature on the nature of contract; Charles Fried's *Contract as Promise* (Cambridge, MA: Harvard University Press, 1981) discusses many of the issues. On the concept of property it is useful to read two essays by A. M. Honoré – "Ownership" (in A. G. Guest (ed.), *Oxford Essays in Jurisprudence*; London: Oxford University Press, 1961) and "Property, Title and Redistribution" (in L. Becker and K. Kipnis (eds), *Property: Cases, Concepts, Critiques*; Englewood Cliffs, NJ: Prentice-Hall, 1984, pp. 162–70). See also Jeremy Waldron's *The Right to Private Property* (Oxford: Clarendon Press, 1986). An excellent work on communitarianism is Charles Larmore's *Patterns of Moral Complexity* (Cambridge: Cambridge University Press, 1987). On feminism, including the issues of patriarchy and the public/private distinction, see Catharine MacKinnon, *Feminism Unmodified* (Cambridge, MA: Harvard University Press, 1987).

Introduction to Selected Readings

The first four readings are from classic documents in the Western political tradition. Plato's *Republic* is about what a society should be like if it is to promote people's good. In the selection included here Plato discusses the basic divisions of a society and the character and education appropriate for those in each class. The selection includes some of Plato's most famous ideas – the idea of the tripartite division of both the human soul and human society and the analogy between them, and the idea that philosopher-kings should rule. Plato's prescriptions are designed to prevent or reduce conflict among the classes in society; out of this, he believes, comes justice.

Hobbes the authoritarian is regarded by some as Hobbes the first liberal thinker in that he regards the state as resting on the consent of the governed and does not think it the role of the state to improve people. The selection from *Leviathan* presents Hobbes's views about the nature of human beings, introduces the idea of a state of nature, and argues that the justification of the state rests on the principles that reason dictates as necessary to avoid the state of nature.

John Locke, whose *Second Treatise on Civil Government* provides the intellectual background for ideas enshrined in the Constitution of the United States, presents a state of nature argument that differs from Hobbes's in apparently small ways and yet yields importantly different conclusions. Whereas Hobbes had no admiration for the rule of law, Locke argues for individual rights that limit the authority of government and for the centrality of an elected legislature rather than an all-powerful monarch. Most of all, Locke is remembered for his powerful argument for natural and complete rights of property.

The selection from *On Liberty* contains John Stuart Mill's famous statement of the boundary between the liberty of the individual and the authority of the state. Mill was one of the earliest philosophers of democracy who saw that a popularly elected legislature was not a complete guarantor of freedom, for unified majorities could always suppress unpopular minorities. Mill coined the phrase "tyranny of the majority" to refer to this phenomenon.

The next two selections discuss legal developments that have had an impact in refining some of the basic political principles on which the United States was founded; the selections have been included to help the reader evaluate the long-term viability of those principles. The selection from a book by George Dargo examines developments regarding property and contracts in the United States in the nineteenth century which affected relationships between the individual and the public. Dargo shows that property rights were modified to some extent to accommodate economic growth. In contracts, on the other hand, the public came to have less and less to say about private arrangements. Charles Reich, in an important 1964 article, coined the phrase "new property" to refer to entitlements, created by government mostly in the twentieth century, that have become for many people their primary form of wealth. He argues that these entitlements should be the functional equivalent of property – people should be secured in possessing them so they can have the same sort of independence from government overreaching that classic property rights provide.

The final selections present two recent movements in political philosophy that are at odds with the traditions represented by Hobbes, Locke, and Mill. In "Morality and the Liberal Ideal" Michael Sandel champions a late twentieth-century version of a prominent nineteenth-century political idea – that people are "constructed" by their societies and that therefore their well-being depends on the character of those societies. Individual rights are, accordingly, not central; the role of government is to focus on people's well-being by promoting the common good.

Finally, in "Impartiality and the Civic Public" Iris Marion Young takes issue with the Hobbes–Locke–Mill political tradition by arguing that it has systematically focused on the perspectives and needs of men to the exclusion of women. The particular deficiency, she holds, is the distinction between the public and the private that is central to liberal political thought. Part of what is meant by the slogan "the personal is political" is that in various ways the realm of the private must become more public – i.e. subject to public norms rather than purely private determinations.

Discussion questions

1   To what extent are Lockean and more public-welfare or common-good ideas involved in many of the issues facing society, such as abortion, pornography, cloning, environmental protection? Identify the principles and try to determine which side has the stronger case.

2   Political philosophies typically involve a conception of human nature – the situation in which we find ourselves is partly a result of our natures, and the solutions that political philosophers offer depend on what they think human beings are like. Compare and

contrast Plato's, Hobbes's, and Locke's ideas about human nature. How do they compare with a Christian conception of human nature? With Karl Marx's (see chapter 8)?

3 Is there an obligation to obey the law? Why or why not? – your answers will differ depending on what political principles you start with. Under what circumstances is a person morally justified in violating the law? If there are such circumstances, should the law itself ever excuse the violators?

4 The United States Constitution forbids taking anyone's property without due process of law. What does due process require when property is taken? A very difficult question is exactly when a person has had property taken. If you have a house, and the part of town in which it is located becomes a historical district, with the result that you are not permitted to put on an addition, has your property been taken? If you run a business that the town council deems harmful to public health, and it is closed down, has your property been taken? Suppose instead that the council deems your business harmful to public morals? If you are grazing cattle on public lands and the government declines to renew the lease under which you use the land, have you suffered a taking?

5 John Stuart Mill's harm principle relies on a distinction between behavior that affects only the actor (self-regarding behavior) and behavior that affects others (other-regarding behavior). Is this a clear distinction? Think about such things as using drugs or prostitution. Think about bungee-jumping. If a clear distinction can't be made, how shall it be decided what we shall be free to do and what the government may regulate or even prohibit?

6 The case of *Bowers v. Hardwick*, decided by the United States Supreme Court in 1987, held that there is no constitutionally protected right to liberty; there are specific rights to be free to do certain things, but no general right to be free to behave as we wish. Because of this, the court said, a legislature does not need a compelling reason to restrict people's freedom – it can do it simply because the majority wants to do it. Do you agree? Why or why not?

7 Is it justifiable for government (state or federal) to regulate aspects of the economy that have considerable impact on the well-being of the community? Think about such issues as wages, working conditions, safety, and environmental impact. What are the applicable principles?

Readings

Plato, *The Republic* (selections)

Book II

[. . .]

I think a city comes to be, I said, because not one of us is self-sufficient, but needs many things. Do you think a city is founded on any other principle? – On no other.

Translated by G. M. A. Grube (Indianapolis: Hackett Publishing Co., 1974), pp. 39–42, 44, 46–9, 80–4, 97–9, 105–6, 108.

As they need many things, people make use of one another for various purposes. They gather many associates and helpers to live in one place, and to this settlement we give the name of city. Is that not so? – It is.

And they share with one another, both giving and taking, in so far as they do, because they think this better for themselves? – Quite so.

Come then, I said, let us create a city from the beginning in our discussion. And it is our needs, it seems, that will create it. – Of course.

Surely our first and greatest need is to provide food to sustain life. – It certainly is.

Our second need is for shelter, our third for clothes and such things. – Quite so.

Consider then, said I, how the city will adequately provide for all this. One man obviously must be a farmer, another a builder, and another a weaver. Or should we add a cobbler and some other craftsman to look after our physical needs? – All right.

So the essential minimum for the city is four or five men. – Apparently.

A further point: must each of them perform his own work as common for them all, for example the one farmer provide food for them all, and spend four times as much time and labour to provide food which is shared by the others, or will he not care for this but provide for himself a quarter of such food in a quarter of the time and spend the other three quarters, one in building a house, one in the production of clothes, and one to make shoes, and not trouble to associate with the others but for and by himself mind his own business?

Perhaps, Socrates, Adeimantus replied, the way you suggested first would be easier than the other.

By Zeus, said I, there is nothing surprising in this, for even as you were speaking I was thinking that, in the first place, each one of us is born somewhat different from the others, one more apt for one task, one for another. Don't you think so? – I do.

Further, does a man do better if he practises many crafts, or if, being one man, he restricts himself to one craft? – When he restricts himself to one.

This at any rate is clear, I think, that if one misses the proper time to do something, the opportunity to do it has gone. – Clear enough.

For I do not think that the thing to be done awaits the leisure of the doer, but the doer must of necessity adjust himself to the requirements of his task, and not consider this of secondary importance. – He must.

Both production and quality are improved in each case, and easier, if each man does one thing which is congenial to him, does it at the right time, and is free of other pursuits. – Most certainly.

We shall then need more than four citizens, Adeimantus, to provide the things we have mentioned. It is likely that the farmer will not make his own plough if it is to be a good one, nor his mattock, nor other agricultural implements. Neither will the builder, for he too needs many things; and the same is true of the weaver and the cobbler, is it not? – True.

Carpenters, metal workers, and many such craftsmen will share our little city and make it bigger. – Quite so.

Yet it will not be a very big settlement if we add cowherds, shepherds, and other herdsmen in order that our farmers have oxen to do their ploughing, and the builders will join the farmers in the use of them as beasts of burden to transport their materials, while the weavers and cobblers will use their wool and hides.

Neither will it be a small city, said he, if it has to hold all these things.

And further, it is almost impossible to establish the city in the kind of place that will need no imports. – Impossible.

So we shall still need other people to bring what is needed from other cities. – We shall.

Now if one who serves in this way goes to the other city without a cargo of the things needed by those from whom he is to bring what his own people need, he will come away empty-handed, will he not? – I think so.

Therefore our citizens must not only produce enough for themselves at home, but also the things these others require, of the right quality and in the right quantity. – They must.

So we need more farmers and other craftsmen in our city. – We do.

Then again we need more people to service imports and exports. These are merchants, are they not? – Yes.

So we shall need merchants too. – Quite so.

And if the trade is by sea, we shall need a number of others who know how to sail the seas. – A good many, certainly.

A further point: how are they going to share the things that each group produces within the city itself? This association with each other was the very purpose for which we established the city.

Clearly, he said, they must do this by buying and selling.

It follows that we must have a market place and a currency for this exchange. – Certainly.

If the farmer brings some of his produce to market, or any other craftsman, and he does not arrive at the same time as those who want to exchange things with him, will he be sitting idly in the market place, away from his own work?

Not at all, he said. There will be people who realize this and engage in this service. In well-organized cities this will be pretty well those of feeble physique who are not fit for other work. They must stay around the market, buying for money from those who have something to sell, and then again selling at a price to those who want to buy.

To fill this need there will be retailers in our city. Do we not call retailers those who establish themselves in the market place for this service of buying and selling, while those who travel between cities are called merchants? – Quite so.

There are some others to serve, as I think, who are not worth admitting into our society for their intelligence, but they have sufficient physical strength for heavy labour. These sell the use of their strength; their reward for this is a wage and they are, I think, called wage-earners. Is that not so? – Certainly.

So the wage-earners complete our city. – I think so.

Well, Adeimantus, has our city now grown to its full size? – Perhaps.

Where then would justice and injustice be in it? With which of the parts we have examined have they come to be?

I do not notice them, Socrates, he said, unless it is in the relations of these very people to one another. [. . .]

Is it not of the greatest importance that matters of war be well performed? Or is fighting a war so easy that a farmer can at the same time be a soldier and so with the cobbler and any other craftsman? Yet no one can become an adequate draughts or dice player if he does not practise at it from childhood and only considers it a sideline. Can a man then pick up a shield or any other arm or instrument of war and on the same day be an adequate performer in a hoplite battle or any other kind? No other instrument makes any man a craftsman or champion by just being picked up, nor will it be of any use except to one who has acquired the necessary knowledge and had sufficient practice.

If instruments could do this, they would be valuable indeed, he said.

Therefore, I said, as the task of the guardian is most important, so he should have the most freedom from all other pursuits, for he requires technical knowledge and the greatest diligence. – I think so.

He also needs a nature which is suited to his pursuit, does he not? – Of course.

It is then our task to select, if we can, the man whose nature is most suited to guard the city. – So it is. [. . .]

So he who is to be a fine and good guardian of our city must be a lover of wisdom, high-spirited, swift and strong by nature. – That is altogether so.

This type of man would be available, as we saw, but how is he to be brought up and educated? The question is highly relevant to our investigation, since our primary purpose is to see how justice and injustice come to be in our city. [. . .]

Do we not start education in the arts before physical training? – Of course.

Under the arts you include literature, or not? – I do.

There are two kinds of discourse, the true and the untrue – Yes.

They must be educated in both, but first in the untrue? – I do not understand your meaning, he said.

Do you not understand, I said, that we first tell stories to children. These are, in general, untrue, though there is some truth in them. And we tell stories to small children before we give them physical training. – That is so.

That is what I meant, that we must deal with the arts before physical training. – Correct.

You know that the beginning of any process is most important, especially for anything young and tender. For it is at that time that it takes shape, and any mould one may want can be impressed upon it. – Very true.

Shall we then carelessly allow the children to hear any kind of stories composed by anybody, and to take into their souls beliefs which are for the most part contrary to those we think they should hold in maturity? – We shall certainly not allow that.

Then we must first of all, it seems, control the story tellers. Whatever noble story they compose we shall select, but a bad one we must reject. Then we shall persuade nurses and mothers to tell their children those we have selected and by those stories to fashion their minds far more than they can shape their bodies by handling them. The majority of the stories they now tell must be thrown out. – Which do you mean? [. . .]

Book III

[. . .] even if the deeds of Cronos and what he suffered from his son were true, I do not think this should be told to foolish and young people; it should be passed over in silence. If there were some necessity to tell it, only a very few people should hear it, and in secret, after sacrificing not a pig but some great and scarce victim, so that as few people as possible should hear it. – Yes, he said, these stories are hard to deal with.

And they should not be told, Adeimantus, I said, in our city. Nor should a young man hear it said that in committing the worst crimes he is not doing anything out of the way, or that, if he inflicts every kind of punishment upon an erring father, he is only doing the same as the first and greatest of the gods. – No by Zeus, he said, I myself do not think these things are fit to be told.

Nor indeed, said I, any tales of gods warring and plotting and fighting against each other – these things are not true – if those who are to guard our city are to think it shameful to be easily driven to hate each other. Certainly stories of battles of giants must not be told nor embroidered, nor all the various stories of gods hating their kindred or friends. If we are to persuade our people that no citizen has ever hated another and that this is impious, then that is the kind of tale we should tell right away to small children, and to old men and women also, and to the middle-aged, and we must compel our poets to follow those guidelines. We shall not admit into our city stories about Hera being chained by her son, or of Hephaestus being hurled from heaven by his father when he intended to help his mother who was being beaten, nor the battle of the gods in Homer, whether these stories are told allegorically or without allegory. The young cannot distinguish what is allegorical from what is not, and the beliefs they acquire at that age are hard to expunge and usually remain unchanged. That may be the reason why it is most important that the first stories they hear should be well told and dispose them to virtue. [. . .]

Very well, I said. Shall we choose as our next topic of discussion which of these same men shall rule, and which be ruled? – Why not?

Now it is obvious that the rulers must be older men and that the younger must be ruled. – Obviously.

And that the rulers must be the best of them? – That too.

The best farmers are those who have to the highest degree the qualities required for farming? – Yes.

Now as the rulers must be the best among the guardians, they must have to the highest degree the qualities required to guard the city? – Yes.

And for this they must be intelligent, able, and also care for the city? – That is so.

Now one cares most for that which one loves. – Necessarily.

And one loves something most when one believes that what is good for it is good for oneself, and that when it is doing well the same is true of oneself, and so with the opposite. – Quite so, he said.

We must therefore select from among our guardians those who, as we test them, hold throughout their lives to the belief that it is right to pursue eagerly what they believe to be to the advantage of the city, and who are in no way willing to do what is not. – Yes, for they are good men. [. . .]

What device could we find to make our rulers, or at any rate the rest of the city, believe us if we told them a noble fiction, one of those necessary untruths of which we have spoken? – What kind of fiction?

Nothing new, I said, but a Phoenician story which the poets say has happened in many places and made people believe them; it has not happened among us, though it might, and it will take a great deal of persuasion to have it believed.

You seem hesitant to tell your story, he said.

When you hear it you will realize that I have every reason to hesitate.

Speak without fear.

This is the story – yet I don't know that I am bold enough to tell it or what words I shall use. I shall first try to persuade the rulers and the soldiers, and then the rest of the city, that the upbringing and the education we gave them, and the experience that went with them, were a dream as it were, that in fact they were then being fashioned and nurtured inside the earth, themselves and their weapons and their apparel. Then, when they were quite finished, the earth, being their mother, brought them out into the world. So even now they must take counsel for, and defend, the land in which they live as their mother and nurse, if someone attacks it, and they must think of their fellow-citizens as their earth-born brothers.

It is not for nothing that you were shy, he said, of telling your story.

Yes, I said, I had very good reason. Nevertheless, hear the rest of the tale. "All of you in the city are brothers" we shall tell them as we tell our story, "but the god who fashioned you mixed some gold in the nature of those capable of ruling because they are to be honoured most. In those who are auxiliaries he has put silver, and iron and bronze in those who are farmers and other workers. You will for the most part produce children like yourselves but, as you are all related, a silver child will occasionally be born from a golden parent, and vice versa, and all the others from each other. So the first and most important command of the god to the rulers is that there is nothing they must guard better or watch more carefully than the mixture in the souls of the next generation. If their own offspring should be found to have iron or bronze in his nature, they must not pity him in any way, but give him the esteem appropriate to his nature; they must drive him out to join the workers and farmers. Then again, if an offspring of these is found to have gold or silver in his nature they will honour him and bring him up to join the rulers or guardians, for there is an oracle that the city will be ruined if ever it has an iron or bronze guardian." Can you suggest any device which will make our citizens believe this story? [. . .]

We must therefore take every precaution to see that our auxiliaries, since they are the stronger, do not behave like that toward the citizens, and become cruel masters instead of kindly allies. – We must watch this.

And a really good education would endow them with the greatest caution in this regard? – But surely they have had that.

And I said: Perhaps we should not assert this dogmatically, my dear Glaucon. What we can assert is what we were saying just now, that they must have the correct education, whatever that is, in order to attain the greatest degree of gentleness toward each other and toward those whom they are protecting. – Right.

Besides this education, an intelligent man might say that they must have the amount of housing and of other property which would not prevent them from being the best guardians and would not encourage them to maltreat the other citizens. – That would be true.

Consider then, said I, whether they should live in some such way as this if they are to be the kind of men we described: First, not one of them must possess any private property beyond what is essential. Further, none of them should have a house or a storeroom which anyone who wishes is not permitted to enter. Whatever moderate and courageous warrior-athletes require will be provided by taxation upon the other citizens as a salary for their guardianship, no more and no less than they need over the year. They will have common messes and live together as soldiers in a camp. We shall tell them that the gold and silver they always have in their nature as a gift from the gods makes the possession of human gold unnecessary, indeed that it is impious for them to defile this divine possession by any admixture of the human kind of gold, because many an impious deed is committed in connection with the currency of the majority, and their own must remain pure. For them alone among the city's population it is unlawful to touch or handle gold or silver; they must not be under the same roof with it, or wear any, or drink from gold or silver goblets; in this way they may preserve themselves and the city. If they themselves acquire private land and houses and currency, they will be household managers and farmers instead of guardians, hostile masters of the other citizens instead of their allies; they will spend their whole life hating and being hated, plotting and being plotted against; they will be much more afraid of internal than of external enemies, and they will rush themselves and their city very close to ruin. For all these reasons, I said, let us say that the guardians must be provided with housing and other matters in this way, and these are the laws we shall establish.

Book IV

[. . .]

Well, I said, listen whether I am talking sense. I think that justice is the very thing, or some form of the thing which, when we were beginning to found our city, we said had to be established throughout. We stated, and often repeated, if you re-member, that everyone must pursue one occupation of those in the city, that for which his nature best fitted him. – Yes, we kept saying that.

Further, we have heard many people say, and have often said ourselves, that justice is to perform one's own task and not to meddle with that of others. – We have said that.

This then, my friend, I said, when it happens, is in some way justice, to do one's own job. [. . .]

Consider then whether you agree with me in this: if a carpenter attempts to do the work of a cobbler, or a cobbler that of a carpenter, and they exchange their tools and the esteem that goes with the job, or the same man tries to do both, and all the other exchanges are made, do you think that this does any great harm to the city? – No.

But I think that when one who is by nature a worker or some other kind of moneymaker is puffed up by wealth, or by the mob, or by his own strength, or some other such thing, and attempts to enter the warrior class, or one of the soldiers tries to enter the group of counsellors and guardians, though he is un-worthy of it, and these exchange their tools and the public esteem, or when the same man tries to perform all these jobs together, then I think you will agree that these exchanges and this meddling bring the city to ruin. – They certainly do.

The meddling and exchange between the three established orders does very great harm to the city and would most correctly be called wickedness. – Very definitely.

And you would call the greatest wickedness worked against one's own city injustice? – Of course.

That then is injustice. And let us repeat that the doing of one's own job by the moneymaking, auxiliary, and guardian groups, when each group is performing its own task in the city, is the opposite, it is justice and makes the city just. [. . .]

We have now made our difficult way through a sea of argument to reach this point, and we have fairly agreed that the same kinds of parts, and the same number of parts, exist in the soul of each individual as in our city. – That is so.

It necessarily follows that the individual is wise in the same way, and in the same part of himself, as the city. – Quite so.

And the part which makes the individual brave is the same as that which makes the city brave, and in the same manner, and everything which makes for virtue is the same in both? – That necessarily follows.

Moreover, Glaucon, I think we shall say that a man is just in the same way as the city is just. – That too is inevitable.

We have surely not forgotten that the city was just because each of the three classes in it was fulfilling its own task. – I do not think, he said, that we have forgotten that.

We must remember then that each one of us within whom each part is fulfilling its own task will himself be just and do his own work. – We must certainly remember this.

Therefore it is fitting that the reasonable part should rule, it being wise and exercising foresight on behalf of the whole soul, and for the spirited part to obey it and be its ally. – Quite so.

Is it not then, as we were saying, a mixture of artistic and physical culture which makes the two parts harmonious, stretching and nurturing the reasonable part with fine speech and learning, relaxing and soothing the spirited part, and making it gentle by means of harmony and rhythm. – Very definitely, he said.

These two parts, then, thus nurtured and having truly learned their own role and being educated in it, will exercise authority over the appetitive part which is the largest part in any man's soul and is insatiable for possessions. They will watch over it to see that it is not filled with the so-called pleasures of the body, and by becoming enlarged and strong thereby no longer does its own job but attempts to enslave and to rule over those over whom it is not fitted to rule, and so upsets everybody's whole life. – Quite so, he said.

These two parts will also most effectively stand on guard on behalf of the whole soul and the body, the one by planning, the other by fighting, following its leader, and by its courage fulfilling his decisions. [. . .]

It is left for us to enquire, it seems, if it is more profitable to act justly, to engage in fine pursuits and be just, whether one is known to be so or not, or to do wrong and be unjust, provided one does not pay the penalty and is not improved by punishment.

But Socrates, he said, this enquiry strikes me as becoming ridiculous now that justice and injustice have been shown to be such as we described. It is generally thought that life is not worth living when the body's nature is ruined, even if every kind of food and drink, every kind of wealth and power are available; yet we are to enquire whether life will be worth living when our soul, the very thing by which we live, is confused and ruined, if only one can do whatever one wishes, except that one cannot do what will free one from vice and injustice and make one acquire justice and virtue.

Thomas Hobbes, *Leviathan* (selections)

Of the Natural Condition of Mankind as Concerning Their Felicity and Misery

Men by nature equal. Nature hath made men so equal, in the faculties of the body, and mind; as that though there be found one man sometimes manifestly stronger in body, or of quicker mind than another; yet when all is reckoned together, the difference between man, and man, is not so considerable, as that one man can thereupon claim to himself any benefit, to which another may not pretend, as well

Edited by Michael Oakeshott (New York: Collier Books, Macmillan Pub. Co., 1962), pp. 98–104, 108, 113–15, 132, 160–3, 169–70.

as he. For as to the strength of body, the weakest has strength enough to kill the strongest, either by secret machination, or by confederacy with others, that are in the same danger with himself. [. . .]

From equality proceeds diffidence. From this equality of ability, ariseth equality of hope in the attaining of our ends. And therefore if any two men desire the same thing, which nevertheless they cannot both enjoy, they become enemies; and in the way to their end, which is principally their own conservation, and sometimes their delectation only, endeavour to destroy, or subdue one another. And from hence it comes to pass, that where an invader hath no more to fear, than another man's single power; if one plant, sow, build, or possess a convenient seat, others may probably be expected to come prepared with forces united, to dispossess, and deprive him, not only of the fruit of his labour, but also of his life, or liberty. And the invader again is in the like danger of another.

From diffidence war. And from this diffidence of one another, there is no way for any man to secure himself, so reasonable, as anticipation; that is, by force, or wiles, to master the persons of all men he can, so long, till he see no other power great enough to endanger him: and this is no more than his own conservation requireth, and is generally allowed. Also because there be some, that taking pleasure in contemplating their own power in the acts of conquest, which they pursue farther than their security requires; if others, that otherwise would be glad to be at ease within modest bounds, should not by invasion increase their power, they would not be able, long time, by standing only on their defence, to subsist. And by consequence, such augmentation of dominion over men being necessary to a man's conservation, it ought to be allowed him.

Again, men have no pleasure, but on the contrary a great deal of grief, in keeping company, where there is no power able to over-awe them all. For every man looketh that his companion should value him, at the same rate he sets upon himself: and upon all signs of contempt, or undervaluing, naturally endeavours, as far as he dares, (which amongst them that have no common power to keep them in quiet, is far enough to make them destroy each other), to extort a greater value from his contemners, by damage; and from others, by the example.

So that in the nature of man, we find three principal causes of quarrel. First, competition; secondly, diffidence; thirdly, glory.

The first, maketh men invade for gain; the second, for safety; and the third, for reputation. The first use violence, to make themselves masters of other men's persons, wives, children, and cattle; the second, to defend them; the third, for trifles, as a word, a smile, a different opinion, and any other sign of undervalue, either direct in their persons, or by reflection in their kindred, their friends, their nation, their profession, or their name.

Out of civil states, there is always war of every one against every one. Hereby it is manifest, that during the time men live without a common power to keep them all in awe, they are in that condition which is called war; and such a war, as is of every man, against every man. For WAR, consisteth not in battle only, or the act of fighting; but in a tract of time, wherein the will to contend by battle is sufficiently known: and therefore the notion of *time*, is to be considered in the nature of war; as it is in the nature of weather. For as the nature of foul weather, lieth not in a shower or two of rain; but in an inclination thereto of many days together: so the nature of war, consisteth not in actual fighting; but in the known disposition thereto, during all the time there is no assurance to the contrary. All other time is PEACE.

The incommodities of such a war. Whatsoever therefore is consequent to a time of war, where every man is enemy to every man; the same is consequent to the time, wherein men live without other security, than what their own strength, and their own invention shall furnish them withal. In such condition, there is no place for industry; because the fruit thereof is uncertain: and consequently no culture of the earth; no navigation, nor use of the commodities that may be imported by sea; no commodious building; no instruments of moving, and removing, such things as require much force; no knowledge of the face of the earth; no account of time; no arts; no letters; no society; and which is worst of all, continual fear, and danger of violent death; and the life of man, solitary, poor, nasty, brutish, and short. [. . .]

It may peradventure be thought, there was never such a time, nor condition of war as this; and I believe it was never generally so, over all the world: but, there are many places, where they live so now. For the savage people in many places of America, except the government of small families, the concord whereof dependeth on natural lust, have no government at all; and live at this day in that brutish manner, as I said before. Howsoever, it may be perceived what manner of life there would be, where there were no common power to fear, by the manner of life, which men that have formerly lived under a peaceful government, use to degenerate into, in a civil war.

But though there had never been any time, wherein particular men were in a condition of war one against another; yet in all times, kings, and persons of sovereign authority, because of their independency, are in continual jealousies, and in the state and posture of gladiators; having their weapons pointing, and their eyes fixed on one another; that is, their forts, garrisons, and guns upon the frontiers of their kingdoms; and continual spies upon their neighbours; which is a posture of war. But because they uphold thereby, the industry of their subjects; there does not follow from it, that misery, which accompanies the liberty of particular men.

In such a war nothing is unjust. To this war of every man, against every man, this also is consequent; that nothing can be unjust. The notions of right and wrong, justice and injustice have there no place. Where there is no common power, there is no law: where no law, no injustice. Force, and fraud, are in war the two cardinal virtues. Justice, and injustice are none of the faculties neither of the body, nor mind. If they were, they might be in a man that were alone in the world, as well as his senses, and passions. They are qualities, that relate to men in society, not in solitude. It is consequent also to the same condition, that there be no propriety, no dominion, no *mine* and *thine* distinct; but only that to be every man's, that he can get: and for so long, as he can keep it. And thus much for the ill condition, which man by mere nature is actually placed in; though with a possibility to come out of it, consisting partly in the passions, partly in his reason.

The passions that incline men to peace. The passions that incline men to peace, are fear of death; desire of such things as are necessary to commodious living; and a hope by their industry to obtain them. And reason suggesteth convenient articles of peace, upon which men may be drawn to agreement. These articles, are they, which otherwise are called the Laws of Nature: whereof I shall speak more particularly, in the two following chapters.

Of the First and Second Natural Laws, and of Contracts

Right of nature what. THE RIGHT OF NATURE, which writers commonly call *jus naturale*, is the liberty each man hath, to use his own power, as he will himself, for the preservation of his own nature; that is to say, of his own life; and consequently, of doing any thing, which in his own judgment, and reason, he shall conceive to be the aptest means thereunto.

Liberty what. By LIBERTY, is understood, according to the proper signification of the word, the absence of external impediments: which impediments, may oft take away part of a man's power to do what he would; but cannot hinder him from using the power left him, according as his judgment, and reason shall dictate to him.

A law of nature what. Difference of right and law. A LAW OF NATURE, *lex naturalis*, is a precept or general rule, found out by reason, by which a man is forbidden to do that, which is destructive of his life, or taketh away the means of preserving the same; and to omit that, by which he thinketh it may be best preserved. For though they that speak of this subject, use to confound *jus*, and *lex*, *right* and *law*: yet they ought to be distinguished; because RIGHT, consisteth in liberty to do, or to forbear: whereas LAW, determineth, and bindeth to one of them: so that law, and right, differ as much, as obligation, and liberty; which in one and the same matter are inconsistent.

Naturally every man has right to every thing. The fundamental law of nature. And because the condition of man, as hath been declared in the precedent chapter, is a condition of war of every one against every one; in which case every one is governed by his own reason; and there is nothing he can make use of, that may not be a help unto him, in preserving his life against his enemies; it followeth, that in such a condition, every man has a right to every thing; even to one another's body. And therefore, as long as this natural right of every man to every thing endureth, there can be no security to any man, how strong or wise soever he be, of living out the time, which nature ordinarily alloweth men to live. And consequently it is a precept, or general rule of reason, *that every man, ought to endeavour peace, as far as he has hope of obtaining it; and when he cannot obtain it, that he may seek, and use, all helps, and advantages of war.* The first branch of which rule, containeth the first, and fundamental law of nature; which is, *to seek peace, and follow it.* The second, the sum of the right of nature; which is, *by all means we can, to defend ourselves.*

The second law of nature. From this fundamental law of nature, by which men are commanded to endeavour peace, is derived this second law; *that a man be willing, when others are so too, as far-forth, as for peace, and defence of himself he shall think it necessary, to lay down this right to all things; and be contented with so much liberty against other men, as he would allow other men against himself.* For as long as every man holdeth this right, of doing any thing he liketh; so long are all men in the condition of war. But if other men will not lay down their right, as well as he; then there is no reason for any one, to divest himself of his: for that were to expose himself to prey, which no man is bound to, rather than to dispose himself to peace. This is that law of the Gospel; *whatsoever you require that others should do to you, that do ye to them.* [. . .]

Covenants of mutual trust, when invalid. If a covenant be made, wherein neither of the parties perform presently, but trust one another; in the condition of mere nature, which is a condition of war of every man against every man, upon any reasonable suspicion, it is void: but if there be a common power set over them both, with right and force sufficient to compel performance, it is not void. For he that performeth first, has no assurance the other will perform after; because the bonds of words are too weak to bridle men's ambition, avarice, anger, and other passions, without the fear of some coercive power; which in the condition of mere nature, where all men are equal, and judges of the justness of their own fears, cannot possibly be supposed. And therefore he which performeth first, does but betray himself to his enemy; contrary to the right, he can never abandon, of defending his life, and means of living.

But in a civil estate, where there is a power set up to constrain those that would otherwise violate their faith, that fear is no more reasonable; and for that cause, he which by the covenant is to perform first, is obliged so to do. [. . .]

Of Other Laws of Nature

The third law of nature, justice. From that law of nature, by which we are obliged to transfer to another, such rights, as being retained, hinder the peace of mankind, there followeth a third; which is this, *that men perform their covenants made*: without which, covenants are in vain, and but empty words; and the right of all men to all things remaining, we are still in the condition of war.

Justice and injustice what. And in this law of nature, consisteth the fountain and original of JUSTICE. For where no covenant hath preceded, there hath no right been transferred, and every man has right to every thing; and consequently, no action can be unjust. But when a covenant is made, then to break it is *unjust*: and the definition of INJUSTICE, is no other than *the not performance of covenant*. And whatsoever is not unjust, is *just*.

Justice and propriety begin with the constitution of commonwealth. But because covenants of mutual trust, where there is a fear of not performance on either part, as hath been said in the former chapter, are invalid; though the original of justice be the making of covenants; yet injustice actually there can be none, till the cause of such fear be taken away; which while men are in the natural condition of war, cannot be done. Therefore before the names of just, and unjust can have place, there must be some coercive power, to compel men equally to the performance of their covenants, by the terror of some punishment, greater than the benefit they expect by the breach of their covenant; and to make good that propriety, which by mutual contract men acquire, in recompense of the universal right they abandon: and such power there is none before the erection of a commonwealth. [. . .]

Justice not contrary to reason. The fool hath said in his heart, there is no such thing as justice; and sometimes also with his tongue; seriously alleging, that every man's conservation, and contentment, being committed to his own care, there could be no reason, why every man might not do what he thought conduced thereunto: and therefore also to make, or not make; keep, or not keep covenants, was not against reason, when it conduced to one's benefit. He does not therein deny, that there be covenants; and that they are sometimes broken, sometimes kept; and that such breach of them may be called injustice, and the observance of them justice: but he questioneth, whether injustice, taking away the fear of God, for the same fool hath said in his heart there is no God, may not sometimes stand with that reason, which dictateth to every man his own good; and particularly then, when it conduceth to such a benefit, as shall put a man in a condition, to neglect not only the dispraise, and revilings, but also the power of other men. The kingdom of God is gotten by violence: but what if it could be gotten by unjust violence? were it against reason so to get it, when it is impossible to receive hurt by it? and if it be not against reason, it is not against justice; or else justice is not to be approved for good. From such reasoning as this, successful wickedness hath obtained the name of virtue: and some that in all other things have disallowed the violation of faith; yet have allowed it, when it is for the getting of a kingdom. [. . .]

And I say it is not against reason. For the manifestation whereof, we are to consider; first, that when a man doth a thing, which notwithstanding any thing can be foreseen, and reckoned on, tendeth to his own destruction, howsoever some accident which he could not expect, arriving may turn it to his benefit; yet such events do not make it reasonably or wisely done. Secondly, that in a condition of war, wherein every man to every man, for want of a common power to keep them all in awe, is an enemy, there is no man who can hope by his own strength, or wit, to defend himself from destruction, without the help of confederates; where every one expects the same defence by the confederation, that any one else does: and therefore he which declares he thinks it reason to deceive those that help him, can in reason expect no other means of safety, than what can be had from his own single power. He therefore that breaketh his covenant, and consequently declareth that he thinks he may with reason do so, cannot be received into any society, that unite themselves for peace and defence, but by the error of them that receive him; nor when he is received, be retained in it, without seeing the danger of their error; which errors a man cannot reasonably reckon upon as the means of his security: and therefore if he be left, or cast out of society, he perisheth; and if he live in society, it is by the errors of other men, which he could not foresee, nor reckon upon; and consequently against the reason of his preservation; and so, as all men that contribute not to his destruction, forbear him only out of ignorance of what is good for themselves. [. . .]

Of the Causes, Generation, and Definition of a Commonwealth

[. . .] *The generation of a commonwealth. The definition of a commonwealth.* The only way to erect such a common power, as may be able to defend them from the invasion of foreigners, and the injuries of one another, and thereby to secure them in such sort, as that by their own industry, and by the fruits of the earth, they may nourish themselves and live contentedly; is, to confer all their power and strength upon one man, or upon one assembly of men, that may reduce all their wills, by plurality of voices, unto one will: which is as much as to say, to appoint one man, or assembly of men, to bear their person; and every one to own, and acknowledge himself to be author of whatsoever he that so beareth their person, shall act, or cause to be acted, in those things which concern the common peace and safety; and therein to submit their wills, every one to his will, and their judgments, to his judgment. This is more than consent, or concord; it is a real unity of them all, in one and the same person, made by covenant of every man with every man, in such manner, as if every man should say to every man, *I authorize and give up my right of governing myself, to this man, or to this assembly of men, on this condition, that thou give up thy right to him, and authorize all his actions in like manner.* This done, the multitude so united in one person, is called a COMMONWEALTH, in Latin CIVITAS. This is the generation of that great LEVIATHAN, or rather, to speak more reverently, of that *mortal god,* to which we owe under the *immortal* God, our peace and defence. For by this authority, given him by every particular man in the commonwealth, he hath the use of so much power and strength conferred on him, that by terror thereof, he is enabled to form the wills of them all, to peace at home, and mutual aid against their enemies abroad. And in him consisteth the essence of the commonwealth; which, to define it, is *one person, of whose acts a great multitude, by mutual covenants one with another, have made themselves every one the author, to the end he may use the strength and means of them all, as he shall think expedient, for their peace and common defence.* [. . .]

Of the Liberty of Subjects

[. . .] *Liberty of subjects consisteth in liberty from covenants.* In relation to these bonds only it is, that I am to speak now, of the *liberty* of *subjects.* For seeing there is no commonwealth in the world, wherein there be rules enough set down, for the regulating of all the actions, and words of men; as being a thing impossible: it followeth necessarily, that in all kinds of actions by the laws prætermitted, men have the liberty, of doing what their own reasons shall suggest, for the most profitable to themselves. For if we take liberty in the proper sense, for corporal liberty; that is to say, freedom from chains and prison; it were very absurd for men to clamour as they do, for the liberty they so manifestly enjoy. Again, if we take liberty, for an exemption from laws, it is no less absurd, for men to demand as they do, that liberty, by which all other men may be masters of their lives. And yet, as absurd as it is, this is it they demand; not knowing that the laws are of no power to protect them, without a sword in the hands of a man, or men, to cause those laws to be put in execution. The liberty of a subject, lieth therefore only in those things, which in regulating their actions, the sovereign hath prætermitted: such as is the liberty to buy, and sell, and otherwise contract with one another; to choose their own abode, their own diet, their own trade of life, and institute their children as they themselves think fit; and the like. [. . .]

The liberty which writers praise, is the liberty of sovereigns; not of private men. The liberty, whereof there is so frequent and honourable mention, in the histories, and philosophy of the ancient Greeks, and Romans, and in the writings, and discourse of those that from them have received all their learning in the politics, is not the liberty of particular men; but the liberty of the commonwealth. [. . .]

But it is an easy thing, for men to be deceived, by the specious name of liberty; and for want of judgment to distinguish, mistake that for their private inheritance, and birthright, which is the right of the public only. [. . .]

Of Systems Subject, Political, and Private

[. . .] *In all bodies politic the power of the representative is limited.* In bodies politic, the power of the representative is always limited: and that which prescribeth the limits thereof, is the power sovereign. For power unlimited, is absolute sovereignty. And the sovereign in every commonwealth, is the absolute representative of all the subjects; and therefore no other can be representative of any part of them, but so far forth, as he shall give leave. And to give leave to a body politic of subjects, to have an absolute representative to all intents and purposes, were to abandon the government of so much of the commonwealth, and to divide the dominion, contrary to their peace and defence; which the sovereign cannot be understood to do, by any grant, that does not plainly, and directly discharge them of their subjection.

John Locke, *Second Treatise on Civil Government* (selections)

Of the Beginning of Political Societies

§. 95. Men being, as has been said, by nature, all free, equal, and independent, no one can be put out of this estate, and subjected to the political power of another,

Edited by C. B. McPherson (Indianapolis: Hackett Publishing Co., 1980), pp. 18–22, 25, 26, 28–9, 52–3, 63–74.

without his own consent. The only way whereby any one divests himself of his natural liberty, and puts on the *bonds of civil society*, is by agreeing with other men to join and unite into a community for their comfortable, safe, and peaceable living one amongst another, in a secure enjoyment of their properties, and a greater security against any, that are not of it. This any number of men may do, because it injures not the freedom of the rest; they are left as they were in the liberty of the state of nature. When any number of men have so *consented to make one community or government*, they are thereby presently incorporated, and make *one body politic*, wherein the *majority* have a right to act and conclude the rest.

§. 96. For when any number of men have, by the consent of every individual, made a *community*, they have thereby made that *community* one body, with a power to act as one body, which is only by the will and determination of the *majority*: for that which acts any community, being only the consent of the individuals of it, and it being necessary to that which is one body to move one way; it is necessary the body should move that way whither the greater force carries it, which is the *consent of the majority*: or else it is impossible it should act or continue one body, *one community*, which the consent of every individual that united into it, agreed that it should; and so every one is bound by that consent to be concluded by the *majority*. And therefore we see, that in assemblies, impowered to act by positive laws, where no number is set by that positive law which impowers them, the *act of the majority* passes for the act of the whole, and of course determines, as having, by the law of nature and reason, the power of the whole.

§. 97. And thus every man, by consenting with others to make one body politic under one government, puts himself under an obligation, to every one of that society, to submit to the determination of the *majority*, and to be concluded by it; or else this *original compact*, whereby he with others incorporates into *one society*, would signify nothing, and be no compact, if he be left free, and under no other ties than he was in before in the state of nature. For what appearance would there be of any compact? what new engagement if he were no farther tied by any decrees of the society, than he himself thought fit, and did actually consent to? This would be still as great a liberty, as he himself had before his compact, or any one else in the state of nature hath, who may submit himself, and consent to any acts of it if he thinks fit.

§. 98. For if *the consent of the majority* shall not, in reason, be received as *the act of the whole*, and conclude every individual; nothing but the consent of every individual can make any thing to be the act of the whole: but such a consent is next to impossible ever to be had, if we consider the infirmities of health, and avocations of business, which in a number, though much less than that of a common-wealth, will necessarily keep many away from the public assembly. To which if we add the variety of opinions, and contrariety of interests, which unavoidably happen in all collections of men, the coming into society upon such terms would be only like *Cato's* coming into the theatre, only to go out again. Such a constitution as this would make the mighty *Leviathan* of a shorter duration, than the feeblest creatures, and not let it outlast the day it was born in: which cannot be supposed, till we can think, that rational creatures should desire and constitute societies only to be dissolved: for where the *majority* cannot conclude the rest, there they cannot act as one body, and consequently will be immediately dissolved again.

§. 99. Whosoever therefore out of a state of nature unite into a *community*, must be understood to give up all the power, necessary to the ends for which they unite into society, to the *majority* of the community, unless they expressly agreed in any number greater than the majority. And this is done by barely agreeing to *unite into one political society*, which is *all the compact* that is, or needs be, between the individuals, that enter into, or make up a *common-wealth*. And thus that, which begins and actually *constitutes any political society*, is nothing but the consent of any number of freemen capable of a majority to unite and incorporate into such a society. And this is that, and that only, which did, or could give beginning to any *lawful government* in the world. [. . .]

§. 119. *Every man* being, as has been shewed, *naturally free*, and nothing being able to put him into subjection to any earthly power, but only his own *consent*; it is to be considered, what shall be understood to be a *sufficient declaration* of a man's *consent, to make him subject* to the laws of any government. There is a common distinction of an express and a tacit consent, which will concern our present case. No body doubts but an express *consent*, of any man entering into any society, makes him a perfect member of that society, a subject of that government. The difficulty is, what ought to be looked upon as a *tacit consent*, and how far it binds, *i. e.* how far any one shall be looked on to have consented, and thereby submitted to any government, where he has made no expressions of it at all. And to this I say, that every man, that hath any possessions, or enjoyment, of any part of the dominions of any government, doth thereby give his *tacit consent*, and is as far forth obliged to obedience to the laws of that government, during such enjoyment, as any one under it; whether this his possession be of land, to him and his heirs for ever, or a lodging only for a week; or whether it be barely travelling freely on the highway; and in effect, it reaches as far as the very being of any one within the territories of that government. [. . .]

Of the Ends of Political Society and Government

§. 123. If man in the state of nature be so free, as has been said; if he be absolute lord of his own person and possessions, equal to the greatest, and subject to no body, why will he part with his freedom? why will he give up this empire, and subject himself to the dominion and controul of any other power? To which it is obvious to answer, that though in the state of nature he hath such a right, yet the enjoyment of it is very uncertain, and constantly exposed to the invasion of others: for all being kings as much as he, every man his equal, and the greater part no strict observers of equity and justice, the enjoyment of the property he has in this state is very unsafe, very unsecure. This makes him willing to quit a condition, which, however free, is full of fears and continual dangers: and it is not without reason, that he seeks out, and is willing to join in society with others, who are already united, or have a mind to unite, for the mutual *preservation* of their lives, liberties and estates, which I call by the general name, *property*.

§. 124. The great and *chief end*, therefore, of men's uniting into commonwealths, and putting themselves under government, *is the preservation of their property*. To which in the state of nature there are many things wanting.

First, There wants an *established*, settled, known *law*, received and allowed by common consent to be the standard of right and wrong, and the common measure to decide all controversies between them: for though the law of nature be plain and intelligible to all rational creatures; yet men being biassed by their interest, as well as ignorant for want of study of it, are not apt to allow of it as a law binding to them in the application of it to their particular cases.

§. 125. *Secondly*, In the state of nature there wants *a known and indifferent judge*, with authority to determine all differences according to the established law: for every one in that state being both judge and executioner of the law of nature, men being partial to themselves, passion and revenge is very apt to carry them too far, and with too much heat, in their own cases; as well as negligence, and unconcernedness, to make them too remiss in other men's.

§. 126. *Thirdly*, In the state of nature there often wants *power* to back and support the sentence when right, and to *give* it due *execution*. They who by any injustice offended, will seldom fail, where they are able, by force to make good their injustice; such resistance many times makes the punishment dangerous, and frequently destructive, to those who attempt it.

§. 127. Thus mankind, notwithstanding all the privileges of the state of nature, being but in an ill condition, while they remain in it, are quickly driven into society. Hence it comes to pass, that we seldom find any number of men live any time together in this state. The inconveniencies that they are therein exposed to, by the irregular and uncertain exercise of the power every man has of punishing the transgressions of others, make them take sanctuary under the established laws of government, and therein seek *the preservation of their property*. It is this makes them so willingly give up every one his single power of punishing, to be exercised by such alone, as shall be appointed to it amongst them; and by such rules as the community, or those authorized by them to that purpose, shall agree on. And in this we have the original *right and rise of both the legislative and executive power*, as well as of the governments and societies themselves.

§. 128. For in the state of nature, to omit the liberty he has of innocent delights, a man has two powers.

The first is to do whatsoever he thinks fit for the preservation of himself, and others within the permission of the *law of nature*: by which law, common to them all, he and all the rest of *mankind are one community*, make up one society, distinct from all other creatures. And were it not for the corruption and vitiousness of degenerate men, there would be no need of any other; no necessity that men should separate from this great and natural community, and by positive agreements combine into smaller and divided associations.

The other power a man has in the state of nature, is the *power to punish the crimes* committed against that law. Both these he gives up, when he joins in a private, if I may so call it, or particular politic society, and incorporates into any common-wealth, separate from the rest of mankind.

§. 129. The first *power, viz. of doing whatsoever he thought for the preservation of himself,* and the rest of mankind, *he gives up* to be regulated by laws made by the society, so far forth as the preservation of himself, and the rest of that society shall require; which laws of the society in many things confine the liberty he had by the law of nature.

§. 130. *Secondly,* The *power of punishing he wholly gives up,* and engages his natural force, (which he might before employ in the execution of the law of nature, by his own single authority, as he thought fit) to assist the executive power of the society, as the law thereof shall require: for being now in a new state, wherein he is to enjoy many conveniencies, from the labour, assistance, and society of others in the same community, as well as protection from its whole strength; he is to part also with as much of his natural liberty, in providing for himself, as the good, pros-perity, and safety of the society shall require; which is not only necessary, but just, since the other members of the society do the like.

§. 131. But though men, when they enter into society, give up the equality, liberty, and executive power they had in the state of nature, into the hands of the society, to be so far disposed of by the legislative, as the good of the society shall require; yet it being only with an intention in every one the better to preserve himself, his liberty and property; (for no rational creature can be supposed to change his condition with an intention to be worse) the power of the society, or *legislative* constituted by them, can *never be supposed to extend farther, than the common good;* but is obliged to secure every one's property, by providing against those three defects above mentioned, that made the state of nature so unsafe and uneasy. And so whoever has the legislative or supreme power of any common-wealth, is bound to govern by established *standing laws,* promulgated and known to the people, and not by extemporary decrees; by *indifferent* and upright *judges,* who are to decide controversies by those laws; and to employ the force of the community at home, *only in the execution of such laws,* or abroad to prevent or redress foreign injuries, and secure the community from inroads and invasion. And all this to be directed to no other *end,* but the *peace, safety,* and *public good* of the people. [. . .]

Of the Extent of the Legislative Power

§. 134. The great end of men's entering into society, being the enjoyment of their properties in peace and safety, and the great instrument and means of that being the laws established in that society; the *first and fundamental positive law* of all common-wealths *is the establishing of the legislative* power; as the *first and fundamental natural law,* which is to govern even the legislative itself, *is the preservation of the society,* and (as far as will consist with the public good) of every person in it. This *legislative* is not only *the supreme power* of the common-wealth, but sacred and unalterable in the hands where the community have once placed it. [. . .]

§. 135. Though the *legislative*, whether placed in one or more, whether it be always in being, or only by intervals, though it be the *supreme* power in every common-wealth; yet,

First, It is *not,* nor can possibly be absolutely *arbitrary* over the lives and fortunes of the people: for it being but the joint power of every member of the society given up to that person, or assembly, which is legislator; it can be no more than those persons had in a state of nature before they entered into society, and gave up to the community: for no body can transfer to another more power than he has in himself; and no body has an absolute arbitrary power over himself, or over any other, to destroy his own life, or take away the life or property of another. [. . .]

§. 136. *Secondly,* The *legislative,* or supreme authority, cannot assume to its self a power to rule by extemporary arbitrary decrees, but *is bound to dispense justice,* and decide the rights of the subject *by promulgated standing laws, and known authorized judges:* for the law of nature being unwritten, and so no where to be found but in the minds of men, they who through passion or interest shall miscite, or misapply it, cannot so easily be convinced of their mistake where there is no established judge: and so it serves not, as it ought, to determine the rights, and fence the properties of those that live under it, especially where every one is judge, interpreter, and executioner of it too, and that in his own case. [. . .]

§. 138. *Thirdly,* The *supreme power cannot take* from any man any part of his *property* without his own consent: for the preservation of property being the end of government, and that for which men enter into society, it necessarily supposes and requires, that the people should *have property,* without which they must be supposed to lose that, by entering into society, which was the end for which they entered into it; too gross an absurdity for any man to own. [. . .]

§. 140. It is true, governments cannot be supported without great charge, and it is fit every one who enjoys his share of the protection, should pay out of his estate his proportion for the maintenance of it. But still it must be with his own consent, *i.e.* the consent of the majority, giving it either by themselves, or their representatives chosen by them: for if any one shall claim a *power to lay* and levy *taxes* on the people, by his own authority, and without such consent of the people, he thereby invades the *fundamental law of property,* and subverts the end of government: for what property have I in that, which another may by right take, when he pleases, to himself? [. . .]

Of Property

[. . .]

§. 26. God, who hath given the world to men in common, hath also given them reason to make use of it to the best advantage of life, and convenience. The earth, and all that is therein, is given to men for the support and comfort of their being.

And tho' all the fruits it naturally produces, and beasts it feeds, belong to mankind in common, as they are produced by the spontaneous hand of nature; and no body has originally a private dominion, exclusive of the rest of mankind, in any of them, as they are thus in their natural state: yet being given for the use of men, there must of necessity be *a means to appropriate* them some way or other, before they can be of any use, or at all beneficial to any particular man. The fruit, or venison, which nourishes the wild *Indian*, who knows no inclosure, and is still a tenant in common, must be his, and so his, *i.e.* a part of him, that another can no longer have any right to it, before it can do him any good for the support of his life.

§. 27. Though the earth, and all inferior creatures, be common to all men, yet every man has a *property* in his own *person:* this no body has any right to but himself. The *labour* of his body, and the *work* of his hands, were may say, are properly his. Whatsoever then he removes out of the state that nature hath pro-vided, and left it in, he hath mixed his *labour* with, and joined to it something that is his own, and thereby makes it his *property*. It being by him removed from the common state nature hath placed it in, it hath by this *labour* something annexed to it, that excludes the common right of other men: for this *labour* being the unques-tionable property of the labourer, no man but he can have a right to what that is once joined to, at least where there is enough, and as good, left in common for others.

§. 28. He that is nourished by the acorns he picked up under an oak, or the apples he gathered from the trees in the wood, has certainly appropriated them to himself. No body can deny but the nourishment is his. I ask then, when did they begin to be his? when he digested? or when he eat? or when he boiled? or when he brought them home? or when he picked them up? and it is plain, if the first gathering made them not his, nothing else could. That *labour* put a distinction between them and common: that added something to them more than nature, the common mother of all, had done; and so they became his private right. [. . .] The *labour* that was mine, removing them out of that common state they were in, hath *fixed* my *property* in them.

§. 31. It will perhaps be objected to this, that it gathering the acorns, or other fruits of the earth, &c. makes a right to them, then any one may *ingross* as much as he will. To which I answer, Not so. The same law of nature, that does by this means give us property, does also *bound* that *property* too. *God has given us all things richly*, 1 Tim. vi. 12. is the voice of reason confirmed by inspiration. But how far has he given it us? *To enjoy.* As much as any one can make use of to any advantage of life before it spoils, so much he may by his labour fix a property in: whatever is beyond this, is more than his share, and belongs to others. Nothing was made by God for man to spoil or destroy. And thus, considering the plenty of natural provisions there was a long time in the world, and the few spenders; and to how small a part of that provision the industry of one man could extend itself, and ingross it to the prejudice of others; especially keeping within the *bounds*, set by reason, of what might serve for his *use*; there could be then little room for quarrels or contentions about property so established.

§. 32. But the *chief matter of property* being now not the fruits of the earth, and the beasts that subsist on it, but *the earth itself*; as that which takes in and carries with it all the rest; I think it is plain, that *property* in that too is acquired as the former. *As much land* as a man tills, plants, improves, cultivates, and can use the product of, so much is his *property*. He by his labour does, as it were, inclose it from the common. [. . .]

§. 33. Nor was this *appropriation* of any parcel of *land*, by improving it, any prejudice to any other man, since there was still enough, and as good left; and more than the yet unprovided could use. So that, in effect, there was never the less left for others because of his inclosure for himself; for he that leaves as much as another can make use of, does as good as take nothing at all. No body could think himself injured by the drinking of another man, though he took a good draught, who had a whole river of the same water left him to quench his thirst: and the case of land and water, where there is enough of both, is perfectly the same. [. . .]

§. 36. The *measure of property* nature has well set by the extent of men's *labour and the conveniencies of life*: no man's labour could subdue, or appropriate all; nor could his enjoyment consume more than a small part; so that it was impossible for any man, this way, to intrench upon the right of another, or acquire to himself a property, to the prejudice of his neighbour, who would still have room for as good, and as large a possession (after the other had taken out his) as before it was appropriated. [. . .]

§. 40. Nor is it so strange, as perhaps before consideration it may appear, that the *property of labour* should be able to over-balance the community of land: for it is *labour* indeed that *puts the difference of value* on every thing; and let any one consider what the difference is between an acre of land planted with tobacco or sugar, sown with wheat or barley, and an acre of the same land lying in common, without any husbandry upon it, and he will find, that the improvement of *labour makes* the far greater part of the value. I think it will be but a very modest computation to say, that of the *products* of the earth useful to the life of man nine tenths are the *effects of labour*: nay, if we will rightly estimate things as they come to our use, and cast up the several expences about them, what in them is purely owing to *nature*, and what to *labour*, we shall find, that in most of them ninety-nine hundredths are wholly to be put on the account of *labour*. [. . .]

§. 42. To make this a little clearer, let us but trace some of the ordinary provisions of life, through their several progresses, before they come to our use, and see how much they receive of their *value from human industry*. Bread, wine and cloth, are things of daily use, and great plenty; yet notwithstanding, acorns, water and leaves, or skins, must be our bread, drink and cloathing, did not *labour* furnish us with these more useful commodities: for whatever *bread* is more worth than acorns, wine than water, and *cloth* or *silk*, than leaves, skins or moss, that is wholly *owing to labour* and *industry*. [. . .]

§. 46. [. . .] Now of those good things which nature hath provided in common, every one had a right (as hath been said) to as much as he could use, and *property* in all that he could effect with his labour; all that his *industry* could extend to, to alter from the state nature had put it in, was his. He that *gathered* a hundred bushels of acorns or apples, had thereby a *property* in them, they were his goods as soon as gathered. He was only to look, that he used them before they spoiled, else he took more than his share, and robbed others. And indeed it was a foolish thing, as well as dishonest, to hoard up more than he could make use of. If he gave away a part to any body else, so that it perished not uselessly in his possession, these he also made use of. And if he also bartered away plums, that would have rotted in a week, for nuts that would last good for his eating a whole year, he did no injury; he wasted not the common stock; destroyed no part of the portion of goods that belonged to others, so long as nothing perished uselessly in his hands. Again, if he would give his nuts for a piece of metal, pleased with its colour; or exchange his sheep for shells, or wool for a sparkling pebble or a diamond, and keep those by him all his life, he invaded not the right of others, he might heap up as much of these durable things as he pleased; the *exceeding of the bounds of* his *just property* not lying in the largeness of his possession, but the perishing of any thing uselessly in it.

§. 47. And thus *came in the use of money*, some lasting thing that men might keep without spoiling, and that by mutual consent men would take in exchange for the truly useful, but perishable supports of life.

§. 48. And as different degrees of industry were apt to give men possessions in different proportions, so this *invention of money* gave them the opportunity to continue and enlarge them. [. . .]

John Stuart Mill, *On Liberty* (selections)

There is, in fact, no recognized principle by which the propriety or impropriety of government interference is customarily tested. People decide according to their personal preferences. Some, whenever they see any good to be done, or evil to be remedied, would willingly instigate the government to undertake the business, while others prefer to bear almost any amount of social evil rather than add one to the departments of human interests amenable to governmental control. And men range themselves on one or the other side in any particular case, according to this general direction of their sentiments, or according to the degree of interest which they feel in the particular thing which it is proposed that the government should do, or according to the belief they entertain that the government would, or would not, do it in the manner they prefer; but very rarely on account of any opinion to which they consistently adhere, as to what things are fit to be done by a government. And it seems to me that in consequence of this absence of rule or principle, one side is at present as often wrong as the other; the interference of government is, with about equal frequency, improperly invoked and improperly condemned.

The object of this essay is to assert one very simple principle, as entitled to govern absolutely the dealings of society with the individual in the way of compul-

Edited by Gertrude Himmelfarb (New York: Penguin, 1974), pp. 67–72.

sion and control, whether the means used be physical force in the form of legal penalties or the moral coercion of public opinion. That principle is that the sole end for which mankind are warranted, individually or collectively, in interfering with the liberty of action of any of their number is self-protection. That the only purpose for which power can be rightfully exercised over any member of a civilized community, against his will, is to prevent harm to others. His own good, either physical or moral, is not a sufficient warrant. He cannot rightfully be compelled to do or forbear because it will be better for him to do so, because it will make him happier, because, in the opinions of others, to do so would be wise or even right. These are good reasons for remonstrating with him, or reasoning with him, or persuading him, or entreating him, but not for compelling him or visiting him with any evil in case he do otherwise. To justify that, the conduct from which it is desired to deter him must be calculated to produce evil to someone else. The only part of the conduct of anyone for which he is amenable to society is that which concerns others. In the part which merely concerns himself, his independence is, of right, absolute. Over himself, over his own body and mind, the individual is sovereign.

It is, perhaps, hardly necessary to say that this doctrine is meant to apply only to human beings in the maturity of their faculties. We are not speaking of children or of young persons below the age which the law may fix as that of manhood or womanhood. Those who are still in a state to require being taken care of by others must be protected against their own actions as well as against external injury. For the same reason we may leave out of consideration those backward states of society in which the race itself may be considered as in its nonage. The early difficulties in the way of spontaneous progress are so great that there is seldom any choice of means for overcoming them; and a ruler full of the spirit of improvement is warranted in the use of any expedients that will attain an end perhaps otherwise unattainable. Despotism is a legitimate mode of government in dealing with barbarians, provided the end be their improvement and the means justified by actually effecting that end. Liberty, as a principle, has no application to any state of things anterior to the time when mankind have become capable of being improved by free and equal discussion. Until then, there is nothing for them but implicit obedience to an Akbar or a Charlemagne, if they are so fortunate as to find one. But as soon as mankind have attained the capacity of being guided to their own improvement by conviction or persuasion (a period long since reached in all nations with whom we need here concern ourselves), compulsion, either in the direct form or in that of pains and penalties for noncompliance, is no longer admissible as a means to their own good, and justifiable only for the security of others.

It is proper to state that I forgo any advantage which could be derived to my argument from the idea of abstract right as a thing independent of utility. I regard utility as the ultimate appeal on all ethical questions; but it must be utility in the largest sense, grounded on the permanent interests of man as a progressive being. Those interests, I contend, authorize the subjection of individual spontaneity to external control only in respect to those actions of each which concern the interest of other people. If anyone does an act hurtful to others, there is a *prima facie* case for punishing him by law or, where legal penalties are not safely applicable, by general disapprobation. There are also many positive acts for the benefit of others which he may rightfully be compelled to perform, such as to give evidence in a court of justice, to bear his fair share in the common defence or in any other joint work necessary to the interest of the society of which he enjoys the protection, and to perform certain acts of individual beneficence, such as saving a fellow creature's life or interposing to protect the defenceless against ill usage – things which whenever it is obviously a man's duty to do he may rightfully be made responsible to society for not doing. A person may cause evil to others not only by his actions but by his inaction, and in either case he is justly accountable to them for the injury. The latter case, it is true, requires a much more cautious exercise of compulsion than the former. To make anyone answerable for doing evil to others is the rule; to make him answerable for not preventing evil is, comparatively speaking, the exception. Yet there are many cases clear enough and grave enough to justify that exception. In all things which regard the external relations of the individual, he is *de jure* amenable to those whose interests are concerned, and, if need be, to society as their protector. There are often good reasons for not holding him to the responsibility; but these reasons must arise from the special expediencies of the case: either because it is a kind of case in which he is on the whole likely to act better when left to his own discretion than when controlled in any way in which society have it in their power to control him; or because the attempt to exercise control would produce other evils, greater than those which it would prevent. When such reasons as these preclude the enforcement of responsibility, the conscience of the agent himself should step into the vacant judgment seat and protect those interests of others which have no external protection; judging himself all the more rigidly, because the case does not admit of his being made accountable to the judgment of his fellow creatures.

But there is a sphere of action in which society, as distinguished from the individual, has, if any, only an indirect interest: comprehending all that portion of a person's life and conduct which affects only himself or, if it also affects others, only with their free, voluntary, and undeceived consent and participation. When I say only himself, I mean directly and in the first instance; for whatever affects himself may affect others through himself; and the objection which may be grounded on this contingency will receive consideration in the sequel. This, then, is the appropriate region of human liberty. It comprises, first, the inward domain of consciousness, demanding liberty of conscience in the most comprehensive sense, liberty of thought and feeling, absolute freedom of opinion and sentiment on all subjects, practical or speculative, scientific, moral, or theological. The liberty of expressing and publishing opinions may seem to fall under a different principle, since it belongs to that part of the conduct of an individual which concerns other people, but, being almost of as much importance as the liberty of thought itself and resting in great part on the same reasons, is practically inseparable from it. Secondly, the principle requires liberty of tastes and pursuits, of framing the plan of our life to suit our own character, of doing as we like, subject to such consequences as may follow, without impediment from our fellow creatures, so long as what we do does not harm them, even though they should think our conduct foolish, perverse, or wrong. Thirdly, from this liberty of each individual follows the liberty, within the same limits, of combination among individuals; freedom to unite for any purpose not involving harm to others: the persons combining being supposed to be of full age and not forced or deceived.

No society in which these liberties are not, on the whole, respected is free, whatever may be its form of government; and none is completely free in which they do not exist absolute and unqualified. The only freedom which deserves the name is that of pursuing our own good in our own way, so long as we do not attempt to deprive others of theirs or impede their efforts to obtain it. Each is the proper guardian of his own health, whether bodily *or* mental and spiritual. Mankind are greater gainers by suffering each other to live as seems good to themselves than by compelling each to live as seems good to the rest.

George Dargo, *Law in the New Republic* (selections)

Private Property and Legal Takings

Eminent domain law, still in its infancy in the immediate postrevolutionary period, already reflected many of the forces pushing and pulling American law in new directions. Although few of the state constitutions adopted in the revolutionary era contained just compensation provisions, the principle was widely recognized: private property could not be appropriated for public use unless the owner was compensated for the taking. The Fifth Amendment to the Constitution put it most succinctly: "nor shall private property be taken for public use without just compensation." The words are simple and straightforward. Even in states with no expressed constitutional provision for just compensation, courts adopted the federal constitutional provision or applied compensation law either as an equitable remedy or by reason of natural justice. Yet despite its "just compensation" predicate, eminent domain became one of the most fertile areas for the undermining of the absolute right to private property. Indeed, the "devolution" of the eminent domain power to "private takers" eroded absolutist conceptions of private property to such an extent that eminent domain law can be said to have prepared the way for the regulatory state.

The difficult questions of eminent domain law were not subject to automatic resolution by reference to fundamental constitutional sources or to simple principles of compensation. Did milldam owners who raised a head of water in order

From *Law in the New Republic: Private Law and the Public Estate* (New York: Alfred A. Knopf, 1983), pp. 30–5, 39–41.

to operate a waterwheel subject an upstream neighbor to an involuntary taking when the latter's land was flooded? Was such a taking by a private party equally compensable as when the taking was by public authority? Did the construction of a milldam constitute a benefit sufficient to satisfy a "public use" test? What if the person whose land was flooded also benefited from the taking? Was his benefit to be "offset" against his loss? How was compensation to be paid, in kind or in money, and if in money, what would be the appropriate measure of damages?

These were serious issues not easily resolved and often not settled in ways indicated by constitutional provisions. In Massachusetts, for example, the 1780 constitution declared that "whenever . . . publick exigencies require that the property of any individual should be appropriated to public uses, he shall receive a reasonable compensation therefor." In *Commonwealth v. Sessions of Middlesex* (1812), however, the Supreme Judicial Court decided that when private land was taken for a public road, if the proprietor's benefit from the construction of the road exceeded his damage from the taking, then no compensation was due because there was no loss. Takings such as this, despite judicial sanction, were recognized as confiscatory by at least some offended contemporaries. As the reporter of the *Middlesex* case noted:

> [T]he justice of the rule is certainly very questionable. The expense of making a highway is a common burden, incurred for the common good; of which burden, each citizen, in proportion to his ability, ordinarily sustains his part, and if one accidentally, whether by dwelling or having his lands near the highway, or from any other circumstance, derives more benefit from it than another, this does not seem to afford any sound reason for imposing a heavier tax upon him merely on that account. Indeed, it would be impracticable, in taxation, to apply the rule generally, and assess the expenses of public works upon each citizen in exact proportion to the supposed benefit he may be expected to derive from them. *Where, then, is the equality or justice of applying the rule in a case like that reported in the text* [emphasis added]?

Thus, courts upheld small individual proprietors against powerful interests when it was not at all clear that the "taking" would result in a genuine public benefit. For example, a Massachusetts case held that

> . . . where private persons or corporations prevail on towns to layout town ways, colorably for the use of the inhabitants, but really for their own benefit, over lands of others who are opposed to the way . . . a jury may discontinue a way thus irregularly obtained; and they ought to do it, whenever they are satisfied that private emolument, and not the interest of the inhabitants, has caused the way to be located.

The emerging ideological commitment to economic growth and development, which the extension of the power of eminent domain enhanced, created a tension with the equally strong social imperative to prevent the abuse of the eminent domain power for purely private ends. The devolution of eminent domain from public authority to private actors was a trend that greatly accelerated after the middle of the nineteenth century; but the trend had begun in the generation following the Revolution, a time when consciousness of the natural rights basis of American constitutionalism was most keenly felt and understood. In short, while the law clearly moved in directions that promoted growth, the law did not simply ratify all of the demands of favored economic interests. Rather it mediated between conflicting values and competing social goods.

Traditional property rights such as quiet enjoyment and just compensation were subjected to other challenges besides the expanded usage of the eminent domain power. Internal improvements and changing technologies necessarily brought values and interests into new sorts of conflicts. If property owners in the eighteenth century enjoyed settled traditions of just compensation and the right to peaceable possession, the opening of the nineteenth century witnessed a growing number of modifications of these customary rules, as builders of roads, canals, bridges, buildings, and mills increasingly interfered with other people's property. The classic example of this development occurred in Massachusetts, a just compensation state whose law was transformed in this period into an instrument for the promotion of economic growth. In 1795 the Massachusetts General Court (the state legislature) passed a milldam act that set up a procedure for compensating riparian landowners whose lands were flooded when a neighbor constructed a dam in order to work a waterwheel. This statute provided for the payment of yearly damages, the damages to be appraised by a jury. The effect of the act was to force a complainant to lease away part of his land in return for an annual rent for as long as the millowner wished to flood. Not only was the plaintiff thereby deprived of the use of his own land, but the award of an annuity rather than a lump sum payment meant that, too often, plaintiffs so situated could not reinvest in alternative resources; nor did they get compensation, in years when no flooding occurred, for the permanent damage to the value of their land.

An important decision of the Massachusetts Supreme Judicial Court, *Stowell v. Flagg*, established that the procedure for awarding annual damages under the 1795 enactment was to be the exclusive remedy. Plaintiffs whose lands were flooded were barred from resorting to more normal legal remedies such as self-help, suits at law for trespass or nuisance, or a petition for injunctive relief. Under self-help, the property owner whose quiet enjoyment had been disturbed could go onto someone else's land and remove the disturbance. Such action would not constitute the wrong of trespass (a serious *intentional tort*) because the complainant had justification. Thus a property owner whose lands were flooded by a neighbor's dam could destroy the dam without incurring liability. At law, such a plaintiff had an alternative remedy, a suit in trespass or nuisance. If the suit were in trespass, the claim to damages would not be limited to the actual value of the loss because the law would seek to deter as well as to compensate. Similarly in a nuisance action, the damages awarded might be higher than the loss. A North Carolina decision summarized the reasons why damages for nuisance ought not to be either light or merely compensatory; the same reasoning would of course apply to the punitive damages available in trespass:

... [I]f the keeping up of the nuisance will afford more profit to the wrongdoer than the small damages assessed by a jury, he will keep it up forever; and thus one individual will be enabled to take from another his property against his consent, and detain it from him as long as he pleases. The damages ought not to be for what the incommoded property is worth, but competent to the purpose in view; that is, a demolition of the erection that occasions the nuisance. Sometimes the profits of such erections as merchant mills for instance, are of much greater value in one year, than the fee simple of the annoyed property. In such cases the object of the law cannot be obtained but by damages equivalent to the profits gained by the erection, or by damages to such an amount as will render those profits not worth pursuing.

Finally, a flooded riparian, under ordinary circumstances, could petition for an injunction blocking either construction of the dam or the millowner's usage of his mill if that disturbed the plaintiff's quiet enjoyment. But the Massachusetts Milldam Act, instead of preserving the *plaintiff's prospective remedy* for preventing damage (i.e., through the injunction), authorized *prospective takings* by the millowner. This represented a major departure from the practice followed in a number of other states where statutes required prior authorization for each dam before it was constructed. Even more significantly, the Milldam Act of 1795, in conjunction with the Supreme Judicial Court's decision in *Stowell v. Flagg*, signified a fundamental incursion into traditional notions about the right to private property.

This departure from customary understandings did not escape the concern of contemporaries. One critic of *Stowell v. Flagg* questioned whether such an "unusual and extraordinary provision of the law" could be constitutional:

I may not seize my neighbor's goods, except by process of law, against his consent, even though I may offer him their full value in return. I may not plough my neighbor's land, even though the thorn and the thistle alone flourish there under the sluggish husbandry of its owner. I may not obscure the light from the ancient cottage window, though poverty and weakness alone may have enjoyed its cheerful influence; nor may I poison the water or air that has, for years, given health and comfort to my neighbor, though the trade I may follow would enrich my coffers, and accommodate the neighborhood. But the ordinary rules of right and wrong, as to the enjoyment of private property, seem not to apply to estates which border upon any of the beautiful and healthy streams which enliven our scenery. They may be sacrificed to the speculating spirit of the manufacturer.

The fundamental right to property guaranteed by the state and federal constitutions was the right not to have property taken even for public use without consent. Unconsented taxation, after all, was the triggering cause of the American Revolution. In this case, however, the law authorized a taking for private use and deprived owners of property "without due process of law." As this writer continued: Through the mill act and *Stowell v. Flagg* the law authorized "the occupation and enjoyment of another's estate *forever*; which . . . is altogether unlike any other assumption of private property usually contemplated by our constitutions." [. . .]

Contract Law

[. . .] In the early nineteenth century, contractual freedom was "privatized". [. . .] The modern theory of contract law is that private individuals are lawmakers who, through the instrument of the bargained-for private agreement, create a legal regime which will govern their future conduct just as if that behavior had been conditioned by statute, regulation, or court order. Behind this "contract theory" stands the psychology of free will and the political philosophy of self-government: mature human beings in a free society are capable of ordering their affairs in ways they best understand.

This has not always been so. In the eighteenth century the law stood as a pervasive "omnipresence in the sky," particularly in the contract area. Parties could enter into a contract (or "covenant") only if the terms of their bargain did not violate group values, rules of social conduct, or community norms. The law of contracts was undeveloped, its rules were traditional, and its design fitted the mold of a stable, premodern society, where relationships were face to face, obligations were undertaken and discharged according to well-established customs, and deviations from the norm were controlled by carefully defined doctrines and procedures.

A contract action brought by a Massachusetts physician a decade before the Revolution illustrates the old law. The doctor's bill was for drugs, travel costs, and medical attention, but not surprisingly, there was no written contract defining the terms of remuneration. Nevertheless, the court decided that these costs "had as fixed a Price as Goods sold by a Shopkeeper. . . . The jury did, according as the Law was laid down to them, and struck off about £7 from the Account, lowering the Charges, probably, to what they thought *'reasonable.'*" The doctor's charges, in other words, were fixed by local custom as established by jurors drawn from the community, who knew what those customs were.

But while many traditional elements of the old law of contracts persisted well into the nineteenth century, by 1820 that law showed signs of rapid change in the direction of modern contract law. The deepest change was the shift away from community values and toward individual intent as the ultimate test of the enforceable agreement. The purpose of the developing rules of contract law was to carry out the will of the parties even when their agreements reflected judgments of value or mandated behavior or performance that ran contrary to accepted custom. For example, courts increasingly allowed the amount of "consideration" to be determined by the parties. Even nominal amounts would be permitted if the parties so intended. This was in contrast to eighteenth century usage, where courts would not enforce contracts where the items exchanged had not been of roughly equivalent value.

Powerful historical forces generated these changes in contract law. The new commercial economy was creating novel products, distant markets, and fluid price structures, plus a whole range of complex commercial relationships among buyers and sellers, employers and workers, producers and consumers. Shifting patterns of trade, the growth of commodity and "futures" markets, greater impersonality in the relations between contracting parties – all forced substantial changes in the rules that governed agreements. In addition, behind the demanding requirements of the new commerce and industry lurked the ideology of private decision making, an ideology rooted as much in political and social attitudes as in hard economic fact. On every level, postrevolutionary legal thought emphasized the lawmaking role of the private individual while it criticized the superintending power of the state. The private contract was, in essence, a private statute; the law of contracts facilitated "private ordering" of markets and resources. In a word, the private contract represented self-government in private law, just as republicanism promoted the representative principle in public law.

The triumph of what has been called "the will theory of contracts" carried the republican impulse to the smallest unit in society – two individuals, who in concert formed a microlegislature and made law. Modern contract law theory brought Americans closer to direct democracy than did their representative political institutions. In practice, however, "liberty of contract" was based upon the illusion that parties entered into agreements on the basis of genuine negotiating equality. In fact the myth of "liberty of contract" eventually became part of an ideological justification for social and economic exploitation. The theory of contracts was sound, but its implementation in a world where wealth and power were not equally distributed inevitably brought distortions in result not unlike the distortions in the legislative process that occurred when powerful interests, or lobbies, corrupted political institutions in the name of representative democracy.

The decline of the eighteenth century's "substantive theory of contracts" meant that the law concerned itself only with the formalities of contract formation. Neither the relative bargaining positions of the parties, nor the substance of what they agreed to was any longer a central issue. This opened the door to widespread abuse by the powerful over the weak, the informed against the ignorant, and too often, the rich against the poor. The emergence of modern contract theory in the nineteenth century was the clearest expression of the tendency of American law to ratify underlying social relationships. Of all the branches of the legal system, the law of contracts became the least responsive to the demands of social justice and economic equality.

Charles A. Reich, "The New Property" (selections)

Property and the Public Interest:
An Old Debate Revisited

The public interest state represents in one sense the triumph of society over private property. This triumph is the end point of a great and necessary movement for reform. But somehow the result is different from what the reformers wanted.

From *Yale Law Journal*, vol. 73, no. 5 (April 1964), pp. 771–4.

Somehow the idealistic concept of the public interest has summoned up a doctrine monstrous and oppressive. It is time to take another look at private property, and at the "public interest" philosophy that dominates its modern substitute, the largess of government.

A. Property and liberty

Property is a legal institution the essence of which is the creation and protection of certain private rights in wealth of any kind. The institution performs many different functions. One of these functions is to draw a boundary between public and private power. Property draws a circle around the activities of each private individual or organization. Within that circle, the owner has a greater degree of freedom than without. Outside, he must justify or explain his actions, and show his authority. Within, he is master, and the state must explain and justify any interference. It is as if property shifted the burden of proof; outside, the individual has the burden; inside, the burden is on government to demonstrate that something the owner wishes to do should not be done.

Thus, property performs the function of maintaining independence, dignity and pluralism in society by creating zones within which the majority has to yield to the owner. Whim, caprice, irrationality and "antisocial" activities are given the protection of law; the owner may do what all or most of his neighbors decry. The Bill of Rights also serves this function, but while the Bill of Rights comes into play only at extraordinary moments of conflict or crisis, property affords day-to-day protection in the ordinary affairs of life. Indeed, in the final analysis the Bill of Rights depends upon the existence of private property. Political rights presuppose that individuals and private groups have the will and the means to act independently. But so long as individuals are motivated largely by self-interest, their well-being must first be independent. Civil liberties must have a basis in property, or bills of rights will not preserve them.

Property is not a natural right but a deliberate construction by society. If such an institution did not exist, it would be necessary to create it, in order to have the kind of society we wish. The majority cannot be expected, on specific issues, to yield its power to a minority. Only if the minority's will is established as a general principle can it keep the majority at bay in a given instance. Like the Bill of Rights, property represents a general, long range protection of individual and private interests, created by the majority for the ultimate good of all.

Today, however, it is widely thought that property and liberty are separable things; that there may, in fact, be conflicts between "property rights" and "personal rights." Why has this view been accepted? The explanation is found at least partly in the transformations which have taken place in property.

During the industrial revolution, when property was liberated from feudal restraints, philosophers hailed property as the basis of liberty, and argued that it must be free from the demands of government or society. But as private property grew, so did abuses resulting from its use. In a crowded world, a man's use of his property increasingly affected his neighbor, and one man's exercise of a right might seriously impair the rights of others. Property became power over others; the farm land-owner, the city landlord, and the working man's boss were able to oppress their tenants or employees. Great aggregations of property resulted in private control of entire industries and basic services capable of affecting a whole area or even a nation. At the same time, much private property lost its individuality and in effect became socialized. Multiple ownership of corporations helped to separate personality from property, and property from power. When the corporations began to stop competing, to merge, agree, and make mutual plans, they became private governments. Finally, they sought the aid and partnership of the state, and thus by their own volition became part of public government.

These changes led to a movement for reform, which sought to limit arbitrary private power and protect the common man. Property rights were considered more the enemy than the friend of liberty. The reformers argued that property must be separated from personality. Walton Hamilton wrote:

> As late as the turn of the last century justices were not yet distinguishing between liberty and property; in the universes beneath their hats liberty was still the opportunity to acquire property.

> . . . the property of the Reports is not a proprietary thing; it is rather a shibboleth in whose name the domain of business enterprises has enjoyed a limited immunity from the supervision of the state.

> In the annals of the law property is still a vestigial expression of personality and owes its current constitutional position to its former association with liberty. (Walton H. Hamilton, "Property According to Locke," *Yale Law Journal* 41 (1932), pp. 877–78)

During the first half of the twentieth century, the reformers enacted into law their conviction that private power was a chief enemy of society and of individual liberty. Property was subjected to "reasonable" limitations in the interests of society. The regulatory agencies, federal and state, were born of the reform. In sustaining these major inroads on private property, the Supreme Court rejected the older idea that property and liberty were one, and wrote a series of classic opinions upholding the power of the people to regulate and limit private rights.

The struggle between abuse and reform made it easy to forget the basic importance of individual private property. The defense of private property was almost entirely a defense of its abuses – an attempt to defend not individual property but arbitrary private power over other human beings. Since this defense was cloaked in a defense of private property, it was natural for the reformers to attack too broadly. Walter Lippmann saw this in 1934:

> But the issue between the giant corporation and the public should not be allowed to obscure the truth that the only dependable foundation of personal liberty is the economic security of private property.

For we must not expect to find in ordinary men the stuff of martyrs, and we must, therefore, secure their freedom by their normal motives. There is no surer way to give men the courage to be free than to insure them a competence upon which they can rely. (Walter Lippmann, *The Method of Freedom*; New York: Macmillan, 1934, p. 101)

The reform took away some of the power of the corporations and transferred it to government. In this transfer there was much good, for power was made responsive to the majority rather than to the arbitrary and selfish few. But the reform did not restore the individual to his domain. What the corporation had taken from him, the reform simply handed on to government. And government carried further the powers formerly exercised by the corporation. Government as an employer, or as a dispenser of wealth, has used the theory that it was handing out gratuities to claim a managerial power as great as that which the capitalists claimed. Moreover, the corporations allied themselves with, or actually took over, part of government's system of power. Today it is the combined power of government and the corporations that presses against the individual.

From the individual's point of view, it is not any particular kind of power, but all kinds of power, that are to be feared. This is the lesson of the public interest state. The mere fact that power is derived from the majority does not necessarily make it less oppressive. Liberty is more than the right to do what the majority wants, or to do what is "reasonable." Liberty is the right to defy the majority, and to do what is unreasonable. The great error of the public interest state is that it assumes an identity between the public interest and the interest of the majority.

The reform, then, has not done away with the importance of private property. More than ever the individual needs to possess, in whatever form, a small but sovereign island of his own.

B. Largess and the public interest

The fact that the reform tended to make much private wealth subject to "the public interest" has great significance, but it does not adequately explain the dependent position of the individual and the weakening of civil liberties in the public interest state. The reformers intended to enhance the values of democracy and liberty; their basic concern was the preservation of a free society. But after they established the primacy of "the public interest," what meaning was given to that phrase? In particular, what values does it embody as it has been employed to regulate government largess?

Reduced to simplest terms, "the public interest" has usually meant this: government largess may be denied or taken away if this will serve some legitimate public policy. The policy may be one directly related to the largess itself, or it may be some collateral objective of government. A contract may be denied if this will promote fair labor standards. A television license may be refused if this will promote the policies of the antitrust laws. Veterans benefits may be taken away to promote loyalty to the United States. A liquor license may be revoked to promote civil rights. A franchise for a barber's college may not be given out if it will hurt the local economy, nor a taxi franchise if it will seriously injure the earning capacity of other taxis.

Most of these objectives are laudable, and all are within the power of government. The great difficulty is that they are simplistic. Concentration on a single policy or value obscures other values that may be at stake. Some of these competing values are other public policies; for example, the policy of the best possible television service to the public may compete with observance of the antitrust laws. The legislature is the natural arbiter of such conflicts. But the conflicts may also be more fundamental. In the regulation of government largess, achievement of specific policy goals may undermine the independence of the individual. Where such conflicts exist, a simplistic notion of the public interest may unwittingly destroy some values.

Michael Sandel, "Morality and the Liberal Ideal"

Liberals often take pride in defending what they oppose – pornography, for example, or unpopular views. They say the state should not impose on its citizens a preferred way of life, but should leave them as free as possible to choose their own values and ends, consistent with a similar liberty for others. This commitment to freedom of choice requires liberals constantly to distinguish between permission and praise, between allowing a practice and endorsing it. It is one thing to allow pornography, they argue, something else to affirm it.

Conservatives sometimes exploit this distinction by ignoring it. They charge that those who would allow abortions favor abortion, that opponents of school prayer oppose prayer, that those who defend the rights of Communists sympathize with their cause. And in a pattern of argument familiar in our politics, liberals reply by invoking higher principles; it is not that they dislike pornography less, but rather that they value toleration, or freedom of choice, or fair procedures more.

But in contemporary debate, the liberal rejoinder seems increasingly fragile, its moral basis increasingly unclear. Why should toleration and freedom of choice prevail when other important values are also at stake? Too often the answer implies some version of moral relativism, the idea that it is wrong to "legislate morality" because all morality is merely subjective. "Who is to say what is literature and what is filth? That is a value judgment, and whose values should decide?"

Relativism usually appears less as a claim than as a question. "Who is to judge?" But it is a question that can also be asked of the values that liberals defend. Toleration and freedom and fairness are values too, and they can hardly be defended by the claim that no values can be defended. So it is a mistake to affirm

From *The New Republic*, vol. 190 (May 7, 1984), pp. 15–17.

liberal values by arguing that all values are merely subjective. The relativist defense of liberalism is no defense at all.

What, then, can be the moral basis of the higher principles the liberal invokes? Recent political philosophy has offered two main alternatives – one utilitarian, the other Kantian. The utilitarian view, following John Stuart Mill, defends liberal principles in the name of maximizing the general welfare. The state should not impose on its citizens a preferred way of life, even for their own good, because doing so will reduce the sum of human happiness, at least in the long run; better that people choose for themselves, even if, on occasion, they get it wrong. "The only freedom which deserves the name," writes Mill in *On Liberty*, "is that of pursuing our own good in our own way, so long as we do not attempt to deprive others of theirs, or impede their efforts to obtain it." He adds that his argument does not depend on any notion of abstract right, only on the principle of the greatest good for the greatest number. "I regard utility as the ultimate appeal on all ethical questions; but it must be utility in the largest sense, grounded on the permanent interests of man as a progressive being."

Many objections have been raised against utilitarianism as a general doctrine of moral philosophy. Some have questioned the concept of utility, and the assumption that all human goods are in principle commensurable. Others have objected that by reducing all values to preferences and desires, utilitarians are unable to admit qualitative distinctions of worth, unable to distinguish noble desires from base ones. But most recent debate has focused on whether utilitarianism offers a convincing basis for liberal principles, including respect for individual rights.

In one respect, utilitarianism would seem well suited to liberal purposes. Seeking to maximize overall happiness does not require judging people's values, only aggregating them. And the willingness to aggregate preferences without judging them suggests a tolerant spirit, even a democratic one. When people go to the polls we count their votes, whatever they are.

But the utilitarian calculus is not always as liberal as it first appears. If enough cheering Romans pack the Coliseum to watch the lion devour the Christian, the collective pleasure of the Romans will surely outweigh the pain of the Christian, intense though it be. Or if a big majority abhors a small religion and wants it banned, the balance of preferences will favor suppression, not toleration. Utilitarians sometimes defend individual rights on the grounds that respecting them now will serve utility in the long run. But this calculation is precarious and contingent. It hardly secures the liberal promise not to impose on some the values of others. As the majority will is an inadequate instrument of liberal politics – by itself it fails to secure individual rights – so the utilitarian philosophy is an inadequate foundation for liberal principles.

The case against utilitarianism was made most powerfully by Immanuel Kant. He argued that empirical principles, such as utility, were unfit to serve as basis for the moral law. A wholly instrumental defense of freedom and rights not only leaves rights vulnerable, but fails to respect the inherent dignity of persons. The utilitarian calculus treats people as means to the happiness of others, not as ends in themselves, worthy of respect.

Contemporary liberals extend Kant's argument with the claim that utilitarianism fails to take seriously the distinction between persons. In seeking above all to maximize the general welfare, the utilitarian treats society as a whole as if it were a single person; it conflates our many, diverse desires into a single system of desires. It is indifferent to the distribution of satisfactions among persons, except insofar as this may affect the overall sum. But this fails to respect our plurality and distinctness. It uses some as means to the happiness of all, and so fails to respect each as an end in himself.

In the view of modern-day Kantians, certain rights are so fundamental that even the general welfare cannot override them. As John Rawls writes in his important work, *A Theory of Justice*, "Each person possesses an inviolability founded on justice that even the welfare of society as a whole cannot override. . . . The rights secured by justice are not subject to political bargaining or to the calculus of social interests."

So Kantian liberals need an account of rights that does not depend on utilitarian considerations. More than this, they need an account that does not depend on any particular conception of the good, that does not presuppose the superiority of one way of life over others. Only a justification neutral about ends could preserve the liberal resolve not to favor any particular ends, or to impose on its citizens a preferred way of life. But what sort of justification could this be? How is it possible to affirm certain liberties and rights as fundamental without embracing some vision of the good life, without endorsing some ends over others? It would seem we are back to the relativist predicament – to affirm liberal principles without embracing any particular ends.

The solution proposed by Kantian liberals is to draw a distinction between the "right" and the "good" – between a framework of basic rights and liberties, and the conceptions of the good that people may choose to pursue within the framework. It is one thing for the state to support a fair framework, they argue, something else to affirm some particular ends. For example, it is one thing to defend the right to free speech so that people may be free to form their own opinions and choose their own ends, but something else to support it on the grounds that a life of political discussion is inherently worthier than a life unconcerned with public affairs, or on the grounds that free speech will increase the general welfare. Only the first defense is available in the Kantian view, resting as it does on the ideal of a neutral framework.

Now, the commitment to a framework neutral with respect to ends can be seen as a kind of value – in this sense the Kantian liberal is no relativist – but its value consists precisely in its refusal to affirm a preferred way of life or conception of the good. For Kantian liberals, then, the right is prior to the good, and in two senses. First, individual rights cannot be sacrificed for the sake of the general good; and second, the principles of justice that specify these rights cannot be premised on any particular vision of the good life. What justifies the rights is not that they maximize the general welfare or otherwise promote the good, but rather that they comprise a fair framework within which individuals and groups can choose their own values and ends, consistent with a similar liberty for others.

Of course, proponents of the rights-based ethic notoriously disagree about what rights are fundamental, and about what political arrangements the ideal of the neutral framework requires. Egalitarian liberals support the welfare state, and favor a scheme of civil liberties together with certain social and economic rights – rights to welfare, education, health care, and so on. Libertarian liberals defend the market economy, and claim that redistributive policies violate peoples' rights; they favor a scheme of civil liberties combined with a strict regime of private property rights. But whether egalitarian or libertarian, rights-based liberalism begins with the claim that we are separate, individual persons, each with our own aims, interests, and conceptions of the good; it seeks a framework of rights that will enable us to realize our capacity as free moral agents, consistent with a similar liberty for others.

Within academic philosophy, the last decade or so has seen the ascendance of the rights-based ethic over the utilitarian one, due in large part to the influence of Rawls's *A Theory of Justice*. The legal philosopher H. L. A. Hart recently described the shift from "the old faith that some form of utilitarianism must capture the essence of political morality" to the new faith that "the truth must lie with a doctrine of basic human rights, protecting specific basic liberties and interests of individuals. . . . Whereas not so long ago great energy and much ingenuity of many philosophers were devoted to making some form of utilitarianism work, latterly such energies and ingenuity have been devoted to the articulation of theories of basic rights."

But in philosophy as in life, the new faith becomes the old orthodoxy before long. Even as it has come to prevail over its utilitarian rival, the rights-based ethic has recently faced a growing challenge from a different direction, from a view that gives fuller expression to the claims of citizenship and community than the liberal vision allows. The communitarian critics, unlike modern liberals, make the case for a politics of the common good. Recalling the arguments of Hegel against Kant, they question the liberal claim for the priority of the right over the good, and the picture of the freely choosing individual it embodies. Following Aristotle, they argue that we cannot justify political arrangements without reference to common purposes and ends, and that we cannot conceive of ourselves without reference to our role as citizens, as participants in a common life.

This debate reflects two contrasting pictures of the self. The rights-based ethic, and the conception of the person it embodies, were shaped in large part in the encounter with utilitarianism. Where utilitarians conflate our many desires into a single system of desire, Kantians insist on the separateness of persons. Where the utilitarian self is simply defined as the sum of its desires, the Kantian self is a choosing self, independent of the desires and ends it may have at any moment. As Rawls writes, "The self is prior to the ends which are affirmed by it; even a dominant end must be chosen from among numerous possibilities."

The priority of the self over its ends means I am never defined by my aims and attachments, but always capable of standing back to survey and assess and possibly to revise them. This is what it means to be a free and independent self, capable of choice. And this is the vision of the self that finds expression in the ideal of the state as a neutral framework. On the rights-based ethic, it is precisely because we are essentially separate, independent selves that we need a neutral framework, a framework of rights that refuses to choose among competing purposes and ends. If the self is prior to its ends, then the right must be prior to the good.

Communitarian critics of rights-based liberalism say we cannot conceive ourselves as independent in this way, as bearers of selves wholly detached from our aims and attachments. They say that certain of our roles are partly constitutive of the persons we are – as citizens of a country, or members of a movement, or partisans of a cause. But if we are partly defined by the communities we inhabit, then we must also be implicated in the purposes and ends characteristic of those communities. As Alasdair MacIntyre writes in his book, *After Virtue*, "What is good for me has to be the good for one who inhabits these roles." Open-ended though it be, the story of my life is always embedded in the story of those communities from which I derive my identity – whether family or city, tribe or nation, party or cause. In the communitarian view, these stories make a moral difference, not only a psychological one. They situate us in the world and give our lives their moral particularity.

What is at stake for politics in the debate between unencumbered selves and situated ones? What are the practical differences between a politics of rights and a politics of the common good? On some issues, the two theories may produce different arguments for similar policies. For example, the civil rights movement of the 1960s might be justified by liberals in the name of human dignity and respect for persons, and by communitarians in the name of recognizing the full membership of fellow citizens wrongly excluded from the common life of the nation. And where liberals might support public education in hopes of equipping students to become autonomous individuals, capable of choosing their own ends and pursuing them effectively, communitarians might support public education in hopes of equipping students to become good citizens, capable of contributing meaningfully to public deliberations and pursuits.

On other issues, the two ethics might lead to different policies. Communitarians would be more likely than liberals to allow a town to ban pornographic bookstores, on the grounds that pornography offends its way of life and the values that sustain it. But a politics of civic virtue does not always part company with liberalism in favor of conservative policies. For example, communitarians would be more willing than some rights-oriented liberals to see states enact laws regulating plant closings, to protect their communities from the disruptive effects of capital mobility and sudden industrial change. More generally, where the liberal regards the expansion of individual rights and entitlements as unqualified moral and political progress, the communitarian is troubled by the tendency of liberal programs to displace politics from smaller forms of association to more comprehensive ones. Where libertarian liberals defend the private economy and egalitarian liberals defend the welfare state, communitarians worry about the concentration of power in both the corporate economy and the bureaucratic state, and the erosion of those intermediate forms of community that have at times sustained a more vital public life.

Liberals often argue that a politics of the common good, drawing as it must on particular loyalties, obligations, and traditions, opens the way to prejudice and intolerance. The modern nation-state is not the Athenian polis, they point out; the scale and diversity of modern life have rendered the Aristotelian political ethic nostalgic at best and dangerous at worst. Any attempt to govern by a vision of the good is likely to lead to a slippery slope of totalitarian temptations.

Communitarians reply, rightly in my view, that intolerance flourishes most where forms of life are dislocated, roots unsettled, traditions undone. In our day, the totalitarian impulse has sprung less from the convictions of confidently situated selves than from the confusions of atomized, dislocated, frustrated selves, at sea in a world where common meanings have lost their force. As Hannah Arendt has written, "What makes mass society so difficult to bear is not the number of people involved, or at least not primarily, but the fact that the world between them has lost its power to gather them together, to relate and to separate them." Insofar as our public life has withered, our sense of common involvement diminished, we lie vulnerable to the mass politics of totalitarian solutions. So responds the party of the common good to the party of rights. If the party of the common good is right, our most pressing moral and political project is to revitalize those civic republican possibilities implicit in our tradition but fading in our time.

Iris Marion Young, "Impartiality and the Civic Public" (selections)

[...] I urge proponents of contemporary emancipatory politics to break with modernism rather than recover suppressed possibilities of modern political ideals. Whether we consider ourselves continuous or discontinuous with modern political theory and practice, of course, can only be a choice, more or less reasonable given certain presumptions and interests. Since political theory and practice from the eighteenth to the twentieth centuries is hardly a unity, making even the phrase "modern political theory" problematic, contemporary political theory and practice both continues and breaks with aspects of the political past of the West. From the point of view of a feminist interest, nevertheless, emancipatory politics entails a rejection of modern traditions of moral and political life. [...]

After two centuries of faith that the ideal of equality and fraternity included women has still not brought emancipation for women, contemporary feminists have begun to question the faith itself. Recent feminist analyses of modern political theory and practice increasingly argue that ideals of liberalism and contract theory,

From *Feminism as Critique*, ed. Seyla Benhabib and Drucilla Cornell (Minneapolis: University of Minnesota Press, 1987), pp. 58, 60–7, 74–5.

such as formal equality and universal rationality, are deeply marred by masculine biases about what it means to be human and the nature of society. If modern culture in the West has been thoroughly male dominated, these analyses suggest, then there is little hope of laundering some of its ideals to make it possible to include women. [. . .]

The Opposition Between Reason and Affectivity

Modern ethics defines impartiality as the hallmark of moral reason. As a characteristic of reason, impartiality means something different from the pragmatic attitude of being fair, considering other people's needs and desires as well as one's own. Impartiality names a point of view of reason that stands apart from any interests and desires. Not to be partial means being able to see the whole, how all the particular perspectives and interests in a given moral situation relate to one another in a way that, because of its partiality, each perspective cannot see itself. The impartial moral reasoner thus stands outside of and above the situation about which he or she reasons, with no stake in it, or is supposed to adopt an attitude toward a situation as though he or she were outside and above it. For contemporary philosophy, calling into question the ideal of impartiality amounts to questioning the possibility of moral theory itself. I will argue, however, that the ideal of normative reason as standing at a point transcending all perspectives is both illusory and oppressive. [. . .]

The ideal of an impartial normative reason continues to be asserted by philosophers as "the moral point of view." From the ideal observer to the original position to a spaceship on another planet, moral and political philosophers begin reasoning from a point of view they claim as impartial. This point of view is usually a counterfactual construct, a situation of reasoning that removes people from their actual contexts of living moral decisions, to a situation in which they could not exist. As Michael Sandel argues, the ideal of impartiality requires constructing the ideal of a self abstracted from the context of any real persons: the deontological self is not committed to any particular ends, has no particular history, is a member of no communities, has no body. [. . .]

Normative reason's requirement of impartiality entails a requirement of universality. The impartial reasoner treats all situations according to the same rules, and the more rules can be reduced to the unity of one rule or principle, the more this impartiality and universality will be guaranteed. For Kantian morality, to test the rightness of a judgement the impartial reasoner need not look outside thought, but only seek the consistency and universalizability of a maxim. If reason knows the moral rules that apply universally to action and choice, then there will be no reason for one's feelings, interests, or inclinations to enter in the making of moral judgements. This deontological reason cannot eliminate the specificity and variability of concrete situations to which the rules must be applied; by insisting on the impartiality and universality of moral reason, however, it renders itself unable rationally to understand and evaluate particular moral contexts in their particularity.

The ideal of an impartial moral reason also seeks to eliminate otherness in the form of differentiated moral subject. Impartial reason must judge from a point of view outside of the particular perspectives of persons involved in interaction, able to totalize these perspectives into a whole, or general will. This is the point of view of a solitary transcendent God. The impartial subject need acknowledge no other subjects whose perspective should be taken into account and with whom discussion might occur. Thus the claim to be impartial often results in authoritarianism. By asserting oneself as impartial, one claims authority to decide an issue, in place of those whose interests and desires are manifest. From this impartial point of view one need not consult with any other, because the impartial point of view already takes into account all possible perspectives.

In modern moral discourse, being impartial means especially being dispassionate: being entirely unaffected by feelings in one's judgement. The idea of impartiality thus seeks to eliminate alterity in a different sense, in the sense of the sensuous, desiring and emotional experiences that tie me to the concreteness of things, which I apprehend in their particular relation to me. Why does the idea of impartiality require the separation of moral reason from desire, affectivity and a bodily sensuous relation with things, people and situations? Because only by expelling desire, affectivity and the body from reason can impartiality achieve its unity.

The logic of identity typically generates dichotomy instead of unity. The move to bring particulars under a universal category creates a distinction between inside and outside. Since each particular entity or situation has both similiarities with and differences from other particular entities and situations, and they are neither completely identical or absolutely other, the urge to bring them into unity under a category or principle necessarily entails expelling some of the properties of the entities or situations. Because the totalizing movement always leaves a remainder, the project of reducing particulars to a unity must fail. Not satisfied then to admit defeat in the face of difference, the logic of identity shoves difference into dichotomous normative oppositions: essence–accident, good–bad, normal–deviant. The dichotomies are not symmetrical, however, but stand in a hierarchy; the first term designates the positive unity on the inside, the second less-valued term designates the leftover outside.

For deontological reason, the movement of expulsion that generates dichotomy happens this way. As I have already discussed, the construct of an impartial point of view is arrived at by abstracting from the concrete particularity of the person in situation. This requires abstracting from the particularity of bodily being, its needs and inclinations, and from the feelings that attach to the experienced particularity of things and events. Normative reason is defined as impartial, and reason defines the unity of the moral subject, both in the sense of knowing the universal principles of morality and in the sense of what all moral subjects have in common in the same way. This reason thus stands opposed to desire and affectivity as what differentiates and particularizes persons. In the next section I will discuss a similar movement of the expulsion of persons from the civic public in order to maintain its unity.

Several problems follow from the expulsion of desire and feeling from moral reason. Because all feeling, inclinations, needs, desires become thereby equally irrational, they are all equally inferior. By contrast, premodern moral philosophy sought standards for distinguishing among good and bad interests, noble and base sentiments. The point of ethics in Aristotle, for example, was precisely to distinguish good desires from bad, and to cultivate good desires. Contemporary moral intuitions, moreover, still distinguish good and bad feelings, rational and irrational desires. As Lawrence Blum argues, deontological reason's opposition of moral duty to feeling fails to recognize the role of sentiments of sympathy, compassion and concern in providing reasons for and motivating moral action. Our experience of moral life teaches us, moreover, that without the impulse of deprivation or anger, for example, many moral choices would not be made.

Thus as a consequence of the opposition between reason and desire, moral decisions grounded in considerations of sympathy, caring and an assessment of differentiated need are defined as not rational, not "objective," merely sentimental. To the degree that women exemplify or are identified with such styles of moral decision-making, then, women are excluded from moral rationality. The moral rationality of any other groups whose experience or stereotypes associate them with desire, need and affectivity, moreover, is suspect.

By simply expelling desire, affectivity and need, finally deontological reason represses them, and sets morality in opposition to happiness. The function of duty is to master inner nature, not to form it in the best directions. Since all desiring is equally suspect, we have no way of distinguishing which desires are good and which bad, which will expand the person's capacities and relations with others, and which stunt the person and foster violence. In being excluded from understanding, all desiring, feeling and needs become unconscious, but certainly do not thereby cease to motivate action and behavior. Reason's task thereby is to control and censure desire.

The Unity of the Civic Public

The dichotomy between reason and desire appears in modern political theory in the distinction between the universal, public realm of sovereignty and the state, on the one hand, and the particular private realm of needs and desires, on the other. Modern normative political theory and political practice aim to embody impartiality in the public realm of the state. Like the impartiality of moral reason this public realm of the state attains its generality by the exclusion of particularity, desire, feeling and those aspects of life associated with the body. In modern political theory and practice this public achieves a unity in particular by the exclusion of women and others associated with nature and the body. [. . .]

Rousseau's political philosophy is the paradigm of this ideal of the civic public. He develops his conception of politics precisely in reaction to his experience of the urban public of the eighteenth century, as well as in reaction to the premises and conclusions of the atomistic and individualist theory of the state expressed by Hobbes. The civic public expresses the universal and impartial point of view of reason, standing opposed to and expelling desire, sentiment and the particularity of needs and interests. From the premises of individual desire and want we cannot arrive at a strong enough normative conception of social relations. The difference between atomistic egoism and civil society does not consist simply in the fact that the infinity of individual appetite has been curbed by laws enforced by threat of punishment. Rather, reason brings people together to recognize common interests and a general will.

The sovereign people embodies the universal point of view of the collective interest and equal citizenship. In the pursuit of their individual interests people have a particularist orientation. Normative reason reveals an impartial point of view, however, that all rational persons can adopt, which expresses a general will not reducible to an aggregate of particular interests. Participation in the general will as a citizen is an expression of human nobility and genuine freedom. Such rational commitment to collectivity is not compatible with personal satisfaction, however, and for Rousseau this is the tragedy of the human condition.

Rousseau conceived that this public realm ought to be unified and homogeneous, and indeed suggested methods of fostering among citizens commitment to such unity through civic celebrations. While the purity, unity and generality of this public realm require transcending and repressing the partiality and differentiation of need, desire and affectivity, Rousseau hardly believed that human life can or should be without emotion and the satisfaction of need and desire. Man's particular nature as a feeling, needful being is enacted in the private realm of domestic life, over which women are the proper moral guardians.

Hegel's political philosophy developed this conception of the public realm of the state as expressing impartiality and universality as against the partiality and substance of desire. For Hegel the liberal account of social relations as based on the liberty of self-defining individuals to pursue their own ends properly describes only one aspect of social life, the sphere of civil society. As a member of civil society, the person pursues private ends for himself and his family. These ends may conflict with those of others, but exchange transactions produce much harmony and satisfaction. Conceived as a member of the state, on the other hand, the person is not a locus of particular desire, but the bearer of universally articulated rights and responsibilities. The point of view of the state and law transcends all particular interests, to express the universal and rational spirit of humanity. State laws and action express the general will, the interests of the whole society. Since maintaining this universal point of view while engaged in the pursuit of one's own particular interests is difficult if not impossible, a class of persons is necessary whose sole job is to maintain the public good and the universal point of view of the state. For Hegel, these government officials are the universal class. [. . .]

I think that recent feminist analyses of the dichotomy of public and private in modern political theory imply that the ideal of the civic public as impartial and universal is itself suspect. Modern political theorists and politicians proclaimed the impartiality and generality of the public and at the same time quite consciously found it fitting that some persons, namely women, nonwhites and sometimes those without property, be excluded from participation in that public. If this was not just a mistake, it suggests that the ideal of the civic public as expressing the general interest, the impartial point of view of reason, itself results in exclusion. By assuming that reason stands opposed to desire, affectivity and the body, the civic public must exclude bodily and affective aspects of human existence. In practice this assumption forces a homogeneity of citizens upon the civic public. It excludes from the public those individuals and groups that do not fit the model of the rational citizen who can transcend body and sentiment. This exclusion is based on two tendencies that feminists stress: the opposition between reason and desire, and the association of these traits with kinds of persons.

In the social scheme expressed by Rousseau and Hegel, women must be excluded from the public realm of citizenship because they are the caretakers of affectivity, desire and the body. Allowing appeals to desires and bodily needs to move public debates would undermine public deliberation by fragmenting its unity. Even within the domestic realm, moreover, women must be dominated. Their dangerous, heterogeneous sexuality must be kept chaste and confined to marriage. Enforcing chastity on women will keep each family a separated unity, preventing the chaos and blood-mingling that would be produced by illegitimate children. These chaste, enclosed women can then be the proper caretakers of men's desire, by tempering its potentially disruptive impulses through moral education. Men's desire for women itself threatens to shatter and disperse the universal rational realm of the public, as well as to disrupt the neat distinction between the public and private. As guardians of the private realm of need, desire and affectivity, women must ensure that men's impulses do not remove them from the universality of reason. The moral neatness of the female-tended hearth, moreover, will temper the possessively individualistic impulses of the particularistic realm of business and commerce, which like sexuality constantly threatens to explode the unity of society under the umbrella of universal reason.

The bourgeois world instituted a moral division of labor between reason and sentiment, identifying masculinity with reason and femininity with sentiment and desire. As Linda Nicholson has argued, the modern sphere of family and personal life is as much a modern creation as the modern realm of state and law, and as part of the same process. The impartiality and rationality of the state depend on containing need and desire in the private realm of the family. While the realm of personal life and sentiment has been thoroughly devalued because it has been excluded from rationality, it has nevertheless been the focus of increasingly expanded commitment. Modernity developed a concept of "inner nature" that needs nurturance, and within which is to be found the authenticity and individuality of the self, rather than in the conformity, regularity and universality of the public.

The civic public excludes sentiment and desire, then, partly in order to protect their "natural" character.

Not only in Europe, but in the early decades of the US as well, the white male bourgeoisie conceived republican virtue as rational, restrained and chaste, not yielding to passion, desire for luxury. The designers of the American Constitution specifically restricted the access of the laboring class to this rational public, because they feared disruption of commitment to the general interests. Some, like Jefferson, even feared developing an urban proletariat. These early American republicans were also quite explicit about the need for the homogeneity of citizens, which from the earliest days in the republic involved the relationship of the white republicans to the Black and Native American people. These republican fathers, such as Jefferson, identified the Red and Black people in their territories with wild nature and passion, just as they feared that women outside the domestic realm were wanton and avaricious. They defined moral, civilized republican life in opposition to this backward-looking uncultivated desire they identified with women and nonwhites.

To summarize, the ideal of normative reason, moral sense, stands opposed to desire and affectivity. Impartial civilized reason characterizes the virtue of the republican man who rises above passion and desire. Instead of cutting bourgeois man entirely off from the body and affectivity, however, this culture of the rational public confines them to the domestic sphere which also confines women's passions and provides emotional solace to men and children. Indeed, within this domestic realm sentiments can flower, and each individual can recognize and affirm his particularity. Because virtues of impartiality and universality define the public realm, it precisely ought not to attend to our particularity. Modern normative reason and its political expression in the idea of the civic public, then, has unity and coherence by its expulsion and confinement of everything that would threaten to invade the polity with differentiation: the specificity of women's bodies and desire, the difference of race and culture, the variability of heterogeneity of the needs, the goals and desires of each individual, the ambiguity and changeability of feeling. [. . .]

Toward a Heterogeneous Public Life

[. . .] The feminist slogan "the personal is political" does not deny a distinction between public and private, but it does deny a social division between public and private spheres, with different kinds of institutions, activities and human attributes. Two principles follow from this slogan: (a) no social institutions or practices should be excluded a priori as being the proper subject for public discussion and expression; and (b) no persons, actions or aspects of a person's life should be forced into privacy.

1   The contemporary Women's Movement has made public issues out of many practices claimed too trivial or private for public discussion: the meaning of pronouns, domestic violence against women, the practice of men's opening doors for

women, the sexual assault on women and children, the sexual division of house-work and so on. Radical politics in contemporary life consists of taking many actions and activities deemed properly private, such as how individuals and enter-prises invest their money, and making public issues out of them.

2   The second principle says that no person or aspects of persons should be forced into privacy. The modern conception of the public, I have argued, creates a conception of citizenship which excludes from public attention most particular aspects of a person. Public life is supposed to be "blind" to sex, race, age and so on, and all are supposed to enter the public and its discussion on identical terms. Such a conception of a public has resulted in the exclusion of persons and aspects of persons from public life.

Ours is still a society that forces persons or aspects of persons into privacy. Repression of homosexuality is perhaps the most striking example. In the US today most people seem to hold the liberal view that persons have a right to be gay as long as they remain private about their activities. Calling attention in public to the fact that one is gay, making public displays of gay affection, or even publicly asserting needs and rights for gay people, provoke ridicule and fear in many people. Making a public issue out of heterosexuality, moreover, by suggesting that the dominance of heterosexual assumptions is one-dimensional and oppressive, can rarely get a public hearing even among feminists and radicals. In general, contem-porary politics grants to all persons entrance into the public on condition that they do not claim special rights or needs, or call attention to their particular history or culture, and that they keep their passions private.

8

Distributive Justice

N. Scott Arnold, "Marx and the Problem of Justice"

Karl Marx. The Granger Collection.

N. SCOTT ARNOLD

Marx and the Problem of Justice

In communist society . . . all the springs of co-operative wealth flow more abundantly — only then can the narrow horizon of bourgeois right be crossed in its entirety and society inscribe on its banner: From each according to his ability, to each according to his needs!
Karl Marx, *Critique of the Gotha Program*

Social philosophers since the time of the ancient Greeks have speculated about what an ideal society might look like. Among the ancients, perhaps the most famous of these are Plato's speculations in the *Republic*. The ideal society he describes is one of harmony and perfect justice. Each individual plays the role in that society which best accords with his or her nature. Other philosophers have had different visions of the good society. A common theme in the writings of many of these authors is that the existing order is not in harmony with human nature or with what God intended and that their vision of the good society is. As in the case of Plato, often this vision is articulated in terms of justice. For example, many nineteenth-century social critics had a vision of the good society in which wealth and income were relatively equally distributed. These egalitarian theories of justice were a reaction to the large inequalities of wealth and income that resulted from the rise of capitalism and the Industrial Revolution.

Contemporary social and political philosophers also possess visions of the good society, which are also defined in terms of justice. John Rawls, perhaps the pre-eminent twentieth-century Anglo-American political philosopher, conceives of his theory of justice as laying down conditions that just social institutions, specifically, a political system and an economic system, must meet. And while Rawls recognizes that there is more to the good society than justice, he nevertheless says: "justice is the first virtue of social institutions . . . laws and institutions, no matter how efficient and well-arranged, must be reformed or abolished if they are unjust" (Rawls 1971: 3). In *Anarchy, State, and Utopia* (1974), the libertarian political philosopher Robert Nozick conceives of just social institutions as providing a framework within which individuals and groups can construct their own utopias.

A common theme, then, in the history of social and political philosophy is a vision of the good society that is animated by the philosopher's views about what justice requires. Political philosophers often conceive of their main task as discovering what justice requires; the subsequent hope is that those in a position to change social institutions will heed the prescriptions of the philosopher or his disciples. It is somewhat surprising, however, to find that Karl Marx, perhaps the most famous and influential social philosopher of the last two hundred years, did not take this approach. Indeed, he explicitly repudiated the idea that the task of the social philosopher and critic is to show why the existing order is unjust and to articulate an ideal that people should try to realize. This chapter seeks to explain Marx's radical critique of the existing order – what he called "capitalist society" – and to explain why he refused to base that critique on the charge that capitalist society is unjust.

1 Karl Marx: Life and Times

Karl Marx was born in 1818 in the German city of Trier. His father was a successful lawyer who expected his son to follow in his footsteps. Marx was sent to the University of Bonn in 1835 to begin his legal studies but found that he had no real interest in the law. The following year, he transferred to the University of Berlin where he took up the study of philosophy. The dominant intellectual figure in Germany at the time was G. W. F. Hegel (1770–1831), and in his studies in philosophy, Marx fell under the influence of a group of Hegel's followers known as the Young Hegelians. Because they were political and cultural radicals, the Young Hegelians were regarded with suspicion by the new king of Prussia, Friedrich Wilhelm IV, who ascended to the throne in 1840. Subsequently, some of the Young Hegelians were dismissed from their academic positions, and the academic careers of many of their students (including Marx) were thwarted. Unable to find a university post, Marx became a writer and then an editor for a succession of radical newspapers. A rising tide of censorship forced him out of journalism for a time and out of Germany as well. In 1843 he married his fiancée, Jenny Westphalen, and they moved to Paris where Marx became acquainted with the leading intellectuals of mid-nineteenth-century Europe. It was here that he met his lifelong collaborator, Friedrich Engels.

Engels was the son of a wealthy manufacturer who owned factories in both Germany and England. Essentially self-taught, Engels had acquired a broad education in the humanities. He also received an on-the-job education in business management from his father and worked intermittently in the family business for most of his adult life. However, he maintained his intellectual interests and wrote extensively on a wide range of subjects. To the modern reader, his prose is generally clearer and more readable than the writings of his more famous collaborator.

In 1845, political intrigue on the part of the Prussian government got Marx expelled from Paris. He went to Brussels where he became affiliated with a workingman's association that was later to become known as the Communist Party (not to be confused with the Bolsheviks, the forerunners of twentieth-century communist parties). Marx and Engels got themselves assigned the task of writing for this workingman's association a statement of purpose and principles, which they called *The Communist Manifesto*. It turned out to be perhaps the most famous and influential political document of the nineteenth century. It was published in London in 1848 on the eve of the series of revolutions that swept Europe that year.

Marx was expelled from Brussels and returned to Cologne, Germany, which had set up a democratic government in the revolution of 1848. He again became a newspaper editor, but after a short time, both democracy and his newspaper were suppressed, and Marx was put on trial for treason. Although he was acquitted, Marx once again had to leave Germany, this time for London where he spent nearly all of the rest of his life.

It is a remarkable fact about Marx that at no time in his life did he have a regular job for any length of time. His journalism career in Germany was brief and intermittent; he did some freelance work after that, including writing a column for the *New York Tribune* as "their man in Europe," but he never consistently earned enough to support himself and his family. He sponged off friends and relatives and squandered a small inheritance. From 1850 to 1870 his family lived on the verge of utter destitution. Finally, in 1870 Engels managed to create an annuity for the Marxes from his personal wealth. This sustained the Marxes for the rest of their lives. Three of their six children died young, and Marx himself suffered from a variety of chronic illnesses. His wife Jenny died in 1882, and Karl died fifteen months later.

By most accounts, Karl Marx was not a pleasant man. Ungracious and ungrateful, he was given to outbursts of anger against friends and was inclined to demonize his opponents. His writings are filled with invective and sarcasm, especially against former allies. It is fair to say that Marx never respectfully disagreed with any of his opponents and never took seriously the ideas of anyone with whom he differed.

Marx's written work is voluminous even by the standards of nineteenth-century German intellectuals, who are notorious for their long-windedness. The collected works of Marx and Engels (most of it written by Marx) run to over 50 volumes. Volume 1 of Marx's *magnum opus, Das Kapital (Capital)*, was first published in 1867. Volumes 2 and 3 of *Capital* had not been completed at the time of Marx's death, so Engels and a collaborator, Karl Kautsky, finished writing and editing these two volumes. *Capital* sets forth Marx's economic theory and his analysis of the capitalist economic system. Important preliminary works written in the 1850s include the posthumously published *Foundations of the Critique of Political Economy* (sometimes referred to as the *Grundrisse*) and *A Contribution to the Critique of Political Economy*. (Full bibliographical information for all works mentioned here is given at the end of this essay.) The Preface to the *Contribution* contains a concise statement of Marx's theory of history, arguably his most important intellectual contribution. A more elaborate statement of it can be found in Book I of *The German Ideology*, which was written in 1845–6 but was not published until 1932. Perhaps Marx's most famous work, co-authored with Engels, is *The Communist Manifesto* (1848). Another important early work is the *Economic and Philosophic Manuscripts*. These manuscripts were written in 1844 but were not published until 1930. They contain a discussion of Marx's conception of human nature and related topics. The influence of Hegel on this work is obvious in both substance and style. Perhaps Marx's most important later work (not counting *Capital*) is the *Critique of the Gotha Program* (1875); this contains the only sustained discussion in all of his writings of his predictions about the nature of post-capitalist society as he believed it would develop.

2   Marx as Radical Critic

In the twentieth century, Karl Marx is perhaps best known as the intellectual forefather of communism. Among nineteenth-century Europeans, he was known as a revolutionary and radical critic of emerging industrial society, which he referred to as capitalism. Although he and Engels authored a number of popular works such as *The Communist Manifesto*, his major works are obscure and often difficult treatises on history, economics, and philosophy. In his mature years, Marx conceived of himself primarily as a social scientist whose main task was to understand the workings of what he called "class societies" in general and capitalist society in particular. His theory of history (usually referred to as Historical Materialism) is really an all-encompassing theory of social development and social change – a sociological theory in today's terminology. Although it has its roots in Hegel's *The Philosophy of History*, this theory represents a fundamentally new approach to the study of human societies and social change. Its influence on social science is comparable to the influence of Darwin's *Origin of Species* on biological science. Among intellectuals in the past three centuries, his influence on the actual course of history is rivaled only by some of the American Founding Fathers (notably, Jefferson and Madison) in the eighteenth century, and in the twentieth century by V. I. Lenin.

Marx's economic theory is an attempt to understand the workings of the capitalist economic system. A capitalist economic system, as Marx understood the term, is any system in which the workers do not own the farms and factories (the means of production, in his terminology) and work for a wage. These individuals are collectively referred to as the proletariat. On the other hand, those who do own the means of production do not derive most of their income from their labor; instead, they get it in the form of profits from the farms and businesses they own. These individuals are called the capitalists or the bourgeoisie. While it is true that some workers own some means of production (e.g. their tools) and some bourgeoisie do work (say, as managers), the main source of income for each group lies with their labor and their capital, respectively.

The capitalist economic system has not always existed. In the Middle Ages, those who worked the land (the serfs) had perpetual obligations to the lord of the manor. Unlike the wage laborer who, at least in principle, can quit at any time, serfs were not free to leave the feudal manor if they so chose. In the late Middle Ages this feudal system began to crumble, and the capitalist system arose to take its place. The rise of capitalism begins around the time of the Renaissance, and it passes out of its infancy around the end of the eighteenth century. The end of the eighteenth century also witnessed the birth of classical economics, the first systematic attempts to understand the capitalist economic system. Classical economics began with the writings of Adam Smith in the late eighteenth century (*The Wealth of Nations* was published in 1776) and ended with the marginalist revolution in economic thought in the late nineteenth century. Marx was very much a part of this intellectual tradition. Though his contributions to economics were perhaps not as pathbreaking as his contributions to sociology, Marx is none the less an important figure in the history of classical economics. He is also widely believed to be a prophet of socialism or communism, but in point of fact he had little to say about what society would be like in the future. He did predict that capitalism would self-destruct, and he explained in general terms how this would happen. But he constructed no detailed blueprints of the new society that he urged his followers to implement. We shall return to Marx's vision of post-capitalist society, such as it was, later in this essay.

Although the mature Marx conceived of himself as a social scientist, this does not mean that he was a dispassionate observer of contemporary society. In point of fact, he conceived of his social scientific writings as providing weapons to be used in a revolutionary struggle to overthrow capitalist society. Moreover, Marx himself was an activist (mostly unsuccessful) in various left-wing organizations through-out his life. Indeed, a guiding idea in Marxist philosophy is the unity of theory and practice as expressed in the famous eleventh of his *Theses on Feuerbach*: "The philosophers have only *interpreted* the world in various ways; the point, however, is to *change* it" (GI, 617).[1]

What unifies theory and practice for Marx is his conviction that something is deeply and irremediably wrong with capitalist society and that fundamental social change is both desirable and possible. To understand this conviction, it is useful to distinguish radical social criticism from moderate social criticism. The moderate critic believes that the social system in which she finds herself is fundamentally sound and/or that her society is basically a good society. Of course, any society falls

---

[1] References to Marx's writings will be given in the text according to the forms given in the Reference section at the end of this essay. For example, this quotation is from page 617 of *The German Ideology*.

short of its ideals, but moderate critics believe that a society can approach more closely its ideals by modifying existing institutions, such as its political or economic system. The promulgation of certain regulations, the creation of a new government agency, the passage of laws to correct various abuses of the system – these are the kinds of changes favored by moderate critics. By contrast, radical critics believe that the problems with existing social institutions are more fundamental. They believe that these problems are rooted in the very structure of social institutions in such a way that attempts to solve them without fundamental institutional change will not succeed. So, for example, nineteenth-century moderate critics of capitalism thought that the poverty and squalor associated with the rise of industrial (i.e. capitalist) society could be alleviated and ameliorated through various reforms (such as those sought by the trade union movement) and by the inauguration of government insurance and welfare programs. Radical critics such as Marx dismissed such ideas. For them, nothing short of a revolutionary change would do. This meant replacing, and not merely fixing, existing institutions. Marx thought that this change was coming to capitalist society, though not because capitalism was objectionable. According to Marx's Historical Materialism, deeper and more powerful social forces were at work – forces that would lead to capitalism's self-destruction. The end of capitalism and the inauguration of a new order, variously called socialism or communism, were coming, Marx believed, and he thought it would be a good thing – but it was not coming *because* he, or anyone else, thought it was a good thing.

Although Marx believed that the institutions of capitalist society were fundamentally flawed, nowhere in his writings does one find a comprehensive discussion of what is wrong with capitalist society. What he had to say on this topic is scattered throughout his writings and is not the subject of any one work. He had even less to say about an alternative to the existing order. Part of the explanation for this is that he was convinced that other social critics of his day spent far too much of their time and energy giving vent to their moral outrage against capitalism and issuing grandiose pronouncements about how a new society should be organized. Marx believed that it would be a better use of his intellectual talents and energies to try to understand the workings of the political and economic system in which he lived and to understand the transformative forces that were at work under the surface of contemporary society. A medical analogy can be used to illuminate Marx's attitude. A doctor who wants to help his patient would do better to try to understand the nature and causes of his patient's illness than to blame someone (e.g. his patient or society at large) for the illness and to describe in detail how good life would be if the patient were cured. Marx saw himself as the doctor who was trying to understand the nature and causes of capitalism's ills (a diagnosis) and what the future would bring (a prognosis). The concrete steps he took to effect a cure consisted of political action informed by his diagnosis of those ills. Even though that political action was largely unsuccessful, it does not follow that he had incorrectly diagnosed and explained the problems of capitalist society.

It is pertinent to ask what exactly Marx thought was wrong with capitalist society. It is surprising to find out that the charge of injustice in the distribution of wealth and income was not part of Marx's critique of capitalist society. As was indicated at the beginning of this essay, a typical complaint against capitalism from its inception down to the present day is that it is unjust because of the huge inequalities in the distribution of wealth and income. Some people have enormous wealth and income, while others are very poor. For many social thinkers, this fact alone is enough to condemn a society as unjust. To hold this view, one need not believe that everyone's income should be equal, but the profound inequalities of capitalism have been the basis of much of the Left's critique of capitalist society from the nineteenth century down to the present. But − and this is the important point here − Marx did not make this complaint. Indeed, not only does he refrain from condemning capitalist society as unjust, in some of his writings he actually affirms that capitalist society is fundamentally a just society!

To understand why Marx thought this, some historical background is in order. In 1875, a unity congress of two left-wing political parties was to be held in the city of Gotha. The union of these two parties resulted in the creation of the Socialist Workers' Party of Germany. The organizers of this union prepared in advance a program and a joint statement of principles (referred to as the "Gotha Program") for the new party. Marx thought that the new party was leading the working-class movement in the wrong direction, and he wrote a scathing critique of this party platform known as the *Critique of the Gotha Program*. One of the main complaints that the authors of the Gotha Program had against the capitalist order was that the distribution of wealth and income was unfair and unjust. In the *Critique of the Gotha Program*, Marx criticized this view when he said, "what is 'a fair distribution'? Do not the bourgeois assert that the present-day distribution is 'fair'? And is it not, in fact, the only 'fair' distribution on the basis of the present-day mode of production?" (CGP, 14).

It is surely puzzling and paradoxical that capitalism's most famous and historically influential left-wing critic seems to have believed in the basic justice or fairness of the distribution of wealth and income under capitalism! This puzzle or paradox serves as a point of departure for the rest of this chapter. An explanation of it will allow us to gain a better understanding of what Marx did think was wrong with capitalism. It will also provide a better understanding of the nature of justice. Finally, it will give us some insights into the foundations of twentieth-century communist thought and practice.

3 Historical Materialism: Ideas and Social Institutions

To address these issues, we need an understanding of some of the details of Marx's Historical Materialism, which is the term used to describe his general theory of society and social change. One of its distinctive elements is a certain view about the relationship between ideas and social institutions. At first glance, one might think that the nature of a society's political and economic system is determined by what its most important thinkers believe it should be like. So, for example, one might think that the nature of America's political and economic system was determined by the Founding Fathers' beliefs about the value and importance of democracy and private property. Not so, says Marx. In fact, just the opposite is true. The Founding Fathers' ideas about democracy and private property were the dominant ideas because those ideas supported the dominant economic and political system and not the other way around. To put the point in general terms, a society's economic system determines a society's dominant ideas about law, politics, and even religion. Marx referred to these normative ideas as a society's *ideology*. What Historical Materialism asserts, then, is that a society's ideology is ultimately determined by its economic system. These ideas serve a variety of social purposes, the most important of which is to give legitimacy to the existing order. For example, the widespread belief in capitalist societies that people should be free to do what they want with the property they control (subject to a few, well-defined limitations and exceptions) serves to legitimate an economic system which is based on private property. A society's ideology helps to insure the stability of the system and serves to justify the actions that the ruling class takes to protect its interests at the expense of subordinate classes. Marx puts this point succinctly when he says: "The ruling ideas of each age have ever been the ideas of its ruling class" (CM, 29). This view has three important philosophical and practical consequences:

Consequence #1: The purpose of the state is to protect and further the interests of the ruling class.

Consequence #2: Justice is relative to a society's basic economic structure. What is just in one kind of society may be unjust in another type of society.

Consequence #3: Attempts to bring about social change by trying to convince people that a society's institutions are unjust are futile and bound to fail.

Let us examine in more detail each of these three general propositions as they apply to capitalist society.

Consequence #1. The two great classes of capitalist society are the capitalists (or bourgeoisie) and the proletariat. As noted above, capitalists own and control the factories and businesses – what Marx calls the *means of production* – and do not labor, whereas the proletariat labor but do not own or control the means of production. Though the workers are free in the sense that they are not owned by the capitalists as slaves, they are nevertheless forced to sell their labor to the capitalists. This is why they are the subordinate class and the capitalists are the ruling class. How does the state serve the interests of the ruling class in capitalist society? First and foremost, the state enforces private property rights. If the workers go on strike and threaten to destroy or take over the factories (i.e. the private property of the bourgeoisie), the state will move in and arrest them. The state also jails or exiles radical critics of capitalist society (such as Marx!). Third, when capitalism seeks to expand to parts of the world where the capitalist mode of production is not yet dominant, the state provides assistance in a variety of ways, ranging from export subsidies to outright conquest (e.g. the British conquest of India).

Sometimes, however, the state seems to work in opposition to the interests of the bourgeoisie, such as when it limits the number of hours in a week that workers are required to work, regulates safety in the workplace, and permits workers to form unions. The Marxist analysis of this legislation is that although the state may be acting against the short-term interests of the ruling class, it is acting in their long-term interests by restraining the greed and rapacity of the capitalists. Without these forms of state regulation, so the story goes, the capitalist system would, in a relatively short time, drive the workers into rebellion and revolution. The state solves what is called a *collective action problem*. While it is in the interests of the capitalists as a class not to do things that would provoke the proletariat into rebellion (e.g. speeding up the pace of work, continually reducing wages, lengthening the working day), individual capitalists would find it in their own self-interest to do all of these things to the workers in their factories, since that would maximize profits. By forcing all capitalists to ease the pressure of their boots on the neck of the working class, as it were, the state ensures the stability of the capitalist system when it apparently acts against the interests of the capitalists.

Finally, although in the conflicts between the proletariat and the bourgeoisie the state is a major player on the side of the bourgeoisie, it maintains the illusion that it is a neutral umpire by proclaiming the equality of all men (and later, women) before the law. A whole host of rights are granted by the state to everyone, including the right to vote, the right to run for office, the right to freedom of thought and expression, and the right to own property. Although everyone has equal rights, these rights are essentially meaningless for everyone except the bourgeoisie. Marxists ask, "What does the right to vote mean when the choice is between individuals and parties all of whom represent the interests of the bourgeoisie? What is the point of the right to run for office or the right to freedom of thought and expression if it is a foregone conclusion that the interests of the ruling class will always prevail and if a worker has neither the leisure nor the resources to develop and present her views? And what is the point of workers having the right to own private property in the means of production if their wages are barely adequate to support themselves and their families?"

Consequence #2. Ideas about justice in the distribution of wealth and income (usually referred to as *distributive justice*) are relative to a society's economic system. This is the basis for Marx's claim in the above-quoted passage from *The Critique of the Gotha Program* in which he agrees with the bourgeoisie that the present distribution of wealth and income is fair. There is no injustice in the fact that the workers do not get the full value of their products, since they have agreed to exchange their labor for a certain wage. Now if the capitalist failed to honor that contract, for example if he shortchanged them at payday, *that* would be an injustice. But the fact that the capitalist is able to make huge profits from the labor of others is no injustice because what is just or unjust is relative to a society's basic economic system, and that system sanctions and indeed celebrates making large profits from the labor of others. Marx's leftist opponents on this point are the authors of the Gotha Program, who believed that one of the principal defects of capitalist society was an unfair distribution of wealth and income. Their proposal was to use the state to redistribute income from the capitalist class to the working class to ensure greater equality between the two classes. Marx regarded this as a pathetic and ineffective proposal to treat the symptoms and not the disease of capitalist society, which leads to the third consequence of Marx's theory of ideology.

Consequence #3. If ideas about justice, law, and politics are determined by a society's economic system, critics of capitalism are likely to have little success in persuading large numbers of people, even and especially members of the working class, of the injustice of capitalism. If the ruling ideas are the ideas of the ruling class, dissident ideas will not be widely disseminated and will fall on deaf ears. Even the workers themselves will not be persuaded of the injustice of the system. Furthermore, to focus on the distribution of income in capitalist society is to miss the point that the fundamental problem with capitalism is to be found not in its distribution of wealth and income but in what Marx calls its *relations of production* – the fact that the capitalists do, and the workers do not, own or control the means of production. The unequal distribution of income is a direct consequence of these relations of production, and the problems this causes cannot be successfully addressed without changing the relations of production themselves.

This third consequence raises an important question for Marx's analysis: if ideas about social injustice are not the basis for social change, what is? As noted earlier, capitalism has not existed for more than a brief span of human history. In Europe anyway, feudalism preceded capitalism and lasted for hundreds of years. In addition, Marx believed that socialism would replace capitalism. These observations raise some profound questions about the causes of social change. What, according to Marx, is the engine of social change if it is not people's beliefs about what is right and wrong in a society? More specifically, how and why did Marx think that capitalism would give way to socialism?

4   Historical Materialism: Forces and Relations of Production

To answer these questions, it is necessary to get into more of the details of Historical Materialism. In particular, it is necessary to answer the more fundamental question of what determines a society's basic economic structure. A society's economic structure is defined in terms of its relations of production – who does and who does not own or control labor and the means of production. Marx's answer to this question is that a society's economic structure is determined by the state of development of the *forces of production*. The forces of production are the things that are used in the process of production. Though a number of things count as forces of production, the most important is technology. Other items in this category include scientific knowledge, labor skills, and the means of production themselves (what we would call capital goods). But technology is the most important element in the forces of production. To oversimplify only a little, one could say that according to Marx, the type of economic system a society has is determined by its state of technological development.

It is a general truth about human societies that the forces of production tend to develop over time, though the rate of development varies from one society to another. This tendency for the forces of production to develop is a consequence of some basic facts about human beings and the human condition: we find ourselves in a world in which not all our wants and needs can be met, and yet we are endowed with a form of intelligence that allows us to transform nature by our labor to meet our needs. This is production. Over time, we get better and better at this, which in general terms is why the forces of production tend to develop over time. All of this happens within a certain economic structure. In the history of a society, a time comes when that structure is no longer appropriate for the further development of the forces of production. When this occurs, Marx says there is a *contradiction* between the forces and relations of production. The existing relations of production fetter the further development of the forces of production. This contradiction compels a change in the economic structure (i.e. in the relations of production) so that the forces of production can continue to develop.

For example, feudalism is characterized by relations of production in which serfs are tied to the land on which they live. They are not the slaves of the lord of the manor, but they cannot leave the land without the lord's consent, and they must labor on the lord's land on a regular basis. They own some of their tools and implements, but they do not fully own their capacity to labor. In the towns, among those who practice a trade, such as glassblowers and blacksmiths, apprentices and journeymen have a similar relationship to master craftsmen. By contrast, under capitalism the workers do fully own their capacity to labor, which they sell to the capitalist for a wage. Even if they must work for some capitalist or other in order to survive, they are not tied to the capitalist for whom they work in the way that the feudal serf, apprentice, or journeyman is tied to his lord or master craftsman.

However, technological developments in the late Middle Ages made possible large-scale manufacturing using relatively unskilled labor. These methods of production were fundamentally incompatible with the feudal system (i.e. feudal relations of production). Parallel developments in shipbuilding resulted in the growth of trade, which created a class of wealthy merchants who owned or bankrolled these new manufacturing operations. These developments created employment opportunities for serfs who were willing to break the law and leave the manor, which many of them did. A self-reinforcing process got underway which led to fundamental changes in the relations of production, ultimately even in agriculture. In the new relations of production, the workers did not own any of the means of production, but they were no longer legally tied to the land or to any particular master. In this way, a contradiction between the forces and relations of production led to revolutionary change in a society's basic economic structure. These changes were accompanied by political revolutions, notably the English Revolution of 1688, the American Revolution of 1776, and the French Revolution of 1789. The aftermath of these revolutions was characterized by the economic and political dominance of the bourgeoisie and the growth of the proletariat – in short, the arrival of capitalism.

The inauguration of capitalism permitted and encouraged phenomenal growth and development of the forces of production. As Marx and Engels say in *The Communist Manifesto,*

> the bourgeoisie, during its rule of scarce one hundred years, has created more massive and more colossal productive forces than have all preceding generations together. Subjection of nature's forces to man, machinery, application of chemistry to industry and agriculture, steam-navigation, railways, electric telegraphs, clearing of whole continents for cultivation, canalisation of rivers, whole populations conjured out of the ground – what earlier century had even a presentiment that such productive forces slumbered in the lap of social labor? (CM, 13–14)

For those who have not studied the writings of Marx and Engels, it is surprising to come across passages such as this which express enthusiastic admiration for the capitalist system. (There are many of them, especially in *The Communist Manifesto.*) This admiration is easily explained by the fact that Marx and Engels believed that capitalism was only a historically transitory mode of production whose historic task was to develop the forces of production to the point where another contradiction between the forces and relations of production would occur. A complete description of how this was supposed to take place would require us to go further into the details of Marx's economic theory than is possible here, but the ultimate consequence of this process is that the workers would eventually see that it is in their collective self-interest to smash the capitalist system. Marx believed this revolution would be violent, though relatively short. The proletariat would seize state power and, ultimately, control of the means of production. In other words, there would be a revolutionary change in the relations of production. In this new world order, the state would once again serve the interests of the ruling class, but this time the ruling class would be the working class. Marx described this situation as a "dictatorship of the proletariat." The main task of the state in this setting would be to protect the new society from its enemies, most especially the former bourgeoisie. In the aftermath of the revolution, many of the latter would become workers and accept the new order. But for those who resisted, the state would deal about as harshly with them as the capitalist state dealt with its radical critics. Marx believed that the first phase of post-capitalist society (hereafter referred to as *socialism*) would be characterized by an economic system in which everyone would be paid in accordance with his or her labor contribution. Since private ownership of the means of production would have been abolished, it would no longer be possible for someone to sit back and collect a return on his or her investment (profit) without laboring. In addition, market forces driven by the desire for profits would no longer guide production. Instead, production would be determined by planning based on human needs.

This type of system would permit the further growth and development of the forces of production, which would eventually bring society to the second or higher phase of post-capitalist society (hereafter referred to as *communism*). Marx describes what life would be like in communist society in the following famous passage from *Critique of the Gotha Program*:

> In . . . communist society, after the enslaving subordination of the individual to the division of labour, and therewith also the antithesis between mental and physical labour, has vanished; after labour has become not only a means of life but life's prime want; after the productive forces have also increased with the all-round development of the individual, and all the springs of cooperative wealth flow more abundantly – only then can the narrow horizon of bourgeois right be crossed in its entirety and society inscribe on its banner: From each according to his ability, to each according to his needs! (CGP, 17–18)

For Marx, a class society is defined as one in which there is differential control of the means of production. In both phases of post-capitalist society, this differential control does not exist because the workers collectively control the means of production and all able-bodied adults are workers (the former bourgeoisie having been turned into workers or repressed, if necessary). This means that socialism and communism are classless societies. Recall that the main purpose of the state is to further the interests of the ruling class in class-divided societies. But since there are no classes in socialist and communist societies, there is nothing for the state to do, at least once the former bourgeoisie have been dealt with and the gains of the revolution have been made secure. According to Marx and Engels, at some time between the onset of socialism and the inauguration of communism, the state would "wither away." This, then, is Marx's vision of post-capitalist society.

It is a misconception to attribute to Marx the view that under communism everyone would be exactly alike or that everyone would be, or would be forced to be, perfect altruists. Nor would it be correct to think of communism as a system of communes that abolish all personal property. Marx has no particular animus against private property in personal items such as cooking utensils, home furnishings, or even privately owned houses – what might be called private property in the means of *consumption*. Rather, his complaint was with private property in the means of *production* – the factories, the farms, and the offices. That is the kind of private property he wanted to abolish and believed would be abolished. Communism is, on Marx's view, profoundly liberating for the individual. Instead of being tied to one boring, repetitive job for all of one's life, communist society, and the wealth that it creates, make it possible for the first time in human history for the masses of people to become well-rounded and to develop their talents and abilities, the kind of development that capitalism stifles.

533

5 The Radical Critique of Capitalism: Exploitation and Alienation

It seems pretty obvious that Marx's main predictions have failed to come true. Capitalist society was not overthrown in the most technologically advanced countries such as Great Britain, the United States, and Germany, as his theory predicted. In point of fact, revolutionary transformations occurred in relatively backward countries such as Russia, Eastern Europe, China, Vietnam, and Cuba. Moreover, these revolutions were not the outcome of a mass uprising of the working class but were instead the handiwork of a relatively small group of professional revolutionaries or, in some cases, outside military force. For most of the twentieth century, Marxist theoreticians have been grappling with these anomalous developments and trying to reconcile them with the basic tenets of Marx's theory of history.

However, the fact that post-capitalist society has not come about in the way Marx thought it would does not invalidate that vision. There may be some other route by which capitalism can be transcended. Perhaps more importantly for our purposes, Marx's vision of post-capitalist society provides a useful perspective for understanding exactly what he thought was wrong with capitalism. Consider the first phase of capitalist society, what we have called socialism. Two of the most important differences between capitalism and socialism are that under socialism, the workers would collectively control the means of production and the distribution of income would be in accordance with labor contribution. By contrast, under capitalism, the capitalists control the means of production, and they receive the lion's share of the income from the farms and factories in the form of profits.

Marx regarded these two facts about capitalism as the basis for the charge that the workers are systematically exploited. They are forced by circumstances to do what is essentially unpaid labor for the capitalists. The capitalists are able to extract some of the value of the products the workers create simply because they (the capitalists) own the means of production. Under socialism, however, since the workers would collectively control the means of production, they would control the disposition of the equivalent of profits, what Marxists call the social surplus. It is true that they would not get back the full value of the products their firms make, since some of the social surplus would have to be deducted to replace capital goods that have been used up and to take care of those who are too young, too old, or otherwise unable to work. And some money would have to be set aside to run the government and to provide for other social services. But, it would be the workers who decide how this money is to be spent. Moreover, in a socialist system, there would be no class of non-workers sitting around collecting income simply because they control the means of production. For these reasons, the systemic exploitation that characterizes capitalism would not exist under socialism.

According to Marx, the second systemic problem with capitalism is that it is responsible for alienation, which manifests itself in four different forms: (1) alienation from labor, (2) alienation from the products of labor, (3) alienation from our human nature (what Marx calls our *species being*), and (4) alienation from others. Let us consider each of these in turn.

Alienation from labor. Because production in capitalist society is determined by the capitalist's desire to make profits (what Marx called "the boundless thirst for surplus value"), work in capitalist society is characterized by extreme fragmentation of task, monotony, speed-ups, forced overtime, etc. In both socialist and communist society, the workers would control the means of production, and planning – not the desire for profits – would guide production. Because of this, work in socialist and communist societies would become the expression of human talents and abilities and not something hateful and demeaning, which is what it is under capitalism.

Alienation from the products of labor. Because the workers do not control the means of production in capitalist society, they also do not control the products of their labor. Those products are under the control of the capitalist who sends them into the stream of commerce by selling them on the market. A recurring phenomenon in capitalist economic systems is the cycle of boom and bust that we now call the business cycle. The depressions and recessions that characterize the troughs of the business cycle are, according to Marx's analysis, the result of the "anarchy of the market." While planning takes place within individual firms, there is no overarching economic plan for the society as a whole. The lack of such a plan is what makes production under capitalism essentially anarchic. Under such a system, the workers' products are like the sorcerer's apprentice or Dr Frankenstein's monster in that the workers create these products but do not control them. And just as in the stories of the sorcerer's apprentice and Frankenstein, these human creations come back to haunt their creators – in this instance in the form of depressions and recessions. Depressions and recessions throw millions out of work, lower the standard of living for most everyone, and create general anxiety. Marx expresses this point vividly in *The German Ideology* when he says:

> trade, which after all is nothing but the exchange of products of various individuals and countries, rules the whole world through the relation of supply and demand – a relation which, as an English economist says, hovers over the earth like the fate of the ancients and with invisible hand allots fortune and misfortune to men, sets up empires and wrecks empires, causes nations to rise and to disappear . . . (GI, 54)

By contrast, in post-capitalist society, the anarchy of the market would be replaced by a system in which production is planned. No longer will the specter of depressions and recessions haunt society. Workers who have painstakingly acquired specialized skills will no longer be cast aside like old typewriters in the computer age. Instead, they would be retrained, and technological changes would be implemented in a more orderly fashion. Production would be under the conscious control of the producers, not the impersonal forces of the market.

Alienation from human nature. For Marx, what fundamentally distinguishes human beings from all other animals is that humans have the capacity to meet a wide variety of needs by first creating something in the imagination which they can then make real through the process of production. This is human labor, the capacity for which Marx regarded as humanity's essence. Under capitalism, however, this capacity is stunted and perverted in the service of production for the sake of profit. Instead of human needs determining production, it is the capitalists' desire for profits that determines all production. The extreme fragmentation of task that characterizes the division of labor under capitalism ties the worker to a few boring, repetitive tasks. By contrast, in post-capitalist society, these undesirable features of human labor would be eliminated. Since the workers would collectively control the means of production, there would be no point in maintaining the perverse forms of labor found under capitalism. At least by the advent of communist society, people would be able to realize their truly human nature. In a famous passage in *The German Ideology*, Marx says:

> for as soon as the division of labor comes into being, each man has a particular exclusive sphere of activity which is forced upon him and from which he cannot escape. He is a hunter, a fisherman, a shepherd, or a critical critic, and must remain so if he does not want to lose his means of livelihood; whereas in communist society, where nobody has one exclusive sphere of activity but each can become accomplished in any branch he wishes, society regulates the general production and thus makes it possible for me to do one thing today and another tomorrow, to hunt in the morning, fish in the afternoon, rear cattle in the evening, criticise after dinner, just as I have a mind, without ever becoming hunter, fisherman, shepherd or critic. (GI, 53)

Alienation from others. Another defect of capitalist society according to Marx is that people are alienated from one another. There are a number of ways in which this is manifested, none of which Marx believed would be present in socialist or communist society. In capitalist society, the state portrays itself as representing the common interests of the community when in fact it represents only the interests of the bourgeoisie. It is essentially a divisive institution. One of its primary functions is the protection of the private property rights (in the means of production) of the bourgeoisie. This cements the inherent conflict of interests between capitalists and proletarians and encourages egoism. The stability of the system is enhanced by the fiction that everyone has equal rights. In addition, because of the competitive forces at work in capitalist society, people think of themselves primarily as isolated individuals instead of members of a community. In a particularly vivid passage from *The Communist Manifesto* Marx and Engels say: "the bourgeoisie . . . has left no other bond between man and man than naked self-interest, than callous 'cash payment.' It has drowned the most heavenly ecstasies of religious fervor, of chivalrous enthusiasm . . . in the icy water of egotistical calculation. It has resolved personal worth into exchange value" (CM, 11).

By contrast, in socialist and communist societies, these sources of egoism would be removed. The state in socialist society would be truly democratic in the sense that effective political power would be widely and evenly spread. Nearly everyone would be a worker, and because of this, the furtherance of the common interest by the state would come closer to reality. Moreover, with the transition to socialist society, there would no longer be private property in the means of production, so a primary function of the state would cease. Finally, the egoism produced and reinforced by a regime of private property and market competition would subside. In communist society, the state itself would cease to exist. The organized use or threat of force would diminish because the conflicts of interests that require coercion would be eliminated. For all these reasons, a major source of alienation of human beings from one another would disappear.

The above provides a thumbnail sketch of what Marx thought was wrong with capitalist society, in part by providing a contrasting vision of post-capitalist society. What unifies this critique of capitalist society is an ideal of freedom – an ideal that he believed would ultimately be realized in communist society. This conception of freedom is not the negative one of the bourgeoisie, who understand freedom solely or primarily in terms of the non-interference of others, especially as it pertains to private property. Instead, freedom is understood in the positive sense of having the ability or capacity to realize one's talents and abilities, one's truly human nature. The workers, a group which now includes virtually everyone, will collectively control their own lives and destinies. The economic system will be geared toward meeting human needs and in so doing will permit the full flowering of our distinctively human capabilities, something that could never happen under capitalism.

6   The Radical Critique of Capitalism: The Circumstances of Justice

Marx's vision of post-capitalist society illuminates what he thought was wrong with capitalist society. Fundamentally, the problems are two: exploitation and alienation, both of which he thought would be eliminated in post-capitalist society. Marx's vision of post-capitalist society also provides the basis for a more complete understanding of why his critique of capitalism is not based on a charge of distributive injustice. Consider once again the function of principles of distributive justice, which are given expression through a society's constitutional and legal system. Marx conceived of such principles as part of a society's ideology. Their purpose was to support or justify existing institutions, which is why different principles of distributive justice apply to different types of societies – and would not apply at all to post-capitalist society.

However, such principles also serve another function, a function Marx seems not to have noticed or appreciated. That function can be understood by noticing that there are some enduring features of the human condition that make concerns about distributive justice important or necessary. These features, which have come to be called *the circumstances of justice*, were first systematically discussed by the eighteenth-century Scottish philosopher David Hume in his *Treatise of Human Nature*. They are *moderate scarcity* and *limited benevolence*. By "moderate scarcity," Hume means that human beings face a condition in which some, but not all, of their wants and needs can be satisfied. By "limited benevolence" he means that our concern for the well-being of others is not unlimited. We care about those close to us more than we care about strangers, and there are limits to what we will do to advance the interests or well-being of others, including those we care about. So, our bene-volence is limited in both its extent and its depth. What Hume means when he says that the circumstances of justice (moderate scarcity and limited benevolence) make principles of justice necessary is this: if scarcity were eliminated, considerations of distributive justice (who gets what through a society's political and economic system) would simply not arise. If we had everything we wanted, or perhaps everything we needed, there would be no need for rules to specify who gets what. Similarly, if our concern for the well-being of others were broader and deeper, considerations of distributive justice would also simply not arise. The twentieth-century American philosopher John Rawls followed up on this point when he said that principles of distributive justice specify how the benefits and burdens of social cooperation are to be distributed. According to Rawls, since people are not indifferent to how these burdens and benefits are distributed, some principles are needed to deter-mine how this should be done (Rawls 1971: chap. 1). This is what principles of justice do.

If concerns about distributive justice are seen as responses to the circumstances of justice, it is possible to see an additional and deeper reason why Marx did not criticize capitalism as an unjust society. Recall that according to Marx's Historical Materialism, the forces of production are no longer fettered and thus continue to develop after a society's relations of production have undergone revolutionary change. This is what happened when capitalism replaced feudalism, and Marx believed that the same thing would happen when socialism, and ultimately communism, replaced capitalism. On his view, the vast increase in social wealth that the new relations of production in post-capitalist society would make possible would serve to diminish the circumstances of justice to the point where considerations of justice would simply not arise.

It is not necessary to suppose that in communist society everyone will drive a Mercedes Benz and live in a big mansion. That reflects a bourgeois conception of abundance or the end of scarcity. What Marx is predicting is an increase in the level of material wealth to the point where everyone's material needs are met. This is why he describes communist society as one that inscribes on its banner: "From each according to his ability, to each according to his needs!" (CGP, 18). So, communist society does not promise people that they can have everything they want, but it will ensure that everyone's needs are met. It will have transcended the condition of moderate scarcity. Moreover, because of revolutionary changes in the economic system, the causes of the excessive egoism we find in capitalist society will also be eliminated. It is not necessary to suppose that everyone will become perfect altruists, but it does seem reasonable to suppose that if communism did in fact increase material wealth to the level Marx envisioned, people would be less concerned to deny others what they need to lead their own conception of the good life. In such a situation, it is fair to say that the circumstances of justice would have been transcended. To summarize, communist society, which is the ultimate standard of comparison against which Marx judged capitalism, is *not* superior to capitalism on the grounds that it is a more just society. Instead, it is a society beyond justice. If Marx were to complain that capitalism is an unjust system, then presumably he would want to say that communism is a just system. But, because communist society has transcended the circumstances of justice, he does not describe it as a just society nor does he complain that capitalism is defective because it is an unjust society.

Similar considerations apply to the concept of rights. Recall that on Marx's view, the most important right in capitalist society is the right to own private property in the means of production. This right is a right of non-interference, which is coercively backed by the state. Marx believed that property rights serve to mark off boundaries between isolated, egoistic individuals in class-divided societies. (He also seems to have thought that this is *all* that private property rights are. To see why this view is seriously incomplete and oversimplified, the reader is directed to the lead essay in the previous chapter of this book.) They are not eternal fixtures of the universe given to us by God, as, for example, John Locke thought. Instead they are one historically conditioned way of organizing production – a way whose time has come and is about to be gone.

Since private property rights in the means of production are a way of dealing with the circumstances of justice and since communism will have transcended the circumstances of justice, under communism there would be no point to private property rights in the means of production; those means would be socially controlled by the community at large. What gets produced and in what quantities would be a collective decision made by the community and not something that emerges willy-nilly out of the independent, self-interested actions of countless firms and individuals.

But what about other bourgeois rights, such as the right to freedom of thought and expression and the rights of political participation? Recall that on Marx's theory of the state, the state maintains a fiction of neutrality but in fact represents the interests of the ruling class. It is an instrument by which the ruling class oppresses the ruled class. The rights the state guarantees in bourgeois society are rights to certain freedoms, though these freedoms are hollow for the reasons indicated earlier. But, by the time communist society arrives, classes will have disappeared and the state will have withered away. The disappearance of the state means the disappearance of all legal rights, obviously enough. However, it does not mean the end to the *freedoms* that those rights supposedly ensured.

Indeed, just the opposite is true. Under communism people will enjoy the freedom to participate in collective decision-making, in particular, in the democratic process which determines what gets produced and in what quantities; they will also have the freedom of thought and expression; and so on. In short, under communism they will have the freedoms but not the corresponding rights because the state – and the need for its coercively backed guarantees of non-interference – will have ceased to exist. Rights, like claims of distributive justice, only have a point or purpose in class-divided societies. They protect isolated individuals from other isolated individuals in the circumstances of justice. When the circumstances of justice have been transcended, these rights will wither away, along with the state.

7   An Evaluation of Marx on Justice

How is Marx's radical critique of capitalist society to be evaluated? Notice that his critique is predicated on a vision of post-capitalist society that has two stages, socialism and communism. He maintains that socialist and communist society would eliminate exploitation and alienation, and, at least in the second stage, such a society will transcend the circumstances of justice to the extent that considerations of justice and rights do not arise. There are serious problems with all three of these elements. Let us consider exploitation and alienation together.

In making his case against capitalism, Marx argues that certain defining features of a capitalist economic system (specifically, private ownership of the means of production and wage labor in the context of a market economy) are responsible for systematic exploitation and for various forms of alienation. He then infers that changes in the defining features of the economic system will result in the disappearance of these social ills. This is a fallacious inference for two reasons. First, some social ill might be overdetermined. What that means is that there might be a number of factors responsible for a given social problem in question, any one of which would be sufficient to cause it. For example, the phenomenon of alienating labor (fragmentation of task, boring and repetitive labor, etc.) might be caused by capitalist relations of production, but it might also be due to the sheer complexity of modern production which makes it impossible for a worker to be involved in every stage of production. So, even if capitalist relations of production were to be eliminated, alienating labor might persist. A second and perhaps more important reason this inference is fallacious is that it might turn out that a socialist or communist economic system would also cause the very same problem Marx has claimed to find in capitalism. This is illustrated in a widely told joke in Eastern Europe before the fall of communism: "*Question*: What's the difference between capitalism and communism? *Answer*: Under capitalism, man exploits man; under communism, it's the other way around." The point is that even if one assumes that Marx's account of the causes of worker exploitation in capitalist society is correct, it simply does not follow that workers would not be exploited under socialism or communism. Under either socialism or communism, it might happen that a majority of the workers would find a way to exploit a minority – or vice versa. What Marx must do – but has not done – in his critique of capitalism is to spell out clearly what a socialist or communist economic system would look like and then explain how or why such a system would prevent the exploitation and alienation he alleges to find in capitalist society. His remarks about the nature of the economic system of post-capitalist society are extremely sketchy, and nowhere in his writings does he make any sustained attempt to explain how or why such a system would preclude the problems he finds with capitalism.

Consider now Marx's belief that socialist or communist society could transcend the circumstances of justice to the extent that considerations of distributive justice would not arise and that the point or purpose of rights would have ceased. Is that really plausible? Certainly, twentieth-century communist societies were not able to transcend moderate scarcity and meet people's needs. Indeed, they made it worse, and it is arguable that their failure to keep up with the capitalist West in dealing with the problem of scarcity was partially responsible for their downfall. But, of course, Marx would say that these societies were not communist as he envisioned communism, and in fact that is true. There remains the question of whether or not socialism or communism, as Marx envisioned it, could transcend the circumstances of justice to the extent just indicated. This is another burden of proof Marx has failed to discharge. Nowhere in his writings does he explain in detail the nature of the economic system of post-capitalist society and argue that such a system could or would transcend the circumstances of justice. There is some suggestion in *The Critique of the Gotha Program* and elsewhere that post-capitalist society would have a centrally planned economy. If indeed that was his view, it would make his burden of proof even heavier in view of the catastrophic economic failures of central planning in the twentieth century. But even if that is not his view, he still owes us a sketch of the basic structure of an alternative economic system – a sketch that is detailed enough to sustain his contention that economic development under social-ism or communism could proceed to the point where moderate scarcity could be effectively overcome. In all of his voluminous writings, this is something Marx did not even attempt to do.

Not only has he failed to execute this task, but this may be a case Marx could not make. The reason is that, arguably, moderate scarcity is a permanent feature of the human condition. To question the possibility of the disappearance of moderate scarcity, it is not necessary to have an inflated conception of human needs so that what we think of as luxuries get defined as things we need, although historically things like indoor plumbing were once considered luxuries but are now considered needs. Those considerations to one side, it is enough to point out that there are certain *positional goods* which are both important and, by their very nature, scarce. Uncrowded parks (both neighborhood and national) would be an example of a positional good. Certain status goods, such as honors and awards, are also necessar-ily scarce. Such goods are often denigrated as appealing to our vanity, but in fact they serve as a social validation of exceptional contributions to society in general or to particular social institutions. Institutional goals, such as teaching and the acquisi-tion of knowledge for universities or efficient production for business enterprises, are obviously important for a society to thrive. Social institutions bestow honors and awards to recognize exceptional contribution to institutional goals and to motivate people to do their best. These status goods are things people fight over in one way or another, and institutional rules are needed both to make sure that the competition is fair and that people get their just deserts.

Putting aside these concerns, there is a more fundamental problem with the idea that moderate scarcity could disappear. In the final analysis, what that would mean is that to accomplish any socially desirable goal, no other socially desirable goal would have to be forgone. In the jargon of economics, it would mean the disappearance of opportunity costs. However, in the real world, if some projects are undertaken, others must be forgone. The disappearance of opportunity costs would mean that there are no other socially useful projects that could be undertaken with the resources used for any project. It is hard even to imagine how a society could develop to that point. Medical research, or more generally medical care, and space exploration, to name just two areas of human endeavor, seem virtually limitless in their potential, including their potential to consume resources.

Let us consider now the other circumstance of justice, limited benevolence. Although it is surely possible that we might be more benevolent than we are, is it really reasonable to believe that a vast increase in material wealth would cause us to be so benevolent as to be indifferent to the distribution of the benefits and burdens of social cooperation? Perhaps, but such an increase in society's wealth might just give people more to fight about. This brings us to a more fundamental and troubling problem for Marx's vision of post-capitalist society: the part about rights. Supposing that not all useful projects involving productive resources can be pursued, society's resources will always be importantly limited. Because of this, there will inevitably be disagreements about how these limited resources are to be allocated. As a result, some people's interests will be furthered and others will be thwarted. Even under the assumption that post-capitalist society is democratic, it would seem to be absolutely vital for individuals to have a whole host of rights – the right to be heard, the right to participate in the democratic process that allocates society's resources, and so on. Rights – including political rights – serve not merely as boundary markers to protect isolated, egoistic individuals as Marx thought but also as essential protections for the interests of minorities and individuals in a democratic society against majoritarian rule. It is true that rights protect certain freedoms in capitalist society. The problem for Marx is that he has simply not explained why comparable freedoms will not require analogously stiff protections in post-capitalist society.

It is fair to say that Marx's vision of post-capitalist society, especially in its higher or communist phase, assumes away a host of problems and features of the human condition that are in fact permanent. The circumstances of justice will always be with us, and the task of social reform is to change our institutions so that they deal better with these permanent features of the human condition and the problems they cause. In this process, it does not help to assume the existence of a future society in which these conditions have disappeared and the associated problems do not come up.

8 Marx's Legacy

There is one final question about Marx's thought that cannot be ignored: to what extent are his ideas responsible for the disaster that was twentieth-century communism? The realities of communist society are not what Marx thought they would be. Is communism as it actually existed, and in places still exists, a complete and total perversion of Marx's ideas or is it a direct consequence of his followers taking his ideas seriously and trying to implement them? On a complex question like this, the truth undoubtedly lies somewhere in between, but that does not mean it lies half-way in between. A case can be made for the proposition that communism, as it actually existed in the twentieth century, is one, though not the only, natural and not surprising outcome of taking Marx seriously. There are at least three elements of Marx's thought that have had a baleful influence on life in the twentieth century.

State power as a weapon in the class struggle

In contrast to the non-Marxist view of the state as a more or less neutral umpire which mediates conflicts among groups and individuals, Marx and his twentieth-century disciples viewed the state as a weapon – and indeed perhaps the ultimate weapon – in the struggle between the bourgeoisie and the proletariat. When the Bolsheviks seized power in Russia and became the Communist Party of the Soviet Union, they thought of themselves as the true representatives of the worldwide working class surrounded by a sea of hostile bourgeois states. It is a short step from this world-view to two propositions: (1) from the point of view of the workers of the world, the larger and more powerful the Soviet state, the better; and (2) opponents of the Soviet state, both internal and external, were enemies of the workers and ultimately of humanity itself. In the former Soviet Union these beliefs legitimated, and were partly responsible for, the bellicosity of the Soviet Union abroad and its repression of dissent at home.

The theory of ideology

According to Marx, ideas about law, justice, morality, and even religion are by-products of the social structure and serve to legitimize the rule of the ruling class. Ideas about these matters are primarily instruments of power, not carriers of truth or falsehood. In light of this, it is not hard to understand how the ideas of Marx (and Lenin) took on this function in the former Soviet Union and other communist countries. The Marxist theory of ideology also led to a completely cynical view among Communists about morality and social justice, since on their view, the function of such ideas is simply to legitimate the rule of one class over another. This also reinforced their belief that dissenters and critics of the regime were witting or unwitting tools of the bourgeoisie or counter-revolutionaries.

Central planning and the role of the state

Lenin and his followers believed themselves to be instituting the first phase of post-capitalist society, what Marx called socialism. According to Marx, socialism would be a dictatorship of the proletariat in which private property in the means of production would be abolished. In its dictatorship, the Communist Party saw itself as the true representative of the working class, and it largely abolished private property in the means of production. When it had to put something in its place, the only feasible alternative was a system of state ownership of the means of production with production coordinated through central planning. The abolition of the market and perhaps the commitment to central planning had their roots in Marx's critique of the market under capitalism. (See the discussion of alienation earlier in this essay.)

However, the abolition of private property and the attempt to centrally plan production led to an economic disaster, which included widespread famine, in a period known as War Communism in the aftermath of the Russian Revolution. While Lenin did retreat from this system in his New Economic Policy in the 1920s, he did not completely abandon the central direction of the economy by the state. When Stalin came to power, he scrapped these reforms and reintroduced fully centralized planning, which remained the basic organizing principle of Soviet (and Eastern European) economic life until the collapse of the Soviet Empire in the late 1980s and early 1990s. Not only was central planning a decisive economic failure, the system concentrated economic and political power in the same hands – the hands of the Communist Party. The totalitarian dangers this posed, which were completely apparent to the regime's opponents, were serious and important, but Marxists had difficulty seeing this, in part because of Marx's belief that the state is always and primarily a tool of the ruling class. Marxists refused to see that there were many distinct centers of power in capitalist society and thus saw no danger in concentrating economic and political power in the hands of the state they controlled.

These observations should not be taken to imply that Marx is primarily to blame for the follies and evils of the former Soviet Union and other communist regimes around the world. Obviously, these are complex phenomena that have many causes and many villains. Under different circumstances, followers of Marx might well have instituted a more decent and humane society. Marx himself was an astute observer of many of the evils of nineteenth-century capitalism, and he both believed and hoped that the future would bring a better society for the working class and ultimately all of humanity. But it is far from the truth to say that Communist parties did what they did in spite of what Marx said; it is much closer to the truth, though not the whole truth, to say that they did what they did because of what Marx said.

References

Works by Marx and Engels

The writings of Marx and/or Engels that are quoted in this chapter are referred to by the abbreviations given in parentheses after the titles. The works are listed in the chronological order in which they were written, though some were first published posthumously. The date in square brackets is the date of first publication; the other date is the current publication date.

Engels, Friedrich. [1878] 1974. "Karl Marx," reprinted in K. Marx, F. Engels, and V. Lenin, *On Historical Materialism: A Collection*. New York: International Publishers.

Marx, Karl. [1930] 1974. *Economic and Philosophic Manuscripts of 1844*. Trans. Martin Mulligan and ed. Dirk J. Struik. New York: Progress Publishers.

—— [1932] 1976. *The German Ideology* (GI). Moscow: Progress Publishers.

—— [1888] 1976. *Theses on Feuerbach*. In *The German Ideology*.

—— and Friedrich Engels [1848] 1948. *The Communist Manifesto* (CM). New York: International Publishers.

—— [1949–50] 1993. *Grundrisse: Foundations of the Critique of Political Economy*. Trans. Martin Nickolaus. New York: Viking Penguin, Penguin Classics.

—— [1859] 1970. *A Contribution to the Critique of Political Economy*. Trans. Maurice Dobb. Moscow: Progress Publishers.

—— [1867] 1992. *Capital*, vol. 1. Trans. Ben Fowkes. New York: Viking Penguin, Penguin Classics.

—— [1885] 1993. *Capital*, vol. 2. Trans. David Fernbach. New York: Viking Penguin, Penguin Classics.

—— [1894] 1993. *Capital*, vol. 3. Trans. David Fernbach. New York: Viking Penguin, Penguin Classics.

—— [1875] 1971. *Critique of the Gotha Program* (CGP). Moscow: Progress Publishers.

Other works cited

Darwin, Charles. [1859] 1969. *The Foundations of the Origin of Species*. Reprint, New York: Kraus.

Hegel, G. W. F. [1899] 1956. *The Philosophy of History*. Trans. J. Sibree. New York: Dover Books.

Hume, David. [1739] 1973. *A Treatise of Human Nature*. Edited by L. A. Selby-Bigge. Oxford: Oxford University Press.

Rawls, John. 1971. *A Theory of Justice*. Cambridge, MA: The Belknap Press of Harvard University Press.

Suggestions for further reading

Good overviews of Marx's work include Allen Wood's *Karl Marx* (London: Routledge & Kegan Paul, 1981), Shlomo Avenieri's *The Social and Political Thought of Karl Marx* (Cambridge: Cambridge University Press, 1968), and Robert Tucker's *The Marxian Revolutionary Idea* (New York: W. W. Norton, 1969). The definitive study of the history of Marxist thought from the precursors of Marx and Engels down through the 1960s is Lezsek Kolakowski's three-volume *Main Currents of Marxism* (Oxford: Oxford University Press, 1981). A student who wished to gain a basic working knowledge of Marx's economics should read Parts I and VII of volume 1 of *Capital*. This could be supplemented by Robert Paul Wolff's *Understanding Marx* (Princeton: Princeton University Press, 1984), which explains Marx's contributions to classical economics. A good discussion of Marx's influence on contemporary sociology and social theory is Frank Parkin's *Marxism and Class Theory* (New York: Columbia University Press, 1985).

In 1978, two books appeared in the English-speaking world which attempted to restate and defend in modern terms Marx's theory of history: G. A. Cohen's *Marx's Theory of History* (Princeton: Princeton University Press) and William Shaw's *Marx and History* (Stanford,

CA: Stanford University Press). Though they differ on some points of detail, Cohen and Shaw give clear and rigorous statements of one interpretation of Marx's theory of history, sometimes called the technological interpretation. This is the interpretation I have followed in the preceding essay. These two books, especially Cohen's, stimulated a large literature by philosophers and social scientists on a variety of topics associated with the theory of history. A guide to this literature and to debates among Marx scholars on other topics can be found in my 1987 survey article, "Recent Work on Marx: A Critical Survey" (*American Philosophical Quarterly* 24: 277–94).

Marx never produced a systematic work on morality and justice. His views on these topics must be inferred from scattered remarks made in widely different contexts. In an article entitled "The Marxian Critique of Justice" published in 1972 (*Philosophy and Public Affairs* 3: 244–82), Allen Wood argued for the view articulated in this essay that Marx was a relativist about justice, that is, that Marx believed that justice is relative to the social and economic system that exists at a given time and place; this implies that the distribution of wealth and income in capitalist society is basically just. Others have challenged this relativist interpretation of Marx's views on justice. The debate is ably summarized in Steven Lukes's *Marxism and Morality* (Oxford: Clarendon, 1985), a short and readable account of some of the issues raised by Marx's views on morality. A more ambitious book on the general topic of Marxism and morality is Kai Nielsen's *Marxism and the Moral Point of View* (Boulder, CO: Westview, 1989). Allen Buchanan's *Marx and Justice* (Totowa, NJ: Rowman & Allenheld, 1982) is perhaps the best treatment of the issues raised by Marx's pronouncements on justice and rights, and it has served as an inspiration for the account of Marx's views on rights and justice given in this essay. This book also contains a useful chapter contrasting Marx's views with those of one of the most important contemporary political philosophers, John Rawls. A selection from Rawls's *A Theory of Justice* (Cambridge, MA: Belknap Press, 1971) is one of the readings in this chapter. Finally, in my *Marx's Radical Critique of Capitalist Society* (New York: Oxford University Press, 1990), I try to give a comprehensive statement and critical evaluation of what Marx thought was wrong with capitalist society. It includes a critical discussion of his view that post-capitalist society could solve the systematic problems he found in capitalist society.

Much has been written on the topic of distributive justice in recent years. Selections from two of the twentieth-century classics are reprinted in this chapter. (More on this shortly.) Overviews of contemporary political philosophy are often substantially devoted to the topic of distributive justice. Some books that the reader may wish to consult are Will Kymlicka's *Contemporary Political Philosophy: An Introduction* (Oxford: Oxford University Press, 1991), John Gray's *Liberalism*, 2nd edition (Minneapolis: University of Minnesota Press, 1992), Raymond Plant's *Modern Political Thought* (Oxford: Blackwell, 1991), *A Companion to Political Philosophy* (Oxford: Blackwell, 1993), edited by Robert Goodin and Philip Pettit, and *Contemporary Political Philosophy: An Anthology* (Oxford: Blackwell, 1997), also edited by Goodin and Pettit.

Introduction to Selected Readings

The selections from the writings of Marx and Engels are mainly about the theory of history, arguably Marx's most important intellectual contribution. The 1859 Preface to *A Contribution to the Critique of Political Economy* contains perhaps the most concise statement of the general principles of Historical Materialism he ever wrote. A more popular statement of the theory of history is given in *The Communist Manifesto*, most of which is reprinted here. Selections from Marx's *Critique of the Gotha Program* are also reprinted. In this work he explains his differences with more moderate left-wing reformers and why his critique of capitalism is not based on a charge of injustice. This is also one of the few places in his writings where Marx makes some predictions about the nature of post-capitalist society.

The second group of readings contains more traditional discussions of the problem of distributive justice. The selections are from two of the most famous and influential twentieth-century books on justice: John Rawls's *A Theory of Justice* and Robert Nozick's *Anarchy, State, and Utopia*. Both assume that the circumstances of justice will not be transcended and that social institutions must face that fact. Rawls conceives of the problem of distributive justice as one of determining how the benefits and burdens of social cooperation are to be distributed. This leads him to propose a social contract theory of justice. He argues that rational individuals in a hypothetical original position would choose two principles of justice to guide the construction (or reform) of social institutions: the Equal Liberty Principle says that each person is to have the most extensive personal and political freedom compatible with a like liberty for all. The second principle, known as the Difference Principle, says that social and economic inequalities are to be permitted so long as they benefit the least advantaged members of society. In other words, there is a presumption in favor of social and economic equality, but departures from equality are permissible provided they benefit the least advantaged. So, for example, if allowing inequality of wealth and income would provide incentives to raise economic output so that the standard of living of the worst off would thereby be improved, such inequalities would be justifiable. Rawls can be thought of as providing a philosophical justification for the welfare state, which takes as one of its main responsibilities ensuring a certain level of well-being for the least advantaged members of society.

The last selection, taken from *Anarchy, State, and Utopia*, articulates Robert Nozick's theory of justice. Nozick begins by assuming that individuals have natural rights, that is, rights that exist independently of any government. These rights include the right to life, liberty, and property. These natural rights, especially the right to private property, prohibit the government from redistributing wealth and income from the haves to the have-nots through the tax and social welfare systems. In part of the selection excerpted here, Nozick criticizes other theories of justice, including implicitly Rawls's theory, on the grounds that they assume that the job of government is to assure some particular distribution of wealth and income or some level of well-being. By contrast, Nozick defends what he calls "the minimal state" – a state whose sole function is to protect and enforce people's rights to life, liberty, and property. Although Nozick's libertarianism has limited appeal in modern society, the idea that government ought to be much more limited in scope than it currently is has become increasingly popular in recent years. This selection from *Anarchy, State, and Utopia* concludes with a discussion of Locke's theory of property rights, a theory that Nozick tentatively endorses but nevertheless finds problematic and troublesome. Further discussion of Locke's theory can be found in chapter 7 of this book.

Discussion questions

1 Explain why Marx's critique of capitalist society is not based on a charge of injustice.
2 What distinguishes the communists that Marx and Engels talk about in *The Communist Manifesto* from other critics of society?

3   What are the principal differences between capitalist society and the first or lower phase of post-capitalist society? – the second or higher phase?
4   What is the basic problem that principles of justice are supposed to solve according to Rawls, and what is his solution to this problem?
5   Contrast and compare Rawls's and Nozick's principles of justice.

Readings

Karl Marx, Preface to *A Contribution to the Critique of Political Economy* (selections)

[. . .] The first work which I undertook to dispel the doubts assailing me was a critical re-examination of the Hegelian philosophy of law; the introduction to this work being published in the *Deutsch-Französische Jahrbücher* issued in Paris in 1844. My inquiry led me to the conclusion that neither legal relations nor political forms could be comprehended whether by themselves or on the basis of a so-called general development of the human mind, but that on the contrary they originate in the material conditions of life, the totality of which Hegel, following the example of English and French thinkers of the eighteenth century, embraces within the term "civil society"; that the anatomy of this civil society, however, has to be sought in political economy. The study of this, which I began in Paris, I continued in Brussels, where I moved owing to an expulsion order issued by M. Guizot. The general conclusion at which I arrived and which, once reached, became the guiding principle of my studies can be summarised as follows. In the social production of their existence, men inevitably enter into definite relations, which are independent of their will, namely relations of production appropriate to a given stage in the development of their material forces of production. The totality of these relations of production constitutes the economic structure of society, the real foundation, on which arises a legal and political superstructure and to which correspond definite forms of social consciousness. The mode of production of material life conditions the general process of social, political and intellectual life. It is not the consciousness of men that determines their existence, but their social existence that determines their consciousness. At a certain stage of development, the material productive forces of society come into conflict with the existing relations of production or – this merely expresses the same thing in legal terms – with the property relations within the framework of which they have operated hitherto. From forms of development of the productive forces these relations turn into their fetters. Then begins an era of social revolution. The changes in the economic foundation lead sooner or later to the transformation of the whole immense superstructure. In studying such transfor-

Translated by Maurice Dobb (Moscow: Progress Publishers, 1970), pp. 20–3.

mations it is always necessary to distinguish between the material transformation of the economic conditions of production, which can be determined with the precision of natural science, and the legal, political, religious, artistic or philosophic – in short, ideological forms in which men become conscious of this conflict and fight it out. Just as one does not judge an individual by what he thinks about himself, so one cannot judge such a period of transformation by its consciousness, but, on the contrary, this consciousness must be explained from the contradictions of material life, from the conflict existing between the social forces of production and the relations of production. No social order is ever destroyed before all the productive forces for which it is sufficient have been developed, and new superior relations of production never replace older ones before the material conditions for their existence have matured within the framework of the old society. Mankind thus inevitably sets itself only such tasks as it is able to solve, since closer examination will always show that the problem itself arises only when the material conditions for its solution are already present or at least in the course of formation. In broad outline, the Asiatic, ancient, feudal and modern bourgeois modes of production may be designated as epochs marking progress in the economic development of society. The bourgeois mode of production is the last antagonistic form of the social process of production – antagonistic not in the sense of individual antagonism but of an antagonism that emanates from the individuals' social conditions of existence – but the productive forces developing within bourgeois society create also the material conditions for a solution of this antagonism. The prehistory of human society accordingly closes with this social formation.

Frederick Engels, with whom I maintained a constant exchange of ideas by correspondence since the publication of his brilliant essay on the critique of economic categories (printed in the *Deutsch-Französische Jahrbücher*), arrived by another road (compare his *Lage der arbeitenden Klasse in England*) at the same result as I, and when in the spring of 1845 he too came to live in Brussels, we decided to set forth together our conception as opposed to the ideological one of German philosophy, in fact to settle accounts with our former philosophical conscience. The intention was carried out in the form of a critique of post-Hegelian philosophy. The manuscript, two large octavo volumes, had long ago reached the publishers in Westphalia when we were informed that owing to changed circumstances it could not be printed. We abandoned the manuscript to the gnawing criticism of the mice all the more willingly since we had achieved our main purpose – self-clarification. Of the scattered works in which at that time we presented one or another aspect of our views to the public, I shall mention only the *Manifesto of the Communist Party*, jointly written by Engels and myself, and a *Discours sur le libre échange*, which I myself published. The salient points of our conception were first outlined in an academic, although polemical, form in my *Misère de la philosophie* . . . , this book which was aimed at Proudhon appeared in 1847. The publication of an essay on *Wage-Labour* written in German in which I combined the lectures I had held on this subject at the German Workers' Association in Brussels, was interrupted by the February Revolution and my forcible removal from Belgium in consequence.

The publication of the *Neue Rheinische Zeitung* in 1848 and 1849 and subsequent events cut short my economic studies, which I could only resume in London in 1850. The enormous amount of material relating to the history of political economy assembled in the British Museum, the fact that London is a convenient vantage point for the observation of bourgeois society, and finally the new stage of development which this society seemed to have entered with the discovery of gold in California and Australia, induced me to start again from the very beginning and to work carefully through the new material. These studies led partly of their own accord to apparently quite remote subjects on which I had to spend a certain amount of time. But it was in particular the imperative necessity of earning my living which reduced the time at my disposal. My collaboration, continued now for eight years, with the *New York Tribune*, the leading Anglo-American newspaper, necessitated an excessive fragmentation of my studies, for I wrote only exceptionally newspaper correspondence in the strict sense. Since a considerable part of my contributions consisted of articles dealing with important economic events in Britain and on the Continent, I was compelled to become conversant with practical detail which, strictly speaking, lie outside the sphere of political economy.

This sketch of the course of my studies in the domain of political economy is intended merely to show that my views – no matter how they may be judged and how little they conform to the interested prejudices of the ruling classes – are the outcome of conscientious research carried on over many years. At the entrance to science, as at the entrance to hell, the demand must be made:

> *Qui si convien lasciare ogni sospetto*
> *Ogni viltà convien che qui sia morta.*[1]

Karl Marx
London, January 1859

[1] Dante, *Divina Commedia*.

> Here must all distrust be left;
> All cowardice must here be dead.

(The English translation is taken from Dante, *The Divine Comedy*, Illustrated Modern Library, Inc., 1944, p. 22.) – *Ed.*

Karl Marx and Friedrich Engels, *The Communist Manifesto* (selections)

A specter is haunting Europe – the specter of Communism. All the powers of old Europe have entered into a holy alliance to exorcise this specter: Pope and Czar, Metternich and Guizot, French Radicals and German police-spies.

Where is the party in opposition that has not been decried as communistic by its opponents in power? Where the Opposition that has not hurled back the branding

The Communist Manifesto (New York: International Publishers, 1948), pp. 8–29.

reproach of Communism, against the more advanced opposition parties, as well as against its reactionary adversaries?

Two things result from this fact:

I. Communism is already acknowledged by all European powers to be itself a power.

II. It is high time that Communists should openly, in the face of the whole world, publish their views, their aims, their tendencies, and meet this nursery tale of the specter of Communism with a manifesto of the party itself.

To this end, Communists of various nationalities have assembled in London, and sketched the following manifesto, to be published in the English, French, German, Italian, Flemish, and Danish languages.

I   Bourgeois and Proletarians

The history of all hitherto existing society is the history of class struggles.

Freeman and slave, patrician and plebeian, lord and serf, guild-master and jour-neyman, in a word, oppressor and oppressed, stood in constant opposition to one another, carried on an uninterrupted, now hidden, now open fight, a fight that each time ended, either in a revolutionary reconstitution of society at large, or in the common ruin of the contending classes.

In the earlier epochs of history, we find almost everywhere a complicated arrangement of society into various orders, a manifold gradation of social rank. In ancient Rome we have patricians, knights, plebeians, slaves; in the Middle Ages, feudal lords, vassals, guild-masters, journeymen, apprentices, serfs; in almost all of these classes, again, subordinate gradations.

The modern bourgeois society that has sprouted from the ruins of feudal society, has not done away with class antagonisms. It has but established new classes, new conditions of oppression, new forms of struggle in place of the old ones.

Our epoch, the epoch of the bourgeoisie, possesses, however, this distinctive feature: It has simplified the class antagonisms. Society as a whole is more and more splitting up into two great hostile camps, into two great classes directly facing each other – bourgeoisie and proletariat.

From the serfs of the Middle Ages sprang the chartered burghers of the earliest towns. From these burgesses the first elements of the bourgeoisie were developed.

The discovery of America, the rounding of the Cape, opened up fresh ground for the rising bourgeoisie. The East Indian and Chinese markets, the colonization of America, trade with the colonies, the increase in the means of exchange and in commodities generally, gave to commerce, to navigation, to industry, an impulse never before known, and thereby, to the revolutionary element in the tottering feudal society, a rapid development.

The feudal system of industry, in which industrial production was monopolized by closed guilds, now no longer sufficed for the growing wants of the new markets. The manufacturing system took its place. The guild-masters were pushed aside by the manufacturing middle class; division of labor between the different corporate guilds vanished in the face of division of labor in each single workshop.

Meantime the markets kept ever growing, the demand ever rising. Even manufacture no longer sufficed. Thereupon, steam and machinery revolutionized industrial production. The place of manufacture was taken by the giant, modern industry, the place of the industrial middle class, by industrial millionaires – the leaders of whole industrial armies, the modern bourgeois.

Modern industry has established the world market, for which the discovery of America paved the way. This market has given an immense development to commerce, to navigation, to communication by land. This development has, in its turn, reacted on the extension of industry; and in proportion as industry, commerce, navigation, railways extended, in the same proportion the bourgeoisie developed, increased its capital, and pushed into the background every class handed down from the Middle Ages.

We see, therefore, how the modern bourgeoisie is itself the product of a long course of development, of a series of revolutions in the modes of production and of exchange.

Each step in the development of the bourgeoisie was accompanied by a corresponding political advance of that class. An oppressed class under the sway of the feudal nobility, it became an armed and self-governing association in the medieval commune; here independent urban republic (as in Italy and Germany), there taxable "third estate" of the monarchy (as in France); afterwards, in the period of manufacture proper, serving either the semi-feudal or the absolute monarchy as a counterpoise against the nobility, and, in fact, cornerstone of the great monarchies in general – the bourgeoisie has at last, since the establishment of modern industry and of the world market, conquered for itself, in the modern representative state, exclusive political sway. The executive of the modern state is but a committee for managing the common affairs of the whole bourgeoisie.

The bourgeoisie has played a most revolutionary role in history.

The bourgeoisie, wherever it has got the upper hand, has put an end to all feudal, patriarchal, idyllic relations. It has pitilessly torn asunder the motley feudal ties that bound man to his "natural superiors," and has left no other bond between man and man than naked self-interest, than callous "cash payment." It has drowned the most heavenly ecstasies of religious fervor, of chivalrous enthusiasm, of philistine sentimentalism, in the icy water of egotistical calculation. It has resolved personal worth into exchange value, and in place of the numberless indefeasible chartered freedoms, has set up that single, unconscionable freedom – Free Trade. In one word, for exploitation, veiled by religious and political illusions, it has substituted naked, shameless, direct, brutal exploitation.

The bourgeoisie has stripped of its halo every occupation hitherto honored and looked up to with reverent awe. It has converted the physician, the lawyer, the priest, the poet, the man of science, into its paid wage-laborers.

The bourgeoisie has torn away from the family its sentimental veil, and has reduced the family relation to a mere money relation.

The bourgeoisie has disclosed how it came to pass that the brutal display of vigor in the Middle Ages, which reactionaries so much admire, found its fitting complement in the most slothful indolence. It has been the first to show what man's activity can bring about. It has accomplished wonders far surpassing Egyptian pyramids, Roman aqueducts, and Gothic cathedrals; it has conducted expeditions that put in the shade all former migrations of nations and crusades.

The bourgeoisie cannot exist without constantly revolutionizing the instruments of production, and thereby the relations of production, and with them the whole relations of society. Conservation of the old modes of production in unaltered form, was, on the contrary, the first condition of existence for all earlier industrial classes. Constant revolutionizing of production, uninterrupted disturbance of all social conditions, everlasting uncertainty and agitation distinguish the bourgeois epoch from all earlier ones. All fixed, fast-frozen relations, with their train of ancient and venerable prejudices and opinions, are swept away, all new-formed ones become antiquated before they can ossify. All that is solid melts into air, all that is holy is profaned, and man is at last compelled to face with sober senses his real conditions of life and his relations with his kind.

The need of a constantly expanding market for its products chases the bourgeoisie over the whole surface of the globe. It must nestle everywhere, settle everywhere, establish connections everywhere.

The bourgeoisie has through its exploitation of the world market given a cosmopolitan character to production and consumption in every country. To the great chagrin of reactionaries, it has drawn from under the feet of industry the national ground on which it stood. All old-established national industries have been destroyed or are daily being destroyed. They are dislodged by new industries, whose introduction becomes a life and death question for all civilized nations, by industries that no longer work up indigenous raw material, but raw material drawn from the remotest zones; industries whose products are consumed, not only at home, but in every quarter of the globe. In place of the old wants, satisfied by the production of the country, we find new wants, requiring for their satisfaction the products of distant lands and climes. In place of the old local and national seclusion and self-sufficiency, we have intercourse in every direction, universal inter-dependence of nations. And as in material, so also in intellectual production. The intellectual creations of individual nations become common property. National one-sidedness and narrow-mindedness become more and more impossible, and from the numerous national and local literatures there arises a world literature.

The bourgeoisie, by the rapid improvement of all instruments of production, by the immensely facilitated means of communication, draws all nations, even the most barbarian, into civilization. The cheap prices of its commodities are the heavy artillery with which it batters down all Chinese walls, with which it forces the barbarians' intensely obstinate hatred of foreigners to capitulate. It compels all nations, on pain of extinction, to adopt the bourgeois mode of production; it compels them to introduce what it calls civilization into their midst, i.e., to become bourgeois themselves. In a word, it creates a world after its own image.

The bourgeoisie has subjected the country to the rule of the towns. It has created enormous cities, has greatly increased the urban population as compared with the rural, and has thus rescued a considerable part of the population from the idiocy of rural life. Just as it has made the country dependent on the towns, so it has made barbarian and semi-barbarian countries dependent on the civilized ones, nations of peasants on nations of bourgeois, the East on the West.

More and more the bourgeoisie keeps doing away with the scattered state of the population, of the means of production, and of property. It has agglomerated population, centralized means of production, and has concentrated property in a few hands. The necessary consequence of this was political centralization. Independent, or but loosely connected provinces, with separate interests, laws, governments, and systems of taxation, became lumped together into one nation, with one government, one code of laws, one national class interest, one frontier, and one customs tariff.

The bourgeoisie, during its rule of scarce one hundred years, has created more massive and more colossal productive forces than have all preceding generations together. Subjection of nature's forces to man, machinery, application of chemistry to industry and agriculture, steam-navigation, railways, electric telegraphs, clearing of whole continents for cultivation, canalisation of rivers, whole populations conjured out of the ground – what earlier century had even a presentiment that such productive forces slumbered in the lap of social labour?

We see then that the means of production and of exchange, which served as the foundation for the growth of the bourgeoisie, were generated in feudal society. At a certain stage in the development of these means of production and of exchange, the conditions under which feudal society produced and exchanged, the feudal organisation of agriculture and manufacturing industry, in a word, the feudal relations of property became no longer compatible with the already developed productive forces; they became so many fetters. They had to be burst asunder; they were burst asunder.

Into their place stepped free competition, accompanied by a social and political constitution adapted to it, and by the economic and political sway of the bourgeois class.

A similar movement is going on before our own eyes. Modern bourgeois society with its relations of production, of exchange and of property, a society that has conjured up such gigantic means of production and of exchange, is like the sorcerer who is no longer able to control the powers of the nether world whom he has called up by his spells. For many a decade past the history of industry and commerce is but the history of the revolt of modern productive forces against modern conditions of production, against the property relations that are the conditions for the existence of the bourgeoisie and of its rule. It is enough to mention the commercial crises that by their periodical return put the existence of the entire bourgeois society on trial, each time more threateningly. In these crises a great part not only of the existing products, but also of the previously created productive forces, are periodically destroyed. In these crises there breaks out an epidemic that, in all earlier epochs, would have seemed an absurdity – the epidemic of over-production. Society suddenly finds itself put back into a state of momentary barbar-ism; it appears as if a famine, a universal war of devastation had cut off the supply of every means of subsistence; industry and commerce seem to be destroyed. And why? Because there is too much civilization, too much means of subsistence, too much industry, too much commerce. The productive forces at the disposal of society no longer tend to further the development of the conditions of bourgeois property; on the contrary, they have become too powerful for these conditions, by which they are fettered, and no sooner do they overcome these fetters than they bring disorder into the whole of bourgeois society, endanger the existence of bourgeois property. The conditions of bourgeois society are too narrow to com-prise the wealth created by them. And how does the bourgeoisie get over these crises? On the one hand, by enforced destruction of a mass of productive forces; on the other, by the conquest of new markets, and by the more thorough exploitation of the old ones. That is to say, by paving the way for more extensive and more destructive crises, and by diminishing the means whereby crises are prevented.

The weapons with which the bourgeoisie felled feudalism to the ground are now turned against the bourgeoisie itself.

But not only has the bourgeoisie forged the weapons that bring death to itself; it has also called into existence the men who are to wield those weapons – the modern working class – the proletarians.

In proportion as the bourgeoisie, i.e., capital, is developed, in the same propor-tion is the proletariat, the modern working class, developed – a class of laborers, who live only so long as they find work, and who find work only so long as their labor increases capital. These laborers, who must sell themselves piecemeal, are a commodity, like every other article of commerce, and are consequently exposed to all the vicissitudes of competition, to all the fluctuations of the market.

Owing to the extensive use of machinery and to division of labor, the work of the proletarians has lost all individual character, and, consequently, all charm for the workman. He becomes an appendage of the machine, and it is only the most simple, most monotonous, and most easily acquired knack, that is required of him. Hence, the cost of production of a workman is restricted, almost entirely, to the means of subsistence that he requires for his maintenance, and for the propagation of his race. But the price of a commodity, and therefore also of labor, is equal to its cost of production. In proportion, therefore, as the repulsiveness of the work increases, the wage decreases. Nay more, in proportion as the use of machinery and division of labor increases, in the same proportion the burden of toil also increases, whether by prolongation of the working hours, by increase of the work exacted in a given time, or by increased speed of the machinery, etc.

Modern industry has converted the little workshop of the patriarchal master into the great factory of the industrial capitalist. Masses of laborers, crowded into the factory, are organized like soldiers. As privates of the industrial army they are placed under the command of a perfect hierarchy of officers and sergeants. Not only are they slaves of the bourgeois class, and of the bourgeois state; they are daily and hourly enslaved by the machine, by the over-looker, and, above all, by the individual bourgeois manufacturer himself. The more openly this despotism proclaims gain to be its end and aim, the more petty, the more hateful and the more embittering it is.

The less the skill and exertion of strength implied in manual labor, in other words, the more modern industry develops, the more is the labor of men superseded by that of women. Differences of age and sex have no longer any distinctive social validity for the working class. All are instruments of labor, more or less expensive to use, according to their age and sex.

No sooner has the laborer received his wages in cash, for the moment escaping exploitation by the manufacturer, than he is set upon by the other portions of the bourgeoisie, the landlord, the shopkeeper, the pawnbroker, etc.

The lower strata of the middle class – the small tradespeople, shopkeepers, and retired tradesmen generally, the handicraftsmen and peasants – all these sink gradually into the proletariat, partly because their diminutive capital does not suffice for the scale on which modern industry is carried on, and is swamped in the competition with the large capitalists, partly because their specialized skill is rendered worthless by new methods of production. Thus the proletariat is recruited from all classes of the population.

The proletariat goes through various stages of development. With its birth begins its struggle with the bourgeoisie. At first the contest is carried on by individual laborers, then by the work people of a factory, then by the operatives of one trade, in one locality, against the individual bourgeois who directly exploits them. They direct their attacks not against the bourgeois conditions of production, but against the instruments of production themselves; they destroy imported wares that compete with their labor, they smash machinery to pieces, they set factories ablaze, they seek to restore by force the vanished status of the workman of the Middle Ages.

At this stage the laborers still form an incoherent mass scattered over the whole country, and broken up by their mutual competition. If anywhere they unite to form more compact bodies, this is not yet the consequence of their own active union, but of the union of the bourgeoisie, which class, in order to attain its own political ends, is compelled to set the whole proletariat in motion, and is moreover still able to do so for a time. At this stage, therefore, the proletarians do not fight their enemies, but the enemies of their enemies, the remnants of absolute monarchy, the landowners, the non-industrial bourgeois, the petty bourgeoisie. Thus the whole historical movement is concentrated in the hands of the bourgeoisie; every victory so obtained is a victory for the bourgeoisie.

But with the development of industry the proletariat not only increases in number; it becomes concentrated in greater masses, its strength grows, and it feels that strength more. The various interests and conditions of life within the ranks of the proletariat are more and more equalized, in proportion as machinery obliterates all distinctions of labor and nearly everywhere reduces wages to the same low level. The growing competition among the bourgeois, and the resulting commercial crises, make the wages of the workers ever more fluctuating. The unceasing improvement of machinery, ever more rapidly developing, makes their livelihood more and more precarious; the collisions between individual workmen and individual bourgeois take more and more the character of collisions between two classes. Thereupon the workers begin to form combinations (trade unions) against the bourgeoisie; they club together in order to keep up the rate of wages; they found permanent associations in order to make provision beforehand for these occasional revolts. Here and there the contest breaks out into riots.

Now and then the workers are victorious, but only for a time. The real fruit of their battles lies, not in the immediate result, but in the ever expanding union of the workers. This union is furthered by the improved means of communication which are created by modern industry, and which place the workers of different localities in contact with one another. It was just this contact that was needed to centralize the numerous local struggles, all of the same character, into one national struggle between classes. But every class struggle is a political struggle. And that union, to attain which the burghers of the Middle Ages, with their miserable highways, required centuries, the modern proletarians, thanks to railways, achieve in a few years.

This organization of the proletarians into a class, and consequently into a political party, is continually being upset again by the competition between the workers themselves. But it ever rises up again, stronger, firmer, mightier. It compels legislative recognition of particular interests of the workers, by taking advantage of the divisions among the bourgeoisie itself. Thus the ten-hour bill in England was carried.

Altogether, collisions between the classes of the old society further the course of development of the proletariat in many ways. The bourgeoisie finds itself involved in a constant battle. At first with the aristocracy; later on, with those portions of the bourgeoisie itself whose interests have become antagonistic to the progress of industry; at all times with the bourgeoisie of foreign countries. In all these battles it sees itself compelled to appeal to the proletariat, to ask for its help, and thus, to drag it into the political arena. The bourgeoisie itself, therefore, supplies the proletariat with its own elements of political and general education, in other words, it furnishes the proletariat with weapons for fighting the bourgeoisie.

Further, as we have already seen, entire sections of the ruling, classes are, by the advance of industry, precipitated into the proletariat, or are at least threatened in their conditions of existence. These also supply the proletariat with fresh elements of enlightenment and progress.

Finally, in times when the class struggle nears the decisive hour, the process of dissolution going on within the ruling class, in fact within the whole range of old society, assumes such a violent, glaring character, that a small section of the ruling class cuts itself adrift, and joins the revolutionary class, the class that holds the future in its hands. Just as, therefore, at an earlier period, a section of the nobility went over to the bourgeoisie, so now a portion of the bourgeoisie goes over to the proletariat, and in particular, a portion of the bourgeois ideologists, who have raised themselves to the level of comprehending theoretically the historical movement as a whole.

Of all the classes that stand face to face with the bourgeoisie today, the proletariat alone is a really revolutionary class. The other classes decay and finally disappear in the face of modern industry; the proletariat is its special and essential product.

The lower middle class, the small manufacturer, the shopkeeper, the artisan, the peasant, all these fight against the bourgeoisie, to save from extinction their existence as fractions of the middle class. They are therefore not revolutionary, but conservative. Nay more, they are reactionary, for they try to roll back the wheel of history. If by chance they are revolutionary, they are so only in view of their impending transfer into the proletariat; they thus defend not their present, but their future interests; they desert their own standpoint to adopt that of the proletariat.

The "dangerous class," the social scum (*Lumpenproletariat*), that passively rotting mass thrown off by the lowest layers of old society, may, here and there, be swept into the movement by a proletarian revolution; its conditions of life, however, prepare it far more for the part of a bribed tool of reactionary intrigue.

The social conditions of the old society no longer exist for the proletariat. The proletarian is without property; his relation to his wife and children has no longer anything in common with bourgeois family relations; modern industrial labor, modern subjection to capital, the same in England as in France, in America as in Germany, has stripped him of every trace of national character. Law, morality, religion, are to him so many bourgeois prejudices, behind which lurk in ambush just as many bourgeois interests.

All the preceding classes that got the upper hand, sought to fortify their already acquired status by subjecting society at large to their conditions of appropriation. The proletarians cannot become masters of the productive forces of society, except by abolishing their own previous mode of appropriation, and thereby also every other previous mode of appropriation. They have nothing of their own to secure and to fortify; their mission is to destroy all previous securities for, and insurances of, individual property.

All previous historical movements were movements of minorities, or in the interest of minorities. The proletarian movement is the self-conscious, independent movement of the immense majority, in the interest of the immense majority. The proletariat, the lowest stratum of our present society, cannot stir, cannot raise itself up, without the whole superincumbent strata of official society being sprung into the air.

Though not in substance, yet in form, the struggle of the proletariat with the bourgeoisie is at first a national struggle. The proletariat of each country must, of course, first of all settle matters with its own bourgeoisie.

In depicting the most general phases of the development of the proletariat, we traced the more or less veiled civil war, raging within existing society, up to the point where that war breaks out into open revolution, and where the violent overthrow of the bourgeoisie lays the foundation for the sway of the proletariat.

Hitherto, every form of society has been based, as we have already seen, on the antagonism of oppressing and oppressed classes. But in order to oppress a class, certain conditions must be assured to it under which it can, at least, continue its slavish existence. The serf, in the period of serfdom, raised himself to membership in the commune, just as the petty bourgeois, under the yoke of feudal absolutism, managed to develop into a bourgeois. The modern laborer, on the contrary, instead of rising with the progress of industry, sinks deeper and deeper below the conditions of existence of his own class. He becomes a pauper, and pauperism develops more rapidly than population and wealth. And here it becomes evident, that the bourgeoisie is unfit any longer to be the ruling class in society, and to impose its conditions of existence upon society as an overriding law. It is unfit to rule because it is incompetent to assure an existence to its slave within his slavery, because it cannot help letting him sink into such a state, that it has to feed him, instead of being fed by him. Society can no longer live under this bourgeoisie, in other words, its existence is no longer compatible with society.

The essential condition for the existence and sway of the bourgeois class, is the formation and augmentation of capital; the condition for capital is wage-labor. Wage-labor rests exclusively on competition between the laborers. The advance of industry, whose involuntary promoter is the bourgeoisie, replaces the isolation of the laborers, due to competition, by their revolutionary combination, due to asso-ciation. The development of modern industry, therefore, cuts from under its feet the very foundation on which the bourgeoisie produces and appropriates products. What the bourgeoisie therefore produces, above all, are its own grave-diggers. Its fall and the victory of the proletariat are equally inevitable.

II   Proletarians and Communists

In what relation do the Communists stand to the proletarians as a whole?

The Communists do not form a separate party opposed to other working-class parties.

They have no interests separate and apart from those of the proletariat as a whole.

They do not set up any sectarian principles of their own, by which to shape and mould the proletarian movement.

The Communists are distinguished from the other working-class parties by this only: 1. In the national struggles of the proletarians of the different countries, they point out and bring to the front the common interests of the entire proletariat, independently of all nationality. 2. In the various stages of development which the struggle of the working class against the bourgeoisie has to pass through, they always and everywhere represent the interests of the movement as a whole.

The Communists, therefore, are on the one hand, practically, the most advanced and resolute section of the working-class parties of every country, that section which pushes forward all others; on the other hand, theoretically, they have over the great mass of the proletariat the advantage of clearly understanding the line of march, the conditions, and the ultimate general results of the proletarian movement.

The immediate aim of the Communists is the same as that of all the other proletarian parties: Formation of the proletariat into a class, overthrow of bourgeois supremacy, conquest of political power by the proletariat.

The theoretical conclusions of the Communists are in no way based on ideas or principles that have been invented, or discovered, by this or that would-be universal reformer.

They merely express, in general terms, actual relations springing from an existing class struggle, from a historical movement going on under our very eyes. The abolition of existing property relations is not at all a distinctive feature of Communism.

All property relations in the past have continually been subject to historical change consequent upon the change in historical conditions.

The French Revolution, for example, abolished feudal property in favor of bourgeois property.

The distinguishing feature of Communism is not the abolition of property generally, but the abolition of bourgeois property. But modern bourgeois private property is the final and most complete expression of the system of producing and appropriating products that is based on class antagonisms, on the exploitation of the many by the few.

In this sense, the theory of the Communists may be summed up in the single sentence: Abolition of private property. [. . .]

The average price of wage-labor, is the minimum wage, i.e., that quantum of the means of subsistence which is absolutely requisite to keep the laborer in bare existence as a laborer. What, therefore, the wage-laborer appropriates by means of his labor, merely suffices to prolong and reproduce a bare existence. We by no means intend to abolish this personal appropriation of the products of labor, an appropriation that is made for the maintenance and reproduction of human life, and that leaves no surplus wherewith to command the labor of others. All that we want to do away with is the miserable character of this appropriation, under which the laborer lives merely to increase capital, and is allowed to live only insofar as the interest of the ruling class requires it.

In bourgeois society, living labor is but a means to increase accumulated labor. In Communist society, accumulated labor is but a means to widen, to enrich, to promote the existence of the laborer.

In bourgeois society, therefore, the past dominates the present; in Communist society, the present dominates the past. In bourgeois society capital is independent and has individuality, while the living person is dependent and has no individuality.

And the abolition of this state of things is called by the bourgeois, abolition of individuality and freedom! And rightly so. The abolition of bourgeois individuality, bourgeois independence, and bourgeois freedom is undoubtedly aimed at.

By freedom is meant, under the present bourgeois conditions of production, free trade, free selling and buying.

But if selling and buying disappears, free selling and buying disappears also. This talk about free selling and buying, and all the other "brave words" of our bourgeoisie about freedom in general, have a meaning, if any, only in contrast with restricted selling and buying, with the fettered traders of the Middle Ages, but have no meaning when opposed to the Communist abolition of buying and selling, of the bourgeois conditions of production, and of the bourgeoisie itself.

You are horrified at our intending to do away with private property. But in your existing society, private property is already done away with for nine-tenths of the population; its existence for the few is solely due to its non-existence in the hands of those nine-tenths. You reproach us, therefore, with intending to do away with a form of property, the necessary condition for whose existence is the non-existence of any property for the immense majority of society.

In a word, you reproach us with intending to do away with your property. Precisely so; that is just what we intend.

From the moment when labor can no longer be converted into capital, money, or rent, into a social power capable of being monopolized, i.e., from the moment when individual property can no longer be transformed into bourgeois property, into capital, from that moment, you say, individuality vanishes.

You must, therefore, confess that by "individual" you mean no other person than the bourgeois, than the middle-class owner of property. This person must, indeed, be swept out of the way, and made impossible.

Communism deprives no man of the power to appropriate the products of society; all that it does is to deprive him of the power to subjugate the labor of others by means of such appropriation. [. . .]

But don't wrangle with us so long as you apply, to our intended abolition of bourgeois property, the standard of your bourgeois notions of freedom, culture, law, etc. Your very ideas are but the outgrowth of the conditions of your bourgeois production and bourgeois property, just as your jurisprudence is but the will of your class made into a law for all, a will whose essential character and direction are determined by the economic conditions of existence of your class.

The selfish misconception that induces you to transform into eternal laws of nature and of reason, the social forms springing from your present mode of production and form of property – historical relations that rise and disappear in the progress of production – this misconception you share with every ruling class that has preceded you. What you see clearly in the case of ancient property, what you admit in the case of feudal property, you are of course forbidden to admit in the case of your own bourgeois form of property.

Abolition of the family! Even the most radical flare up at this infamous proposal of the Communists.

On what foundation is the present family, the bourgeois family, based? On capital, on private gain. In its completely developed form this family exists only among the bourgeoisie. But this state of things finds its complement in the practical absence of the family among the proletarians, and in public prostitution.

The bourgeois family will vanish as a matter of course when its complement vanishes, and both will vanish with the vanishing of capital.

Do you charge us with wanting to stop the exploitation of children by their parents? To this crime we plead guilty.

But, you will say, we destroy the most hallowed of relations, when we replace home education by social.

And your education! Is not that also social, and determined by the social conditions under which you educate, by the intervention of society, direct or indirect, by means of schools, etc.? The Communists have not invented the intervention of society in education; they do but seek to alter the character of that intervention, and to rescue education from the influence of the ruling class.

The bourgeois claptrap about the family and education, about the hallowed co-relation of parent and child, becomes all the more disgusting, the more, by the action of modern industry, all family ties among the proletarians are torn asunder, and their children transformed into simple articles of commerce and instruments of labor.

But you Communists would introduce community of women, screams the whole bourgeoisie in chorus.

The bourgeois sees in his wife a mere instrument of production. He hears that the instruments of production are to be exploited in common, and, naturally, can come to no other conclusion than that the lot of being common to all will likewise fall to the women.

He has not even a suspicion that the real point aimed at is to do away with the status of women as mere instruments of production.

For the rest, nothing is more ridiculous than the virtuous indignation of our bourgeois at the community of women which, they pretend, is to be openly and officially established by the Communists. The Communists have no need to introduce community of women; it has existed almost from time immemorial.

Our bourgeois, not content with having the wives and daughters of their proletarians at their disposal, not to speak of common prostitutes, take the greatest pleasure in seducing each other's wives.

Bourgeois marriage is in reality a system of wives in common and thus, at the most, what the Communists might possibly be reproached with is that they desire to introduce, in substitution for a hypocritically concealed, an openly legalized community of women. For the rest, it is self-evident, that the abolition of the present system of production must bring with it the abolition of the community of women springing from that system, i.e., of prostitution both public and private.

The Communists are further reproached with desiring to abolish countries and nationality.

The workingmen have no country. We cannot take from them what they have not got. Since the proletariat must first of all acquire political supremacy, must rise to be the leading class of the nation, must constitute itself *the* nation, it is, so far, itself national, though not in the bourgeois sense of the word.

National differences and antagonisms between peoples are vanishing gradually from day to day, owing to the development of the bourgeoisie, to freedom of commerce, to the world market, to uniformity in the mode of production and in the conditions of life corresponding thereto.

The supremacy of the proletariat will cause them to vanish still faster. United action, of the leading civilized countries at least, is one of the first conditions for the emancipation of the proletariat.

In proportion as the exploitation of one individual by another is put an end to, the exploitation of one nation by another will also be put an end to. In proportion as the antagonism between classes within the nation vanishes, the hostility of one nation to another will come to an end.

The charges against Communism made from a religious, a philosophical, and, generally, from an ideological standpoint, are not deserving of serious examination.

Does it require deep intuition to comprehend that man's ideas, views, and conceptions, in one word, man's consciousness, changes with every change in the conditions of his material existence, in his social relations and in his social life?

What else does the history of ideas prove, than that intellectual production changes its character in proportion as material production is changed? The ruling ideas of each age have ever been the ideas of its ruling class.

When people speak of ideas that revolutionize society, they do but express the fact that within the old society the elements of a new one have been created, and that the dissolution of the old ideas keeps even pace with the dissolution of the old conditions of existence.

When the ancient world was in its last throes, the ancient religions were overcome by Christianity. When Christian ideas succumbed in the 18th century to rationalist ideas, feudal society fought its death-battle with the then revolutionary bourgeoisie. The ideas of religious liberty and freedom of conscience, merely gave expression to the sway of free competition within the domain of knowledge.

"Undoubtedly," it will be said, "religion, moral, philosophical, and juridical ideas have been modified in the course of historical development. But religion, morality, philosophy, political science, and law, constantly survived this change.

"There are, besides, eternal truths, such as Freedom, Justice, etc., that are common to all states of society. But Communism abolishes eternal truths, it abolishes all religion, and all morality, instead of constituting them on a new basis; it therefore acts in contradiction to all past historical experience."

What does this accusation reduce itself to? The history of all past society has consisted in the development of class antagonisms, antagonisms that assumed different forms at different epochs.

But whatever form they may have taken, one fact is common to all past ages, viz., the exploitation of one part of society by the other. No wonder, then, that the social consciousness of past ages, despite all the mutiplicity and variety it displays, moves within certain common forms, or general ideas, which cannot completely vanish except with the total disappearance of class antagonisms.

The Communist revolution is the most radical rupture with traditional property relations; no wonder that its development involves the most radical rupture with traditional ideas.

Karl Marx, selections from *Critique of the Gotha Program*

1. "Labour is the source of all wealth and all culture, *and since* useful labour is possible only in society and through society, the proceeds of labour belong undiminished with equal right to all members of society."

First Part of the Paragraph: "Labour is the source of all wealth and all culture."

Labour is *not the source* of all wealth. *Nature* is just as much the source of use values (and it is surely of such that material wealth consists!) as labour, which itself is only the manifestation of a force of nature, human labour power. The above phrase is to be found in all children's primers and is correct in so far as it is *implied* that labour is performed with the appurtenant subjects and instruments. But a socialist programme cannot allow such bourgeois phrases to pass over in silence the *conditions* that alone give them meaning. And in so far as man from the beginning behaves towards nature, the primary source of all instruments and subjects of labour, as an owner, treats her as belonging to him, his labour becomes the source of use values, therefore also of wealth. The bourgeois have very good grounds for falsely ascribing *supernatural creative power* to labour; since precisely from the fact that labour depends on nature it follows that the man who possesses no other property than his labour power must, in all conditions of society and culture, be the slave of other men who have made themselves the owners of the material conditions of labour. He can work only with their permission, hence live only with their permission.

Let us now leave the sentence as it stands, or rather limps. What would one have expected in conclusion? Obviously this:

"Since labour is the source of all wealth, no one in society can appropriate wealth except as the product of labour. Therefore, if he himself does not work, he lives by the labour of others and also acquires his culture at the expense of the labour of others."

Instead of this, by means of the verbal rivet "*and since*" a second proposition is added in order to draw a conclusion from this and not from the first one.

Second Part of the Paragraph: "Useful labour is possible only in society and through society."

According to the first proposition, labour was the source of all wealth and all culture; therefore no society is possible without labour. Now we learn, conversely, that no "useful" labour is possible without society.

One could just as well have said that only in society can useless and even socially harmful labour become a branch of gainful occupation, that only in society can one live by being idle, etc., etc. – in short, one could just as well have copied the whole of Rousseau.

And what is "useful" labour? Surely only labour which produces the intended useful result. A savage – and man was a savage after he had ceased to be an ape – who kills an animal with a stone, who collects fruits, etc., performs "useful" labour.

Critique of the Gotha Program (Moscow: Progress Publishers, 1971).

Thirdly. The Conclusion: "And since useful labour is possible only in society and through society, the proceeds of labour belong undiminished with equal right to all members of society."

A fine conclusion! If useful labour is possible only in society and through society, the proceeds of labour belong to society – and only so much therefrom accrues to the individual worker as is not required to maintain the "condition" of labour, society.

In fact, this proposition has at all times been made use of by the champions of the *state of society prevailing at any given time*. First come the claims of the government and everything that sticks to it, since it is the social organ for the maintenance of the social order; then come the claims of the various kinds of private property, for the various kinds of private property are the foundations of society, etc. One sees that such hollow phrases can be twisted and turned as desired.

The first and second parts of the paragraph have some intelligible connection only in the following wording:

"Labour becomes the source of wealth and culture only as social labour," or, what is the same thing, "in and through society."

This proposition is incontestably correct, for although isolated labour (its material conditions presupposed) can create use values, it can create neither wealth nor culture.

But equally incontestable is this other proposition:

"In proportion as labour develops socially, and becomes thereby a source of wealth and culture, poverty and destitution develop among the workers, and wealth and culture among the non-workers."

This is the law of all history hitherto. What, therefore, had to be done here, instead of setting down general phrases about "labour" and "society," was to prove concretely how in present capitalist society the material, etc., conditions have at last been created which enable and compel the workers to lift this social curse.

In fact, however, the whole paragraph, bungled in style and content, is only there in order to inscribe the Lassallean catchword of the "undiminished proceeds of labour" as a slogan at the top of the party banner. I shall return later to the "proceeds of labour," "equal right," etc., since the same thing recurs in a somewhat different form further on.

> 2. "In present-day society, the instruments of labour are the monopoly of the capitalist class; the resulting dependence of the working class is the cause of misery and servitude in all its forms."

This sentence, borrowed from the Rules of the International, is incorrect in this "improved" edition.

In present-day society the instruments of labour are the monopoly of the landowners (the monopoly of property in land is even the basis of the monopoly of capital) *and* the capitalists. In the passage in question, the Rules of the International do not mention either the one or the other class of monopolists. They speak of the *"monopoliser of the means of labour, that is, the sources of life."* The addition, *"sources of life,"* makes it sufficiently clear that land is included in the instruments of labour.

The correction was introduced because Lassalle, for reasons now generally known, attacked *only* the capitalist class and not the landowners. In England, the capitalist is usually not even the owner of the land on which his factory stands.

> 3. "The emancipation of labour demands the promotion of the instruments of labour to the common property of society and the co-operative regulation of the total labour with a fair distribution of the proceeds of labour."

"Promotion of the instruments of labour to the common property" ought obviously to read their "conversion into the common property"; but this only in passing.

What are "proceeds of labour"? The product of labour or its value? And in the latter case, is it the total value of the product or only that part of the value which labour has newly added to the value of the means of production consumed?

"Proceeds of labour" is a loose notion which Lassalle has put in the place of definite economic conceptions.

What is "a fair distribution"?

Do not the bourgeois assert that the present-day distribution is "fair"? And is it not, in fact, the only "fair" distribution on the basis of the present-day mode of production? Are economic relations regulated by legal conceptions or do not, on the contrary, legal relations arise from economic ones? Have not also the socialist sectarians the most varied notions about "fair" distribution?

To understand what is implied in this connection by the phrase "fair distribution," we must take the first paragraph and this one together. The latter presupposes a society wherein "the instruments of labour are common property and the total labour is cooperatively regulated," and from the first paragraph we learn that "the proceeds of labour belong undiminished with equal right to all members of society."

"To all members of society"? To those who do not work as well? What remains then of the "undiminished proceeds of labour"? Only to those members of society who work? What remains then of the "equal right" of all members of society?

But "all members of society" and "equal right" are obviously mere phrases. The kernel consists in this, that in this communist society every worker must receive the "undiminished" Lassallean "proceeds of labour."

Let us take first of all the words "proceeds of labour" in the sense of the product of labour; then the co-operative proceeds of labour are the *total social product*.

From this must now be deducted:

First, cover for replacement of the means of production used up.

Secondly, additional portion for expansion of production.

Thirdly, reserve or insurance funds to provide against accidents, dislocations caused by natural calamities, etc.

These deductions from the "undiminished proceeds of labour" are an economic necessity and their magnitude is to be determined according to available means and forces, and partly by computation of probabilities, but they are in no way calculable by equity.

There remains the other part of the total product, intended to serve as means of consumption.

Before this is divided among the individuals, there has to be deducted again, from it:

First, the general costs of administration not belonging to production.

This part will, from the outset, be very considerably restricted in comparison with present-day society and it diminishes in proportion as the new society develops.

Secondly, that which is intended for the common satisfaction of needs, such as schools, health services, etc.

From the outset this part grows considerably in comparison with present-day society and it grows in proportion as the new society develops.

Thirdly, funds for those unable to work, etc., in short, for what is included under so-called official poor relief today.

Only now do we come to the "distribution" which the programme, under Lassallean influence, alone has in view in its narrow fashion, namely, to that part of the means of consumption which is divided among the individual producers of the co-operative society.

The "undiminished proceeds of labour" have already unnoticeably become converted into the "diminished" proceeds, although what the producer is deprived of in his capacity as a private individual benefits him directly or indirectly in his capacity as a member of society.

Just as the phrase of the "undiminished proceeds of labour" has disappeared, so now does the phrase of the "proceeds of labour" disappear altogether.

Within the co-operative society based on common ownership of the means of production, the producers do not exchange their products; just as little does the labour employed on the products appear here *as the value* of these products, as a material quality possessed by them, since now, in contrast to capitalist society, individual labour no longer exists in an indirect fashion but directly as a component part of the total labour. The phrase "proceeds of labour," objectionable also today on account of its ambiguity, thus loses all meaning.

What we have to deal with here is a communist society, not as it has *developed* on its own foundations, but, on the contrary, just as it *emerges* from capitalist society; which is thus in every respect, economically, morally and intellectually, still stamped with the birth marks of the old society from whose womb it emerges. Accordingly, the individual producer receives back from society – after the deductions have been made – exactly what he gives to it. What he has given to it is his individual quantum of labour. For example, the social working day consists of the sum of the individual hours of work; the individual labour time of the individual producer is the part of the social working day contributed by him, his share in it. He receives a certificate from society that he has furnished such and such an amount of labour (after deducting his labour for the common funds), and with this certificate he draws from the social stock of means of consumption as much as costs the same amount of labour. The same amount of labour which he has given to society in one form he receives back in another.

Here obviously the same principle prevails as that which regulates the exchange of commodities, as far as this is exchange of equal values. Content and form are changed, because under the altered circumstances no one can give anything except his labour, and because, on the other hand, nothing can pass to the ownership of individuals except individual means of consumption. But, as far as the distribution of the latter among the individual producers is concerned, the same principle prevails as in the exchange of commodity equivalents: a given amount of labour in one form is exchanged for an equal amount of labour in another form.

Hence, *equal right* here is still in principle – *bourgeois right*, although principle and practice are no longer at loggerheads, while the exchange of equivalents in commodity exchange only exists *on the average* and not in the individual case.

In spite of this advance, this *equal right* is still constantly stigmatised by a bourgeois limitation. The right of the producers is *proportional* to the labour they supply; the equality consists in the fact that measurement is made with an *equal standard*, labour.

But one man is superior to another physically or mentally and so supplies more labour in the same time, or can labour for a longer time; and labour, to serve as a measure, must be defined by its duration or intensity, otherwise it ceases to be a standard of measurement. This *equal* right is an unequal right for unequal labour. It recognises no class differences, because everyone is only a worker like everyone else; but it tacitly recognises unequal individual endowment and thus productive capacity as natural privileges. *It is, therefore, a right of inequality, in its content, like every right.* Right by its very nature can consist only in the application of an equal standard; but unequal individuals (and they would not be different individuals if they were not unequal) are measurable only by an equal standard in so far as they are brought under an equal point of view, are taken from one *definite* side only, for instance, in the present case, are regarded *only as workers* and nothing more is seen in them, everything else being ignored. Further, one worker is married, another not; one has more children than another, and so on and so forth. Thus, with an equal performance of labour, and hence an equal share in the social consumption fund, one will in fact receive more than another, one will be richer than another, and so on. To avoid all these defects, right instead of being equal would have to be unequal.

But these defects are inevitable in the first phase of communist society as it is when it has just emerged after prolonged birth pangs from capitalist society. Right can never be higher than the economic structure of society and its cultural development conditioned thereby.

In a higher phase of communist society, after the enslaving subordination of the individual to the division of labour, and therewith also the antithesis between mental and physical labour, has vanished; after labour has become not only a means of life but life's prime want; after the productive forces have also increased with the all-round development of the individual, and all the springs of co-operative wealth flow more abundantly – only then can the narrow horizon of bourgeois right be crossed in its entirety and society inscribe on its banner: From each according to his ability, to each according to his needs!

I have dealt more at length with the "undiminished proceeds of labour," on the one hand, and with "equal right" and "fair distribution," on the other, in order to show what a crime it is to attempt, on the one hand, to force on our Party again, as dogmas, ideas which in a certain period had some meaning but have now become absolete verbal rubbish, while again perverting, on the other, the realistic outlook, which it cost so much effort to instil into the Party but which has now taken root in it, by means of ideological nonsense about right and other trash so common among the democrats and French Socialists.

Quite apart from the analysis so far given, it was in general a mistake to make a fuss about so-called *distribution* and put the principal stress on it.

Any distribution whatever of the means of consumption is only a consequence of the distribution of the conditions of production themselves. The latter distribution, however, is a feature of the mode of production itself. The capitalist mode of production, for example, rests on the fact that the material conditions of production are in the hands of non-workers in the form of property in capital and land, while the masses are only owners of the personal condition of production, of labour power. If the elements of production are so distributed, then the present-day distribution of the means of consumption results automatically. If the material conditions of production are the co-operative property of the workers themselves, then there likewise results a distribution of the means of consumption different from the present one. Vulgar socialism (and from it in turn a section of the democracy) has taken over from the bourgeois economists the consideration and treatment of distribution as independent of the mode of production and hence the presentation of socialism as turning principally on distribution. After the real relation has long been made clear, why retrogress again? [. . .]

I come now to the democratic section.

A. *"The free basis of the state."*

First of all, the German workers' party strives for "the free state."

Free state – what is this?

It is by no means the aim of the workers, who have got rid of the narrow mentality of humble subjects, to set the state free. In the German Empire the "state" is almost as "free" as in Russia. Freedom consists in converting the state from an organ superimposed upon society into one completely subordinate to it, and today, too, the forms of state are more free or less free to the extent that they restrict the "freedom of the state."

The German workers' party – at least if it adopts the programme – shows that its socialist ideas are not even skin-deep; in that, instead of treating existing society (and this holds good for any future one) as the *basis* of the existing state (or of the future state in the case of future society), it treats the state rather as independent entity that possesses its own *intellectual, ethical and libertarian bases.*

And what of the riotous misuse which the programme makes of the words *"present-day state," "present-day society,"* and of the still more riotous misconception it creates in regard to the state to which it addresses its demands?

"Present–day society" is capitalist society, which exists in all civilised countries, more or less free from medieval admixture, more or less modified by the special historical development of each country, more or less developed. On the other hand, the "present–day state" changes with a country's frontier. It is different in the Prusso–German Empire from what it is in Switzerland, it is different in England from what it is in the United States. The "present–day state" is, therefore, a fiction.

Nevertheless, the different states of the different civilised countries, in spite of their manifold diversity of form, all have this in common, that they are based on modern bourgeois society, only one more or less capitalistically developed. They have, therefore, also certain essential features in common. In this sense it is possible to speak of the "present–day state," in contrast with the future, in which its present root, bourgeois society, will have died off.

The question then arises: what transformation will the state undergo in communist society? In other words, what social functions will remain in existence there that are analogous to present functions of the state? This question can only be answered scientifically, and one does not get a flea-hop nearer to the problem by a thousandfold combination of the word people with the word state.

Between capitalist and communist society lies the period of the revolutionary transformation of the one into the other. There corresponds to this also a political transition period in which the state can be nothing but *the revolutionary dictatorship of the proletariat.*

Now the programme does not deal with this nor with the future state of communist society.

Its political demands contain nothing beyond the old democratic litany familiar to all: universal suffrage, direct legislation, popular rights, a people's militia, etc. They are a mere echo of the bourgeois People's Party, of the League of Peace and Freedom. They are all demands which, in so far as they are not exaggerated in fantastic presentation, have already been *realised*. Only the state to which they belong does not lie within the borders of the German Empire, but in Switzerland, the United States, etc. This sort of "state of the future" is a present-day state, although existing outside the "framework" of the German Empire. [. . .]

John Rawls, selections from *A Theory of Justice*

Justice as Fairness

The role of justice

Justice is the first virtue of social institutions, as truth is of systems of thought. A theory however elegant and economical must be rejected or revised if it is untrue; likewise laws and institutions no matter how efficient and well-arranged must be

A Theory of Justice (Cambridge, MA: The Belknap Press of Harvard University Press, 1971), pp. 3–7, 11–21, 60–5, 75, 78, 100–4, 136–9.

reformed or abolished if they are unjust. East person possesses an inviolability founded on justice that even the welfare of society as a whole cannot override. For this reason justice denies that the loss of freedom for some is made right by a greater good shared by others. It does not allow that the sacrifices imposed on a few are outweighed by the larger sum of advantages enjoyed by many. Therefore in a just society the liberties of equal citizenship are taken as settled; the rights secured by justice are not subject to political bargaining or to the calculus of social interests. The only thing that permits us to acquiesce in an erroneous theory is the lack of a better one; analogously, an injustice is tolerable only when it is necessary to avoid an even greater injustice. Being first virtues of human activities, truth and justice are uncompromising.

These propositions seem to express our intuitive conviction of the primacy of justice. No doubt they are expressed too strongly. In any event I wish to inquire whether these contentions or others similar to them are sound, and if so how they can be accounted for. To this end it is necessary to work out a theory of justice in the light of which these assertions can be interpreted and assessed. I shall begin by considering the role of the principles of justice. Let us assume, to fix ideas, that a society is a more or less self-sufficient association of persons who in their relations to one another recognize certain rules of conduct as binding and who for the most part act in accordance with them. Suppose further that these rules specify a system of cooperation designed to advance the good of those taking part in it. Then, although a society is a cooperative venture for mutual advantage, it is typically marked by a conflict as well as by an identity of interests. There is an identity of interests since social cooperation makes possible a better life for all than any would have if each were to live solely by his own efforts. There is a conflict of interests since persons are not indifferent as to how the greater benefits produced by their collaboration are distributed, for in order to pursue their ends they each prefer a larger to a lesser share. A set of principles is required for choosing among the various social arrangements which determine this division of advantages and for underwriting an agreement on the proper distributive shares. These principles are the principles of social justice: they provide a way of assigning rights and duties in the basic institutions of society and they define the appropriate distribution of the benefits and burdens of social cooperation.

Now let us say that a society is well-ordered when it is not only designed to advance the good of its members but when it is also effectively regulated by a public conception of justice. That is, it is a society in which (1) everyone accepts and knows that the others accept the same principles of justice, and (2) the basic social institutions generally satisfy and are generally known to satisfy these principles. In this case while men may put forth excessive demands on one another, they nevertheless acknowledge a common point of view from which their claims may be adjudicated. If men's inclination to self-interest makes their vigilance against one another necessary, their public sense of justice makes their secure association together possible. Among individuals with disparate aims and purposes a shared conception of justice establishes the bonds of civic friendship; the general desire for justice limits the pursuit of other ends. One may think of a public conception of justice as constituting the fundamental charter of a well-ordered human association.

Existing societies are of course seldom well-ordered in this sense, for what is just and unjust is usually in dispute. Men disagree about which principles should define the basic terms of their association. Yet we may still say, despite this disagreement, that they each have a conception of justice. That is, they understand the need for, and they are prepared to affirm, a characteristic set of principles for assigning basic rights and duties and for determining what they take to be the proper distribution of the benefits and burdens of social cooperation. Thus it seems natural to think of the concept of justice as distinct from the various conceptions of justice and as being specified by the role which these different sets of principles, these different conceptions, have in common. Those who hold different conceptions of justice can, then, still agree that institutions are just when no arbitrary distinctions are made between persons in the assigning of basic rights and duties and when the rules determine a proper balance between competing claims to the advantages of social life. Men can agree to this description of just institutions since the notions of an arbitrary distinction and of a proper balance, which are included in the concept of justice, are left open for each to interpret according to the principles of justice that he accepts. These principles single out which similarities and differences among persons are relevant in determining rights and duties and they specify which division of advantages is appropriate. Clearly this distinction between the concept and the various conceptions of justice settles no important questions. It simply helps to identify the role of the principles of social justice.

Some measure of agreement in conceptions of justice is, however, not the only prerequisite for a viable human community. There are other fundamental social problems, in particular those of coordination, efficiency, and stability. Thus the plans of individuals need to be fitted together so that their activities are compatible with one another and they can all be carried through without anyone's legitimate expectations being severely disappointed. Moreover, the execution of these plans should lead to the achievement of social ends in ways that are efficient and consistent with justice. And finally, the scheme of social cooperation must be stable: it must be more or less regularly complied with and its basic rules willingly acted upon; and when infractions occur, stabilizing forces should exist that prevent further violations and tend to restore the arrangement. Now it is evident that these three problems are connected with that of justice. In the absence of a certain measure of agreement on what is just and unjust, it is clearly more difficult for individuals to coordinate their plans efficiently in order to insure that mutually beneficial arrangements are maintained. Distrust and resentment corrode the ties of civility, and suspicion and hostility tempt men to act in ways they would otherwise avoid. So while the distinctive role of conceptions of justice is to specify basic rights and duties and to determine the appropriate distributive shares, the way in which a conception does this is bound to affect the problems of efficiency, coordination, and stability. We cannot, in general, assess a conception of justice by its distributive role alone, however useful this role may be in identifying the concept of justice.

We must take into account its wider connections; for even though justice has a certain priority, being the most important virtue of institutions, it is still true that, other things equal, one conception of justice is preferable to another when its broader consequences are more desirable.

The subject of justice

Many different kinds of things are said to be just and unjust: not only laws, institutions, and social systems, but also particular actions of many kinds, including decisions, judgments, and imputations. We also call the attitudes and dispositions of persons, and persons themselves, just and unjust. Our topic, however, is that of social justice. For us the primary subject of justice is the basic structure of society, or more exactly, the way in which the major social institutions distribute fundamental rights and duties and determine the division of advantages from social cooperation. By major institutions I understand the political constitution and the principal economic and social arrangements. Thus the legal protection of freedom of thought and liberty of conscience, competitive markets, private property in the means of production, and the monogamous family are examples of major social institutions. Taken together as one scheme, the major institutions define men's rights and duties and influence their life-prospects, what they can expect to be and how well they can hope to do. The basic structure is the primary subject of justice because its effects are so profound and present from the start. The intuitive notion here is that this structure contains various social positions and that men born into different positions have different expectations of life determined, in part, by the political system as well as by economic and social circumstances. In this way the institutions of society favor certain starting places over others. These are especially deep inequalities. Not only are they pervasive, but they affect men's initial chances in life; yet they cannot possibly be justified by an appeal to the notions of merit or desert. It is these inequalities, presumably inevitable in the basic structure of any society, to which the principles of social justice must in the first instance apply. These principles, then, regulate the choice of a political constitution and the main elements of the economic and social system. The justice of a social scheme depends essentially on how fundamental rights and duties are assigned and on the economic opportunities and social conditions in the various sectors of society. [. . .]

The main idea of the theory of justice

My aim is to present a conception of justice which generalizes and carries to a higher level of abstraction the familiar theory of the social contract as found, say, in Locke, Rousseau, and Kant. In order to do this we are not to think of the original contract as one to enter a particular society or to set up a particular form of government. Rather, the guiding idea is that the principles of justice for the basic structure of society are the object of the original agreement. They are the principles that free and rational persons concerned to further their own interests would accept in an initial position of equality as defining the fundamental terms of their association. These principles are to regulate all further agreements; they specify the kinds of social cooperation that can be entered into and the forms of government that can be established. This way of regarding the principles of justice I shall call justice as fairness.

Thus we are to imagine that those who engage in social cooperation choose together, in one joint act, the principles which are to assign basic rights and duties and to determine the division of social benefits. Men are to decide in advance how they are to regulate their claims against one another and what is to be the foundation charter of their society. Just as each person must decide by rational reflection what constitutes his good, that is, the system of ends which it is rational for him to pursue, so a group of persons must decide once and for all what is to count among them as just and unjust. The choice which rational men would make in this hypothetical situation of equal liberty, assuming for the present that this choice problem has a solution, determines the principles of justice.

In justice as fairness the original position of equality corresponds to the state of nature in the traditional theory of the social contract. This original position is not, of course, thought of as an actual historical state of affairs, much less as a primitive condition of culture. It is understood as a purely hypothetical situation characterized so as to lead to a certain conception of justice. Among the essential features of this situation is that no one knows his place in society, his class position or social status, nor does any one know his fortune in the distribution of natural assets and abilities, his intelligence, strength, and the like. I shall even assume that the parties do not know their conceptions of the good or their special psychological propensities. The principles of justice are chosen behind a veil of ignorance. This ensures that no one is advantaged or disadvantaged in the choice of principles by the outcome of natural chance or the contingency of social circumstances. Since all are similarly situated and no one is able to design principles to favor his particular condition, the principles of justice are the result of a fair agreement or bargain. For given the circumstances of the original position, the symmetry of everyone's relations to each other, this initial situation is fair between individuals as moral persons, that is, as rational beings with their own ends and capable, I shall assume, of a sense of justice. The original position is, one might say, the appropriate initial status quo, and thus the fundamental agreements reached in it are fair. This explains the propriety of the name "justice as fairness": it conveys the idea that the principles of justice are agreed to in an initial situation that is fair. The name does not mean that the concepts of justice and fairness are the same, any more than the phrase "poetry as metaphor" means that the concepts of poetry and metaphor are the same.

Justice as fairness begins, as I have said, with one of the most general of all choices which persons might make together, namely, with the choice of the first principles of a conception of justice which is to regulate all subsequent criticism and reform of institutions. Then, having chosen a conception of justice, we can suppose that they are to choose a constitution and a legislature to enact laws, and so on, all in accordance with the principles of justice initially agreed upon. Our social situation is just if it is such that by this sequence of hypothetical agreements we would have contracted into the general system of rules which defines it. Moreover, assuming that the original position does determine a set of principles (that is, that a particular conception of justice would be chosen), it will then be true that whenever social institutions satisfy these principles those engaged in them can say to one another that they are cooperating on terms to which they would agree if they were free and equal persons whose relations with respect to one another were fair. They could all view their arrangements as meeting the stipulations which they would acknowledge in an initial situation that embodies widely accepted and reasonable constraints on the choice of principles. The general recognition of this fact would provide the basis for a public acceptance of the corresponding principles of justice. No society can, of course, be a scheme of cooperation which men enter voluntarily in a literal sense; each person finds himself placed at birth in some particular position in some particular society, and the nature of this position materially affects his life prospects. Yet a society satisfying the principles of justice as fairness comes as close as a society can to being a voluntary scheme, for it meets the principles which free and equal persons would assent to under circumstances that are fair. In this sense its members are autonomous and the obligations they recognize self-imposed.

One feature of justice as fairness is to think of the parties in the initial situation as rational and mutually disinterested. This does not mean that the parties are egoists, that is, individuals with only certain kinds of interests, say in wealth, prestige, and domination. But they are conceived as not taking an interest in one another's interests. They are to presume that even their spiritual aims may be opposed, in the way that the aims of those of different religions may be opposed. Moreover, the concept of rationality must be interpreted as far as possible in the narrow sense, standard in economic theory, of taking the most effective means to given ends. I shall modify this concept to some extent, but one must try to avoid introducing into it any controversial ethical elements. The initial situation must be characterized by stipulations that are widely accepted.

In working out the conception of justice as fairness one main task clearly is to determine which principles of justice would be chosen in the original position. To do this we must describe this situation in some detail and formulate with care the problem of choice which it presents. These matters I shall take up in the immediately succeeding chapters. It may be observed, however, that once the principles of justice are thought of as arising from an original agreement in a situation of equality, it is an open question whether the principle of utility would be acknowledged. Offhand it hardly seems likely that persons who view themselves as equals, entitled to press their claims upon one another, would agree to a principle which may require lesser life prospects for some simply for the sake of a greater sum of advantages enjoyed by others. Since each desires to protect his interests, his capacity to advance his conception of the good, no one has a reason to acquiesce in an enduring loss for himself in order to bring about a greater net balance of satisfaction. In the absence of strong and lasting benevolent impulses, a rational man would not accept a basic structure merely because it maximized the algebraic sum of advantages irrespective of its permanent effects on his own basic rights and interests. Thus it seems that the principle of utility is incompatible with the conception of social cooperation among equals for mutual advantage. It appears to be inconsistent with the idea of reciprocity implicit in the notion of a well-ordered society. Or, at any rate, so I shall argue.

I shall maintain instead that the persons in the initial situation would choose two rather different principles: the first requires equality in the assignment of basic rights and duties, while the second holds that social and economic inequalities, for example inequalities of wealth and authority, are just only if they result in compensating benefits for everyone, and in particular for the least advantaged members of society. These principles rule out justifying institutions on the grounds that the hardships of some are offset by a greater good in the aggregate. It may be expedient but it is not just that some should have less in order that others may prosper. But there is no injustice in the greater benefits earned by a few provided that the situation of persons not so fortunate is thereby improved. The intuitive idea is that since everyone's well-being depends upon a scheme of cooperation without which no one could have a satisfactory life, the division of advantages should be such as to draw forth the willing cooperation of everyone taking part in it, including those less well situated. Yet this can be expected only if reasonable terms are proposed. The two principles mentioned seem to be a fair agreement on the basis of which those better endowed, or more fortunate in their social position, neither of which we can be said to deserve, could expect the willing cooperation of others when some workable scheme is a necessary condition of the welfare of all. Once we decide to look for a conception of justice that nullifies the accidents of natural endowment and the contingencies of social circumstance as counters in quest for political and economic advantage, we are led to these principles. They express the result of leaving aside those aspects of the social world that seem arbitrary from a moral point of view. [. . .]

The merit of the contract terminology is that it conveys the idea that principles of justice may be conceived as principles that would be chosen by rational persons, and that in this way conceptions of justice may be explained and justified. The theory of justice is a part, perhaps the most significant part, of the theory of rational choice. Furthermore, principles of justice deal with conflicting claims upon the advantages won by social cooperation; they apply to the relations among several persons or groups. The word "contract" suggests this plurality as well as the condition that the appropriate division of advantages must be in accordance with principles acceptable to all parties. The condition of publicity for principles of justice is also connoted by the contract phraseology. Thus, if these principles are the outcome of an agreement, citizens have a knowledge of the principles that others follow. It is characteristic of contract theories to stress the public nature of political principles. Finally there is the long tradition of the contract doctrine. Expressing the tie with this line of thought helps to define ideas and accords with natural piety. There are then several advantages in the use of the term "contract." With due precautions taken, it should not be misleading. [. . .]

The original position and justification

I have said that the original position is the appropriate initial status quo which insures that the fundamental agreements reached in it are fair. This fact yields the name "justice as fairness." It is clear, then, that I want to say that one conception of justice is more reasonable than another, or justifiable with respect to it, if rational persons in the initial situation would choose its principles over those of the other for the role of justice. Conceptions of justice are to be ranked by their acceptability to persons so circumstanced. Understood in this way the question of justification is settled by working out a problem of deliberation: we have to ascertain which principles it would be rational to adopt given the contractual situation. This connects the theory of justice with the theory of rational choice.

If this view of the problem of justification is to succeed, we must, of course, describe in some detail the nature of this choice problem. A problem of rational decision has a definite answer only if we know the beliefs and interests of the parties, their relations with respect to one another, the alternatives between which they are to choose, the procedure whereby they make up their minds, and so on. As the circumstances are presented in different ways, correspondingly different principles are accepted. The concept of the original position, as I shall refer to it, is that of the most philosophically favored interpretation of this initial choice situation for the purposes of a theory of justice.

But how are we to decide what is the most favored interpretation? I assume, for one thing, that there is a broad measure of agreement that principles of justice should be chosen under certain conditions. To justify a particular description of the initial situation one shows that it incorporates these commonly shared presumptions. One argues from widely accepted but weak premises to more specific conclusions. Each of the presumptions should by itself be natural and plausible; some of them may seem innocuous or even trivial. The aim of the contract approach is to establish that taken together they impose significant bounds on acceptable principles of justice. The ideal outcome would be that these conditions determine a unique set of principles; but I shall be satisfied if they suffice to rank the main traditional conceptions of social justice.

One should not be misled, then, by the somewhat unusual conditions which characterize the original position. The idea here is simply to make vivid to ourselves the restrictions that it seems reasonable to impose on arguments for principles of justice, and therefore on these principles themselves. Thus it seems reasonable and generally acceptable that no one should be advantaged or disadvantaged by natural fortune or social circumstances in the choice of principles. It also seems widely agreed that it should be impossible to tailor principles to the circumstances of one's own case. We should insure further that particular inclinations and aspirations, and persons' conceptions of their good do not affect the principles adopted. The aim is to rule out those principles that it would be rational to propose for acceptance, however little the chance of success, only if one knew certain things that are irrelevant from the standpoint of justice. For example, if a man knew that he was wealthy, he might find it rational to advance the principle that various taxes for welfare measures be counted unjust; if he knew that he was poor, he would most likely propose the contrary principle. To represent the desired restrictions one imagines a situation in which everyone is deprived of this sort of information. One excludes the knowledge of those contingencies which sets men at odds and allows them to be guided by their prejudices. In this manner the veil of ignorance is arrived at in a natural way. This concept should cause no difficulty if we keep in mind the constraints on arguments that it is meant to express. At any time we can enter the original position, so to speak, simply by following a certain procedure, namely, by arguing for principles of justice in accordance with these restrictions.

It seems reasonable to suppose that the parties in the original position are equal. That is, all have the same rights in the procedure for choosing principles; each can make proposals, submit reasons for their acceptance, and so on. Obviously the purpose of these conditions is to represent equality between human beings as moral persons, as creatures having a conception of their good and capable of a sense of justice. The basis of equality is taken to be similarity in these two respects. Systems of ends are not ranked in value; and each man is presumed to have the requisite ability to understand and to act upon whatever principles are adopted. Together with the veil of ignorance, these conditions define the principles of justice as those which rational persons concerned to advance their interests would consent to as equals when none are known to be advantaged or disadvantaged by social and natural contingencies.

There is, however, another side to justifying a particular description of the original position. This is to see if the principles which would be chosen match our considered convictions of justice or extend them in an acceptable way. We can note whether applying these principles would lead us to make the same judgments about the basic structure of society which we now make intuitively and in which we have the greatest confidence; or whether, in cases where our present judgments are in doubt and given with hesitation, these principles offer a resolution which we can affirm on reflection. There are questions which we feel sure must be answered in a certain way. For example, we are confident that religious intolerance and racial discrimination are unjust. We think that we have examined these things with care and have reached what we believe is an impartial judgment not likely to be distorted by an excessive attention to our own interests. These convictions are provisional fixed points which we presume any conception of justice must fit. But we have much less assurance as to what is the correct distribution of wealth and authority. Here we may be looking for a way to remove our doubts. We can check an interpretation of the initial situation, then, by the capacity of its principles to accommodate our firmest convictions and to provide guidance where guidance is needed.

In searching for the most favored description of this situation we work from both ends. We begin by describing it so that it represents generally shared and preferably weak conditions. We then see if these conditions are strong enough to yield a significant set of principles. If not, we look for further premises equally reasonable. But if so, and these principles match our considered convictions of justice, then so far well and good. But presumably there will be discrepancies. In this case we have a choice. We can either modify the account of the initial situation or we can revise our existing judgments, for even the judgments we take provisionally as fixed points are liable to revision. By going back and forth, sometimes altering the conditions of the contractual circumstances, at others withdrawing our judgments and conforming them to principle, I assume that eventually we shall find a description of the initial situation that both expresses reasonable conditions and yields principles which match our considered judgments duly pruned and adjusted. This state of affairs I refer to as reflective equilibrium. It is an equilibrium because at last our principles and judgments coincide; and it is reflective since we know to what principles our judgments conform and the premises of their derivation. At the moment everything is in order. But this equilibrium is not necessarily stable. It is liable to be upset by further examination of the conditions which should be imposed on the contractual situation and by particular cases which may lead us to revise our judgments. Yet for the time being we have done what we can to render coherent and to justify our convictions of social justice. We have reached a conception of the original position. [. . .]

The Principles of Justice

Two principles of justice

I shall now state in a provisional form the two principles of justice that I believe would be chosen in the original position. In this section I wish to make only the most general comments, and therefore the first formulation of these principles is tentative. As we go on I shall run through several formulations and approximate step by step the final statement to be given much later. I believe that doing this allows the exposition to proceed in a natural way.

The first statement of the two principles reads as follows.

> First: each person is to have an equal right to the most extensive basic liberty compatible with a similar liberty for others.
>
> Second: social and economic inequalities are to be arranged so that they are both (a) reasonably expected to be to everyone's advantage, and (b) attached to positions and offices open to all.

[. . .] By way of general comment, these principles primarily apply, as I have said, to the basic structure of society. They are to govern the assignment of rights and duties and to regulate the distribution of social and economic advantages. As their formulation suggests, these principles presuppose that the social structure can be divided into two more or less distinct parts, the first principle applying to the one, the second to the other. They distinguish between those aspects of the social system that define and secure the equal liberties of citizenship and those that specify and establish social and economic inequalities. The basic liberties of citizens are, roughly speaking, political liberty (the right to vote and to be eligible for public office) together with freedom of speech and assembly; liberty of conscience and freedom of thought; freedom of the person along with the right to hold (personal) property; and freedom from arbitrary arrest and seizure as defined by the concept of the rule of law. These liberties are all required to be equal by the first principle, since citizens of a just society are to have the same basic rights.

The second principle applies, in the first approximation, to the distribution of income and wealth and to the design of organizations that make use of differences in authority and responsibility, or chains of command. While the distribution of wealth and income need not be equal, it must be to everyone's advantage, and at the same time, positions of authority and offices of command must be accessible to all. One applies the second principle by holding positions open, and then, subject to this constraint, arranges social and economic inequalities so that everyone benefits.

These principles are to be arranged in a serial order with the first principle prior to the second. This ordering means that a departure from the institutions of equal liberty required by the first principle cannot be justified by, or compensated for, by greater social and economic advantages. The distribution of wealth and income, and the hierarchies of authority, must be consistent with both the liberties of equal citizenship and equality of opportunity.

It is clear that these principles are rather specific in their content, and their acceptance rests on certain assumptions that I must eventually try to explain and justify. A theory of justice depends upon a theory of society in ways that will become evident as we proceed. For the present, it should be observed that the two principles (and this holds for all formulations) are a special case of a more general conception of justice that can be expressed as follows.

> All social values – liberty and opportunity, income and wealth, and the bases of self-respect – are to be distributed equally unless an unequal distribution of any, or all, of these values is to everyone's advantage.

Injustice, then, is simply inequalities that are not to the benefit of all. Of course, this conception is extremely vague and requires interpretation.

As a first step, suppose that the basic structure of society distributes certain primary goods, that is, things that every rational man is presumed to want. These goods normally have a use whatever a person's rational plan of life. For simplicity, assume that the chief primary goods at the disposition of society are rights and liberties, powers and opportunities, income and wealth. (Later on in Part Three the primary good of self-respect has a central place.) These are the social primary goods. Other primary goods such as health and vigor, intelligence and imagination, are natural goods; although their possession is influenced by the basic structure, they are not so directly under its control. Imagine, then, a hypothetical initial arrangement in which all the social primary goods are equally distributed: everyone has similar rights and duties, and income and wealth are evenly shared. This state of affairs provides a benchmark for judging improvements. If certain inequalities of wealth and organizational powers would make everyone better off than in this hypothetical starting situation, then they accord with the general conception.

Now it is possible, at least theoretically, that by giving up some of their fundamental liberties men are sufficiently compensated by the resulting social and economic gains. The general conception of justice imposes no restrictions on what sort of inequalities are permissible; it only requires that everyone's position be improved. We need not suppose anything so drastic as consenting to a condition of slavery. Imagine instead that men forgo certain political rights when the economic returns are significant and their capacity to influence the course of policy by the exercise of these rights would be marginal in any case. It is this kind of exchange which the two principles as stated rule out; being arranged in serial order they do not permit exchanges between basic liberties and economic and social gains. The serial ordering of principles expresses an underlying preference among primary social goods. When this preference is rational so likewise is the choice of these principles in this order. [. . .]

The fact that the two principles apply to institutions has certain consequences. Several points illustrate this. First of all, the rights and liberties referred to by these principles are those which are defined by the public rules of the basic structure. Whether men are free is determined by the rights and duties established by the major institutions of society. Liberty is a certain pattern of social forms. The first principle simply requires that certain sorts of rules, those defining basic liberties, apply to everyone equally and that they allow the most extensive liberty compatible with a like liberty for all. The only reason for circumscribing the rights defining liberty and making men's freedom less extensive than it might otherwise be is that these equal rights as institutionally defined would interfere with one another.

Another thing to bear in mind is that when principles mention persons, or require that everyone gain from an inequality, the reference is to representative persons holding the various social positions, or offices, or whatever, established by the basic structure. Thus in applying the second principle I assume that it is possible to assign an expectation of well-being to representative individuals holding these positions. This expectation indicates their life prospects as viewed from their social station. In general, the expectations of representative persons depend upon the distribution of rights and duties throughout the basic structure. When this changes, expectations change. I assume, then, that expectations are connected: by raising the prospects of the representative man in one position we presumably increase or decrease the prospects of representative men in other positions. Since it applies to institutional forms, the second principle (or rather the first part of it) refers to the expectations of representative individuals. Neither principle applies to distributions of particular goods to particular individuals who may be identified by their proper names. The situation where someone is considering how to allocate certain commodities to needy persons who are known to him is not within the scope of the principles. They are meant to regulate basic institutional arrangements. We must not assume that there is much similarity from the standpoint of justice between an administrative allotment of goods to specific persons and the appropriate design of society. Our common sense intuitions for the former may be a poor guide to the latter.

Now the second principle insists that each person benefit from permissible inequalities in the basic structure. This means that it must be reasonable for each relevant representative man defined by this structure, when he views it as a going concern, to prefer his prospects with the inequality to his prospects without it. One is not allowed to justify differences in income or organizational powers on the ground that the disadvantages of those in one position are outweighed by the greater advantages of those in another. Much less can infringements of liberty be counterbalanced in this way. Applied to the basic structure, the principle of utility would have us maximize the sum of expectations of representative men (weighted by the number of persons they represent, on the classical view); and this would permit us to compensate for the losses of some by the gains of others. Instead, the two principles require that everyone benefit from economic and social inequalities. It is obvious, however, that there are indefinitely many ways in which all may be advantaged when the initial arrangement of equality is taken as a benchmark. How then are we to choose among these possibilities? The principles must be specified so that they yield a determinate conclusion. [. . .]

Democratic equality and the difference principle

The democratic interpretation is arrived at by combining the principle of fair equality of opportunity with the difference principle. [. . .] Assuming the framework of institutions required by equal liberty and fair equality of opportunity, the higher expectations of those better situated are just if and only if they work as part of a scheme which improves the expectations of the least advantaged members of society. The intuitive idea is that the social order is not to establish and secure the more attractive prospects of those better off unless doing so is to the advantage of those less fortunate. [. . .]

To illustrate the difference principle, consider the distribution of income among social classes. Let us suppose that the various income groups correlate with representative individuals by reference to whose expectations we can judge the distribution. Now those starting out as members of the entrepreneurial class in property-owning democracy, say, have a better prospect than those who begin in the class of unskilled laborers. It seems likely that this will be true even when the social injustices which now exist are removed. What, then, can possibly justify this kind of initial inequality in life prospects? According to the difference principle, it is justifiable only if the difference in expectation is to the advantage of the representative man who is worse off, in this case the representative unskilled worker. The inequality in expectation is permissible only if lowering it would make the working class even more worse off. Supposedly, given the rider in the second principle concerning open positions, and the principle of liberty generally, the greater expectations allowed to entrepreneurs encourages them to do things which raise the long-term prospects of the laboring class. Their better prospects act as incentives so that the economic process is more efficient, innovation proceeds at a faster pace, and so on. Eventually the resulting material benefits spread throughout the system and to the least advantaged. I shall not consider how far these things are true. The point is that something of this kind must be argued if these inequalities are to be just by the difference principle. [. . .]

The tendency to equality

I wish to conclude this discussion of the two principles by explaining the sense in which they express an egalitarian conception of justice. Also I should like to forestall the objection to the principle of fair opportunity that it leads to a callous meritocratic society. In order to prepare the way for doing this, I note several aspects of the conception of justice that I have set out.

First we may observe that the difference principle gives some weight to the considerations singled out by the principle of redress. This is the principle that undeserved inequalities call for redress; and since inequalities of birth and natural endowment are undeserved, these inequalities are to be somehow compensated for. Thus the principle holds that in order to treat all persons equally, to provide genuine equality of opportunity, society must give more attention to those with fewer native assets and to those born into the less favorable social positions. The idea is to redress the bias of contingencies in the direction of equality. In pursuit of this principle greater resources might be spent on the education of the less rather than the more intelligent, at least over a certain time of life, say the earlier years of school.

Now the principle of redress has not to my knowledge been proposed as the sole criterion of justice, as the single aim of the social order. It is plausible as most such principles are only as a prima facie principle, one that is to be weighed in the balance with others. For example, we are to weigh it against the principle to improve the average standard of life, or to advance the common good. But whatever other principles we hold, the claims of redress are to be taken into account. It is thought to represent one of the elements in our conception of justice. Now the difference principle is not of course the principle of redress. It does not require society to try to even out handicaps as if all were expected to compete on a fair basis in the same race. But the difference principle would allocate resources in education, say, so as to improve the long-term expectation of the least favored. If this end is attained by giving more attention to the better endowed, it is permissible; otherwise not. And in making this decision, the value of education should not be assessed solely in terms of economic efficiency and social welfare. Equally if not more important is the role of education in enabling a person to enjoy the culture of his society and to take part in its affairs, and in this way to provide for each individual a secure sense of his own worth.

Thus although the difference principle is not the same as that of redress, it does achieve some of the intent of the latter principle. It transforms the aims of the basic structure so that the total scheme of institutions no longer emphasizes social efficiency and technocratic values. We see then that the difference principle represents, in effect, an agreement to regard the distribution of natural talents as a common asset and to share in the benefits of this distribution whatever it turns out to be. Those who have been favored by nature, whoever they are, may gain from their good fortune only on terms that improve the situation of those who have lost out. The naturally advantaged are not to gain merely because they are more gifted, but only to cover the costs of training and education and for using their endowments in ways that help the less fortunate as well. No one deserves his greater natural capacity nor merits a more favorable starting place in society. But it does not follow that one should eliminate these distinctions. There is another way to deal with them. The basic structure can be arranged so that these contingencies work for the good of the least fortunate. Thus we are led to the difference principle if we wish to set up the social system so that no one gains or loses from his arbitrary place in the distribution of natural assets or his initial position in society without giving or receiving compensating advantages in return.

In view of these remarks we may reject the contention that the ordering of institutions is always defective because the distribution of natural talents and the contingencies of social circumstance are unjust, and this injustice must inevitably carry over to human arrangements. Occasionally this reflection is offered as an excuse for ignoring injustice, as if the refusal to acquiesce in injustice is on a par with being unable to accept death. The natural distribution is neither just nor unjust; nor is it unjust that persons are born into society at some particular position. These are simply natural facts. What is just and unjust is the way that institutions deal with these facts. Aristocratic and caste societies are unjust because they make these contingencies the ascriptive basis for belonging to more or less enclosed and privileged social classes. The basic structure of these societies incorporates the arbitrariness found in nature. But there is no necessity for men to resign themselves to these contingencies. The social system is not an unchangeable order beyond human control but a pattern of human action. In justice as fairness men agree to share one another's fate. In designing institutions they undertake to avail themselves of the accidents of nature and social circumstance only when doing so is for the common benefit. The two principles are a fair way of meeting the arbitrariness of fortune; and while no doubt imperfect in other ways, the institutions which satisfy these principles are just.

A further point is that the difference principle expresses a conception of reciprocity. It is a principle of mutual benefit. We have seen that, at least when chain connection holds, each representative man can accept the basic structure as designed to advance his interests. The social order can be justified to everyone, and in particular to those who are least favored; and in this sense it is egalitarian. But it seems necessary to consider in an intuitive way how the condition of mutual benefit is satisfied. Consider any two representative men A and B, and let B be the one who is less favored. Actually, since we are most interested in the comparison with the least favored man, let us assume that B is this individual. Now B can accept A's being better off since A's advantages have been gained in ways that improve B's prospects. If A were not allowed his better position, B would be even worse off than he is. The difficulty is to show that A has no grounds for complaint. Perhaps he is required to have less than he might since his having more would result in some loss to B. Now what can be said to the more favored man? To begin with, it is clear that the well-being of each depends on a scheme of social cooperation without which no one could have a satisfactory life. Secondly, we can ask for the willing cooperation of everyone only if the terms of the scheme are reasonable. The difference principle, then, seems to be a fair basis on which those better endowed, or more fortunate in their social circumstances, could expect others to collaborate with them when some workable arrangement is a necessary condition of the good of all.

There is a natural inclination to object that those better situated deserve their greater advantages whether or not they are to the benefit of others. At this point it is necessary to be clear about the notion of desert. It is perfectly true that given a just system of cooperation as a scheme of public rules and the expectations set up by it, those who, with the prospect of improving their condition, have done what the system announces that it will reward are entitled to their advantages. In this sense the more fortunate have a claim to their better situation; their claims are legitimate expectations established by social institutions, and the community is obligated to meet them. But this sense of desert presupposes the existence of the cooperative scheme; it is irrelevant to the question whether in the first place the scheme is to be designed in accordance with the difference principle or some other criterion.

Perhaps some will think that the person with greater natural endowments deserves those assets and the superior character that made their development possible. Because he is more worthy in this sense, he deserves the greater advantages that he could achieve with them. This view, however, is surely incorrect. It seems to be one of the fixed points of our considered judgments that no one deserves his place in the distribution of native endowments, any more than one deserves one's initial starting place in society. The assertion that a man deserves the superior character that enables him to make the effort to cultivate his abilities is equally problematic; for his character depends in large part upon fortunate family and social circumstances for which he can claim no credit. The notion of desert seems not to apply to these cases. Thus the more advantaged representative man cannot say that he deserves and therefore has a right to a scheme of cooperation in which he is permitted to acquire benefits in ways that do not contribute to the welfare of others. There is no basis for his making this claim. From the standpoint of common sense, then, the difference principle appears to be acceptable both to the more advantaged and to the less advantaged individual. Of course, none of this is strictly speaking an argument for the principle, since in a contract theory arguments are made from the point of view of the original position. But these intuitive considerations help to clarify the nature of the principle and the sense in which it is egalitarian. [. . .]

The Original Position

The veil of ignorance

The idea of the original position is to set up a fair procedure so that any principles agreed to will be just. The aim is to use the notion of pure procedural justice as a basis of theory. Somehow we must nullify the effects of specific contingencies which put men at odds and tempt them to exploit social and natural circumstances to their own advantage. Now in order to do this I assume that the parties are situated behind a veil of ignorance. They do not now how the various alternatives will affect their own particular case and they are obliged to evaluate principles solely on the basis of general considerations.

It is assumed, then, that the parties do not know certain kinds of particular facts. First of all, no one knows his place in society, his class position or social status; nor does he know his fortune in the distribution of natural assets and abilities, his intelligence and strength, and the like. Nor, again, does anyone know his conception of the good, the particulars of his rational plan of life, or even the special features of his psychology such as his aversion to risk or liability to optimism or pessimism. More than this, I assume that the parties do not know the particular circumstances of their own society. That is, they do not know its economic or political situation, or the level of civilization and culture it has been able to achieve. The persons in the original position have no information as to which generation they belong. These broader restrictions on knowledge are appropriate in part because questions of social justice arise between generations as well as within them, for example, the question of the appropriate rate of capital saving and of the conservation of natural resources and the environment of nature. There is also, theoretically anyway, the question of a reasonable genetic policy. In these cases too, in order to carry through the idea of the original position, the parties must not know the contingencies that set them in opposition. They must choose principles the consequences of which they are prepared to live with whatever generation they turn out to belong to.

As far as possible, then, the only particular facts which the parties know is that their society is subject to the circumstances of justice and whatever this implies. It is taken for granted, however, that they know the general facts about human society. They understand political affairs and the principles of economic theory; they know the basis of social organization and the laws of human psychology. Indeed, the parties are presumed to know whatever general facts affect the choice of the principles of justice. There are no limitations on general information, that is, on general laws and theories, since conceptions of justice must be adjusted to the characteristics of the systems of social cooperation which they are to regulate, and there is no reason to rule out these facts. It is, for example, a consideration against a conception of justice that, in view of the laws of moral psychology, men would not acquire a desire to act upon it even when the institutions of their society satisfied it. For in this case there would be difficulty in securing the stability of social cooperation. It is an important feature of a conception of justice that it should generate its own support. That is, its principles should be such that when they are embodied in the basic structure of society men tend to acquire the corresponding sense of justice. Given the principles of moral learning, men develop a desire to act in accordance with its principles. In this case a conception of justice is stable. This kind of general information is admissible in the original position.

The notion of the veil of ignorance raises several difficulties. Some may object that the exclusion of nearly all particular information makes it difficult to grasp what is meant by the original position. Thus it may be helpful to observe that one or more persons can at any time enter this position, or perhaps, better, simulate the deliberations of this hypothetical situation, simply by reasoning in accordance with the appropriate restrictions. In arguing for a conception of justice we must be sure that it is among the permitted alternatives and satisfies the stipulated formal constraints. No considerations can be advanced in its favor unless they would be rational ones for us to urge were we to lack the kind of knowledge that is excluded. The evaluation of principles must proceed in terms of the general consequences of their public recognition and universal application, it being assumed that they will be complied with by everyone. To say that a certain conception of justice would be chosen in the original position is equivalent to saying that rational deliberation satisfying certain conditions and restrictions would reach a certain conclusion. If necessary, the argument to this result could be set out more formally. I shall, however, speak throughout in terms of the notion of the original position. It is more economical and suggestive, and brings out certain essential features that otherwise one might easily overlook.

These remarks show that the original position is not to be thought of as a general assembly which includes at one moment everyone who will live at some time; or, much less, as an assembly of everyone who could live at some time. It is not a gathering of all actual or possible persons. To conceive of the original position in either of these ways is to stretch fantasy too far; the conception would cease to be a natural guide to intuition. In any case, it is important that the original position be interpreted so that one can at any time adopt its perspective. It must make no difference when one takes up this viewpoint, or who does so: the restrictions must be such that the same principles are always chosen. The veil of ignorance is a key condition in meeting this requirement. It insures not only that the information available is relevant, but that it is at all times the same. [. . .]

Robert Nozick, "Distributive Justice"

The minimal state is the most extensive state that can be justified. Any state more extensive violates people's rights. Yet many persons have put forth reasons purporting to justify a more extensive state. It is impossible within the compass of this book to examine all the reasons that have been put forth. Therefore, I shall focus

From *Anarchy, State, and Utopia* (New York: Basic Books, 1974), pp. 149–53, 155–64, 174–5, 177–80.

upon those generally acknowledged to be most weighty and influential, to see precisely wherein they fail. In this chapter we consider the claim that a more extensive state is justified, because necessary (or the best instrument) to achieve distributive justice.

The term "distributive justice" is not a neutral one. Hearing the term "distribution," most people presume that some thing or mechanism uses some principle or criterion to give out a supply of things. Into this process of distributing shares some error may have crept. So it is an open question, at least, whether *re*distribution should take place; whether we should do again what has already been done once, though poorly. However, we are not in the position of children who have been given portions of pie by someone who now makes last minute adjustments to rectify careless cutting. There is no *central* distribution, no person or group entitled to control all the resources, jointly deciding how they are to be doled out. What each person gets, he gets from others who give to him in exchange for something, or as a gift. In a free society, diverse persons control different resources, and new holdings arise out of the voluntary exchanges and actions of persons. There is no more a distributing or distribution of shares than there is a distributing of mates in a society in which persons choose whom they shall marry. The total result is the product of many individual decisions which the different individuals involved are entitled to make. Some uses of the term "distribution," it is true, do not imply a previous distributing appropriately judged by some criterion (for example, "probability distribution"); nevertheless, despite the title of this chapter, it would be best to use a terminology that clearly is neutral. We shall speak of people's holdings; a principle of justice in holdings describes (part of) what justice tells us (requires) about holdings. I shall state first what I take to be the correct view about justice in holdings, and then turn to the discussion of alternate views.

The Entitlement Theory

The subject of justice in holdings consists of three major topics. The first is the *original acquisition of holdings*, the appropriation of unheld things. This includes the issues of how unheld things may come to be held, the process, or processes, by which unheld things may come to be held, the things that may come to be held by these processes, the extent of what comes to be held by a particular process, and so on. We shall refer to the complicated truth about this topic, which we shall not formulate here, as the principle of justice in acquisition. The second topic concerns the *transfer of holdings* from one person to another. By what processes may a person transfer holdings to another? How may a person acquire a holding from another who holds it? Under this topic come general descriptions of voluntary exchange, and gift and (on the other hand) fraud, as well as reference to particular conventional details fixed upon in a given society. The complicated truth about this subject (with placeholders for conventional details) we shall call the principle of justice in transfer. (And we shall suppose it also includes principles governing how a person may divest himself of a holding, passing it into an unheld state.)

If the world were wholly just, the following inductive definition would exhaustively cover the subject of justice in holdings.

1   A person who acquires a holding in accordance with the principle of justice in acquisition is entitled to that holding.
2   A person who acquires a holding in accordance with the principle of justice in transfer, from someone else entitled to the holding, is entitled to the holding.
3   No one is entitled to a holding except by (repeated) applications of 1 and 2.

The complete principle of distributive justice would say simply that a distribution is just if everyone is entitled to the holdings they possess under the distribution.

A distribution is just if it arises from another just distribution by legitimate means. The legitimate means of moving from one distribution to another are specified by the principle of justice in transfer. The legitimate first "moves" are specified by the principle of justice in acquisition. Whatever arises from a just situation by just steps is itself just. The means of change specified by the principle of justice in transfer preserve justice. As correct rules of inference are truth-preserving, and any conclusion deduced via repeated application of such rules from only true premises is itself true, so the means of transition from one situation to another specified by the principle of justice in transfer are justice-preserving, and any situation actually arising from repeated transitions in accordance with the principle from a just situation is itself just. The parallel between justice-preserving transformations and truth-preserving transformations illuminates where it fails as well as where it holds. That a conclusion could have been deduced by truth-preserving means from premises that are true suffices to show its truth. That from a just situation a situation *could* have arisen via justice-preserving means does *not* suffice to show its justice. The fact that a thief's victims voluntarily *could* have presented him with gifts does not entitle the thief to his ill-gotten gains. Justice in holdings is historical; it depends upon what actually has happened. We shall return to this point later.

Not all actual situations are generated in accordance with the two principles of justice in holdings: the principle of justice in acquisition and the principle of justice in transfer. Some people steal from others, or defraud them, or enslave them, seizing their product and preventing them from living as they choose, or forcibly exclude others from competing in exchanges. None of these are permissible modes of transition from one situation to another. And some persons acquire holdings by means not sanctioned by the principle of justice in acquisition. The existence of past injustice (previous violations of the first two principles of justice in holdings) raises the third major topic under justice in holdings: the rectification of injustice in holdings. If past injustice has shaped present holdings in various ways, some identifiable and some not, what now, if anything, ought to be done to rectify these injustices? What obligations do the performers of injustice have toward those whose position is worse than it would have been had the injustice not been done? Or, than it would have been had compensation been paid promptly? How, if at all, do things change if the beneficiaries and those made worse off are not the direct parties in the act of injustice, but, for example, their descendants? Is an injustice done to someone whose holding was itself based upon an unrectified injustice? How far back must one go in wiping clean the historical slate of injustices? What may victims of injustice permissibly do in order to rectify the injustices being done to them, including the many injustices done by persons acting through their government? I do not know of a thorough or theoretically sophisticated treatment of such issues. Idealizing greatly, let us suppose theoretical investigation will produce a principle of rectification. This principle uses historical information about previous situations and injustices done in them (as defined by the first two principles of justice and rights against interference), and information about the actual course of events that flowed from these injustices, until the present, and it yields a description (or descriptions) of holdings in the society. The principle of rectification presumably will make use of its best estimate of subjunctive information about what would have occurred (or a probability distribution over what might have occurred, using the expected value) if the injustice had not taken place. If the actual description of holdings turns out not to be one of the descriptions yielded by the principle, then one of the descriptions yielded must be realized.

The general outlines of the theory of justice in holdings are that the holdings of a person are just if he is entitled to them by the principles of justice in acquisition and transfer, or by the principle of rectification of injustice (as specified by the first two principles). If each person's holdings are just, then the total set (distribution) of holdings is just. To turn these general outlines into a specific theory we would have to specify the details of each of the three principles of justice in holdings: the principle of acquisition of holdings, the principle of transfer of holdings, and the principle of rectification of violations of the first two principles. I shall not attempt that task here. (Locke's principle of justice in acquisition is discussed below.) [. . .]

The general outlines of the entitlement theory illuminate the nature and defects of other conceptions of distributive justice. The entitlement theory of justice in distribution is *historical*; whether a distribution is just depends upon how it came about. [. . .] *Historical principles* of justice hold that past circumstances or actions of people can create differential entitlements or differential deserts to things. An injustice can be worked by moving from one distribution to another structurally identical one, for the second, in profile the same, may violate people's entitlements or deserts; it may not fit the actual history. [. . .]

The entitlement principles of justice in holdings that we have sketched are historical principles of justice. To better understand their precise character, we shall distinguish them from another subclass of the historical principles. Consider, as an example, the principle of distribution according to moral merit. This principle requires that total distributive shares vary directly with moral merit; no person should have a greater share than anyone whose moral merit is greater. (If moral merit could be not merely ordered but measured on an interval or ratio scale, stronger principles could be formulated.) Or consider the principle that results by substituting "usefulness to society" for "moral merit" in the previous principle. Or instead of "distribute according to moral merit," or "distribute according to useful-ness to society," we might consider "distribute according to the weighted sum of moral merit, usefulness to society, and need," with the weights of the different dimensions equal. Let us call a principle of distribution *patterned* if it specifies that a distribution is to vary along with some natural dimension, weighted sum of nat-ural dimensions, or lexicographic ordering of natural dimensions. And let us say a distribution is patterned if it accords with some patterned principle. (I speak of natural dimensions, admittedly without a general criterion for them, because for any set of holdings some artificial dimensions can be gimmicked up to vary along with the distribution of the set.) The principle of distribution in accordance with moral merit is a patterned historical principle, which specifies a patterned distribu-tion. "Distribute according to I.Q." is a patterned principle that looks to informa-tion not contained in distributional matrices. It is not historical, however, in that it does not look to any past actions creating differential entitlements to evaluate a distribution; it requires only distributional matrices whose columns are labeled by I.Q. scores. The distribution in a society, however, may be composed of such simple patterned distributions, without itself being simply patterned. Different sectors may operate different patterns, or some combination of patterns may operate in different proportions across a society. A distribution composed in this manner, from a small number of patterned distributions, we also shall term "patterned." And we extend the use of "pattern" to include the overall designs put forth by combinations of end-state principles.

Almost every suggested principle of distributive justice is patterned: to each according to his moral merit, or needs, or marginal product, or how hard he tries, or the weighted sum of the foregoing, and so on. The principle of entitlement we have sketched is *not* patterned. There is no one natural dimension or weighted sum or combination of a small number of natural dimensions that yields the distribu-tions generated in accordance with the principle of entitlement. The set of hold-ings that results when some persons receive their marginal products, others win at gambling, others receive a share of their mate's income, others receive gifts from foundations, others receive interest on loans, others receive gifts from admirers, others receive returns on investment, others make for themselves much of what they have, others find things, and so on, will not be patterned. Heavy strands of patterns will run through it; significant portions of the variance in holdings will be accounted for by pattern-variables. If most people most of the time choose to transfer some of their entitlements to others only in exchange for something from them, then a large part of what many people hold will vary with what they held that others wanted. More details are provided by the theory of marginal productiv-ity. But gifts to relatives, charitable donations, bequests to children, and the like, are not best conceived, in the first instance, in this manner. Ignoring the strands of pattern, let us suppose for the moment that a distribution actually arrived at by the operation of the principle of entitlement is random with respect to any pattern. Though the resulting set of holdings will be unpatterned, it will not be incompre-hensible, for it can be seen as arising from the operation of a small number of principles. These principles specify how an initial distribution may arise (the principle of acquisition of holdings) and how distributions may be transformed into others (the principle of transfer of holdings). The process whereby the set of holdings is generated will be intelligible, though the set of holdings itself that results from this process will be unpatterned.

The writings of F. A. Hayek focus [more] than is usually done upon what patterning distributive justice requires. Hayek argues that we cannot know enough about each person's situation to distribute to each according to his moral merit (but would justice demand we do so if we did have this knowledge?); and he goes on to say, "our objection is against all attempts to impress upon society a deliberately chosen pattern of distribution, whether it be an order of equality or of inequality." However, Hayek concludes that in a free society there will be distribution in accordance with value rather than moral merit; that is, in accordance with the perceived value of a person's actions and services to others. Despite his rejection of a patterned conception of distributive justice, Hayek himself suggests a pattern he thinks justifiable: distribution in accordance with the perceived benefits given to others, leaving room for the complaint that a free society does not realize exactly this pattern. Stating this patterned strand of a free capitalist society more precisely, we get "To each according to how much he benefits others who have the re-sources for benefiting those who benefit them." This will seem arbitrary unless some acceptable initial set of holdings is specified, or unless it is held that the operation of the system over time washes out any significant effects from the initial set of holdings. As an example of the latter, if almost anyone would have bought a car from Henry Ford, the supposition that it was an arbitrary matter who held the money then (and so bought) would not place Henry Ford's earnings under a cloud. In any event, *his* coming to hold it is not arbitrary. Distribution according to benefits to others *is* a major patterned strand in a free capitalist society, as Hayek correctly points out, but it is only a strand and does not constitute the whole pattern of a system of entitlements (namely, inheritance, gifts for arbitrary reasons, charity, and so on) or a standard that one should insist a society fit. Will people tolerate for long a system yielding distributions that they believe are unpatterned? No doubt people will not long accept a distribution they believe is *unjust*. People want their society to be and to look just. But must the look of justice reside in a resulting pattern rather than in the underlying generating principles? We are in no position to conclude that the inhabitants of a society embodying an entitle-ment conception of justice in holdings will find it unacceptable. Still, it must be granted that were people's reasons for transferring some of their holdings to others always irrational or arbitrary, we would find this disturbing. (Suppose people always determined what holdings they would transfer, and to whom, by using a random device.) We feel more comfortable upholding the justice of an entitlement system if most of the transfers under it are done for reasons. This does not mean necessar-ily that all deserve what holdings they receive. It means only that there is a purpose or point to someone's transferring a holding to one person rather than to another; that usually we can see what the transferrer thinks he's gaining, what cause he thinks he's serving, what goals he thinks he's helping to achieve, and so forth. Since in a capitalist society people often transfer holdings to others in accordance with how much they perceive these others benefiting them, the fabric constituted by the individual transactions and transfers is largely reasonable and intelligible.[1] (Gifts to loved ones, bequests to children, charity to the needy also are nonarbitrary components of the fabric.) In stressing the large strand of distribution in accordance with benefit to others, Hayek shows the point of many transfers, and so shows that the system of transfer of entitlements is not just spinning its gears aimlessly. The system of entitlements is defensible when constituted by the individual aims of individual transactions. No overarching aim is needed, no distributional pattern in required.

To think that the task of a theory of distributive justice is to fill in the blank in "to each according to his ＿＿" is to be predisposed to search for a pattern; and the separate treatment of "from each according to his ＿＿" treats production and distribution as two separate and independent issues. On an entitlement view these are *not* two separate questions. Whoever makes something, having bought or contracted for all other held resources used in the process (transferring some of his holdings for these cooperating factors), is entitled to it. The situation is *not* one of something's getting made, and there being an open question of who is to get it. Things come into the world already attached to people having entitlements over them. From the point of view of the historical entitlement conception of justice in holdings, those who start afresh to complete "to each according to his ＿＿" treat objects as if they appeared from nowhere, out of nothing. A complete theory of justice might cover this limit case as well; perhaps here is a use for the usual conceptions of distributive justice.

So entrenched are maxims of the usual form that perhaps we should present the entitlement conception as a competitor. Ignoring acquisition and rectification, we might say:

> From each according to what he chooses to do, to each according to what he makes for himself (perhaps with the contracted aid of others) and what others choose to do for him and choose to give him of what they've been given previously (under this maxim) and haven't yet expended or transferred.

This, the discerning reader will have noticed, has its defects as a slogan. So as a summary and great simplification (and not as a maxim with any independent meaning) we have:

> *From each as they choose, to each as they are chosen.*

---

[1] We certainly benefit because great economic incentives operate to get others to spend much time and energy to figure out how to serve us by providing things we will want to pay for. It is not mere paradox mongering to wonder whether capitalism should be criticized for most rewarding and hence encouraging, not individualists like Thoreau who go about their own lives, but people who are occupied with serving others and winning them as customers. But to defend capitalism one need not think businessmen are the finest human types. (I do not mean to join here the general maligning of businessmen, either.) Those who think the finest should acquire the most can try to convince their fellows to transfer resources in accordance with *that* principle.

How Liberty Upsets Patterns

It is not clear how those holding alternative conceptions of distributive justice can reject the entitlement conception of justice in holdings. For suppose a distribution favored by one of these non-entitlement conceptions is realized. Let us suppose it is your favorite one and let us call this distribution D_1; perhaps everyone has an equal share, perhaps shares vary in accordance with some dimension you treasure. Now suppose that Wilt Chamberlain is greatly in demand by basketball teams, being a great gate attraction. (Also suppose contracts run only for a year, with players being free agents.) He signs the following sort of contract with a team: In each home game, twenty-five cents from the price of each ticket of admission goes to him. (We ignore the question of whether he is "gouging" the owners, letting them look out for themselves.) The season starts, and people cheerfully attend his team's games; they buy their tickers, each time dropping a separate twenty-five cents of their admission price into a special box with Chamberlain's name on it. They are excited about seeing him play; it is worth the total admission price to them. Let us suppose that in one season one million persons attend his home games, and Wilt Chamberlain winds up with $250,000, a much larger sum than the average income and larger even than anyone else has. Is he entitled to this income? Is this new distribution D_2, unjust? If so, why? There is *no* question about whether each of the people was entitled to the control over the resources they held in D_1; because that was the distribution (your favorite) that (for the purposes of argument) we assumed was acceptable. Each of these persons *chose* to give twenty-five cents of their money to Chamberlain. They could have spent it on going to the movies, or on candy bars, or on copies of *Dissent* magazine, or of *Monthly Review*. But they all, at least one million of them, converged on giving it to Wilt Chamberlain in exchange for watching him play basketball. If D_1 was a just distribution, and people voluntarily moved from it to D_2, transferring parts of their shares they were given under D_1 (what was it for if not to do something with?), isn't D_2 also just? If the people were entitled to dispose of the resources to which they were entitled (under D_1), didn't this include their being entitled to give it to, or exchange it with, Wilt Chamberlain? Can anyone else complain on grounds of justice? Each other person already has his legitimate share under D_1. Under D_1, there is nothing that anyone has that anyone else has a claim of justice against. After someone transfers some-thing to Wilt Chamberlain, third parties *still* have their legitimate shares; *their* shares are not changed. By what process could such a transfer among two persons give rise to a legitimate claim of distributive justice on a portion of what was transferred, by a third party who had no claim of justice on any holding of the others *before* the transfer? To cut off objections irrelevant here, we might imagine the exchanges occurring in a socialist society, after hours. After playing whatever basketball he does in his daily work, or doing whatever other daily work he does, Wilt Cham-berlain decides to put in *overtime* to earn additional money. (First his work quota is set; he works time over that.) Or imagine it is a skilled juggler people like to see, who puts on shows after hours.

Why might someone work overtime in a society in which it is assumed their needs are satisfied? Perhaps because they care about things other than needs. I like to write in books that I read, and to have easy access to books for browsing at odd hours. It would be very pleasant and convenient to have the resources of Widener Library in my back yard. No society, I assume, will provide such resources close to each person who would like them as part of his regular allotment (under D_1). Thus, persons either must do without some extra things that they want, or be allowed to do something extra to get some of these things. On what basis could the inequalities that would eventuate be forbidden? Notice also that small factories would spring up in a socialist society, unless forbidden. I melt down some of my personal possessions (under D_1) and build a machine out of the material. I offer you, and others, a philosophy lecture once a week in exchange for your cranking the handle on my machine, whose products I exchange for yet other things, and so on. (The raw materials used by the machine are given to me by others who possess them under D_1, in exchange for hearing lectures.) Each person might participate to gain things over and above their allotment under D_1. Some persons even might want to leave their job in socialist industry and work full time in this private sector. I shall say something more about these issues later. Here I wish merely to note how private property even in means of production would occur in a socialist society that did not forbid people to use as they wished some of the resources they are given under the socialist distribution D_1. The socialist society would have to forbid capitalist acts between consenting adults.

The general point illustrated by the Wilt Chamberlain example and the example of the entrepreneur in a socialist society is that no end-state principle or distributional patterned principle of justice can be continuously realized without continuous interference with people's lives. Any favored pattern would be transformed into one unfavored by the principle, by people choosing to act in various ways; for example, by people exchanging goods and services with other people, or giving things to other people, things the transferrers are entitled to under the favored distributional pattern. To maintain a pattern one must either continually interfere to stop people from transferring resources as they wish to, or continually (or periodically) interfere to take from some persons resources that others for some reason chose to transfer to them. (But if some time limit is to be set on how long people may keep resources others voluntarily transfer to them, why let them keep these resources for *any* period of time? Why not have immediate confiscation?) It might be objected that all persons voluntarily will choose to refrain from actions which would upset the pattern. This presupposes unrealistically (1) that all will most want to maintain the pattern (are those who don't, to be "reeducated" or forced to undergo "self-criticism"?), (2) that each can gather enough information about his own actions and the ongoing activities of others to discover which of his actions will upset the pattern, and (3) that diverse and far-flung persons can co-ordinate their actions to dovetail into the pattern. Compare the manner in which the market is neutral among persons' desires, as it reflects and transmits widely scattered information via prices, and coordinates persons' activities.

It puts things perhaps a bit too strongly to say that every patterned (or end-state) principle is liable to be thwarted by the voluntary actions of the individual parties transferring some of their shares they receive under the principle. For perhaps some *very* weak patterns are not so thwarted. Any distributional pattern with any egalitarian component is overturnable by the voluntary actions of individual persons over time; as is every patterned condition with sufficient content so as actually to have been proposed as presenting the central core of distributive justice. Still, given the possibility that some weak conditions or patterns may not be unstable in this way, it would be better to formulate an explicit description of the kind of interesting and contentful patterns under discussion, and to prove a theorem about their instability. Since the weaker the patterning, the more likely it is that the entitlement system itself satisfies it, a plausible conjecture is that any patterning either is unstable or is satisfied by the entitlement system. [. . .]

Locke's Theory of Acquisition

[Now] we must introduce an additional bit of complexity into the structure of the entitlement theory. This is best approached by considering Locke's attempt to specify a principle of justice in acquisition. Locke views property rights in an unowned object as originating through someone's mixing his labor with it. This gives rise to many questions. What are the boundaries of what labor is mixed with? If a private astronaut clears a place on Mars, has he mixed his labor with (so that he comes to own) the whole planet, the whole uninhabited universe, or just a particular plot? Which plot does an act bring under ownership? The minimal (possibly disconnected) area such that an act decreases entropy in that area, and not elsewhere? Can virgin land (for the purposes of ecological investigation by high-flying airplane) come under ownership by a Lockean process? Building a fence around a territory presumably would make one the owner of only the fence (and the land immediately underneath it).

Why does mixing one's labor with something make one the owner of it? Perhaps because one owns one's labor, and so one comes to own a previously unowned thing that becomes permeated with what one owns. Ownership seeps over into the rest. But why isn't mixing what I own with what I don't own a way of losing what I own rather than a way of gaining what I don't? If I own a can of tomato juice and spill it in the sea so that its molecules (made radioactive, so I can check this) mingle evenly throughout the sea, do I thereby come to own the sea, or have I foolishly dissipated my tomato juice? Perhaps the idea, instead, is that laboring on something improves it and makes it more valuable; and anyone is entitled to own a thing whose value he has created. (Reinforcing this, perhaps, is the view that laboring is unpleasant. If some people made things effortlessly, as the cartoon characters in *The Yellow Submarine* trail flowers in their wake, would they have lesser claim to their own products whose making didn't *cost* them anything?) Ignore the fact that laboring on something may make it less valuable (spraying pink enamel paint on a piece of driftwood that you have found). Why should one's entitlement extend to the whole object rather than just to the *added value* one's labor has produced? (Such reference to value might also serve to delimit the extent of ownership; for example, substitute "increases the value of" for "decreases entropy in" in the above entropy criterion.) No workable or coherent value-added property scheme has yet been devised, and any such scheme presumably would fall to objections (similar to those) that fell the theory of Henry George.

It will be implausible to view improving an object as giving full ownership to it, if the stock of unowned objects that might be improved is limited. For an object's coming under one person's ownership changes the situation of all others. Whereas previously they were at liberty (in Hohfeld's sense) to use the object, they now no longer are. This change in the situation of others (by removing their liberty to act on a previously unowned object) need not worsen their situation. If I appropriate a grain of sand from Coney Island, no one else may now do as they will with *that* grain of sand. But there are plenty of other grains of sand left for them to do the same with. Or if not grains of sand, then other things. Alternatively, the things I do with the grain of sand I appropriate might improve the position of others, counterbalancing their loss of the liberty to use that grain. The crucial point is whether appropriation of an unowned object worsens the situation of others.

Locke's proviso that there be "enough and as good left in common for others" (*Second Treatise*, sect. 27) is meant to ensure that the situation of others is not worsened. [. . .] Is the situation of persons who are unable to appropriate (there being no more accessible and useful unowned objects) worsened by a system allowing appropriation and permanent property? Here enter the various familiar social considerations favoring private property: it increases the social product by putting means of production in the hands of those who can use them most efficiently (profitably); experimentation is encouraged, because with separate persons controlling resources, there is no one person or small group whom someone with a new idea must convince to try it out; private property enables people to decide on the pattern and types of risks they wish to bear, leading to specialized types of risk bearing; private property protects future persons by leading some to hold back resources from current consumption for future markets; it provides alternate sources of employment for unpopular persons who don't have to convince any one person or small group to hire them, and so on. These considerations enter a Lockean theory to support the claim that appropriation of private property satisfies the intent behind the "enough and as good left over" proviso, *not* as a utilitarian justification of property. They enter to rebut the claim that because the proviso is violated no natural right to private property can arise by a Lockean process. The difficulty in working such an argument to show that the proviso is satisfied is in fixing the appropriate baseline for comparison. Lockean appropriation makes people no worse off than they would be *how?* This question of fixing the baseline needs more detailed investigation than we are able to give it here. It would be desirable to have an estimate of the general economic importance of original appropriation in order to see how much leeway there is for differing theories of appropriation and of the location of the baseline. Perhaps this importance can be measured by the percentage of all income that is based upon untransformed raw materials and given resources (rather than upon human actions), mainly rental income representing the unimproved value of land, and the price of raw material *in situ*, and by the percentage of current wealth which represents such income in the past.[2]

We should note that it is not only persons favoring *private* property who need a theory of how property rights legitimately originate. Those believing in collective property, for example those believing that a group of persons living in an area jointly own the territory, or its mineral resources, also must provide a theory of how such property rights arise; they must show why the persons living there have rights to determine what is done with the land and resources there that persons living elsewhere don't have (with regard to the same land and resources). [. . .]

A theory which includes this proviso in its principle of justice in acquisition must also contain a more complex principle of justice in transfer. Some reflection of the proviso about appropriation constrains later actions. If my appropriating all of a certain substance violates the Lockean proviso, then so does my appropriating some and purchasing all the rest from others who obtained it without otherwise violating the Lockean proviso. If the proviso excludes someone's appropriating all the drinkable water in the world, it also excludes his purchasing it all. (More weakly, and messily, it may exclude his charging certain prices for some of his supply.) This proviso (almost?) never will come into effect; the more someone acquires of a scarce substance which others want, the higher the price of the rest will go, and the more difficult it will become for him to acquire it all. But still, we can imagine, at least, that something like this occurs: someone makes simultaneous secret bids to the separate owners of a substance, each of whom sells assuming he can easily purchase more from the other owners; or some natural catastrophe destroys all of the supply of something except that in one person's possession. The total supply could not be permissibly appropriated by one person at the beginning. His later acquisition of it all does not show that the original appropriation violated the proviso. [. . .] Rather, it is the combination of the original appropriation *plus* all the later transfers and actions that violates the Lockean proviso.

Each owner's title to his holding includes the historical shadow of the Lockean proviso on appropriation. This excludes his transferring it into an agglomeration that does violate the Lockean proviso and excludes his using it in a way, in coordination with others or independently of them, so as to violate the proviso by making the situation of others worse than their baseline situation. Once it is known that someone's ownership runs afoul of the Lockean proviso, there are stringent limits on what he may do with (what it is difficult any longer unreservedly to call)

---

[2] I have not seen a precise estimate. David Friedman, *The Machinery of Freedom* (N.Y.: Harper & Row, 1973), pp. xiv, xv, discusses this issue and suggests 5 percent of U.S. national income as an upper limit for the first two factors mentioned. However he does not attempt to estimate the percentage of current wealth which is based upon such income in the past. (The vague notion of "based upon" merely indicates a topic needing investigation.)

"his property." Thus a person may not appropriate the only water hole in a desert and charge what he will. Nor may he charge what he will if he possesses one, and unfortunately it happens that all the water holes in the desert dry up, except for his. This unfortunate circumstance, admittedly no fault of his, brings into operation the Lockean proviso and limits his property rights. Similarly, an owner's property right in the only island in an area does not allow him to order a castaway from a shipwreck off his island as a trespasser, for this would violate the Lockean proviso. [. . .]

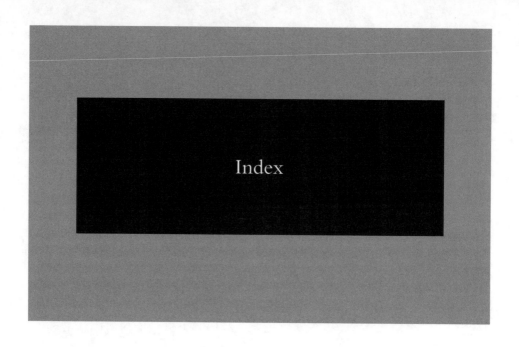

Index

MAI